STORIES OF INDIAN SAINTS

Stories of Indian Saints

Translation of Mahipati's Marathi ***Bhaktavijaya***

JUSTIN E. ABBOTT
and
NARHAR R. GODBOLE

An Introduction by
G.V. TAGARE

Parts I & II
(Bound in One)

MOTILAL BANARSIDASS PUBLISHERS
PRIVATE LIMITED • DELHI

7th Reprint: Delhi, 2014
Fourth Edition: Pune, 1933

ISBN: 978-81-208-0469-2

MOTILAL BANARSIDASS
41 U.A. Bungalow Road, Jawahar Nagar, Delhi 110 007
8 Mahalaxmi Chamber, 22 Bhulabhai Desai Road, Mumbai 400 026
203 Royapettah High Road, Mylapore, Chennai 600 004
236, 9th Main III Block, Jayanagar, Bengaluru 560 011
Sanas Plaza, 1302 Baji Rao Road, Pune 411 002
8 Camac Street, Kolkata 700 017
Ashok Rajpath, Patna 800 004
Chowk, Varanasi 221 001

Printed in India

by RP Jain at NAB Printing Unit,
A-44, Naraina Industrial Area, Phase I, New Delhi–110028
and published by JP Jain for Motilal Banarsidass Publishers (P) Ltd,
41 U.A. Bungalow Road, Jawahar Nagar, Delhi-110007

FOREWORD

BY

J. F. Edwards

How the *Bhaktavijaya* was Translated

This book contains the first published English translation of Mahipati's *Bhaktavijaya* which consists of forty thousand lines of beautiful Marathi poetry and is rightly regarded as one of the classics of a language spoken by over twenty-one million people in present-day India. Who Mahipati was will be found on another page and each of his joint-translators speaks for himself in his own separate Preface. Since one of these joint-authors is no more, and the other is a self-effacing Indian Pandit, our first task in this Foreword is to introduce their work to English readers by indicating some of the limitations under which this work has been prepared. This English translation of one of the great Marathi classics is published under the provisions of the last will and testament of the late Dr. Justin E. Abbott who passed away at Summit, New Jersey, United States, on June 19, 1932. Born at Rahuri in the Ahmednagar District on Christmas Day 1853, it was as a loyal son of Maharashtra that he took in hand the translating into English of important sections of the lives and writings of the Poet Saints of Maharashtra. Eight volumes had been published when he died, and the ninth volume entited *Ramdas* we published a year ago. The present work is planned to appear in two volumes, the second being already in the Press. The foundation for these two volumes had been well and truly laid in the completion of the first draft translation by Dr. Abbott before the final stages of his physical weakness. On this task the patient scholar spent about eighteen months of the last two years of his life. His method of work during those last months was to follow the Marathi text from a volume placed on a movable book-rest attached to his couch or bed, while he dictated his translation into a dictaphone whenever he felt fit for work, a lady attendant (see page xx) afterwards typing off the translation as repeated by the dictaphone. Though kept to his bed continuously for several weeks during this period, sometimes in a serious condition, he nevertheless pursued his task with his usual cheerfulness. When we stayed with him in New Jersey for a month in early 1930 it was quite clear that daily fellowship with the Poet Saints was a great comfort in his loneliness. And as we have worked over this translation which was produced under such conditions of physical disability, we have done so with the feeling that we were permitted to gaze upon a monument of heroic industry and endurance.

The Editor's Task

Let us emphasize at the outset that our own share in this undertaking has been strictly editorial. It need hardly be said that this editorial task has been no sinecure. Knowing Dr. Abbott's passion for exactitude, and knowing also that his translation had been committed to paper under the peculiar conditions just now indicated, which included the important factor that the typist neither knew Marathi, nor how to spell or pronounce Marathi proper names, nor could her copy be corrected by the translator–in view of these and similar facts we felt there was no alternative but to compare the entire translation with Mahipati's original of ten thousand Marathi verses of four lines each. This we began during the last hot weather at Mahableshwar and completed in the weeks following under the competent guidance of Pandit N. R. Godbole who is rightly given his place on the title-page as joint-author of the book (see page xx). Dr. Abbott's punctilious care even in his growing weakness is shown by the fact tnat no more than a hundred lines had been overlooked by him in translating the forty thousand lines of Mahipati's entire work, the major portion of the alterations that were necessary having arisen from the confusion caused by the three stages of sound in the typing of the manuscript, viz., the voice of the person dictating, the sound as emitted by the dictaphone, and the word-sound as understood and typed by the non-Marathi typist. For all errors of proof-correction we must bear final responsibility. Following on two proofs read by the Pandit, ours was the task of reading the third or fourth proof of every page throughout the book, sometimes a fifth being necessary. In this connection we owe a heavy debt of gratitude to the manager and workmen at the Aryabhushan Press for their uniform patience and courtesy.

Dr. Abbott's English Style

A word seems necessary about Dr. Abbott's English style in his translation, in view of a stray opinion that has mingled here and there with the high praise bestowed on preceding volumes. His aim throughout the series has been to let the Marathi Poet Saints speak for themselves as far as that is possible through the medium of a translation. This is the answer to an observation made by one reviewer, a well known Englishman, that the translation is 'painfully literal, jerky, disjointed.' That Dr. Abbott's translation is 'literal' may be regarded as one measure of its success, for this was one of his chief aims in order to let English readers see what the Poet Saints themselves actually say. That it is also 'jerky' and 'disjointed' is due to the attempt to turn oriental poetry, and that Mahipati's difficult *ovi* poetry, into occidental prose. As Dr. Abbott himself remarked to the present writer in a personal letter dated 1926 regarding this series: 'Anyone wishing to make a further study of these Marathi Poet

Saints will know where to turn for material. By translating Mahipati, I kill two birds with one stone. I make Mahipati known, as a graphic interesting writer; and I show his characters, his heroes and heroines, not in my language, or from my point of view, but through the Indian eye.' That Dr. Abbott has succeeded in this worthy aim is shown by the appreciative remarks made by the same reviewer referred to above. See also a later reference by the same pen on this subject given below.

Mahipati's Place in Literature

What claim on our time and study has this Mahipati, one of whose masterpieces is translated in this book ? Unquestionably his first claim arises from the rare quality of the Marathi literature he has given us. For evidence on this point turn to two of Mahipati's students in the ranks of the Indian Civil Service. Mr.L.J. Sedgwick, I. C. S., who when he passed away a few years ago had just completed his able survey as 1921 Indian Census Superintendent for the Bombay Government, wrote in *The Journal of the Royal Asiatic Society, Bombay Branch* (1910, volume 23, No. 65, pp. 109–110): ' Viewed from any standpoint of criticism the *ovi* poems of Mahipati, and the *abhangs* of Namdev, Eknath, Tukaram and Ramdas must be placed among the finest of the poetic productions of the world.' Another acknowledged authority on Marathi literature among the ranks of the Indian Civil Service is the Hon. C. A. Kincaid, I. C. S., joint author with Rao Bahadur D. B. Parasnis of a three-volume *History of the Maratha People* and who in his interesting *Tales of the Saints of Pandharpur* (pp. 3–4) affirms: ' Had Mahipati used a linguistic medium more widely known than Marathi, he would have ranked high among the world's poets. Even a foreigner can appreciate the easy flow of his stanzas; his musical rhymes and above all his unrivalled imagery.' No one can work steadily through the *Bhaktavijaya* of Mahipati without being driven to the same conclusion. It is one of the most fascinating of religious story-books. By the title *Bhaktavijaya* is meant *Triumphs of the Saints*, and concerning Mahipati's entrancing poetical narratives of the saints the late Narayan Vaman Tilak once said he was 'reminded of Foxe's *Book of Martyrs*.' Though a critical estimate compels the conclusion that the *Bhaktavijaya* conveys an 'atmosphere rather than exact history,' supplying rich 'biographical material rather than biography,' and though many of Mahipati's embellishments can only be viewed as beautiful 'legends,' yet he has so thoroughly succeeded in investing with the true *bhakti* (devotional) spirit the daily life of rich and poor, high caste, low caste and out-caste alike, among the Marathi-speaking people, that ever since he died in 1790 this work has rightly been regarded as one of the source-books concerning the Marathi Saints who lived from the 13th to the 17th centuries. On his trustworthiness see pp. xxiii–xxviii.

How To Understand the Indian Heart

A translation such as this is, of one of the incomparable portions of India's religious literature, enables all who wish to understand the heart of India to do so without the laborious task of acquiring a strange language. If this applies to all across the seas who desire to acquaint themselves with India's religious point of view, it applies with double force to all those from other lands who come to India for whatever purpose. In a recent speech H. H. The Maharajah of Mysore observed: 'There are diverse religions in this land of ours and frequently there exists a most irreligious hostility between them. This being so, the creed and custom of each religion among us is surely worthy of reverent study by the followers of every other.' If such an attitude is desirable on the part of all foreigners in India, it is nothing less than a sacred duty on the part of those foreigners who come to India for the purpose of helping its people religiously. Surely one of the first duties of a missionary should be to become acquainted with the religious point of view of the people of the land, and a book such as this enables this to be done even before the language has been acquired. As the Chaplain of Simla, the Rev. P. N. F. Young M. A., said in a thoughtful address before the Simla Y. M. C. A. recently: 'I think the Christian should be keen to learn about and understand other religions, firstly because they are worthy of study, and because they are the result of a sincere search after God. Secondly, because we can best commend our own faith if we appreciate sympathetically those who differ from us. And thirdly, because there is a real bond between all those who in these secularised days hold to a spiritual interpretation of the Universe.'

India's Insurrection Against Religion

Mahipati's matchless stories make a distinctive contribution in the direction indicated by H. H. The Maharajah Gaikwar of Baroda at the conclusion of his eloquent address at the opening of the Second World Parliament of Religions at Chicago in September this year when he said: 'Let us humbly and in the spirit of partnership combine against the common enemies: ignorance, selfishness and materialism.' In the second chapter of his wonderful Marathi poem entitled *Christayan*, Narayan Vaman Tilak ascribes to India the glowing phrase, 'enthroned as *guru* of the earth.' If this high place is to be won and retained by India, her educated people need to guard against the growing tendency to leave the heart's throne empty after having dethroned whatever false gods may have occupied it hitherto. Every one of us must welcome every sign of insurrection against any form of religion that may be false and unworthy, and no doubt much of the religious rebellion in India to-day is against degrading and unworthy ideas of God. But some aspects of India's insurrection against religion are against religion in any form both false and true. They are like that South Indian paper called *Revolt*: they revolt 'against both heaven and hell, both God and Satan.' That the shrine in the soul of young India to-day is too often an empty shrine was shown by Gandhiji not long ago when he said he was 'inundated with letters from young men...about the void that their unbelief has made in their lives.' As an able Indian barrister remarked some time ago: 'The kirk I stay away from is Hinduism.' An Indian Christian educational leader of Bengal, the Rev. S. K. Chatterji of Bishnupur, stated some two years ago: 'The rising generation in India is inclined to throw over religion altogether. In its place they want to put Secularism. They seem to think that it is religion and faith in God which has made India effeminate and weak, and that no independence and progress are possible so long as there is religion in this land. These secularists are not mere materialists, in the sense that they believe only in wealth and power; no, a great many of them believe in social reform, in the emancipation of women, and in education. What they do not seem to believe in, is *God*. They do not seem to have any use for religion or religious practices. We shudder to think of a god-less India; yet we find her on the very brink of it.'

Why do we call attention to this state of things? Because Mahipati and his *bhakti* saints had just the very opposite ideal of life to the secular ideal which shuts God out. Also because there is so much in them calculated to call back those who are drifting into the anti-religious attitude. Though from our standpoint to-day these poet-saints may have had a defective ideal, yet we need to remind ourselves of the state of things that prevailed in their days. In an age when the worship of the Unseen was almost entirely through stocks and stones, these *bhaktas* in Mahipati's pages urged upon their hearers the total inefficacy of the customary modes of purification and of the attainment of God, such as pilgrimages, vows, fasts, penances and sacrifices. These *bhakti* poets also inculcated upon their readers 'the omnipresence of God, and His being neither stock nor stone.' In their teachings they further placed 'a special emphasis upon purity of heart, humility, self-surrender, forgiveness, and the love of God they severely condemned religious practices which concerned the body only, and all mechanical rites and cermonies; and they strongly enforced the absolute necessity of striving for the attainment of pure devotion to God.'

The Nationalizing and Democratizing Value of *Bhakti*

There is another reason why Maharashtra in these days may well turn its mind from being anti-religious to Mahipati and his *bhaktas*, and the reason is that these provide a unifying, nationalizing and democratizing, and larger purifying, influence in these days of national aspiration. Justice Ranade in his *Rise of the Maratha Power* shows how 'the *bhakti* movement tended to unite the hearts of the Marathas in the cause of establishing the independence of their motherland. and how the Maharashtra mystics were a source of living moral inspiration and influence over the people and how they by their example, preachings and writings, through the medium of the spoken language of the country, kindled the warlike fire in the heroic race of the Maratha people and infused and awakened the long slumbering sense of the patriotic spirit in them .... The political revolution was in fact to some extent caused by a religious and social upheaval which moved the entire population.'

Untouchability Still In Vithoba Worship

We wish we could get all the citizens of the Maharashtra of today to see with clearness that these things have a practical application to India's great fight against Untouchability, a fight in which some of India's greatest and noblest have dedicated themselves. One of these incomparable stories of Mahipati tells of how the untouchable Mahar poet Chokhamela was turned out of the temple of Vithoba *because he was a Mahar*. See the story in full on pages 377–384, and remember that one of the chief boasts in connection with Vithoba worship has been its democratic character and that *all* castes have been welcomed by it. But even yet, in this enlightened 20th century, Vithoba worship has not become democratic enough to welcome the *out*-caste. For the benefit of any who may be inclined to doubt this we will quote a moving appeal made in that Brahmin newspaper, the *Kesari*, whose Marathi editorial of October 14, 1932 we translated as follows in our *Dnyanodaya* English columns of a few days later on October 27:—

More than 500 years ago there lived a simple Maharashtrian saint named Chokhāmelā who it seems was not allowed to take the vision of Vithoba. After him were hundreds and thousands of Mahars, Mangs and Chambhars who became Varkaris, the chief devotees of Vithoba at Pandharpur. They played their instruments, lifted high their banners, founded their guilds, and in the very vicinity of the god built even their schools. *But* these were all compelled to satisfy their hungering hearts by bathing in the sacred river Chandrabhaga near by and by gazing from a distance at the spires of Vithoba's temple. Why should not this three hundred years' penance of gazing at the temple spires now have its due reward? Why should they not now be permitted to look into the holy of holies where the god abides in serene contemplation, standing on the sacred brick with hand on hip, beneath those spires on which they have feasted their eyes for generations past? May not Vithoba himself be weary with the long vigil as he beholds their distress?

Why should not these untouchables now be reckoned to have completed their long probation?

India's Yearning For a Personal God

But there is more than the democratizing influence of *bhakti* to be learned from Mahipati's *Bhaktavijaya* stories. They show how wide and deep has been India's revolt against the deadening philosophy of the Hindu Vedanta. Many of these stories illustrate the truth that while Vedantism may fascinate and enthral the metaphysical type of mind, it is not a religion by which common people may live. These stories in the *Bhaktavijaya* disclose how passionately India wants a personal God, that she will re-refuse to be satisfied until she finds such a God, or is found by Him, as the New Testament affirms; and that for a thousand years past India 'has been driven by the inner urge of the heart to a conception of a Personal Lord or *Ishwar* which the most strenuous efforts have not been able to reconcile with the older philosophy. No more convincing demonstration of the inability of the human mind and heart to be content with non-personality as Supreme, has been given the world, than by India. The Vedanta still gets lip-service; but it is the Personal God as pictured by the *Ramayana* of Tulsi Das, the Hymns of Tamil and Maratha saints, and the school of Ramanuja, etc., that receives the heart's devotion of India. The "God" of which Gandhiji and other educated modern Hindus speak is not by any means the "Brahma" of the Upanishads, but a Personal Being toward whom many Hindus feel the deepest love and devotion.' It is because all these important matters receive impressive illustration on every page of Mahipati's *Bhaktavijaya* that such practical value attaches to the translation appearing in the present work, especially for missionaries and for all who would understand the yearnings of the Indian heart and do something to satisfy those yearnings. That distinguished Hindu editors recognize the existence of deep religious yearnings in present-day India is impressively illustrated concerning another part of India in *The Indian Review* for December 1933. An Indian writer is there quoted as referring to the Tamil Saint Thayumanavar whose date largely synchronized with that of Mahipati. The article states:

The great realities of religion called for his zealous pursuit of them. He began to ask seriously : .... What is sin ? What is the way to freedom ? How am I to get knowledge which will free me from fear both in this life and the next ? When I think of birth and death my heart is terrified. Both my eyes become sleepless. My body melts day and night like gold in fire. What is the cause of all these ? If Thou dost not grant me the blessed stage of *nishta*, because of my soul's thirst, I will be destroyed. If I die before realising this, what shall I do, O God ? He gives expression to his restless mind thus :

When I, the way of love not knowing,
Was moved and stirred to love by Thee,
My spirit with love-languor fainted.
Thy doing all, for whom love-longing
I pine, and pining gain no rest.
Thou comest not, I cry for comfort;
Unpitied and alone I live.

Mysticism In Maharashtra

Literature dealing with Marathi *bhakti* has been greatly enriched during the present year (1933) by the appearance of a substantial volume of 500 pages on *Mysticism in Maharashtra*, the seventh volume in the *History Of Indian Philosophy*. This new volume on Maharashtra Mysticism is by Professor R. D. Ranade, Professor of Philosophy in the University of Allahabad, and was preceded by four 'source-books' giving selections illustrating the main theme of the larger work. To enter upon a discussion of Professor Ranade's great effort would take us far beyond the purpose of this Foreword, and happily this has been rendered unnecessary by an able review from the competent pen of the Rev Alexander Robertson, formerly of Poona and now of Nagpur, in the *N. C. C. Review* for October this year. Professor Ranade expresses warm appreciation of 'the panorama of Marathi Literature' exhibited by Dr. Abbott in this series on the 'Poet Saints of Maharashtra.' In one of the December Indian magazines to hand just as this Foreword goes to press. Professor Ranade's book on *Mysticism* is reviewed, though not with equal competence, by the English reviewer we have mentioned above who repeats his earlier criticism by observing: 'Dr. Abbott's translations must rank among the worst–in style and language–of any translations ever published;' adding also: 'His industry in execution was not paralleled by felicity of expression.' We have already given reasons for showing that to have aimed at 'felicity of expression' from the English language point of view would have been to rob the Poet Saints of the opportunity of largely speaking for themselves, uncouth though they may be from the standpoint of our later day. As for the first remark, its last five words (' of any translations ever published') are rich indeed. For the real question is: How *many* translations of the Poet Saints of Maharashtra have been 'published' with which to institute such a comparison? The *Bhaktavijaya* for example, translated in the present work, has never appeared before as a whole in an English dress. If the comparison is with certain poetical versions of Marathi that have appeared in English, the answer is that it is widely accepted that very much more has occasionally been *put into* such translations than appears in the Marathi original, resulting in religious interpretations rejected by certain schools of Marathi scholarship. In view of this state of the case it is encouraging to note that the same critical reviewer in another place can say of this Poet Saints series: 'which I have found very useful.' As for the departed scholar whose latest work is found in this book, he himself would say of any critic : 'Of course my translation is very imperfect; please do not argue in its defence; whatever merits it may have, let them speak for it.' And let it be remembered that the Mystics of Maharashtra differ as much among themselves as do their present-day interpreters and critics.

The Heart A Safer Guide Than the Head

As we are desirous of avoiding anything of the nature of controversy we cannot better conclude this Foreword than by quoting something Dr. Abbott wrote to us in a personal letter a few years ago as follows:— 'Oh! that the eyes of good men, who want to help this sad world, could be opened to see that the path of controversy is the wrong path. The head, however well or logically directed, however historically correct, however true to doctrines traditional or new, has *never* made the heart better, nobler, Christlike. Emphasis therefore should be on the *heart*, to move it to love and kindness and gentleness, unselfishness, tolerance and all the virtues idealized in Christ. Controversy stirs anger, unkind thoughts, divisions. Controversy has been the curse of Christendom through all its history, and the great cause of putting back the Kingdom of Christ in India and other lands. The battle *about* Christ, the contentions on doctrines *relating to Him*, are as far away from *Him* as are the horrors of war from the peace of a home where the Christ-spirit lives.'

United Theological College
of Western India,
7 Sholapur Road, Poona,
December 7, 1933

J. F. Edwards

CHIEF AUTHOR'S PREFACE

Mahipati was born in the little village of Taharabad, in the Ahmednagar district, in the year 1715, and died in the year 1790. He was a Brahman by birth, and the first we hear of him is that he was employed as the town-scribe of Taharabad. The story told of him is that one day he was summoned by an official of the town to come at once. When the messenger arrived he was sitting performing the worship of God. He replied to the messenger that he was 'busy with his worship and could not come now, but would come later.' The messenger, however, would not take 'No' for an answer and insisted that he should come with him. Mahipati finally agreed to go, but mentally resolved to give up his secular employment and devote himself wholly to the religious life. He went with the messenger, performed his duty, and returned vowing never again to use his pen in secular employment. He resigned from his office and devoted himself solely to religion.

Naturally he became interested in the lives of those who had given up their secular lives, because they had become indifferent to its attractions. He then began to write the stories connected with the lives of the *bhaktas* (those who with love and devotion worshipped God) who were known in Maharashtra (the great nation, meaning the Marathi country included in the Bombay Presidency).

He evidently began at once to accumulate the books that told of the lives of those saints. He mentions some of them, such as the work of Nabhaji and Chidghan. He possessed the *Gathas* (poems) of one Nama Vishnudas. For if we compare the stories told by that Nama we find indisputable evidence that Mahipati used them in writing his own account. It is to be presumed that other books were available, but are now non-existent, through time, rats, white ants and other enemies of manuscripts Whether the stories of the different saints are real or legendary, matters little, but from them we learn what was popularly considered their conception of God, and their way of approach to Him. That they considered an image of an *avatar* like Rama or Krishna a way of approach cannot be doubted. Tukaram's enthusiasm before the image at Pandharpur and the devotion of Ramdas to images of Rama give abundant evidence. But it should also be remembered that the approach by way of the idol was not their only way. They practised and taught what is called *manas puja*, that is, worship with the mind alone. It was their way of going as it were into their inner chamber and closing the door to pray in secret to God, whom they called Mother and Father. If Hindus of the present day would follow the ideas of their saints, they need not seek approach to God through an idol but can use the method of *manas puja* (mental worship).

Not all the *bhaktas* in these stories held to the ideal of *bhakti* and *Vairagya* (renunciation) as did Tukaram and Ramdas. Many were sincere *bhaktas* while carrying on their worldly business, but they had the spirit of *Vairagya*; that is, their indifference to worldly things (or their *Vairagya*) was one of spirit. It meant that they did not look upon their riches as acquired for their own happiness, but to help the needy. They understood that they should not lay up the temporary riches of this world, but those supreme spiritual riches that are eternal.

Saints like Eknath, Tukaram and Ramdas tried to live the life of *complete* indifference to worldly things. They obeyed literally the precepts, ' Give to him who asketh of thee,' ' Take no thought for the morrow; what ye shall eat or drink, nor yet for your body, what ye shall put on.'

They trusted God for everything. But as I have elsewhere intimated they did not press this upon others unless others so chose it. Others were to continue in the business of life, doing their respective duties, but always with the unselfish spirit of *Vairagya* or of indifference to worldly things.

As will be noticed on the title-page, Pandit Narahar R. Godbole will appear as a collaborator with me in the production of the remaining books of the 'poet saints of Maharashtra' series. He has translated a portion of this book and will help me in that same manner in completing the remaining three. The knowledge he has acquired of the language and style of the ancient writings he is making available for me in the laborious work of translating such large books as the *Bhaktaviiaya* and the *Bhaktalilamrit*.

As on former occasions my thanks are due to the Rev J. F. Edwards for reading the final proofs of this book.

Included in my physical weakness is my inability to use a pen. Anyone who has helped me in typing my translation deserves special thanks and a public acknowledgment of it. My nurse, Miss Joan Maree, has learned the art of typing in order to help me, and to her I owe a debt of gratitude.

Pandit N. R. Godbole has been fortunate in obtaining for comparision a rare manuscript of the *Bhaktavijaya*. He has discovered that the printed versions have omitted several passages that are found in this manuscript. It has seemed to me therefore worth while to publish these passages, and so give the book the form that possibly it originally had.

Summit, N. J., U. S. A.
October 1931

Justin E. Abbott

PANDIT'S PREFACE

The Preface to this book has already been written by the Late Dr. Abbott, for the Manuscript of the translation of the *Bhaktavijaya* was just completed in his lifetime. On the title-page the learned Doctor has put my name under his as the second author. Nobody need remind me that I do not deserve this high honour, for I know better than anyone else my inability and unworthiness. But he treated me all along with a motherly indulgence, and my joint authorship with him is one consequence of it. I had the boldness to request him to drop my name from the title-page but in reply he commanded me to accept his decision.

While working for Dr. Abbott I was often impressed by the meagreness of my knowledge of Marathi, and I have often found that his English translation has enabled me to elucidate the meaning of the Marathi text. This fact I told several Marathi scholars whose comparisons of his English translation with the original text often filled them with admiration. Some of them therefore urged me to make known to the public the learned doctor's masterly knowledge of Marathi, which I would have done very readily had it not seemed like trumpeting the fame of my master whose salt I was eating. I am still eating his salt but as he is not living I cannot now be accused of flattery. Many times have I asked him in letters if the Husband of Rukmini had given him the correct interpretation of some difficult Marathi sentence in a dream. On one occasion I wrote a letter to him in the form of Marathi verse and to my great astonishment he sent his reply to me in Marathi verse. In May 1928 I presented copies of Dr. Abbott's first and second publications to the learned Shri Shankaracharya, Dr. Kurtakoti, who was so delighted with them that he was pleased to confer on their author the high title of *Bhashabhushan* (' an ornament to the language ')

Great, however, as was his scholarship and learning, his character was greater still. Mahipati says that ' Saints conquer their opponents by the strength of peace and forgiveness' and Dr. Abbott has strikingly exemplified this in the case of some harsh critics. By nature unassuming and unpedantic, Dr. Abbott was a very thorough and God-fearing Christian, and higher praise than that I feel I cannot bestow.

627 Sadashiv Peth, Poona 2 *N. R. Godbole*

INTRODUCTION

MAHIPATI : THE BIOGRAPHER OF THE POET SAINTS

Birth and Early Influences

Mahipati's father Dadopant is said to have been in the service of the Mughals, but where, when and in what capacity is not known. At the age of forty he retired from service, and came to live in Taharabad, his native place in the Ahmednagar District. He was a regular *warkari* pilgrim of Pandharpur and the hereditary village accountant of Taharabad. This state of things continued until he was sixty-four years old, but being without an issue he felt naturally anxious lest the regular visits to Pandharpur would be discontinued after his own death. He therefore prayed to God to grant him a son, and a son was born to him in 1715 A. D. (*Shaka* era 1637). This son he named Mahipati, who was destined to become the biographer of saints. Mahipati was handsome and of a sharp intellect. In his very boyhood he was devoted to God and he went as a pilgrim to Pandharpur at the age of sixteen. It seems Mahipati was well educated. His handwriting was good. That he had a good knowledge of Sanskrit is proved by his translations into Marathi. Besides Marathi, his mother tongue, he knew Hindi. At the age of sixteen Mahipati's father died and the burden of supporting the family fell on him at that early age. Aside from his household responsibilities, he had to work as village accountant, an office hereditary in the family. Taharabad was then a part of a *jaghir* of a Muhammadan to whose court Mahipati had to go in his official capacity. Well substantiated is the story to which Dr. Abbott has alluded in his Preface, that once after bathing Mahipati was performing the worship of his household gods when a messenger from the Muhammadan came to summon him to court on business Mahipati sent word in return that he would be at his service after he was through his daily devotion. Nevertheless there was another and a very peremptory call to appear in court at once. Reluctantly he went, but on his return he took his pen from behind his ear and laying it before the god he vowed never to use it again in any official capacity. This vow was adhered to rigidly by his descendents and is to continue until the seventh generation.

Mahipati's Literary Sources and Methods

Mahipati had two sons, Vitthal and Narayan. Mahipati's *guru* was Tukaram from whom he received the mystic *mantra* in a dream. It is said Tukaram at the same time commanded Mahipati to write the lives of saints. Like most of the great writers, Mahipati is very modest, quotes some of his sources, and admits without reserve that he derived information from Nabhaji of North India and Uddhav Chidghan of Mandesh, both biographers of the saints. In Chapter 1.37–39 of the present work Mahipati says: 37. 'Perhaps you may say that I myself have composed this book, founding it on my own imagination and according to my own fancy, but sirs, that is truly not so. Have no doubts regarding this. 38. In the country to the North there was one by the name of Nabhaji, an *avatar* of Brahmadev. He wrote a great book containing the stories of saints. He wrote it in the Gwalior language. 39. And in Mandesh there was one Uddhavchidghan. He also wrote the stories of the saints. Uniting the stories of both, I have begun this book, the *Bhaktavijaya*.' Mahipati wrote the following biographical works: The *Santalilamrit* in 1757, the *Bhaktavijaya* in 1762, the *Kathasaramrita* in 1765, the *Bhaktalilamrit* in 1774, and finally the *Santavijaya*. Until recently the *Santavijaya* was supposed to have been incomplete with 26 chapters only but it is now found in a complete form (27 chapters) and is in the possession of the *Bharat Itihas Sanshodhak Mandal, Poona.* Besides his biographical works Mahipati also wrote several minor works. He died in 1790 at the age of seventy-five

Mahipati An Honest Author

Writing under this heading in his own *Life and Teaching of Tukaram* (pp. 70–72) in 1921, the editor of this present work (the Rev. J. F. Edwards) quoted the following statement which Dr. Abbott had drawn up at his request regarding Mahipati's trustworthiness. Dr. Abbott stated :— 'Is Mahipati's account true to facts ? Tukaram died in 1649 (traditional date) and Mahipati wrote his account in 1774, or 125 years after Tukaram's death. Not very long, but long enough for legends to grow. I regard Mahipati as an honest writer, that he used honestly the material at his disposal. He was not a "higher critic", but used as truth whatever came to him in the form of MSS or oral traditions. I think I can produce convincing evidence of this honesty. He had evidently a good library of manuscripts. I have the names of some he possessed, or was more or less familiar with. I find this list in his own writings. But as a poet he avows the principle of expanding the facts at his disposal, "as a seed expands into a tree." This is indeed a habit of Indian poets. What MSS or what oral tradition did Mahipati use ? This is as yet an unsolved problem, with this exception, that a few sources are known. Among the MSS he uses are the *Abhangs* by Tukaram's brother Kanhoba (see *Bhaktalilamrita* ch. 40.198 and following) and *Abhangs* of Rameshwar (*Bhaktalilamrita* ch. 40.209). There is also now published Niloba's *Gatha.* Niloba was a (posthumous) disciple of Tukaram's. He gives some account of Tukaram, and Mahipati knew of Niloba, so probably knew of his *Abhangs* (*Bhaktalilamrita*, ch. 40.238.) The last part of Mahipati's chapter 40, which describes Tukaram's "ascension," mentions many individuals who must have passed on to the next generation their knowledge of Tukaram. It still remains true that all modern accounts of Tukaram's life are to be traced to Mahipati as the practically sole source of information. Perhaps some time Mahipati's sources will be better known. This being so we cannot now know what are facts and what are fiction in Mahipati's account. It will not do merely to deduct the manifestly legendary, and call the balance facts, as seems to be the general practice. The only honest way for any modern writer is to give Mahipati credit for the account the writer gives, and give it as Mahipati gives it, legend and all, leaving it to the future, for possible discoveries to settle what are the real facts. Much of Mahipati's account may be facts, but I think events in Tukaram's life should not be recorded *as facts*, until they can be substantiated from other and clear sources.'

Mahipati's Historical Material

(b) 'As I have before remarked I regard Mahipati as an honest historian. He wrote from books before him, and from oral tradition. He anticipated the charge that he drew from his own imagination and says in *Santalilamrita* (1.67-69): "You will raise this doubt in your mind and say: You have drawn on your own imagination. This is not so. Listen. Great poet-saints have written books in many languages. It is on their authority that I write this *Santalilamrita.* If I wrote on my own authority my statements would not be respected. The Husband of Rukmini is witness to this, who knows all hearts." In *Bhaktavijaya* (1.37) he says: "You will say I have compiled this book on my own authority. This indeed is not so. Hold no doubts in your minds." He then quotes Nabhaji and Uddhav Chidghan as authorities: "Joining these two together, *Bhaktavijaya* was begun" (1.39). For a list of saints with whose names and books Mahipati was familiar see *Bhaktavijaya* (1.19), *Bhaktavijaya* (57.169–201) and *Bhaktalilamrita*, chap. 51, where there are 127 saints mentioned by name. His story of Dnyaneshwar in *Bhaktavijaya* (chap. 8) he took from *Dnyandevachi Adi* (Dnyandev's Origin) by Namdev. His story of Mirabai in *Bhaktavijaya* (chap. 38) he took from *Mirabaiche Charitra* (Life of Mirabai) by Namdev. His story of Gora Kumbhar in *Bhaktavijaya* (chap. 17) he took from *Goroba Kumbharache Charitra* (Life of Goroba Kumbhar) by Namdev. So far as evidence goes he conscientiously used his sources, as an honest recorder of what he believed to be true. If he expanded meagre statements into fuller detail it was not to add facts but to give a fuller understanding of them. To use his own words he "expanded facts just as a tree is the expansion of a seed." By this I understand that he embellished but did not add imaginary accounts, that what he wrote he felt he had good authority for. The faithfulness of Mahipati in recording the traditions received by him, either through books or oral sources, does not ensure the truth of these traditions, which must be established on other grounds, but it is satisfaction that one can depend with good assurance on his honesty as a writer, and that he did not draw on his imagination more than he felt necessary for poetic reasons.'

Mahipati's Trustworthiness

(c) Following on the above, Mr. Edwards concludes as follows in page 72 of *The Life and Teaching of Tukaram*:– 'In addition to the above from Dr. Abbott on the honesty and trustworthiness of our chief authority, Mahipati, we shall do well to note a striking illustration of Mahipatis' candour as provided by his faithful account of the attitude adopted towards caste by one of his Brahman saints. Dr. Sir R. G. Bhandarkar has pointed out that Mahipati makes " one of his Brahman saints declare that there is no caste among devotees of God and represents him to have drunk the holy water given to him by a *chambhar* or leather-worker." That Mahipati, a "Rigvedi Vasistha Gotri Deshasth Brahman," should have faithfully recorded that another Brahman winked at caste in relation to religious matters and should have portrayed him as receiving water at the hands of one of the lowest of India's out-castes is a remarkable illustration of Mahipati's honesty as an author. He sometimes even revises an earlier account of his own.' An interesting example of this is found in Mahipati's story in his earlier *Bhaktavijaya* that a poor old Brahman woman came to Tukaram and begged of him some clothes, whereas in telling the same story in his later *Bhaktalilamrit* Mahipati corrects himself by saying it was Rukhumai the goddess who came in the guise of a Maharani.

MAHIPATI—A GENERAL SURVEY

By Dr. G. V. Tagare

Here is Mahipati's *magnum opus*, The *Bhakta-Vijaya* (Victory of the devotees of the Lord), so excellently rendered into English as *Stories of Indian Saints* by Abbot and Godbole. Since its last edition in 1933, a great deal of research has been done both about the Bhakti-movement and the works and biographies of the saints described by Mahipati. Although Mahipati had a second-hand knowledge of Nābhāji's *Bhakta-māl*, (a work in dialectal Braj) in depicting the legends about saints in northern India, he had painstakingly studied the works of the saints of Maharashtra, visited their places, contacted their descendants and culled together the legendary stories from different sources before presenting them poetically in his work. Mahipati is not a historian in the strict sense of the term, as his motivation was spiritual. He believed in the *Advaita* (non-difference) between God and His devotees and thought that glorification of the saints or devotees of God is equally meritorious like singing the glories of the Lord. His passion for describing the spiritual exploits of saints was so strong that even at the fag-end of his life he undertook another work *Santa-Lilāmṛta*.

It is now generally accepted that the Bhakti movement in mediaeval India was a powerful integrating force which brought together Hindus (including Harijans) and Muslims as brothers on the same spiritual platform, engendered *esprit de corps* among the masses irrespective of castes and communities and inspired hope and confidence in the hearts of the downtrodden and the sufferers from foreign invasions as well as from intolerant orthodoxism. A reference to this work will show how Mahipati treats with equal veneration Muslim saints like Kabir, Kamal, Shaikh Mohammad, Harijan saints like Chokhā Melā, Bankā, Rohidās and Senā, non-Brahmin saints like Nāmadeva, Tukārāma and Brahmin saints like Jñānadeva, Ekanātha and Rāmadāsa. Mahipati was aware that under the physical, mental and temperamental differences of these saints, there is absolutely no distinction among the saints in the quality of their mystical or intuitive realization of God. And this awareness of the internal oneness of all saints is the *sine qua non* of the Viṭṭhala cult. "Though saints appear different (outwardly), they are one (internally) due to their oneness with God," remarks Rāmadāsa. And Rāmadāsa does not belong to the Viṭṭhala cult technically. In chapter 47 of this work, Mahipati records the legend that when Rāmadāsa, the staunch devotee of Rāma, visited Pandharpur, god Viṭṭhal manifested himself as Rāma to him. There had been no conflicts between Śaivites and Vaiṣṇavites in Maharashtra as in the South and there were no distinct currents (*Dhārās*) of the devotees of Rāma and of Kṛṣṇa as in the North India. Nāmadeva, Eknātha, Tukārāma—in fact all saints who followed the Viṭṭhala cult—glorified the importance of the name of Rāma along with that of Kṛṣṇa or Viṭṭhala.

This synthesis of Vaiṣṇavism and Śaivism is symbolised in the idol of Viṭṭhala. Though regarded as Viṣṇu, the icon is not a four-handed deity but pastoral Kṛṣṇa with his two arms placed on his waist and a *Śivaliṅga* on its head as its crest. Iconographically this icon is still a puzzle. Though saints in Maharashtra regard Viṭṭhal as the Buddha, the ninth incarnation of Viṣṇu, the image is positively not that of the Buddha or of Avalokiteśvara as is believed by some. Curiously enough its erect pose with both of its hands on the waist resembles *Birkuār*, the god-let of Ahīrs (Ābhīras) of western Bihar. The Ahīrs regard *Birkuār* as a form of Kṛṣṇa as we do in the case of Viṭṭhala. *Birkuār*-type idols are found in some parts of Maharashtra and Karnataka. Ahīrs or Ābhīras settled in ancient Maharashtra and their speech Ahirāṇī, a dialect of Marathi, is still current in northern Maharashtra. "Ābhīra", according to Sanskrit lexicons, means a cow-herd. It means that the majority of Ābhīras followed that pastoral profession in ancient times. According to the X Skandha of the *Bhāgavata Purāṇa*, Kṛṣṇa, in his boyhood, was brought up in a cow-herd community and all saints of the Viṭṭhala cult sing of this part of Kṛṣṇa's life prominently. This Kṛṣṇa opposed the tradition of offering a sacrifice to the Brahmanical god Indra then in vogue in his cow-herd community. He advocated instead the worship of cows and Govardhana hill that offered fodder to the cows (Bhāgavata Purāṇa X.34. 13-30).

Pandharpur, the centre of the Viṭṭhala cult, devoutly revered as *Bhū-Vaikuṇṭha* (the residence of god Viṣṇu on the earth), is in the Sholapur district of Maharashtra. It is, however, mentioned as "Paṇḍarige" in the famous "Cauryaiṁśicā Śilālekha"—a stone-inscription dated Śaka 1195 (A.D. 1223) in the Viṭṭhala Temple at Pandharpur and as "Pāṇḍuraṅga-pallī" (a small village called Pāṇḍuraṅga) in the Copperplate of Rāṣṭrakūṭa Avidheya of A.D. 516. Both the names show Dravidian influence in the area. The names however, do not shed any light on this cult. The fact that the most important *Yātrā* of this cult is on the eleventh day of the bright half of Āṣāḍha (July-August)—a period of rainy season in this part of the country when farmers should be busy with their farming operations suggests that this traditional *Melā* should be dated to the era of food-gathering economy. It has survived down to the period of food-growing economy just as pagan festivals survived in Christian Europe. But this information merely shows that Pandharpur was a place where the mass-*melā* of Indo-Aryan and Dravidian speakers traditionally met on that occasion since times immemorial.

The traditional founder of the deity is Puṇḍalīka who is said to be a *Koḷi*, a descendent of pre-Aryan Kolla settlers of Maharashtra. This traditional founder is reported to have been visited by god Viṭṭhala not due to his merits of Brahmanical rituals but due to his devotional service to his parents. Puṇḍalīka is credited to have thrown a brick to the God to stand upon as he was then busy serving his parents. And the God stood waiting, with both of his hands on his waist.

Such is the popular etymology of the name Viṭṭhala which is traced to *viṭa* "a brick" in Marathi. As a matter of fact, Viṭṭhala, Viṭhu, Viṭṭhu—Viṣṇu is due to the tendency of pronouncing Sk.—Ṣṇ—as-ṭṭh—current in Karnataka and Maharashtra at least since the 8th Century A.D. The other name of the deity, next in popularity to Viṭhu or Viṭṭhala is Pāṇḍuraṅga (white-complexioned one). The name is most inappropriate to the idol of Viṭṭhala, which is made of black stone. But as Hemacandra (12th Cent. A.D.) records in the *Deśi-nāma-mālā* (6.23) Pāṇḍuraṅga is the epithet of Śiva. The application of the names of Viṣṇu and Śiva to one and the same deity is not surprising as iconographically the image represents both the deities as seen above. The prevalence of the Hari-Hara cult and images representing both the gods (though in a different way than in the Viṭṭhala idol) were found in other parts of India also.

Though the period of Puṇḍalīka is not certain, the saint who gave a philosophical basis to this cult and is regarded as the founder* was Jñānadeva, (A.D. 1275 ?—1296) the victim of the intolerant centrifugal Hindu society which excommunicates its followers on the flimsiest pretext. Jñānadeva was, however, salvaged by a Śavite sect which retained the catholicity and *Karuṇā* of its Buddhistic predecessor. It is, however, noteworthy that Jñāndeva does not mention the name of Viṭṭhala or Pāṇḍuraṅga in his philosophical treatises—the *Bhāvārtha-Dipikā*, a commentary on the *Bhagavad-Gitā* now popularly known as *Jñāneśvari* and his mystic poem *Anubhavāmṛta*. It is only in *Abhaṅgas* attributed to him that we find him teaching the Viṭṭhala cult. The real credit of popularising the devotion to Viṭṭhala should rather be given to saints from the masses contemporaneous with Jñānadeva like Nāmadeva and others. These saints from practically all castes and communities preached a simple religion—faith

---

*ज्ञान देवें घातला पाया । रचियेलें देवालया ॥

—Bahinā Bāi

and devotion unto God, *Japa* of His Name, and fast on the eleventh day of each fortnight and an annual pilgrimage to Viṭṭhala at Pandharpur

The personalities who are draped in miraculous and fascinating legends by Mahipati in this work, were historically outstanding philosophers, social and religious reformers and eminent *litterateurs* of their age. All of them were 'mystics' (as R. D. Ranade designates them) who unanimously advocated the Bhakti cult and carried on a sustained struggle against discrimination between man and man and mal-practices in the name of religion.

Jayadeva (circa 1150-1250 A.D.) is the author of that supremely musical poem *Gīta Govinda* which became the source of inspiration to Fine Arts in medieval India. On the spiritual side, he was the exponent of *Madhurā Bhakti* long before the birth of Caitanya Mahāprabhu. Jñānadeva (A.D. 1271 or 1275—1296) was a revolutionary genius in more than one ways. When sacred works like the *Bhagavadgītā* (B.G.) were scrupulously protected from the "pollution" of the language of the masses, Jñānadeva wrote his *Bhāṣya, Bhāvārtha-dipikā,* in Marathi. His interpretation of the B.G. supplied a sound philosophic base to the Viṭṭhala cult.

Though he propagated his Yogic tradition separately and also entertained disciples of all caste to the *Bhakti sampradāya*, his selection of Nāmadeva to lead the *Sampradāya* and requisitioning his association in his (Jñanadeva's) pilgrimage to sacred places in North India, showed his farsightedness. Yogic back-ground, scholarship, *Karuṇā* for the dumb, and the downtrodden masses so deeply impressed his contemporaries that they and the later followers of the Viṭṭhala cult regard Jñanadeva as an incarnation of Viṣṇu.

Mahipati devoted the highest number of chapters to Nāmadeva (A.D. 1279-1350). Though elder to Jñānadeva, he was the disciple of Jñānadeva's disciple Visobā Khechar and is called the "servant" (*Kiṁkara*) of Jñānadeva by Bahinābāī. But long before he met Jñānadeva, he was an ardent devotee of Viṭṭhala. As recorded by non-Maharashtrian saints like Narsi Mehta (Gujarat) and Kabir (U.P.), it was reported that god Viṭṭhala drank the milk from the hands of child Nāmadeva, repaired the roof of his house and made the temple of god (Āvaḍhyā Nāganātha) turn round to enable the deity to have Nāmadeva in front of him. (Narsi Mehta—*Hāramālā* vv. 53, 82; also in Nāmadeva's *Mukhabāni* in *Ādi-Grantha* what is not known to Mahipati and to a large number of people in Maharashtra is Nāmadeva's work in the Punjab. We owe it to Sikh Guru Arjan Singh (A.D. 1561-1606) who, while compiling the *Ādi grantha* (Granth Sāhib) of Sikhs, included 61 poetic compositions of Nāmadeva in a mixed Braj-like dialect, as his *mukhabāni.* Hindi scholars like Vinay Mohan Sharma[1], Bhagirath Mishra and others call it "Hindi". After a prolonged dispute, it has now been established that Nāmadeva, the contemporary of Jñānadeva in Maharashtra is the same person who went to the Punjab probably in Circa A.D. 1325 and stayed there for 20 years. He had his headquarters at Ghoman in Gurudaspur Dist., though he spent most of his time in touring from place to place, preaching the efficacy of the name of the Lord.

Textual similarity between Nāmadeva's *Mukhabāni* in the *Ādi-grantha* and his Marathi *Abhaṅgas* (poems), identity in their teachings and glorification of god's name, sometimes of Rāma and at other places of Bī (vī) ṭhalu—(the latter is a loan-word from Marathi, the Panjabi form would have been Biśan), to lives or spiritual exploits of both Nāmadeva's are the same viz.: Viṭṭhala idol drinking milk from Nāmadeva's hand, repairing of the roof of his house by Viṭṭhala, bringing

1. i) Vinay Mohan Sharma—हिंदी को मराठी संतों की देन
   ii) S. P. Joshi—पंजाबातील नामदेव
   iii) Bhagirath Mishra and Rajnarayan Maurya—संत नामदेव की हिंदी पदावली (Poona University 1964).
   iv) नामदेव दर्शन Pub. Namadeva Samajonnati parishad, Kolhapur 1976.

back to life a dead cow in the Durbar of a Sultan. These and other factors have led to establish the identity of these two Nāmadevas'.

This identity makes Nāmadeva the first exponent of *Santamata* as Ramananda, Kabir, Nanak seem to have got inspiration from his work. He is probably the second Nirgunia after Jñānadeva who synthesized both the *Saguṇa* and *Nirguṇa* types of Bhakti. His associates and disciples included Brahmins, as well as men from goldsmith, potter, barber, Harijans communities.

Bahinābāī rightly gives the credit of extending the temple of Bhakti to this "servant" of Jñānadeva.[1]

Though Mahipati did not observe a chronological sequence in the arrangement of chapters, the next important saint is Ekanātha (A.D. 1533 ?—1599). He was the greatest scholar-philosopher-saint-poet *cum* social reformer of the 16th Century Maharashtra. But as we have already written in details about him[2], we may pass on to the towering personalities of the 17th Century (Maharashtra) viz. Tukārāma and Rāmadāsa.

Next to Nāmadeva, Tukārāma is respected by *Vārakaris* (followers of the Viṭṭhala cult). As stated above, Mahipati studied his literature, visited this native place Dehu and based his chapters on Tukārāma on the legends he got from Gopāla Bābā, the great-grandson of Tukārāma. Being a product of a credulous age (as many of us are even today), Gopāla Bābā thought that it is not his literature and piety but attribution of miracles that would enhance the greatness of Tukārāma, and Mahipati believing in them as historical facts depicted them in a highly poetic way. Modern researchers, however, have established that Tukārāma was not a destitute nor a simpleton. Though he discontinued his hereditory *Mahājanaship* and money-lending profession, he owned a big house,

---

1. नामा त्याचा किंकर । त्यानें केला हो विस्तार —Bahinā Bāi
2. Introduction to J. E. Abbot's *The Life of Ekanath* (Motilal Banarsidass, Delhi, 1980)

had his private Viṭṭhala temple with a land-grant of 15 *Bighas*, had sufficient landed property other than this land-grant. Hence he could condemn begging in the strongest terms.[1]

Bahiṇābāī, his spiritually advanced disciple who stayed at Dehu to the end of Tukārāma's life, does not record him to be a *Vārakarī* but notes that he spent most his time in *Sādhanā* in his private Viṭṭhala Temple. She does not record the formation of *Ṭālkaris* at the time of his *Kīrtana* and hints that Tukārāma wrote his *Abhaṅgas* himself, the manuscript of which due to the absence of Tukārāma's wife and children from Dehu for 25 years after his death, is now irrecoverably lost. As a miracle, she records that God preserved the Abhaṅga-books of Tukārāma dry in water, for 13 days. People still believe that Tukārāma went to Vaikuṇṭha physically (in his mortal body). Bahiṇābāī states that Tukārāma suddenly passed away in the presence of all.[2]

The epithet *Caitanya* in the names of the two spiritual predecessors of Tukārāma misled many to link up Tukārāma to the Caitanya *Sampradāya* of Bengal.[3] It is true that Nimāī or Gaurāṅga Prabhu came to Pandharpur where he was initiated in Kṛṣṇa cult by Īśvara Purī and he spent some six years in the Deccan before he went to Orissa. But philosophically, (if we are to believe Baladeva, the Commentator of the *Brahma Sūtras* as per Caitanya's Cult), Caitanya was a *Dvaiti*, a follower of Madhva. In his *Prameya Ratnāvali* which Baladeva regards as the summary of the nine *Prameyas* (proved propositions) of Caitanya, the world is regarded as real and

---

1. भिक्षापात्र अवलंबणे । जको जिणें लाजिरवाणे ॥
2. तुकारामा तंव देखतां देखत । आले अकस्मात मृत्युरूप

(Abhaṅg No. 74)

V. S. Bendra—तुकाराम महाराज यांचे सांगाती pp. 83-108. The whole book is worth perusal (Mauj Pub. Bombay 1958)

3. For example M. T. Kennedy—*The Chaitanya Movement*, p. 42 Pub. Y. M. C. A., Calcutta

that difference (of souls etc.) is real. This is against the teachings of Tukārāma—in fact against the teachings of all saints of the Viṭṭhala cult (and of Rāmadāsa as well). A reference to any standard catalogue of Sk. MSS. will show a number of authors bearing the epithet Caitanya but having absolutely no relation with Gaurāṅga Prabhu.

Mahipati bases Viṭṭhala's manifestation as Rāma to Rāmadāsa on the basis of his own Abhaṅga at the sight of Viṭṭhala. It shows his realization of oneness of Rāma and Viṭṭhala, if not an attempt to mobilise the followers of Viṭṭhala to the cause of Shivaji.

A lot of research has been carried out on Hindi and Gujrati saints like Kabir, Tulasīdās, Sūrdās, Narsī Mehtā. But Mahipati had only a second-hand knowledge about them through the works of Nābhājī and Uddhava Cidghana. In fact our knowledge about many Maharashtrian saints described by him is still very limited. We owe gratitude to him for preserving for us their names and legends for further research.

This is not a critique of Mahipati, but an attempt to present succinctly the research on these saints since 1933. Mahipati deserves our gratitude for presenting these legends in a fascinating, poetic style. The very fact that he devoutly describes the legends of all saints irrespective of caste, language, state or community shows that he had imbibed the fundamental tenet of philosophy of Bhakti:

ekaṁ sad, viprā bahudhā vadanti |

that difference (jatyadi etc.) is real. This is against the teachings of Tukārāma—in fact against the teachings of all saints of the Vitthala cult (and of Rāmadāsa as well). A reference to any standard catalogue of the MSS will show a number of authors bearing the epithet Caitanya but having absolutely no relation with Kṛṣṇa Caitanya.

In the same way, Vitthala's manifestation as Rāma to Rāmadāsa on the basis of his own Abhanga "The sight of Vitthala" shows his realization of oneness of Rāma and Vitthala; it is not an attempt to proselytise the followers of Vitthala to the cause of Shivaji.

A lot of research has been carried out on Hindi and Gujarati saints like Kabir, Tulsidas, Sūrdās, Narsi Mehta; but Mahipati had only a second-hand knowledge about them through the works of Nabhaji and Uddhava Cidghana. In fact our knowledge about many Maharashtrian saints described by him is still very limited. We owe gratitude to him for preserving for us their names and legends for further research.

This is not a critique of Mahipati, but an attempt to present succinctly the research on these saints since [illegible]. Mahipati deserves our gratitude for preserving these legends in a fascinating poetic style. The very fact that he devoutly describes the legends of all saints irrespective of caste, language, state or community shows that he had imbibed the fundamental tenet of philosophy of Bhakti.

[illegible]

BHAKTAVIJAYA

BY

MAHIPATI

CHAPTER I

INVOCATION

OBEISANCE TO SHRI GANESH

1. Obeisance to Shri Sarasvati (goddess of speech). Obeisance to my *guru*. Obeisance to Rukmini and Pandurang. Victory, Victory, to Thee whose place of enjoyment is the bank of the Bhima river, Lover of Thy *bhaktas*. Ocean of mercy, Who, although pervading all the animate and inanimate, art different from them, and dost extend far beyond all existing things. 2. Yet assuming the form of Ganesh and Sarasvati, Thou hast appeared as if existing in many forms. Therefore, at the beginning of this book I have bowed to Sarasvati and Ganesh. 3. Let us bow to the *sadguru* Tukaram, who discarded the illusions of this worldly existence, showed me love for his name; and removed me from this earthly existence. 4. Now let us bow to the great poets, Vyasa, the *Muni* Vālmiki, Bhargav, Shuka, Narada, and the poets Ushana, and Jaimini, who are the first to be bowed to. 5. Now let us bow to saints and good men, whom Hari (God) loves with all his heart, and who in this *Kali Yuga* came to save the dull, the fools and the ignorant. 6. I have begun this book, the *Bhaktavijaya*, but in order that it may be carried to completion, all of you must help. Just as when in a poor man's house some function is planned, his rich neighbours assist him. 7. Just as a man, full of kindness and endowed with sight, enables a blind man to visit sacred places, so do

you by your gift of kindness make these verses acceptable to the hearers. 8. I am mentally dull and ignorant. I have never studied the art of poetry. I have never read the books known as *Puranas.* I do not know the divine (Sanskrit) language. 9. But here there is one special thing that Hari (God) is fond of, the stories of His *bhaktas*, so the God Shiva has said in the *Bhavishyottar Purana.* 10. And therefore a desire has arisen in my mind out of intense love for the stories of the *bhaktas*, but the attempt is like that of the water bird, the *titavi*, saying to itself, 'I will drink the ocean dry.' 11. Who am I to attempt to describe the attributes of Hari (God)? For when the *Vedas* attempted to describe Him even they had to be absolutely silent. The attempt made the serpent Shesha's tongue to be cloven, and it made itself into a couch for Hari. 12. Since Brahmadev, Indra and Shiva do not know His limits, how can I describe His attributes, I a poor miserable sinner? 13. When an infant obstinately insists on anything, the mother supplies it at once; so He, the Merciful to the Lowly, will grant me my obstinate longing. 14. The child Dhruva desired to sit on his father's lap, and Hari gave him an everlasting seat. 15. When Upamanyu asked for a cup of milk, He gave him the whole ocean of milk. So, I know that He, the Merciful to the Lowly, will supply my intense desire. 16. The *bhaktas* who descended to the earth during the *Krita*, *Treta*, and *Dvapara Yugas*, they are the very ones who in this *Kali Yuga* have become manifest as saviours of mankind. 17. I have felt intense joy in relating the stories connected with them, so now, my hearers, be careful to give close attention to me. 18. I am neither a clever nor a wise man. I have read but little of Vedantic books. know nothing of the Sanskrit language. This the glorious husband of Rukmini knows. 19. Long ago Eknath wrote his version of *Ramayana* at the inspiration of the saints, but I have neither those words of blessing, nor any inspiration. 20. Namdev and Mukteshwar described Vishnu in the *Bharata*, but I have no inspiration like them. 21. In the commentary by Vaman on the glorious *Bhagavata* and in the *Harivijaya* composed by Shridhar their words carry blessing, but in my attempt to speak such words of blessing I have not been able to use them. 22. In the *Bodharaja* composed by Ramdas, he pleads in his verses with the Giver of salvation, but in my attempt to speak words of blessing I have failed. 23. Ganeshnath, Keshavaswami, Salaya, are all well known in the world for their sweet compositions (in Marathi) while Kabir wrote in Hindustani, the language of his own country. 24. Such were the good saints whose books make the ignorant wise: this is a most remarkable fact. 25. In Pratishthan (Paithan), Dnyaneshwar made a male buffalo repeat the *Vedas*. To such saints, merciful in character I bow at the beginning of this book. 26. Just as when a little stream of water acquires holiness when it flows into the river Ganges and becomes the very same in nature; or just as iron becomes a golden ornament for the rich man the moment it comes in contact with the touchstone (the *paris*); 27. or as when any one sings the praise of kings the sons of the minister regard that praise as rightly given: so as I relate the stories of the saints good men are delighted. 28. As in the case of a river that is not distinguished by being mentioned, it receives the reverence of men when it joins the sea; or as when a man sits in the shadow of a wish-tree, neither poverty nor disaster harms him; 29. so, although I am so dull-minded, yet when I relate the character and deeds of God's *bhaktas* the Merciful One will have pity on me. 30. I bow to the ground before Vasishtha in whose family line I was born. May He in his mercy cause this book to reach completion. 31. And now let me bow to my mother and father, to whom I give honour higher than to all the sacred places, through whom by my good fortune I gained this human body.

32. As I bow to the Husband of Rukmini who is the family deity of both my maternal and paternal family lines, surely all the gods feel satisfaction. 33. Just as when one worships the sea, the hearts of all rivers are made happy; or as when one looks at the moon, all stars become visible; 34. or as when one travels round the world rapidly, that journey must include all sacred places; or as the worship of the Son of Vinata (Eagle, the vehicle of Vishnu) is the same as the worship of all birds; 35. so when I worship the deity Pandurang (Krishna) all the gods are made happy. The function of supporting all things rests on Him, Pandharinath, the God Supreme. 36. He, Vishnu, is the giver of all intellect. In whatever manner he may cause me to compose my verses, saints and other good men must with reverence and love listen to them.

SOURCES AND ENCOURAGEMENT

37. Perhaps you may say that I myself have composed this book, founding it on my own imagination and according to my own fancy, but sirs, that is truly not so. Have no doubts regarding this.

38. In the country to the North there was one by the name of Nābhāji, an *avatar* of Brahmadev. He wrote a great book containing the stories of the saints. He wrote it in the Gwalior language. 39. And in Māndesh there was one Uddhvachidghan. He also wrote the stories of the saints. Uniting the stories of both, I have begun this book, the *Bhaktavijaya*. 40. The Husband of Rukmini who abides on the bank of the glorious river Bhima, has given me the needed encouragement, and he has caused me to write this profound book. So good people, listen with love. 41. A child speaks in broken words, but its mother

expresses her delight. So my very uncouth language I think you will accept. 42. Or as a streamlet flows into the river Ganges, the river makes it like itself; so by making you friendly to me my verses will be acceptable. 43. If clay should become one with the fragrant musk, it will arrive at value; so you will accept my commonplace language. 44. Or as when a tiny drop of water falls into milk, it makes the drop like itself; so through your kindness my words will become acceptable to you. 45. That you are saints, the very image of God, is the firm conviction of my mind. Therefore, I, Mahipati, bow to you in reverence.

EVILS OF THE KALI YUGA

46. And now listen with attention. At the end of the *avatarship* of Shri Krishna during the *Kali Yuga*, when the offering of sacrifices and giving of benevolent gifts had ceased, 47. Brahmans had neglected their religious obligations, and the Kshatriyas had given up rational thinking. *Sannyasis* had abandoned their duties and Brahmans (earth-gods) had ceased to observe the duties of the fourth stage of life. 48. Sons would not listen to the commands of their parents. Disciples would not serve their religious teachers. Husbands listening to the wishes of their wives, went to live in the homes of their fathers-in-law. 49. No one cared to go to sacred places. No one listened with reverence to the reading of the *Puranas*. And giving up the Hari-praise-services, they delighted in watching indecent dramatizations. 50. Brahmans cast aside the Shaligram and installed in their homes the idols of inferior deities. They threw away the rosary made of the *tulsi* and *rudrāksha* and wore around their necks garlands made of glass beads. 51. Rich persons disliked to make gifts. Those in health had no desire for religious acts. Kings had no love for their subjects, and justice and morality were put aside. 52. Women of noble birth

became slaves of others. Parents sold their daughters just as they sold horses. Muhammadans slaughtered cows as the king Kali became powerful. 53. Many spoke falsehood and insulted *Sadhus* (godly *Sannyasis*). They declared as true, things that were false; they gave a false witness. 54. The repeating of *Gayatri* (a prayer to the Sun) ceased. Magical formulas took their place. Evil men, pretending to be trustworthy to the pious, murdered them. 55. The images of deities would be mere stones, and then Muhammadans would smash them to pieces. The visiting of sacred places would be taxed. Thus the *Kali Yuga* (the evil age) brought trouble to men. 56. There is no sin equal to that of falsehood. There is no virtue equal to truth, but *Kali Yuga* caused all truth to disappear and evil deeds multiplied without limit. 57. When Rahu (the monster that swallows the sun, creating an eclipse) arises, darkness fills the sky; or when death approaches, a multitude of diseases attack the body; 58. or when night falls, ghosts leave the cemeteries; or when an unfortunate person sees himself without good fortune, pains and poverty come upon him; 59. or as when a teacher becomes angry the result is ignorance, or when the period of youth arrives, pride fills the heart; 60. or when men of crooked life come into an assembly, they naturally indulge in insults ; thus during the existence of *Kali Yuga* unlimited sins appeared. 61. *Rishis* went away to Badrikashram, while Brahmans neglected their religious duties. When this was once happening, an earthquake took place. 62. Then Shri Hari (God) in heaven thought over the sad conditions of His *bhaktas*. He saw terrible sins committed on earth among mortals. 63. All sacrifices and offerings had ceased. Brahmans had cast aside the doing of good deeds. Ignorant men sank in the sea of sorrow. 64. As the Husband of the Daughter of the Ocean (God) thought of what was to be done, all His *bhaktas* joined their hands palm to palm and stood before Him. 65. Then they said to Him, 'Vishnu, give us some command.' Then He who enjoys dwelling on the ocean of milk (Vishnu) spoke thus to His *bhaktas*: 66. 'Long ago I became an *avatara* and killed evil demons, setting free the whole world from enemies. I am now carrying on the Buddha *Avatara*. 67. Now I wish you all to become *avatars* in the world of mortals, in as many places as I have an abode, and in the ancient sacred places. 68. For example, in the forest called Dindir there is a place named Pandhari. Uddhav should become an *avatar* and turn the inhabitants of the southern country (Deccan) to worship me. 69. Akrur should become an *avatar* at Mathura and Gokulvrindavan, and by his preaching turn all their inhabitants to my worship. 70. The *bhakta* Daruk should become the *avatar* Ramdas in the Western country, and cause the whole country to worship me. 71. In the East at Jagannath, Vyas should become an *avatar*. He should cause men to listen to my extraordinary deeds. 72. In Hastināpur (ancient Delhi) the well known sacred place, Vālmīki should become an *avatar* and turn everyone to worship me with extreme reverence. 73. I became the Ram *avatar*, and at that time you became monkeys. I killed Ravan, and delivered Indra together with all the other gods. 74. They were the very ones who in the time of Krishna's *avatar* became cowherds, and others became loving Yadavas. He slaughtered Kansa and other demons and protected cows and Brahmans. 75. And now becoming Buddha I am remaining quiet. Who dares to sing my praises to men, except you? 76. For your sake I took human form with visible qualities. Otherwise who would have paid attention to me? Aside from my *bhaktas* I see no one dear to me.' 77. While thus the Husband of Kamala (Vishnu) spoke, the *bhaktas* shouted 'Victory, Victory', adding 'Thou art God, Merciful to the Lowly. This we have now fully understood. 78. As the rays proceed from the sun, as gold comes out of clay, so we Thy *bhaktas* are purified by Thee, Shri Hari. 79. Or as trees develop from water, or as clusters of stars arise in the heaven, so we Thy *bhaktas* are (dependent on) Thee, Shri Hari. 80. As cloth comes from threads, as light comes from lamps, so we Thy *bhaktas* are purified by Thee, Shri Hari. 81. As fishes develop from water, as honey comes from flowers, so we Thy *bhaktas* seem important because of Thee. 82. As the bracelet is made of gold, as the wind comes out of the sky, so we Thy *bhaktas* have become *avatars* on earth with human qualities. 83. As the dolls of the juggler are made to dance by pulling a string, so Thou noble Ram, didst cause us to capture Ceylon. 84. A fife gives out a sweet sound, but it must be played by one who knows how to play it; so during the *avatarship* of Krishna, Thou didst perform great deeds through us. 85. According to Thy will, everything, Brahmadev and the other gods included, come into existence and then disappear. At Thy will, Thou hast created an infinite number of universes, and then Thou dost destroy them. 86. So according to Thy command, O Vishnu, we will hasten and turn mankind to Thy worship.'

VISHNU ALLOTS AVATARSHIPS

87. Having heard their reply, the Husband of Kamala (Vishnu) replied to Uddhava, 'I wish you to become an *avatar* by name of Namdev in the family line of a tailor. 88. And in becoming that *avatar* on earth in the sacred city of Pandhari, cause men to hear the infinite number of my names. 89. The deeds which I showed you in my *avatars* as Ram and Krishna, I wish you to make known to the ears of mankind. 90. In the *Kali Yuga* my name is the Only Saviour.' Thus spoke the Husband of Rama to Uddhava. 91. Vishnu then said to Shuka, 'I wish you to become an *avatar* in the family of a Muhammadan, and I will give you birth in an unusual way. 92. Become my *bhakta* Kabir. Go there as my representative and proclaim widely

the extraordinary power of my name.' 93. Then Vishnu said to Vālmīki, 'I wish you to become the Brahman Tulsidas and cause men to realize in this *Kali Yuga* an intense love for worship. 94. You composed the *Ramayana*, a thousand million verses in which you spoke of the future You should describe the same glory in the vernacular (Hindi) language, and turn men to worship me.' 95. 'Daruka, I wish you to become at once at Dakur the Brahman Ramdas, and in return for your devotion for me I will rush to your aid from Dvaraka.' 96. The Creator of the universe said to Shiva, 'I wish you to become Narsi Mehta and cause the inhabitants of Junagad to hear the stories connected with the path of devotion. 97. I wish you to hasten before me. I also will soon follow you in the form of Dnyaneshwar. I shall explain the meaning of the *Bhagavadgita*. 98. Brahmadev will become Sopan; Sadashiv will become Nivritti; Adimaya will become Muktabai; and descend to the earth as *avatars*.' 99. So spoke Vishnu and all clapped their hands with cries of 'Victory, Victory,' and the gods showered flowers upon them. The immortals rejoiced. 100. They said, Blessed is this day; the Life of the World has been pleased with us. We will now descend to the world of mortals and carry on our work of salvation. 101. The world of mortals seems to us to be superior to the heavens, Vaikuntha and Kailas. Here both sin and righteousness are harvested, as also sacrifices and offerings. 102. As the fruit of good deeds done in the world of action comes to an end in heaven, souls are pushed back to the world of action. 103. In this world of mortals it is possible to be united to the feet of Hari. In this world of mortals, one can attain to Hari's heaven. Through birth here, the praise of Hari falls on the ears of every one. 104. Therefore, we gods will become *avatars*.' Thus speaking the gods returned to the heaven of Indra. 105. The noble *Vaishnavas* will now become *avatars* as we shall see, in order to save the world. Let your ears now listen to the stories of saints.

106. Perhaps you will say in your mind, that these stories are not in the *Puranas* composed by Vyas. By bringing this into your mind, you will fall into the forest of doubts. 107. Still, in the latter part of the *Bhavishya Purana*, Vyas himself declared that in the *Kali Yuga* the *bhaktas* in heaven will become *avatars* voluntarily among a race of inferior beings. 108. They will perform in men's sight the most remarkable deeds and cause Vishnu Himself to be subject to them. They will proclaim the glory of God's name and be filled with the knowledge of the Vedanta. 109. I have already related what *avatarships* the Vaishnavas, *bhaktas* of God, were to assume. This I have already related in detail. Do you, good people, listen to it with pleasure. 110. In the next chapter there will be a relating of the story of Shri Jayadev, a man absolutely pure. Mahipati herewith states, 'Let all saints and good men give close attention to me.' 111. *Svasti.* This book is the *Bhaktavijaya.* The Lord of the earth will be pleased as he listens to it. Let the pious, God-loving *bhaktas* listen. This is the first delightful chapter

———

CHAPTER II

JAYADEV

Obeisance

Obeisance to Shri Ganesh. Obeisance to Shri Krishna who appeared among the cowherds.

1. After this Vishnu said, 'Vyas, what you have said in the *Purana* is not understood in the *Kali Yuga* by ignorant men, because of its difficulties. 2. I wish you to become an *avatar* in the form of Jayadeva, and bring about the salvation of mankind.' Having thus heard the wish of Vishnu, Vyas prostrated himself on the ground before Him. 3. In accordance with Vishnu's wish, Vyas became a full *avatar* in a Brahman family, in a town by the name of Tundubilva, near the sacred city devoted to Jagannath, Lord of the universe. 4. The Brahman belongs to the highest caste. He is chief among the four castes. Here Vyas descended voluntarily as an *avatar*. 5. Day by day he grew in stature. His mother and father invested him with the sacred thread. Without the effort of study he became skilled in all the sciences. 6. As the moon cannot be hidden among a multitude of stars, or as the eagle among birds, or as the god Indra among other gods; 7. or as God Shiva (Shankar) among ascetics, or as the Husband of Rukmini (Krishna) among the Yadavas, or as a jewel in the midst of gold; 8. or as a hero in an army, or as the sun in the sky, or as an ocean above all ponds; 9. or as a clever listener among the ignorant, or as a speaker in a Hari Kirtan, or as a royal swan among birds–these the wise can recognize from afar; 10. or as a prince among paupers, or as pure devotion among all the other means of worship; so Jayadeva appeared amongst the Brahmans as a great orator.

11. He studied the Vedas and the Shastras. He went through all the *Puranas.* He discovered that in the *Kali Yuga* the praising of God was the chief means of salvation.

JAYADEV'S GITA--GOVINDA AND KING SATVIK

12. The Husband of Rukmini (Krishna) said to Uddhav, 'In the *Kali Yuga* I wish you to worship me by singing my praise.' Therefore, the poet Jayadev composed the poetic work called *Gita-Govinda.* 13. The theme of this poem is from the *Padma Purana*, about the love-actions of the Lord of the Universe with Radha, and also His voluntary plays in Gokul in his Krishna *avatar.* 14. The actions of Shri Hari are already enchanting; and moreover Jayadev has sung them in a beautiful manner in the form of a poem. This is like setting a diamond in a golden bracelet. 15. He composed a book called *Gita-Govinda* which everyone copied and took away with him. They joyfully committed it to memory and sang it in every house. 16. Flowers may be in one place, but their fragrance spreads everywhere. So this book, the *Gita-Govinda* became known throughout the world. 17. There was a King in Jagannath whose name was Satvik. He also composed a book similar to that of Jayadev. 18. He had copies made of his book, sent them to people and ordered it to be read by all. 19. When the *pandits* heard this news, they were very angry. These wise ones assembled at Jagannath and said to the King, 20. 'You have composed a book which is pleasing to yourself. You have even put it on an equality with that of Jayadev, and are therefore talking nonsense. 21. But those who are really wise never praise their own works with their own lips. But you are telling all men to commit your book to memory. 22. If you shout out, "Take this knowledge, take this divine service, this mantra of a particular *guru*, and this knowledge of *Brahma*, this garland, and this great diamond," it loses its

value. 23. With your own lips to praise your own cleverness and the beauty of your own poetry, is as foolish as it is to praise the musk, the sandalwood of Mount Maila, or saffron, or the odorous testicle of a wild cat. 24. If you also try to fix the value of a daughter or a pearl, of a book or a rich cloth, of black *ambergris* or the wind on the Mount of Malaya, it is really lowering their true value.' 25. The Brahmans continued, 'O King, you have composed this book in vain. You are holding pride in your heart. This is not pleasing to God.' 26. The king replied, 'Bring both books here at once, and we will place them for the night before the idol of Jagannath. 27. Jayadev sang the praises of God's goodness, and I also did the same. The book that is not acceptable to God, He will throw out of the temple.' 28. Both books were immediately brought and placed before the idol. The doors were locked, and the priests came out of the temple. 29. On the next morning early all the Brahmans assembled together, and at the time of wickwaving all the priests also came into the temple. 30. There they saw the superior book of Jayadeva. This book was placed near Him, by the Supreme Being. The king's book was treated with contempt and tossed outside the temple. 31. Hands were clapped with shouts of 'Victory, Victory.' The assembled Brahmans rejoiced and the king had to hang his head in shame. 32. The *pandits* said to the king, 'Milk and water have now been separated. How can a book on the Vedanta philosophy and an immoral book be placed on an equality? 33. How can a royal swan and a crow, or a learned *pandit* and an out-caste Mang, or tinplate and pure gold be considered as of equal value? 34. How can the babhul tree and the sandlewood tree, the sandalwood on Mount Maila and the fruit *hingan*, a good man and a bad man, be considered equal?' 35. How can a saint and a reviler, a deceiver and a pious man, the god Indra and a pauper, be evenly matched? 36. So your poem and the *Gita-Govinda* of Jayadev, could not be brought to any equality, and yours was therefore thrown out by Jagannath.' 37. When the king heard them say this he was greatly ashamed. He went and stood before the image of Jagannath. 38. Joining his hands palm to palm, he said to God, 'O Jagannath, I now understand the meaning of the names you bear. 39. Your name is Purifier of the Sinful. I think this is not true in that you discard one, and call another your own. 40. You are alike to every being, pervading everything, O God. One who is a *bhakta* and one who is not a *bhakta* both live by Thy power. 41. The sun shines in every vessel. Just as water is to a cow and a tiger, so Thou, O Lord of the Yadavas, art alike to every being. 42. Just as to a locust and an eagle all space is the same, so art Thou, O Lord of the universe, alike to every living being. 43. A child is the same to its mother, whether ignorant or wise; so Thou, O Purifier of the Fallen, art alike to all. 44. The moon is the same to both king and despised pauper; so Thou, O Husband of Rukmini, art alike in every one. 45. O Jagannath, Thou didst cause Jayadev to utter his poem in the world. Then, O Infinite One, tell me who is the mover of *my* heart. 46. This being so, O Jagannath, you threw my book outside. I therefore shall now commit suicide.' Thus spoke the king. 47. As God heard his pleading words, He was pleased and He took from the king's book twenty-four verses 48. The Life of the World then wrote them down in Jayadeva's book. By doing so the King was comforted.

JAYADEV'S MARRIAGE

49. There was a Brahman in the sacred city of Jagannath with sacrificial duties. He had a jewel of a daughter born to him by name of Padmavati. 50. Her beautiful

form seemed like that of Lakshmi's. Therefore the noble Brahman gave her the name of Padmavati. 51. The Brahman thought to himself, 'My daughter is a mountain of beauty and goodness, so I must with reverence offer her to Jagannath.' 52. When Brahmans came to ask her in marriage, seeing her beauty, he would tell them that she had been offered to Krishna. 53. Every one understood this, and she grew up day by day. The Pervader of the World came to the Brahman in a dream. 54. Jagannath said to the Brahman, 'You offered your daughter to me, but I live in the *Kali Yuga* in the form of Buddha. 55. Now the poet Jayadev is a portion of me, an *avatar* of mine. You should give her to Jayadev with all her ornaments' 56. Waking from this dream, the Brahman was exceedingly happy. And after inviting Jayadev *Swami* to his house, an agreement for marriage was made. 57. The Brahmans examined their horoscopes. They showed a value of thirtysix points. All preparations were made, including ornaments. 58. The deity presiding over marriage was installed; the Brahmans were feasted; and the god Ganpati (Destroyer of obstacles) was worshipped. The Brahmans held the marriage curtain. The words of blessing were pronounced by the priest. 59. 'O Keshav, O Narayan, O Madhav, O Govinda, O Gopal, O God Supreme, O Slayer of Madhu, O Madhav, protect this bride and bridegroom. 60. O Krishna, Vishnu, Vaman, Ram, O Advocate of Thy *bhaktas*, O Home of all goodness, O Imprisoner of Bali, O Trivikram, protect this bride and bridegroom. 61. O Protector of the cowherds, Dweller in Dwarka, O Lord of Pandhari, O Krishna, Protector of the World, O Thou mountain of goodness, protect this bride and bridegroom. 62. O Thou who dwellest in the heaven Vaikunth, O Husband of Rukmini, Dweller in the ocean of milk, Recliner upon the serpent Shesha, O Protector of the *bhaktas*, O Mine of goodness, protect this bride and bridegroom. 63. O Ram, who dwellest in Ayodhya, and who protects his *bhaktas* in time of distress.' These were the verses the Brahmans uttered as they performed the wedding ceremony. 64. Suddenly there was one great shout of 'Victory, Victory.' Innumerable musical instruments were sounded. For four days the festival lasted and the wedding parties were honoured. 65. Jayadev *Swami* continued to live in Jagannath. He continued praising God daily with great love. He performed the services of praise.

THE PIOUS MERCHANT

66. There was a merchant there, who was a God-loving pious man and exceedingly generous. Jayadev seeing that he was worthy of being initiated made him his disciple. 67. One should not be accepted as a disciple who is unfaithful and miserly, who is always looking for faults in others, one who is desirous of the property of others. 68. One should not be accepted as a disciple who is an evil-doer and a great rascal, who hates his father and mother, whose ways are filthy, who lives an immoral life. 69. One should not be accepted as a disciple who is very loquacious and extremely garrulous, who does not enjoy singing the praises of God, who preaches the doctrine of Brahma without any experience of it himself. 70. One should not be accepted as a disciple who does not believe in the *Vedas* and *Shastras*, who will not listen to the words of the saints, who has no campassion on living beings.

71. Such a one this merchant was not. He was supremely pious, exceedingly generous, always alert to serve his *guru* with body, speech and mind. 72. One day he invited Jayadev *Swami* to come to his home. He seated the *Swami* in a carriage and brought him into the city. 73. It is impossible to attain to the praise of the goodness of God or to thoughts of the doctrine of Brahma without fellowship with the good. 74. Pardon,

peace, mercy, unselfishness, sacrifices, benevolences, cannot be attained without association with the good. 75. Generosity, courage, faith, knowledge, postures for breathings, can never be attained without association with the good. 76. It was for this purpose that the merchant took Jayadev to his home, and there served him day and night with great zeal. 77. Jayadev *Swami* performed the services of praise day and night in that city. He helped the dull-minded, the ignorant and the doers of evil to a life of devotion to God. 78. He remained there a month. He then said to the merchant, 'Give me permission now to return to Jagannath.' 79. The merchant said to Jayadev, 'Place thy hands upon my head. Let thy favour be on me as thy servant for ever.' 80. The merchant then seated him on a golden chair and worshipped him with great love. Meanwhile he was thinking in his mind what he should give to his *Guru* as his religious gift? 81. 'Jewels, silver and gold are like earth to the *Swami*, so I will send some money to the *Guru's* wife.' 82. So without the knowledge of the *Swami* he placed in a carriage many kinds of brilliant diamonds, garlands of pearls and golden ornaments. 83. After that, having properly arranged a seat, he placed Jayadev in the carriage with reverence, sent a clever man along with him, and thus saw him off for some distance. 84. He said to his man at that time, 'Go to his home and tell Padmavati that I bow at her feet. 85. Without the knowledge of the *Swami*, I have given raiments and ornaments. Offer them to the *Guru's* wife and quickly return.' 86. After accompanying Jayadev for some distance the merchant returned to his own city. Now that day there were two thieves who came walking behind Jayadev. 87. These thieves learned the news that Jayadev had gone from the city and that the merchant had made a secret gift. Therefore the two thieves walked behind Jayadev. 88. The merchant had given a man to accompany Jayadev. He said to Jayadev, 'It is very necesary that I return to my home, I have some urgent business there.' 89. Hearing this remark Jayadev said to him, 'Return to your home and carry your business to completion. 90. A female slave, a male slave, a wife, a beast, a tree, an insect, an ant, as they wander about in this life, have to endure the life of subordination.' 91. Therefore Jayadev felt compassion in his heart. Having given this man permission to leave he sent him back to his home. 92. And so he went through the forest quite alone, driving the cart himself. Suddenly the two thieves appeared walking behind him. 93. They waited for an opportunity and coming near him the thieves made him a *namaskar* (obeisance), just as a crane on the banks of the Ganges sits waiting for the prey. 94. Then suddenly the two thieves walked along on both sides of the cart. Jayadev now understood the purpose of these thieves. 95. The wise man recognises from afar the crooked, the deceivers, the evil doers, the crafty, the thief, an immoral man, an impious man, a reviler, and a bad man. 96. Jayadev understood their movements, so he said to them, 'O what is it you wish? I will give it to you now. 97. You are aware that on this cart are many kinds of brilliant diamonds, rich clothes and ornaments. I offer them to you. 98. Great evils are associated with money. For money, men will kill others.' So Jayadev left the cart and quickly walked forward. 99. The thieves thought to themselves, 'Jayadev has left his cart. He will inform the merchant and cause us to be punished. 100. So let us kill him and take his cart.' Thus saying, they rushed towards him. 101. But a moment later the two men thought to themselves that they ought not to kill him. So they cut off both his feet and hands and threw him into a pit. 102. They then took the cart and at once returned to the city. In the meantime Jayadev was thinking of God, remembering Him with feelings of love. 103. Thinking of this subject with true perception, he said to himself, 'It is only the body that can be killed. The soul is not touched thereby It is quite separate from happiness and pain. 104. The body is the home of all diseases. The body is the root of lust and anger. The unhappy changes of the three *gunas* arise out of the body.' 105. Therefore Jayadev quickly becoming unconscious of his body thought of God, who finds His pleasure on the Ocean of milk.

THE DEVOUT KING OF KRAUNCH

106. On a certain day the King of Kraunch came into the forest to hunt, and night fell while he was wandering there. 107. Seeing a light in the pit, the king walked rapidly towards it to see what it was. 108. There he saw this worshipper of Vishnu in a posture of contemplation, supremely bright and refulgent, and repeating the names of God: 'Ram, Krishna, Govinda!' 109. The king seeing him in this position, he bowed prostrate before him. Looking at him closely he saw that his hands and feet had been cut off. 110. The king was frightened and said to Jayadev, 'How is it that you are in this condition?' 111. Jayadev replied to the king, 'I was born this way without hands and feet. I am quite separate from all my bodily organs.' 112. The king thought to himself that this *bhakta* of Vishnu seemed a very learned man. So he seated the *Swami* in a palanquin and took him back to the city. 113. Seating him on a golden throne he worshipped him lovingly. Coming humbly before Jayadev, he received the *mantra* making him his disciple. 114. Having seated Jayadev on his throne he said to his attendants, 'You must carry out my command and serve the *Swami* every day.' 115. The attendants said, 'O King, our star of fortune has arisen. We have seen a saint. We shall now listen

to the praise-services of God, and to the stories of His deeds.' 116. One day the king thought to himself, 'Let me ask today of the *Swami* the means which I must adopt for my salvation.' 117. So when Jayadev was seated on the throne, the king with hands joined palm to palm said, 'Please ask of me some act of service.' 118. Jayadev said, 'O king, you should worship saints. There is no better means (for attaining *Paramartha*). 119. When saints or other good men come to your home, you must feast them with such food as they enjoy. You should give to them the raiments, money, gold ornaments which they ask of you. 120. If you worship the saints in that way, God will be pleased. God is fond of those who serve His saints. They are more to Him than Lakshmi herself.' 121. The king said to the *Swami*, 'How shall I recognise saints? I do not at all know how, because I live in a condition of ignorance.' 122. The Husband of Padmavati (Jayadev) said to him, 'Listen to the marks of a saint. On his forehead are the three upright marks, and twelve other marks on his body. On his neck he wears the ornament of a *tulsi* garland. 123. Such are the outer marks of a follower of Vishnu. You must go to him alone as a suppliant.' The king hearing this replied, 'I certainly will do so.' 124. Honouring his *Guru's* command, the king served the saints. *Vaishnavas* heard of this, and came to his home. 125. Just as travellers come to sit in the shade when they see a tree, or as when birds see some food and joyfully come there; 126. or just as beggars come rushing when they hear the news of some generous giver; or as an ant seeing sugar, runs towards it with great joy; 127. or as when a cow comes back from feeding in the forest, the calf rushes to meet her; or as a cloud sends down rain joyously, when it sees a high mountain; 128. or as a peacock dances in ecstasy when it hears the thunder in the cloud; or as the warrior seeing a battle rushes towards it with eagerness and courage; 129. so good people came to see the marks of the king's *bhakti*. They first met Jayadev and then went to see the king. 130. When the king saw these saints he prostrated before them on the ground. He was accustomed to take them into his home for four months of the year and to feast them after their own hearts. 131. Whatever these *Vaishnavas* asked for, the king was accustomed to give them. He gave them limitless garments, ornaments and money when they asked for them.

THIEVES WHO FEIGNED AS SAINTS

132. The thieves who cut off the hands of Jayadev learned that this was the case. 133. They said, 'Let us pretend to be saints and go and see the king, and so plan that we shall obtain an abundance of money.' 134. They did not know that Jayadev was there. These deceivers then dressed themselves as saints. 135. Taking *gopichandan* (a sort of clay) they decorated their persons with the twelve marks of a *Vaishnava*. They wore a garland of *tulsi* around their necks. They appeared very brilliant. 136. As the meditation of a crane (sitting with eyes closed while intending to seize fish) looks more beautiful than that of a great *muni*; or as a *sher* tree looks brighter than a banana tree from a distance; 137. or as tin appears brighter than gold from a distance, or as the colour of *patang* wood looks better than saffron; 138. or as the singing of indecent songs is liked more than the songs of a *Haridas* (who sings God's praises); or as a shell in the sun shines brighter than silver from afar; 139. so these thieves from a distance seemed perfect saints, but no one knew that in their hearts there was deception. 140. The two thieves came into the city and hastened to meet the king. They had a rosary in their hands and pretended to be indifferent to earthly things. 141. As they went into the king's palace and

looked in front of them they suddenly saw Jayadev sitting on the throne. 142. The fire of alarm burned within them. The two made signs with their eyes, implying that by their own act they had fallen into this furnace of fire. 143. 'Jayadev, the poet whose hands and feet we cut off, is here. Our deception has at once come to its fruitage. 144. A hunter once went to shoot a dove and its mate when a great serpent bit his heel. Such seems to be our case now.' 145. As the two came forward Jayadev recognized them from afar. As soon as their eyes met they understood one another. 146. Jayadev naturally lived without enmity towards every creature, as forgiveness and peace were personified in him. 147. Enemies to him were like friends. He ignored the faults or merits of others. All mankind was to him in the form of Brahma. Such is the characteristic of saints. 148. Hearing that thieves had robbed him of his property and wealth, it brought comfort to his heart. Such is the characteristic of saints. 149. Pity either for one's own crying child or for the crying child of another is the characteristic of saints. 150. Whether a king gives him ornaments, or a common man brings him vegetables and greens, both please him alike. Such is the characteristic of saints. 151. Jayadev *Swami* leaped down from his throne when he saw these enemies near him. 152. They hastened to grasp the feet of Jayadev. Seeing this, the Husband of Padmavati embraced them. 153. Jayadev said to his servants, 'Some saints have come to the city. Go and say to the king that they should receive special honour.' 154. Hearing this remark the servants went and told the king, who came at once and bowed to them. 155. The king worshipped them. Using the many kinds of materials used for worship he gave them to each and then made the following request. 156. He said, 'As long as you may desire, spend your time in this my home.' Hearing this they said, 'We shall surely remember to do so.' 157. When it was night the two thought as follows: 'What will be the end of all this? We feel uneasy at the hospitality shown to us'. Then they said to one another, 158. 'In a town of cruel Muhammadans men are deceived and then fed. Then finally they murder them. Such will be the case with us, we think. 159. Just as a parrot comes and sits on a trap, and then falls into the cage, this is going to happen to us it would seem. 160. Seeing the bait a fish is deceived. It swallows it and the hook pierces its throat. Such will happen to us today, so it seems.' 161. By continually worrying, the bodies of these so-called saints began to waste away as if they were seized with tuberculosis.

162. One day the king said to Jayadev, 'O my *Swami*, I have a request to make at your feet. 163. Other saints come to my house and the *Swami* worships them at a distance. Why did you bow prostrate before these? 164. Although I am constantly using many kinds of worshipping materials on them, yet their bodies are becoming thin day by day.' 165. Jayadev replied, 'O king, the saints are not fond of enjoying the objects of the senses. To those who are indifferent to worldly things, the illusions of the world and selfish enjoyment seem like poison. 166. Other *Vaishnavas* come, but these are more indifferent to worldly things than the others. Your fortune is good, therefore they have remained here. 167. If they should say to you, 'Give us permission to go,' give them as much money as they may of their own choice request.' 168. The king replied, 'I will certainly do that.' And with this he bowed to his *Swami*. One day these thieves who pretended to be saints asked permission to go. 169. 'We live at a sacred city. We wish to go back to our home.' The king said to them, 'Ask me for whatever you wish.' 170. To this reply of the king's the pretending saints said, 'Fill two carts with money for us.

171. The king replied, 'Your request is my authority. I will give you whatever you ask.' So he gave to these pretending saints garments and ornaments. 172. He filled two carts with these costly things and gave two soldiers to go with them. He joined his hands palm to palm, in a very humble manner. 173. After taking leave of Jayadev these pretending saints started on their way. When they were in the forest some distance away, soldiers asked them a question. 174. 'Many *sadhus* and saints come to our palace, but it seems the *Swami's* special favour has been bestowed on you rather than on others. 175. We have this doubt, therefore we ask the *Swami* for an answer to our question.' The pretending saints replied to the soldiers, 176. 'Some time ago, while in the former stage of life, we and your *Swami* (Jayadev) lived with a king who was a very bad man. 177. He had a minister Jayadev by name. We were his servants. Because of some fault he committed, the king was very angry with him. 178. In anger the king gave us a command to take him far away into the forest and there behead him. 179. Having received this command we immediately carried him to the forest and instead of killing him, we cut off his hands and feet. 180. We threw him into a pit and returned to the city. From that day we became indifferent to worldly things. 181. We gave up serving the king, and have become worshippers of Vishnu. Wandering from sacred city to sacred city, we arrived at your city. 182. As soon as we entered the palace we recognised one another. We saved the life of Jayadev and for that reason he was full of thankfulness. 183. Because we had saved his life he prostrated himself before us. He told the king our story and caused him to serve us.' 184. As they said these things the earth began to tremble. There is no sin in this world equal to that of untruth. 185. The earth quickly opened her mouth and the pretending saints disappeared into it.

This caused great wonderment to the soldiers. 186. They said, 'This is a great catastrophe. What ought we to do? The king will punish us.' It caused them great alarm. 187. One said, 'Let us be courageous and truthfully relate what has occurred.' Saying this the servants returned to their city. 188. Coming to Jayadev *Swami* they told him all the news. Tears then flowed from the lotus eyes of Jayadeva. 189. He said, 'O Krishna, Purifier of the sinner, Dear to the *bhaktas*, Husband of Rukmini, why have you taken my enemies to hell, O Life of the World? 190. Ravan who was the enemy of the *bhaktas* was given a home in the highest spiritual state. Why didst Thou, O Enchanter of the heart, take my enemies to hell? 191. Shishupal committed hundreds of faults, yet Thou wast favourable to him, but my enemies Thou didst take to hell. Why was this, O Merciful One? 192. Kans, Chanur, and Putana, to these Thou gavest the highest spiritual state, but my enemies, O Slayer of Madhu, Thou hast taken to hell.' 193. Listening to this moving plea, the Life of the World was delighted. At once Vishnu came and met Jayadev. 194. God Narayan became pleased with him and appeared before Jayadev in His *sagun* form with four arms. Immediately afterwards, Jayadeva's hands and feet sprouted from him like the branches of a tree. 195. A chariot of light, Pushpaka by name, was sent. And the pretending saints were taken to Vaikuntha (the heaven of Vishnu). Such is the power of a *bhakta* which even Bramhadev and the other gods cannot understand. 196. The husband of Rukmini said to Jayadev, 'Blessed is your devotion. Forgiveness, mercy and peace dwell in you. 197. To whom an enemy and a friend are alike, even I *Hrishikeshi* (Lord of the heart) to him am subordinate. Thus saying, the Dweller in Vaikuntha became invisible. 198. The king, seeing that the hands and feet had sprouted from Jayadeva, then thought it a wonderful miracle, and joining his hands together palm to palm he spoke with him. 199. Jayadev then related to the King the story mentioned above. The *Vaishnavas* shouted aloud the names of God.

PADMAVATI, THE WIFE OF JAYADEV

200. At that time the king sent a palanquin and had Padmavati brought. This dutiful wife was a mine of beauty, the *avatar* of Indira (Lakshmi, wife of Vishnu). 201. The king gave to her (the wife of his *Guru*) ornaments, jewellery and garlands of pearls. The king with reverence bowed before this honoured mother. 202. The king going into his private apartment said to his wife, 'The queen of Jayadev, Padmavati, is our honoured mother. 203. I desire that you should personally serve her day and night with all your heart.' Hearing her husband's remark, his lovely wife replied, 'I shall certainly do so.' 204. The king thus thinking to himself, he sent his servants away, and personally began to serve Jayadev.

205. Now it happened on a certain day that the king's wives were seated together. Padmavati, a mine of virtues, shone from her *dais* (the chief seat). 206. Like the noble Bhagirathi among the rivers, or like Savitri among faithful wives, or as the *Gayatri mantra* among all other *mantras*, she shone as the chief ornament. 207. Like the musk among all other fragrant perfumes, like a necklace of glass beads among ornaments, so Padmavati seemed when sitting on the chief seat. 208. Suddenly a message arrived announcing that the queen's brother Sujan had passed away. 209. Thinking of her husband in her heart, his (Sujan's) wife started to burn herself on his funeral pyre. The young women hearing this were overcome and wondered about it. 210. Padmavati sat quietly. Seeing her so, all thought it strange, and all the queens with folded hands requested her as follows: 211. 'Thinking of her husband at heart, the dutiful wife

started to immolate herself. How is it that hearing this news you feel no surprise? 212. Abandoning all ties of affection, a dutiful wife who starts to burn herself alive with her dead husband has the same husband during her seven births'. 213. Hearing this Padmavati said, 'Why should a wife burn herself alive? When her husband goes before her, I do not know when they will meet one another again. 214. When one hears of the death of one's husband, one should immediately commit suicide; just as when the sun sets, the rays disappear.' 215. As Padmavati said these things the queens were astonished. They said, 'She speaks without experience.' They therefore took it as false. 216. (But she continued):— 'Just as the knowledge of Brahma without experience of it, just as a body without life in it, so to speak without the favour of God seems a vain thing.' 217. As a house without a master, as a face without a nose, as the doing of anything without authority seems in vain; 218. as the beauty of a barren woman and the friendship of a money loving person are in vain, and as a town without trees looks frightful; 219. as God without His *bhaktas*, or a king without his army, so a pure purpose without the means of fufilling it is good for nothing.' 220. While Padmavati was saying this, her thoughts seemed false to the queen. She called the minister and communicated to him her plan. 221. She said, 'Listen to one thing. Speak an untruth for my sake, that Jayadev *Swami* is dead and send this news to the city'.

222. On a certain day the king went into the forest to hunt. He seated Jayadev in a palanquin, and took him with him to the forest. 223. The minister now sent a messenger into the city to say that a tiger had killed Jayadev. 224. Some garments were dipped in the blood and sent later by the minister. Hearing this news the queen wept. 225. Making a pretence, the queen came weeping and

running to the place where the beautiful Padmavati was. 226. Said she, 'A catastrophe has happened. Jayadev *Swami* has been killed by a tiger.' Padmavati questioned her, 'Is this really true?' 227. The other replied, 'It is absolutely true. Jayadev has been really killed.' On hearing this news Padmavati gave up her life. 228. Just as when the sun sets, its rays set with it; or as when a lamp is put out its light disappears; 229. just as the moon's phases wane in succession after the full moon, or as flowers lose their fragrance when crushed between the hands; 230. so as soon as she heard of the death of Jayadev she gave up her life. When the king returned to the city, he saw what a catastrophe had fallen. 231. He asked of the minister what had happened, and he listened to all the story. Said he, 'I would like to kill my wife, but that would be murdering a woman. 232. So by being burnt to death on burning wood, I will give up my own life.' Therefore outside the city he immediately made a great bonfire, 233. and came there to make a *namaskar* to Jayadev *Swami*, saying, 'O *Swami*, a great disaster has occurred through me.' 234. By his inner sight Jayadev understood all the news. He comforted the king and told him not to give up his life. 235. Jayadev came near to the corpse of Padmavati, bringing cymbals and the *vina* (the lute) in his lotus hands. He began to sing the Radhavilas. 236. Jayadev sang twenty-four of the eight-feet verses well known to the world. Then singing God's loving names, he danced in the place of the *kirtana*. 237. 'O Keshava, Narayana, Mukunda, Lover of the *Bhaktas*, O Source of joy, Protector of the Cowherds, praised by the world, come quickly to my help. 238. Hearing the pleading cry of Gajendra, Thou, Life of the World, didst hasten to his help. O Protector of Pralhad, O Thou Enchanter of the heart, hasten to my help. 239. Thou who didst protect Draupadi from shame, Protector of the Pandavas, Slayer of

Madhu, Delight of the mind of the cowherdesses, hasten to my help. 240. Helper of the helpless, Husband of Rukmini, Dweller on the bank of the Bhima, Thou whose garment is all space, Purifier of the sinners, Saviour of the world, hasten to my help.' 241. Hearing this plea, God came at once to his help. He embraced Jayadev and gave him this boon. 242. 'Whoever sings your verses, or listens to them with fondness, the Husband of Lakshmi (Vishnu) stands at his side with hands joined palm to palm.' 243. Having given him this blessing, the Life of the world embraced Padmavati and brought her to life. 244. As soon as the corpse came to life there was a united cry of 'Victory, Victory,' and the gods sitting in their chariots of light showered flowers upon her. 245. Everyone was greatly delighted. The noble Vaishnavas shouted in their love, and the king with reverence made a *namaskar* to Jayadev *Swami.* 246. Pious men both sing and listen to this exceedingly interesting story of Jayadev. If they are in trouble and remember the Husband of Rukmini, He will come to their aid immediately. 247. I have related to the best of my ability this sin-purifying story of the perfect *avatar* of Vyas, to whom an enemy and a friend were alike.

NABHAJI OF GWALIOR

248. In the province of Gwalior there lived a well-known Nāgar Brahman by name of Nabhaji, a chief jewel amongst the *Vaishnavas* and the perfect *avatar* of Brahmadev. 249. He wrote the very extraordinary history of the *bhaktas*. After reading his verses I wrote this book in Marathi. 250. Just as the dolls of the jugglers dance when pulled by the strings; in the same way my lips have uttered the story of Jayadev. 251. The Husband of Rukmini, who dwells on the banks of the Bhima, gave Pundalik this promise. The Advocate of His *Bhaktas*, the Life of the World is the real composer of this book.

252. In the next chapter the very special story of Tulsi das the *bhakta* of Vishnu will be told. But the composer and the relater will be God. Listen with attention, you pious folk. 253. Krishna is standing with both hands on His hips. I, Mahipati, am singing of His goodness in the praise services.

254. *Svasti.* This book is the *Bhaktavijaya.* God will be pleased as He hears it. Listen therefore, you God-loving pious *bhaktas.* This is the second delightful chapter.

CHAPTER III

THE LIFE OF TULSIDAS

Obeisance to Shri Ganesh. Obeisance to Shri Krishna.

God's Care of His **Bhaktas.**

1. Victory, Victory, to the lover of His *bhaktas*, root of all joy, the Supreme Being, Sachchidananda, Saviour of the world, worthy of the worship of the world, beautiful in His dark features, Govinda. 2. Victory to Him Who lives near the banks of the Bhima, Giver of the promise to Pundalik, King of the Yadavas, Who stands with his hands upon His hips, waiting for His *bhaktas*. 3. Many sinners, thieves, adulterers, haters of Brahmans, killers of cows have been saved by mere sight of Him. 4. Gajendra the elephant, wholly ignorant, remembered Thee when in distress. Thou didst listen to his pitiable cry and send Thy disk to save him. 5. Thou didst punish the crocodile and didst come to meet Gajendra. Thou didst seat him in a chariot of light. The crocodile laughed at Thee. 6. The crocodile said to Thee, 'Thy name is the Purifier of the sinners, and yet Thou didst cast me aside and didst depart taking Gajendra. 7. So drop Thy reputation of being the Purifier of the sinners, O Krishna.' Hearing this remark of the crocodile, Thou didst take him also in Thy chariot of light. 8. Thou gavest both *bhakta* and non-*bhakta* a home in the Final Deliverance. In thus attempting to describe Thy goodness and good deeds the serpent Shesha became wearied. 9. Indra and other gods have never acquired the nectar of the stories of Thy goodness and good deeds. But Thou gavest the nectar of Thy stories to those God-loving *bhaktas* who came to Thee with entire reverence. 10. Just as a loving mother, seating her child by her side puts the morsel of food into its mouth, feeling a sense of great love

for it, 11. so Thou didst rain down the nectar of Thy stories, and didst place morsels of it in the mouths of Thy *bhaktas*, O Life of the world, Thou who dost attract the heart, O Govinda. 12. So seating Thy *bhaktas* by Thy side Thou feedest them with the nectar of Thy stories. And at this time therefore I also, a beggar, have arrived in order to receive food. 13. As Thy *bhaktas* were fed with the nectar of Thy stories, they ate to their satisfaction, and now, O Lord of the world, whatever they left in their plates, send to me, a helpless one. 14. O Merciful to the lowly, O Husband of Rukmini, hearing an account of Thy extraordinary deeds, I Mahipati have been waiting eagerly. Show me Thy love.

15. In the *Kali Yuga* there were very many God-loving *bhaktas*. O Cloud-dark Govinda, I will describe their exceedingly delightful stories, as Thou mayest make me relate them.

TULSIDAS

16. Now listen, O hearers. While Narayan was reclining on the serpent Shesh in the sea of milk, some of His *bhaktas* arrived. 17. Uddhav, Akrur, Vālmiki, Dhruva, Pralhada and Shuka coming near Him paid their reverence to the Lord of the Yadavas. 18. The Saviour of the world said to Vālmiki, 'In the *Kali Yuga* sins have become intolerable. I wish you to become an *avatar* among mortals and bring about the salvation of men. 19. The *Ramayana* which you composed, in which you sang my name, goodness and good deeds, was in the Sanskrit language which the ignorant people of the *Kali Yuga* did not understand. 20. So becoming an *avatar* among mortals, set them to worshipping me.' Vālmiki hearing Him say this made obeisance to Him. 21. In the northern country, in the city of Hastanapur (Delhi) in the house of a Kanoja Brahman, the *Rishi* Vālmiki became a voluntary

avatar. 22. The Brahman bore the name of Atmaram. He became a man devoted to religion and of perfect good deeds. Akbar was king at that time, and he was in the service of Akbar. 23. Atmaram was a wise Brahman and he enjoyed the King's favour. It was in his family that Vālmiki became an *avatar.* 24. The good Brahman, Atmaram, performed rituals of birth and naming of his son. He was named Tulsidas. The father lovingly played with him. 25. Day by day he grew in stature. His parents invested him with the sacred thread. And he was kept as a *Brahmachari* (a celibate) for twelve years. 26. He daily performed his baths and devotions. They made him study the *Vedas* according to the prescribed rules. After searching out a bride for him his marriage took place. 27. As his childhood passed away, and he became a young man, the two were united in love. They never could endure separation. 28. Both gave themselves up to enjoying many kinds of rich clothes and ornaments, garlands of pearls and brilliant jewels, saffron, musk, sandal and flowers, yellow betelnut leaves, 29. cardamons, cloves and nutmeg; but Tulsidas could not endure being without his wife. 30. The name of Tulsidas' wife was Devi Mamata. As a dutiful wife she served him with full reverence.

31. It happened one day, that King Akbar was going on a tour. Tulsidas immediately joined him and went with him. 32. Just then a messenger arrived from her mother's home asking her to come there. He said, 'Your mother is seriously ill. 33. Let her have a sight of you and then you can return.' On hearing this she wept aloud. 34. Hearing that her mother was seriously ill, she became hysterical. The messenger therefore said to her, 'We have told you what is false. 35. It is many days since you have visited your mother. Tulsidas refuses to send you, therefore we told you a falsehood.' 36. Mamata replied to them, 'My husband has gone on the royal

tour. In the meantime I shall go to my mother's. Having visited her I will immediately return.' 37. Obtaining leave from mother and father-in-law Mamata went to visit her own mother. That very day, by evening Tulsidas returned. 38. He questioned his mother and learned all the news. Said he, 'My dear one, why have you left me and gone away?' 39. At night on his bed he was unable to sleep. So he started at once, and by walking ten miles that night he arrived at the house of his father-in-law. 40. Two watches of the night had already passed away. All the doors were closed. Tulsidas looked all about him. 41. Just then he saw a great poisonous serpent hanging down from above. He seized it with his hand and ascended to the upper storey. 42. As he entered the house the servants were awakened, and as they looked about they saw Tulsidas. 43. Mamata, that mine of beauty, awoke just at that moment. Seeing her husband there, she arose astonished. 44. The husband said, 'You mine of beauty, why did you leave me and come here? I have had to walk ten miles, in order to come for you.' 45. The wife replied, 'The Yamuna river is full of flood. I cannot understand how you were able to enter the house.' 46. Tulsidas replied, 'Your love for me is so great that you threw a rope from above and I crossed holding on to it.' 47. The dutiful wife hearing this replied, 'Why do you speak an untruth? I never threw a rope from the upper storey.' 48. As she did not know what was true or false, she said, 'Show me the rope.' Taking her servant with her and lighting a lamp they looked for it. 49. Just then they saw this great enormous serpent hanging down from above. All were frightened. It seemed so strange a thing. 50. Holding her husband by the hand the wife entered into the house and said to her husband, 'O Lord of my life, listen to me. 51. You call yourself wise and clever, but you have no common sense. You are always intoxicated with your ignorance. 52. Why did you leave your mother, father, brother, and friends, your wealth, and property, and come for me at such a time of night? 53. If this great serpent had bitten you, you would have lost your life. O Lord of my life, you know nothing about the transitory concerns of this life. 54. With desire to see me you came rushing by night. Many have lost their lives in running after women. 55. When Indra saw the beautiful Ahalya he was overcome by her charms. Many have lost their lives by running after women. 56. Ravan lost life by running after Sita. Many have lost their lives by running after us women. 57. Seeing the brightness of the light, the moth loses its life. So many have lost their lives by running after women. 58. Not recognizing God in their hearts, they seek to satisfy sensual desire. These evil ones do not recognize Shri Ram, the place of rest for every one. 59. Men love their sons, wives, wealth, and properties, more than their own lives. If men remembered the feet of Shri Hari (God) their lives would have value.' 60. Through these words of Mamata, Tulsidas experienced a change of heart. 'What you say, Oh mother, is true,' and as he (Tulsidas) said this, he bowed to his wife. 61. 'When a child puts out its hand to grasp a live ember of the *khadir* wood, the mother at once protects it. So to-day you have done me a great favour.' 62. Speaking thus to her, he immediately left. He remembered all he had done in his former births. 63. Said he, 'I am the *Vaishnava* Vālmiki. I have become an *avatar* in this world of mortals, that I may sing with my lips the story of Ram, and that I may turn men to devotion to Him. 64. I was entangled in the enjoyment of temporary sensual joys.' With this change of heart he came to Anandvan (Benares). 65. After bathing in the Bhagirathi, he adopted severe austerities. He rejected cooked food and fruits and he lived on the fallen leaves. 66. After bathing in the early morning he was accustomed to pray to Shri Ram. He used to say, 'O Dweller in Ayodhya, O Husband of Janaki, show me manifestation of Thyself.' 67. In order to wash himself he was accustomed to go into the forest. If any water was left in his vessel he poured it on the roots of the trees. 68. Twelve years he continued with these austerities. He was always repeating God's names. He never ceased for a single moment.

69. It happened one day that Tulsidas went into the forest to wash himself. The water that remained in his vessel he poured upon the roots of the tree. 70. Suddenly he saw a most terrifying demon. His two hands were joined together as he stood before Tulsidas. 71. He said to Tulsidas, 'I am pleased with you. Whatever blessing you may ask, I will give it to you.' 72. Tulsidas said to him, 'Tell me who you are, and why you have become pleased with me? I do not understand why?' 73. The other replied, 'I am a demon. I have been here for a long time. I drink the water which you pour on the roots. 74. We have no permission to drink water from wells, tanks, rivers, or the sea, so I am very thirsty. 75. You have supplied me with water for these twelve years. I will give whatever you ask for.' 76. Tulsidas with an astonished mind, said to himself, 'I was wishing for a visible manifestation of Shri Ram. The result of that desire has been the favour of this ghost. 77. I planted a mango tree, and bore the fruit of the Vrindavan tree. So the performance of these austerities have brought me the favour of this ghost. 78. I was wishing for a wish-cow. Instead of her a pig appeared. So failing a manifestation of Shri Ram it is this ghost who is showing this favour to me. 79. Having made a ring of sugar around a tree, there sprung out of it a bitter squash. So although my austerities have been good, it is this ghost who is pleased with me. 80. I was looking

at a beautiful royal swan coming towards me, when suddenly I saw a crow instead. So instead of meeting Shri Ram it is this ghost that is pleased with me. 81. It is like looking for association with the good, and then seeing a reviler coming forward. So instead of meeting the Husband of Janaki, this has become pleased with me. 82. While seeking philosophic knowledge, sensual stories may fall on one's ears. So instead of meeting with Ram, it is this ghost that is pleased with me. 83. It is like one, desiring the shade of the wish-tree, should immediately see a forest of Sindi trees. So, instead of meeting with Ram, it is this ghost who is pleased with me. 84. So one has the desire for scientific knowledge and suddenly one listens to some heretical story. So instead of meeting with Ram this ghost is pleased with me. 85. While one desiring a garland of pearls, a pile of crystals fell before him, so instead of seeing the Husband of Janaki this ghost has been pleased with me. 86. While desiring to see the ocean of milk, one suddenly sees instead a pool of water, so instead of meeting the slayer of Ravana it is this ghost that is pleased with me.' 87. After listening to him the demon said, 'You seem to be a wonderfully clever man. So ask of me a gift worthy of me to give. Do not hesitate. 88. One should never call that great or little by which our purposes are carried out. If one refuses to use borax, gold will not melt in the melting pot. 89. If one refuses to use fine thread, he will not be able to string a garland of flowers. And without an iron needle one will not be able to sew a coat. 90. One should not refuse to use the broom because it is made of *sindi*. A wise man is willing to use common things to carry out his purpose.' 91. So Tulsidas said to him 'You have become pleased with me, you say. I have no further desire in my heart than that you should help me to meet Shri Ram.' 92. As the name of Ram was heard by the demon he stepped back and said; 'If I should repeat His name by my lips it will mean my destruction. 93. If you really wish to meet Him, Maruti is His servant. I can cause him to manifest himself to you.' 94. Tulsidas replied, 'Where is Maruti? Show him to me at once. He will fulfil my desire.' 95. The demon answered, 'You are constantly listening to the *puranas*. An aged Brahman is accustomed to come there. It is he who is Maruti. 96. If you ask who he is I will tell you how he may be recognised. He comes and sits before anyone else. He leaves after every one has gone. 97. He has a staff in his hand and a cap on his head. He wears an old garment and a loin cloth. If you see a form like that, you will know that he is the head of the monkeys.' 98. Thus speaking the demon became invisible, and Tulsidas returned to his hermitage. 99. The next day after taking his bath, and repeating God's name as usual, he hastened to go where the *purana* was being read. 100. When suddenly an aged Brahman appeared and seated himself there. Tulsidas saw that his appearance was just as described by the demon. 101. After the reading of the *purana* was finished, and all the listeners had gone, the aged Brahman in silence started to go. 102. Tulsidas followed along with him. When he got outside the city, Hanuman (Maruti) was going very rapidly. 103. Seeing himself all alone with him, he held the Brahman by his feet and said to him, '*Swami*, have compassion on me, Thou Mighty One.' 104. The Brahman said to him, 'Hallo, who are you? Why have you held my feet? I am a poor helpess lowly one.' 105. Tulsidas replied to him. 'You are Maruti, the *bhakta* of Ram.' Thus speaking he again fell at his feet. 106. Maruti thought to himself, 'He is the *muni* Vālmīki who has descended as an *avatar*.' He at once gave him an embrace, thus expressing his love. 107. Maruti said to Tulsidas, 'I am pleased with you.' The other replied, 'My mind desires a gift by your favour. 108. I want you so to act that I may have a manifestation of Shri Ram.' Saying, 'I will do so,' he (Hanuman) became invisible. 109. Maruti said to Shri Ram, 'Listen to this my request. The *bhakta* Tulsidas is a full *avatar* of Vālmīki. 110. I want you to give him a visible manifestation of yourself. This is my desire, so complete the wish of my heart, O *Swami*.' 111 Hearing Maruti's words Ram replied, 'I will do so.' So he called together all the monkeys and took the army with him. 112. The Holder of the bow (Ram) passed in front of the hermitage of Tulsidas, but he did not recognise Him. He said to himself, 'Some Muhammadans are passing by.' 113. The monkeys seemed heroic and Shri Ram seemed to be the king of the Muhammadans. Seeing them thus, Tulsidas made them a *namaskar*. 114. After that Maruti came to the hermitage of Tulsidas and said to him, 'Ram has fulfilled your desire.' 115. The other replied, 'O Maruti, I have not met Shri Ram.' Maruti replied 'Why? He has just passed by your hermitage.' 116. Tulsidas said, 'The one who passed by my hermitage was truly a Muhammadan. I did not see Ram. My desire still remains unfulfilled.' 117. Maruti remarked, 'A wish-cow came to your house, and you wise fellow drove it away, thinking it was a goat. 118. As you were once walking along the road you suddenly saw a touchstone, how is it that you, a wise man, should throw it away, thinking it was a mere pebble? 119. A very wise clever parrot happened to come to your hermitage. It seemed to you to be a dove, therefore you did not care for it. 120. You meet the forest of wish-trees, but they seem to you like *sindi* trees. So when Shri Ram was passing by, you did not recognize him. 121. On a day of great festival a Brahman came to your house. You thought him a herder of goats, and so you turned him away. 122 You saw a garland of pearls and you thought them made of glass. So Ram passed by you and you did not recognize Him. 123. A flock of royal swan passed by you and they seemed to you like crows, so Shri Ram passed by and you made no obeisance to Him. 124. As if Lakshmi should come without an effort into a pauper's kitchen and he should discard her as a slave, in the same way you have acted. 125. An unfortunate man, while digging the foundation of a house, found a golden coin. He thought it was a pebble and discarded it. 126. The pure sandalwood of Mount Maila, has seemed to you like *hingan*-wood. So when Ram passed by you, you did not recognize Him. 127. The Holder of the Pinak bow, the Husband of Parvati (Shiva), came in the form of a beggar, you gave him no gift. So you have done now.' 128. Tulsidas replied, 'O *Swami*, you accuse me unjustly, but Ram who fills all space and pervades the universe, is invisible. 129. A bracelet is made of gold, but the ignorant man does not call it gold. Milk comes from water, but one should not call water milk. 130. All water is the same, but the *chatak* bird will not drink the water that is on the earth. So the worshipper of Ram does not consider Him as appearing in many forms. 131. The Dweller in Ayodhya, the Life of Janaki, was holding His bow and arrow in the same way as Vālmīki described Him. Show me that appearance.' 132. When Maruti heard him say this, he smiled and said, 'Shri Ram will fulfil the desire of your heart.' 133. Saying this, Maruti became invisible, and bringing the image of Shri Ram into his imagination he began his loving praise: 134. 'Victory, Victory, O Dweller in Ayodhya, Husband of Sita, Slayer of Ravan, Holder of the bow, Purifier of the sinner, Saviour of the humble, Slayer of demons, O Shri Ram.' 135. Shri Ram replied, 'Maruti, why this special praise today? What is the special desire of your heart, that you have begun this loving praise?' 136. Maruti replied, 'Shri Ram, Wish tree of the desires of the *bhaktas*, Thou a visible form, dark as thick cloud, I desire Thee to visit Tulsidas.' 137. Hearing Maruti's request Ram said, 'How can he have a direct manifestation in this *Kali Yuga* ?' 138. Maruti replied, 'O Lord of the heart, he is an *avatar* of the *rishi* Vālmiki. It was Thou who gavest the command that he should turn men to Thy worship.' 139. Hearing this remark of Maruti's Ram said, 'I will listen to your request. I never break my word.' 140. So Shri Ram with Sita and Lakshman, taking the form of visible *avatars*, walked along with Maruti. 141. The *bhakta* Maruti went forward and informed Tulsidas. Said he, 'Shri Ram will today fulfil your heart's desire.' 142. Hearing Maruti's remark, Tulsidas was full of joy. Just then he saw before him the Lord of Ayodhya. His joy now was without limit. 143. A brilliant crown adorned his head. He wore a yellow garment. His complexion was that of a dark cloud. In His hand was a bow and arrow. In this form he saw Shri Ram. 144. With deep reverence Tulsidas bowed prostrate on the ground. And the merciful Shri Ram embraced his *bhakta* Tulsidas. 145. Maruti said to him, 'You are a very fortunate man. With your eyes you have seen the form of Ram. You must now proclaim to all men God's deeds which you formerly described. 146. In this *Kali Yuga* the means of salvation are not *yoga* practices, nor sacrifices, nor the study of the *Vedas*. So proclaim the might of God's names and turn men to the worship of God.' 147. Maruti said to Ram, 'Place your hand on his head.' Ram listened to his request and gave Tulsidas the blessing of his assurance. 148. After giving him this blessing the Husband of Sita (Ram) became invisible, and Tulsidas continued with love his description of Shri Ram's good deeds. 149. All the inhabitants of Benares listened to his services in the praise of God, and they built a hermitage for Tulsidas.

150. There were wealthy and pious men to whom Tulsidas gave the *mantra* and made them his disciples. They used to bring a variety of things and place them in the hermitage. 151. A thousand Brahmans daily dined along

with Tulsidas. Any poor person, any beggar, anyone without food, if he came there, went away satisfied. 152. His reputation became great among the people. They brought him unlimited amounts of money, great, great, golden plates and an unlimited and innumerable amount of silver. 153. Some gave and some took away. Some reviled him and some praised him. But Tulsidas was untouched by them. He had neither joy nor sorrow. 154. Just as in the heavens the three seasons have their beginning, yet the sky is free from the fault of association with them. 155. After the feast of the Brahmans, there followed the enthusiasm of the praise-service. Pious people came in large numbers in order to repeat God's names. 156. People left their doors open while all went to sleep. Thus they thought of the feet of Shri Ram, when dreaming and in dreamless sleep. and when awake. 157. Two thieves therefore considered the situation carefully. 'We see no one in the hermitage of Tulsidas who would refuse us admission. 158. We can go there without fear, and take away a load of golden plates. We can take away as much as our hands are able to carry.' 159. After the praise-service of God was over, all the audience went to sleep. Just then the two thieves came and began to steal. 160. They gathered up the golden plates with their hands and tied them up in a bundle. They placed the load on their heads and started to leave hurriedly. 161. As they came near the gate they found two men seated there with bows and arrows, very stout-looking men. 162. The astonished mind of the thieves said to them, 'A while ago there was no sentinel here to protect the place.' So they turned back quickly and arrived at the northern gate. 163. They suddenly saw a person with shining countenance with a crown and ornaments. In His hand were a bow and arrow. The thieves saw him from afar and became ashamed. 164. Then they went to the south door, but there also sat the door-keepers. The thieves thought this very strange and came back and sat down. 165. The two thieves thought to themselves, 'These men holding the bow will soon get up and go away. Then we will quickly take away these golden plates.' 166. Thus remarking to one another, the thieves sat quietly for four *ghatikas* and then they went to the gate and looked. 167. And there they saw the two men seated with bow and arrows in their hands, with the string drawn to their ears, and standing in a position to shoot. 168. The thieves became frightened, threw down the gold plates and went to the gate, but they were not allowed to pass. 169. The night passed in great anxiety of mind. The sun now arose, and all the *bhaktas* arose when the wicks were lighted for waving. 170. After the early morning repetition of God's names, Tulsidas came out of his hermitage. Just then the two thieves came and fell at his feet. 171. The thieves filled with emotion said to him. 'Forgive us our fault.' Tulsidas said to them, in reply, 'Tell me who you are.' 172. They replied, 'We are thieves, who had come to rob you. But there were soldiers of the bow seated at the gate and they would not let us pass. 173. We had made a bundle of your golden plates, and were waiting in your hermitage. It was a great fault on our part, forgive us, you merciful one. 174. You are, a *bhakta* of Ram, supremely generous. At night you leave your door open. Therefore we thieves came in without fear.' 175. Tulsidas had many disciples. He therefore asked them, 'Who is at the gate protecting us? Why have you placed them there without my knowledge? 176. I have already told you that it was alike to me whether anyone gave to me or took away. Worship Shri Ram with love.' 177. The disciples replied with an oath, 'We swear by your feet that we do not know who is guarding the door.' 178. The thieves replied, 'His face was brilliant. He wore a crown and ornaments. He was dressed in a yellow robe. His complexion was dark. He is seated there even now.' 179. All were astonished, and coming near to the gate they looked, but they saw nothing and thought this very strange. 180. Tears now came to the lotus eyes of Tulsidas. He said to himself, 'Ram and Lakshman have now become my doorkeepers at this time: 181. what I could not obtain by adopting the severest postures in *yoga* practices, what visits to sacred places would not give me; for I have as my doorkeeper Ram the Dweller in Ayodhya; 182. Husband of one wife, who does not require a second to accomplish his purpose, whose determination was as he promised; He the Slayer of Ravan, Shri Ram, has become my doorkeeper. 183. When His feet touched the stone-slab, it brought about the salvation of Ahalya. He who with supreme generosity is the Giver of. eternal life. He has become my doorkeeper.' 184. He then exclaimed, 'Victory, Victory to the noble Ram, the Supreme Being, the Supreme Generous one, Friend of the blue-necked Shiva, the Saviour of the world, Ram Krishna. 185. Thou art the Husband of Lakshmi, supremely generous. When Upamanyu asked Thee for a little milk, Thou didst listen to his request and gavest him the ocean of milk. 186. When his father would not permit him to sit on his lap, the infant Dhruva went away in a sulk. Then Thou, the Husband of Sita, gavest him an eternal place in a wonderful way. 187. Bibhishan was loved by Thee, so Thou gavest him a golden city. So when the thieves began to take away the golden vessels Thou didst become a great miser.' 188. Tulsidas then said to the thieves, 'Whatever your heart may desire, take it away to your homes. Do not feel any hesitation.' 189. When they heard him say this, the thieves fell at his feet. They cried out, 'Have mercy on us, and place your assuring hand upon us. 190. We are sinful, evil men. We were encircled by ignorance, but by the power of association with you, we have seen a manifestation of Ram. 191. The natural virtue of the touchstone turns iron into gold; so through giving you trouble we have had a sight of Shri Ram. 192. The moment we beheld you, our evil heart left us; just as when the day dawns, the darkness can no more be seen.' 193. Tulsidas said to them, 'Your good fortune is very great. Without any efforts on your part, Shri Ram gave you a manifestation of Himself. 194. You are like one who, collecting herbs in the forest, finds the vine that gives immortality, or as a man while gathering pebbles near the town, happens to find a touchstone. 195. Or as one begging for gruel from house to house, finds in his possession the nectar juice. Or as when one is labouring over a lamp, the sun itself shines into the house. 196. Or as when examining *Kokashastra*, a book on the *Vedanta* comes to hand. Or when stringing beads of glass, a necklace of pearls comes to one's hand. 197. Or as when searching for *babhul*-wood in a forest, one should see the sandal-wood tree of Mount Maila. Or as when one should go in search of the city of Yama, one should see the city of Heaven.' 198. Hearing him say this, the thieves made him a *namaskar* and putting aside their evil minds, constantly remained in Tulsidas' hermitage. 199. In the *Shri Bhagavat Purana* the Lord Krishna told Uddhava the meaning of His deep thoughts. 'He who desires to attain Me he must associate himself with the good. 200. By association with the good the praises of God fall on one's ears.' So these thieves, who had been evil men and adulterers became good men. 201. They began to listen to the praises of God constantly, and to repeat His names. These things continued for many days, and then a very strange thing happened.

202. Some Brahmans were seated eating in the hermitage of Tulsidas. A great variety of food cooked

with butter and sugar was spread before them. 203. As Tulsidas was about to make the offering to the gods, and as the Brahmans were repeating the words, 'This is an offering to the Supreme *Brahma*,' suddenly a Brahman appeared at the gate. Listen to what he said. 204. First repeating the names of Sita and Ram, he said, 'I am a great killer of Brahmans, Give me some of the food you give to those who ask for it.' This was what he said. 205. When the Brahmans who were present heard him, they were all filled with wonder. Tulsidas came outside and embraced him. 206. He took the Brahman by the hand and seated him by his side. He then said to him. 'O *Swami*, personification of mercy, listen to my request. 207. The moment you utter the words Sita and Ram, sins like that of killing Brahmans and similar sins are burnt up as if they were straw.' 208. So saying to him, he then said to the Brahmans, 'Begin now to eat.' Hearing him give this invitation, the Brahmans replied to him. 209. These Brahmans, skilled in the six *shastras*, said to Tulsidas, 'On what authority have you seated this Brahman-killer in our line?' 210. Tulsidas replied to them, 'There is one authority for it. How can the sin of killing a Brahman remain, when uttering the name of Ram? 211. In the *Shri Bhagavat Purana* the Lord Krishna revealed his ideas to Uddhava, that in the *Kali Yuga* the power of God's name would be manifested to an extraordinary degree. 212. When performing one's bath and devotion one has first to repeat the names Keshav and Narayan. If he is faulty in any of his religious deeds, it would be remedied by repeating the names of Vishnu. 213. In order to carry out properly the worship of ancestors, the whole rite is finally offered to Janardana (feeder of the universe). No rite is properly performed, unless the name of Hari is pronounced. 214. When determining upon a marriage, the horoscopes of the bride and the bridegroom agreeably resulting in thirty-six points, the marriage will not take place without repeating the names of the Husband of Lakshmi. 215. When about to die and taking the penance, the name of God is repeated at that final moment. The Husband of Parvati (Shiva) the Lord of Kailas, lovingly repeats the name of Ram. 216. That great sinner, Pingala Ganika (prostitute) spoke to her parrot, calling him Raghu (parrot). In doing so the straw of her great faults was burnt up by the flames of the names of God. 217. The Brahman Ajamil became exceedingly depraved, when he was at the point of death, and when he called to his infant son Narayan, immediately all his sins were burnt up.' 218. The Brahmans wanting explanation said, 'This does not seem to our minds to be true. Show us some evidence, and our doubts will disappear.' 219. Tulsidas said to the Brahmans, 'What kind of evidence do you ask for?' The Earth-gods (Brahmans) said: 'Make an offering to the stone bull. 220. The Lord of the Universe, the Lord of Kailas (Shiva's heaven), Nandikeshvar, stands in front of it. Fill a plate with food and offer it to the stone bull. 221. If the stone image of the bull eats the offering from your hands in sight of us, then we shall allow this killer of Brahmans to sit amongst us at this time. 222. Using many instances you tell us much of the power of God's names. If you will give us this evidence to our sight, our minds will accept it. 223. Not merely by telling us of the sweetness of sugar will our tongue's love of the sweet be satisfied. You tell us of the great power of the names of God, but our doubts do not leave us. 224. The experts pierce coins by their instrument in order to test their genuineness. So show us good evidence and remove our doubts. 225. Just as the jewels in the serpent's head are wound around with a string, and then thrown into the fire and examined, so show us the certainty of experience of the names of God. 226. A diamond is placed on an anvil, and tested by striking it with a hammer. So you, wise man, show us the power of God's name at this time.' 227. Hearing the Brahmans' remarks, Tulsidas was very pleased. He at once took a plate of food and went into the temple of Vishveshvar, the Lord of the Universe. 228. All the Brahmans now arose and followed him. They stood in the assembly hall and all looked with curiosity 229. With a plate of food in his hand Tulsidas came to the great door of the temple. He joined his hands palm to palm, and bowed prostrate on the ground. 230. Said he, 'Victory, Victory, to Thee Who wearest the moon on Thy head, blue-throated one, Holder of the Khatvanga bow, Husband of Parvati, Enemy of the demon Tripur, listen to the request of the lowly one. 231. Just as Thou didst drink the virulent poison, and Thy whole body became inflamed, then Thou didst repeat the names of Ram. 232. By merely repeating the two-lettered name of Ram, Thou didst become cool, O Lord of the Universe. If that be true, then let this stone bull eat this offering.' 233. As soon as the prayer was heard a very strange thing happened. The stone bull arose and began to breathe violently. 234. After eating all the offering he ate up the whole leaf-plate. All saw this miracle. Blessed was that time and happy day. 235. Having shown this miracle, the stone bull sat quietly. Neither the *Vedas* nor the *Shastras* understand the most extraordinary power of a *bhakta*. 236. The noble *Vaishnavas* all shouted out, 'Victory, Victory.' While repeating the names of God all the twice-born made a *namaskar* to Tulsidas. 237. They said, 'Blessed are you noble *Vaishnava*. You are very wise in the spheres of the knowledge of eternal truths. Now we know that you are truly a full *avatar* of Vālmīki. 238. Just as the moon stands supreme among the clusters of stars, just as the eagle is supreme among birds, just as Vishnu is supreme among the gods; so you are supreme among the *Vaishnavas*. 239. Just as Shiva is supreme among ascetics, just as *muni*

Vyas is supreme among the *rishis*, just as Mother Rukmini was supreme among the cow-herdesses, so you are supreme among the *Vaishnavas*. 240. As the Husband of Janaki is supreme among the Holder of Bows, as the ocean of milk is supreme among all oceans, as the Son of Anusaya is supreme among those who had attained Godhead, so you are supreme among the *Vaishnavas*. 241. As the fourth stage of deliverance among the four stages, as the father of Brahmadev among the Yadavas, as the expounder of the *Vedas* among *Pandits*, are each supreme, so you are supreme among *bhaktas*. 242. As the sun among the nine planets, as Ushana among the great poets, and as mount Meru among mountains, are each supreme, so you are the noblest *Vaishnava* among the *Vaishnavas*.' 243. Thus having praised Tulsidas, all the Brahmans came back to the hermitage. They allowed the Brahman-killer to sit at their side and all dined together. 244. Thus all the people of Benares began to repeat the names of God. They gave up their pride and came to listen to the deeds of Hari.

TULSIDAS RESTORES JAITPAL TO LIFE

245. Some time after these things had happened a very wonderful event took place. There was a merchant by name of Jaitpal. He suddenly passed into a state of peace (i. e., he died). 246. His dutiful wife, abandoning everything that was dear to her with the Lord of her Life in her heart, started to burn herself with him. 247. In a cleared forest by the bank of the Ganges, they lighted a great funeral pyre. She arranged herself for the occasion in the spirit of one already possessing a husband, and walked gaily along. 248. Just then she walked by the cave of Tulsidas. She came alone in order to make him a *namsakar*. 249. Tulsidas was repeating the names of God. She bowed prostrate on the ground. He gave her this blessing, 'May you have eight sons.' 250. The good

woman said to the *bhakta* of Vishnu, 'My husband has reached the state of eternal sleep. And I am on the way to accompany him, abandoning all that is dear and my own. 251. You have given me this blessing that I should become the fortunate mother of eight sons, and be endowed with a husband. That word of yours will prove true, and yet I have my doubts.' 252. He said, 'I spoke without knowing your condition, but Ram will make it true. When the good woman heard him say this, she bowed before him. 253. When she went near the corpse she found her husband sitting up. This gave great joy to all, and all cried out, 'Victory, Victory.' 254. She took her husband by the hand, and leading him to the hermitage, there she again made to Tulsidas loving obeisance. 255. All the inhabitants of Benares sang the praise of Tulsidas. They exclaimed, 'Blessed is this *Vaishnava.* He is a complete Saviour for us dull-minded men. 256. He caused the stone bull to eat food, and by his word of blessing brought a corpse to life.' Then someone went and carried the news to the king.

AKABAR SENDS FOR TULSIDAS TO TEST HIM

257. King Akbar was at Delhi where somebody in-informed him. He then made an attempt to see the miracle. 258. He called his wise ministers and informed them of his thoughts. He said, 'I want you to bring about a meeting with the *Vaishnava* Tulsidas. 259. I wish you to send a messenger, who is exceedingly learned in the knowledge of *Brahma* who is a remarkably clever speaker, and who will incline Tulsidas' mind to come here. 260 Take a palanquin and carriage and bring him here quickly. I wish to see for myself what I have heard by the ear.' 261. The minister said to him, 'Your command is my authority.' He took some wise and clever speakers along with some of his army, and arrived at Benares. 262. Coming to the

hermitage of Tulsidas they remained there that day. The news was conveyed to him that the king had called him. 263. They said, 'The king has heard of you, as a most extraordinary God-loving *Vaishnava bhakta.* The king has sent us because of his desire to see you. 264. Hearing this request, Tulsidas thought to himself, 'I must turn all the inhabitants of that country to repeating God's name. 265. If the noble *Vaishnavas* are free from selfish desire, why should they wander from country to country ? Because it is truly Hari's command that they should save mankind. 266. Evil and ignorant men are surrounded by dark ignorance. In order to save them, good men wander about. 267. The king as we have seen has sent a messenger and every one has heard the news.' Tulsidas the God-loving *bhakta* at once started. 268. Enthusiastically repeating the names of Hari, he quickly arrived at Delhi. The king came forward and fell at his feet. 269. The king then seated Tulsidas on his throne and whispered a command to his servants, not to allow him to return. 270. He worshipped him with the sixteen materials for worship. The King said to Tulsidas, 'I have heard of your wonderful power and that you have got yourself made into a God. 271. You made the stone-bull eat food. In the giving of a blessing, you brought a corpse to life. Your deeds seem impossible to me. I do not understand your power.' 272. Tulsidas said to him, 'It is all the doing of Shri Ram. I am but a helpless person who has placed his heart at the feet of Ram.' 273. Hearing this the king said to him, Cause me to meet Ram. If you do not do so, I shall surely not allow you to go from here.' 274. Thus speaking, the king went into his palace. He said, 'If he will show me a manifestation of Ram, then only will I regard Tulsidas as a noble *Vaishnava.*' 275. While

Tulsidas sat on the throne the servants said to him, 'You are not to be allowed to go from here. 276. Without losing a moment give the king a sight of Shri Ram. If you do not grant this, he certainly will not allow you to leave here.'

MARUTI'S VENGEANCE

277. Hearing them say this, he began to praise Maruti, and Maruti at once came and met Tulsidas. 278. Tulsidas said, 'I am in extreme distress and, therefore, I have thought of you. And now remove this distress and increase the glory of the names of God.' 279. Maruti then performed a wonderful miracle. He called together his army of monkeys and many mighty heroes started from Heaven. 280. Just as during the rainy season clouds appear in the sky; or as when the rain falls on the earth the grass begins to sprout; 281. or as during the time of famine a cloud of locusts appears in the sky; so suddenly this army of monkeys ten thousand in number appeared. 282. The monkeys bowed to Maruti, and said to him, 'Please tell us what your command is.' 283. Maruti replied to them, 'I have called you together in order that you may show to the king some of your natural characteristics.' 284. As soon as they received this command, the monkeys became full of action. They climbed upon the roofs and began to destroy the tiles. 285. They pulled up great trees by the roots, and threw them at men. There was a great alarm felt in Delhi, and a great outcry. 286. They broke the noses of some and cut off their ears, they twisted off the necks of some. They grabbed some by the legs and started upwards. 287. As women were going to the river Jamna, with water-jars on their heads, they snatched their clothes from them, and threw them into the river. 288. As fathers-in-law and mothers-in-law were passing out of the alleys, the monkeys seized them, and fastening their beards and braids of hair together, they ran away.

289. Those who did not worship Shri Ram, or persecuted the *bhaktas* of Vishnu, the monkeys lifted them up and threw into the stinking drains. 290. The evil-minded merchants never gave food to anyone; the monkeys broke open their store-rooms and carried away their contents. 291. There was a great outcry in the city. Then they entered into the palace of the king and cut off noses and ears. This also made a great outcry. 292. The five hundred wives of the king were all seated in the company of his concubines. The monkeys came and threw dirty water on them. 293. They suddenly seized all evil men who were thieves, adulterers, and crooked in their lives. They lifted them up and took them from the palace, and threw them down from above. 294. They seized the garments and ornaments, and flew with them into the sky and then with great pleasure gave them to the poor or those who lacked food. 295. They made the poor rich. They robbed the merchants. They beat those who spoke untruth. 296. The servants of the king hastened to inform him what was taking place. They said, 'An army of monkeys has arrived, and they are destroying everything. 297. Just as when a cloud pours down a heavy rain, the sky is dense with clouds, so Delhi seems crowded with this army of monkeys. 298. The monkeys show great anger, and there is a great outcry in the city.' The king remarked, 'The time for destruction of all things seems to have arrived.' 299. There were some wise men present who said to the king, 'Tulsidas is a *Vaishnava*. You should not persecute him. 300. If the monkeys increase in their anger,they will turn the whole city of Delhi upside down.' The king thought all this very remarkable, and confessed that he had committed a great fault: 301. 'When Durvas persecuted Ambarisha, he had to be humiliated. So it has happened to me. I am reminded of my injustice.' 302. So he came to Tulsidas and there joining his hands

palm to palm, he stood before him. 303. Akbar said to him, ' O *bhakta* of Vishnu, restrain this army of monkeys. I persecuted you, because in my ignorance I did not know what I was doing. 304. Duryodhan suffered humiliation when he attempted to persecute the good Draupadi. So it has happened to me by my persecuting you.' 305. Hearing this pity-arousing request, Tulsidas said to him, 'You were wishing to see Shri Ram. It is His army that has arrived. 306. Just as when the sun arises at dawn, and its light spreads all over the world, so this great hero has come with an advance guard, O king. 307. Hearing produces desire. Meditation produces devotion to listening, and a direct manifestation of God produces in one a desire to know more of Him. 308. So the monkeys are arriving first, and Ram is following them. An army of eighteen billions are following these monkeys. 309. These eighteen billion monkey warriors will be followed by Ram. Your good fortune has no limit. Shri Ram is coming to see you.' 310. Hearing this, the king said, 'I have already seen enough of Ram.' So saying, he grasped him by his feet and said, 'I did not understand His power. 311. If an army of ten thousand monkeys has wrought such destruction, then if the army of eighteen billion should come it would mean the end of the world.' 312. Hearing the king's pity-arousing request, the monkey army became invisible and all men worshipped the feet of Tulsidas.

313. Tulsidas remained here for a year, and in great love he daily sang the praises of the extraordinary deeds in Shri Ram's life. 314. All the inhabitants in Delhi began now to repeat constantly the names of God. And the ignorant and dull-minded became wise through association with him.

TULSIDAS GOES TO MATHURA

315. Tulsidas nowtook leave of Akbar and went

went to see and worship Shri Krishna at Mathura. 316. At first he came to Gokul and bathed by the bank of Jumna river. Having seen and worshipped Shri Krishna he departed from there. 317. From there he came to Vrindavan. There he made an obeisance to Krishna. He remained there a month, and danced in the praise-services devoted to Hari. 318. From there he came to Mathura. He bathed by the banks of the Jumna. He saw and worshipped Shri Krishna, and met there many *Vaishnavas.* 319. In Mathura, Gokul, and Vrindavan, live many *Vaishnavas* (those who worship only Vishnu as the One God). They are constantly engaged in singing the praises of Hari, and are always repeating His names day and night.

320. There was a Brahman citizen by name of Priyadas of supreme piety, and a *Vaishnava. Bhakti*, knowledge and indifference to worldly things, were his characteristics.

RAM HIMSELF WRITES TULSIDAS' LIFE

321. This Priyadas wrote a book in Sanskrit, describing the extraordinary deeds of *bhaktas* of Vishnu in this *Kali Yuga.* 322. Tulsidas heard that he had written this book containing the stories of saints. So on a certain occasion he came to visit Priyadas. 323. He said, ' O *Swami*, you have written the stories of saints. I have not listened to them. Bring me the book and show it to me. ' 324. Priyadas replied, ' I have described the *bhaktas* belonging to the four *yugas.* But I have not written in this book the noble story of Tulsidas.' 325. Even the *Vaishnava bhaktas* of *Kali Yuga* were described in that book. Therefore he (Priyadas) felt very much troubled. Just then a very wonderful thing happened. 326. Unknown to Priyadas, Shri Ram came there and with His own hands wrote the story of Tulsidas. 327. In order to listen to the book, all the *Vaishnavas* assembled and sat in the assembly hall by the great door of the temple. 328. Clever and wise *pandits* also sat down

to listen. Priyadas the God-loving *bhakta* read aloud from the book. 329. All the *Vaishnavas* admired the book that was written by Priyadas. It was Tulsidas who said to him that it was Shri Hari who spoke through his lips. 330. Hearing this remark made by the saint (Tulsidas), Priyadas said to them, ' Ram came and wrote the whole history of Tulsidas. ' 331. All the noble *Vaishnavas* now examined the handwriting of Ram. The power of *bhaktas* is great. Neither *Vedas* nor *Shashtras* are able to describe it. 332. In attempting to describe the characteristics of Shri Hari the eighteen *Puranas* had to remain silent. And the six *Shastras* had to ackowledge that they did not understand His power. 333. If one constantly listens to this explanation of the book with pleasure he will certainly have a sight of Shri Ram. 334. Thus the beloved of Shri Ram, the full *avatar* of Vālmīki, had his story recorded by Ram's own hand. 335. Priyadas' first book was in the Sanskrit language. After that, Nabhaji wrote in the Gwalior language. 336. After listening to its verses I have written this book in the Marathi tongue, just as the milkman adds a little water to his milk. 337. As in setting a diamond in a gold ornament, lacquer is used in the act of placing it, so, you saints and good people, have listened to my uncouth language. 338. It is God Himself who is describing the life of Tulsidas; listen to it, therefore, with reverence. Those who do so, assume the form of Shri Ram. 339. The Husband of Rukmini, Dweller by the banks of the Bhima, is the real Author of this book. Mahipati's name appears in these verses, but the real writer is Ram.

340. *Svasti.* This book is the *Bhaktavijaya.* In listening to it, the Lord of the world is pleased. Listen therefore you God-loving, pious *bhaktas.* This is the third delightful chapter.

CHAPTER IV

LIFE OF NAMDEV

Obeisance to Shri Ganesh. Obeisance to the Beloved of the Gopis.

1. Victory, Victory, to Thee, Pervader of the Universe the Saviour of the world, Father of Cupid, beautiful with His dark complexion, loved by the mind of the blue-throated One (God Shiva), Lord of all, Govinda, 2. Victory to Thee who lived at Gokul, Protector of the cows, the Child of Yashoda, Father of Brahmadev, Slayer of Kanas, Preserver of the universe, Lord of the senses. 3. Victory to Thee who dwellest at Dwaraka, who has in His hand the Sharang bow, generous in the extreme in the giving of Final Deliverance, beloved by the daughter of the sea (Lakshmi, the goddess of wealth), Lord of the Universe and Ruler of the world. 4. Victory to Thee who delightest the heart of Radhika, the one who findest Vaikunth the place of Thy pleasure, the Life of the world, the Slayer of Putana, the Killer of Kaliya, Destroyer of this worldly existence, O Shri Hari, 5. Victory to Thee, Giver of the promise to Pundalik, Husband of Rukmini, Deliverer of Draupadi from humiliation, Lover of Thy *bhaktas*, Cloud of mercy, Victorious King Shri Ram. 6. Victory to Thee Lover of Thy *bhaktas*, Lord of Pandhari, Pervader of the universe, Husband of Lakshmi, Thou, the Infinite One, be my Helper, and enable me to compose this book.

NAMDEV AND KABIR AS AVATARS OF UDDHAV AND SHUKA

7. Now listen to Nama's story, you good hearers. Narayan invited Uddhav and Shuka to see Him on the ocean of milk. Said he to them, ' I wish you to become *avatars* in the world of mortals. ' 8. They replied to Him who

dwells on the Ocean of Milk, 'We do not wish to be born in the natural way, O Vishnu, give us birth in an unnatural way.' 9. Listening to them, the Life of the world turned them into infants, put them in shells, and dropped them down from raining clouds. 10. One fell into the Bhagirathi river. One fell in the Bhimarathi river. As they flowed along with the stream they repeated the names of God. Listen to what they said. 11. The one in the shell that fell in the Bhagirathi river repeated the name 'Ram, Ram.' The other who fell in the Bhimarathi river cried in his delight, 'Vitthal, Vitthal.' 12. So Shuka became the worshipper of Ram, and Uddhava became the worshipper of Pandurang (Vitthal). Listen to the wonderful things that happened as they flowed along. 13. There was one Damaji a tailor, a *Vaishnava*, supremely pious, pure through good deeds, and perfect in his devotion to God, his knowledge, and his indifference to worldly things. 14. After bathing in the Chandrabhaga, he went to worship Pandurang. After completing this, it was his regular custom to take his morning meal. 15. His wife Gonai was supremely pious and a dutiful wife. They both lived at Pandhari and were constant in repeating the names of the Lord of the World. 16. Gonai had no child of her own, so she said to her husband, 'Go to Pandurang and ask for a son.' 17. Damaji said to her, 'You are an ignorant woman. We are both now aged. Why should we expect God to give us a child? 18. If insects have eaten the seeds, there is no use of expecting a crop when sown. So are you not ashamed to ask for a son ? 19. What is the good of wishing that clouds would pour down rain, after the rainy season ? So you ought to be ashamed to wish for a son. 20. The mango tree does not bear fruit in the month of Shravan. So are you not ashamed to ask for a son ? 21. After the oil and wick in the lamp have been consumed, only darkness will prevail. It is like that when you wish for a son of which you are not ashamed.' 22. The wife replied, 'Lord of my life, you blame me for being unreasonable, but God's power is supreme. Now I know that you are ignorant. 23. When Ram was an *avatar*, He made stones float on the sea. What difficulty has He in giving us a child although we are aged? 24. When Brahmadev carried away the calves, He himself became cows and cowherds. What difficulty can He have, therefore, in giving us a son?' 25. Damaji said to his wife, 'I will go now to the temple and tell God the wish you hold in your mind.' 26. He therefore went to the great door of the temple and there prostrated himself before God.He said, 'My wife desires a son. Be pleased to give one, Shri Hari.' 27. After saying this, he immediately fell asleep. The Life of the world came to him in a dream and said, 'I have given you the gift of a son.' 28. When at sunrise you go to bathe on the bank of the Bhima, a son will come floating down the stream. Take the babe up, and hasten back to your home with it. 29. The *avatar* of Uddhav will fill the three worlds with the glory of his deeds. He will be a saviour of the world, and a supreme *Vaishnava*.' He carries my name. 30. Hearing this in his dream, he hurried back to his home. There he told his wife just what had happened. 31. The next day Damaji came early to the bank of the Bhima. He quickly bathed and performed his daily devotions. 32. Just then he suddenly noticed a shell floating down the Bhima. He waded into the river, and took up the shell. 33. When he opened the shell his eyes fell on a beautiful babe, just as if at that very moment it had come from the womb of its mother. 34. As he saw it his mind was troubled, for he said, 'Who will nurse it?' He wrapped up the infant in his garment, and brought it to his home. 35. He said to his wife, 'God has given us a son.' Gonai took the child, and immediately her breast filled with milk.

36. Both of them thought it very strange, that in her old age she should be able to nurse the child. She bathed the infant, and with great love fed it at her breast. 37. Because they had made God pleased with them, and had asked for a son from the dark-complexioned One, they therefore called him Nama, and they had intense love for the child.

THE IMAGE OF GOD EATS NAMDEV'S OFFERING OF FOOD

38. Day by day the child grew in stature. Now listen to what happened. Damaji went to the market, and he sent Nama to the temple. 39. Gonai gave him an offering to take to the temple. The mother said to Nama, 'Show this offering to the god and come back.' 40. Taking with him all necessary things for worship, Nama came into the temple. He bowed prostrate before the god, and worshipped with all the materials he had brought. 41. He bathed the image. He clothed it in a yellow robe. He offered sandalwood paste and flowers, and presented incense and lamps. 42. He then placed the plate of food for offering before the image. He joined his hands together palm to palm, and said, 'Be pleased now to eat.' 43. Nama had always conceived the idea that God always ate these offerings. He had no doubt about it in his mind. It was his firm conviction. 44. He said, 'Victory, Victory to Thee, Merciful One. Thou, Lord of Pundalik, must be angry because of my delay in bringing the offering. 45. But Damaji Thy *bhakta* has gone early to the market, and has sent me here to present this offering of food. 46. If Thou dost not eat this offering of food, my mother will be angry with me. What wrong have I done, O Lord of the world, that Thou dost not eat this offering of food?' 47. Nama had no question in his mind, as to how a stone image could eat, therefore he began to sob aloud, and said, 'O God, eat this offering.' 48. Seeing Nama's pure thoughts, God Supreme became pleased. He caressed Nama, and embraced him. 49. God manifested

his love by eating the offering which Nama had brought. Hari said to Nama, 'By no means tell anyone about this event.' 50. After making obeisance to God, Nama returned to his home. His mother said to him, 'Whom did you give that offering to?' 51. Nama said, 'O mother, the god ate the offering.' Now next day Damaji returned from the market. 52. After inquiring of his wife what had happened he heard the whole story about the offering. Damaji became much perplexed; it seemed to him a very extraordinary thing. 53. He said to Nama, 'How was it that the god ate? Let us both go to the temple, and show me what took place.' 54. They took with them the materials for worship, and both came to the great door of the temple. There they bowed to the Saviour of the world, and began at once to worship. 55. They worshipped the god, with the sixteen forms of worship, and fittingly offered incense and lights. Nama said to the eagle-bannered One, 'Be pleased to eat.' 56. The god said to Nama, 'Damaji has come with you; I shall never appear to his sight. I will meet with you.' 57. Nama said to God, 'Thou art a deceiver, Thou sayest Thou wilt not meet with my father. Thou seemest to me, O God, to use deception.' 58. Hearing Nama's remark, the Life of the world began to laugh. He gave Damaji a sight of Him and ate the offering. 59. The father said to Nama, 'You have been born in my family line, therefore God in His love has given me this vision.' 60. Thus satisfying his doubts, the father bowed prostrate before the god. He took Nama by the hand, and returned to their home. 61. He told the whole story to his wife. 'The Lord of Heaven truly ate the offering. We must no longer call Nama a relative, because he is God's *bhakta.*' 62. Gonai then said, 'God had mercy upon you, and gave you a son, though born in an unnatural way.'

NAMDEV'S MARRIAGE

63. Thus with their doubts settled, they bestowed great love on Nama. After searching for one who would be a helpmate, he was married.

64. When Nama was growing up he had a son. For the naming of the child on the twelfth day, the Life of the world Himself brought the gifts. 65. Gonai said to God, 'Nama has now a son. What name shall I give him, O God, tell me.' 66. Listening to what she said, the Life of the world replied, 'Call him Narayan, and play with him in love and joy.' 67. The Brahmans were then invited, both men and women, and the *Punyāhavāchan* then began. It was the Life of the world who in His love gave gifts to Nama. 68. He gave *sari* and jackets to Gonai and gave the child a garment and a cap. God Himself gave them and then went back to His home in Heaven. 69. Gonai said to Nama, 'Both of us are now aged. You are engaged in the contemplation of God. Day and night you meditate. 70. Your thoughts are always occupied with His name and form. Not for a moment do you think of yourself. You are holding the Lord of Pandhari in your heart. He has persecuted you extremely. 71. In your domestic life we require every sort of thing. But you, my son, have become one indifferent to worldly things. What can I now do?' Such was Gonai's exclamation. 72. 'There are many *Vaishnavas* who carry on at the same time their domestic affairs and their religious life. It seems to me that your condition is quite different from theirs. 73. In your domestic life you have children, but you have very little food and few garments. The evil-minded laugh at you, what are we to do?' 74. At these words of his mother's he felt grieved about himself. He went to the temple and bowed prostrate before God. 75. Said he, 'O Shri Hari, who dwellest at Pandhari, why didst Thou put

me in this domestic life? Why hast Thou deserted me in the sad sea of this worldly existence?' 76. Hearing Nama's piteous plea, God said to him, 'Who is it that is troubling you?' He lovingly embraced him, and wiped his eyes. 77. Nama replied, 'Oh God, it is my mother, Gonai, who is troubling me, but I am continually remembering Thy feet. Cause the shadow of Thy mercy to cover me.' 78. God said to Nama, 'You should always remain with me, then the illusion and seductions of the world will never touch you. 79. You are a portion of Myself. And I am in your form. Just as salt gathered from the sea is not different from the salt water to the eyes of knowledge; 80. and as the sun and its rays are not different from one another; so your life and My life are united, O Nama. 81. A lamp and its light, although they are one, yet they seem different. So your love and Mine are the same. 82. You cannot separate sweetness from sugar. So your thoughts and Mine are not different, O Nama. 83. A diamond and its brilliancy, although not different, are spoken of as different. So let your heart regard your love and Mine, O Nama. 84. Or only as the most precious pearl is spoken of as different from its lustre, so you, God-loving *bhakta*, are not different from Me, O Nama. 85. Ordinary water and the water of the Ganges are never different, so I, of dark complexion, am not different from you, O Nama. 86. Gold and the ornaments made from it are surely not different, so your thoughts and Mine are not different, O Nama. 87. When sound proceeds from a bell, it becomes really one with the bell itself. So, considering our oneness, you must destroy the thought of duality.'

NAMDEV AND GOD CONVERSE

88. Nama said to God, 'What is this knowledge that Thou art teaching me? If Thy name is on the tip of one's tongue, who would pay any attention

to the sorrow of this worldly existence? 89. If Thy form is reflected in my heart, where would there be any room for the sorrows of this worldly existence? If Thou art mother and father in this worldly existence, no sorrow can come upon me. 90. Thou art God. I am Thy *bhakta*. I will sing Thy praises with my lips. I ask this blessing of love in every future birth of mine. Give it to me. 91. Thou speakest of the supremacy of the joy that comes from the deliverance from rebirths. But I do not agree with that.' Hearing this remark of Nama's, God smiled. 92. The Life of the world said to Rukmini, 'Nama is desirous of seeing Me in visible form. If he is taught philosophic knowledge it does not satisfy him.' 93. Thus saying, God drew Nama to His heart. He embraced him, and held him close to Him. 94. The Dweller in Heaven (Vaikunth) said to Nama, 'What is your manner of life at home? Tell Me. Do not be ashamed to do so.' 95. Hearing this, Nama replied, 'If one has Thy blessing what could there be lacking? Thy home is the Heaven of Vaikunth. We live in a broken down hut. 96. The eight *Siddhis* (accomplishments personified) are Thy slaves. In our home rats live. Thou art clothed with the divine garments, my children have no clothes to wear. 97. Thou reclinest on the serpent Shesha in the ocean of milk, but we cannot obtain even a seat made of straw. Thou hast platters of gold; we have leaves to eat on. 98. Thou hast gold and silver in Thy home, but our comfort is Thy name.' Hearing this remark, Krishna laughed.

GOD DISGUISED AS KESHAVSHET

99. Turn now to Nama's wife. She experienced much trouble in her home, and said to her mother-in-law, 'For me you have given birth to a pure crystal. 100. But now my garments are torn and exceedingly old. I have not enough to eat. I have, therefore, come to your house to

live my poverty-stricken life. 101. He whom I serve with devotion has been persecuting me. I see no way of bettering our domestic state.' 102. As Nama's wife was in great trouble in her own home, the Lord of Pandhari, Helper of the helpless, had mercy on her. 103. Without Nama knowing it, God became a merchant by name Keshava. This was because of his great love for His *bhakta*. In their distresses He at once came to their relief. 104. He filled a bag with gold coins, and he said to His Eagle, 'Take the form of an ox, and come to the house of Nama.' 105. He took the bag of money along with him, and on His way he said to the people, 'Will some one tell me the way to Nama's house?' 106. Hearing this question the townspeople laughed. They said, 'There is no food to eat at Nama's house. Who can this guest be that has arrived?' They added, 107. 'Do you see yonder *tulsi* altar with many *tulsi* plants around it? Many bright banners adorn the altar. That is Nama's house.' 108. Krishna said to Rajai, 'Some guests have come to your home. Come outside at once and give them a place to sit down.'

109. Hearing these words, Rajai was perplexed. 'Where could a guest come from? I do not know who this is whose coming will humiliate me.' 110. She therefore attempted to send him away, and said to him, 'The master of the house is not here, therefore I wish you to go back.' 111. To the neighbours who assembled she said, 'These guests have nearly taken my life, what am I I to do? 112. Just listen to the strange things that are happening. Innumerable *sadhus* have come into my house. They carry cymbals and *vinas* and dance in their love. 113. They put aside all thought of shame and public praise. They put aside all thoughts of caste difference. They hold the Chief of Yadavas in their heart and dance in their delight 114. The master of my house has told me that I must feed

every saint that comes to the house. Now I have not the least bit of food in the house, but he does not know this.' 115. Shri Hari was standing at the door listening to that conversation. He said to Rajai, 'Come outside quickly.' 116. She asked from behind the door, 'Where are you from, and who are you? And tell me your name.' 117. Hearing her question the Lord of the world replied, 'My name is Keshav Shet; I love Nama dearly, and I have come to visit him. 118. I have heard the news that you have no food in your house. Nama is a friend of mine, and therefore I have brought him some gold coins.' 119. Hearing this answer of His, Rajai came outside in crder to bring and give him a seat. 120. Seeing that she spoke harshly to Him, and then spoke with reverence, amused the Lord of the world, and smiling He remarked, 121. 'You saw the money I have brought, and now you speak very friendly, therefore one should not ever go anywhere empty-handed. 122. One should never go to a marriage, without carrying a wedding gift. One should never go to see the king without money in his hand. 123. One should never go to visit one's daughter or sister empty-handed. So during the time of distress one should not go to visit at the house of a relative or an evil-minded person. 124. One should never visit sacred places at festivals empty-handed. One should not go empty-handed when going to a temple to worship God. 125. When going to see and pay worship to a *sadhu* or *guru* you should at least take a *tulsi* leaf as Sudama, with great reverence, gave me a handful of parched rice. 126. Everybody is selfish, and I pay them as they deserve. Nama alone worships me without a selfish desire.' 127. So God said to Rajai, 'Do not do anything now to trouble Nama. 128. I have brought a bag full of money. Store it in your house, and when it is all spent, call on me for more. 129. Give Nama my kind regards and tell him that his friend had called.' Nama's wife having heard this said to Vithoba (Krishna), 130. 'Do not be angry with me, because I spoke harshly to you. I did not know that you were a friend of the master of the house. 131. Eat therefore and then go on your way.' The Lord of Heaven replied, I will not eat without the presence cf Nama.' 132. So saying Vithoba hastened to go away. He came to Rukmini and told her all the news.

GONAI'S COMPLAINT TO GOD

133. Now Rajai felt very much comforted at heart and said, 'My husband served God and He has been pleased.' 134. She tore open the bag and took out a lapful of gold coins. She went at once to the market and gave it to the grocer. She said to him, 135. 'You know what materials are needed for one's domestic life. Send them to my house.' 136. After saying this to him, she hastened back to her home. The merchant was perplexed, but said to himself, 'God must be helping him.' 137. He sent to Nama's house various garments and ornaments, melted butter, rice, sugar, and other materials. She (Rajai) could not contain herself for joy. 138. Gonai had gone out, and she knew nothing of what had occurred. She had gathered some grain and was returning to her house. 139. She thought to herself, 'Nama has sulked and gone off. I will go to the temple, console him, and bring him back. 140. Thus saying, she hastened to the great door of the temple. She bowed to God on the eagle-platform, and then came into the assembly hall. 141. As she looked she saw God standing before her sight. He put Nama behind Him when he saw Gonai. 142. Gonai said, 'O God, turn Thy face this way towards me. Thou hast made Nama love Thee greatly, and so we are lacking in our worldiy affairs. 143. By association with Thee, O Govinda, he has neglected his home and business. In his worldly affairs he is suffering distresses,

because he has no taste for things that please the senses. 144. Giving up all ties of affection, he has firmly grasped Thy feet. By our lack of things in our domestic life, we are laughed at by the evil-minded. 145. Putting aside all thoughts of himself, he enjoys perfect satisfaction. It is Thou who hast turned his mind to non-duality, and he has no longer thoughts of worldly things. 146. Those who become associated with Thee, Thou makest like Thyself, I have never seen, nor heard anyone associated with Thee coming back to his domestic life. 147. Thou hast purposely brought about ill feeling between us, and put Nama behind Thee. His wife is in great distress at home, but O God, Thou hast no pity. 148. Thou art destroying my life by taking pity on Nama. I will no longer hold Thee in reverence, O Husband of Rukmini. 149. With great love I bore him for nine months, but Thou, O God, hast made me hopeless. Thou hast divided us in our worldly affairs. 150. Thou callest Thyself generous, but tell me what and whom Thou hast given anything? O Life of the world, I do not believe in the praise that is given Thee. 151. Thou didst take Sudama's handful of parched rice, and for it Thou didst give him a city of gold. Thou never comest to the aid of one, unless he gives Thee something. 152. Seeing Ravan's power Thou didst turn Bibhishana against him and taking advantage of this domestic division, Thou gavest him the gift of Ceylon. 153. When Draupadi was in great distress, Thou didst first take from her a vegetable leaf (to satisfy Thy own hunger), and then feasted the *rishis*, and thus Thou didst proclaim Thy generosity. 154. In describing Thy bad qualities, the serpent Shesha grew weary in his writing. I have had some reverence for Thee, therefore Thy divinity has remained.' 155. Hearing Gonai's reply, God laughed and said, 'You are needlessly angry with me. 156. Your crazy Nama who cares not for himself, insisted on clinging to My feet. If you have a false coin, why quarrel with another about it ? 157. With love in your heart you look to Nama from the point of view of his being a son. You try to divide us and seek to reproach us with your lips. 158. If you have any love, take away your son from here. Do not needlessly place upon Me the wrong you charge. 159. A fruit has ripened on a stem, the wind blew against it and it fell down. And so in the case of Nama, you have brought a false charge against Me. 160. I am the Unborn, the Imperishable, the Unconquerable, and have no relation with the three *gunas* (*satva*, *raja*, and *tama*). Out of love for Nama I assumed a form and visible attributes. 161. I was formless when there existed no space, no air, no water, no earth, no light, no fire, when even Brahmadev, Vishnu and Shiva did not exist, and everything was without form. 162. Then Nama has been my associate, and my love has been intense. And why you want to quarrel with me, I do not understand. 163. Just as when a tree bears fruits, the gardener plucks and takes them away. The tree could not enjoy them itself. This separation has been caused by its own bad deeds (in its former birth). 164. So consider Me as a tree in the form of the universe, and the loving Nama was the nectar fruit on it. You have plucked off that fruit, and I feel troubled thereby !' 165. Gonai replied, 'O God, Thou art talking very proudly. Thou dost compel me to swallow pebbles (for lack of grain), and makest a separation between us. 166. The farmers with various efforts raise crop from the earth. The king comes along and exacts a penalty, and becomes lord of the division. 167. Suffering much I have raised Nama from childhood to adult age, and now Thou dost claim to be his owner in a very wrong way.' 168. Hearing Gonai's reply the Life of the world laughed and said to Himself, 'I must explain it all to her plainly. 169. If I do not do so, she will ruin my reputation.' Therefore the Husband of Rukmini replied to her. 170. The dark-complexioned One said to Gonai, 'Your good deeds are entirely pure in motive, therefore this God-loving *bhakta* came to your womb. 171. As the great *Vaishnava* Narad was born to Bramhadev and Savitri, so is it with you and the fortunate *bhakta* Damashet, through whom Nama has descended as an *avatar*. 172. Just as in the line of demons, the *bhakta* Pralhad became an *avatar* by being born to Kayadhu, so Nama the servant of Vishnu has been born from you for the salvation of the world. 173. Among the sixty-five million Yadavas, Udhhava was the most distinguished *Vaishnava*. So in the line of tailors Nama has become an *avatar*. 174. Just as among saints, *sadhus* and *yogis*, the son of Anusaya was the most distinguished, so you seem the most fortunate of women, that you have had such a jewel of a son in Nama. 175. Or just as the king Uttanacharan had as his distinguished wife Suniti, and she gave birth to their son Dhruva and he made me subservient to him. 176. Or as Maruti was born in the race of monkeys from his mother Anjani (a female eagle) so Nama, the embodiment of virtue, has been born to you. 177. O Gonai, blessed is your devotion, for this *Vaishnava* has come to your womb. Who can describe your fortune, in that you should become the nurse of Nama? 178. Taking Nama to your bosom, you rested with him on your bed. I cannot sufficiently describe your great good fortune. 179. While eating with Nama you ate taking him to your side. You only are cognizant of the great number of your good deeds, dear friend. 180. I who am above every other being, and unconquered, am the one who is describing your good character. You alone have the fortunate blessing of having Nama as your son.'

181. Gonai replied, 'O Life of the world, O Pervader of the universe, the Delight of the heart, give me my son Nama, and let his love of worship still remain.' 182. After hearing her say this, God looked up and saw that she would influence Nama to engage in worldly affairs. Therefore He was very much troubled. 183. As the Life of the world remained silent, Gonai understood its meaning. The power of reason is the highest kind of knowledge. So say the wise men. 184. While studying about the fourteen spheres of knowledge and every form of wisdom coming to one's hand, if the mind has no reasoning power these fourteen spheres are entirely useless to him. 185. One may show learning in the king's assembly; justice and morality may be discussed, and the replies may depend on the assembly which appears before him; still there must be the power of reason. 186. In arranging a matrimonial connection, or in one's business relations with others, or in the reading of books, there must be the knowledge of reasoning. 187. In forming friendship with someone whom to trust when revealing a secret, or when writing a book, there is necessary the knowledge of reasoning. 188. To be able to give a gift to a worthy person, or to give the right medicine to the sick, to perform the praise service suitable to the asssembly present, the power of reasoning is necessary.

GONAI'S APPEAL TO SATYABHAMA AND KALINDI

189. In the story already related, it was stated that the Life of the world remained silent. So Gonai called Rahi and Rukmini and told them her story. 190. She lovingly called the good Satyabhama and Kalindi. Gonai said to them, 'Listen to what I have to say. 191. Your Husband is merciful to the lowly, of whom the *Vedas* and *Shastras* speak in praise. So why has He been pleased to cause my child to possess the condition of one unconscious of

his own body ? 192. My child is my only-begotten, yet God has turned him to worshipping Him all the time. Such is this false actor as you all know. 193. Shuka, Sanaka, and other distinguished *sadhus*, saints, and other leading *yogis* are familiar with the fact that He has ruined my home. 194. We are weak, helpless and lowly. We have no garments or food at our home. He has turned Nama to the contemplation of Himself. Please understand this. 195. I have seen and heard of many gods. A fastidious person is known at dinner, but I have never seen anyone quite so reserved as this man is. 196. He calls Himself a family deity at whose feet I should always fall, but He needlessly employs deception and needlessly troubles us. 197. Until to-day I have paid him reverence, and so His high reputation remains. But if he carries matters to the extreme, I shall lose regard for him before the public. 198. At His sight, one's own life is destroyed. He has turned my only-begotten son to His contemplation. Friends, what am I to do ? 199. You have all heard my story. Beseech the dark-complexioned One and tell Him to free me from my trouble. 200. All you wives, coming together, should bring Krishna to my house, and there ask Him what He has in His mind to do, friends.'

GONAI REBUKES GOD

201. She then turned to Nama and said to him, 'Why are you sitting here ? I will take you away by force in the very presence of the god. 202. Nama, you are a thief as regards our domestic life. This Enchanter of the world is our enemy. He stands on the brick and destroys the domestic life of others. 203. O this false Saviour of the world, Pundlik gave Him a place to stay, therefore you do not come home, and have brought our domestic affairs to ruin. 204. So I will never leave this place without taking you with me. I am determined to swallow the whole of Pandhari. 205. O You of

beautiful form, and wise one, reply to me. You Lord of the Yadavas are sitting silent, O Vitthal, You Destroyer of the house.' 206. Gonai said to him, 'O Life of the world Pervader of the universe, Ornament of *bhaktas*, why does my plea not come to your mind? O Cloud of mercy, 207. give back Nama to me, and thus may Thy fame increase in the world.' Hearing her say this, the Husband of Lakshmi spoke as follows:— 208. 'Listen to me, Gonai, take your son and go away. You are making a vain attempt to found a charge against me.' 209. Vitthal said to Gonai, 'Take your son Nama by the hand, and lead him away. Take your son to your house even now. 210. He has put aside all ties of affection, but the charge of wrongdoing has needlessly been cast on me. Take your son and go back to your home. Why do you continue such useless charges?' 211. Thus speaking, the Husband of Lakshmi brought Nama and placed him in her hand, and Gonai then at once started for her home. 212. As they walked along the road his mother said to Nama, 'You have deserted your business and have gone to the Lord of Pandhari as a suppliant.' 213. Hearing this charge of Gonai, Nama hung his head and tears of love flowed from his eyes. 214. So the mother taking Nama by the hand returned to their home. Just then Rajabai started to do her cooking in her part of the house.

NAMDEV SICKENS AT FORTUNE'S SIGHT

215. She prepared many kinds of delicious food including nine kinds of cooked food saying to herself, 'The Life of the world has done a very remarkable thing,' and she was full of joy. 216. But Nama saw with great displeasure the various pots and vessels, and the garments and ornaments which had been given to his wife. 217. Just as when a deer that has been ensnared in a net becomes distressed, so Nama by holding these rich vessels experienced the same distress; 218. or

as when a strong wind blows upon a light, it at once loses its brightness; so Nama's sad mind lost its happiness in seeing these riches; 219. or just as a beautiful person, when he finds himself a victim to leprosy, feels disgusted in his mind, so *Vaishnava bhaktas* feel disgusted at the sight of wealth; 220. or as when the sun is in eclipse it seems to be without any brightness, so, when he saw this illusory wealth, his face turned sad; 221. or as when a south wind strikes a cloud, it melts away in every direction; so in Nama's heart there was dejection. 222. As when a king hears of a defeat he finds his mind full of perplexity, so this *bhakta* of Vishnu became full of concern. 223. Or as Shuka sat performing his austerities, he was troubled at the sight of Rambha, so Nama seeing this wealth became sad at heart. 224. He asked his mother lovingly, 'Where has all this wealth come from?' Gonai replied, 'I surely do not know.' 225. Nama's wife said to him, 'You are very late in eating, so perform your bath at once, and sit down and enjoy the food which God has bestowed as a favour.' 226. Nama wondered to himself, 'Why is she speaking so humbly to-day? It must be because my wife feels great comfort in seeing all this wealth and grain in the house.' 227. When there is no money in one's possession, even a brother calls one an enemy, and the evil-minded and wrongdoers laugh, and this is what is called affection. 228. Seeing her son unable to acquire money, even his father is disgusted with him and says, 'In being born to us, you have brought us a bad reputation.' 229. The neighbours are displeased with him and say, 'He seems to us to idle away his time, so when he goes to visit his daughter or sister they feel ashamed to see him. 230. A wife will not embrace a husband who is so weak.' His sons say, 'He has put us all into debt.' 231. Thus all enjoy association with one in happy circumstances, but in time of his distress they turn away from him. Nama had love for the Brother of the helpless, the Husband of Rukmini. 232. Nama said to his wife, ' Where did you bring this bagful of wealth from ? ' But she maintaining silence uttered not a word. 233. She thought to herself, 'If I inform him of it just now, he will distribute it off-hand.' Therefore knowing he would do so she said nothing in reply. 234. Just then Jani, Nama's maidservant, hastened near to Nama, bowed at his feet, and told him what had occurred. 235. She said, ' Rajabai was greatly troubled. God quickly came to her help. He became a merchant by name of Keshavshet and forced this bag of wealth upon her. 236. The Lord of Heaven became a Kanarese Lingayat, and standing in front of her house informed her that He had come as her guest.' 237. Rajabai said to Him, ' Tell me your name. ' Hearing her, the Cloud of mercy replied. 238. The lotus-eyed One, in kindly words said, ' Nama is my greatest friend. You ask Me My special name. I am spoken of as one whose complexion is that of a dark cloud. 239. Hearing that there was a lack here of food and raiments, I have come with a bag full of coins. 240. When this bag of money is spent I will bring some more. So that from to-day no one should trouble Nama. 241. The Husband of Rukmini let the bag down from the ox's back, and he has only just gone.' At this point tears flowed from Nama's eyes.

NAMDEV DISTRIBUTES HIS FORTUNE

242. He cried, ' O Krishna, Purifier of the sinner, Lover of the *bhaktas*, the Ornament of Thy saints, Ocean of mercy, Life of the world, the Delight of the heart, Shri Vitthal. 243. Thou who art the Unborn, the Unconquered, the Imperishable, Unaffected by *maya*, Void of any pain, Helper of the helpless, the Home of compassion, why hast Thou wearied Thyself on my behalf ? 244. Thou

never comest to the sight of those who practise rigorous austerities. But to-day Thou becamest the merchant Keshavshet for my sake. 245. O Thou Merciful to the lowly, Mother Krishna, it was not I who gave Thee this trouble, and yet Thou didst rush to my help on foot. 246. *Bhaktas* with desire in their hearts worship Thee, but Thou dost not give them the wealth they seek. But without my asking Thee, O Husband of Rukmini, Thou didst rush to my aid out of love. 247. If a cloud pours down rain on the ocean, of what use is that? So, O God, the gold Thou gavest me I regard as of no value. 248. Casting aside the *Riddhis* and *Siddhis* (female deities, presiding over accomplishments), royal wealth, the four forms of final deliverance, including that of *Salokata*, I think, O God, of Thy feet alone day and night. 249. I know nothing about sacred places, religious rites, the practices of *yoga*, mystic formulas, or austerities. I sing only of Thy name day and night with love.' 250. Praising God in these words, he then called the Brahmans of the town and gave to these twice-born the money, the garments, and the ornaments. 251. And now Nama without any hindrance worshipped the Good Being with reverence. Even Brahmadev was ignorant of Nama's love.

252. This book containing the history of the saints may be thought of as the ancient sacred city of Pandhari. The pure-minded and the good *Vaishnavas* come to visit it. 253. Those who are suffering from fever cannot bear the taste of cooked food. So those desiring wealth and wives will not enjoy these stories. 254. But those who worship without the desire of worldly things and are indifferent to them, they will enjoy this book. Those who are inclined to evils and are not *bhaktas* will feel a distaste for these stories. 255. Crows want meat for their food, so why would they come to the ocean of milk? So be well assured that those

who are not *bhaktas* will not find this book at all to their taste. 256. The good-natured swans will like my saying as delicious. So those who have love in their hearts are without disturbing thoughts.

257. In the next chapter we shall have the wonderfully delightful tale of the *bhakta* Kabir, the *avatar* of Shuka. May *bhaktas* in love listen to these delightful stories. 258. I will write their lives somehow or other just as they happened. In fact, it is the doing of saints who caused me, Mahipati, to write my name in these verses.

259. *Swasti* (Peace!). This book is the *Shri Bhaktavijaya*. In listening to it the Lord of the world will be pleased. May the pious, God-loving *bhaktas* also listen. This is the fourth delightful chapter.

CHAPTER V

KABIR'S BIOGRAPHY

Obeisance to Shri Ganesh, Obeisance to Shri Krishna

1. Listen now, my hearers, to a story that is very interesting and very purifying. In thinking of its sweetness it is sweeter than nectar. This comparison even seems inadequate. 2. I undertake to describe its purity. It seems to be superior to the river Ganges. If I look at the great extent of its influence, I have nothing with which to compare it. 3. If I look to its depths of meaning, it looks deeper than the sea. It is more generous than the generous wish-tree to whom a prince and a pauper are alike. 4. If I think of how it brings coolness, a comparison of it with the moon is inadequate. Although the lustre of a diamond is most precious, still the light of this story would dim it. 5. If I look to the honour paid to it, it is sung by the five-faced god (Shiva). An equal would be impossible to find, so Indra and other gods search for it. 6. Such being the holy story of a saint, listen, you pious folks, with reverence.

KABIR AS AVATAR OF SHUKA

In a former chapter, I have related the story which all of you have heard, 7. namely, that a shell came floating down the river Bhima, and from it Gonai received the *bhakta* Nama. The shell fell into the Bhagirathi river, and was floating down exceedingly fast. 8. This very obstinate *avatar* of Shuka was not born in the natural way, and floating down the river Ganges landed at the Manikarnika *ghat* of Benares. 9. Becoming one with human attributes, through his unnatural form of birth, he continued repeating the names of God with his lips. From the shell a sound was continually coming out. It was of

'Ram, Ram.' 10. Just then Kamal the Muhammadan weaver came down to wash his thread. As he looked down he happened to see the shell. 11. He waded in the water, opened the shell and looked in. There his eyes beheld a babe, and his heart was full of joy. 12. It was as if a man without making any efforts finds a hidden store of wealth; or as if one hunting for a pool of water should suddenly see the ocean of milk; 13. or as if when stringing glass beads, one should find them to be pearls; or as when picking up shells, one should find there a jewel; 14. or as when hunting for the city of Yama (god of death), one should find the city of Vishnu; or as when hunting for a hut habitable to live in, one should find himself entering a golden palace; 15. or as when seeking to hear some obscene music, one should hear a service of praise of God; or as when one might go to watch a quarrel, it should turn out to be a song from the *Sama Veda*; 16. or as when spending one's energy on the *shindi* palm (wine yielding) tree, he should come across a wish-tree in his compound; or as when beginning to associate with a thief or immoral person, suddenly one's religious teacher should come to visit him; 17. so, while merely carrying on his daily business, Kamal found this babe in the Ganges river. This child was the *avatar* of Shri Shuka in this *Kali Yuga*, the universal Saviour, a world-Guru. 18. He wrapped the babe up in his garment, and hastened to his home. With heart overflowing with joy he said to his wife, 19. 'I have found a babe in the Ganges, of perfect beauty, endowed with thirty-two qualities. My dear wife, take care of it.' 20. Hearing this, his wife's breasts swelled with milk. She nursed the child and her joy overflowed. 21. A great *Vaishnava* was born in a Muhammadan family, therefore the name of Kabir was given to him. His father and mother loved him intensely. 22. Even while a babe it repeated God's name, and listening to it every one was astonished. They said, ' We wonder what good deeds this orthodox Muhammadan named Kamal performed in his former birth. 23. How is it that this Vishnu-*bhakta*, already distinguished by his religious characteristics, should be born to this Muhammadan ?' One replied, ' It was because fate was favourable to him. 24. If fate is favourable to anyone, why does one need the power of knowledge ? Madmen, born in a low caste, are often praised by all men, through the power of fate. 25. So this man's good fortune is extraordinary. A *bhakta* of Vishnu has come to birth through him. ' Such was the talk amongst all the people of that sacred city.

KABIR'S INDIFFERENCE TO WORLDLY THINGS

26. Well, because he had done some good deeds in his former births, Kabir was born to him (this Muhammadan) Day by day he grew in stature and his parents had him married. 27. The mother and father taught Kabir how to carry on his avocation, but he would not take it to heart. He would give no attention to a business life. 28. He could not distinguish what belonged to him and what belonged to others. He did not know what was joy and what was sorrow. He paid the same respect to a Brahman, a prince, or a pauper. 29. If he saw a heap of money fall before him, he had no desire to pick it up. If a thief came to rob him of his money, he did nothing to protect himself. 30. Because Kabir worshipped in this way, his business declined. The evil-doers and evil-minded laughed as they saw Kabir's conduct. 31. If a banana tree and a *bor* tree are planted in the same place it will not be happy for either. How can fire and water dwell together in friendship ? 32. How can a prostitute and a dutiful wife, a miser and a generous giver, a reviler and a man of intelligence, live together in peace ? There will be enmity between the one and the other. 33. How can a fly and dainty food get on well together ? A goat-herd and a

pandit cannot live together in friendship. 34. How can the demon Rahu and the moon, a moth and a flame, the sea and the *rishi* Agasti, dwell in love ? 35. While the story of Shri Krishna was being read, Shishupal was unwilling to listen. When Ravan heard of the might of Shri Ram he did not feel happy. 36. As there is perpetual enmity between poison and nectar, so there is always a mental, opposition between worldly riches and the supreme spiritual riches.

RAM WEAVES FOR KABIR

37. Well, enough of this long digression. Kabir continued his worship of God, while his business prosperity grew less. The evil-minded laughed at him. 38. 'You have taken God to your heart, and so has come about this condition of self-neglect. It does not appear how you will continue to carry on your domestic affairs.' 39. Having that day rubbed paste on the threads, Kabir was made to sit at the loom, but he was not able to think of himself. He was entirely lost in the worship of Ram. 40. Bringing the image of Ram to his imagination, he closed both his eyes. His full attention was given to the form and name of God. He no longer remembered his own bodily condition. 41. His mother came to him, and tried to awaken him. She said, 'Kabir, I do not know what has happened to you now.' 42. Believing that his mother would whip him, he came to self-consciousness and being now awake he wove a hand-breadth of cloth. 43. But just then he again became unconscious and the image of Shri Ram appeared in his heart. Seeing this to be the case, the Lord of Ayodhya (Ram) Himself sat down to weave. 44. Rama said to himself, ' He has lost himself in contemplating Me. His mother will give him a beating. ' So thinking, the Holder of the Bow (Ram), sat down to weave the *shela* (gold scarf). 45. He who finds his pleasure in the ocean of milk, Lord of

the universe, Dweller in the Heaven *Vaikuntha*, He sat down at Kabir's loom in order to weave. 46. *Yogis* sit on spiked beds and yet He does not quickly come into their imagination, but seeing Kabir's *bhakti* He sat down to weave the scraf. 47. He who cannot be attained by the study of the *Vedas* and *Shastras*, by wandering from sacred places to sacred places, He, Dweller at Dwaraka, Ornament of His *bhaktas*, sat down to weave the scarf. 48. He whom Sanak and other *munis* bring continually into their contemplation, even He, Hari, sat down to Kabir's loom and wove the scarf. 49. He whom the daughter of the ocean serves, holding His feet to her heart, He who is the dear ornament of Shiva, even He sat down to weave the scarf.

50. Now awaking, however, Kabir regained his consciousness and after a moment's thought he hastened to begin to weave. 51. But he was no more than awakened when the Husband of Janaki (Ram) came into his imagination. Kabir's mind attained its calmness, and beheld that it was Krishna who sat weaving. 52. Whenever Kabir lost self-consciousness then Krishna began to weave. When self-consciousness began to return Krishna would stand at a distance amused. 53. Thus Kabir and Krishna both together, wove the garment; just as when the water of the Saraswati joins the water of the Ganges, the two are no longer different; 54. so God and His *bhakta* together wove the garment. Kabir folded it up, came into the house and gave it to his mother. 55. The mother now said to Kabir, 'Go now into the market and quickly sell the scarf and come back bringing me the money.' 56. Saying 'I will do so,' Kabir started from his home, taking the scarf in his hand, and sat down in the *bazaar*. 57. He closed his eyes and brought to his mind the form of Shri Ram. He lost self-consciousness and continued singing the praise of Ram with his lips. 58. He forgot entirely

that he had come to sell the scarf. Holding God in his heart, he continued repeating the names of Ram in his love for Him. 59. Merchants came into the *bazaar* and Kabir sat down beside them, but no customers appeared for the purpose of buying the *shela*.

MIRACLE OF THE SHELA (SCARF)

60. Because the hand of God Supreme, Lord of the Heaven *Vaikunth*, had touched it, it seemed to would-be purchasers as they looked at it from a distance, as being too costly for them. 61. If buyers wished to purchase a garment within five rupees, it seemed to them that it was of twice that value. If they thought they would buy it for ten rupees, it appeared to them as if it were worth twenty rupees. 62. Those who would purchase it for twenty-five rupees, seemed to see it worth more than fifty. Those people who were in search of one worth fifty rupees, saw it as worth double that amount. 63. Purchasers who wished to spend five hundred or a thousand rupees seemed to see it as worth more than a thousand. Because it seemed of such high value, people merely glanced at it from a distance. 64. They said to themselves, 'Even if we ask him the price, we have no money with which to purchase it.' Some wealthy merchants passed by. It seemed to them to be worth more than a hundred thousand rupees. 65. Looking at one another, customers passed into the *bazaar* saying to one another, 'This *bhakta* Kabir weaves very costly garments. 66. As we have no money, our coming to the *bazaar* is useless.' Thus saying, men and women hastened back to their homes. 67. The value of the scarf seemed to exceed the financial ability of the customer. So no customer came to ask Kabir his price. 68. The garment that seemed to customers of the value at which they were willing to purchase it, that garment seemed to become double such value.

Just as in every living being the soul exists, just so it was in this case. 69. Having planted mustard, an onion, sugarcane, or any seed, and having given it water its sap gets the same characteristic as the plant. 70. When many musical instruments are being loudly played, space seems to take their very form; so Kabir's cloth seemed of a different nature to every one looking at it. 71. Or one might think of gold as being homogeneous, but ornaments made from it seem of various kinds; or just as a flame seems in size according as one piles on the wood; 72. or just as the beholder sees himself as he is in a looking glass held before him by a barber; so Kabir's scarf seemed to the customer. 73. Looking at it from a distance they said to themselves, 'We have not the ability to pay for it, and not having sufficient money with which to purchase it, why needlessly go and ask him the price? 74. Thus saying to themselves, customers went forward aimlessly into the *bazaar*. In the meantime the *bhakta* Kabir full of love continued his worship of Shri Ram. 75. As the sun began to set, the *bazaar* people began to dwindle. Kabir now opened his eyes and looked about him. 76. Said he, 'All the people have gone to their homes, and the scarf has no customer. If I go back to my home, my mother will give me a whipping.' 77. So saying, this *bhakta* of Vishnu continued sitting calmly. Just then he suddenly noticed an empty house.

GOD AS A BRAHMAN TESTS KABIR

78. Kabir quickly arose and went and sat inside, and continued his worship of Ram with love and affection. 79. Just as a daughter-in-law hides herself saying, 'My mother-in-law will treat me roughly,' so Kabir out of fear of his mother sat alone in this deserted house. 80. Or just as when Dhruva was kicked by his mother, and sulking went into the forest,

so this *bhakta* Kabir became indifferent to worldly things, and went and sat down in this vacant house. 81. Just as *sannyasis* attain their highest order by abandoning every form of action, so Kabir became indifferent to his domestic affairs, and sat down in this vacant house. 82. The servant of Vishnu having entered this deserted house for that purpose, the Pervader of the universe, seeing his devotion, came to test the truth of it. 83. He took the form of a very aged Brahman, with old and torn clothes. The cold was intense, just as it is in the months of *Paush* (January) and *Magha* (February). 84. In order to test the generosity of Kabir, the Life of the world entered shivering. As he sat there worshipping, this Brahman arrived. 85. Just as the son of Gadhi arrived to give trouble to the King Harischandra, or as the Lord of Kailas, assuming the form of a guest, came to trouble Shriyal; 86. or as the *Muni* Durvas, having heard of the goodness of Ambarish, came to trouble him; or as when God assuming the form of Vaman came to test Bali with his own eyes. 87. In that way this Brahman spoke to Kabir in a distressed voice, 'I am old, helpless and poor. I have no clothes to wear. 88. You are the *bhakta* of Vishnu and exceedingly generous. It is intensely cold; if you have any garments, give me some.' 89. As the Dweller in the Heaven Vaikunth said thus, Kabir thought to himself, 'If I say No to this Brahman, it will be to the harm of my desire to be good.' 90. So he tore his scarf in half and gave one piece to the Brahman. Kabir then full of love continued his worship. 91. Krishna then put on this garment and came immediately outside. Then he thought to Himself, 'I will go in again, and see what is happening.' 92. Thus saying, Krishna became a *fakir* in the guise of a Muhammadan. His head was adorned with a mass of hair. On his feet was an ornament made of crystal. 93. Carrying in his hands a rosary and opening wide his blood-shot eyes, the cloud-dark-One rushed violently into the house to test the truth about Kabir. 94. When gold is seen to be dimmed in lustre it is rubbed on a testing stone. Or when a coin is suspected of being false, it is forcibly punctured by an instrument. 95. Or when a valuable diamond is under consideration, the expert hammers it on an anvil. So, God became a Muhammadam *fakir* in order to test the mind of Kabir. 96. In a violent laughter He stood at the door and called Kabir. He said to Kabir, 'Give me at once a garment. 97. God is without form and without qualities. You have forgotten this. Why do you leave Him and worship Ram?' 98. Hearing this harsh voice, Kabir replied in soft tones. He said, 'To be without form and at the same time possess qualities, both can exist without any difference between them. 99. If butter is hardened or melted, it does not thereby lose its character of being butter. Or when an ornament is made of gold it does not thereby lose its lustre. 100. So, the Unmanifested, Eternal Being has taken form. The Pervader of the universe has assumed visible form for the purpose of His *bhaktas*.' 101. To these words of the noble *Vaishnava* the *fakir* said in reply, 'If you have got any garment, give it to me quickly.' 102. Kabir hastened to remove the half of the scarf which remained with him and gave it to the *fakir*. He then continued to sit there without any concern and the *fakir* hastened away. 103. Just as when the rainy season has passed away the sky looks clear; or as when the soldering is tested it turns out to be brilliant gold; 104. just as when the python has left the mount Maila, or as when Rahu has let go the moon, so Kabir sat down to his worship with quietness of mind. 105. Or as the water of the Ganges appears clear after the flood has ceased; or as when mount Mandara was drawn out of the ocean its roar ceased; 106. so, the concern which Kabir felt, when no customer appeared for the purchase of the scarf, disappeared from his mind. Kabir was now in a state of joy. 107. So thus satisfied in his mind, he sat worshipping Shri Ram. The Life of the world hearing this did something which I ask you to listen to.

GOD DISGUISED AS A BRAHMAN REPORTS TO KABIR'S MOTHER HIS INDIFFERENCE

108. In the guise of a Brahman, Krishna went to Kabir's house. He called to his mother and told her what had happened. 109. He said, 'Kabir sat in the *bazaar* and customers came and asked the price of the scarf, but he would not reply to them and kept silence. 110. A great number of customers came and he could give them no reply, but bringing the Husband of Sita to his mind he continued his worship. 111. When the whole bazaar was empty, he called to a Brahman, tore his scarf in half, and gave it to him, mother. 112. A *fakir* then called for the remainder of the garment, and Kabir at once gave him the other half of the scarf. 113. He saw there an empty house, and is seated there now performing his worship. I saw from a distance what was happening, and have hastened here to tell you. 114. It is the earnest wish of my heart that you may be prospered, but mother, Kabir will not put his mind to worldly affairs.' 115. As the Dweller in the Heaven Vaikunth said this, Kabir's mother grew very angry. She said to herself, 'When he comes home I will give him a sound beating.' 116. As the Delight of the mind (Ram) heard her say this, He exclaimed, 'He will not come home quickly. After a scorpion has completed its wrong doing by stinging, it hides itself in some other place. 117. Come along with me, I will show you where he is sitting.' Then taking the old woman by the hand, Krishna walked rapidly with her. 118. Both soon arrived where Kabir was seated, repeating the names of God. The Life of the world pointed him out to the old woman from a distance. 119. From the house in which Kabir was seated, there issued

the sound of Ram's name. Just as Narad seated the *Muni* Valmiki for the purpose of repeating the name of Ram; 120. or as Sita sat in Ashoka forest and with love worshipped Ram; or as Jatayu worshipped Ram when harassed by Rawan; 121. in that same manner Kabir sat, and bringing the form of Shri Ram into his imagination, with his lips he sang the praises of Ram, having lost his self-consciousness. 122. Losing all thought of whether he was honoured or dishonoured, losing all pride of public recognition, losing all thought of objects of sense, he continued singing the praises of Ram with his lips. 123. Just then his mother entered the house, and the Lord of the Heaven Vaikunth pointed Kabir out from a distance. He then stood outside, and saw the amusing scene of the *bhakta* Kabir.

KABIR'S MOTHER PUNISHES HIM

124. The mother said to Kabir, 'Bring the scarf and show it to me. If you do not bring it at once, I shall punish you.' 125. He would, however, give her no reply. Keeping his mind steady in the worship of Ram he did not recognize the fact that his mother and a noble Brahman had arrived. 126. His mind was entirely taken up with the form and name of God, and so he lost all self-consciousness. His mother became angry and said to her son, 127. 'In a stupid manner you are sitting here, lovingly worshipping Ram.' Hearing her say this, the Lord of the Heaven Vaikunth said to the old woman, 128, 'You have used harsh language with your lips, but you have love for him in your heart. Now take a cane in your hand and punish your son.' 129. Hearing Him say this, Kabir's mother said, 'I see nothing with which to whip him.' God then produced a cane, and put it in her hand. 130. Growing angry she struck Kabir on his back, but he had no bodily consciousness, being lost in the

worship of Ram. 131. Now you wise *bhaktas*, listen to the amusing event that took place. As she continued to strike Kabir on his back, Shri Hari stood outside trembling with the pain. 132. He said to her, 'You are beating your child, but the welt appears on My back. Now that beating is quite sufficient.' So said the dark complexioned One. 133. Just as when the edge of an axe strikes the root of a tree, the tree violently trembles, so as she continued punishing the *bhakta* Kabir, the Saviour of the world trembled. 134. Or as when a child is troubled by some bad person, its mother suffers the pain, so as she continued whipping Kabir with the cane, God trembled with the pain. 135 Or as when an army lessens in number a king becomes depressed; so when this God-loving *bhakta* was being troubled it was this One, the Merciful to the lowly, who trembled with pain. 136. Or as when a young deer is caught in a trap, the mother deer feels the pain; so in the whipping of His *bhakta*, God trembled with the pain. 137. Or as when the sea saw the *rishi* Agasti it trembled in its heart, so the Dweller in the Heaven Vaikunth trembled with pain as the mother continued to beat Kabir. 138. Finally the Husband of Rukmini exclaimed, 'That is sufficient now, O mother,' and then the Infinite One added, 139. 'I went to trouble Bali. I ended in being His door-keeper. So in the end my deception had its positive result. 140. I have had many noble and pious *bhaktas*, but no one has ever given me a beating. Now I recognize the fact that the *bhakta* Kabir is superior to Myself.' 141. Then said the Husband of Sita to Himself, 'I must show him My visible form, and because I troubled him in the guise of a Brahman, so he did not recognize Me.'

RAM (WITH SITA) MANIFESTS HIMSELF TO KABIR

142. So he cast aside His Brahman guise, and in His hand took His bow and arrow. A dazzling crown

adorned His head. His large eyes gave brightness to his face. 143. In his ears were the most brilliant ear-rings. His chest was broad, but His waist was slender. Around His neck was the purest of jewels, the Kaustubh, and the Vaijyanti garland adorned His neck. 144. Around His waist was an embroidered yellow garment. On His feet were the *Vanki* and the *Todar* ornaments. The Husband of Janaki thus presented Himself together with Sita. 145. Kabir opened his eyes and looked. It was as if a billion of suns had arisen. Seeing such a form as that, he embraced His feet. 146. The Dweller in Vaikunth then said, 'You have stood My test. I shall never forget you, just as a mother never forgets her child. 147. Just as experts pierce coins with their instruments, and then string them together; or as they test diamonds by hammering them on an anvil, and then store them in their treasury; 148. so I have put you to the test. Now I will put you in the depths of My heart, always looking on you with the eye of favour.' So spoke God. 149. The Life of the world then gave Kabir's mother a loving embrace, and said, 'Your good fortune, because of Me, can never be fully described.' 150. As God said this, the mother felt great joy. She drew Kabir to her heart, and gave him a caress of love. 151. Said she to him, 'It is because you have become my son that I have had a sight of Shri Ram.' The mother then took Kabir by the hand and led him back to their home. 152. And the Husband of Sita said to them, 'Keep thoughts of Me in your heart.' Thus speaking, the Life of the world became invisible.

153. This book relating the stories of the saints is the lake Manas. Listeners who are wise, and *bhaktas* of good fortune come to it. 154. The royal swans, who want pearls as their food, sit by this lake. Crows, who are not *bhaktas*, who are haters, and who have no faith in their

hearts, they revile these royal swans. 155. They gladly eat pebbles, because they dislike pearls. So there is no sense of worship aroused in those who are not *bhaktas.* They hold in their minds irrational thoughts. 156. But now good people, let that thought pass. Give me your attention. Just as when an infant uses prattling words, its mother rejoices to hear them. 157. The blind grope their way behind those who have sight, by listening to their footsteps. So through your favour I speak to you in my uncouth language. 158. It is you who are making my thoughts clear, and causing me by your love to write this book. As the author of the book my name, Mahipati, appears in the beginning. But the book is being written through your favour.

159. *Swasti* (Peace !). This book is the *Shri Bhaktavijaya.* The Lord of the universe is pleased as He listens to it. So let all God-loving pious *bhaktas* listen also. This is the fifth sweet chapter.

CHAPTER VI

KABIR AND HIS SON KAMAL

Obeisance to Shri Ganesh, Obeisance to Shri Krishna

1. To-day the festival of lights and the *Dasara* festival have arrived, bringing joy to every sense. Among these the ear of the listener possesses the highest good fortune. 2. The moon shines for all alike, but the *Chakor* bird first satisfies itself with it. So when reading the stories of the saints, it is the ear that seems more fortunate; 3. or as when at marriage a great number of guests assemble, it is the bridegroom's mother who has the highest honour paid her; or as when the sun has arisen in the sky, it is the lotus that is the first to open; 4. or as when a cloud brings moisture to the sky it is the *Chatak* bird that first satisfies itself with it; or as the bee is the first one to supply itself from the sweet honey of the flower; 5. or as when uttering sacred words there is first the worship of Ganpati; or as when Shiva distributed the fourteen jewels (churned out of the ocean), he gave the first honour to Vishnu; 6. so when offering to you, a fortunate assembly, this delightful composition, giving the story of the *bhaktas*, it is the ear that satisfies itself; so it seems to me. 7. As the result of hearing is thinking, and after thinking there comes study, then the experience of it comes and the seeker after truth becomes complete in his knowledge; 8. so in the acquisition of knowledge, it is the ear that is the most important among the organs of sense. Therefore if one wishes to place an ornament in the ear, it should be the precious jewel of the story of the saints, set in a golden setting. 9. I will therefore make an ear-ring of a beautiful form, and place it in my listeners' ears. It will shine with the light of knowledge of philosophic truth. 10. Then the Husband of

Rukmini will be pleased, and give them an everlasting blessing. In describing the good deeds of his saints I have held this purpose steadily in my mind.

THE HAPPY HOME OF KABIR

11. Now listen, you pious God-loving people. The story to be told is a very delightful one. After the dark-complexioned One had embraced Kabir, he went back to his home. 12. When Kabir's mother had whipped him it was done in ignorance. After that event had brought to her the sight of Shri Ram, she became comforted. 13. She was in the habit of persecuting him, but now she said nothing to him. When one has the favour of the Pervader of the universe, all troubles pass away. 14. Those who have the king's favour are honoured by the king's ministers. If a mother-in-law is fond of her daughter-in-law, no one ever reviles her. 15. Those who have the favour of their *guru* are never troubled by rebirths. If Sarasvati (goddess of speech) is favourable, heretics do not enter into discussion with them. 16. Those who have obtained nectar are not troubled by disease; or if Ganpati is favourable to anyone, hindrances do not come into his way; 17. so Kabir's mother having received the favour of the Lord of Ayodhya (Ram), no longer persecuted him. And having received divine knowledge, she gave herself to the worship of Hari. 18. Her mind became indifferent to worldly things. In order to conform to public custom she carried on her daily routine in her domestic concerns, but in her heart she was continually repeating the names of God, full of love. 19. Although she had not in her home any food or raiments, her mind felt no anxiety. Kabir's dutiful wife was like the good Anusaya. 20. A lamp and its light are without difference from one another; so also there is no difference between a word and its meaning; and in the same way Kabir and

his wife were one. 21. Lightning and a cloud both exist in unity, so the two, Kabir and his wife, lived in perfect harmony. 22. Just as sweetness and sugar never exist apart from one another, so their love* was strong like the phases of the moon. 23. Kabir in his domestic life considered joy and sorrow as both alike. In the same way his wife behaved resolutely in union with her husband.

KAMAL'S BIRTH AND PILGRIMAGE

24. Kabir's wife was great with a child who became a statue of devotion, knowledge, and indifference to worldly things, and in the ninth month a son was born to Kabir by her. 25. At the moment of his birth his nature was one indifferent to worldly things. In matters of cleanliness he was extremely pure. He was generous, wise, and one of fixed determination. His mind suffered no disturbance. 26. When he was twelve days old he was given the name of Kamal. As he heard his father sing the praises of God, so he imitated him in the same worship. 27. When seven years old he said to his father in a humble voice, 'Give me permission to go to Dwarka.' 28. Hearing his son's request, Kabir said to him, 'Go and fulfil the desire of your heart and then hasten back.' 29. While still young he had the desire to visit sacred places. Seeing this, Kabir's mind was full of joy. 30. Just as when a king's son wishes to conquer the whole world, the father feels joyous, so it was with Kabir; 31. or as the tide of the sea reaches its fulness when it sees the full moon, so when Kamal started to go to visit sacred places, the *bhakta* Kabir rejoiced; 32. or as when Ganpati danced, the five-headed

---

* The reading translated in the text for the latter half of verse 22 is that of the Indu-Prakash edition, 1888, edited by Lakshman Babu Gokhale. Another reading in the *Abhinava Bhaktavijaya*, 1930, edited by Dinadas is translated: 'Just as the phases of the moon wax *and wane*.'

One (Shiva) nodded His head in His joy ; or as when Brahmadev rejoiced when listening to the singing of Sarasvati ; 33. so seeing his son full of the spirit of indifference to worldly things, both were filled with joy. Kamal made an obeisance to his father and mother and then started. 34. As he walked along the easy path, he sang of the names and praiseworthy deeds of God. The shame of worldly life never came into his mind. 35. He had no liking for clothes or ornaments. His tongue had no liking for the best of food. He had no desire for the hypocritical meeting with the king. All he cared for was the worship of Ram. 36. Every one knew the *bhakta* Kamal as the son of Kabir. As he entered into cities, people heard of his coming and went out to meet him. 37. Just as the *rishi* Narad, the son of Brahmadev, continually devoted himself to the singing of God's praises, so Kamal day and night gave himself up to the worship of Ram. 38. The townspeople, seeing him, would take him into the town with marks of honour. He would remain there a night and perform a *Hari-kirtan*. 39. In this way, with full experience of knowledge, he hastened to Dwarka. Suddenly there appeared before him the sacred pond of Gomati. His mind at the time was full of repentance.

PILGRIMAGE FUTILE WITHOUT REPENTANCE

40. If a man wanders from one sacred city to another without repentance in his heart, his going and coming will be in vain. Why should anyone who has no son seek to lay up a fortune ? 41. If you have no money, why uselessly go to the market ? If you have no love of God in your heart, why sing the praises of God ? 42. If you do not mix salt in your food it will have no good taste. The wealth of a miser does not reach those who are worthy of a gift. 43. If a warrior has no bravery, why

should he in vain carry a weapon? In making friendship with a miser, one will never find joy. 44. If one does not know the *Gayatri mantra* why call himself a Brahman? Although loaded with ornaments, still that is all useless if without the *Mangalasari* ornament. 45. If one has not the knowledge of reasoning, the sixty-four crafts are useless to him. If one has no compassion for living beings, why prate with his lips over his own knowledge? 46. Or if one has not the favour of God, one has composed his verses in vain. So if one has not full repentance in his heart, his wandering from one sacred place to another results in no advantage to him. 47. Lust, anger, pride, and envy are the worst faults of a person. If there is no repentance in his heart, these sins will not be washed away by bathing at these sacred places. 48. As the son of Kabir now stood on the banks of the Gomati he made obeisance and with feelings of love praised God. 49. He then waded in the water and bathed with his clothes on. He prayed, 'Oh Ganges, wash away my faults, and end my re-births.' 50. Having bathed in this way and made the twelve marks on his forehead with clay, and having placed around his neck the *tulsi* garland, 51. and having brought into his mind the Lord of Dwarka, he mentally worshipped (*manas-puja*) and with love in his heart, entered into the temple to see Him. 52. At the great door of the temple he bowed prostrate on the ground. Then entering the inner shrine, he embraced the feet of Shri Krishna. 53. Now lovingly opening his eyes, he brought the image of Shri Krishna before his imagination, and singing His names and great deeds he waved auspicious lights.

A MERCHANT GIVES KAMAL A DIAMOND

54. Living in this way, the *bhakta* Kamal remained four months at Dwarka and in love composed

poetry describing the good deeds of Hari. 55. Having completed four months at Dwarka in the acquisition of knowledge, by association with the good, and three times a day entering into the temple to see and worship God, he left that place. 56. He made his obeisance to the image of Krishna, prostrating himself on the ground. With love he prayed, 'O God, give me again the opportunity of coming here to see and worship Thee.' 57. Thus praying, he immediately started on his way. As he walked along he saw the town of Chitrakut which he entered. 58. There was a merchant by name Vishnudas (a worshipper of Vishnu), supremely pious and generous. He came and with feelings of love made obeisance to Kamal. 59. Having a great desire to welcome him he took the *bhakta* Kamal to his home, lovingly washed his feet and placed a meal before him. 60. For the night a *Hari-kirtan* was arranged, and all the people of the town assembled. They listened with love and their minds became absorbed in the theme. 61. The merchant then thought to himself, 'What shall I give him? If I should place before him a heap of money, he would not care for it.' 62. In his treasure-house he had a diamond which he quickly brought. He seated Kamal and placed it at his feet. 63. He said to him, 'This little brilliant diamond will dim the lamps; take it to your home and place it in your house. 64. At night-time if you place it before you, there will be no darkness.' Kamal replied, 'Kabir will be very angry with me on account of his indifference to worldly things. 65. Diamonds and crystals look alike to my sight. Why do you give it to me and urge me to take it? 66. Money should be offered to Brahmans. Diamonds and other jewels should be offered to kings, and food and gifts should be given to living beings. You know this, for you are a wise man. 67. One should give to rope-dancers, jugglers, and players, the old clothes. One should give dry provisions of food to the holy men who are performing austerities. 68. One should give daintily cooked food to *Sannyasis.* They should be given the yellow robe and the loin cloth. We are worshippers of Vishnu, indifferent to worldly things, with minds always satisfied. 69. Having no desires in my heart, why do you force me to take this diamond? Why serve a meal to those already satisfied? Why not give it to those in distress from hunger? 70. A great cloud may rain upon the sea, but the sea has no need of it, so you have uselessly brought and given me this diamond.' 71. As the *bhakta* Kamal thus replied to him, the merchant prostrated himself on the ground before him, and unknown to Kamal, the merchant tied the diamond in Kamal's garment.

UNWORTHINESS OF ACCEPTING GIFTS FOR 'KIRTANS'

72. He soon left that place and came back to Benares. He entered into his home and embraced the feet of Kabir. 73. His son placed the diamond before Kabir, and related the things that had happened to him. Kabir was overcome by the recital and at once fainted away. 74. His heart was full of repentance, and he wept aloud. His wife immediately came out and grasped her husband by his feet. 75. The dutiful wife said to Kabir, 'Why are you so troubled to-day? What have you seen to-day of evil omen that has aroused the feeling of repentance in your mind?' 76. Turning his back towards his son, he said to his wife, 'It seems to me that our whole family line has been sunk in shame. 77. Our Kamal has sold our good name, and brought back this diamond, and therefore, my good wife, I have fallen into this sea of sorrow. 78. It is as if one had scattered musk in the bazaar, and tied up ashes in his garment; or as if one had driven away a well-versed person in the *Shastras*, and in his stead had brought a *Mang* into his home; 79. or as if one should throw away a

bottle full of the sacred water of the Bhagirathi and should take in its stead water from a washerman's pot or as if one should drive away from his home the Dweller in the sacred place and put a thief there instead; 80. or as if abounding in the worship of Vishnu, one should resort to a cemetery and worship Vetal there; or as if giving away books on the *Vedanta* philosophy, one should bring back immoral books; 81. or as if one should give away the sandalwood of mount Malaya, and bring back instead the stinking *hingan*; or like giving to crooked dealers a place in your neighbourhood, and driving away those of religious character; 82. or like giving away the horse of the sun and taking the washerman's donkey; or like giving away the sweet nectar, and taking curdled milk in his vessel. 83. So, O wife, I think to myself that my son, with a secret desire, has committed a wrong. He has sold the name of Ram and has brought here this diamond. 84. Therefore my heart is full of grief, and I fell to the ground in a faint.' Hearing his father's words, Kamal started from there, 85. and going back to where the merchant was, he returned the diamond. Then he came back to his home and bowed to his mother and father. 86. He told them all that happened. When Kabir heard his story he was full of joy. Just as a good *guru* rejoices when his disciple becomes indifferent to earthly things; 87. or as when a mother sees her child free from its illness, she overflows with joy; or as when Shri Ram was delighted when he heard of the bravery of Lava and Kusha; 88. so seeing Kamal free from hindrances, Kabir at once embraced him. And he (Kamal) embracing Kabir's feet, gave himself up to the worship of Shri Ram.

KABIR AND KAMAL AS ROBBERS

89. It now happened on a certain occasion, that a large company of saints who lived at sacred places came to

Kabir's house. 90. It was at the first watch of the night that these saints came to Kabir's house. Both father and son came forward and prostrated themselves on the ground. 91. Kamal hastened to bring a woollen blanket for them to sit upon, and he said to the saints, 'O *Swamis*, seat yourselves on it.' 92. When the saints saw what was being done, the three parties felt joy, just as Indra felt joy when he saw Sanak and the others; 93. or just as after many days of drought, a great number of clouds should pour down rain, making men happy, so Kabir felt joy; 94. or it was as if one should give to a sick person nectar to drink; or as when a *Chatak* bird drinks nectar from the moon; or as when wick and oil are placed in the lamp, it is seen to give bright light; 95. or as when the God-loving *bhaktas* full of joy, nod their heads in gladness while listening to a *kirtan*; or as when the daughter of Janaka (Sita) was full of joy when she met Maruti in the forest of Ashoka; 96. so Kabir felt great joy as he saw these great saints. Going aside he said to his wife, 'We must give these saints something to eat. 97. These *bhaktas* of Vishnu who reside at sacred places have come to our home. If we permit them to sleep here hungry, our reputation for goodness will be lost.' 98. Now there was not the least bit of food in the house, so the distress of the couple was intense; but now listen to what the wife said, when she heard her husband's remark. 99. She said to Kabir, 'O lord of my life, I do not see what is to be done. If we go to our neighbours to borrow, they will give us nothing whatever 100. We could go into the bazaar and buy, but we have no money. So take your son with you and go and steal something. 101. Break open the shop of the merchants who seem to have an abundance of materials for food and bring back the food which you steal, and serve a meal to these saints.' 102. The *bhakta* Kabir assented to this.

He took a sword, and the *bhakta* Kamal took a crowbar, and they hastened to go. 103. They came into the bazaar, and broke open the shop of the merchant. He put the son inside the shop, and he himself remained outside. 104. It was now midnight, and the merchant was in heavy sleep. Kabir called to his son from outside that he should hasten in what he had to do. 105. When Kamal looked into the shop he saw piles of money, garments and ornaments. Seeing them he felt a sense of disgust. 106. The son brought out of the shop flour, rice, sugar, split peas, melted butter, crystallized sugar, and gave them to Kabir.

HONESTY EVEN IN THEFT

107. He also brought out termeric, assafoetida, cummin seed, salt and vegetables and plates of leaves, just sufficient to provide what was needed for the saints. 108. Just as when a thirsty man, though he sees an abundance of water in the Ganges, drinks just enough to quench his thirst, and then comes out of the river; 109. or as when a hungry man has a dish offered him with a great abundance of food on it, still he eats only sufficient for his stomach's need; or as when *Sannyasis* beg food on their open palm and will not eat more than a morsel; 110. or as when Vaishnava *bhaktas* when listening disregard faults in the *kirtan*, and accept its good points; or as when a royal swan sits in the water and separating the milk in it from the water, drinks it; 111. so although Kamal saw with his eyes garments, ornaments and a heap of money he rejected them all, and took with him only the materials needed for cooking. 112. As he hastened to come out of the house a thought came into his mind, 'The grocer is fast asleep, I ought to waken him. 113. If one's enemy is fast asleep, and one kills him in that state, or if one reviles anyone behind his back, he will fall into the horrors of hell. 114. If in a battle anyone pursues a fleeing enemy; or if

anyone steals fearlessly, or if one sets fire to a house inhabited by men, he will fall into the horrors of hell. 115. Now I am a wise *bhakta* of Vishnu and I know what is wrong and what is right. So I will waken the grocer and quickly run away from here.' 116. Then taking courage he moved quickly to the side of the grocer, and slapped him on his back, saying, 'You ought to be awake. 117. We are two thieves who have broken open your shop. We are going away with the materials for cooking, I tell you this.'

KAMAL ASKS HIS FATHER TO CUT OFF HIS HEAD

118. The grocer sat up, but Kamal started to run away. As he was passing through the narrow opening both his feet got caught. 119. When half his body was outside, the merchant seized him. It was as if a deer, escaping from a snare, should find itself in a forest full of hunters; 120. or as if a royal swan should go to lake Manas and there should be suddenly seized by a falcon; or as when a parrot in its ignorance finds itself in a trap; 121. or as when the king of the Kauravas arranged his army in a circle and in it was caught the child of Subhadra (Abhimanyu); or as when the *kokil* bird, while flying about in the flower garden, is caught by a hunter; 122. so Kamal, as he hastened to run away, had both his feet seized by the grocer. The child Kamal then called out to his father. 123. He said, 'As the Son of the wind (Maruti) was carrying away mount Dron for the aid of Ram, while on his way Bharat wounded him and threw him down, that is just happening to us. 124. The grocer will now come outside and shout in the bazaar. When the people of the town hear him, they will come rushing to see what the matter is. 125. All the men and women will regard us as the thieves of the town, so you cut off my head and hurry back to our home. 126. If you hold in your mind any idea of love (that I am yours), it will be to the loss

of your reputation for goodness. If people hear the story of your stealing, saints will not come and sit in your house; 127. just as when dutiful wives, hearing a statement that there are prostitutes present, get up and go away; or as when the Mang (out-caste) comes into a house, those learned in the *shastras* and *pandits* will not remain present; 128. or just as when a wise person hears his good *guru* reviled, he gets up and goes away; so hearing the story of your stealing, saints and *sadhus* will get up and depart; 129. so, O *bhakta* of Vishnu, ocean of peace, complete in all good qualities, now listen to me. Put aside all ideas of love and of my belonging to you, and cut off my head with your own hand.' 130. Listening to what his son said, Kabir was pleased in his mind. He took the sword in his hand and cut off his son's head. 131. He then made the bundle of materials for cooking, and taking it up, hurried back to his home. There he told his wife what had happened.

SAINTS FED IN KABIR'S HOME

132. In lovingly relating this courageous act of Kabir's, my whole mind is overcome with wonder; so I, Mahipati, will seek for illustrations of it and give them to you who are listeners. 133. Just as when the Dweller in the Kailas (Shiva) came as a guest into the palace of Shriyala and asked to be served with human flesh, he (Shriyal) killed his own son; 134. so this noble *Vaishnava* did the same thing. But this illustration will not be adequate because the Husband of Parvati (Shiva) persecuted Shriyal, and therefore he killed his own son. 135. But in the present case no saint asked Kabir for a meal, and yet he killed his own son. Therefore the illustration I have used seems deficient, as all clever and wise men will recognize. 136. Where is anything to be found as solid as the earth? Where elsewhere is to be found the vast extent of space? Where is a tree to be seen as

worthy of worship as the *Pimpal* tree ? 137. There is truly no bird like the eagle. There is no river mightier than the Bhagirathi river. As for depth, no other collection of water surpasses that of the sea. 138. What fruit is there equal to that of the wish-tree ? Or what cow is superior to the wish-cow ? One might search through the three worlds and not find a mother equal to Anasuya. 139. What planet is there in the heavens equal to the brilliancy of the moon ? In all the line of demons there was no such generous giver as Bali. 140. What poet has there ever been equal to Valmiki, who declared future events out of his own mind ? If one searched throughout the three worlds, one would not be able to find or see a monkey equal to Maruti. 141. What is the use of using too many illustrations ? Illustrations really belong only to those to whom they apply. I might hunt everywhere and not find so noble a *bhakta* as Kabir.

142. Kabir put the bundle down on the floor and gave Kamal's head to his wife. Her love for him overwhelmed his mother, and tears flowed from her eyes. 143. 'O my child, you are one of great good fortune. You have sacrificed your body for saints. Coming into this worldly existence you have made Shri Ram your own. Thus you have saved our whole family line.' 144. Saying this, Kabir's wife restrained her feelings by the force of her courage. She took the cooking materials and started to cook. 145. She mixed the nine different kinds of materials into a dainty dish and served the meal to the saints, saying as she served them, 'This is a blessed day. I have seen the feet of saints.' 146. Kabir gave them straw mattresses to sit on, and served these saints. It was now sunrise and these *sadhus* at once arose.

KAMAL'S BODY IMPALED

147. After their early morning devotions, these *Vaishnavas* went to their bath. Meanwhile the grocer came out

of his house and shouted aloud. 148. Hearing the shouting, all the people came there in a hurry. They came to where the thief was, and looked at his condition. 149. They said, 'His head has been cut off and taken away. Who can now recognize him?' They remarked to the grocer, 'Your fate works most curiously. 150. One of the thieves has killed this man and taken away his head. The God of all has protected you. If it had not been for that, you would have truly met with calamity. 151. When one has a great deal of money with one he should not sleep alone. In the possession of money, there is great and continual danger. 152. If one loves his money, his friends and brothers become his enemies. Money works in two ways. It both saves and kills. 153. If one is confined by the king's court, money can procure his release. The beheading of this thief must have been done for the sake of his money. 154. You have laid up good deeds from former births, and therefore your life has been preserved. Perhaps they were not thieves; they must have been very good men. 155. There was a pile of money in your shop. How is it that they left the garments and ornaments, and took away only a little cooking materials? This seems very strange to us.' 156. Thus the different classes of people discussed the subject, and expressed their various opinions. The grocer, however, hurried away and reported the matter to the king. 157. He said, 'Two thieves came and broke open my shop. I caught them in the act of taking away the materials of food. 158. One of the thieves cut off the head of the other and took it away.' Hearing him say this, everyone present laughed. 159. The king, however, became very angry and gave the command to his officers, saying, 'Impale the thief. He must be punished.' 160. Hearing this command, the officers hurried in their anger and impaled Kamal's body. 161. To bestow punishment upon a dead body, to enter into discussion with a person of great mental ability, to pick up a quarrel in a foreign country, are all bad actions in wise people.

KAMAL RESTORED TO LIFE BY THE SAINTS

162. The saints and *sadhus* had gone to the river-bank to bathe. They performed their worship of God and returned to Kabir's hermitage. 163. Finally taking leave of Kabir, these dwellers in sacred places started on their way. Kabir made a *namaskar* to these saints, and accompanied them to see them off. 164. The wife was bitterly weeping. She prostrated herself on the ground before these saints, and said, 'When shall I see your feet again?' 165. Speaking thus humbly to these saints, the two accompanied the saints to see them off. As they came out of the city an extraordinary event took place. 166. As the company was hurriedly walking along the path, they suddenly saw a headless corpse impaled upon a stake. The saints saw it from afar. 167. As they stood still for a moment to look at the sight, a most extraordinary thing took place. Kamal joined his hands together and made a *namaskar* to the saints and *sadhus*. 168. The men and women expressed their astonishment as they saw this most unusual act. It seemed to them extraordinary that a headless corpse should make a *namaskar*. 169. The saints and *sadhus* said to Kabir, 'The corpse is making a *namaskar* to us. How is it that life has been preserved in a body without head? 170. When a tree is cut down what would make its branches suddenly show signs of life? If the feathers of a bird are plucked from it, what would enable it to fly in the air? 171. If the strings of a *vina* are broken, how can it be played upon? So, seeing a corpse with life in it, seems to our minds a most unusual thing.' 172. Kabir joined his hands palm to palm, and said to the saints, 'Bhishma fell on the bed of arrows, and yet his life was preserved in his body.

173. Abhimanyu, in order to relate to Arjun his sorrows when he fell on the battlefield, had his life preserved in his body with courage. 174. Also when Ravan was making trouble for Jatayu his body was overwhelmed with pain, his desire to see Shri Ram preserved life in his body. 175. So this thief was a *Vaishnava.* He had a great desire to make a *namaskar* to your feet. Therefore his life remained in him. 176. The desire of his heart has been fulfilled. He has seen you. Now he will leave his perishable body and live in his everlasting home.' 177. Hearing him say this, the saints replied, 'Who indeed was this thief ?' Then Kabir related to the saints the whole story. 178. The *Vaishnavas* then said, 'Although we had not asked for food, how is it that Kabir should kill so good a son as Kamal ?' 179 Hearing them say this, the noble *Vaishnava* answered, 'All earthly things are perishable. Whatever is seen to have a form must in the end disappear.180. Suppose I had not killed Kamal, would he thereby have remained immortal ?' Listening to this remark, a sense of compassion arose in the hearts of the saints. 181. The saints said to Kabir's wife, 'Hasten and bring the head and show it to us. Hearing this remark, she hastened back to her home. 182. She took her son's head and brought it back to the saints. When the compassionate saints saw it they were moved with emotion. 183. They took the corpse down from the stake and placed the head upon it. The men and women looked on with wonder. Listen now to the strange thing that happened. 184. As the saints placed their hands upon the head of Kamal, he came to life, arose and made a *namaskar* to the saints. 185. All the inhabitants of Benares now prostrated themselves on the ground before Kabir. Said they, 'This *Vaishnava* is supremely wise, a complete saviour for all dull-minded beings.' 186. The saints gave him their blessing and started on their way to sacred places.

Listen now to the delightful story which will be related in the next chapter. 187. This book containing the history of the saints might be considered as a beautiful temple in the sacred city of Pandhari; where the eternally loved, dark-complexioned One for ever stands on a brick; 188. where *sadhus* and *Vaishnavas* sing His praises out of love, and there I, a sinner and an ignorant person, have come to see and worship Him. 189. With reverence I take in my hand these verses, like *tulsi* leaves and flowers. I, Mahipati, fall at His feet in order to ask Him for His beneficent love.

190. *Swasti* (Peace !). This book is the *Shri Bhaktavijaya*. The Lord of the world will be pleased if you listen to it. Therefore listen, you God-loving pious *bhaktas*. This is the sixth very delightful chapter.

CHAPTER VII

KABIR CHOOSES RAMANANDA AS HIS GURU

Obeisance to Shri Ganesh. Obeisance to Shri Krishna.

1. Listen now. The book that contains the stories of the saints may be considered as the ocean of milk, in which water-animals in the form of illustrations rush hither and thither in the water, in their love of it. 2. Waves of joy arise heavenward and seek to split the space above, the space that is knowledge. Pious clouds come rushing over the sea, and drink the water of these stories. 3. Then they go and rain down the water-joy upon those who have become heated by the fever of this earthly existence. 4. The favour of Shri Pandurang is the full moon, which when it rises in its love, produces the tide on the limitless sea, a tide that cannot be resisted. 5. He who will bathe in the sea of this book at the time of a festival, when a praise service is being held, will find severe diseases of this earthly existence certainly disappear.

KABIR WEEPS AT THE SOUND OF A GRINDING MILL

6. In the previous chapter there was the holy story of how the saints raised the son of Kabir to life. Let the hearers now listen to the holy story of what happened afterwards. 7. Once upon a time the father of Kamal went into the bazaar at night. He was worshipping Shri Ram at that time full of love. 8. He took a *vina* (lute) in his hand and sang the praises of God in his sweet voice. He brought to his imagination the form of Shri Ram, and sang with a heart full of love. 9. His mind discarded desires, affections, honour, pride and wrong wishes. He put aside egoism and the thought of 'I' and 'thou,' and gave himself to contemplating Shri Ram. 10. There was a grocer's wife in the

bazaar sitting there grinding. When the *bhakta* Kabir saw her grinding, his heart was overcome with emotion. 11. He stood there and wept aloud. The men and women in the bazaar seeing him do this, laughed and wondered why he did so. 12. One of them said to Kabir, 'Why are you crying here ? Who has been giving you trouble ? Tell us.' 13. A great many people said the same thing to him, but he would not reply to any of them, for he thought to himself, 'These people cannot remove my sorrow. 14. If one tells his grief to one already in sorrow, one feels his pain all the more. If a frog makes a friend of a serpent, the serpent will not give him the least joy. 15. A wise *Pandit* will not ask a drunkard any questions on good thoughts and morals; just as a thoughtful man will never take medicine from the hand of a sick man; 16. just as the *chatak* bird will not drink the water of the river, even if it be intensely thirsty; or as the *chakor* bird finds no satisfaction until the moon arises; 17. or as an orator will never speak with love and enthusiasm to wicked and ignorant hearers; or as the royal swan will never bring to mind pearls made of quick silver; 18. or as when a twice-born (Brahman), seeing a Mang at a distance, will not pronounce a blessing, or as a clever and wise man will not talk in private with a reviler.' 19. So when these avaricious lovers of wealth asked Kabir that question, he would not give them any answer, but continued crying bitterly. 20. The various classes of people said to one another, 'Kabir has gone crazy. He is crying for nothing in this bazaar.'

KABIR CONSOLED BY NIPAT NIRANJAN

21. Just then a *sadhu*, named Nipat Niranjan, happened to come there. He at once said to Kabir, 'Why are you manifesting such grief ?' 22. When Kabir opened his eyes and looked, he saw an ocean of knowledge before him

Then taking courage he replied to him. 23. He thought to himself, 'If I tell him the truth, he will remove at least a part of my trouble.' Thus thinking to himself the *bhakta* Kabir spoke as follows: 24. 'A sick person feels great joy in his mind when telling of his pain to a good physician.' Just as a daughter-in-law does not hesitate to tell of her sorrows to her own mother; 25. or as a good disciple, if he has doubts in his mind, tells them to his *guru*; so the father of Kamal told the reason of his crying to the *sadhu* Nipat Niranjan. 26. Kabir said to him, 'O good *guru*, my heart is full of repentance. You, kind sir, have questioned me in affectionate terms, so listen, and I will tell you why I am crying. 27. As I saw the mill being turned, I saw the grains of wheat turn to flour. Just such is my condition. I have fallen between the millstones of this earthly existence. 28. I was therefore seized with fear, and have manifested this violent grief. Who besides you can remove the sorrows of this earthly existence?' 29. Hearing this, Nipat said to him, 'Why do you mourn in vain? As you saw the mill turning, your mind felt a sense of repentance 30. So, O *bhakta* of Vishnu, I will remove your doubts on this question. It is when you discard the central prop and wander about that you become as it were flour in the mill of *Kal* (death). 31. Just as grain in the mill adhering to the central prop, is not turned to flour, so those who are devoted to the worship of Shri Ram are not caught in the cycle of death. 32. You are courageous on account of your righteousness, and indifferent to earthly things. You are a mountain of peace and forgiveness; you see the fearsome things in a dream. Why do you in vain fear them?' 33. Hearing him say this, Kabir was awakened to the truth, and the two embraced one another with feelings of love. 34. These noble *Vaishnavas* made loving *namaskars* to one another. Kabir then hastened to leave there, and returned to his hermitage. 35. There in many forms of verses he continually sang the praises of Hari. He continually performed *kirtans* full of joy and love.

ONE WITHOUT GURU IS WITHOUT LIFE

36. He said to himself one day as his mind was thinking about it, 'If one does not have a *guru* while in this earthly existence, he should be called a man without life. 37. It is useless to have a domestic life without a wife, and a home without children, and ornaments without the saffron mark on the forehead of a woman (indicative of her husband living). 38. If a tree grows, but yields no fruit; or if a king is born without possessing valour; or if one should cook a meal without the use of salt, its saltlessness will make that food useless; 39. or like a youthful body with no life in it; or a banker without money; or an officer without authority; of what value are these? 40. The rainy season without a cloud, a great lake without water, a festival without a sacred place and observed in a miserable village, 41. a corn-cob without grain on it; of what value are they? A home seems empty without a master; a praise service without love is like the singing of obscene songs. 42. As friendship without any regard, or as knowledge without any compassion, so why should one accept the state of a *sannyasi* without repentance? 43. There can be no enjoyment without money, no religious observance without some rule, and why should those without peace be called saints? When a great man possesses no peace of heart, why do people needlessly call him a great man? 44. Just as the *chatak* bird seems to be without beauty until the moon arises; so this human body has experienced many rebirths in vain if it has not had a good *guru*.45. So I must go with feelings of reverence as a suppliant to the *sannyasi swami* Ramananda.' Having decided this in his mind, he remained with that

determination. 46. When after seeing many kings with her own eyes, and carefully considering the matter, Sita saw the form of Shri Ram, her heart chose him at once. 47. When the daughter of king Bhimaka (Rukmini) heard of the beautiful form of Shri Krishna, she sought to win him as her husband. So it was that Kabir held the desire for the dust of Ramanand's feet. 48. Finding himself alone one day, he at once arose and went to the hermitage of Ramanand and lovingly embraced his feet. 49. Standing first at a distance, Kabir besought Ramanand saying, 'Your greatness must show me compassion. 50. When Ramanand heard Kabir's voice, he put his fingers in his ears, went into a cave and sat alone on his mat. 51. Kabir stood outside and said in his soft sweet voice, 'A lowly and helpless one, I stand at your door. Give me your assurance and satisfy my desire.' 52. Ramanand said to Kabir, 'You were born in a Muhammadan family. I have, therefore, no authority whatever to give you instruction. 53. All wise men recognize that seed should be sown in a field after the examination of its soil. In making a gift, one should first seek someone worthy of it. When giving a daughter in marriage one must choose the proper bridegroom.' 54. Kabir replied, 'I have determined to come to your feet. I have not spared body, speech or mind in doing so. 55. The moon loves the *chakor* bird, but even if the love may not be exclusive, yet God in His pleasure rains nectar on it for its devotion. 56. Should the sun not express its intense love for the lotus by rising, still it will not open by an attachment for something else. 57. In the making of an earthen image of Dron, the reverence of the Koli (Ekalavya) bore fruit. So I have embraced the *swami's* feet with body, speech and mind.' 58. Thus speaking, Kabir again with love prostrated himself on the ground before the *Swami*. He then hastened back to his home with his mind full of intense love.

59. One day while sitting alone he thought to himself, I must hear the sound of Ram's name from the lips of my *swami*. 60. What methods shall I adopt that the dust of his feet may cling to me ?' He then dug a ditch in the path and laid down in it. 61. The lotus in the lake Manas closes its petals at night time, and says to itself, 'When will the sun arise ? It will make my heart rejoice.' 62. Or as when the *chatak* bird is exceedingly thirsty it longs for a cloud, so the *bhakta* Kabir lay in the ditch waiting for his *guru*. 63. Just as on the beautiful day of the full moon the *chatak* bird wishes for the sight of the moon. Or as a child overcome with hunger, waits for the coming of its mother. 64. Or as when an excessive drought having taken place men long for the clouds, so the *bhakta* Kabir in his love waited for the coming of Ramanand. 65. Now it happened that there were four *ghatikas* remaining of the night, and *swami* Ramanand was on his way to bathe in the river Ganges. 66. As he was rapidly walking, his foot touched Kabir and he exclaimed, 'Ram, Ram! Whom has my foot touched ?' 67. The *bhakta* Kabir having heard him say this, stood up and said, 'You, *swami*, have done me a great favour today. 68. Your feet accidentally touched my forehead, and I heard the mantra, "Ram, Ram." I see no one as fortunate as myself in all the three worlds. 69. All the good deeds that I may have committed during the infinite number of my rebirths, have now come to their fruitage. Today birth and death have ceased for me through the touch of the feet of my *guru*. 70. If fate comes to one's aid, grains of sand may become brilliant diamonds. If the water of a well contains salt, fate can make it like nectar.' 71. So the *bhakta* Kabir, in his love, danced before the *Swami* Ramanand. His heart felt intense joy, because it was full of happiness. 72. It was like that of a hungry man receiving dainty food. Or as when a cloud rains upon a withering tree; or as when the

husband of Shachi gave nectar to drink to one who had no longer to live; 73. or as when a poor man finds a heap of money; or as when a sick man receives a divine medicine; or as when a man seeking final-deliverance becomes associated with the good, he cannot contain the joy that he feels; 74. or as when a girl who is living with her mother-in-law meets her own mother; or as when a poor person obtains a wish-cow; or as when a king through his power gains his seat on the throne. All these have joy. 75. As when the *muni* Gautam arrived at the river Godavari his mind was full of joy; or as when Bhagiratha brought the Bhagirathi river–these felt joy in their hearts; 76. or as when the son of the Wind (Maruti) was in the forest, he suddenly met Shri Ram; or as when Narad, seeing Vyas, became full of joy; 77. so the heart of Kabir was now comforted. *Swami* Ramanand smiled, astonished at what was taking place.

RAMANAND TESTS KABIR

78. He kept silence, however, and went on to perform his bath, saying to himself, 'I have never seen one so determined as Kabir seems to be. 79. So I will give him a little suffering, and so give his mind a test, as experts melt and examine inferior kind of gold; 80. or as experts seek to discover the true diamond by placing it upon the anvil and striking it with a hammer; or as when they test the jewel in the serpent's head by winding thread around it and throwing it into a blazing fire; 81. or as when Vishvamitra gave Harischandra's mind a severe test; or as when Shiva came as the uninvited guest to Shriyal; 82. or as when Karna fell on the pile of arrows when Krishna went to him for some gift; so I will assume an outward anger and test Kabir's mind.'

83. On a certain day Kabir went into the bazaar singing and dancing with joy. Tears of happiness flowed from

his eyes in the fulness of his love. 84. As he danced in his love he said to himself, 'By holding in my heart the lotus feet of my *guru* Ramanand my mind has joy.' 85. As he was thus singing in his love, Ramanand heard from a distance. He took off his wooden sandals and said angrily to Kabir, 86. 'You call yourself my disciple without any reason for it. When did I give you instructions? What witness have you employed to prove that you are my disciple? Tell me.' 87. So saying he struck Kabir on his head with his sandal, just as a mother outwardly manifests anger to her child; 88. or again as a mother outwardly pretending anger gives her daughter instructions; or as a teacher punishes his pupil in order that he may gain knowledge; 89. or just as men forcibly brand their cattle to drive away all diseases; or as an expert melts the gold to test it; 90. so in order to test the determination of Kabir, Ramanand struck him on the head with his sandal. Blood flowed freely, but Kabir was full of joy. 91. Said he, 'Give attention to what I say. When you gave me the instructions that made me your disciple, there was no witness present, therefore, O *Swami*, you could treat me with contempt. 92. Now in the presence of everyone, you gave my head a blow with your sandal. That act proclaims to the people that everyone should know that I am your disciple. 93. I have appointed as my witnesses water, the earth, air, space, light and God, that I have placed my service at your feet.' 94. As the *bhakta* said these things the good *guru* was very pleased. He went up to Kabir and placed his hand on his head. 95. Saying, 'Seeing your determination, my test of you has satisfied my mind. Now constantly repeat the *mantra*, "Ram Krishna" and sing their praise day and night.' 96. As the *sadguru* said these things, Kabir became full of joy, and composing verses of various kinds, he sang of the goodness of Shri Ram. 97. Putting aside all wrong desires, all hopes for popular honour, putting aside all sensual desires, putting aside all pride of knowledge, he continually sang God's praises. 98. All the people of Benares said to Kabir, 'Blessed are you.' Such high reputation became intolerable to the evil-minded persons.

KABIR'S PUBLIC PERSECUTION

99. When evil-minded persons hear the praises given to the good, they have doubts arisen in their hearts; just as when the sun arises, owls become ashamed and go in hiding; 100. or as when thieves are intensely troubled when they see the moon arise; or as when a miser hears the great praise given to a donor his mind burns with malice; 101. or as when a prostitute becomes angry, as she hears praise given to a dutiful wife; or as when hearing from anyone an exposition of the *vedanta*, a heretic becomes irritated; 102. so, as soon as Kabir's high reputation spread, revilers sought to find some fault in him. These evil-minded persons then met together in private and discussed the matter, 103. 'Through the unusual service rendered by the *bhakta* Kabir to saints, his reputation has vastly increased. But he killed his own son with his own hand, and the saints raised him to life. 104. From that day everyone bows to him. So now unknown to Kabir, let us bring here a company of saints and good men. 105. Let us write letters to them, and some day bring a company of *Vaishnavas* here. When Kabir sees with his own eyes the great number of saints, he will run away. 106. If a very great gathering of these saints should once take place, Kabir would become disgusted with them. Then the saints will curse him and no blame will be attached to us. 107. Starting a quarrel between the demons and the gods, the son of Brahmadev(Narad) watched the fun; or as having started a fight between the Kauravas and the Pandavas, Shakuni watched them from a distance; 108. so let us

invite a vast number of saints, and dishonour the *bhakta* Kabir.' Such was the plan which these evil-minded persons formed at that time. 109. Writing letters in the name of Kabir, they sent them to Hardwar, Mathura, Gokul and Vrindavan, and to the city of Dwarka as well. 110. All the *Vaishnavas* were invited to come on a certain day in a certain month. They also sent messengers, inviting all the mendicants who lived in the sacred cities. 111. They decided among themselves not to let Kabir know of this. If these saints came unawares, what would he do? 112. If there should be a great gathering of a hundred thousand or more on some special date, who was there so foremost in doing good that he would provide them all with food? 113. So they spent their own money in inviting these *Vaishnavas.* The evil men arranged for Kabir's discomfiture, that they might bring out his faults. 114. Just as Duryodhan endangered his merit and sent the *yogi* Durvas to the Pandavas, so, with evil thoughts in their mind, these people invited an innumerable number of saints.

SAINTS SERVED BY GOD IN VARIOUS FORMS OF KABIR

115. Having listened to the reading of Kabir's letters' the saints bowed their heads in his praise, and on the day appointed in the letters, they arrived. 116. An innumerable number of saints arrived from east, west and south. Kabir bowed to them and lovingly embraced them. 117. Seeing this enormous gathering of *Vaishnavas,* the saint Kabir was full of joy. Said he, 'A happy day has arisen to-day. for with my own eyes I have seen the *Vaishnavas.*' 118. The crooked-minded men began to wag their heads in derision; 'Now let us see what is going to happen.' Looking at one another they clapped their hands. 119. Noticing this difficult situation the Dweller in Ayodhya, the Life of Janaki (Ram), said to Himself, 'I cannot bear to have any lack found in my *bhakta* on my

account. 120. Kabir is one entirely detached from the thinkings of this world. Now that this innumerable gathering of saints has taken place, I must be his helper and protect him.' 121. The *Vaishnavas* of the sacred cities suddenly arrived and encamped on the banks of the Ganga river. The Lord of the world seeing this, arrived to relieve Kabir in his distress. 122. He became a Kabir to as many of the noble *Vaishnavas* as had arrived. The Holder of the Bow (Ram) assumed for the occasion an infinite number of forms. 123. Hari took the form of Kabir in various ways and served these *bhaktas*. The evil-minded sought to see the fun, but seeing the astonishing sight, 124. and taking one another by the hand, they went into the gathering to investigate. When they saw with their eyes an infinite number of Kabirs, their mind was filled with amazement. 125. God felt great pleasure in serving His saints. In assuming these infinite forms His wonderful power of creating appearances was seen. 126. As men and women looked about to see the fun they everywhere saw the *bhakta* Kabir. Each Kabir was serving the saints with reverence and caring for them. 127. One washed their feet, one gave them a bath, one prepared the sandalwood paste used in the worship of God. 128. One stood before them with hands joined palm to palm. One massaged their feet. One held their wooden sandals. Such were the illusory forms of Hari. 129. One sang before them and another gave them to eat. The Life of the world gave them *pan-supari*. 130. He helped some to lie on beds, and himself sat by them. To some of them Krishna spoke in tender tones. 131. Krishna powdered *bhang*, and gave to some. To some He gave the *kusumba* juice to drink. He filled the pipes of some and gave them to smoke. 132. The Saviour of the world said to some, 'Let us hasten to the temple.' To some He was constantly saying, 'Show me your favour.' 133. On the foreheads of some he made the marks with the paste of white clay. Making a garland of *tulsi* He would put it on them and hold a mirror before them. Shri Ram put these on with His own hands. 134. The Lord of the world sat before some, rubbing them with the saffron and sandalwood paste. He put musk on the foreheads of some, and gave beauty to their eyebrows. 135. The Life of the world put on raiment and ornaments on some. Some He took aside and requested them to teach Him the knowledge of the soul. 136. He took the sandals of some, and with feelings of reverence held them on His head. Before some of them the wonder-working Hari sang songs. 137. The Life of the world prepared straw mats for some and laid them down to sleep. To those who had a hankering for opium, He brought and gave it to them. 138. Innumerable people sat down to eat and there the Lord of the world served them. In His love He gave some water to drink. 139. In some places Krishna was making garlands of *tulsi* and placing them around their necks. In some places He had taken fans in His hands and was delighting people with the cool breeze. 140. In some places the Life of the world made the saints lie down, and He sat by them massaging them. In some places He lovingly sat to listen to books being read. 141. When some went to bathe, the Lord of the heart went with them. The Dweller in the heaven Vaikunth would say to some, 'Tell me something I can do for you.' 142. He sat near some and gave them a light lunch. The Husband of Rukmini waved the whisk on some. 143. Just as the one sun is reflected in all vessels of water and is still untouched by the water, so the all-pervading Krishna manifested Himself in the form of Kabir. 144. Long ago when Krishna was a child, the cow-herdesses took him by the hand and came to complain to Yashoda. He then suddenly manifested Himself in numberless forms. 145. While the daughter of Drupad was serving a meal to a gathering of Kauravas some evil-minded men gave her trouble. He then appeared before each one's plate in the form of Draupadi and reproached Duryodhan. 146. So Krishna, seeing the loving devotion of Kabir, assumed innumerable forms. Men and women saw the amazing sight and wondered at it.

147. The *Vaishnava bhaktas* remained there in the sacred city of Benares for three nights. During all these times, the Lord of the heaven Vaikunth lovingly served them. 148. The Lord of the heart with His own hands gave to every one garments and ornaments. Whatever anyone desired, he obtained. 149. The Husband of Sita, having seen these *Vaishnavas* on their way, He became invisible.

PERSECUTORS OF KABIR REPENT

Then all these evil-minded men came to Kabir and embraced his feet. 150. They said to him, 'You are a *bhakta* of Vishnu, we have troubled you greatly, but Ram has been your helper, and increased your extraordinary praise. 151. Moths try to put out the bright flame of a lamp, but it is not put out. The hatred of the fire-fly cannot hide the brightness of the sun. 152. Although the Kauravas sought to burn down the Pandavas in the lacquer houses, they could not burn them. The internal fire of the ocean seeks to burn up the ocean, but it can never be burned up.' 153. Thus saying they again prostrated themselves upon the ground. They put aside their unreasonable anger, and lovingly sang the praises of his goodness and good name.

THEME OF THE NEXT CHAPTER

154. In the next chapter, the Husband of Rukmini, who is the ornament of *bhaktas*, an Ocean of Mercy, will be described as *avatar* in the form of Dnyaneshwar in this mortal world. 155. That story, with its nine sweet juices,

I will serve on the plates of those who are anxious for it. Those who are fortunate, God-loving, and who hunger for it, can eat and drink it with love. 156. The wise *bhaktas* drive away the flies in the form of doubts to a distance and enjoy the fragrance of this story. Mahipati, your servant beseeches you lovingly to take it.

157. *Swasti* (Peace !) This book is the *Shri Bhaktavijaya*· The Lord of the world is pleased when He hears it read. So you, God-loving pious *bhaktas*, listen. This is the seventh very delightful chapter.

CHAPTER VIII

DNYANDEV AND HIS GRANDPARENTS

Obeisance to Shri Ganesh, Obeisance to Shri Krishna

1. To-day is the very happy day on which we have seen the book relating the stories of the saints. Both hearers and speakers have received its nectar with love. 2. To speak, however, of the stories of the *bhaktas* as nectar seems to be a comparison that is deficient. The Husband of Shachi drank the nectar of immortality, but did He gain final deliverance from rebirths? 3. On the contrary, those who drink the nectar of these stories attain final deliverance. Therefore, listening to the stories of the saints causes rebirths and deaths to cease. 4. One might compare these stories to the river Ganges, but the saving merit of the Ganges cannot be weighed in the same balance as one weighs the meritorious nectar of these stories; for, in order to gain final deliverance through the Ganges one needs to be sawn asunder at the confluence of the three rivers (Ganges, Jumna and Saraswati). 5. Such are not the praises of Hari. Men become pure in heart by merely listening to them. Therefore clever and wise people speak of these stories as nectar. 6, God loving *bhaktas* regard these stories as more brilliant than the sun, and as making men feel a coolness greater than that of the moon, and regard them as purer than space itself.

DNYANESHWAR'S ANCESTRY

7. Now give me your attention. Brahmadev and Shiva suddenly appeared on the Ocean of Milk to see and worship Hari. 8. The Husband of the daughter of the Ocean of Milk (Hari) said to them, 'Let us become *avatars* in the world of mortals, in the form of Nivritti, Sopan and Dnyaneshwar, and manifest such deeds as may please us.

9. We will take birth at the same place, as three brothers Muktabai, the Primal Maya, will become our sister.'

10. On the bank of the Ganga (Godavari) there is a celebrated sacred place named Apegaon known all over the world. The town clerk was Govindpant. He was a *bhakta* of Vishnu. 11. His wife Nirabai was a supremely pious and dutiful woman. Being with child she greatly desired a son. 12. The personification of indifference to worldly things came into her womb. Nine months as ninefold devotion were completed, and she gave birth to a son.

DNYANDEV'S FATHER VITHOBA

13. When the mother and father saw the son born to them as the personification of *bhakti*, knowledge and indifference to worldly things, they were full of joy. 14. On the twelfth day they named him Vithoba. When he had fully completed his eighth year, he was invested with the sacred thread. 15. Vithoba studied the *Vedas* and *Shastras* and became proficient in grammar and poetry. He now entertained a wish to visit the sacred places. 16. With repentance in his heart, he asked leave of his mother and father and said to them, 'Give me permission to go to the sacred place of Pushkar (in Rajputana).' 17. Hearing him say this his parents were pleased. Vithoba bowed to them, and at once left. 18. If the heart does not attain indifference to earthly things, the study of the *Shastras* is in vain. If a deaf man should have very large ears, of what use would they be to him? 19. The peacock looks as if it had eyes all over its body, but what use are they if they lack sight? 20. Of what use is the enlarged growth on the neck of a goat? Of what use is a dense forest of *Sawri* trees? Of what use is the sweet singing of those who sing love songs? Of what use is a widow in her youth? 21. All these are like a face without a nose; or an officer without authority; or as a grown up man without manliness is good for nothing.

22. So although the *Shastras* may be profoundly studied, yet without the heart experiencing repentance, of what use are they ? It would be like a crane who sits apparently performing some religious act but really to swallow fishes.

VITHOBA'S WANDERINGS

23. So with repentance in his heart, Vitoba started on his wanderings to sacred places. Putting aside love and affection for earthly things, he gave himself up to the worship of Hari. 24. He came first to Dwaravati, and there he bathed in the Gomati river. Seeing there an image of Krishna, he lovingly prostrated himself before it. 25. He then hastened to the place where God became an *avatar* in the form of a fish, who both killed and saved the monster Shankha and is the Home of, Final Deliverance. 26. From there he went to Pindaraka. From there he visited Mangalahuda. He saw the domes of Dwarka, and then proceeded again on his way. 27. After a visit to Sudampuri (now Porebunder) he came to Mulmadhav where King Bhishmak gave Rukmini in marriage to Krishna. 28. He paid his respects to the sacred place Bhaluka, where Shri Krishna ended His avatarship. From there he hastened on to Prabhaslinga. 29. He worshipped at Sorati-Somnath (a sacred place in Kathiawar); then hurried on from there, and saw the kind of a cave in which Muchakund had lived. 30. He saw the place where Kalayavan was burnt to ashes by Muchakund. Then coming to Dhawalpuri he visited that cave which was Muchakund's place of rest. 31. He paid his respects to all the great sacred places along his route described in the *puranas* and known the world over. He then came to Saptashringi. 32. He paid his respects here to Adimaya and bathed in the Arunawaruna. From there he travelled eastward to the Godavari river, the sight of which gave him great joy. 33. He saw Kapileshwar with his own eyes and then arrived

at Trimbak. He bathed in the Kushavart pond and paid his respects to Gangadwar (the source of the Ganga). 34. He circumambulated the Brahmagiri mountain, keeping it to his left, this gave him great joy. He came to Bhimashankar where through his repentance he became pure in heart. 35. Every day as he walked along he sang the praises of Hari with his lips. From there he soon came to Alandi.

VITHOBA MARRIES THE BRAHMAN SIDHOPANT'S DAUGHTER

36. After bathing in the Chakratirth, he sat down to worship God. Just then the Brahman Sidhopant came there to bathe. 37. Seeing a *Brahmachari* before him, Sidhopant prostrated himself on the ground. 'Tell me your name,' he said. 'Where have you come from?' 38. The Brahmachari replied, 'I belong to a family in good circumstances at Apegaon on the banks of the Godavari. So the elders speak of us. 39. My aged mother and father live there. I have been to Dwarka and all other sacred places, and now I have arrived at Alandi.' 40. The Brahman replied, 'Blessed is the day in which you, my *Swami*, have come here. Now come to my house and by your presence make my home holy.' 41. Thus saying, Sidhopant took him at once to his own house. He gave him a meal of delicious food, and made him lie down to sleep. 42. In a dream Shri Pandharinath came to Sidhopant and said, 'Give your daughter, adorned with jewelry, to this Brahmachari.' 43. The moment he heard this in his dream he felt great satisfaction. After finishing his usual bath and devotions, he reported what had been told him in the dream. 44. The Brahmachari replied, 'What you say is absolutely true, but Pandharinath has given to me no command whatever.' 45. Sidhopant replied, 'Then remain here over this day. If what I say is true, you will most certainly have the same dream.' 46. The Brahmachari then arranged his bedding

near the *tulsi* altar, and at once went to sleep. While all sorts of thoughts, wise and foolish, were passing through his mind, the saw the following in a dream. 47. Pandharinath, the Pervader of the universe, was telling the young Brahmachari in a dream, 'Four *avatars* will be born to you by her. 48. So bow your head to My command and accept the gift of his daughter.' The Brahmachari after seeing this in this dream woke up. 49. A Brahman astrologer was consulted, and their horoscopes agreed in thirty-six points. The wedding day was appointed, and all the marriage arrangements were made. 50. The gods were installed; the Brahmans were feasted. Ganesh who removes hindrances was worshipped. Sweet music was played and the auspicious ceremony of *Punyahavachan* (blessing the day) was performed. 51. All kinds of dainty food were cooked and given to the Brahmans. The bridegroom was worshipped by the bride's father at the town line, and Brahmans recited the eight verses of blessing. 52. 'Victory, Victory to Mukund, the Enemy of Mura (Krishna), the Eternal Being, the Enemy of Madhu, and Kaitabha, the Ornament of His *bhaktas*. In every way protect the bride and bridegroom. 53. Victory, Victory to Thee, Slayer of the Demon Shankha. Victory, Victory to Thee, Who took the form of a tortoise, churner of the ocean, who took the form of a wild boar, Slayer of Hiranyaksha, protect this bride and bridegroom. 54. Victory, Victory to Thee, half-man half-lion, Protector of Pralhad. Victory to Thee, in the form of Vaman, the Troubler of Bali. Victory to Thee, Holder of the axe, Slayer of the thousand-armed One, protect this bride and bridegroom. 55. Victory to Thee, son of Dasharath and Slayer of demons. Victory to Thee who played His pranks at Gokul, Son of Nand. Victory to Thee, in the form of Buddha, O Janardan, protect this bride and bridegroom ! 56. Victory to Thee, in the form of Kalki *avatar*, Slayer of despised foreigners, Founder of religion, Life of the world. Victory to Thee, Giver of blessing to Pundalik, Husband of Rukmini, protect this bride and bridegroom.'

57. After reciting these verses of blessing, the Brahmans repeated the word '*Savadhan*' (Beware!) Many musical instruments were now played, and the ceremony of taking one another by the hand (marriage) was completed.

VITHOBA AND SIDHOPANT GO TO PANDHARPUR

58. After the four days of the marriage festival, they made their bow to Sidhopant and said, 'We must go to Pandhari in the month of *Ashadh* (July) to see and worship Shri Pandurang.' 59. Then Sidhopant with his family took him (Vithoba) and his wife on a pilgrimage to Pandhari. He bathed in the Chandrabhaga, and worshipped Shri Pundalik.

60. If Pandhari is compared to other sacred places, any such comparison seems deficient. No one sees a planet in the sky as brilliant as the moon. 61. What metal is superior to gold? Whose praise is greater than that given to Vishnu? One may search as one will, and not find a diamond as brilliant as the Kaustubh. 62. What bull is superior to the *nandi* of Shiva? What performer of austerities equals Shiva? What *Shastra* is superior to the *Bhagavadgita*? One might hunt through the three worlds and not find its equal. 63. One has never seen or known a *mantra* superior to that of the names 'Ram, Krishna.' There is no other religious teaching superior to that taught by the *Bhagavat*. 64. So there is no other sacred city to be seen by one's lotus eyes in all this round earth like that of Pandhari. The moment it is seen it burns up mountains of sins. 65. You may say, 'How can Pandhari be superior to *Saptapuri* (the seven great sacred cities, Ayodhya,

Mathura, Maya, Benares, Kanchi, Avantika, Dwarka), the givers of final deliverance from rebirths. ' There takes place the destruction of pride, and egoism does not remain. 66. Moreover, by bathing at other sacred places one's pride especially grows, but Pandhari, if seen even from the distance, moves evil men to repentance.

67. Well, this praise of Pandhari's greatness must suffice, for to say more would greatly increase the length of our story. Sidhopant with his son-in-law remained in the sacred city of Pandhari. 68. They played on the cymbals and *vina* and drum, and as *Vaishnavas* danced and sang with love, even the Lord of the heaven Kailas (Shiva) seeing that interesting sight, nodded His head in joy and love. 69. After the party had circumambulated the city, they came to the great door of the temple. By the eagle platform Vitthal bowed prostrate on the ground before God. 70. Sidhopant took both his daughter and son-in-law by the hand and placed them at the feet (of Vithoba). 71. After embracing the god, they tightly held His feet. When the great festival was over Sidhopant 72. taking his daugeter, his wife and all his attendants returned to Alandi.

VITHOBA VISITS RAMESHWAR

Vithoba now said to Sidhopant, 'I wish to go to Rameshwar, but will return quickly.' 73. Recognizing his motive, Sidhopant gave him permission, saying, 'Quickly perform that pilgrimage and come back to my home.' 74. He made his bow first to Pandurang, and then quickly started, visiting one after another the chief places described in the *Puranas*. 75. He saw Mount Shaila, Mallikarjuna, and Nivritte Sangam; their power is unfathomable. The moment they are seen a heap of sins turns to ashes. 76. As Vitthal hurriedly walked along the path, he kept thinking in his mind of the image of Vitthal and with his lips he sang the praises of God's name with love. 77. After seeing Ahobal, Narsinha, Vasudev and Lord Vyankat in Mount Giri and Mount Arun, he worshipped Chidambar. 78. After visiting those places he saw Gokarna. He bathed at Hatakeshwar, and then hurried from there. 79. He saw with his own eyes the mountain from which Hanumant flew in search of Sita. From there he hurried forward. 80. After seeing Janardan he arrived at Rameshwar. He there accomplished his purpose and then started to return. 81. He came to Kolhapur and there bathed on the Panchaganga. He saw and worshipped Lakshmi. Then he started on his way from there. 82. He came into the valley of the Krishna river, and there bathed at Mahuli Sangam. Continuing from there he returned to Alandi. 83. With supreme love he embraced Sidhopant, bowing before him prostrate on the ground and at his feet.

VITHOBA RETURNS TO HIS PARENTS

84. After remaining there four nights, he said to Sidhopant, 'I feel I ought to go and see my mother and father. 85. If you will give me permission I will go at once.' Sidhopant assented and said to him, 86. 'Go with your wife and visit your parents. I will also accompany you in order to meet them.' 87. Sidhopant then took with him his daughter and son-in-law, and went to Apegaon, and there he met Govindpant. 88. Vitthal bowed to his mother and father and embraced them, and Sidhopant told them in detail the story of their son. 89. When Nirabai heard his explanation she was very glad. Just as the daughter of Janak rejoiced when Ram, after his marriage, came to Ayodhya; 90. and seeing Shri Ram and Sita before her, his mother Kausalya could not contain her joy; so, Vithoba's mother, seeing her son and daughter-in-law, was extremely happy. 91. It was just as Kunti was full of joy when Arjun, the brother of Bhima, won the bet and brought Draupadi. Such was the case now. 92. In order to honour

'the parents, Sidhopant gave them garments and ornaments. Then after obtaining leave from them, he returned to Alandi.

VITHOBA GOES TO ALANDI WITH SIDHOPANT

93. Now it happened on a certain day that both father and mother left their bodies and went to the heaven Vaikunth. 94. Vithoba never entertained disgust for the concern which his domestic duties gave him; just as when the three seasons come, they are accepted by every one; 95. or as when the rivers are in flood they do not increase the water in the ocean; or as when in the hot season water evaporates, one does not notice the lack of it; 96. so Vithoba considered both joy and sorrow as alike. Sidhopant then learned of this state of Vithoba's mind. 97. Feeling that his son-in-law would be experiencing sorrow, he felt he should visit him and comfort him. So then he returned to Apegaon. 98. He said to his son-in-law, 'You are one indifferent to earthly things, and yet all kinds of things are needed in one's domestic life for the daily and occasional necessities. 99. Therefore do me the favour of coming with me now to Alandi. It is Hari who cares for you, but your conduct is contrary to popular custom.' 100. Vithoba assented and Sidhopant took with him his daughter and son-in-law and very quickly returned to Alandi. 101. Residing in this sacred city was a great comfort to Vithoba's mind. He daily performed praise-services in praise of Hari, and continually met *sadhus.*

VITHOBA BECOMES A SANNYASI

102. On the eleventh day of the month Ashadh (July) and Kartik (November) he was accustomed to go on a pilgrimage to Pandhari. Many days passed but they saw no signs of a child being born to them. 103. Vithoba now said to his wife, 'My mind has become dejected. I want to go to Benares in order to join the order of the *sannyasis.*

104. This is the way my mind feels, and I ask your' permission to go.' Rakhumabai gave him no reply, because her mind was so troubled. 105. She hurried to her father and told him the whole affair. She said, 'The lord of my life asks my permission to join the order of *sannyasis*. 106. Sidhopant said in reply to her complaint, 'So long as a man has no child, he should never enter the order of *sannyasis*, such is the command of the *Vedas*. 107. Beware, lest you give him permission.' Having received this reply from her father, Rakhumabai was always careful to watch what she said.

108 It so happened on a certain day that Vithoba said to his wife, 'Give me your permission to go and bathe in the Ganga.' 109. Very carelessly she assented. He was satisfied with her reply, and went to Anadavan (Benares). 110. Just as when a cobra escapes from the juggler and crawls into an ant-hole in the forest; or as when a parrot escapes from its cage and goes and sits on the tree; 111. or as when a *sadhu* finds comfort in leaving an assembly of crooked men; or as when a dutiful wife runs away privately from a company of prostitutes; 112. or as a deer runs away from the clutches of a tiger; or as when a saint leaves a town of revilers and goes to a great sacred city; 113. or as the *muni* Shuka ran far away from Rambha; or as the ocean came out of the womb through the action of the *rishi* Agasti; 114. so with that same satisfaction in his heart Vithoba came to Benares. He bathed at the junction of the Triveni, and there experienced repentance of heart. 115. After worshipping (Bindu) Madhav (Krishna), he went to Prayag in the month of Magh (February) to bathe. From there he returned and came to Pushkar (a sacred place in Rajputana). 116. At this place there lived an innumerable number of saints, *sadhus* and *Vaishnavas*. Here while

listening to the explanations of the *Bhagvadgita*, he heard of the principles of the order of *sannyasis*. 117. He said to himself, 'It is difficult to endure the difficulties created by *Maya*. I must take thought how to escape the ever-returning births and deaths. 118. He therefore went as a suppliant to a *sannyasi* named Shri Ramashram. Vithoba embraced his feet and said, 'Initiate me into the order of the *sannyasis*.' 119. The *sannyasi* asked him in reference to what previous order he belonged, and whether he had a wife, a son, brothers and other relatives? 120. He replied, 'I am all alone. I have no snare of wife or children. Therefore, as soon as I have experienced repentance I have come with reverence as a suppliant to you, my *swami*.' 121. Seeing that this saint seemed one free from all wordly passions, the *sadguru* said, 'I agree.' So he gave him the *mantra* that initiated him, and he entered into the order of the *sannyasis*.

122. After Vitthal had thus entered the fourth stage at Benares, Sidhopant indirectly heard this news regarding him. 123. Hearing that her husband had become a *sannyasi*, Rakhumabai became deeply concerned in her mind. Said she, 'O lord of my life, why have you cast me away in the wilderness of this world?' 124. Just as the good Draupadi felt at separation from the Pandavas, or as Damayanti wept when separated from Nal, or as Taramati was scorched by the fire of sorrow when she found herself without Harischandra, 125. or as when death approached Satyavan, Savitri sought to commit suicide, or as when hearing of the death of Jayadev, Padmavati fell in a faint, 126. so the faithful wife of Vithoba cried aloud when she heard the news of his becoming a *sannyasi*. But being comforted by her mother and father, she restrained her mind with courage. 127. After completing her domestic duties it was her custom to

worship the pimpal-tree. By her very many austerities all her faults were destroyed.

VITHOBA'S DISLOYALTY TO HIS WIFE FOUND OUT

128. Shripad, the head of the *sannyasis*, who had admitted her husband to that order, happened to come to Alandi. Rakhumabai seeing him there approached him to make him a *namaskar*. 129. Shripad had seated himself at the time on the stone platform surrounding the pimpal-tree. Rakhumabai made a *namaskar* very reverently. 130. Very graciously he gave her a blessing: 'Be the mother of eight sons, and one possessing a husband.' Hearing him say this she was exceedingly astonished. 131. As Rakhumabai smiled to herself, Shripad questioned her. He said, 'Mother, why do you regard what I said as a matter to laugh at?' 132. She replied, 'Because you gave me the blessing that I should always have a husband, and be the mother of sons. But oh chief of the *sannyasis*, how can this result without my husband? 133. My husband has left me, and with repentance has entered the order of the *sannyasis*. Therefore, when you gave me your blessing, I thought it a very strange thing. 134. To sow seed in a fireplace, or for a cloud to rain down upon a rock, such is your blessing given to me, without asking me any questions. 135. It is like showing a mirror to a blind man, or singing before a deaf man, or giving dainty food to a sick man, without giving the deed a thought. 136. Just as it is useless to blow the fire when there are no live coals, or bringing a lamp without oil in it; or as it is in vain that a beggar pleads with a miser; 137. or as it is useless to sow the seeds in the ground when the clouds have poured down no rain; or of what use is it for a physician to give the royal medicine to a man destined not to live? 138. When the moon is in its dark half, why should an astrologer allow the bride to

marry ? Or after the sun has set, of what use are the gifts given in worship? 139. So you did not bring the facts (of my case) to your mind, and yet gave me your blessing. A promise that *you* utter cannot prove untrue, however, and that is why it amused me.' 140. While Rakhumabai spoke Shripad felt great surprise. He thought to himself, 'It will be necessary to prescribe a penance to the one who admitted Vithoba to the order of the *sannyasis.* 141. If a disciple abandons his young wife when as yet she had no offspring, and enters the order of the *sannyasis*, then for both disciple and *guru* the *Shastras* have prescribed a penalty. 142. When one speaks in a mine, the echo comes back to him; so although I asked him his condition, yet my mistake has come back to me. 143. It is like the moon laughing at the stars, when it itself has spots; or as if the ocean should blame the Ganges, when itself is salty; 144 or as when a man finds fault with dainty food when his mouth tastes bitter; or as when a person blind from his birth should blame the sun; 145. or as when a person without a straight nose should get angry with his mirror; or as when a lamp has darkness underneath it, but shows light to others; 146. so I have done what is wrong and needlessly blame others. I feel that the injury I have caused her will destroy my good deeds.' 147. So he asked Rakhumabai, 'Who are your relatives here?' She stood before him with hands joined palm to palm, and replied in a humble tone of voice: 148. 'I have a mother, father, brothers and sisters, but because of my separation from my husband I seem like one without a protector.' 149. Shripad then commanded her to invite her father and bring him there. She hastened to her home and brought Sidhopant. 150. When he saw this chief of *yogis* he made him a prostrate obeisance. He worshipped him by the use of flowers and perfumes and washing his feet, and ended by giving him to eat. 151. He stood before him with hands joined and asked, 'Where have you come from, my *swami*? And where are you going to from here? Kindly tell me.' 152. Shripad replied, 'My home is at Benares. With intention of going to Rameshwar I have reached this southern country. 153. Your daughter has told me all about herself. I must therefore now hasten back to Benares.' 154. Shripad further added, 'According to scripture authority my good deeds will go for nothing, because of the fault committed against her. 155. Bring Rakhumabai with you, and let us go to Benares.' When he said this, Sidhopant fell at his feet, and said, 156. 'You are merciful. Let us hasten to go.' He took his daughter with him and started. 157. Arriving at Benares, Shripad went to his hermitage. He called Chaitanya [as Vithoba was now called in the order] before him, and asked him again about his former condition of life. 158. 'Tell me now. Did you have a wife or did you not in your home when you were a householder? You told me an untruth. Now keep nothing whatever back. 159. Tell me the whole truth.' And with that, he placed his assuring hand upon him. Hearing the *sadguru* say this, Chaitanya (Vithoba) replied in the same way as does 160. a child when it has committed a fault and its mother speaks to it with anger; it timidly confesses to its mother; so Vithoba confessed to his *guru*. 161. When a subject has done what is wrong and the king has punished him, he very timidly tells him what had happened, just so it was with this *sannyasi* Chaitanya (Vithoba); 162. or as when a sick man eats some indigestible food and the physician in anger asks him about it, the sick man tells the truth from fear of further sickness; 163. or as when the youngest of the daughters-in-law in the performance of her domestic work fails in some matter that has been told her, and she confesses timidly when the mother-in-law becomes aware of it; 164. so Vithoba replied very timidly to his *sadguru*, feeling in his heart great fear lest this chief of the *yogis* should curse him. 165. He said: 'I did truly abandon my young wife while yet without offspring.'

VITHOBA AS HOUSEHOLDER AGAIN

Shripad hearing him say this, called Rakhumabai. 166. He now said to Chaitanya (Vithoba), 'Take back your wife, return at once to your own country, and live according to the rules that apply to you. 167. If you hold the fear of doing what is forbidden and have no doubts in your mind, then my command to you is your authority to obey, and God will be your Helper.' 168. Having received this blessing, Chaitanya (Vithoba) worshipped his feet. He took his wife by the hand and started for his own country; 169. just as the Vindhya mountain range accepted Agasti's command, and fell down upon the earth; so accepting his *sadguru's* wish, Chaitanya (Vithoba) hastened on his way.

170. Thus Sidhopant arrived at home bringing with him his daughter and son-in-law. When the people heard the news, all the evil-minded began to laugh at them. 171. They said, 'How is it that after entering the *sannyasi* order he has now become a householder?' One said, 'He has done what is improper, because he is a man of faulty life.' 172. Another one remarked, 'He must be sensually inclined.' A third remarked, 'He is a miser and a vile hateful fellow.' Still another remarked, 'We should never even look into his face. 173. As one who first drinks nectar and then takes intoxicating drinks, abandoning his connection with the *sannyasis*, he has become absorbed in earthly things. 174. It is like one who at first carefully studies the *Vedas*, and then takes in his hand some obscene book. So, determined to cast aside indifference to earthly things, he has returned to the sorrows of the domestic life. 175. He has left off the worship of Vishnu and has brought

upon himself the favour of devils; or as if one should leave his residence in a sacred city, and come and live in some miserable village; 176. or as if one should give up association with Brahmans and set his affection upon the unnamables (untouchables), so he has abandoned the gain from indifference to worldly things and fallen into the maze of domestic life.' 177. So everyone now began to revile him, but Vithoba had peace of mind; just as when a cloud rains upon a mountain it is never washed away; 178. just as an eagle will never fly away out of fear of a serpent; or as an elephant is never frightened by the barking of a dog; 179. when the sea roared, Agasti was not frightened; and when the sun sees a firefly with its eye it is not troubled. 180. so when the waves of trouble came upon Vithoba he drank deeply of peace; he stopped the entrance of desire and anger; his action was unusual and beyond comparison. 181. The Brahmans turned him out of caste. His relatives abandoned him. He built a hut in the forest and there lived with his wife. 182. In order to provide for his wife he obtained food by begging. Day and night, never ceasing for a moment, he repeated the names of God. 183. He spent his time in listening to and contemplating the *Bhagavadgita* and *Bhagwat*, with a mind continually at peace.

THE BIRTH OF DNYANDEV

In this way twelve years passed and then children were born to them, 184. three sons and one daughter; these were their children. And by merely listening to their names dullards and fools are purified. 185. The first one born was an *avatar* of (Shiva) the Husband of Mridani (Parvati); they gave him the name of Nivritti. The *avatar* of Vishnu came to birth in this world and was given the name of Dnyandev. 186. Sopan was the *avatar* of Brahmadev. Adimaya (the primal force of the universe) took the form of Muktabai. In their births Rakhumabai took great comfort.

MAHIPATI AS GOD'S DRUM

187. And now, fortunate hearers, listen with reverence to the next chapter with its delightful story. Just as the *chakor* bird, drinking the nectar of the moon, looks at it with close attention; 188. or just as a deer enraptured over music forgets itself, so do you hearers listen with reverence. 189. Or as the *chatak* bird, when thirsty, longs for the rain from a cloud, so with fondness listen to the story with its nine sentiments [love, heroism, compassion, surprise, mirth, wrath, fear, disgust, peace]. 190. The stories of these *bhaktas* have a depth of meaning indescribable by words. It is the Husband of Rukmini who is really relating it. Just as the sound proceeds from a drum, but it will not sound unless one plays upon it, 191. so my mouth has as it were a skin stretched over it, and it is God who makes me compose this book. Mahipati is a mere instrument in God's hand, as all wise saints know.

192. *Swasti* (Peace !) This book is the *Shri Bhakta-vijaya.* In listening to it, the Lord of the earth will be pleased. Listen therefore, you God-loving, pious *bhaktas.* This is the eighth very delightful chapter.

CHAPTER IX

LIFE OF DNYANDEV (Continued)

Obeisance to Shri Ganesh. Obeisance to the Husband of Rukmini

BENEFITS FROM THE STORIES OF THE SAINTS

1. Blessed is this day on which the stories of the saints are related. Those who listen to them are fortunate possessors of love and *bhakti*. 2. Listen now to the words in which the story of the saints is related. As it enters into the heart through the door of the ear, peace and forgiveness move in them as they become indifferent to earthly things. 3. As one listens to the story through the ear, compassion for every creature arises in the heart. Through the eye of knowledge wrong thinking at once flees away. 4. He who makes a collection of such books at his home, hindrances in his life flee far away. Shri Hari with a disk in His hand protects him in every way. 5. Those who continually sing the stories of God's *bhaktas*, the Husband of Rukmini will meet with them and the longings of these hearers will at once be fulfilled.

BRAHMANS REFUSE TO INVEST VITHOBA'S CHILDREN WITH THE SACRED THREAD

6. In the previous chapter, attentive hearers learned the fact that Nivritti, Dnyandev, Sopan descended as *avatars*, and Muktabai as the primal force (of the universe). 7. But everyone reviled them, saying, 'One should not even look into their faces. Those children have been born among the low caste and brought a stain on their Brahmanhood.' 8. Day by day they grew and appeared as youths. As their mother and father became concerned regarding them, 9. the wife said to her husband, 'I have great concern in my mind. We must ask permission

of the Brahmans, and invest our sons with the sacred thread.' 10. On a certain day therefore, Chaitanya (Vithoba) gathered together an assembly of Brahmans and joining his hands he pleaded with them: '*Swamis*, forgive me my transgression Listen to the pleading of a humble person. 11. Consult the *Shastras* that contain the religious principles and prescribe a penance for us.' Saying this, Vithoba prostrated himself on the ground before the Brahmans. 12. The eldest son, Nivritti, then said to them, 'Merely by seeing you, we have become free. Prescribe at once penance for us six persons.' 13. The *pandits* skilled in the *Shastras*, and the highest rank of the Brahmans, consulted the books and replied, 'There is no other penance for you except death.' 14. The Brahmans said, 'Put yourselves under a saw, or burn yourselves to death with repentance. 15. Aside from these penances there are no other prescribed for you.' Hearing this reply of the Brahmans, Vithoba's mind was filled with repentance. 16. He made a *namaskar* to the Brahmans and quickly started away leaving his wife, his sons, his daughter and his home. 17. He did not even glance backward, much to the astonishment of the Brahmans, and they remarked, 'He has burnt up all his sins by bathing in the sacred waters of repentance. 18. The *Shastras* speak of no penance superior to that of repentance. Through the favour of his *sadguru* he has become pure.' 19. Nivritti then said to the Brahmans, 'Tell us what we are to do, what penalty do the *Shastras* prescribe for us?' 20. Hearing his question the Brahmans said to him, 'Go now to Pratishthan (Paithan) and bring from there a letter declaring you to be pure.' 21. Nivritti said to the Brahmans, 'What shall we go and tell them? We have no authority to tell them regarding our caste or family. 22. We are neither Vaishyas, Kshatriyas, nor Brahmans. We are of the imperishable, the ancient of days, the eternal, the self-knowing perfect one. 23. We are neither water, light, the heavens, the earth, the wind, nor the original elements. Nor can we be said to possess the divine form of the universe. 24. We are not god-attendants of Shiva, nor are we celestial beings such as *Yakshas* and *Kinnars.* We are neither *rishis* nor demons. We do not possess attributes, nor are we unchangeable. We should not be called formless.' 25. Nivritti said to Dnyaneshwar, 'Such being our ancestry, if we do go to Paithan, what are we to tell the Brahmans there?' 26. Dnyandev replied, 'The man who acts contrary to scripture commands is worthy of blame, such is the teaching of the *Shastras.* 27. Although the man who has knowledge becomes a *jivanmukta* (free while living), he should not leave the rules that are prescribed for him. Moreover, those who are *sadhus* should show others the right way by themselves walking in it. 28. To act contrary to what is prescribed in the scriptures should be recognized as the supreme fault. Whatever one's special duties are, they should be performed. So have spoken the Brahmans learned in the *Vedas.*' 29. Dnyandev then said, 'Nivritti, this is what the *Shastras* have to say regarding one's duties. I have therefore replied to you because of our close friendship.' 30. Sopan then spoke, Of what value is caste or family? Without *bhakti* the feet of Shri Hari can never be attained. 31. Durvas, the *muni* Vasishtha, Gautama, Vyas, Valmiki, and the great Agasti and the Pandavas, in what scripture are the familes of all these declared noble? 32. Alhough one may be born in the noblest families, and although he may have studied profoundly the *Vedas*, still, unless he has *bhakti*, all this is in vain. The *Shastras* do not praise such. 33. If one places one's *bhakti* on God, of what necessity is there of being of high caste?' Such were the words that Sopan addressed to Dnyandev. 34. After this discussion among themselves, they gave an answer to the Brahmans.

DNYANDEV AMONG PAITHAN BRAHMANS

After making them a *namaskar* they at once started on their way to Paithan. 35. After reaching the banks of the Godavari they performed all the duties devolving upon the pilgrims to sacred waters, and then entering into Brahmapuri, they made their bow to the twice-born (the Brahmans). 36. They collected an assembly of Brahmans and told them plainly just what had happened. The Brahmans of the highest rank after listening to them said, "It is evident that you have fallen from your high state.' 37. When they read the letter (from the Brahmans at Alandi), the whole affair became known, and they remarked, 'These are the children of a *sannyasi*. There is no penance that can avail them. 38. If a *Shudra* is bathed in the Ganges, will he thereby become a pure Brahman? If a touchstone is applied to a piece of pottery, it will never turn to gold. 39. If one should give water to seed that has been baked, it will never sprout. If one gives medicine to one whose life is about to end why look for his recovery? 40. So these can never be made pure by sacred waters or religious observances or by any number of penalties.' Such was the decision of the whole assembly of Brahmans. 41. They said, 'According to the opinion of the *Shastras* there is only one remedy. If they do that, what necessity is there of penance? 42. They should go as suppliants to Shri Hari (God) and worship every existing thing. Donkeys, dogs, elephants and the like should be worshipped as if they were the same. 43. They should bow with the same reverence to a hog and an out-caste with the thought that God is in them all; they should bow to them in love'. 44. After listening to this reply, Nivritti was highly pleased. Dnyandev and Sopan also felt supreme joy. 45. They remarked, 'This rule of religion and morals is just as it was in our hearts.'

Muktabai also accepted the decision with pleasure. 46 Listening to their (strange) names, the Brahmans manifested great surprise and said, 'Why should we call you Dnyandev ? 47. How can we call you Dnyandev ? Have you lovingly studied the *Vedas* or become acquainted with the *Puranas* ? 48. If one has no efficiency, of what good is it to speak of one's self as a great person ? If a cow has no milk in her udder, of what value are her long horns ? 49. A great eye without sight, or the assuming of responsibilities without being respected, or a man without manliness, what use is there for such to exist ? 50. Divine knowledge without compassion for creatures, singing without enthusiasm, food cooked without salt, never produces a good taste. 51. If one has no courage, why go on to the battlefield ? If one has not lost desires, why should he be called indifferent to earthly things ?'

DNYANDEV MAKES A BUFFALO REPEAT THE VEDAS

52. While they were thus speaking and saying among themselves, 'What is in a name ?' one of the Brahmans remarked, 'A young male buffalo with a leather waterskin on his back is coming towards us. 53. His name also is Dnyan.' Listening to this remark of the Brahman, Dnyandev joined his hands palm to palm, and said, 'Listen to my words. 54. I cannot see the least difference between this male buffalo and myself. The *atma* (soul) that pervades every body is alike in every creature. 55. If an infinite number of jars are filled with water, the sun would be reflected in all of them. So the All-pervading, the Holder of the disk (Krishna) is alike in every creature. 56. There might be eighteen kinds of vegetables, but the water that feeds their roots is the same for each. Just so the Lord of Rama (Krishna) is alike in every existing thing. 57. The gold is the same in all ornaments, but the ornaments are seen to be different

So God pervades all existing things alike. 58. One thread is used in the weaving, but the cloth woven appears in different forms. So the Holder of the disk (Krishna) pervades all existing things alike.' 59. A Brahman hearing him say this remarked, 'You are needlessly talking too much.' Then taking a whip in his hand, he angrily struck the buffalo. 60. That made Dnyaneshwar violently tremble, and the welt appeared on his own back. When the twice-born (Brahmans) saw this, they exclaimed, 61. 'If there is no difference between you and the buffalo, then let it recite the *Vedas*.' Hearing these words of the twice-born (Brahmans), the *bhakta* who knew no differences did as follows. 62. He went up to the buffalo, and placed his hand upon its head, saying, 'Recite at once the *Rigveda*, and satisfy these earth-gods (Brahmans). 63. As soon as he said this a most extraordinary thing happened. The young buffalo recited the *Vedas* with proper intonation. 64. The buffalo then recited all four of the *Vedas* and gave pleasure to the Brahmans. They exclaimed, 'No one has ever seen so wonderful a thing in this world of mortals. 65. When a sick man drinks nectar, his disease immediately disappears. If the poor man has the favour of a wish-cow, he is no longer despondent. 66. If the sun shows favour to the blind man, what will he not be able to see? Or if Sarasvati (goddess of speech) kindly gives her blessing to a dumb man, will he not speak? 67. If Ganpati shows His favour, the *fourteen sciences will become as plain as the lines on one's palm. By association with the Husband of Mridani (Shiva), *yoga* in its eight forms can be acquired. 68. So by the hand of the Giver of blessing, Dnyandev made the buffalo recite the *Vedas*.' All the Brahmans were full of astonish-

* The four *Vedas*, the six *angas* (grammar, prosody, astronomy, pronunciation, interpretations of unusual terms, the Hindu ritual), the eighteen *Puranas*, *mimansa* or theology, *nyaya* or logic, and *dharma* or law.

ment, and they felt repentance in their hearts. 69. They remarked, 'We have studied the *Vedanta* and all those parts called *Upanishads*, but God has never given to us such great power. 70. What has never been heard of before, our eyes have seen today in our very presence. What Brahmadev could not perform, that seemingly impossible thing in this universe has taken place. 71. These three are evidently the *avatars* of the three gods, and Muktabai is the *avatar* of *Adimaya* (primal force of the universe). No penance is of value to them. Just as the river Ganges cannot be defiled (so they cannot be defiled). 72. We preach to others freely, but we do not act according to it. Wishing for wealth and honour among men, we have spent our life in vain. 73. We have not seen in this world such noble Brahmans as these.' This is what all the twice-born (Brahmans) said, adding, 74. 'Blessed are their mother and father. Both of them must have performed good deeds in their former births.' With these expressions of astonishment the Brahmans remained silent. 75. But Dnyandev said to them, 'O *Swamis*, what I have done is through your power, I am truly an ignorant person. It is your feet that manifest this power.' 76. All the people of Paithan were moved with much love and reverence. They exclaimed, 'Blessed are these *bhaktas* of Vishnu, who in this earthly existence are entirely indifferent to earthly things.' 77. They now began daily to bathe in the Godavari, to listen to the explanations of the *Vedanta*, and the stories in the *Puranas*. At night time there were *kirtans* in praise of Hari, and every one came to listen. 78. Seeing the extraordinary miracle they had performed every one showed them respect. After many days passed in this way another most extraodinary thing happened.

ANCESTORS COME TO THE FEAST AT WHICH THEY ARE WORSHIPPED

79. On a certain day, the owner of the house where,

Nivritti, Dnyandev and Muktabai were staying began the ceremony of worshipping his ancestors. 80. When he went to invite the twice-born (Brahmans) to be present, they said to him, 'You have kept in your house the children of a *sannyasi.* 81. Therefore we cannot come to your house to eat.' Hearing their words the man was deeply concerned. 82. He hurried back to his home and sat down depressed in mind. Dnyandev asked him what had happened. 83. 'Why are you so troubled today and sitting so silent ?' Hearing this question, 84. the Brahman replied, 'Today is the holy ceremony in honour of ancestors, but the Brahmans will not come to the feast. Therefore my mind has become sad and I am sitting here silent.' 85. Dnyandev then said to the Brahman, 'Do not be troubled in your mind. The ancestors will come to the feast in visible form. 86. Calm your mind, and do the necessary cooking in your house.' Hearing this prediction the man was astonished 87. After finishing his bath and devotions and thus purifying himself he prepared and served many kinds of dainty food on leaf plates. 88. Dnyandev sprinkled the rice and brought down the ancestors in visible form. He worshipped their feet and gave them seats in the chief place. 89. He gave them garments, ornaments, adornments, *tulsi* leaves, garlands of flowers, the twelve forehead-marks, the beautiful sacred thread, and gifts of gold. 90. In this way having worshipped them he offered to them an abundance of incense and lights. The twice-born (Brahmans) thought this very strange and in their minds they expressed their astonishment. 91. When Dnyandev made the offering to God in the form of the ancestors in visible form' these ancestors very graciously began to eat the food. 92. He served to them whatever pleased their taste until all of them were satisfied. He gave them water to wash their hands, then offered them the *pan-supari*, and gifts of money.

93. When it was said to them, ' Return to your abodes, these ancestors became invisible, and all the Brahmans of Paithan discussed the matter among themselves. 94. They said, ' Dnyandev has done a wonderful thing. He has feasted the ancestors in their actual visible form. We have never seen nor heard so great a miracle in this world of mortals. 95. Through our obstinate pride we rejected the invitation to the feast. So the ancestors came in person and took away the gifts. 96. Just as Shiva devoured the offering, and the guardian of the idol remained silent, so it seems it has happened to us. 97. It is as if the sun came in person and took away the image of the sun, and the astrologer whose mind was full of expectations remained chewing his cud. 98. The guardian of the scared city has taken away the victim that was placed near the altar of sacrifice. The keeper of the treasures strongly objected, but his opposition was of no avail. 99. Just as when Indra and those with Him came in person and took away the materials offered in sacrifice, the fire itself remained silent, so it has happened to us. 100. Just as when ghosts come in visible form and take away what has been offered to them, and the sorcerer, thinking what is done as of no value, remains hungry; 101. so these ancestors have taken away the gifts of gold and the dainty food. Because we were filled with pride, we have lost everything. 102. Blessed are these: Nivritti, Dnyaneshwar, and Sopan, noble *Vaishnavas*, and Muktabai who is the visible *avatar* of *Adimaya* (the primal force). 103. A penance cannot be of any value to these three divine beings. They are world *gurus*, uninfluenced by their bodies, and *jivanmuktas* (free while living).'

104. They therefore wrote a letter to that effect and gave it into the hand of Sopan. 'The young male buffalo has recited the *Vedas*, and in the same way it is still reciting them.'

105. When a touchstone touches iron, it always turns it to gold, so this buffalo was day and night long reciting the philosophic teachings of the *Vedanta.* 106. Hari gave to Dhruva an immovable place. His seat will never be removed. In that same way Dnyandev gave to this buffalo the everlasting knowledge. 107. Upamanyu was seated by the ocean of milk and continued without ceasing to drink the milk. Just so Dnyandev made the buffalo recite the *Vedas* without ceasing. 108. Just as *Yogis* sit on seats of spikes and yet feel unceasing joy, so this buffalo is absorbed in the knowledge of the *Vedanta.*

DNYANESHWAR WRITES HIS 'DNYANESHWARI' AND 'AMRITANUBHAV'

109. Dnyaneshwar realized the truth of the above, and discussed the matter with Nivritti. He said, 'Through this continually recited knowledge of the buffalo, the Way of Works will be destroyed. 110. The deep inner meaning of the *Vedas* is a secret. If it is plainly divulged to people, it will drive away the misunderstandings of those devoted to the Way of Works. There will then be nothing left of sacrifices.' 111. After explaining this to Nivriti, he made a *namaskar* to the Brahmans, and having asked their permission to take away the buffalo, they obtained leave from the Brahmans and started on their way. 112. As they left the town the Brahmans walked with them to see them off. Tears filled their eyes, and they lovingly embraced them. 113. With hearts stirred with emotion they conversed with one another. The Brahmans remarked, 'The time has been well spent in our association with Dnyaneshwar'. 114. The men and the women of the town accompanied them for one mile. And then Dyaneshwar pleaded with them to return to their homes. 115. They then made a *namaskar* and returned, while Nivritti, Sopan and Dnyaneshwar, with their sister Muktabai, 116. walked along the road full of joy. With love they sang

the praises of Hari (God) and composed wise verses containing the nine emotions. 117. When they arrived at the sacred town of Mahalaya (modern Nevasa), they remained there. They bathed in the sacred waters of the Pravara river, and there met with the Lord of Mohani. 118. There Dnyaneshwar composed his Marathi commentary on the *Bhagavadgita*, and showed an easy way for the dull-minded, the fools and all ignorant persons. 119. To begin with, it is like the brilliant gold on which is the setting for diamonds; it is like dainty food prepared from grain in order to give to the tongue the pleasant taste; 120. or like a golden ornament that adorns a beautiful body; or like the scattering of very small seeds, that finally show their beauty in flowers and fruit; 121. or like the power of the wish-tree which is made to appear beautiful through the imagination; or like the full moon raining down nectar for the *chakor* bird. 122. Dnyandev composed this Marathi book to make plain the deep meaning of the *Bhagavadgita*, in order that the wise, God-loving, pious men might have true knowledge. 123. Nivritti, who was Dnyandev's *sadguru*, said lovingly to him, ' From your own thoughts on the subject, compose the *Amritanubhav*. ' 124. Replying that he would do so, he placed his head at his *sadguru's* feet. Then giving thought to his own spiritual experiences, he composed the *Amritanubhav*. 125. In order to destroy the pride of Brahmadev, Krishna created cows and calves, and Dnyandev composed the *Amritanubhav* to answer the proud heretics who talked in vain out of their own imaginations.

126. After having lovingly made a *namaskar* to the primal-power, Mhalasa, the party hastened from there to come back to their own part of the country. 127. As the four walked along the path, they lovingly repeated the names of God. At night they lodged in some town and performed a *kirtan* in honour of Hari. 128. Having left

all thoughts of love and affection, of honour and dishonour, and all pride of body, they looked upon every creature, from Brahmadev to insects, as the same. 129. One day while walking along the path, they encamped in the forest belonging to Alandi. Here the animal that recited the *Vedas* died. 130. Having placed it in a tomb, they caused it to reach the state of final deliverance. Saints are always merciful mines of compassion and givers of assurance 131. After worshipping the tomb, they smeared it with *shendur*. That place is still called Mhasoba.

132. From there they hastened to return to the town of Alandi. Muktabai said to Nivritti, 'We must see the place where we were born' 133. When all arrived at Alandi, all people there felt very happy. With feelings of love they worshipped their feet and embraced them. 134. The people had already heard what had happened at Paithan. In addition Sopan showed to the Brahmans the letter he had brought with him. Listening to it, all were amazed. 135. It was clearly written in the letter that the three brothers were the *avatars* of the gods. Hearing this, the Brahmans were lost in wonder. 136. And so after listening to the letter from Paithan all the Brahmans accepted its contents, and acted just as Indra and the other gods act in obedience to the command of Brihaspati; 137. or as *pandits* acknowledge the authority of the *Puranas* uttered by the lips of Shri Vyas; or as a good disciple studies philosophic subjects at the command of his *guru*;. 138. or as clouds move in the same direction as the wind; or as our sense organs act in accordance with the desire of our minds; 139. or just as a sun-flower turns to wherever the sun may be; or as when water is in the form of a stream it flows by reason of its fluidity; 140. in whatever direction the wind blows the banners wave and musical instruments sing in harmony with songs sung giving due attention to the stops; 141. just so, the Brahmans

of Alandi worshipped the three brothers according to the suggestion of the Brahmans of Paithan. They said to one another, 'Truly three gods have descended as *avatars*.' 142. And as they lovingly performed *kirtans*, all the people came to listen to them. They remarked, 'These *sadgurus* have become *avatars* for our sake.'

DNYANESHWAR AND HIS OPPONENT VISOBA CHATI

143. There was a very hateful Brahman there, whose name was Visoba Chati. He was continually reviling these four children. 144. He exclaimed, 'These are the children of a *sannyasi*. One should not look into their faces.' He was continually muttering these revilings. 145. Just as the moth in accordance with its character should seek to put out the light; or as the fire-fly should say, 'I will utterly destroy the sun;' 146. or as when Hiranyakashipu muttered to himself in rage when he saw Prahlad; or as Duryodhan was filled with anger when he heard of the praises given to Dharma; 147. or as the ten-necked monster (Ravan) was filled with wrath when he heard the story of Ram's heroism; or as *pandits* with feelings of hatred rebuke authors when they see books written in Marathi; 148. or as when thieves see the full moon they revile it; or as astrologers with hatred oppose the teachings of Sahadev; 149. in that same way Visoba Chati continually looked at them with his wrathful eyes; if he saw them anywhere he felt greatly troubled. 150. He would remark, 'These are children of a *sannyasi*. One should never even look into their faces. If we look at them, they will make us the same as themselves.' 151. Now it happened on a particular occasion that the festivals of Dasara and of lights were being celebrated. Nivritti said to Muktabai, 152. 'Prepare some very excellent pancakes for us, and give them to us to eat.' Assenting at once, she collected the materials necessary for the

cooking. 153. In order to bake these cakes she went to the potters' factory for an earthen pan. As she went along the street, she suddenly observed Visoba. 154. Seized with fear, Muktabai hid herself behind something. He at once rushed towards her, and said to her, 155. 'For what purpose are you hastening? Tell me at once.' When Muktabai heard him say this, she trembled violently. 156. For just as the lotus flower has fear aroused in its heart when it sees an elephant, or just as the *kokil* bird (cuckoo) trembles violently at seeing a falcon, 157. or as when a deer searching for water in a forest, sees a hunter in the distance; or as when a cow sees a tiger, she trembles violently with fear; 158. so with extreme fear she replied, 'I am going to the potters' field to purchase an earthen pan. 159. Nivritti has told me to make at once some pancakes.' Hearing her reply, Visoba broke out into a laugh. 160. He struck Muktabai, and then went and told the potter that if he gave the earthen pan to her, he would punish him at once. 161. 'I have lent you money and I shall demand it at once.' Hearing this threat the potter was very troubled. 162. If one gets no profit from any source but has to pay money on the debts he owes people, or when one has a severe illness; one should recognize it as due to the anger of God. 163. If one lives in a poverty-stricken home, or if one mourns over a son dying in adult age, or if people revile one who is honoured by others, this also should be recognized as due to the anger of God. 164. Or one may have studied a subject all one's life and yet on an occasion may not remember the right reply while many wrong thoughts arise in the mind; this also should be recognized as due to the wrath of God. 165. Or an enemy discovers one of our secrets and then everyone speaks alike in reference to it, anger then grows in the heart; this should be recognized also as due to the anger of God. 166. A householder (lover of his family) when travelling is greatly disturbed from his lack of food and at his home his wife bitterly complains of the same; this also should be recognized as God's anger. 167. If in one's old age one's limbs are without strength, or if none of his sons come and inquire for his welfare, or if his wife speaks harshly to him, that should be regarded as due to God's anger. 168. Well what is the use of any further illustrations ? A man enjoys or suffers according to his own acts. So when he heard Visoba's threat the potter remained silent. 169. Just then Muktabai arrived and said to the potter, ' Give me at once an earthen pan on which to bake my cakes. ' 170. The potter answered her, ' We have not yet prepared the earthenware for baking. After I have baked them, then you may come and take away an earthen pan.' 171. Hearing his reply, Muktabai returned to her home very much concerned and weeping with a pitiful voice. 172. Just then Dnyaneshwar returned to his hermitage after performing his bath, and suddenly there fell on his ear Muktabai's pitiful cry. 173. Dnyandev drew her close to himself and with his hand caressed his sister. He said to her, 'Why are you sad ? Tell me at once.' 174. She said, ' I was on my way to the potter's house to bring an earthen pan for baking cakes and Visoba met me on the way and angrily struck me. 175. He went and said to the potter, " Do not give the earthen pan to Muktabai. " I then returned home and am sitting here weeping. 176. Nivritti gave me the command to make the cakes to-day with my own hands. Therefore I am sitting here disconsolate. What shall I do ? 177. Just then Visoba Chati began to look at them from a distance through a window, and in order to hear everything they said in detail he stood outside. 178. Dnyandev then said to Muktabai, ' Why are you being troubled for nothing ? I wonder what I should do in view of his character.

DNYANESHWAR'S POWER OF 'YOGA'

179. Dnyandev then made use of his powers of *yoga*. He kindled his internal fire and flames came out of his mouth. His eyes were seen to be blood-hot. 180. Like gold when heated, so his back became bright red. Visoba stood outside and viewed the wonderful sight. 181. Dnyaneshwar then said to Muktabai, 'Bake the cakes on my back.' She immediately brought together the materials for the cakes and properly rolled them out. 182. In a moment the cakes were baked and ready, and Dnyandev put out his internal fire. 183. She served the milk of *bhakti* and love in a cup of joy. Then for sugar she used the joy of peace, whose sweetness is unlimited. 184. Into this milk she broke the cakes of experience and the four sat down together to eat them, Nivritti, Dnyandev, Sopan, and the sister Muktabai. 185. As all four partook of the first morsel they exclaimed, 'Shri Hari is the real enjoyer of this meal.' All this time Visoba stood outside watching the wonderful sight. 186. Then with a repentant heart he thought to himself, 'These are really divine persons. I have needlessly troubled them. I have not taken proper thought. 187. I found a mine of jewels and diamonds, and I thought they were glass beads, and so by a careless thought I took a sling in my hand and slung away wish-jewels. 188. I saw a wish-tree, but thinking it to be a mere *hivar* tree I applied the axe to it. Before a blind man the most precious diamonds are but like common stones. 189. Ganges water when put into a bottle, a drunkard understands as intoxicating liquor; or it is as when an unfortunate man comes near a pile of jewels, and it should seem to him to be merely a fire; 190. or as when Duryodhan thought to himself, " Shri Krishna the *avatar* of the Supreme Brahm (God) is my brother-in-law and I thought wrongly regarding him and needlessly troubled him." ' 191. Having thus repented, Visoba said

to himself, ' I must go as a suppliant to them. I must take by force what they leave on their plates, and thus bring about my well-being.' 192. Thus thinking, Visoba rushed into their home and came into the room where they were sitting eating. 193. Dnyandev hid his plate behind him, but Visoba forcibly swooped down on it and grabbed from it a morsel of food. 194. As he put his morsel into his mouth, Dnyaneshwar said to him, ' Why are you becoming a scavenger bird ? Go away from here at once.' 195. Hearing this, Visoba took that thought to his heart, and no language can describe his state. 196. Whatever is beyond description in words was here united into one person, and the darkness of his ignorance then entirely disappeared. 197. A sound comes out of a bell, then disappears in the same place, so becoming united with Brahm's essential form, Visoba remained without any duality in his nature. 198. Then joining his hands together palm to palm, he placed his head on Dnyandev's feet. Dnyandev understood his thought and gave him the blessing of assurance. 199. Just as Valmiki put aside his evil nature as soon as he saw Narad, so by association with Dnyandev, Visoba gained a character of goodness, 200. because Dnyandev said to him, ' Why are you eating like a scavenger bird ?' From that time he was called Visoba Khechar.

201. The story to be told in the next chapter is exceedingly interesting. Hearers must listen to it attentively. As it falls on their ears, they become regardless of other things and all faults disappear. 202. Just as when the sun arises the darkness sets, so when the *Bhaktavijaya* falls on anyone's ears ignorance is driven away. 203. When the touchstone touches iron its name and form at once change. So the moment one hears the stories of saints, the thought of all earthly affairs disappears. 204. The history of the saints cannot be fully described in

words, but the real relator of it is the Husband of Rukmini. To Mahipati has come the office of being His attendant in order that He might use him as His instrument.

205. *Swasti* (Peace !) This book is the *Shri Bhakta-vijaya.* In listening to it, the Lord of the earth will be pleased. Listen to it, you God-loving pious *bhaktas.* This is the ninth deeply delightful chapter.

CHAPTER X

LIFE OF DNYANDEV (Continued)

Obeisance to Shri Ganesh. Obeisance to the Husband of Shri Rukmini.

THE STORIES OF SAINTS SWEETER THAN NECTAR

1. To-day good fortune has arisen for those who have listened to the *Bhaktavijaya.* This joy cannot be described in words. What then shall I say with my lips ? 2. It is as if a wish-tree sprang up in the garden and bore wish-jewels as its fruit; or as if an abundant rain of nectar should fall on the earth; 3. or as if twelve suns, becoming cool, should shine at the same time; or as if all rivers began to flow over the earth with nectar as their waters; 4. or as when a mine has been opened containing precious stones, diamonds and wish-jewels, a fortunate man should wholly drive away his laziness and take them away with him; 5. or as if in a moment's time sand itself should become like diamonds and precious stones; or as if common stones should become eternal wish-jewels. 6. All kinds of right and wrong thoughts and poverty have fled away. Therefore listeners have received waves of the nectar of love. 7. I think that the sweetness of love is superior to nectar. The immortals who drink nectar, long for the nectar of love. 8. The gods that drink nectar perish at the end of the ages, but those who drink of the supreme spiritual nectar they exist for all eternity. 9. Therefore give close attention and listen to the stories, you God-loving *bhaktas.* As the stories fall on your ears all your sins in half a moment's time are destroyed.

DNYANDEV AND NAMA GO TOGETHER ON PILGRIMAGE

10. It came to pass on a certain day that Dnyandev came to Pandhari and conceived the desire of meeting Namdev.

11. As he entered into the house of Nama he saw him from a distance. Namdev prostrated himself on the ground before him and lovingly embraced him. 12. He worshipped him with the usual materials and said to him, 'My good fortune has arisen to-day, because the king of wise men has kindly come to my home. 13. My good deeds in a former birth have come to their fruitage. I have met Pandurang in visible form. 14. In order to save those who are entangled in the deeds of this earthly life, and those ignorant men intoxicated by the seductions of this life, you, O *Swami*, have become an *avatar*.' Saying this he again prostrated himself on the ground before him. 15. Dnyandev then said to Nama, 'Your good fortune is a special one. God is near you without ceasing. I see no limit to your good fortune. 16. You have received the joy and sweetness of His love. Desire and thirst for the things of this life have passed away. The family in which you were born has a holy ancestry. 17. If you will listen I will tell you one of the secrets of my heart.' He then took Nama by the hand, and led him into the interior of the house. 18. He said, 'Although a *Jivanmukta* (free while living) has become free from sin, he should not leave off the worship of his *guru*, of God or of sacred places. I desire to see all the sacred places on the surface of this earth in your company. 19. With this purpose in mind I have come to meet you. Tell me whether the desire of my heart will be fulfilled or not. 20. Having heard this remark Nama became very sad and said, 'Why should I abandon the sacred city of Pandhari, and wander to sacred bathing places? 21. That is like throwing nectar away and going from house to house begging for gruel; or it is like throwing away the precious *kasturi* (musk), and like carrying ashes in one's cloth. 22. Why should one leave the shade of the wish-tree and search for a forest of *shindi* (palm) tree? Why leave untouched the

dainty food on a plate, and eat fallen leaves? 23. Why drive the royal swan away and in its place bring a crow to one's house ? Why fling away diamonds and precious stones and fill one's cloth with sand ? 24. Why leave off listening to the hymns of the *Samaved*, and listen to sensual songs ? Why drive away the wish-cow and bring home a goat?' 25. Having decided the matter in his mind, Nama said to Dnyandev, 'I am not master of myself.' So saying he bowed at his feet. 26. 'I am subject to him who has cared for me and supported me, and I call myself His in body and speech Who is the beloved life of Rukmini, and the giver of the promise to Pundalik. 27. I am subject to Him with all my heart. You go and ask Him. If He gives me the command to go with you, I will respect His words.' 28. Dnyandev replied to Nama, 'I understand your purpose ; you are clever, wise, and generous, and the home of *bhakti* and knowledge.' 29. Then giving him an embrace he took Nama by the hand and said to him, 'Let both of us go to the temple and ask God to give His command.' 30. So taking Nama with him, Dnyandev came to the great door of the temple. He lovingly bowed prostrate on the ground near the eagle-platform. 31. He then came to the inner shrine and there he saw God standing on the brick. He embraced the god and with sincere feeling worshipped His feet. 32. The secret thought which he had in his mind he told the god, and as God heard his wish he began to smile. 33. The One dark as a cloud said to Dnyandev, 'You are intelligence itself in visible form. You are as pure as crystal. You are untouched by the association of desires. 34. You are absolutely in the form of soul. Why do you want to wander to sacred bathing-places ? Why apply a paste to the surface of the sun ? 35. Why again and again use means to make the moon cool ? For what purpose should one turn the ocean of milk into a guest ? 36. Why does the moon need the gentle cooling breeze of a fan? What paste should one use to cool the moon? 37. It is not necessary to teach Ganpati. It is not at all necessary to teach Sarasvati the sixty-four arts. 38. Just so, Dnyandev, why do you want to wander to sacred bathing-places with useless thoughts in your mind? Why wander about uselessly?' 39. The other replied, 'True, true. What you say is perfectly right, but I want association with such a God-loving *bhakta* as Nama is. 40. I want the joy of association with him, and so make my life worth living.' Thus saying he lovingly placed his head on the god's feet.

41. Then the Lord of Pandhari smiled and looking towards Nama He said to him, 'Dnyandev, who is actually God supreme, desires your company. 42. So, go with him at once and come back again soon. Accomplish whatever purpose you have in your mind. 43. But whether sitting or lying down or walking do not forget me. And Nama, life of my life, let your love of Me continue.' 44. Thus speaking, God's throat choked with emotion. Then turning towards Dnyandev, He said, 45. 'You are wise and the very image of joy. I have one thing to ask you. Let the remembrance of it continue in your heart. 46. Nama grew up by My favour; I have always loved him. For once I might bear separation from Rumā (Lakshmi) but I could never be separated from Nama. 47. You have put Me into a dilemma, for I do not like to go against your wish. There is no one dearer to Me than Nama.' 48. God then took Nama by the hand, and gave him into the hand of Dnyandev, saying, 'Never neglect him, lovingly care for him. 49. You are putting Me in a great difficulty in asking Me for the beautiful jewel (Nama) around my neck. So take care of this uncouth, innocent, crazy Nama. 50. Never have I been separated from Nama, but because of My respect for you, I am sending him with you.' 51.

Thus speaking the Husband of Rumā was moved with emotion. Tears filled His eyes. 52. Dnyandev then placed his head at God's feet and immediately started, taking Nama by the hand. They came first to the bank of Chandrabhaga river. 53. After both had bathed they walked round the tomb of Pundlik. They made a *namaskar* before his feet and then crossed over to the other side of the river. 54. After seeing Nama off, Krishna returned to His own temple. Just then Rukmini came with a golden vessel to wash his feet. 55. When she gazed into His face she saw His eyes were filled with tears and His whole body was wet with perspiration. The Mother of the world was astonished. 56. Rukmini placed Her head upon His feet and said to Him, 'Your condition today seems very strange. I feel very surprised.' 57. Hearing Rukmini's question the Life of the world said, 'My heart has been broken by the arrow of separation from Nama. 58. I love him greatly and therefore I feel very sad. By no method of joy does My mind become quieted. 59. Aside from Myself, Nama has no close friends and relatives. I feel great concern as to how he will keep alive without Me? 60. Dnyandev came as a beggar and has carried away the wealth I had stored up, miserly as I am, in the form of God-loving Nama who is a mine of *bhakti*. 61. Nama is the child of My old age, and I am very fond of him all the time. But Dnyandev has forcibly dragged him away from Me, and taken him away to wander to sacred bathing-places. 62. I am, as it were, a tree in the form of the earth, and Nama is the moisture of My roots. Dnyandev, a water-deity as it were, has drawn it away. 63. As I was watering the tree, Nama gave it moisture like a cloud of joy. Dnyandev coming like a tornado carried it far away.' 64. Hearing Him say this, Rukmini replied, 'Weeping, pain, and desires do no injury to those whose lips repeat Thy name.' 65. Hearing her, the Life of the world answered, 'You have spoken the truth, but I cannot endure a single moment without My *bhakta*. 66. I am the unmanifested and the formless but have assumed attributes for the sake of my *bhaktas*. I have created the Heaven of *Vaikunth* for My *bhaktas* to dwell in. 67. My *bhaktas* alone have the right to become sharers in my good fortune. I alone know their necessities. 68. Aside from My *bhaktas* no one knows my heart's secrets.' This the Lord of Heaven said to Rukmini with great emotion. 69. 'These *bhaktas* of mine put aside all pride, and become one with Me in essence, just as there is no difference between a lamp and its light; 70. or just as the sun and its rays are always united; or as gold and brilliancy are always found together. 71. Nama is the dust of the feet of the chiefs of the *bhaktas*, who have the experience of soul-knowledge. I am separated from him to-day and therefore I am sad.' 72. Thus saying, the god fainted away and fell on the ground. Mother Rukmini, the Mother of the world, was greatly alarmed. 73. But regaining her courage, she awakened the god from his faint. She then invited all *bhaktas* to come there and told them what had happened. 74. She said, 'The Holder of the disk (Krishna) suddenly gave a great sob and fell down in a faint. Do something to help. Come near Him and tell Him.' 75. The *bhaktas* fanned Him with their clothes and asked Him, 'O Ocean of mercy, Saviour of the world, why art Thou so overcome to-day?' 76. Hearing the words of His *bhaktas*, He aroused Himself by force of will. The Life of the world awakened from His faint and said with emotion, 77. 'There is nothing that I am more fond of than Nama. I feel as though I must hold him to My heart in an embrace. 78. I am always working to meet the needs of My *bhaktas*. I am ashamed to say so. But Nama has never put me into difficulty in working for him. 79. I have not given him the four chief ends of the existence of man. After his birth he made Me his debtor through service. 80. Slaughtering those powerful enemies, lust, anger, pride and envy by his heroic deeds he conquered the difficulties of this earthly existence. 81. He put envy and conceit far from him. He freed himself from those enemies such as illusion and earthly attachment. And Nama has no fondness for exalting the inferior deities. 82. Nama will not bow to any other God than Myself. He has not seen one moment's rest for his soul except in Me. 83 As he walks along the path, he must often be weary. Who will ask him whether he is hungry or thirsty ? This is what severely troubles me.' 84. As God said this, the *bhaktas* shouted out, 'Victory, victory,' and overflowing with joy and love they prostrated themselves at His feet. 85. From there they came to the eagle-platform, dancing with joy. They again prostrated themselves here before Him. 86. Seeing them do this, the Life of the world became slightly conscious.

NAMDEV'S DOUBTS AND DNYANDEV'S REPLIES

In the meantime Nama looked back very often. 87. He cried, 'O, God, Thou hast forsaken me. Thou hast not come to see me off.' Thus speaking he fainted away. 88. Just as a child cries aloud when separated from its mother; as a young deer feels when losing sight of its mother-deer hunts for her in every direction; 89. and as a man overcome with hunger, suffers from lack of food; and as one overcome with thirst hunts for water; and as the *chatak* bird, in its thirst, watches for a cloud; 90. and as a *chakor* bird, on the first day of the month, searches for the moon; and as a fish in the hot season is troubled by lack of water; 91. and as when a young turtle is hungry and does not see its mother within sight; so by separation from Pandurang, Nama was overwhelmed with grief. 92. He said to himself, 'I find myself in a forest overcome with anxiety. I see no one who is near and dear to me. Thou art my father and mother. O God, rush to my help. 93. O

Lord of Pandhari, Thou alone art my dearest friend, my brother and my uncle. O Shri Vitthal, Helper of the helpless, Thou alone art my family deity. 94. Thou alone art the means for my gaining final deliverance. Thou, O Cloud of intelligence, who knowest the thoughts of the heart, who knowest whether my words are true or false, O Shri Vitthal. 95. O Ocean of mercy, supreme Lord of the earth, Nama is in great trouble without Thee. Look upon him with the eye of mercy, and let him be in the chamber of Thy heart. 96. Thus Nama, overcome with grief, used moving words. Dnyandev then addressed him. Listen to what he said. 97. 'With streams of love in your heart, why are you sad? God being in your heart, you are needlessly troubled. 98. O chief of *bhaktas*, think for a moment. Your joy is in your heart. You yourself without question are the visible God with attributes. 99. The fragrant perfume, existing as it does in the navel of the deer itself, the latter needlessly wanders through a forest in search of it, so you, ignorant of your own spiritual nature, are overcome by the pain of separation. 100. It is as if untold wealth lay buried in the house of an unfortunate man; he does not see it and therefore he goes hungry. Such is your case.' 101. Hearing his words, Nama replied, 'Show me God Supreme before my eyes, and possessing attributes, with His feet parallel on a brick, 102. clothed around His waist with a yellow robe, with both hands on His hips. Show me this Advocate of *bhaktas*, and Saviour of the world. 103. Show me the object of contemplation for Sanak and the others, the precious ornament of Shiva, the Husband of Rukmini, the Life of the world. 104. Show me at once Him of whom Narad and Tumbaru with love sing day and night, the Giver of the promise to Pundalik. 105. I know nothing of the means adopted in the *yoga* philosophy. My resting place is the Life of the world. O Dnyandev, if I do not meet Him, my life will desire to depart. 106. Dnyandev replied,' O God-loving *bhakta*, there is no place empty of God. Abandon the idea of any difference in nature and recognize in your heart the One Being who is without a second.' 107. Nama hearing this replied, 'The *chatak* bird will not drink water out of a river, he will only drink gladly of streams of water from the skies. 108. So God fills the whole universe, this seems to me as a false theory, just as a dutiful wife will not listen to the story of anyone aside from her husband.' 109. In reply to this, Dnyandev said, 'The Being who is imperishable and One only, whom the wise worship, it is He who is in your heart.' 110. To this Nama replied, 'I am fond of a form that has attributes. For to look at it, is refreshing to the eye. I feel as if I wish to listen to songs in His praise.'

DNYANESHWAR ASKS ABOUT 'BHAKTI' FROM NAMDEV

111. Dnyandev seeing Nama's firm resolve, said, 'Blessed is your pure faith.' In this manner they exchanged their experience every day. 112. They tested their discussion by experience. Thereby they felt extremely happy, and that brought them joy which their hearts could not contain. 113. Dnyandev further said to Nama, 'Explain to me in detail the way of *bhakti*, by which you have made God subject to yourself. 114. In what way should one worship God? How should one listen and contemplate? What is study? What is the way of gaining courage? 115. What is that we should call peace? Tell me this in detail. For many days I have had it in my mind to ask you. 116. Tell me of the means of deliverance which you have obtained through your own experience.' Dnyandev with hands joined together palm to palm, thus pleaded with Nama. 117. Having listened to his words, Nama tightly embraced Dnyandev's feet. His voice choked with emotion, and he said, 118. 'I do not

know much about philosophy, and so I have been consigned to your care. The Husband of Rukmini placed my hand in yours. 119. I know little. I am very ignorant, and yet you ask me metaphysical knowledge. It is as if the wish-tree should become a beggar and go to the house of a miser. 120. Or as if the Himalayas should become heated and call out, " Fan me with your garment;" or it is like the sun saying to anyone, " Light a lamp and bring it to my house; " 121. or it is as if the sky should say, " Give me an extended place in which to live;" or as if the earth should come to the king, and ask him for a written deed of land; 122. or as if the ocean should wish to go and bathe in a pond; or as if a wish-cow should ask of a common cow to permit her to drink her milk; 123. so you, humbling yourself, are asking me for metaphysical knowledge.' Thus speaking, Nama held Dnyandev by the feet. 124. Dnyandev said to him, ' Have no doubts in your heart. Abandoning all feelings of duality, speak out of your own experience. 125. Nama, your clear speech seems to me deeper than the sea. The collection of the moisture of the supreme divine joy is always cool, and refreshing. 126. My ears are hungry to listen to it immediately, so let the nectar of divine knowledge at once rain down on them. 127. You are a refuge of rest, and therefore I have sought your company. Nama, you are God's loved one, you have made even Him subject to you. 128. Aside from the emotion of love, why does one need any deep knowledge ? Just as the great and the little stars wander all night long in the starry heaven, 129. the north polar star (Dhruva) looks very small; still it is placed where it is ever unmoved; so Nama, you must never speak of your knowledge as little. 130. If a fire becomes a great flame it does not spread an entirely pure light in the house; tell me how it can claim equality with the pure light of the lamp. 131. A lion's body seems small, but no elephant can endure its gaze. So Nama, your knowledge is superior by means of the brightness of your courage. 132. One may have collected a large quantity of medicines but it cannot be the equal of nectar, so even learned men have no knowledge equal to yours. 133. The flower of the cotton plant is without fragrance; yet from king to common citizen it is regarded as an adornment. So Nama, your knowledge is seen to be what would savë the universe. 134. To listen to it my mind is filled with intense desire and love. Now cease your silence and supply my longing.'

NAMDEV'S TEACHING TO DNYANESHWAR ON 'BHAKTI'

135. To this request of Dnyaneshvar, Namdev gave reply, 'Listen then with reverence to my experience, O *Swami*. 136. One should have the determination to be indifferent to all earthly passions. One should have unchanging compassion on every creature. One should not have the troublesome thought of 'I' and 'thou'. One should not have any perplexities about the earthly life. 137. As soon as one reaches this condition his worship may be called pure. And if he does not have these characteristics, why adopt useless means of acquiring them ? 138. One can bow outwardly and at the same time remember the faults of the person bowed to; just as a man with keen appetite may eat dainty food along with a fly in it. 139. Not to have in mind (any idea of) the superior and the common, that should be regarded as unceasing worship, for there is no cessation of the supreme divine joy in the heart. 140. God fills the universe, He pervades the universe. With that fixed thought, one should keep his mind steady. This is called contemplation, and it is an everlasting cloud of joy. 141. Now you have asked how one should listen. Just as a deer, absorbed by the sound of music, forgets all about itself; 142. just so with one's mind lost in the subject, one

should listen to services of praise in honour of God. To this the wise and experienced give the name of *bhakti* through listening. 143. Just as a miser, giving his whole attention to his business stores up money; so take thought for what is for your good. This is called contemplation. 144. Now as to study, it is like a woman giving her love to a man (who is not her husband but) who lives in her house according to popular custom. 145. The *chatak* bird lives on the earth, but it is always giving attention to the clouds in the heaven. The lotus remains in a pond, but its thought is towards the sun. 146. While a cow is feeding on the hillside, it has its thought fixed on her calf; a miser with his mind placed on his wealth wanders about in the bazaar; 147. a goldsmith fixing his attention on the stealing of gold, forms it into an ornament; the *chakor* bird though far away gazes at the moon; 148. a woman taking a water vessel on her head, walks along with uncumbered hands giving her attention to the vessel on her head, and at the same time gossiping; 149. a bee fixing its thought on a flower yet lives humming in the air; so while performing one's domestic duties in their outward form, God should be in one's heart. 150. Vitthal should be wholly in one's heart, but His form should be seen in every creature. One should entirely cast aside all wrong activities and thoughts and have love in one's heart. 151. He is called great who disassociates himself from worldly things and, standing alone with a character of goodness, wisdom and courage, devotes himself entirely to the loving *bhakti* of one God. 152. One should regularly sit down by himself and perform services of song in praise of God. All means that are employed contrary to this should be considered as bondage. 153. Thus I have told you my experience regarding body, speech and the feelings of the mind. But the one who is really telling this is the Lord of Pandhari, the Husband of Rukmini, Shri Vitthal.' 154. Hearing

Nama's words, Dnyandev was greatly amazed. He said, 'There are many *bhaktas*, of Vishnu, and in the future also there will be an innumerable number, 155. but Nama's teaching is most unusual. One should not speak of it as being in the least out of the way. To-day a rain of nectar has fallen upon us. 156. This unlimited joy and peace hardly ever takes place in anyone. So consider it in your mind and let its cause and effect remain in your mind; 157. There have been many writers of the *Shastras* and there have been many wise minds that have become well known. There have been many learned men devoted to the performance of deeds, and there have been great men reverenced by others. 158. Though a man may understand the art of poetry, though he may be clever in all the arts, though he may become very active and a ready speaker, though he may have become a reader of the *Puranas* and a seeker after salvation, still I cannot see him as the equal of Nama. 159. There may be *jivanmuktas* (free while alive), who have the knowledge of the soul and acquainted with the *yoga* philosophy, and who sit down absorbed in contemplation, but I see no one among them like Nama. 160. *Yogis* sit on iron spikes and live amongst men indifferent to earthly things, but in the whole three worlds one like Nama cannot be found. 161. Nama's method of *bhakti* is never understood by others, except by the Husband of Rukmini, the Lord of Pandhari who stands on a brick.'

DNYANESHWAR AND NAMDEV VISIT DELHI

162. Such were their daily and occasional discussions, as they walked along full of joy. Suddenly in their wanderings to sacred places they arrived at Hastanapur (Delhi). 163. Namdev in his love was singing of God's goodness. As he came near the city every one looked at him. 164. As they listened to Nama's most unusual expression of love, they prostrated themselves before him,

and taking cymbals, *vina* and drums they danced while singing songs of praise. 165. Having heard of Nama's *kirtans* an innumerable number of people gathered together. They carried musical instruments and banners and organized a great assembly. 166. Flags on which was the design of an eagle were waved, and musical instruments made a great sound. Joy filled Hastinapur and cries of 'Victory, victory,' called out aloud the names of God.

THE DELHI KING KILLS A COW WHICH NAMDEV RESTORES TO LIFE

167. The Muhammadan king who lived in the city heard of the affair. He was told that the *bhakta* Nama was on his way to visit sacred bathing-places and had arrived from Pandhari. 168. 'He is performing *kirtans* in the city and these have absorbed the interest of the men and women.' When the king heard of this his heart became full of anger; 169. just as when the moon arises, the thieves curse it in their hearts; or as at the sight of the thousand-eyes (the sun) the night-wanderers (evil spirits) become enraged; 170. or as heretics curse in their minds after listening to the knowledge of the *Vedas*; so an intense hatred arose in the king's heart. 171. But he said to himself, 'I must go and see for myself Nama's recitation of Hari's deeds. If I am not convinced by it, I shall call it a heretical production.' 172. Thus thinking to himself, this evil-doer came to the *kirtan*; as if a Mang (an out-caste) should suddenly intrude into an assembly of Brahmans; 173. or as if a dog should enter into a Brahman's kitchen and touch his food; or as if that terrible disease (leprosy) should attack one in his youth; 174. so this evil-minded man came suddenly and sat down in the *kirtan*. Just then Nama was filled with a sense of love, as he was describing the attributes of Shri Hari. 175. The sky reverberated with the sound

of the cymbals, the drum and the *vina.* To that was added the loud hand-clapping. The enthusiasm was without limit. 176. Now what did that Muhammadan do in the midst of the enthusiastic *kirtan*? He killed a cow. And he said to Nama, ' What is it you are singing, you heretic? 177. If you will raise this cow again to life I shall regard your songs as true. If you do not bring the cow to life, I shall kill you with my own hand.' 178. When this evil-doer said this, the men and women became greatly concerned. Their minds were thrown into confusion and the enthusiasm of love melted away; 179. as when dainty food has been served on plates and suddenly poison should fall on it; or as when reading a book, a moth should put out the light; 180. or as if a poor man should find a mine of wealth, and then a ghost be created there; or as when one is singing with a clear voice, and suddenly his throat should fill with phlegm; 181. or as when a field of grain should grow ripe and bear fruit a hundred thousand fold, locusts should attack it; or as when performing an auspicious ceremony in one's home it should at that moment be visited by death; 182. or as when the *chakor* bird is gazing at the moon, the monster Rahu should come in between; or as when Agasti was drinking up the ocean, all the water animals were thrown into confusion; 183. such was the confusion felt that night by all the listeners. They sat silent in their places, for they could do nothing else before the king. 184. The Muhammadan king said to Nama, ' When are you going to raise this cow to life? Give me some evidence of your truth, and then go on praising Hari.' 185. The noble *Vaishnava* having heard him replied, ' O king, it will certainly take me four days from today to do it.' 186. Having heard him say this, the king went back to his palace. Namdev brought Hari to his mind, and earnestly asked Him to come to his help. 187. ' Victory to Thee, Merciful to the lowly, Purifier of the sinner, Lover of His *bhaktas*, Cloud of compassion, Witnesser of the thought of the heart, Mine of goodness, Ornament of His *bhaktas*, Govinda. 188. Victory to Thee, Father of Brahmadev, Dweller on the ocean of milk, Thou whose form has attributes, Lord of the heart, Giver of blessing to Pundalik, Lord of Pandhari, Victory to Thee, the Indestructible, the Guru of the world. 189. Victory to Thee, Ram, Slayer of Ravana, Giver of joy to Nand, Slayer of Kans, Destroyer of the pride of the Kauravas, Protector of the Pandavas, Shri Krishna. 190. Victory to Thee, Ocean of goodness, Cloud of joy, Thou who didst protect Draupadi from shame, Husband of Rukmini, lotus-eyed One, the Ornament of His *bhaktas*, Pandurang.' 191. Thus Nama filled with enthusiasm of love expressed his mournful thoughts in the midst of the *kirtan*. His throat choked with emotion. Tears flowed from his eyes. 192. The large assembly of those who came to hear him began also to weep. For a whole day they sat there. 193. When the sun arose they got up and went to their homes; just as when in a time of famine the hypocritical donors send away those who come to them to beg; 194. or as when the organs of sense become weakened, men of gay life discard sensual things; or as when contractors see a loss coming to them and desert their province and country; 195. or as when the cool season arrives, the clouds vanish from the sky; or as when the rays of the sun fall on the colour of the *patang* wood and makes it fade; 196. or as when a king falls on the battlefield, his army deserts him and flees away or as when the life of a creature is passing away it has to leave its body; 197. or as when a poor man comes to a well-to-do man, evil-minded relatives send him away or as when old age comes, the organs of sense cease to function properly in a man, 198. so as men listened to Namdev's *kirtan*, and saw his extreme distress, they all got up and left. 199. Nama took the head of the cow in his lap and wept. He cried out and said, ' O Lord of Pandhari, Shri Hari, come quickly to my aid. 200. Hast Thou been sleeping near to Rukmini, and therefore been much delayed in coming ? Or hast Thou been sitting listening to *kirtans* of the God-loving *bhaktas* ? 201. Or hast Thou, O Krishna, got entangled in the thoughts of *Yogis* ? Or has anyone put Thee into difficulties and so Thou art remaining entangled in them ? 202. Or, O Vishnu, hast Thou been sitting receiving the worship of those who regard Thee as possessing attributes ? Or has Indra taken Thee along with Him for the purpose of drinking nectar ? 203. Or have pilgrims who belong to Thy *bhaktas* arrived at Pandhari to see and worship Thee ? And therefore, O Lord of the Heart, Thou hast long delayed coming to my help ? 204. Rich people worship Thee, providing many kinds of ornaments, garments and adornments and perhaps absorbed in these Thou hast forgotten all about *me*.' 205. Thus for four days, day and night he cried to God to come and help him. The earth was sprinkled by the tears that fell from his eyes. 206. He cried, ' O God, hasten quickly, for *kal* (death) has come to swallow Thy Nama. I am overcome with concern, like fish out of water. 207. Hearing these moving words the Holder of the disk (Krishna) immediately came, and manifested Himself in Nama's heart. 208. He immediately raised the cow to life and then said to Nama, ' Awake to consciousness.' Nama seized Him tightly by the feet, and now listen to what he said. 209. ' O God, in what business hast Thou been entangled ? O eagle-bannered One, for four days Thou hast put me to an extreme test. ' 210. God replied, ' O Nama, it was you who made a needless promise. Why did you needlessly say that it would take four days to raise the cow to life ? 211. If you had only replied to the king that you would immediately raise the cow to life, I should certainly have rushed to your aid. 212. It is your own mistaken thought that has borne fruit. Why do you needlessly blame Me? For I, God, am subject to you, and I naturally act through My love to you. 213. I accept as My duty the words that fall from the lips of My *bhaktas*. The prophetic words which Valmiki used compelled Me to follow them. 214. When a seer looks into a mirror he sees himself just as he is. So when a man conceives of Me in his heart, I, the Saviour of the world, am just as he conceives Me. 215. Just as a crystal assumes the colour of the thing on which it is placed, so I, who am subject to My *bhaktas* become just as they would like Me to be.' 216. Speaking thus, the Holder of the disk (Krishna) became invisible. Nama opened his eyes and looked, and the cow was sitting there raised to life. 217. Seeing this amazing thing, the people reported the matter to the king. Hearing this most extraordinary news, the Muhammadan king arrived on the scene. 218. Seeing the cow whose head he had cut off now raised to life, the king made a *namaskar* to Nama. 219. All the people felt great joy and exclaimed, 'Blessed is the *Vaishnava* Nama, whose love for God, Brahmadev and the other multitude of gods are unable to fully describe.' 220. Hands were clapped accompanied by cries of, 'Victory, victory.' The assembly of *bhaktas* rejoiced. Nama then arose and reverently worshipped Vanamali (Krishna). 221. As the, final hymns of praise were sung, all shouted, 'Victory, victory.' Blessed is this noble *Vaishnava*, for he has made the Holder of the *sarang* bow (God) subject to him.

222. Listeners must now give attention, and become absorbed in the stream of these stories; just as the Ganges river in its love becomes one with the ocean; 223. or as the royal swan comes to lake Manas and there chooses the milk out of the water, so discard the waters of wrong thinking and drink the nectar of love. 224. If you give good attention, great enthusiasm will come in their

recitation, and then Pandurang, rendering His favour, will bring about the destruction of the sorrows of this life belonging to His servants. 225. The Merciful to the lowly, the Husband of Rukmini, will cause me further to describe their lives in this book. Mahipati who is as it were His stamp, conveys this message to you listeners.

226. *Swasti* (Peace !) This book is the *Shri Bhaktavijaya.* When the Lord of the earth hears it He will be pleased. Listen therefore, you God-loving, pious *bhaktas.* This is the tenth very delightful chapter.

CHAPTER XI

NAMDEV, KABIR AND DNYANDEV

(Continued)

Obeisance to Shri Ganesh. Obeisance to Shri Krishna

THE STORIES OF THE SAINTS ARE LIKE NECTAR

1. Dear hearers, listen now with attention. You are now offered a drink of nectar, in that these stories of the *bhaktas*, with their deep and marvellous significance, have blossomed like flowers through their being related in the Marathi tongue. 2. Just as a dainty food prepared in a Brahman's house is eatable by every caste; or as ornaments of gold remarkably adorn any beautiful form; 3. or as garments woven in cotton protect all from the cold; or as pure melted butter when stored by itself never spoils; 4. or as jewels in a golden setting are useful for all wearers of adornments; or as when the seed of the nectar plant is sown in the ground and spreads a million fold; 5. or as when stones are chiselled and a temple erected in which the image of Shiva (Jashvanila) is placed; so this easily understood book has become available for all. 6. But if anyone has a contrary opinion and says, 'How much are you going to boast of yourself ?' I reply, 'I have spoken to you as to an intimate friend with thoughts of love. 7. Though you needlessly blame me, do not neglect the *Bhaktavijaya*. Disregard its faults and accept its good qualities. You have the right to do this. 8. On the other hand I Mahipati and dullness come in the same schedule of analogy. Let it be firmly understood in your minds that the Husband of Shri Rukmini is the composer of this book. 9. How can the dolls dance when the cords that move them are broken ? If the wind ceases to blow, the trees will never wave.' 10. It was rela-

ted in the former chapter how Namdev raised a cow to life, and how the king came and worshipped his feet and every one rejoiced. 11. After performing this miracle he took leave of all, and as he walked along by day and night he was continually repeating the names of God. 12. In whatever country he visited the sacred bathing places he composed verses in the same manner there. In their various languages he described the priceless qualities of God. 13. If I should mention in detail these sacred bathing places in the various countries, this book will be extended too much. Namdev visited all of them and finally came to Anandavan (modern Benares). 14. He bathed in the Bhagirathi river He saw and worshipped Vishveshwar (the Lord God of the universe). Having thus carried out his purpose, his mind was full of supreme joy.

KABIR'S WIFE AND THE REPENTANT GROCER

15. Namdev remained there for four months, and then a very extraordinary thing happened. There suddenly came some saints to Kabir's house. 16. It was midnight when they arrived and all in the house were asleep. But suddenly Kabir noticed the arrival of the noble *Vaishnavas.* 17. Kabir and his wife both arose and made them a prostrate obeisance. Their house was in a dilapidated condition and very old. The wattle walls were in a broken state. 18. There was not a bit of food in the house. The children had gone to bed hungry. They removed the matting from underneath the children, and gave it to the saints to rest upon. 19. Kabir said to his wife, 'We must make them an offering.' She said to her husband, 'That is true, but I am troubled in mind. 20. There is no grain in the house and no one in the city will lend us any.' Then taking courage into her heart she went alone into the bazaar. 21. As she walked rapidly along the street

she worshipped Shri Ram in words that fell from her lips. Said she, 'If I do not get food after this effort it will bring loss to my good deeds.' 22. Having arrived at the row of grocer shops she looked about her and spied in one shop a grocer who was awake. 23. Coming to the shop she spoke to him in her sweet voice, 'Some saints have come to our house as guests, arriving from visits to sacred places. 24. They need to be given provisions of food. Do not delay giving them to me. Whatever price you may name I will bring it to you.' 25. The grocer said to her, 'Whose wife are you, and who are you?' She replied sweetly, 26. 'The noble *Vaishnava* who was born in a Muhammadan family, Kabir, is my husband. Get up quickly and give me the materials I need. The saints are hungry.' 27. As this beautiful woman said this the grocer became enamoured of her, just as when Indra saw Ahilya he had a wrong thought; 28. or as when Bhasmasur was overcome with desire when he saw the beautiful Parvati; or as Ravana looked upon the Mother of the universe with a sinful eye; 29. or as Duryodhan entertained an evil desire about faithful Draupadi the wife of the Pandavas; so this sinful-minded grocer spoke to the wife of Kabir. 30. 'If you will do for me as I wish I will give you the materials. I will give you as many garments and adornments as you may ask of me. 31. If you have any hesitation in your mind then go back to your home.' Hearing the words of this evil man she thought to herself, 32. 'If I say *No* to him, where else can I obtain any food? The saints will go hungry and that will be a loss to my good deeds. 33. Act according to circumstances; give a reply as occasion demands; perform a *kirtan* after judging the character of the audience; and sow seed according to the nature of the soil. 34. King Harischandra of the noble character carried water at an out-caste's house and his queen Taramati suffered great mortification.

35. Chaff should be blown away in the direction of the wind. When one is sinking, one may seek the support of an out-caste. In time of famine, beggars have to ask for food even of a miser. 36. In order to carry on their domestic affairs Brahmans may have to serve Muhammadans. When the king of the *Kali Yuga* (evil age) comes to power at times, he compels men to do something unusual. 37. The *Shastras* have spoken to men of what is their duty and what is not their duty. But if by doing what is not one's duty, one is thereby united to the feet of Shri Hari, one should do it. 38. One's mother and father are as it were sacred bathing places. To an elder brother honour is due just as to them. The command of one's family *guru* and that of a guest is one's authority for action. 39. If Bharat had listened to the wish of his mother, how would he have been united to the feet of Shri Ram? Because Prahlad turned against his father, Narahari was pleased with him. 40. Bali would not listen to the words of Shukra, and he offered to Vaman as much land as His three steps would cover. The cow-herdessess deserted their husbands and became absorbed in the form of Krishna. 41. Violating the commands of their husbands, the wives of the *rishis* carried food (to Krishna). If they had obeyed the commands of the *Shastras* they would have been separated from the feet of Shri Hari. 42. And now, if I should consult the *Shastras*, my guests who are saints and *sadhus* will remain hungry. So I will give my promise to the grocer and thus accomplish my purpose. 43. Then since I respect the names of God, the Dweller in Ayodhya, the Life of Janaki, who sees the thoughts of the heart and is a Cloud of intelligence, will deliver me from all my troubles.' 44. Kabir's wife then courageously replied to the grocer, 'First give me the materials for cooking, then I will truly come. 45. The night is now far spent and the saints at my home are hungry. If

I am delayed, these *Vaishnavas* will have gone to sleep.' 46. The grocer heard her but did not think she was telling the truth; just as in Duryodhan's sight no one was good. 47. A blind man thinks everyone is blind. To a thief the moonlight seems filthy. The sick exclaim, 'What made you cook this bitter food?' 48. A miser has no compassion towards other lives. How can a meat-eater feel any love? One ill with tuberculosis does not even in his dreams see himself with a beautiful body. 49. How can an evil man possess a feeling of love? A reviler does not see anyone as good. A low caste man does not believe that a Brahman's conduct is ever true. 50. So this grocer would not accept the promise of Kabir's wife as worthy of belief. So he said, 'If you will give me a definite promise, I shall regard it as true.' 51. Listening to the words of this evil-minded one, by the strength of her courage she controlled her mind. She thought to herself, 'If I do not give him the promise I shall not receive the materials' 52. So she gave him the promise and took in her garments the materials she needed. She hastened back to her home, and prepared these materials for cooking. 53. The saints then said to Kabir's wife, 'We wish to do the cooking ourselves.' The *Vaishnavas* then very lovingly took the cooking vessels and began to cook. 54. With great pleasure they prepared many various kinds of dainty food which was served on plates, and Kabir and his wife began the ceremonies of the saints' worship. 55. They offered to them perfume, rice, garlands of flowers, fragrant ointments, incense, and bowed to them with reverence. 56. The saints had their appetites satisfied with such food as they liked. Kabir's wife then called her husband into a private room. 57. The wife said to Kabir, 'You must remain with the saints. I gave a definite promise to the grocer, and was thus able to bring home quickly the cooking materials. 58. Give me your permission to fulfil the desire of the grocer. If I delay any longer the day will dawn, and that will mean loss of my character for truthfulness.' 59. Kabir the *bhakta* listening to what she said replied, ' I also will come along with you. The grocer's kindness towards us has been very great. 60. The saints have been able to-day to obtain food. This will be credited to him as a good deed. We have no way of repaying his kindness. 61. You have thought of a good way of doing this and have offered your own body in the service of the saints, so I will take you on my shoulder and carry you there. 62. A heavy rain is falling, a dense terrible darkness has settled on this night and I am afraid to let you go alone.' 63. Thus speaking, Kabir made his wife sit on his shoulder and immediately hurried along to the bazaar. 64. As they passed along the street both of them lovingly worshipped Shri Ram. They exclaimed, ' Blessed is this happy day, which brought the *Vaishnavas* to our home ' 65. Thus conversing with one another they quickly arrived at the shop. Kabir then said to his wife, ' I will now go back home. 66. The saints are still at our home and might suddenly leave. I must hasten to go to them to serve at their feet. 67. Do not hesitate in the least. Carry out the wishes of the grocer.' Having thus spoken, the *bhakta* Kabir hastened homeward. 68. The grocer with his evil desires was sitting waiting for her. He thought to himself, ' She came alone tonight, and deceiving me, she has gone away.' 69. As this evil-doer was thus talking to himself he saw before him the wife of Kabir. It made him happy to see that she had kept her promise. 70. Sitting in his usual place the grocer said to her, 'The clouds are pouring down rain without limit, how is it that your feet are not covered with mud ? 71. This fact perplexes me, so you, good woman, tell me the truth. ' The good woman having heard him say this replied to the grocer, 72. ' Listen to me, you good sir. I will tell you exactly what happened. After having given you my promise I supplied the wants of the saints. 73. The *Vaishnavas* were well satisfied. That good deed will go to your credit. Your great kindness to us can never be repaid. 74. I call myself a faithful wife. The command of my husband is my authority for action. I gave you that promise because of the distress in which I was. 75. I told Kabir, the lord of my life, what had happened. He carried me on his shoulder and brought me to you. 76. He then went back. Now put aside your doubts and do whatever your mind wishes.' 77. This mass of goodness having thus spoken, the grocer became repentant. He said to himself, 'I have come to the state of a human body, but I have not accomplished anything thereby. 78. After wandering for eight million four hundred thousand births I have suddenly attained this human body. Now I have taken no proper thought, and have allowed my mind to incline to sensual things. 79. Kabir is indifferent to earthly passions and generous, and I have cruelly troubled his wife; just as if a man should take in his hand an axe and cut down a *tulsi* plant; 80. or as if one should take a hoe and forcibly tear down a sacrificial building; or as if one should push aside all worship of Shiva and belabour His emblem with kicks; 81. or as if one purposely spilled a jar of nectar; or as if one purposely crushed the Shaligram (emblem of Vishnu); or seeing a banyan tree or *pimpal* tree, should cut them down with an axe; 82. or as if one should cross the Ganges without bathing in it; or as if one should revile the *Shri Bhagwat*; I have committed just those kinds of faults in causing this trouble to the *bhakta* Kabir. 83. I have never seen any other husband who would thus lend his wife to the use of another man. Blessed are you, O mother, mine of good qualities, the first mother, mother of the world.' 84. Thus repentant in heart he made her a *namaskar* and said, 'I am your child, you are my mother. Do not keep in your mind my transgression. 85. In my ignorance I, who know but little, have troubled you. Forgive me all I have done and give me your blessing. 86. Take me as your child by the hand and place me at Kabir's feet.' Thus speaking, he placed his hands on her feet again and again. 87. Hearing him say these moving words, she exclaimed, 'O grocer, blessed is your mind. I see it as soft as butter. 88. The greatest men have expressed the opinion of the *Shastras*, that though one may have constantly committed very many evil deeds, if finally repentance is aroused in the heart, those sins at once disappear. 89. It is as if one should eat poison and then should receive a drink of nectar. By that he escapes harm, so all wise men say. 90. So listen to me, you courageous man. Just as soon as your heart felt repentance, the disease of sin in this earthly life ran away from you. 91. I will now at once cause you to meet Kabir.' Hearing her say this, the grocer was filled with supreme joy. 92. He put aside pride and conceit. He abandoned all evil qualities. He left seductive illusions and firmly held to qualities that are characterized by goodness. 93. And so becoming pure in heart, and bright with light, he left his shop. He hastened from there, having cut through the net of illusions. 94. In company with Kabir's wife he arrived at her home in less than a minute, and with feelings of reverence and love he made Kabir a prostrate *namaskar*. 95. He said, 'I am an ignorant, stupid child. I have truly committed an infinite number of transgressions. You must forgive me, your slave, and lay your hand upon me and give me your blessing.' 96. Kabir was a perfect reader of inward thoughts and he recognized in the grocer the feeling of repentance. He then embraced the grocer and saying 'Fear not' he gave him his blessing. 97. Such was the God-loving *bhakta* Kabir, always trusting, believing, understanding, and as for himself he was indifferent to all earthly things but full of compassion towards others. 98. The grocer having thus repented he began to worship Shri Ram. Such is the greatness of association with a saint. Even the *Vedas* and *Shastras* cannot understand its full power.

KABIR MEETS DNYANDEV AND NAMDEV

99. Namdev heard of the very extraordinary reputation of Kabir. He told Dnyandev of it and the two came to visit Kabir. 100. When Kabir saw Dnyandev and Namdev he made a prostrate *namaskar* at their feet. Kabir seemed very happy and embraced them with love. 101. He spread a straw mat on the floor for them to sit upon and the eyes of both of them became filled with nectar of love.

102. Dnyandev said to Namdev, 'Remember what happened long ago, how God whose home is on the ocean of milk gave you a command. 103. You are in reality Uddhav, and this *bhakta* Kabir is the *avatar* of Shuka, and both of you descended into this world of mortals as *avatars* in the heart of a shell. 104. The *bhakti marga* (the way of devotion) has become soiled. All mankind was sunk in worldly concerns, and you came to this world of action to save them.' 105. When Dnyandev had thus spoken they bowed to one another. There was a mutual recognition of the facts of their inner condition. 106. Dnyandev said to Kabir, 'The sacred city of Pandhari lies in the country of the South. It was there that the Dweller in the Heaven Vaikunth came to visit Pundalik. 107. Though in the absolute form of the supreme Brahm, He took on a human form. He performed miracles of various kinds. He is the Life of the world. He is Nama's Life of love and remains standing on a brick. 108. Some day you must come and see that ancient sacred city with your own eyes.' Hearing Dnyandev's remark, Kabir fell at his feet.

109. Kabir said to Dnyandev, 'I shall surely come to see and worship Him on the eleventh day of the bright half of the month of *Kartik* (November).' Such was his promise. 110. Dnyandev and Namdev now took leave of Kabir, and at once started from there. And now, you good people must listen with reverence to the delightful story which will now be related. 111. Just as the thirsty man drinks water, or a hungry man eats delicious food, so giving your mind's attention to these stories of the *bhaktas*, listen with reverence, you pious folk. 112. If you have this feeling of love in your heart, it will bring infinite gain. This is Mahipati's plea to his listeners. May you have joy and happiness.

113. *Swasti* (Peace!). This book is the *Shri Bhaktavijaya*. In listening to it the Lord of the earth will be pleased. Listen, you God-loving pious *bhaktas*. This is the eleventh very delightful chapter.

CHAPTER XII

NAMDEV AND DNYANDEV (Continued)

Obeisance to Shri Ganesh. Obeisance to Shri Gopal Krishna.

THE STORIES OF THE SAINTS SATISFY THE HEART

1. To-day the three worlds are in the happiness of plenty. For the cloud, the *Bhaktavijaya*, has moistened the soil from the sky above. It has thundered aloud from the heaven of intelligence, and has poured down the water of Brahm-joy. 2. The true-hearted ones who may be likened to the *chatak* bird have already satisfied their thirst. For other men, with minds both good and bad, there have grown many kinds of grain. 3. For the evil-minded, brute-like men there are plenty of weeds. The water which has soaked down deep into the soil has become useful for many. 4. On the rocky soil of those without any desire to listen the rain flowed away as it fell. Those surplus streams, however, flow on and remain in the sea of knowledge. 5. It is there that the wise and pious men swim about as fishes. And as the stream of water comes towards them in the form of waves of joy they play about with love and happiness.

DNYANDEV GETS WATER FROM A DEEP WELL

6. In the previous chapter the story was told of the meeting of Kabir and Nama (and Dnyandev). They remained by the bank of the Ganges for four months and then retraced their steps. 7. They visited Gaya and Prayag (Allahabad) and from there journeyed to Ayodhya. Then making rapid visits to Mathura and Gokul they arrived at Dwarawati. 8. As they were returning they had to pass through the desert of Marwad, and being overcome with thirst they searched about for water to drink. 9. Suddenly they spied a deep well and as they looked down

into it they could not determine its depth. They were puzzled to know what device to adopt to obtain some water. 10. Then Dnyandev said to Nama, 'There is a method which is possible for me.' Saying this he reduced his own size through his *yoga* powers and went down into the well. 11. Having drunk the water he quickly came out again.

WATER COMES IN ANSWER TO NAMDEV'S PRAYER

Nama was now extremely thirsty but could think of no way of obtaining the water. 12. Dnyandev then said to him, 'Why is your heart troubled? I will bring the water and give it to you at once. 13. You know nothing of the methods of the mystic *yoga* power by which one can reduce his size. No longer hold in your mind the feeling of duality, and drink the water. 14. Do not refuse to drink the water taken from my hand, for the soul which is a Cloud of intelligence is one and pervades every living being alike.' 15. Nama replied, 'Vitthal is the soul in every heart, so, O *Swami*, why will he not put away my distress far from me? 16. Have patience for a moment and see a miracle.' He then closed his eyes and brought the Lord of the Yadavas (Krishna) to his mind. 17. Nama brought into his imagination the image of Pandurang and thus prayed to him. 'Rush to my aid, O Husband of Rukmini. Why hast Thou forsaken me? 18. Thou only art my mother, my father, my dearest friend, my brother and uncle. Thou alone art my family deity. Why hast Thou forsaken me to-day? 19. Thou art my wealth and my property. Thou art my philosophic knowledge. Thou art my accomplishment of *yoga*. I recognize no other source. 20. Now hurry to my aid, lest Thou shouldst see my end. O Thou merciful One, Helper of the helpless, be the Helper of Thy lowly one.' 21. As he was saying these things tears flowed from his lotus-eyes. Said he 'O God, my courage will not hold out any longer.

Without Thee my life is in great trouble. 22. I Thy ignorant child am Thine in body, speech and mind. I am overpowered with thirst today. To whom shall I go for help ? 23. O Giver of blessing to Pundalik, O Husband of Rukmini, from birth I call myself one cared for by Thee. And now, O Cloud of mercy, if Thou forsakest me, who will be the one to be ashamed ? 24. For in the *Vedas* and *Puranas* Thou art described as the Helper of the helpless, and if Thou forsakest me it will become evident at once that Thy noble reputation is false. 25. When the crocodile seized the Gajendra (the noble elephant) Thou, O God, Lord of the heart, didst hasten to help him; with the same speed come to my help to-day. 26. When Draupadi was in distress, Thou didst quickly come to her aid, but it would seem that Thou hast forgotten all Thy compassion. 27. O Husband of Rukmini, when sending me to visit sacred bathing places, Thou didst give me into Dnyandev's hands. Why art Thou regardless of me today, O merciful One, and dost refuse to come ? 28. Thou compassionate One, Lord of the earth, do not give me this trouble. But hasten to the aid of Nama, overcome with thirst, and despondent without Thee. 29. If Thou dost not come here today all evil-minded men will laugh at me. So hasten to my help and care for me who am Thy lowly one.' 30. (In this connection) let us think now of Pandharpur, that heaven upon earth where Shri Hari lives in His temple and where His heart's love for His *bhaktas* is the same for ever. 31. For while this compassion was moving in His heart, the Lord of the earth said to Rukmini, 'If I can only see Nama once more, I will never separate him from me.' 32. Rukmini said, 'Dear God, why is it that today this tender love has come to thee ? What trouble has come to Nama, that Thou shouldst be so sad ?' 33. Hearing her, the Life of world replied, 'Today my left eye throbs and my left arm twitches. I therefore feel concerned. 34. I feel greatly troubled as to which of My *bhaktas* is in distress. I am unable to find out.' So said Krishna. 35. 'May the howling wind not affect them, my dear *bhaktas*. I cannot understand which of them is affected by thirst or hunger.' 36. After Rukmini had listened to His remark, she began to give close attention to the thought and just then the mournful cry of Nama fell on her ears. 37. Said she, 'O God supreme, Nama is overcome with thirst and is crying to Thee for help. Rush quickly to his aid. Do not delay a moment.' 38. The moment He heard her suggestion He hastened more quickly than thought. Just then the well with a rumbling noise became filled, and began to overflow. 39. As Dnyandev saw this miracle, he thought to himself, 'This is a most remarkable deed. I do not understand how Nama has made God his debtor.' 40. Then awakening Nama to consciousness he lovingly embraced him and said, 'Krishna has come to your aid, and has shown us this seemingly impossible miracle. 41. The monkey made stones float on the water. Vashishtha heated his staff. And the son of Gadhi (Vishwamitra) created a new world by his own power. 42. Bhagirath with great effort brought the Bhagirathi river down to the surface of the earth. After making Shiva favourable to him, Gautam brought down the Godavari river. 43. But in a more wonderful way at Hastinapur he (Nama) raised a dead cow to life (see Chapter X) and now when overcome with thirst he has brought up the Ganga from the regions below.' 44. In thus speaking to Nama he brought back somewhat of his consciousness. Then drinking of the water freely Nama said to Dnyandev, 45. 'God always supplies that which I earnestly request of Him. When I see the *tamal* dark One then only my eyes become cool.' 46. To this Dnyandev replied, 'I have seen *yogis* sitting in contemplation but in seeing them my mind never attained a sense of peace.

47. To you alone my sense of love has become infinite. I cannot think of anything else but you. You, a *bhakta* of Vishnu's personification of love, have made the Husband of Rukmini subject to yourself. 48. Krishna the Supreme Spirit is beside you. Blessed, O Nama, is your family line. I feel the same happiness that a cow feels on seeing its little calf. 49. In seeing your noble qualities my mind has become filled with the joy of love. As I listen to your praise of God, I no longer care for pilgrimages and sacred places. 50. The *Vedas*, *Smritis* and the *Puranas* are fully enamoured by the qualities of Hari. And seeing your love, the *yogis* have cast aside their contemplation.51. The crowd of *Rishis*, *Gandharvas* (celestial singers), Brahmadev, Indra and other deities sought with feelings of love to fathom the formless One, 52. yet they were unable to attain God. But you made Him subject to yourself.' Having said this, Dnyandev embraced Nama's feet. 53. That well, where Nama became overwhelmed with thirst, still flows today in that very place in the Marwad country. Pilgrims assemble there in the month of *Margashirsh* (December) 54. If I should stop to relate the glory of that sacred bathing place, it would vastly increase the size of this book. Dnyandev and Nama now departed from that spot.

DNYANDEV AND NAMA ON PILGRIMAGE

55. They saw many sacred bathing places in the different countries through which they hastened. They visited Badrikashram in the Himalayas and arrived in the Himalaya mountains. 56. They visited Jagannath of Odhya where God lives in the form of Buddha; and even in the *Kali Yuga* seemingly impossible miracles still take place here today. 57. After visiting Onkar and Amaleshwar they went on to Kedar. From there they visited Mahakaleshwar at Ujjain. 58. After seeing that place, they came back

and after visiting Paralivaijanath they arrived at Soratisomnath. 59. Their next place was the mountain of Shri Shaila where the Husband of Parvati lives (in a Shiva temple). For sixty years He had been waiting for these *bhaktas* to come there. 60. After visiting this place they hastened on to see Ghrishneshwar. I am not able properly to describe the great glory of the sacred bathing place Seval. 61. From there they came to Nasik and Trimbak where they bathed in the Kushavart pond. After worshipping the five-faced One (Shiva) they departed from there (see page 88 of Nama's *Gathas*). 62. They had a view of the western ocean and then arrived at Bhimashankar where they worshipped Janardan. From there they started for Rameshwar. 63. Thus taking one after another the most important sacred bathing places on the surface of this earth, among which the most distinguished of them are mentioned as well known and with high reputation in the *Puranas*. 64. Ayodhya, Mathura, Kanti, Benares, Dwarawati, Avanti and Maya, the seven cities as givers of salvation, were lovingly visited with repentant hearts. 65. To this may be added the celebrated twelve *Jyotirlingas*. I have mentioned only these; still there are many on the earth which remain to be mentioned, but to what length should I go in speaking of them in this book? 66. Just as when one looks at the moon, the eye without any effort sees the stars; or if one dug up a tree and gave it to anyone, the branches would naturally go with it; 67. or as when drinking nectar it includes every medicine; or as when studying the *Vedanta*, one thereby understands the meaning of the *Vedas*; 68. or as when worshipping the *Ashvattha* tree, it is the same worship given to eighteen bhars (a bhar is 8000 tolas) of vegetables; or as when one sees the serpent on which the earth rests, he has seen practically all other serpents also; 69. or as when offering a garland of *tulsi* leaves to Vishnu, there is included in it the sixteen materials of worship; or as when having seen the Husband of Mridani (Shiva) one has seen all *yogis*; 70. or as when one sees the elephant *Airavat*, he has really seen every elephant on earth; or as when the Husband of Shachi (Indra) becomes pleased, the other gods are pleased also; 71. or as when the son of Vinata (the eagle, Vishnu's vehicle) comes in to one's sight, that includes all birds; or as when one sees the Himalaya mountains, the whole stable creation becomes known; 72. so, in describing the greatness of the seven salvation-giving cities, and the greatness of the twelve *lingas*, one has naturally met with the names of the other sacred bathing places on the earth.

NAMA AND DNYANDEV AT NAGNATH

73. After visiting Rameshwar both returned from there. The God-loving *bhaktas*, Nama and Dnyandev, finally arrived at Nagnath. 74. The fourteenth of the dark half of the moon in the month of *Magh* (February) is the special night for the festival in honour of Shiva. On such an occasion Nama and Dnyandev arrived at that place. 75. Just as on the first day of the bright half of the moon in the month of *Chaitra* (April) the cycle of sixty years comes to one's home; or as when on the second day of the bright half of the moon in the month of *Magh*, Dharmarao (god of death) comes to His home; 76. or as when on the third day of the bright half of the moon in the month of *Vaishakh* one's host of ancestors come as one's guests; or as when the elephant-faced god (Ganesh) arrives on the fourth day known as *Ganesh Chaturthi*; 77. or as on the fifth day of the bright half of the moon in the month of *Shravan* (August) the great serpent comes to one's home; or as when the Husband of Mhalasa (Khandoba) is to be met in the month of *Margashirsh* (December); 78. or as when on the seventh of

the bright half of *Magh* (February) the sun comes as a guest; or as when the king of the Yadavas (Krishna) comes at the time of *Janmashtami* (or *Gokul Ashtami*) to occupy His cradle; 79. or as when the son of Kausalya (Ram) on Ramnavami day (the ninth of the month of *Chaitra* or April) suddenly arrives playing; or as when on the tenth of *Vijaya* (the month of *Ashvin* or October) the Mother of the world (Parvati) comes hastening home; 80. or as when on the eleventh of *Ashadh* (July) one sees the image of Shri Vitthal as seen by the God-loving *bhaktas*, who look upon Him with great pleasure and feel a joy which their hearts cannot contain; 81. or as when on the twelfth day of the bright half of the moon in the month of *Kartik* (November) Shri Krishna comes to Vrindavan; or as when on the thirteenth of the month in the evening, the Husband of Mridani (Shiva) returns at the time of the evening worship; 82. or as when on the new moon day of the month of *Shravan* (August) Nandikeshwar comes back to the cows' stable; just so, Nama and Dnyandev arrived on *Shivaratri* (Shiva's festival). 83. The *bhaktas* speak of the holy city Avandhanagnath as a second Kailas (heaven). At this place and at this time of the festival both arrived with joy of love. 84. After bathing in the sacred waters and performing their usual rites of worship, they prostrated themselves before the great door of the temple with feelings of love. 85. Then in their affection they entered into the inner shrine in order to see and worship God. Here again they prostrated themselves before Nagnath. 86. They said to the god, 'O Helper of the helpless, Husband of Parvati, Dweller in the cemeteries, Holder of the *khatvang* (sword), Lord of Kailas, Digambar, Lord of the earth, King of the universe.' 87. Having thus spoken they touched the god's head with the palm of their hands, and knowing their love, Shiva was much pleased in His mind.

NAMA'S *KIRTAN* BEFORE NAGNATH

88. Namdev then stood before the great door of the temple and began a *kirtan*. He took in his hands the cymbals and *vina* and loudly shouted the names of God. 89. Bringing into his mind the image of Vitthal he closed both his eyes. He had no longer the least consciousness of possessing a body. 90. He put aside the thoughts of honour and insult and the proud ways of men. He put aside every form of desire and in his love performed the *kirtan*. 91. He put aside all idea of distinctions. He cut off from himself the idea of duality. He broke through the bonds made by the snare of desires and danced in his joy and love. 92. Accompanying the sound of cymbals, drum and *vina*, he performed a *kirtan* with feelings of love. A great crowd of people came with the desire to listen. 93. Just as at the time of the full moon the Husband of Rohini (the moon) looks beautiful in its various phases, and the ocean seeing it swells with the joy of love; 94. or as when the oil-wick is pushed far forward the flame is increased; or as at a Brahman's oblation the sun feels happy; 95. or as when drinking nectar, one's body becomes immortal; or as when a generous man distributes his wealth, beggars rejoice; 96. or as when the rain falls, the grass grows in desert places; or as when Brahmans receiving sweet delicious food they become supremely happy; 97. so, in listening to Nama's *kirtan* all good listeners became happy. In listening to God's goodness, in their joy of love, tears fell from their eyes. 98. Their throats choked with emotion, their hair stood on end, and the hearers for the time being lost all consciousness of body. 99. When a king throws aside the glory of courage, his army naturally does the same. If the mind drops all shame of sensual things, then the organs of sense forget their functions. 100. So when

Namdev cast aside his consciousness of body the very same thing happened to his listeners. As they listened to the character and deeds of Shri Hari they all lost consciousness of body. 101. As they brought into their minds the Lord of the world, they clapped their hands in joy, they shouted aloud the names of Vitthal, and their minds were unable to contain their happiness.

BRAHMANS ANGRY WITH NAMA

102. Brahmans just then came from bathing, having rubbed ashes all over their bodies. Around their necks they had placed garlands of *rudraksha.* Their *dhotars* were wet. 103. Their hands held the water and the sixteen materials intended for their worship. In order to bathe the god they came to the big door of the temple. 104. Here Nama was performing his *kirtan*, singing and dancing in the joy of love. An enormous number of people were assembled there and the Brahmans could see no way of getting through them. 105. Outwardly they had performed their devotions and baths, but their minds within were defiled with wrong thoughts. They said to the people, 'Look out or you will touch us ; get off to one side.' 106. A bad man who has anger in his heart thinks that everybody is impure. And as he is fallen into the net of wrong thought, he does not see anyone as pure. 107. In the praise-services in honour of Hari there is no such thing as being defiled by one another, so in going into an assembly of Brahmans to see and worship Shiva and Vishnu, no one should think of defilement. 108. Anyone who says the *Bhagavadgita* or the *Bhagwat* are defiled by touch is a heap of sin. He who finds fault with the *Vedanta* should be considered the same. 109. Not recognizing the truth of this, these Brahmans were possessed with envy. They were filled with anger and spoke roughly to the people. 110. They shouted at them, 'Why are you singing here

uselessly, clapping your hands and shouting aloud? Such doings are acceptable at Pandhari only. Nagnath does not enjoy such things. 111. Every one should be addressed as he likes. Why should salt be put into milk ? If you add sugar to vegetable, you never increase the good taste. 112. If you hold a perfume to the ear, it cannot smell it. Why tell stories to the eyes ? 113. Show a mirror to your tongue and it cannot see itself. If you show to your eyes some sweet tasting juice, they cannot partake of it. 114. So the Lord of Kailas (Shiva), the Husband of Uma, is not fond of these *kirtans* in honour of Hari. Go off to Pandhari and dance *there* putting aside all shame.' 115. When the Brahmans said this, the listeners replied, 'You ought to bear in mind that Hari and Hara (Vishnu and Shiva) are not different from one another; 116. just as the water of the sacred bathing place and the common element of water are not in the slightest degree different; sweetness and sugar are not to be distinguished from one another; 117. a lamp and its light, a flower and its honey, are not different; the sun and its rays are not different; 118. one should not say that a cloud and water are different; one should never try to separate brilliancy from a jewel; 119. how can one point out unlikeness between delicious food and its taste ? A musical instrument and its sound are always without any difference; 120. so all wise people speak of Shiva and Vishnu as really one. As the Slayer of Madan (Shiva) listened to the praises of Vishnu, He lovingly wagged His head in joy.' 121. The Brahmans hearing this reply of the listeners, grew very wrath, and said, 'These low people, with pride in their hearts, are preaching to us, 122. even to us Brahmans who are of the highest caste and who have authority to explain the *Shastras* with full knowledge. We do not approve of the principles preached by Nama. 123. Now get away from here at once; if not, we shall punish you.'

To this threat of the Brahmans no one replied. 124. 'We have already been delayed in our worship of Shiva and there is no way open for us to go into the temple,' said one. Another said, 'Beat out Nama at once. 125. If anyone of *these* people touches us, we shall have to go again and take a bath with our clothes on.' Saying this, two of them forced themselves into the midst of the audience. 126. Just as when gifts are given to those who are worthy of them, those who are unworthy are driven away by envy, so these Brahmans suddenly walked into the midst of Nama's *kirtan*. 127. They said angrily to Nama, 'Why are you needlessly making all this noise here? There is no way open to us for going through the crowd in order to see and worship Shiva. 128. You have cast aside bodily consciousness and made everyone else like yourself. In giving these men your principles you have hindered the performance of our rites. 129. Now go and stand at the back of the temple, and there you may sing without any shame.' Namdev having listened to their demand, bowed to the Brahmans. 130. He replied, 'I will do so'. And the noble *Vaishnava* went away from there. The enthusiasm of the *kirtan* immediately melted away; 131. just as when some intoxicating liquor should fall into a jar full of holy water; or as when salt is put into milk it immediately spoils it; 132. or as when the paste of sandalwood has been prepared, there should fall garlic into it; or as when *assafoetida* is mixed with musk, it naturally destroys the latter; 133. so when the servant of Vishnu (Nama) arose to go the enthusiasm of the *kirtan* melted away. Seeing this the hearts of the listeners felt extreme sorrow; 134. just as when delicious food is served on plates, and a crow snaps it up; or as when one comes back from a journey and he is robbed by thieves on the way; 135. so the crowd with troubled minds went away from here and all followed Nama. 136. In company with

Namdev they retired behind the temple of Shiva, and there sat down for the continunance of the *kirtan.* 137. When the sun sets, its rays go with it; when the king goes into the wilderness, his army also accompanies him; 138. in whatever direction the wind blows, the clouds also move along the same path; so all the listeners followed Nama. 139. With joy and shouting they clapped their hands at the name of Hari, and tears flowed down from the lotus-eyes of the servant of Vishnu (Nama). 140. Nama cried out, 'O Purifier of the sinner, Helper of the helpless, Husband of Rukmini, hasten to my help. O Life of the world, why hast Thou deserted me in this foreign land? 141. It is to-day as if a doe had discarded her young; or as if a bird had forgotten her fledglings; or as if a mother had abandoned her child in a jungle; 142. or as if the *chatak* bird were forgotten by the clouds; or as if the moon were angry with the *chakor* bird; or as if the sun were angry with the lotus; 143. today it is as if the soul has abandoned the body; or as if sight had turned against the eye; or as if the five vital airs had discarded life; such is our unhappy condition to-day. 144. O Dweller in Pandharpur, Vithabai, family goddess, how is it Thou hast forgotten me? 145. I have wandered all over the sea around the continents and with my own eyes have seen all the sacred bathing places, but I have nowhere seen a god such as Thee. 146. With feet parallel, with hands upon the hips, beautiful in form, delightful to look at, as one sees and contemplates the unclad idol, consciousness entirely melts away. 147. While the cymbals, the *vina* and the drum are sounding, and the eagle banners create a beautiful sight; as one looks at them the eyelids forget their activity of winking.' 148. Thus Nama, choked with emotion, thought of the Husband of Rukmini. Just then a most extraordinary thing happened. Listen to it, you holy, pious ones. 149. Nine hundred thousand banners came down from heaven like lightning and suddenly stood upright where the *kirtan* was being performed. 150. They were not merely nine hundred thousand flags; they were the fruit of the nine forms of *bhakti*; or as if the nine sentiments becoming personified entered the *kirtan* performance. 151. Seeing this marvel, all men were amazed, and gazing with their eyes, stood astonished with no thought of their possessing a body. 152. This so filled with joy the servant of Vishnu (Nama) that he shouted with enthusiasm the names of Vitthal, and in his love he danced in the midst of the *kirtan*. 153. The night was one in the dark half of the moon; it was intensely dark, but the banners filled with their light every available space. 154. The joy was great in Nama's heart. The sound of the clapping of hands filled the sky. The gods rained down an abundance of flowers. The marvel was one beyond conception. 155. The people in their joy raised their hands aloft and made the sound of handclapping and of the snapping of their fingers. The sixty-four arts, personified, seemed to be standing there watching the marvel in astonishment.

NAMA'S PRAYER

156. Nama then thought to himself, 'Everything seems to be favourable here, and made so by the Lord of Pandhari, but there seems to be one thing lacking. 157. Nagnath is facing the other way. He has turned His back on this *kirtan* in honour of Hari. I do not know what wrong has been committed by me. 158. Were the temple of Shiva before us, the enthusiasm of the *kirtan* would have been great. Why does not the Husband of Rukmini come to my aid? Why does He hold His anger against me? 159. Victory to Thee, O Thou who delightest in Thy home on the sea of milk, Husband of Lakshmi, most generous One, Helper of the helpless, compassionate One, come swiftly to

my help. 160. Victory to Thee, the One who didst free Gajendra (the elephant), Home of mercy, Father of Brahmadev, King of the Yadavas, put aside Thy *maya* as I utter Thy name, and do Thou hasten to help me. 161. Upamanyu made Thee an obstinate appeal, and Thou gavest to him the ocean of milk. In the same way be merciful to me and hasten to my aid. 162. In order to protect Draupadi from shame, Thou didst make her four-handed. Be merciful to me and come to my help. 163. The Muhammadan king killed the cow in the midst of the *kirtan* and I then put Thee in trouble, O Master. Thou didst immediately come to my help and in a moment raised the cow to life. 164. When I was thirsty in the wilderness Thou didst immediately come to my assistance, but now having a hardened heart, Thou dost not quickly come, O Vitthal. 165. Shiva is sitting in His temple, with His back turned towards me. Now look upon me with the eye of mercy and come to my help, O Lord of the universe.' 166. Thus Nama, full of love, mournfully pleaded in the midst of his *kirtan*. Suddenly an extraordinarily wonderful thing happened. Listen to it, you pious *bhaktas*.

THE TEMPLE FACING EAST TURNS WEST

167. The temple that had faced the east, suddenly turned around to the west. All expressed their astonishment. Blessed was that time and day. 168. In the joy of love they clapped their hands. The whole assembly of *bhaktas* rejoiced. They cried out, ' He who wears the moon on His forehead (Shiva) has certainly come to the help of Nama. ' 169. Hearing Nama's *kirtan* the Husband of Parvati (Shiva), together with the temple, turned their faces to the west and listened with love. 170. Seeing how great was the *bhakti* of Nama, the listeners became full of joy. Nama remarked to them, ' The doer of this is the merciful Shri Hari. ' 171. This most extraordinary *kirtan* of

Nama was seen as being performed in front of the temple with the joy of love. 172. After the Brahmans had performed their worship they came outside the temple, and lo! the *kirtan* of Nama was being performed in front of the temple with the joy of love. 173. After bathing in the holy water early in the morning, they sought to make oblation to the sun. Then they remarked, 'The sun seems to have arisen in the west, 174. or else we have lost all sense of direction. Or perhaps by keeping awake, we have fallen into some misconception. Or if not that, it would seem as though Shiva had become especially pleased with Nama.' 175. After further thought they looked about them, then they glanced to see if the sacred bathing place was still the same, but they did not see it there. 176. It was the temple alone that had turned and was now facing Nama. And those many divine banners shone like lightning.

PENITENT BRAHMANS

177. Seeing this, the Brahmans were astonished and remarked, 'Even Brahmadev and the other gods could not understand the limits of Nama's power. 178. Being proud of our own deeds, we have needlessly persecuted him.' Thus repentant in heart they came into the place where the *kirtan* was being performed. 179. The Brahmans remarked to Nama, 'Blessed are you, God-loving noble *Vaishnava*, the full *avatar* of Uddhav. This we now truly understand. 180. You have performed and shown to us what the ear has never heard before, nor the eye has ever seen. O Nama, blessed is your mother. This assembly is fortunate indeed. 181. May your extraordinary praise spread throughout the three worlds, so long as the earth, the moon and the sun are seen with a form. 182. Until then, may the holy *bhaktas* sing of your life by their lips, for the ears which will listen to it will become holy in a moment.

183. Thus speaking, the Brahmans made a *namaskar* with reverence and remarked to Nama, 'Neither Brahmadev nor the other gods could comprehend the limits of your power. 184. Durvas, filled with pride, persecuted Ambarish. The Life of the world knowing his distress bore the sufferings of birth. 185. When the Brahmans of Pratishthan (Paithan) persecuted Dnyaneshwar, then he made the buffalo repeat the *Vedas*. 186. In the same way you have done a seemingly impossible thing. You have actually turned the temple of Shiva round.' Nama then opened his eyes and became choked with emotion. 187. Then with love he recited the hymn of praise and waved lights over the Husband of Rukmini. He lovingly made a prostrate *namaskar* and then distributed the sweetmeats. 188. At that moment the banners flew off, and at once went to their home in the Heaven *Vaikunth*. The people lifted up their faces and watched the wonderful sight. 189. The temple of Shiva that was turned round about at that time is even today the same. Shri Hari, who is proud of His *bhaktas*, Himself puts away their distresses. 190. Among the gods, the Husband of Rukmini is the most supreme. Among all *Vaishnavas*, the *bhakta* Nama stands first. One cannot see in the three worlds anyone fit to make a comparison with Nama. 191. What juice is there which can be used to make a comparison with nectar? What river can be mentioned that would do for a comparison with the ocean?

192. In the next chapter the Husband of Rukmini will cause this book to be written with its extraordinary interest. Mahipati simply bears His stamp, and here comes to the saints as a suppliant.

193. *Swasti* (Peace!) This book is the *Shri Bhaktavijaya*. In listening to it the Lord of the earth will be pleased. Listen to it, you God-loving pious *bhaktas*. This is the twelfth very delightful chapter; it is an offering to Shri Krishna.

CHAPTER XIII

NAMDEV'S PILGRIMAGE ENDS

Obeisance to Shri Ganesh. Obeisance to Shri Gopal Krishna.

GOD REJOICES IN THE STORIES OF HIS *BHAKTAS*

1. O hearers, listen to these strange and extraordinary stories. To-day your tongues receive supreme nectar, so that I see none as fortunate as you are. 2. Among the gods, the Lord of the heaven *Vaikunth* is superior to all. He is also fond of His loving *bhaktas*. And now these stories of the *bhaktas*, very extraordinary as they are, have become known for your good fortune. 3. The Husband of Rukmini feels very happy as the stories of the saints are being sung and listened to; just as when the moon arises the sea of milk rejoices; 4. or as when one praises the elephant-faced deity (Ganesh), Shiva and Parvati are pleased; or as a *sadguru* wags his head with love when his disciple acquires knowledge; 5. or when one sings the praises of a child the mother feels happy; or as when describing Narad's indifference to worldly things, Brahmadev rejoices; 6. just so, the Lord of the world rejoices when the stories of the saints are praised, and becoming pleased He gives an everlasting home to both listeners and speaker. 7. Therefore it is that I have called you fortunate. What gain can be greater than the home of Vishnu? I can see nothing greater anywhere.

DNYANDEV AND NAMDEV GO TO PANDHARI

8. In the former chapter there was the delightful story of how the temple of Avandhya Nagnath was turned round, and how when all the Brahmans saw the marvel they were overcome with amazement. 9. After Dnyandev and Namdev had made a *namaskar* to the Lord of the heaven *Kailas*, both left that place and returned

to Pandhari; 10. just as when a daughter who is living with her mother-in-law returns to her mother's home her mind is full of joy, so it was with Nama; 11. or as when a cow and her calf having been separated the calf suddenly sees its mother, and rushes towards her, so it happened to Nama; 12. or as when a child is playing in the street, and then goes back into the house to its mother, its heart is full of joy, so it happened to Nama; 13. or as when a young deer has wandered away for the purpose of playing about, and then comes back to its mother deer, its heart overflows with joy, so it happened to Nama. 14. Thus rejoicing at heart the two, Namdev and Dnyandev, walked rapidly along. As they approached Pandhari, they saw the dome from a distance. 15. As soon as they saw Pandhari, they made a prostrate *namaskar*. They embraced one another and both felt very happy. 16. Then taking cymbals and *vina* in their hands, they lovingly performed a *kirtan* in honour of Hari. As they approached the main door of the temple, they again made a prostrate *namaskar*. 17. Just as one lets go of a stick and it falls to the ground, so Nama becoming unconscious of his body fell on the ground. 18. Dnyandev raised him up and brought back a little of his consciousness. He took his hand in his and walked forward. 19. When they came to the god's bedroom and made their bow, the Life of the world descended from His throne and came forward to meet them. 20. The Lord of the world being moved with emotion drew Nama to His heart and removed all his calamities by waving a torch over him. 21. Nama also was filled with emotion and tears flowed from his eyes. He placed his head on the lotus-feet of the god and spoke with a sweet voice. 22. 'O Lord of the world, I am very weary. Look upon me with Thy mercy. Without Thee I am in deep distress. I cannot see what the end will be.'

PANDURANG AND NAMDEV MEET

23. 'My mind was in ignorance, and therefore I wandered from house to house, but I have seen no place even in my dreams as happy as Pandhari. 24. There are very sacred bathing places with high reputation, but my mind is attached to the Chandrabhaga, for, O Merciful to the lowly, O Pandurang, Thou causest this earthly existence of Thy servants to cease. 25. O Lord of the Yadavas, scruple arises in my mind as I see a god without eagle banners. 26. As I looked at them with my eyes, I was sorrowful at not seeing Thee, but bringing Thy form into my mind I remained quiet. 27. Thou art my dearest friend, brother and relative, and Thou alone art my family deity.' Thus speaking, Nama remained perfectly still. 28. To this the Husband of Rukmini replied, 'I was very sorrowful, I could not sleep day and night, while waiting for you. 29. When you, Nama, were far away, Pandhari seemed a desolate city. But My heart never forgot you a single moment. 30. And now, My dear loving *bhakta*, do not separate yourself from my sight. Fasten your eye upon My form and sit quietly down. 31. I love you infinitely, and you also love Me as sweetness never leaves sugar; it is the same with the sweetness of love. 32. Just as the lotus and the sun are fond of one another, so certain is our love for each other, O Nama; 33. or as the *chatak* bird and the cloud never forget one another, so great is your love and Mine, O Nama. 34. The moon and the ocean love one another infinitely; so, O Nama, to My mind is association with you. 35. A mother loves her infant child and never forgets it; so in our minds the idea of duality does not enter even in our dreams. 36. Whenever I happened to see an itinerant pilgrim, I would ask him about you, "Did you see My Nama ? Was he well ?" 37. If he should be thirsty or hungry, who aside from Myself would know it ? Whom would he tell of his soul's secrets ?

38. Perhaps he is in sorrow, and is calling for My help, He knows of no other object of contemplation day or night. 39. Aside from Me, who will ask Nama whether he is weary ? In whose shade will he sit, and rest for a moment?' 40. Thus the Lord of the world spoke His secrets to the saints. 'It may be that Nama may be in distress without Me and is just holding on to life.' 41. Then the Lord of the world bending His arm gave Nama an embrace, caressed his face, and with His hands wiped his eyes. 42. He took off from Himself His garland of flowers and *tulsi*, and put it around the neck of Nama. This dark complexioned One looked all over the person of Nama with close attention.

43. Just then some noble *Vaishnavas* came to see Him ; Nivritti and Dnyaneshwar, Sopan, Visoba Khechar and Narahari the goldsmith. 44. Assembling there at this time they prostrated themselves on the ground. They embraced Nama and shouted, 'Victory, victory.' 45. and wagged their heads in the joy of love. 46. The crowd of *Rishis* and *Gandharvas* (choristers), Brahmadev, Indra and other gods also came there at that time, in order to rejoice at the sight. 47. Just then Rukmini hastened there, bringing the five-lamp platter in her hand, and in her love she waved it over these *bhaktas* of God. 48. Holding Nama by the chin she looked upon him with compassion. The Lord of the world again said to Nama :—

NAMA TOLD TO GIVE A FEAST TO BRAHMANS

49. 'O Nama, listen, you have seen all the sacred bathing places; in coming to this birth you have accomplished your good, and have satisfied the desire of your heart. 50. Now in order to complete your pilgrimage, bring your rites to a close by feeding the Brahmans. Perform what is prescribed and thus wholly complete your purpose. 51. You have suffered many things. They

will bear good fruit. Listen, O Nama, to what I have said.' So God spoke to him in love. 52. 'Although one may have wandered to many sacred places, yet if the final rites have not been performed, it will be as if the most delicious food had been cooked, and then finally not eaten; 53. or as if one should listen to the reading of many *Puranas*, yet unless they are meditated upon it goes for naught; or like ornaments beautifully formed but useless if not worn; 54. or as if one in order to have a healthy body should take medicine, O Nama, but if he did not eat digestible food, the medicine would not prove of use; 55. so you may have seen many sacred bathing places, including *Sapta-puris* [seven cities, givers of final deliverance:—Ayodhya, Mathura, Maya, Kashi, Kanchi, Avantika, Dwarawati], and yet if you do not perform the final rites, your wandering will be in vain. So say the *Shastras*. 56. This holy city of Pandhari is a heaven upon earth, far famed, and for comparing it nothing animate or inanimate exists. 57. It is a place where if one offers food to Brahmans it satisfies to the end of the ages. So collect all the Brahmans who live in the sacred city and bring them to the feast. 58. Worship them with the proper materials and give them a feast of delicious things. Offer them also with reverence the *pansupari* and gifts of money.' 59. After saying this, Krishna took Nama by the hand and led him into the inner shrine.

60. Then with a smiling face the merciful One and Holder of the *Sharang* bow (Krishna) said to Rukmini, 'My love for Nama is very great, I can never be separated from him. 61. After having visited many sacred bathing places, he is going to complete the final rites to-day.' The Life of the world having said this, the Mother of the world replied, 62. 'O Lord of the universe, Thy most beloved friend Nama has put aside all other loves and affections, and in deep love is worshipping Thee alone.

63. He has abandoned every business enterprise. Who then will perform the final rites? By serving Thee he has made Thee his debtor, casting aside pride and affection. 64. Having passed through a great number of births he has accumulated some good deeds. All these he has lovingly offered at Thy feet. 65. Just as rivers in great volumes of water pour into the sea, so Nama has followed Thee with singleness of devotion. 66. And so it falls to Thee to perform Thyself everything in Thy affection for him.' Hearing her say this, *Shrirang* (Krishna) smiled. 67. Rukmini added, ' O good Being, Nama's love is extraordinary. Brahmadev would not be able to describe it by His lips. It is always new and beyond comparison. 68. So Thou, O Holder of the disk, must now go taking Nama with Thee and after inviting the Brahmans come back quickly. 69. If all the *siddhis* are favourable, one will not have to worry; if Thou, Lord of Pandhari, hast the wish to do a thing, what canst Thou not do? 70. The calf of the wish-cow does not have to go into the mountains to feed. The sun never has to light a lamp to cause brightness. 71. The ocean does not have to worry as to whether it will rain or not. A person who drinks nectar continually, what does he have for digestible food? 72. Why should the moon make an effort to become cool? How can it be difficult for Sarasvati to compose poetic verses? 73. The elephant-faced (Ganesh) does not have to labour to put away hindrances. Why does one want a mirror to see the bracelet on one's hand? 74. So, O Life of the world, it will not take much effort to feast Brahmans for Nama.' Hearing her say this, the king of *Vaikunth* started on his way.

KRISHNA GOES TO INVITE BRAHMANS

75. Taking Nama's lotus-hand, Krishna walked along. He assembled and took along with Him with great ceremony

a crowd of *bhaktas.* 76. Among them were Nivritti and Dnyandev, Sopan, Visoba Khechar, Chokhamela, Narahari the goldsmith,and Vanka the woodcutter. 77.Sanaka and the others walked on each side, watching the wonderful sight. Behind Nama, the Lord of the Yadavas walked in His love.78. I will tell you the reason why He walked behind Nama. It was because the Life of the world wished to take the dust of Nama's feet.

79. Hearing this remark, my listeners may raise a doubt: ' How is it that God could wish for the dust of the feet of a *bhakta* ?' 80. Know then that in the book called *Tirthavali*, the Lord of the world said this very thing through His own lips. Taking that as my authority I have written the same thing. 81. The Life of the world said with His own lips that He was the object of the suppliant. What cannot the Ocean of mercy, the Cloud of compassion, do ? 82. The Brother of the lowly, Helper of the humble, is known world-wide as to His reputation. Therefore you listeners should never have a doubt in your mind.

83. Why should I speak any more on this subject ? The *bhaktas* of Vishnu understand its meaning. The Husband of Rukmini hastened to give invitations to the Brahmans. 84. In order that the Life of the world might carry to completion the ambition of His servant He acted as a householder, a merchant, a Brahman, and a host for His *bhaktas.* 85. The king of the Yadavas, along with the *Vaishnavas*, first circumambulated the sacred city, and as he saw the Brahmans, the king of *Vaikunth* arrived on the sands of the river. 86. As soon as he saw the Brahmans, He, the Helper of the helpless, the Husband of Rukmini, the merciful One to the lowly, the Ocean of compassion, reverently made them a *namaskar*. 87. The *Pandits*, the *Vedic* Brahmans, the good and expert listeners, seeing the Life of the world, were amazed. 88. The Life of

the world had taken the form of a citizen, and yet the marks of His six glorious elements [all-sovereignty, all-goodness, all-glory, all-opulence, all-knowledge, all-dispassionateness] were not hidden; just as when gold is mixed with brass, it can never be hidden. 89. Pure silver in the midst of tin a God-loving *bhakta* in the midst of a business life, or the touchstone among other stones, can never be hidden. 90. Just as the *tulsi* plant among other plants; or as the Ganges among other rivers; so among His *bhaktas*, the Dweller in the heaven *Vaikunth* could not possibly remain hidden. 91. As the diamond can be prominently seen in diamond dust, as nectar can be seen in a plate of delicious food, and as the moon appears brilliant in the midst of clusters of stars, 92. so in this assembly of *Vaishnavas*, the Brahmans were astonished to see the Holder of the *Sharang* bow (Krishna). Then with a great joy they spoke very sweetly to Him. 93. 'In seeing Thy form, the three kinds of afflictions [that is, from deities, or from devils, or from fate] have departed. Tell us Thy name, and where hast Thou come from? 94. What is Thy occupation? What business dost Thou conduct? Whereabouts are Thy lodgings? Let us have an answer to these questions.' 95. Hearing these questions of the Brahmans, the Holder of the disk (Krishna) replied, 'Both my family and occupation are known to these *bhaktas*. 96. I am the unconquered One, and the Unassociated, but in all my infinite number of rebirths I have been associated with these in close acquaintance. 97. And now making your feet my witness, I am speaking the exact truth. I am the dear friend of Nama. 98. If you still have any doubts in your minds, then present your sacred thoughts to these saints. With your doubts removed you must come to the feast. 99. I have taken lodgings in the temple. If you ask me my name, it is *Ananta* (the infinite One). Perform the right of bathing and come quickly to the feast.' 100. Hearing this nectar reply, the Brahmans rejoiced in mind. Replying that they would come at once, the cooking of the feast was completed.

GOD FAR AWAY FROM ALL PRIDE

101. The Life of the world, having heard their reply, returned to the temple, and told Rukmini of the things that had happened. 102. He said, ' O Beloved of my life, listen to me, I have returned after inviting the Brahmans, but some of the conservative and proud did not recognize Me. 103. They saw the glory of My form, and they felt so happy. They asked Me of my family and of My occupation and I told them everything. 104. I spoke to them with My own lips that I was accompanying the saints and that Nama was My dearest friend. 105. The Brahmans asked Me where I lodged and I told them that I lodged in the temple. They asked me my name, and I told them it was *Ananta* (the infinite One). 106. I told them the signs by which they could recognize Me. But they could not make Me out. ' Thus speaking, the Life of the world smiled. 107. Rukmini said to Krishna, 'He who always has the idea of differences in his mind, together with pride in his own knowledge, will never meet with the Saviour of the world. 108. He who says his caste and family are pure, has no repentance in his heart; then how can he ever meet with the Holder of the disk (Krishna) ? 109. To one who has jaundice, the colour of the moon seems yellow. He whose body is racked with fever says that food is bitter. 110. So those who have pride of their conservative opinions, the knowledge of *bhakti* will not be to their taste. Without reverence towards Thee Thou cannever be seen by them. 111. Through their good fortune, O God of gods, Thou hast been found as the storehouse of *Vaikunth*. Today by the good fortune of Nama he is made prosperous.

KRISHNA'S GIFTS TO NAMDEV

112. While the Mother of the universe was thus speaking, a very novel thing occurred at that moment. In order to prepare the feast, all the eight *siddhis* (accomplishments personified) arrived. 113. Merely by their own wish they came to the great door of the temple. They prepared all the materials for a feast and sprinkled the ground with water mixed with sandalwood paste. 114. Having sprinkled them all according to the rules of the *Bhagwat* they raised banners on the altar of *tulsi*. They planted flags of nine different designs as nine forms of *bhakti* [hearing, reading, calling to mind, washing, outward worship, adoration, service, cultivating friendship, consecration of one's self] in the heavens and made this miracle visible to the eye. 115. Having decorated the houses, they remarked, 'What holy deeds this servant of Vishnu (Nama) has done that by it he has made crazy with love the One without qualities !' Every one was astonished at the sight. 116. Squares of pearls were designed, and decorations of various coloured powders were drawn. Illuminations were made. In short, for the sake of the loving *bhakta* (Nama) an unforeseen ceremony was started. 117. There was a very loud cry of joy. Sweet musical instruments proclaimed their happiness. The *bhaktas* shouted out 'Victory, victory' full of joy. 118. Then they gave Nama a bath, and began to repeat the *mantras* according to religious rites, and commenced the day-blessing (*punyahavachan*) ceremony. 119. Satyabhama, Rai, and Rukmini came bringing their gifts, and they flashed with lightning in the home of the clouds. 120. Then Krishna with His own hands gave gifts to this servant of Vishnu. In His love He put on him garments and ornaments without limit. 121. With supreme joy men and women gazed at the beautiful and joyful sight, and with sincerity they waved the lights over the servant of Vishnu. 122. The One whose complexion is dark as a cloud

(Krishna) with His own hands honoured His servant. This Helper of the helpless, this supreme Being, this Ocean of mercy for all the lowly, did this. 123. And all said to Nama, 'Blessed is your *bhakti*. The happiness which you have attained is unattainable even by Brahmadev.' 124. In the meantime the feast had been cooked and all Brahmans were invited to it. As they came to the great door of the temple they were given seats.

CEREMONY AT COMPLETION OF PILGRIMAGES

125. In order to worship the Brahmans, Krishna Himself sat amongst them; just as when the gods coming together in the heavens said to one another, 126. 'We have been deceived; these *bhaktas* of Vishnu have robbed us of our joy; we drink good nectar, it is true, but we miss the nectar of love; 127. just as if one experienced the deliverance called *Salokata* [living in the same place as the Deity], but further on missed the deliverance called *Sayujyata* [absorption into the Deity]; or as through intimacy with a studied poetic composition, one may miss the blessing of it; 128. or as while doing one's regular religious duties, one may easily fail in doing the occasional ones; or as when one obtains the means of having a desire fulfilled, the means slips away for acquiring a desireless mind which had been attainable; 129. or as if one should visit all the sacred bathing places on the surface of the earth, but should fail in the service that should be rendered to his mother; or as one may serve the inferior deities and yet the possible worship of Vishnu ceases; 130. or as in giving a feast to invited Brahmans, the uninvited guests had to be turned away; so, sitting in the place of the gods we have lost the love of *bhakti*.' 131. Thus the gods in the sky conversed with one another. In the meantime Krishna seated the Brahmans at the great door of the temple for the purpose of worshipping them. 132. He placed broad seats on which were golden designs inlaid

with jewels and seated the Brahmans on them. 133. Then with His own hands the Husband of Rukmini washed the feet of the Brahmans. The Life of the world wiped their feet with His yellow robe and in love drew them to His heart. 134. He touched His eyes with their great toes and seated the Brahmans in their proper line. In his love the Lord of the heaven *Vaikunth* then drank the holy water in which their feet were washed and rejoiced in the act. 135. He rubbed on them a paste made of eight different perfumes. He put garlands of *tulsi* round their necks. The Lord of the world placed on their forehead the mark made with musk-paste. 136. The Lord of *Vaikunth* (Krishna) worshipped them with love. He waved before them incense made of ten different kinds. In His love He waved before them the lighted lamps in a plate inlaid with jewels. 137. Then arranging them in two lines he placed golden plates before them. In her undivided love the good Rukmini served them. 138. She served with four kinds of divine food. Then calling to Nama, the offerings to the gods were made through him. 139. The *bhaktas* shouted aloud, ' Victory, victory, the Husband of Rukmini is the enjoyer of this feast.' Thus remarking, they made offerings to the five vital airs (*pran, apan, vyan, udan, saman*). 140. The chief Actor, God Himself, became the Fulfiller, the Enjoyer, and the Causer of others to act, so there was nothing lacking in all that heart could wish. 141. In the feast of the sun from whence would darkness come ? When listening to the singing of Saraswati, drowsiness will not come to anyone. 142. If the ocean is married, need one be concerned about the water ? In the hot season what need has the moon of a fan ? 143. If a touchstone is placed on an iron anvil, it would not be necessary to guild the anvil. No one becomes afflicted with disease who lives in the heaven of Indra. 144. If one looks to find something that is doubtful in the perfect book, the *Dnyaneshwari*. he will not find it there. So in the feast given by Nama there was nothing lacking. 145. The Husband of Rukmini frequently prayed, and as the Brahmans listened to His sweet voice they were made happy. 146. They said, 'With every morsel one should take the name of God, in that way a man's eating will result in happiness.' 147. Thus in the feast the minds of all became filled with joy. The Life of the world Himself gave to the Brahmans water for the washing of their hands. 148. Having seated the Brahmans in their places, He gave them *pansupari* made of thirteen ingredients At that moment it seemed as if the loving desire itself assumed a concrete form. 149. Or one might say, 'By the good fortune of Vishnu, it became visible in form and came to visit Nama; so that in its love the joy with Intelligence (God Himself) was enticed.' 150. Then joining His hands palm to palm, the Holder of the *Sharang* bow (Krishna) said to the Brahmans, 'I feel as though I wanted to take your blessing (in the form of dinner) in your presence. 151. This is what I would love to do. Therefore I request the *Swamis* to sit for a moment in quietness of mind. 152. After I have finished dining, I shall quickly make the gifts of money. Accept them with satisfied minds and then depart for your homes.' 153. Shri Krishna thought to himself, 'If I should place in their hands the gifts of money before the feast ends, they would not remain sitting here, but would depart without taking leave; 154. just as the relatives do not leave the marriage festival until the marriage gifts have been made; or just as the beggars are not satisfied in their minds until they have taken the charitable gifts.' 155. So thinking in His mind, Shri Krishna said to the Brahmans, 'Through Nama I have been able to serve you. 156. You are the *Vedas* incarnate, worthy of worship by Brahmadev and others, so look upon Me with the eye of mercy. Take care of Me, O noble Brahmans.' 157. As Krishna thus spoke, it seemed to the Brahmans that it was a nectar voice. Then rejoicing in their minds, they were full of happiness. 158. The earth-gods (Brahmans) replied to Him, 'Thou hast worked very hard, and while Thou hast been worshipping the Brahmans, Thy own dinner has been delayed. 159. Thou didst everything Thyself, and it was very successful. Though we might look to see if anything was lacking, we would never see such a thing. 160. We have today seen a new thing; when we look at the *Swami's* novel reverence, his humility and the respect paid to us, they seem beyond all comparison.' 161. Then the Brahmans learned in the four *Vedas*, repeating the great *mantras* over the rice, threw it on His head as their blessing. 162. 'Mayest Thou be victorious for ever, and be our protector, and mayest Thou live until the end of the ages in the home of the universe.' 163. Then taking rice in His yellow garment, He sprinkled it on Nama's head saying, 'May this love remain for ever in your heart.'

JOYOUS INTERDINING OF GOD AND HIS *BHAKTAS*

164. (The Brahmans replied): 'Now take these *Vaishnavas* to Thy side and eat, O heap of good qualities. We will quiet our minds and sit beside Thee.' 165. To these words of the Brahmans Krishna replied, 'I will do so.' Just then Rukmini arrived with various kinds of food served on golden plates. 166. Then Satyabhama came quickly with a golden vessel in her hand, and having given them water to sip, a most extraordinary thing happened. 167. The Holder of the *Sharang* bow (Krishna), then called to His side Uddhav and Akrur, Narad and Tumbar as companions in His line of guests. 168. Nama who was standing at the great door of the temple was called also. But he had lost consciousness of body and his heart overflowed with love. 169. Pandharinath by His

inner light saw him filled with supreme Brahm-joy and rushed to his aid; just as a cow, seeing her young one, hastens towards it with her teats full of milk. 170. The Life of the world lifted Nama up with His four hands and gave him a loving embrace. He brought him back to consciousness and caressed him. 171. Then taking him by the hand, He seated him by His plate that he might eat. As Nama began to sob, the Lord of the world caressed him. 172. As he put each joyous morsel into his mouth, he saw him as the same Supreme Element as Himself, and at once in the form of intelligence He assumed the same form. 173. Then seizing a flag on the eagle-platform, He told Nama one of His secrets. Said He, ' My dearest friend, putting aside the shame of considering ourselves as different, speak to me. 174 When you turn to the secrets of the heart, it is as clear as the heavens without any back or front; so Nama, you are in the closest relation to Me. 175. This is what you recognize in Me, and I recognize the same in you. Recognize in your heart that we are of one essence, O Nama 176. Turn your attention to Me, and in your heart see that I am your dearest friend, I, who am the Unmanifested, am yourself, so I consider. 177. Open your eyes and see this extraordinary performance of the completion of pilgrimage rites on your account, O loving *bhakta*, for you have with you the lamp of knowledge. 178. The chief of *bhaktas* have come to visit you. Speaking to them nectar wards, give them the feast of joy. 179. Nivritti is the personification of supreme joy, and here is Dnyandev the associate of all joy. 180. Over there yonder is Sopan, a ferry to take men into their Beyond. O fortunate one, pay him reverence in nectar words.' 181. Saying this, the Husband of Rukmini gave Nama His assuring hand, and he in reverence placed his head on His feet.

NAMDEV ASKS FOR THE BOON OF LOVE

182. Said he, ' In all my rebirths, give me the gift of love to Thee. ' Hearing him say this, the Life of the world smiled. 183. Thus this Lover of *bhaktas* placed morsels of food in Nama's mouth, and Gopal Krishna, the Mereciful to the lowly, wiped away the perspiration of weariness of His servant. 184. The hand of assurance which Hari placed on the head of Sanak and the others, that very hand of the Enemy of Putana (Krishna) caressed Nama. 185. Vanamali (Krishna) said to Nama, ' Drop all your concern, I am near you to give you rest. I shall always care for you. 186. You laboured hard on your journey, and your body has become emaciated by separation from Me; your moon-face has lost its glow; your eyes lack lustre for want of sleep. 187. No one has paid attention to your thirst or hunger from the time that you went away from Me. Aside from you My eyes have seen nothing to please Me. 188. As I could not control Myself My eyes turned to the ten different directions. I said to Myself, " When will Nama the servant of Vishnu return to Me ?" 189. Becoming in My mind impatient I looked for you at the eagle-platform. Not seeing you there, I used to look for you at the great door of the temple on the banks of the Bhima. 190. If you were not at the sacred bathing place at Padmatirtha, then I looked for you at the Venunad, but not seeing you anywhere I was very sorrowful. 191. As I, the Life of the world, sat down to eat or as each day I took My drink of nectar, I remembered you, saying to Myself that you would hasten to come; 192. that in your impatience you would rush to meet Me ; that in your love you would give Me an embrace ; and that you would tell Me the secrets of your heart. This was the wish I kept in My heart.' 193. As the compassionate One said these things, there was a full tide of feelings of mercy, just as the mother rejoices, when she sees her loved child ; 194. in

the same way the king of the heaven *Vaikunth* rained down His love on Nama. Anyone who drinks that divine juice never finds it distasteful. 195. In this way, the Holder of the disk (Krishna) supplies the wish of His *bhaktas*. Then at that moment He performed a wonderful deed. Listen to it, you pious folk.

KRISHNA SHOCKS THE BRAHMANS

196. Krishna ate with a feeling of fondness what Nama had left on his plate. Seeing this, all the Brahmans were astonished, and feeling shocked they hung their heads down. 197. The Brahmans considered it a strange act, and discussed it among themselves: 'What are we to think about it? He has truly violated the caste's religious rules. 198. His wives served the food, and we know not of what caste they are. They were neither *Kshatriyas* nor Brahmans, neither *Vaishnavas* nor *Shudras*. 199. His doings are unfathomable. He seemed different from the four castes. How is it that we forgot this when seeing His acts that are beyond comparison? 200. Now we must regard this as certain that He is Nama's mother and father, and that He loves him in body, mind and speech. 201. He took the rice in His yellow garment and sprinkled it over Nama's head, and when the offering of food to the god was to be performed He made him the leader in it. 202. Disasters are continually being created, and such have happened now. Now let no one discuss with any other regarding this or ever speak of it.'

203. In the next chapter the Holder of the *Sharang* bow (Krishna) will speak to Brahmans. You wise listeners, learned in the *siddhanta* (established facts), give your attention. 204. Just as when a diamond is sunk in an anvil it comes out at the sight of the diamond dust, so fortunate saints, through knowledge gained by experience, know the secrets of God. 205. Hunger is sweeter than

food, therefore it satisfies the desire for food. If there was no desire in the heart to listen to the stories of Hari, they would not seem sweet to anyone. 206. The relator of this version of the *Tirthavali* [see verse 80] is the Husband of Rukmini. Mahipati in his love speaks of himself as His slave and servant.

207. *Swasti* (Peace!) This book is the *Shri Bhaktavijaya.* In listening to it the Lord of the world will be pleased. Listen, you God-loving, pious *bhaktas.* This is the thirteenth deeply delightful chapter; it is an offering to Shri Krishna.

CHAPTER XIV

NAMDEV'S LIFE

(Continued)

Obeisance to Shri Ganesh. Obeisance to Gopal Krishna.

THE RITE COMPLETING NAMA'S PILGRIMAGES

1. My mind is very happy to-day in relating the rite connected with the completion of Nama's wanderings, and I have invited you, good people, to sit down in lines for the feast. 2. On the golden plates of joy, the delicious food composed of the nine juices has been served. The *Vaishnava bhaktas* partake of its sweetness and become eternal. 3. You may ask who are sitting at this feast. Nivritti, Dnyandev, Sopan, Gora the potter, all *Vaishnavas*; also Savata and Narahari, 4. Uddhav, Akrur, Narad, Tumbar, and the limitless number of noble *Vaishnavas*, all of whom Krishna seated in lines. 5. As they tasted the delicious divine juices, all the saints were satisfied. That which they left on their plates has unexpectedly fallen into our mouths. 6. As soon as we had the great and wonderful favour an extraordinary thing occurred, inasmuch as the priceless stories of God's *bhaktas* out of love came to our lips. 7. Just as whatever seed is planted in the earth, it later yields fruit just like itself, so through the favour of the saints we have received the stories of their lives.

KRISHNA ACCUSED OF BREAKING CASTE

8. Now listen, you hearers. In the previous chapter there was described how the Life of the world ate with intense delight what remained on Nama's plate. 9. When the Brahmans saw him do this their minds were filled with astonishment and they said, 'We do not recognize who this violator of caste-rules may be. 10. In eating food at his house we have fallen from our religious duty.

Now let us never accuse one another. 11. When making a journey, if anyone eats what he has begged for, or if in time of famine one has eaten the food of a *Shudra*, or if in the age of ignorance one has performed some immoral deed, one should never tell of it. 12. If a friend tells you something in private, or if a miser sees a pile of wealth, or if one's domestic life is going on badly, one should never speak of it. 13. If while giving a feast to a thousand Brahmans a dog should accidentally touch the food, a wise person who sees this act should never speak of it.' 14. Then one of the good Brahmans spoke up and said, 'If we have not observed our religious duties, why should we perform another evil act, and hide our true duty? 15. If ignorantly some fault attaches itself to us, some penance may be performed. After we have confessed our wrong deeds to men, our fault does not remain a single moment. 16. If we have any faults, we should tell them to others, but with repentance. If any one reviles us for doing so, that very act destroys our fault. 17. So now without any hesitation we should turn him out of caste and repeating the *Gayatri-mantra* we shall remain pure. 18. Things done in the confusion of ignorance are not called a sin. In the *Dharma Shastra* this remedy is open to every one.' 19. Thinking of it this way, the noble Brahmans went silently away and the Holder of the *Sharang* bow (Krishna) then invited them to him. 20. The Husband of Rukmini said to them, 'Why is your heart in doubt? With sad faces you are all hurrying away. 21. What doubt have you in your heart? Kindly tell Me, and in telling Me the secrets of your heart do not hold them back in the least degree.' 22. The Life of the world said this, and then gave them gifts of diamonds, precious jewels and gold mixed with the leaves of *tulsi*, as a means of pacifying them. 23. He then lifted Nama up and put him at the feet of the Brahmans saying,

'Be favourable to him.' This is what the Enemy of Mura (Krishna) said, 24. and He added, 'If you have any other natural doubts, tell them to Me.' As the eagle-bannered One spoke these words, the Brahmans said to Him, 25. 'They say that Nama is a tailor. This has been plainly said to us. How is it that you sat down with him in the same line? 26. Putting aside your duty, you ate with him. You ate what was left on his plate without giving the matter a single thought. 27. What feelings of love have you held in your mind that you should have given your love to Nama? We certainly do not understand this extraordinary action of your compassion. 28. As we thought of the matter you seem to us one whose actions are merely outward, for your extraordinary and strange deeds seem to change moment by moment. 29. We do not see in you any observance of the law relating to the different castes. Although we have thought over the matter, we certainly do not understand it. 30. It would seem that in your eyes praiseworthy and unpraiseworthy seem to be alike. The idea of a difference never seems to have touched your mind. 31. You are acting on the understanding that the inhabitants of the world are just as you are; just as to the touchstone, iron and gold are alike. 32. To the ocean the water of the Ganges and that of a little streamlet are both alike. Water regards the tiger and a cow as equal. 33. Three seasons, the cold, the hot and the rainy seasons, are the same to the sky. To the cloud, a street gutter, a river and a streamlet are all the same. 34. To the wish-tree, a prince and a pauper are equal. The sandalwood of Mount Maila is cooling to everyone alike. 35. The sun shines alike on thieves, on immoral men and on good men. So also it would seem that praiseworthy men and those to be despised are the same to you. 36. Every one thinks that others are like themselves, just as when King Dharma searched for an evil person he could not find one. 37. You wore the appearance of a Brahman and we pinned our faith on that. But your inner purpose, O *Swami*, we do not clearly understand. 38. Every one should seek his own good and should raise the question in his mind regarding what is wrong and what is right; he should establish the truth of the *Vedas* by acting according to the prescribed rules. 39. You seem to be learned in all knowledge. You seem an expert in all the *Shastras.* Now pay respect to the commands of the *Vedas* and observe their prescribed forms. 40. You have cast aside the principles of the *Shastras* and shown great love for Nama. This we see now for a certainty.'

KRISHNA ANSWERS THE ACCUSATION

41. The Husband of Rukmini, after listening to the remarks of the noble Brahmans, said, 'Do not blame Me for having had Nama dine along with Me. 42. The Soul that is the Mover and the Pervader of all things, how can it be spoken of as either praiseworthy or worthy of being despised? Neither holiness nor sin is able to touch Me. 43. I am Pure Intelligence without spot, the All-Pervading Soul, the Internal Witnesser, undefiled by anything. 44. Nama's body is that of a tailor, and is made up of the five primary elements [earth, water, light, wind and space]; just as when the sky is covered with clouds there does not seem to be any separate clouds. 45. What member of Nama's body makes him Namdev? Give Me your careful opinion. 46. If in your eyes there are faults in light, water, earth, air or space, then it must be of your own creation. 47. You are Brahmans who repeat the *Vedas*; you are learned in all *Shastras*; but you have not yet reached the condition of divine knowledge. 48. Your illusion regarding essential distinctions has not yet left you, but the doubts have grown in your minds. When Nama made the offering of food to the gods, you did not take this into

consideration. 49. And you did not tell Me that you had no right to partake of the food of a tailor, therefore I pleaded with you again and again and told you the secret of action. 50. By means of this occasion with Nama, I have been able to serve you to-day. Although you heard Me say this, you have not understood Me. 51. The rice over which *mantras* were recited was given me as a favour, and I threw it on the head of Nama. I am independent of all, yet you have called Me dependent. I am desireless, yet you have attributed desires to Me. 52. Though I am really not a doer, yet you have made Me a doer. And though you have heard this explanation of Mine, you still do not recognize Me. 53. You partook of the feast without any doubts in your mind, and I accepted what remained on your plates.· Now tell me what is the prescribed penalty for this in the scripture lawbooks? 54. I have this one purpose, to take on Me the dust from the feet of this servant of Hari (Nama), and to drink the water in which your feet are washed, that I may for ever be purified. 55. Aside from these means all religious rites, austerities and gifts seem to be in vain '. Thus spoke the Life of the world who continued thus: 56. ' Only these will I regard as true means. Nor shall I ever forget My *bhaktas* or men in their trouble; just as a mother never forgets her infant child; 57. and as a miser does not forget his wealth; and as a doe never forgets her young; and as the *lava* bird is always thinking of her little ones; 58. and as fishes never forget the water; so My *bhaktas* are always in My mind, O noble Brahmans. 59. *Bhaktas* are My very heart. In their good fortune they don the garment of knowledge and continually partake of the juice of love, namely, *bhakti* and indifference to worldly things. 60. Association with one another is to saints their life-giving nectar; wearing the steel armour of love they are ever without fear. 61. My true *bhaktas* do not bring to their sight the four chief ends of the existence of man [namely, the acquisition of merit, the pursuit of fame, the enjoyment of the pleasures of sense, and the seeking and working out of final deliverance]; even the four kinds of deliverance are matters for their minds to despise. 62. To sing My name with joy, this is their eternal musical instrument. And the well-known platter of their aim has the lights lighted on them. 63. They regard the happiness of Indra's dignity as perishable; just as when the wise men see the shadow made by a cloud, they do not regard it as perpetual; 64. and just as one seeking lodgings and seeing a royal palace does not take refuge there; and just as when wise men see a flood in a mirage, they regard it as false; 65. so (My *bhaktas*), becoming indifferent to worldly passions, have no desire for the home of the immortals. For this reason I dwell for ever in their hearts. 66. In searching for such a *bhakta* I have seen only Nama the tailor; one who has experienced My love in his heart. 67. Therefore it was in My love for him that I ate what was left on his plate. In comparing it (My love), all comparison with divine juices is a faulty one.'

KRISHNA'S GLORIFICATION OF PANDHARI

68. (Krishna added): 'Pandharpur, the sacred city for deliverance, is the treasure-house of all the sacred bathing-places, and if one should look all over the world, another like it cannot be seen. 69. A *jivanmukta* (one free while living) and a wise man and chief among the *bhaktas* was the *Muni* Pundalik. He sat down for contemplation of the most supreme Krishna. 70. And this Bhima river flowing towards the south gives the nectar of immortality. She is the mistress of an abundant joy and shines with the water of that supreme joy. 71. Anyone who sees this Chandrabhaga river from a distance will not have to return to rebirths. When the Bhagirathi river looked at her (the Chandrabhaga) she

felt ashamed and hid away. 72. The Bhagirathi feeling a sense of fear joined with the ocean, and the Bhogavati hastened with extreme speed to the lower regions. 73. In such a sacred city my servants have lived continually day and night, and in the joy of their love they unceasingly shout my names. 74. With joy filling his heart Nama danced in the *kirtans* in the name of Hari. When one goes in search through the three worlds for such joy he will not see it anywhere else.' 75. The good Being also said to the Brahmans, ' He who with his lips repeats My name, whether with some desire in his heart or without a desire, such an one is my dearest friend and relative. 76. I love him more than I love Myself and I will not put him away. He is My family deity whom I worship in reverence. 77. I *Vanamali* (Krishna), *Sacchidanand* (truth, intelligence and joy), am attracted by the family of the servants of Hari. In this world My widespread reputation dwells in the assembly of *bhaktas*. 78. I am quite crazy over My *bhaktas*, and the remnants which are left on their plates I put into My mouth as I very gladly stand before the saints. 79. I think them exceedingly delicious and as I partake of them they seem tasty and sweet. By taking these remnants that remain on their plates My body becomes eternally plump. 80. The brilliant childlike lustre of My body, My eternal victory and wealth, My prosperity, plumpness and satisfaction, are the constant result of My partaking of the food of the *bhaktas*. 81. These saints visit Me like relatives and create for Me the joyous festival of *Divali* (the festival of lights); just as when the *chakor* bird sees the moon, it is full of happiness through the joy of love. 82. Therefore it was that with a very longing heart I had Nama dining along with Me. This is exactly as it happened. Now what is your next thought ?'

NECESSITY OF KRISHNA OBEYING VEDIC RULES

83. The Husband of Rukmini having said this, the Brahmans replied, 'We now understand perfectly that you are an ocean of goodness. 84. But the duties which have been prescribed in the *Vedas* should be performed by You. According to a man's condition should be a man's conduct. 85. The first duty is the observance of caste rules. The rule of constantly keeping himself clean and speaking the truth, is the rule applicable to a Brahman. 86. Forgiveness and control of one's sense are his austerities. He must have perfect compassion for all creatures. He should give thought unceasingly to the contemplation of Brahma. 87. In addition to his religious bath, his devotions, his worship of God and his constant sacrifices, he should study the *Vedas* with a satisfied mind. 88. He should perform well the worship of fire and of uninvited guests and the offering of food to God and he should give such an oblation to God, to *Rishis*, and to ancestors whereby God may be pleased. 89. In this way having performed the prescribed rules, he should then eat and in the third watch of the day he should listen with a satisfied mind to the *Puranas*. 90. With a mind full of joy he should put his trust in the words of the *Vedas*. You are equipped with all knowledge of goodness. Now think for yourself what is for your good. 91. If you throw aside what is your special duty, how can mankind be saved ? If animals that live in the water leave it, then what way have they for remaining alive ? 92. If an infant does not take its nourishment from its mother's breast, it can have no other way of obtaining food. If a bird discards the space where can it go ? 93. If the lotus will not look at the sun, how will it flower ? If the bee does not partake of honey, how can it be made happy ? 94. If a fly leaves the heap of sugar, how can it meet with happiness ? So if a

Brahman discards his own special duties, one sees disaster before him. 95. So putting aside your pride, make your mind pure through repentance. Perform those acts which your reputation will increase in both worlds. 96. Go to the Chandrabhaga river, and there bathe accompanied by the rites of repeating the *mantras.* Give gifts of gold to the Brahmans and perform the *punyahavachan* (day-blessing ceremony). 97. Listen, you wise and expert One, and circumambulate the sacred city. By doing so, your family will become holy. 98. Only by doing this will your fault of eating what was left on Nama's plate be put away.'

FOUR KINDS OF BATHING

Hearing these words of the Brahmans, the Soul of the universe replied, 'I certainly will do so.' 99. *Hrishikeshi* (the Lord of the heart, Krishna) then said to the Brahmans, 'Your command is My authority, but I have one request to make with my whole body and speech.' 100. The One who is dark as a cloud (Krishna) further said to the Brahmans, 'Take care of Nama. Though I have searched, I have found no God-loving *bhakta* equal to him. 101. You are righteous teachers of the *Vedas.* The stream of your words has the form of sacred waters. O *Swamis*, I have already well bathed in the water of your truthful words. 102. I am the Beginning, the Unconquered and the *Adhokshaja* (the Pervader of earth and sky). But I have faith in you. You are worthy of My supreme worship. Indeed, you are My supreme deity. 103. You tell me to perform a bath. Bathing is of four different kinds. I will explain this clearly to you. 104. Know that to hear and meditate on the *Puranas* and *Hari-kirtans* is superior to all forms of bathing. 105. No one has ever declared that any bathing was of more value than experience, than study, or than the vision of the supreme Spirit. 106. The second form of bathing is that of making oneself clean within and without. Anyone who has the good fortune to accomplish this, does not require any other means. 107. The third form of bathing is to put all your organs of sense under control and to destroy all desire. If anyone performs this bathing, why should he need other rites ? 108. The fourth form of bathing superior to all others, is to have compassion on all creatures. Seldom can there be found one good man out of a thousand who has performed this bath. 109. If anyone should ask Me regarding the fifth form of bathing it is the bathing with water. This bathing is spoken of as merely for the public eye. 110. Lust, anger, avarice, caste-feeling, seductions and hypocrisy are hereditary in one's body. They do not leave one by bathing in water. 111. So they must first be driven out by means of right thinking, and by a heart indifferent to earthly things. This purification of the heart must be obtained through association with saints. 112. The fact of the infinite number of rebirths is itself called a penance for the person who has the regular rule of repeating the names, Ram, Krishna, Govinda. 113. Exactly as your mental state is, so will you reap its fruit. To My mind Nama seems spotless.'

KRISHNA UNDERGOES A PENANCE

114. Having said this, the God of gods made the following request to the Brahmans, 'Put aside all your doubts in your feelings. 115. Let us, *bhaktas* of Vishnu, you and all of us, hasten to the Chandrabhaga river, and I will accept whatever penance you may prescribe for Me.' 116. The Husband of Rukmini, who enjoys the drama of His own *līlā* (acts), the loved Ornament of His *bhaktas*, accomplished before His *bhaktas* marvellous deeds of *Maya*. 117. Then *Vanamali* (Krishna), taking Nama's hand and pressing it against His lotus-heart, hastened

to the Chandrabhaga river with a crowd following. 118. Men and women came there to see the marvellous deed. Indra and Brahmadev and the other gods stood by looking on. 119. The Holder of the disk (Krishna) with a crowd of saints walked in front of the procession, and the noble Brahmans hastened along in the rear. 120. In this way the Lord of the heaven *Vaikunth* arrived at the Chandrabhaga and made a *namaskar* to Pundalik, and the servants of Vishnu shouted aloud God's name. 121. Krishna then walked around the noble Brahmans and began the bathing prescribed in the scriptures. He whom the Husband of Mridani (Shiva) is unable to contemplate, He took in his hand *til* seed, the sacred *darbha* grass and flowers. 122. As the Brahmans repeated the *mantras* prescribed in the *Vedas*, He rubbed on Himself cowdung and ashes. Then the Life of the world, Wearer of the yellow robe, showed a wonder to His servants. 123. He let down His curled hair on His back. With very wide and lotus-eyes, the Lover of Rukmini, the One dear to His *bhaktas*, showed them a marvel. 124. This Life of the world, the Dweller upon the sea of milk, for whose sake many forms of austerities and postures in *yoga* are practised, He lovingly took the penance. 125. He whose name alone destroys faults and delivers His *bhaktas* from rebirths, the Giver of the promise to Pundalik, the Lord of the world, even He gladly took the penance. 126. One might search through the *Vedas* and *Shastras* and yet not understand His power—even to that blameless One it was that the Brahmans gave the penance. 127. He from whose big toe the holy Ganges started, Him they stood in the water and gave Him the penance. 128. He who is the Immoveable, the Changeless, the Eternal, the perfect One, the Pervader of the Universe, the Mass of Intelligence, they gave Him the penance of being rubbed over with cowdung and ashes. 129. The Dweller in *Vaikunth*, *Hrishikeshi* (the Lord of the heart), the Ornament of His *bhaktas*, ths Lord of the world, although blameless, was charged with sin and given penance. 130. After having properly bathed He clothed Himself with the yellow garment. He drank the water in which the Brahmans' feet were washed, and in love bowed His head to them. 131. The Lord of the world then worshipped His *bhaktas*, and having bathed and worshipped He thus finished the regular ceremonies. 132. After worshipping the Brahmans, he gave them gifts according to the prescribed rules, and then the Life of the world said to the Brahmans, 'You have now patronised Me. 133. I have accomplished your most cherished desire. From now on, never bring into your minds any doubtful thoughts regarding Me. 134. I have accomplished all you have asked Me to do. Now consider Me as yourselves.'* Listen to what the eagle-bannered One did after thus speaking.

KRISHNA RETURNS TO HIS TEMPLE

135. He gave the Brahmans leave to depart and Him-

---

*Three different readings are found in the *Bhaktavijaya*, Ch. XIV 134, as follows:—

(1) आतां अगत्यरूप माना मज. This is the reading in all printed editions, and would apper to be quite meaningless.

(2) आतां आत्मरूप माना मज. This reading is found in the Taharabadkar and Naik Mss. and is translated as 'Now consider Me as yourselves.'

(3) आतां अगत्यरूप नामा मज. This reading is adopted by Lakshman Babu Gokhale in the Induprakash Edition of 1888, and may be translated as ' Now Nama is the most essential thing to me.'

(4) आतां आत्मरूप नामा मज. This is a fourth possible reading and it is tempting to regard it as correct in accordance with the widely accepted principle in dealing with ancient documents, viz., the unusual reading is often the correct one. This reading would be translated, ' Now Nama is My own Self.'

self returned to His temple, accompanied by all the *bhaktas* who in joy shouted aloud His name. 136. Then Satyabhama, Radha and Rukmini brought different kinds of food, and served it before them. Krishna lovingly sat down in the assembly of His *bhaktas* to eat. 137. Just as the moon is glorious with all the clusters of stars around it, so the Husband of Rukmini in His joy sat down in the assembly of *Vaishnavas.* 138. In His love the Life of the world put morsels of food in the mouths of each one, and on His yellow robe in His affection caught whatever food fell from their mouths. 139. Having completed His love-feast, He gave to the *bhaktas* the *pansupari.* Then the Husband of Rukmini laid down on His bed of ease. 140. The *Vaishnavas* took leave of Him and went to their homes. With joy and love they worshipped Him in their heart.

NARAD VISITS KRISHNA

141. Just then Narad arrived in haste with a *brahmavina* in his hand. He was singing with his sweet voice in very delightful words. 142. The God-loving *bhakta* arrived singing of the pure and blessed name of God, then hastened to approach Pandurang, and bowed to Him. 143. The Husband of Rukmini suddenly saw Narad, the statue of indifference to earthly things, possesser of the joy of love. 144. Krishna lovingly gave him an embrace, and said to this son of Brahmadev, 'Your singing seems to Me beyond all comparison.' 145. Hearing Him say this, Narad was choked with emotion. Tears fell from his eyes. Then with joy he sang of Krishna's good deeds and name. 146. Victory to Thee, who gavest the promise to Pundalik, Helper of the helpless, Dweller on the banks of the Bhima, Husband of Rukmini, Ocean of mercy, overflowing with joy, Thou didst personally protect Thy *bhaktas.* 147. Victory to Thee, lotus-eyed *Shrirang* (Krishna), Ornament of Thy *bhaktas*, eternally unchangeable, O Saviour of the universe,

Pandurang, associated with what has no associate, and for ever the same. 148. Victory to Thee, Enjoyer of the sea of milk, Father of Brahmadev, King of the Heaven *Vaikunth*. Through repeating Thy name alone, Thou drivest away illusory thought from Thy *bhaktas*. 149. Victory, victory to Thee, Ocean of compassion, Lord of the earth. Thou dost stand upon the banks of the Bhima, and when pious *bhaktas* come to visit Thee, Thou dost protect them with Thy look of mercy.' 150. Narad sang His praises in this way, and then performed over the Husband of Rukmini the waving ceremony. Having finished this song of praise, he prostrated himself before Him. 151. The god then hung around Narad's neck a garland made of *champaka* flowers and the *tulsi*. The son of Brahmadev having worshipped God, departed.

RADHA PERPLEXED BY THE CHARGE AGAINST KRISHNA

152. Radha came to Rukmini and whispered to her, 'I am feeling exceedingly strange in my lotus-heart. 153. What fault has the Friend of the *bhaktas* committed today, that He had to take penance and purify Himself? 154. I have this doubt in my mind. Therefore I ask you. How can the Unmanifested One commit a fault as to what is duty and not duty? 155. The unusual has happened today, such as would be the confining of the sun in darkness, or of sinking the ocean in a pool of water, or of imprisoning the Ganges in a well, 156. or like the moon growing warm, or like the confining of the wind in a cage. How could Agasti tremble with fear seeing the ocean? 157. How could the sun be hidden by the light of the stars? How can nectar die with disease? 158. If all space could be confined in a jar, or a mountain make adamant tremble, then only could the Lord of the heart be in any bondage to duties, so I think. 159. If seed that had been roasted and then sown can grow luxuriously, then

only could the Lord of our life be entangled in the bondage of duties. 160. Tell me everything. Who has been troubling the dark-complexioned One? You are all knowing and my elder. Tell me, because I am ignorant.' 161. Rukmini replied, ' O noble One, the eagle-bannered One has put away all shame of lowering His greatness and has accepted the performance of penance for Nama's sake. 162. Listen, you intelligent One but ignorant of facts! This Krishna, Helper of the helpless, has been attracted through the *bhakti* rendered to Him and He cannot bear separation from Nama. 163. This *Sachchidananda* (Krishna) has become confused through His love for Nama, and so has accepted duties that are auspicious and non-auspicious. 164. Notice the power of affection. What will one not do through it? This is the universal experience. O mother, I will describe it to you. 165. A child might be blind, lame, dumb and of lisping speech, but its mother because of her love always has sympathy with it. 166. Crazy for her child through her love, she plays only with it. A child of another might be more beautiful, but she pays no attention to it. 167. She pays no attention to any malformation in her child, so she says to herself, ' Perhaps an evil eye will fall upon it.' So she takes that away (by waving her hands over it, and cracking her knuckles) and kisses it on the face. 168. Just so with love in his heart, the Holder of the disk (Krishna) cares for his *bhaktas*. He pays no respect to their caste or family. He loves them more than He does His own life. 169. This debt of love, through His love of body, mind and speech, has come down from the infinite rebirths of the past. 170. God loves him deeply. He has never been separated from Him. Keshav (God) has always held this love for His dearest Nama. ' 171. Hearing Rukmini say this, Radha was quite satisfied. In silence she bowed to her, and then went to her home.

NARAD VISITS SATYABHAMA

172. In the meantime, Narad arrived at the house of Satyabhama. The beautiful one paid him her respects and seated him on a couch of ease. 173. The wife of Shri Krishna (Satyabhama) said to him, 'I consider it very strange that the King of *Vaikunth* (heaven) should put aside His greatness and dance in the midst of the *kirtan*. 174. In what past birth did He become a debtor to Nama, so that now the One dark as a cloud carries out his many wishes? 175. Though His love for Pundalik, *Shrirany* (Krishna) stood on a brick. Twenty-eight ages have already passed since then, but He is not weary of it. 176. Although Pundalik made the Saviour of the world stand on the brick, He never turned his back on that position. The cruel one (Pundalik) does not even speak to Him, although the Saviour of the universe was made to suffer. 177. Although it was thus, the Holder of the *Sharang* bow (Krishna) stood upon the brick, and without giving thought to it, continued to protect the door of Bali. 178. Seeing their love for Him, He protected the Pandavas in many ways. He felt no shame in His heart while carrying out the purposes of His *bhaktas*. 179. Thus Madhav (Krishna) personally performed very marvellous deeds, and to fulfil the purposes of His *bhaktas* He wearied His own body, without any necessity for doing so. 180. There must be in this age on the surface of the earth a great number of His *bhaktas*. How can I give you the whole list of their names? 181. Therefore I feel much troubled in my mind that His *bhaktas*, exciting His love, weary Him through acts expressing it.'

SATYABHAMA'S DOUBT ABOUT KRISHNA DISPELLED

182. As Satyabhama thus spoke, Narad replied, 'Listen, O mother, to what I am going to tell you. You must regard it as true. 183. This Being without form, this Life

of the world, had as His only reason for becoming an *avatar*, the purpose of protecting His *bhaktas* through many forms of activities. And for this reason He came in bodily form. 184. It was as if the earth took form in order to bear the weight of things animate and inanimate; or it was as if the sun descended to give light to men; 185. or as if the internal digestive fire descended to burn and digest the food; or as if grass was made to grow for the purpose of removing the hunger of the cow; 186. or as if *Hrishikeshi* (the Lord of the heart) had created the space for birds to fly about in; or as if He had created the night in order to give mankind rest; 187. or as if divine jewels had been formed to provide the bodies of the beautiful ones with ornaments; or as if nectar had been created to save the life of those whose life has come to an end; 188. so *Adhokshaja* (the Pervader of earth and sky) became a Being with qualities that He might carry out the purpose of His *bhaktas*. In dropping His greatness He is not ashamed and he manifests His *līlā* (sports) with ease. 189. O you wise one, you know that this Helper of the helpless, Lover of the *bhaktas*, Ocean of compassion, Merciful to the lowly, this dark-complexioned One, preserves His reputation by so doing. 190. The Lord of the heart personally suffered births in Ambarishi's place and at the same time being indifferent to earthly things He guarded the door of Bali without feeling ashamed of doing so. 191. He became a slave, and with body, mind and speech this merciful Husband of yours protected the Pandavas. 192. Becoming the son of Nanda He protected the cows in Gokul, and taking the food left on the plates by the cowherds He tasted it in love. 193. Seeing a great danger approaching, He threw Himself into the midst of it and broke the bondage of His *bhaktas*. Such are His praiseworthy deeds. 194. All we His *bhaktas* are entirely portions of Him, but today He has become a complete *avatar* for

Nama's sake, in a visible form, with qualities.' 195. The *Muni* Narad, having explained these things to Satyabhama, quickly left.

KRISHNA'S SECRETS REVEALED TO RUKMINI

Just then Rukmini came to the bed on which the Holder of the disk (Krishna) was lying and worshipped Him. 196. With reverence she placed her head on His feet, and said to Him, 'O Lord of Pandhari, tell me what You like above everything else. 197. O Lover of His *bhaktas*, Lord of *Vaikunth* (heaven), remove this anxious doubt from me. Your mind is not where the eight forms of *yoga** are through which the *Yogis* obtain their salvation. 198. Where the *Yogi* sits in contemplation, there Your mind does not take pleasure. You have no love for *Vaikunth* (heaven). This I clearly recognize. 199. Your mind has no fondness for the happiness and enjoyments of heaven. Your mind is always depressed. Tell me why this is so. 200. In giving final deliverance to the *Yogis*, You have absorbed them into that which is without qualities, and I know of no one closer to You than they. 201. Your four-faced son (Brahmadev) worships You in His wise way. And the four *Vedas* and the eighteen *Puranas* describe Your attributes. 202. But unable to express them fully, they say, " It is not this. It is not that." The question is discussed in the six *Shastras*, but your incomparable reputation is unknown to them.' 203. Hearing Rukmini say this, the Lord of the heart said to her, ' You call yourself a wise

---

*The eightfold *yoga*:—1.यम = Restraint or government of the senses. 2. नियम = A religious observance. 3. आसन = Posture or attitude. 4. प्राणायाम = Breathing. 5. प्रत्याहार = Withdrawing or restraining the organs from the objects of sense. 6. धारणा = Suspending the breath, abstracting the mind, and restraining all natural wants. 7. ध्यान = Profound and abstract contemplation. 8. समाधि = Deep and devout meditation; restraining the senses and confining the mind to contemplation; abstracted or absorbed state.

woman, but you do not know the secret of My heart. 204. Now I will tell you the secret of My heart, that in body, speech and mind, dear Nama is for ever in My thoughts. 205. I tell you these secrets of My heart today. It is they whom I love, these pious, dear *bhaktas.* 206. I am the formless One, One without attributes, and yet for the purpose of My *bhaktas* I have come, assuming form and name. 207. My soul loves My *bhaktas.* My *bhaktas* are the resting-places of the wise. Know this that the *bhaktas* are the storehouse of My love. 208. Know well that My *bhaktas* are the ornaments of My good fortune. The *bhaktas* are the treasure–house of My goodness. I am always subject to them. 209. The *bhaktas* are My victory and praiseworthy deeds. They are My happiness. When I meet them they provide all the desires of My heart. 210. Know this, that I and My *bhaktas* will never be separated to the end of time. The *bhaktas* alone know the joy of worshipping Me. 211. I repeat the names of My *bhaktas.* I contemplate their form in My imagination and it is My pleasure from time to time to look to the joy of My *bhaktas.* 212. It is My *bhaktas* alone who are always thinking of My feet. It is they who sing of My good qualities, and worship Me with desireless minds. 213. If I give them the four chief earthly gifts, including the four forms of deliverance, they will not so much as touch them with their hands. The *bhaktas* never put on Me the burden of supplying their domestic wants. 214. I am the heart of My *bhaktas.* They are My nearest relatives. Considered from every side, My *bhaktas* seem more generous than I am. 215. Therefore, I Keshav (Krishna) have no desire to go away from being near to Nama's heart.' 216. While the Husband of Rukmini was saying this, the sun arose. What then happened further, listen with reverence, you wise *bhaktas.*

MANY LANGUAGES BUT ONE MEANING

217. This delightful story of *bhakti* without comparison has been related in this fourteenth chapter, just as in the eleventh section of the *Bhagwat* Shri Krishna spoke to Uddhava. 218. In that book the delightful chapter is the twenty-ninth. In it are poured out nothing but divine juices. So in this *Bhaktavijaya*, it is the fourteenth that does this. 219. You may say, 'Your verses are in Marathi, and you yet compare them with that supreme *Gita*.' But that is not truly so. Listen to my observation on this point. 220. In the *Tirthavali*, Shri Dnyaneshwar has spoken with his own lips. I have taken his words as my authority and described things as he does. 221. When you turn to the meanings of words, the Marathi and Sanskrit are considered by men as conveying the same sense, just as the cow has two names, *gautami* (Sanskrit) and *gaya* (Marathi) but she gives only one kind of milk. 222. You use two words in speaking of the ocean, *paycbdhi* and *sagar*, but there is no difference in their waters, therefore *pandits* must not speak of a Marathi book as being inferior.

223. In the next very delightful chapter the Holder of the disk (Krishna) will be the composer of the book. Mahipati having received His gift of assurance will always be without fear.

224. *Swasti* (Peace !) This book is the *Shri Bhaktavijaya*. As the Lord of the world listens to it He will be pleased. Listen, you God-loving pious *bhaktas*. This is the fourteenth very delightful chapter.

CHAPTER XV

NAMDEV'S LIFE

(Continued)

Obeisance to Shri Ganesh. Obeisance to Rukmini and Pandurang

BHAKTAVIJAYA IS FOR LOVERS OF SAINTS

1. Listen with reverence, you hearers. Today the Husband of Rukmini is especially pleased with you. Therefore He has made the stories of His *bhaktas* widely known and in detail over the whole of the earth. 2. When a cloud has rained for the sake of the *chatak* bird; or when the moon has arisen for the *chakor* bird; or as fishes rejoice when the ocean is stirred up for their sake; 3. or as the sandalwood descended in order to cool the body of good men; or as the sun arises to make the whole world happy; 4. or as if a limitless forest of *tulsi* should spring up in order to complete fully the worship of Vishuu; or as when the *bilva* tree grows up to make glad the Husband of Uma (Shiva); 5. or as when in the spring-time flowers appear in order to give pleasure to the nostrils; or as when a cloud rains upon the earth in order to make mankind happy; 6. or as when the Godavari river came down on the surface of the earth in order to wash away the sins of Gautam; or as if the nectar should appear in the ocean in order to satisfy the gods; 7. so, for you who listen with fondness, these stories of the saints have been composed. Listen with reverence, you pious folk, to a summary of the previous chapter. 8. The Holder of the *Sharang* bow (Krishna) had said to Rukmini, 'I intensely love all My *bhaktas*, but I always feel a limitless love for Nama more intense than for others.'

KRISHNA AND HIS *BHAKTAS* MEET

9. While the Holder of the disk (Krishna) was carrying on this conversation (with Rukmini) the sun

arose. Just then all the *bhaktas* arrived for worship. 10. They shouted aloud the names of Krishna, and with loud cries of 'Victory, victory', they prostrated themselves before Him. Just as the bee lovingly buzzes over the lotus flower; 11. or just as the little child, seeing its mother, comes to her; or just as when the doe sees her young, she cannot contain the joy in her heart; 12. or just as when a miser finds some hidden wealth, his mind rejoices in his love of it; so these *Vaishnavas* were made happy as they looked upon the form of this dark-complexioned One. 13. This form which they saw for their contemplation they fixed in their minds. By it they had waves of joy and tears flowed from their eyes 14. In trying to describe the experience of their joy, words fail the poets, and in order to illustrate it how can they find the words, though they should hunt all over the world? 15. No one can describe the characteristics of sugar, unless he has tasted of its sweetness, so it is by experience alone that the *Vaishnavas* know of the joy of fellowship with Vishnu. 16. *Vanamali* (Krishna) then embraced His *bhaktas* and drew them to His heart, and with reverence for them He protected all His *bhaktas* by His look of mercy. 17. And these *bhaktas* of His, as they looked upon His lotus-eyes and His cloud-dark complexion, enjoyed an incomparable happiness that cannot be expressed in words.

KRISHNA THINKS OF FEEDING BRAHHANS

18. Thus the God of gods in His generosity told Rukmini of His feelings, that with love and reverence He should invite the earth-gods (Brahmans) to a feast: 19. 'I went yesterday to the bank of the Chandrabhaga river, and there took penance. It was there that the thought came to Me of inviting the Brahmans to a feast. 20. The Brahmans who live in the sacred city and fulfil their religious duties, I wish to invite them all and bring

them here to My temple. 21. By merely looking at them, sin and affliction are burned up and all desires are fulfilled. They rain a very joy of soul. 22. Giving them delicious feast, I wish to take away all doubts from their minds, and showing them My four-armed form to perform marvellous deeds before them. 23. The influence of association with saints is very great, and the praise of it will greatly increase in the world.' Such was the Holder of the *Sharang* bow's (Krishna's) explanation to Rukmini in His love. 24. The Mother of the world assented: 'Why do you worry over the giving of the invitation to the Brahmans when all the *siddhis* (accomplishments personified) are favourable to you?' 25. The Lord of Pandhari smiled and then said to Nama. 'Listen to My words. It will be your duty to perform the marvel.'

KRISHNA AND NAMA CONVERSE

26. As the Life of the world said this, Nama replied, 'O Krishna, I alone know the secrets of Your heart.' 27. The Holder of the disk (Krishna) said to Nama, 'Embrace Me, dear friend, and from now on never go away from Me. 28. As I see your love, My mind is not too well satisfied. As I look at you with a full gaze, it is a comfort to My eye. 29. My mind is absorbed in you. This is a debt acquired during many rebirths. Therefore this bond of love cannot be broken. I Govinda, am filled with love. 30. I am not aware of what good deeds you have performed, what rites, austerities or religious ceremonies you have carried out, whether you have put your body to the saw, or visited sacred bathing places; 31. whether you have rejected all illusions, and held your mind in control. You have made Me, however, subject to you, and you hold Me in your heart. 32. Although I might search through the three worlds, I see nothing which I could give to you in return. 33. Dear *bhakta*,

you have made a sacrifice of your body and mind and have done many unselfish acts for Me. 34. I *Shrirang*, call Myself your slave, but you have no need of anything.' 35. Nama replied, 'Thou art the Helper of the helpless, the Advocate of Thy *bhaktas*, therefore, O God, it is Thy good pleasure to bestow Thy love upon me.'

KRISHNA CONFORMS TO CEREMONIAL RITES

36. Then the lover of His *bhaktas*, *Hrishikeshi* (the Lord of the heart), with His own mind free from fear, took His *bhaktas* with Him and started to give the invitations. 37. This object of contemplation by the *Yogis*, the object of worship for all gods, arrived at the *kundal* bathing pool. 38. All the earth-gods (Brahmans) had assembled there, great and small. They said among themselves, 'Our host does not come quickly to see us. 39. When taking the penance yesterday, he promised to give the Brahmans a feast, but even the invitation has not yet arrived.' 40. Just then *Vanamali* (Krishna), along with the assembly of *bhaktas*, arrived, and seeing the Brahmans with His lotus-eyes, He prostrated Himself on the ground before them. 41. The Life of the world said to them, 'Discarding all doubts and without hesitation you must come to the feast. 42. You gave Me your assurance that I should not fear. You must fulfil My wish. Complete your bathing and devotions and quickly come.' 43. Hearing this kindly worded invitation, the Brahmans were pleased. Listen now with reverence to the reply they made: 44. 'Regarding it as perfectly true that we live under Thy protection, in living in this sacred city we give Thee our blessings. 45. Thou art always protecting cows and Brahmans. Every one speaks of Thee that Thou, O *Swami*, art merciful to the lowly. 46. Thou art King of kings; we Brahmans are Thy priests, and with Thy look of mercy Thou constantly carest for us. 47. In describing with Thy lips Thy rever-

ence for us, we can truly make no comparison. It is Thy good pleasure always to show respect for the commands of the *Vedas.* 48. Thou, O God, in all good faith, must keep Thy promise. Thou must grant love to Nama's mind through Thy favour.' 49. Hearing this, the Brother of the helpless, the Root of every life, the Ocean of happiness for all His *bhaktas*, the Joy of *Yogis*, 50. with a mind overflowing with joy, quickly returned to His temple, and with exceeding love told Rukmini of all that happened. 51. 'This day is a blessed one, a golden day has arisen. I have therefore arranged it as a festival to My *bhaktas*, which will truly be without comparison.'

BRAHMANS FEASTED BY KRISHNA

52. The Life of the world said to Rukmini, 'I have invited all the Brahmans. As soon as they perform their bathings and devotions, they will come quickly to the feast. 53. Today's novel and incomparable marvel is the glorification of humility.' Thus speaking, the God of gods smiled. 54. *Hrishikeshi* (the Lord of the heart) said to Rukmini, 'Their good deeds have come to their fruitage. Therefore without effort on their part you will be seen by the noble Brahmans.' 55. The noble Brahmans, having completed their regular ceremonial duties, came to the temple. The Holder of the *Sharang* bow (Krishna) made them a *namaskar* and gave them seats. 56. Then Krishna took the lead in worshipping the Brahmans. With His own hands He washed their feet and bowed His head to the water in which their feet were washed. 57. The dark-complexioned One lovingly gave the Brahmans sandalwood paste and the black paste, the garlands of flowers, incense and lights, the fragrant black powder, the *tulsi* and many kinds of perfumes. 58. *Shrirang* (Krishna) having put plates before them, served

them with solid and liquid foods. Taking water, He made the offering of food to God. 59. He gave to the noble Brahmans water to sip and then praying to them, the Dweller in *Vaikuntha* (Heaven) said to them, 'As you eat, remember Govinda (God) at every morsel. 60. He who remembers God with every morsel that he takes into his mouth, although he has dined yet he will be regarded as having fasted.' So said the Husband of Rukmini to the Brahmans. 61. All the Brahmans were full of joy and all were satisfied. Water to wash their hands and the *pansupari* were given to all by Krishna. 62. Then *Shripati* (Krishna) waved over the Brahmans lights in a platter inlaid with jewels as they sat in lines on their own seats. 63. The Holder of the *Sharang* bow (Krishna) then joined both His hands together and said to them, 'The event of today will never occur again. 64. Through the millions of good deeds belonging to My credit I have met you here today, and the universe is filled with supreme joy.' Thus spoke the Lord of the world. 65. 'Now I Myself and the saints will sit down in one line and eat. Put your minds at rest, and sit quietly for a moment.' 66. Thus speaking, the Performer of the marvellous deeds called to Him the assembly of the *bhaktas*, and the Brahmans saw at that time a remarkable wonder. 67. Brahmadev and other gods sitting in their chariots of light, and Indra with many other gods, also arrived. 68. The *Yogis* were disturbed in their minds saying, 'We have not the joy of *bhakti* which the Husband of Rukmini, pleased with Nama, has given him with love.'

KRISHNA WORSHIPS HIS *BHAKTAS*

69. The Holder of the *Sharang* bow (Krishna) then invited to His own line Nivritti, Dnyaneshwar, Sopan, the great *bhakta* Savata, Jagmitra who was (Krishna's) very dear friend, 70. the great *bhaktas* Asand, and Sudama, the

God-loving *Vaishnav* Visoba Khechar, also Savata and Narahari the goldsmith, all of whom came to the feast; 71. Chokhamela and Vanka and Janaka who is as dear to Him as His life, and for whom the Lord of the Yadhavas had never-ending love. 72. Then there was the potter Gora, who was a veritable Mount Meru of indifference to every form of earthly things, whom the Holder of the *Sharang* bow (Krishna) used to call His dearest child. 73. So the Lord of the *bhaktas*, having invited all of them, great and small, worshipped them in His love. 74. He who is the Life of the world, superior to everything, even He worshipped His *bhaktas*. Nama was amazed at this and lovingly questioned Him: 75. 'O God, my mind feels surprised at this. It is as if the ocean worshipped the river; or as if the moon circumambulated the stars; 76. or as if the Eagle (Vishnu's vehicle) should sit down to worship other birds; or as if the Husband of Parvati (Shiva) should pray to the *Nandi* (the bull, Shiva's vehicle); 77. or as if a king should worship his subjects; or as if Indra should pray to the gods; in that very same way, Thou, O Life of the world, dost pay respect to Thy servants.' 78. The Husband of Rukmini smiled and said, ' It is you who have ascribed greatness to Me. If rivers were not created, how would the ocean have grown to its present size ? 79. If there were no stars around the moon it would not have its present beauty. If the birds had not been created, no one would have called the Eagle the noblest of birds. 80. If *Nandi* had not been created, who would have been Shiva's vehicle ? If there had not been three hundred and thirty million gods, from whom would Indra have received reverence ? 81. It is the subjects who make the king great. So it is you who have given Me My name and form.' Hearing Him say this, the hearts of His *bhaktas* were overcome with amazement.

KRISHNA DINES WITH HIS *BHAKTAS*

82. Just then Satyabhama, Rahi and Rukmini brought many kinds of food and served it before them. You may ask in what way Krishna shone in the midst of His *bhaktas*. 83. It was like the ocean of milk in the midst of the seven oceans, or as the moon among the stars, or as the *Kaustubh* jewel stands chief in all ornaments; so He was effulgent through His own form and brilliance. 84. Just as gold among the eight chief metals, or as a jewel in the midst of a lime heap, so the Life of the world appeared in the assembly of His *bhaktas*, glorious in His six great characteristics [see ch. 13 verse 88, p. 211]. 85. The Husband of Rukmini put morsels of food into the mouths of all, and whatever fragments of food fell from their mouths He caught them on His robe. 86. As Brahmadev saw that happiness He licked His chops and said, The Lord of the world is pleased with Nama and does not even look at us.' 87. In this friendly way the feast was soon over, and all the saints were satisfied with the divine juices. 88. The gods then sitting in their chariots of lights shouted 'Victory, victory' in their joy, and rained down an abundance of flowers.

BRAHMANS CONVERSE ABOUT KRISHNA

89. The whole sky was unable to contain their perfume. The Brahmans were astonished and said, 'Injury to life (from the abundance of perfume) seems to have come. 90. Extraordinary enthusiasm has arisen. This is not the way of knowledge. This is not an evil indifference to earthly things. It is the goodness of *bhakti* that has taken form.' 91. One of them said to the other, 'What you say is true. This is truly Pandurang Himself. How can a human being possess great and seemingly impossible good fortune? 92. He is absolutely free from the three qualities. He is free from actions. How

can He be given penance? 93. An outcaste and a Brahman both bathe in the Ganges, but one must never say that the Ganges has been defiled thereby. 94. There are various castes in the world and they have voluntary relations with one another. They have no division of inferior and superior. The Holder of the *Sharang* bow (Krishna) is like that. 95. He is like the sun when it arises. It gives equal light to all. So this Life of the world is the same. 96. When the rain falls upon the earth, the land and the mountains are the same to it; just so, this noble Yadav is alike to all creatures. 97. So this Holder of the *Sharang* bow (Krishna) in His quality-less form has no recognition of "mine" and "thine." He has no thought whatever of caste or family. 98. When considering His relation to the six enemies of the soul [lust, anger, covetousness, affection, pride, envy], they never apply to Him. Even the very words "Wrong thinking" have no relation to Him. 99. In body, mind and speech He is the dearest relative of the lowly. With His generous mind He loves His *bhaktas* without limit. 100. If anyone follows Him He breaks his net of illusions, and he does not allow His God-loving *bhaktas* to get entangled in the net of worldly affairs. 101. The mother of Nama in our very presence entered into much discussion and became greatly troubled in her mind. 102. The *Hrishikeshi* (Lord of the heart), the Performer of wonders, held Nama to His heart and embraced him. 103. As one looks upon His beautiful form, one forgets one's own body. As one remembers His feet, the mind becomes fully absorbed in Him. 104. He who goes to Him as a suppliant with an undivided heart, has his rebirths ended.' The Life of the world, hearing these words of noble Brahmans, smiled.

GOD IN HIS *SAGUN* FORM

105. Then He changed His form from that of a

citizen, and showed the form in which His attributes are manifested. He gave Nama an embrace and lovingly held him to His heart. 106. *Hrishikeshi* (the Lord of the heart) gave the Brahmans His blessing and showed them also His true form. Even Sharada (the goddess of learning) finds it impossible to describe the beauty of that form. 107. The noble Brahmans looked upon Him with a crown of jewels on His head, with a mark of the musk-paste on His forehead, dark-complexioned, and beautiful to look at. 108. He wore a head-dress of peacock feathers, and beautiful earrings shaped like crocodiles hung from His ears. This Husband of Rukmini looked with compassion on all His saints. 109. He who having seen the abundance of Pundalik's good deeds, took a *sagun* form. This Enjoyer of the ocean of milk, this Dweller in the heaven *Vaikunth*, God supreme, 110. His pure face was smiling. His teeth sent forth a lustre like that of jewels. This dark-complexioned Form gives peace to the eyes of those who look at it. 111. The God-loving *bhaktas* alone have authority to possess that joy. As they bring into their imagination the Lord of the Yadus, they acquire many forms of joyous love. 112. This Merciful to the lowly wore the *Kaustubh* jewel and the *Vaijayanti* garland. 113. On His breast was the *Shri Vatsa* mark which was his ornament of love. His dark-skinned body had been rubbed over with sandalwood paste. His lotus-eyes were beautiful. 114. He had in His hand the conch-shell and the disk. His hands were placed on His hips. His dark-complexioned body was clothed in a yellow robe. It is this appearance which rests in the hearts of His *bhaktas*. 115. Shri Hari along with His wife Lakshmi had His feet placed parallel on the bricket. The limitless number of foot-ornaments were, so to speak, so many demons (named *daityas* and *danavas*). 116. When this divine light manifested itself, it lighted up the whole universe. Even the sun, seeing that light hid itself. 117. The saints and all the Brahmans quietly stood and looked upon that four-armed *sagun* form.

KRISHNA IN HIS UNIVERSAL FORM

118. The noble twice-born (Brahmans) looked about and saw birds, insects, animals, men, rocks and trees, and all seemed to them in the form of Vitthal. 119. As the Brahmans looked on water, light, the heavens, the earth, the air, in all these five elements they saw the form of Vitthal. 120. The many kinds of animal life, the sun, the moon, all the stars, the many and wonderful deities, all appeared in the form of Vitthal. 121. The hall of assembly, the slab before the god, the door-keepers, Jaya and Vijaya, the pillar with the Eagle, and the great door of the temple, all these appeared in the form of Vitthal. 122. The Eagle-banners, the dome of the temple, the cymbals, the drums, the shouting aloud of God's name, the steps, and the pilgrims' outhouses, appeared in the form of Vitthal to the noble Brahmans. 123. As they brought to their minds the three *gunas* : *raja, tama, satva* [life, intelligence and mind], they all appeared in the form of Vitthal. 124. It was as if a single seed of the banyan tree was sown, and then taking root it spread out into an infinite number of forms, just as the light of the sun alone spreads over the whole of the earth; 125. and just as there is water in every juice ; and just as there is but one air that pervades the universe; or as in all living bodies the digestive fire fills them. 126. There are infinite numbers of eyes, but sight is one; one tune, but many notes; the mind pervades the ten organs of sense as it appears to one's sight; 127. likewise the one Being, the Husband of Rukmini, appeared in many forms. And as the noble twice-born (Brahmans) looked at Him, they were overwhelmed with astonishment. 128. The Life of the world took the form of the universe. Who else can be

found out to give an illustration of this except Krishna, the Lover of the heart who was encircled by the *Gopis*? 129. When they came (to complain) to Yashoda, they saw Krishna in an infinite number of forms. Just so the Brahmans saw Him in the form of the universe. 130. The Lord Keshav (Krishna) alone pervaded the universe and no other was to be seen They naturally lost the consciousness of body, and any shame of being so left them. 131. The knowledge of supreme joy manifested itself. Every one felt the joy. The whole idea of duality was put aside, and every one had his heart filled with gladness. 132. Looking from outside, He pervaded the three worlds. But looking into the heart, the form of Shri Krishna had hidden itself there.

BHAKTI ALL-POWERFUL

The Brahmans looked with love at Him who is the *Yogi's* happiness and rest. 133. With feelings of love the saints and good men embraced one another. They were full of love and shouted out 'Victory, victory.' 134 Every one, seeing this limitless joy and rest, became absorbed in it. *Shripati* (Krishna) made His servants experience the divine joy in His love for them 135. The Life of the world brought to consciousness those twice-born (Brahmans) who had lost consciousness of body. He raised Nama up and placed him at their feet 136. This Lover of His *bhaktas*, this Lord of the world, looked with compassion on every one. And sitting closer to the Brahmans, He whispered to them His secret thoughts. 137. *Keshavraj* (Krishna) said to the Brahmans, 'Listen to the secrets of My heart. My *bhaktas* have put aside their earthly concerns and have followed Me. 138. Becoming their debtor through their service rendered Me, I am fully bound to them. Being subject to My *bhaktas*, I have no independence of My own. 139. Nivritti, Dnyandev and Sopan worship Me in every creature. Paying very little regard to their bodies, they have made Me subject to them. 140. This *Jagamitra* (Friend of the world) here, giving up all worldly things, has become my supreme friend. Hiding Me in the temple of his heart, the consciousness of body does not come any more to him. 141. This servant of mine, Savata, the gardener, putting his faith in My worship, in his love sees Me alone in every creature. 142. When this Vasara, was twelve days old his mother threw him in *Venunad*, and the child realizing the non–iduality of his nature began to worship Me. 143. These My *bhaktas*, Visoba Khechar, the goldsmith Narahari and Gora the potter, have worshipped Me without interruption. 144. Leaving home, wife and everything else, each has torn away from him the net of illusions. And so this God–loving bhakta, Sudama, is the object of my compassion. 145. Chokhamela, Vanka and Janaka, are My loving *bhaktas*. They have no close friends aside from Me. 146. They have put aside every other association, and with a feeling of unity with Me have followed Me. Aside from Me, they have no love for any other deity. 147. To what extent can I recount the kindness of each one?' Thus remarked the Holder of the *Sharang* bow (Krishna) to the Brahmans in describing the joy of His love.

BRAHMANS REPENT

148. The twice-born (Brahmans), hearing that the God-loving and chief of all *bhaktas*, Nama, was the dust of the feet of all the *bhaktas*, were astonished. 149. They, a full ocean of good fortune, said very sweetly, 'O Vitthal, Thou hast become our real mother-home. 150. And now O Lord of Pandhari, we have only this to ask of Thee, that Thou break from us the desire of earthly things, and so help us, that we may never be separated from Thy feet. 151. We

do not need any earthly enjoyments or the different forms of final deliverance. We want neither money nor property, but give us, O *Shripati* (Krishna), association with the good during all our re-births. 152. Even while studying the *Vedas* and *Shastras,* our minds have turned to the objects of sense, and pride has unsteadied our hearts. 153. Should one not understand Thy secret of love, down, down with such knowledge. If it were not for Thy mercy, public honour deserves to be set on fire. 154. We are Brahmans of the highest caste. We have been seized by that illusion. Thereby we have been separated from the sweetness of Thy love. The bondage of pride is very great. 155. O Lord of Pandhari, all this illusion is of Thy creation which has deceived us. We have needlessly been swept along by it, but now, O Lord God, Thou hast delivered us. 156. We have committed very many millions of transgressions, but Thou, O Lord of Pandhari, merciful One, hast become our Protector. 157. Thou hast been called the Helper of the lowly, and Thou hast made true that reputation today. Thou hast given us a sight of Thyself, and hast saved us sinners. 158. Because of our good deeds stored in our numberless rebirths, Thou hast given this sight of Thyself, and has spoken to us in Thy love. 159. These accumulated seeds of deeds were sown, and on them was sprinkled the water of association with saints, so that now, O Lord God, these seeds have grown to maturity, and have produced an infinite number of fruits. 160. Thou hast torn the exceedingly strong net of seduction and made us conform to Thy beautiful essential form. In attempting to describe Thy *lila* (sports) the *Vedas* and *Shastras* have found it beyond their power. 161. The three forms of affliction were burning us up like a forest fire, but Thou didst quickly put it out. O *Swami,* Thou didst forcibly feed us needy ones with the nectar of Thy love. 162. Now, O Lord of the world, we have only this to ask of Thee, that we may always see Thy form as it is now, and that we may constantly meet with the saints. It is this desire that we hold in our hearts. 163. May Thy love be continually in our hearts. May we love to worship Thee, then we shall never grow weary of our rebirths. 164. Thou alone, Lord of the infinite universe, art the Doer, and the One who causes others to act. The *Vedas* and *Shastras* wearied themselves in describing properly Thy goodness. 165. So now, O *Hrishikeshi* (the Lord of the Heart), do not keep in mind our faults. Call us Thy own, and give us into the care of the saints, O merciful One. 166. May we become the servants of Thy servants. We have no other wish in our hearts. So make it that the dust of their feet shall rest upon us. 167. This in itself will take the place of our austerities, religious ceremonies and deeds. May we love Thy worship and repeat Thy names with affection.'

BHAKTI THE SUPREME SECRET

168. Hearing this reply of the twice-born (Brahmans), the Holder of the *Sharang* bow (Krishna) was pleased. He showed His limitless compassion and embraced all of them. 169. After embracing the Brahmans, the Dweller in *Vaikunth* (heaven) said, 'Whatever Dnyandev may tell you, keep his thoughts in your mind. 170. This Dnyandev is My very soul, O chief of all knowing ones. Whatever he may tell you of the experience of his heart, hold to it with reverence. 171. If you trust to him, those thoughts will naturally be easier for you. So, hold tightly in your heart what he tells you, and carefully preserve it. 172. If that knowledge is kept close to you, you will not have to wander to sacred bathing places; you will never have to study the *Vedas* and *Shastras*. 173. You will not need the austerities of the *Yogis*. You will not have to torture your body, if you

pin your faith on association with saints. Your faults will be destroyed in a moment. 174. You will not have to sit on iron spikes. Such efforts are in vain. You will not have to live in the caves of the mountains. 175. Why perform cruel austerities? The repeating of *mantras* is not at all necessary. Through association with the saints the three forms of affliction will all disappear in a moment. 176. You will not have to cover your body with ashes. You will not have to grow long matted hair. You will never have to act as hypocrites before men. 177. One should be filled with kindness towards all creatures. One's tongue should have the nectar of God's name; in less than a moment's time the mind will come back to its true state. 178. One may make the effort of performing one's duties, but without love in one's heart one becomes disgusted with them. This is not the way to the knowledge of the soul. That is a needless effort for those who cling to the old way. 179. This is a very easy way, without having to use the various means. Praise God with love and repeat 'Ram, Krishna, Govinda.' 180. What are sacred bathing places, religious rites and severe austerities? Poor things compared with the singing of God's praise. Putting aside their pride of greatness, all of them have to hide their heads in shame. 181. This well-known and royal road is superior to all. One should therefore, without ceasing, hold to the association with saints and keep the name of God on his lips. 182. Do not let a course of wrong thinking come into your minds. With all your heart and reverence go as suppliants to the saints.' 183. Thus the Lord of the earth whispered His secret to the Brahmans. The Brahmans assented, and worshipped the feet of God. 184. The Husband of Rukmini said to Dnyandev, 'I have left these twice-born (Brahmans) in your care. Place your hands upon their heads, and give them the everlasting blessing.' 185. Dnyaneshwar replied, 'I will do so,' and in reverence he bowed to the Husband of Rukmini. I am truthfully telling you of the experience which the chief of *rishis* possessed.

NAMDEV'S LIFE THE CREAM OF *BHAKTI*

186. This supreme secret should be considered as the secret knowledge of the *Vedas*, the life of indifference to earthly things, and as the characteristic of the sphere of intelligence. 187. It is the mystic power of pure knowledge, the seed of final deliverance, the king of all *mantras*. the treasure-house of joy manifested in the world. 188. Nama's extraordinary love was for a time hidden in his heart, but his story has made it known world-wide. 189. This story of Nama's is the height of hearing the highest contemplation for the mind, and the loved object of meditation. 190. It is the summing up of thought, the centre of one's intelligence, the revelation of one's essence to the world. 191. It is the marvellous doing of *bhakti*, the soul of reverence, the glorification of honour manifested in the world. 192. It is the noble light of victory, it is life beyond the beyond, the extending of God's praise coming to stand before us. 193. It is the life of all religious duties, it is the purifier of the pure, or the storehouse of joy. 194. It is the nectar of *yoga* accomplishment, the joy of *bhaktas* and the full life of desirelessness. 195. It is the festival of God and His *bhaktas*. It is nectar brought to its perfection. He who will drink of it with fondness will without effort go to everlasting life. 196. Those who listen to this story of the *Tirthavali* [Nama's wanderings to sacred bathing places] will not have to be born again. Therefore, you should listen to its description. 197. One must not speak of it as a common story. It is not memorized poetry. In it the substance of the *Upanishads* and the manifestation of the divine sweetness appear. 198. Here is not the place where that knowledge is to be recognized which none should claim for themselves. One should

leave the desire for pedantry and listen with reverence. 199. This is the method adopted by the good. The enjoyers of it are the saints. Such is the substance of the words Dnyandev has written in the *Tirthavali.* 200. Bringing his verses to my mind, I have written in my own uncouth way; so the wise should not find fault with it.

201. In the next chapter there will be the exceeding delightful and significant story of the life of Kurmadas. Listeners must keep their minds in a quiet state and listen with attention. 202. The Pervader of the universe, the Husband of Rukmini, the Life of the world, is the One who relates the story and the One who causes it to be related. This holy book the *Bhaktavijaya* is being composed at His desire. 203. When oil and a wick are placed in a lamp, a brilliant light appears; so the eagle-bannered One, giving light to the mind causes this book to be composed by His love. 204. He who is the Purifier of the sinner, the Helper of the helpless, He has saved an innumerable number of the dull-minded. Mahipati is His stamp and he worships Him with love.

205. *Swasti* (Peace !) This book is the *Shri Bhaktavijaya.* In listening to it the Lord of the earth is pleased. Listen, you God-loving, pious *bhaktas.* This is the fifteenth deeply delightful chapter; it is an offering to Shri Krishna.

CHAPTER XVI

KURMADAS THE CRIPPLE

Obeisance to Shri Ganesh. Obeisance to Shri Krishna.

STORIES OF *BHAKTAS* THE CREAM OF GOOD DEEDS

1. Today is a happy day of blessing. For if anyone reads the love-inspiring stories of God's *bhaktas* he reaps without special effort the blessing which can be had by visiting the sacred bathing places and by observing the festival days. 2. That is equal to three hundred and sixty performances of ceremonial rites, according to the prescribed rules; or as if one hundred horse-sacrifices had been made with hearts free from desires and full of devotion; 3. or as if many rigorous austerities had been performed; or as if all the deities had been prayed to; or as if in time of famine gifts of food had been made without effort on their part to the hungry; 4. or as if one had adopted the life of a *sannyasi* according to the prescribed rules; or as if one had given water to drink to those suffering from thirst; or as if one had given full service with an abundance of love to one's mother and father. 5. All the good deeds mentioned above have been received today by hearers of the stories of God's *bhaktas* without effort on their part, and *Hrishikeshi* (the Lord of the Heart) being pleased thereby gives them eternal life. 6. Therefore all wise men must give their attention to me and in their love wag [or nod] their heads; just as serpents do when they hear the piping of the juggler; 7. or as when a deer absorbed in listening to a song, forgets all thought of its body; thus the Life of the world is Himself pleased in listening to the stories of the *bhaktas*.

KURMADAS LONGS FOR PANDHARI

8. There was a Brahman by name of Kurmadas, a man of supreme piety. He had neither hands nor feet.

He lived at Pratishthan (Paithan). 9. He was the *avatar* of the charioteer of the sun, who in order to worship Hari became a full *avatar* in a Brahman family. 10. He was born without hands or feet. Gradually he grew up to manhood. One day hearing the *kirtan* he hastened there to listen. 11. Hearing there the cymbals, the *vina* and the drum giving out their music, the *Vaishnavas* singing with love, his own heart had great feeling of great joy and he sat down with love to listen. 12. The *Haridas* (preacher) was describing in his love the delightful glory of Pandhari, and as Kurmadas listened his mind was filled with happiness. 13. Then joining together both hands he spoke sweetly to the singers, 'If I should go to Shri Pandhari, I should see the Husband of Rukmini.' 14. Hearing him say this all the people began to laugh. 'You have neither hands nor feet. We cannot understand how you could go. 15. If a bird has no wings, how can it fly through the air? If a man has no eyes, how can he climb a mountain? 16. If a man cannot hear, how can he perform a *Hari-kirtan*? If one's voice becomes hoarse, how can he sing? 17. If one possesses no money, those who beg of him cannot be made happy. If one has not acquired knowledge, how can he receive the respect of men? 18. If the mind is not under self-control, how can it perform the *yogic* practices? If one does not have the entire favour of his *sadguru*, he cannot attain self-knowledge. 19. So, you have no hands nor feet, and yet you talk of going to Pandhari. Hearing you say this, our minds become somewhat perplexed. 20. We had sufficient wealth, our bodies were in good health, and yet we have never been on pilgrimage even up to our old age. 21. And yet you have conceived this desire, which we do not feel confident you can carry out. How will you be able to go? As you have no hands or feet we do not understand.' 22. Kurmadas replied to them, 'Without any effort on my part I have obtained this human body. Now if I do not go to Pandhari, I cannot escape the eighty-four million rebirths.'

KURMADAS CRAWLS FOR FOUR MONTHS TO PANDHARI

23. Therefore with a penitent mind, he at once set off and crept along for two miles beyond his village. 24. He went first into the temple of Maruti and there lodged for the night. He became very hungry and thirsty and his mind was full of concern. 25. He then prayed, 'O Lord of Pandhari, Husband of Rukmini, care for me, the helpless one. Aside from Thee, I can see no one to be a brother or uncle, a mother or father. 26. Thou art the life of my heart. Who can provide for me in my hunger and thirst ?' Hearing the pitiful cry of Kurmadas, the Life of the world approached him. 27. The Lord of Pandhari in the form of a merchant suddenly approached him. The Lord of *Vaikunth* (heaven) then spoke to Kurmadas. 28. 'You have neither hands nor feet. Where are you journeying to ? Tell me what your name is.' 29. Kurmadas replied, 'I have the desire to go to Pandhari. You ask me my name. It is Kurmadas.' 30. Hearing this, Shripati (Krishna) was highly pleased and said, 'Without any effort on your part your good fortune has brought me into your company.' 31. Kurmadas replied, 'I am without hands and feet, how can my company be of any use to You ? 32. Tell me where You are going. And tell me Your name.' Hearing him say this, the Lover of the heart replied, 33. 'The whole world speaks of Me as the merchant Vithoba. My shop is at Pandhari, and I must go there.' 34. Kurmadas said to him, 'You will be able to go rapidly. I cannot quite understand how I can keep in company with You.' 35. The Holder of the *Sharang* bow (Krishna) said to him, 'We are going slowly. We do business on the way in buying and selling. 36. After going a mile or two, we

lodge quietly for the night. I will not allow myself to be separated from your company.' 37. At this reply of the Holder of the disk (Krishna), Kurmadas was made very happy. Preparing the evening meal, He (the merchant) gave him to eat. 38. The lotus--eyed One gave Kurmadas a garment to wear and said, 'Holy *bhaktas* live in the sacred city of Pandhari.' 39. During the night the Lord of the universe whispered His secret thoughts to Kurmadas: 'You have become tired by walking a long way and you cannot start at once. 40. Wherever you go tomorrow, we also shall come there. Do not be at all troubled about food and drink. 41. We wander about for this very reason, to remove the weariness of the helpless and lowly who are going on pilgrimage, and to enquire regarding their hunger and thirst.' 42. Thus replied the Husband of Rukmini. The sun now arose. He lovingly awakened Kurmadas and said to him, 43. 'I will point out to you the path. Hasten your going. We shall certainly come to your lodgings at eventide.' 44. The Husband of Rukmini having said this, He suddenly became invisible and Kurmadas started on his way. 45. Kurmadas crept along until sunset, and having come near a village he waited there for the Brahman. 46. Quickly the cloud-dark complexioned One arrived and began to care for him as usual. In this way the Merciful to the lowly cared for him. 47. If there was no town near by, He created a new village. God would not allow His *bhakta* to become weary. 48. In this way Kurmadas crept along for four months. Finally in the month of *Kartik* (November) he arrived at Lahul. 49. It was on the tenth of *Kartik* and the pilgrims were going on to Pandhari. Kurmadas seeing this band of pilgrims, he was greatly troubled in his mind. 50. 'I shall not be able to arrive in time for the festival on account of my being without hands and feet. He who is the Merciful to the lowly is now lost to me.

51. Tomorrow is *ekadashi* (the eleventh of the month). The *Vaishnavas* will move along rapidly. I am lame and am alone in this foreign land. 52. Had I but hands and feet, I would have gone along with this pilgrim band.' Such was the deep anxiety of his mind. 53. A lame man cannot walk along with those who are able to walk quickly. A miser is never able to give with the lavishness of one who is generous. 54. How can a sick man eat with the same appetite as a hungry man? How can the moon equal the sun in brilliance? 55. How can any other metal equal gold in value? How can badly cooked food seem to the taste like daintily prepared food? 56. The ordinary animal cannot possess the glory of the wishcow. How can an ordinary tree equal the wish-tree?

KURMADAS SENDS A MESSAGE BY PILGRIMS

57. It was because Kurmadas was unable to walk along with the same rapidity as the band of pilgrims that his mind became troubled. 58. Thinking over the matter he decided to send a message. 'Tell the Husband of Rukmini that I send to Him my reverential *namaskar*. 59. I am a lowly, helpless man without a protector. I am without hands and feet. I see no possibility whatever of seeing You on the eleventh. 60. From Lahul, Pandhari is fourteen miles. I shall have to travel seven days in order to reach Pandhari. 61. O Lord of the world, protect me by Thy look of compassion. My heart is indeed troubled that I cannot meet Thee (on the eleventh). 62. Just as the *chatak* bird wishes for a cloud, or just as the *chakor* bird looks towards the moon, so I without ceasing look to meet Thee. 63. Just as the calf seeks for the mother cow, and just as the little fledging looks towards the mother bird; so I, Kurmadas, am thinking of Thee in my heart. 64. I have not the support of a family or of any wealth. Aside from Thee, I have no one, O Vitthal. I see no wealth of money or

property except in Thee. 65. O Holder of the *Sharang* bow (Krishna), Thou callest Thyself the Helper of the helpless; O Sea of compassion, come as far as this and save Thy lowly one.' 66. So he sent a piteous message, requesting the band of pilgrims to convey it to the Holder of the *Sharang* bow (Krishna) and to send Him back there as soon as possible. 67. The *Warkaris* [pilgrims of a special order] replied that they would carry the message, and started to walk along rapidly to Pandhari. As they walked they shouted aloud the names of Vitthal.

NAMDEV'S *KIRTAN* AT PANDHARI

68. At that time Namdev happened to be performing a *kirtan* at the great door of Pandhari. With cymbals in his hand and love in his heart and accompanied by a band of singers he danced and shouted aloud in his joy. 69. Using the beloved names of Ram and Krishna, and becoming unconscious in body, he sang of the goodness of Shri Hari. 70. He laid aside every thought of pride and holding his ears he danced. He kept in his heart the appearance of the image of Vitthal. 71. Lovingly he brought to his mind the noble qualities of Shri Hari, His birth, His name and His deeds, and sang them in joy. 72. He who is naturally the resting-place of His *bhaktas*, He who is the secret of the wise and the root of final deliverance, and who is called the Giver of deliverance; 73. Krishna, the cloud-dark complexioned One, Mukunda, Murari, the good Being, Achyuta, Narahari, the cloud-dark complexioned One, O victorious Ram, O Raghupati. 74. Victory, victory to Thee, Saviour of Mount Govardhan, Victory, victory, to Thee who takest compassion upon the *bhaktas*, Saviour of the lowly, Pandurang. 75. Victory, victory to Thee who hast in Thy hand the giving of every blessing, Breaker of the bonds of sin, O *Hrishikeshi* (Lord of the heart), Lord of the gods, Lord of all,

Possessor of eternal guise, Thou whom destruction cannot reach. 76. Thou who art Supreme Joy, O Shripati, Thou art the beginnng and the middle and the end, Thou art the joy and the wealth of goodness unattainable except through Thee. 77. O Brother of the lowly, O Lord of Pandhari, Thou art my hearer as well as the speaker, Thou art the giver of joy founded on love, given to me a helpless one.' 78. Thus Nama at that time brought to his mind Shri Hari and said, 'O Shri Hari, O Govinda, quickly remove me from the sorrows of this earthly life.' 79. Then the Husband of Rukmini was pleased. With His four arms He embraced Nama with His lotus-hands. He caressed Nama's face and thus the Life of the world addressed Nama.

KRISHNA'S *BHAKTAS*

80. The cloud-dark complexioned One said to the saints, 'He has been given the name of Namdev. He has experienced my love and according to the laws of the heart he has obtained peace. 81. Moreover I love the saints and the *Vaishnavas* more than I love my own life. They have plunged into my form and become united with me. 82. Nama, I see that your good qualities are superior to those of all the others, and the joyful cloud of the nectar of love is seen more and more in you. 83. This Dnyandev here also is my very life. He is the ornament of theoretical and experimental knowledge. Nivritti my servant is a mountain of *vairagya*. 84. This noble *bhakta* Sopan is the full sea of soul-knowledge. My *bhaktas* also are Rohidas, Visoba Khechar, and Gora the potter. 85. My *bhaktas* are also Paramanand Joga and this Jagamitra Naga Vinatarama, Vateshvar Changa. I, Krishna, am very fond of the saints. 86. I am especially fond of Asand, Sudama, Keshavdas, the goldmith Narahari, and Bhanudas. Still there is no limit to my love for you. 87. Bhishma, Rukmangad, Akrur, Uddhav, Arjun, Pralhad, the noble Druva, Narad

and Tumbar, know my heart. 88. They are for ever indifferent to every earthly thing, and without effort will become *Jivanmuktas* (free while living); but O Nama, I see your most unusual and fortune-blest glory. 89. All these love me dearly. They have accompanied me all through their infinite rebirths. But your devotion appears to my heart as superior to that of all others.'

90. While Hari was carrying on this conversation, suddenly the bands of *Warkari* pilgrims arrived. There were musical instruments and banners in their hands, and they were shouting out 'Victory, victory.' 91. With them were a great number of banners, with the design of an eagle upon them. Innumerable drums were being sounded, and loud shouting of God's name, making the banks of the Bhima reverberate. 92. The God-loving *bhakta* Pundalik understood the pure joy of such an occasion. Just as the *chakor* bird alone enjoys the nectar of the moon; 93. or just as it is the infant alone that understands the joy of taking the nourishment from its mother's breast; or just as no one aside from Upamanyu can understand the glory of the sea of milk; 94. or just as the royal swan is able to separate the milk that has become mixed with water; or just as the wise understand by experience the praise of *bhaktas* who are God-loving; 95. or as it is the bee alone that understands how to drink the honey in the lotus-flower; so it was the *bhakta* Pundalik who enjoyed the supreme joy of the sacred city of Pandhari.

PILGRIMS CONVEY THE MESSAGE OF KURMADAS

96. With feelings of love the *Warkari* pilgrims prostrated themselves at the great door of the temple. In their love they embraced one another. 97. Then as they gazed, they saw the idol of the Holder of the *Sharang* bow (Krishna). Both His hands were on His hips and He was clothed in a yellow robe. 98. As the Life of the world

was thus standing, these *bhaktas* rejoiced. They embraced one another in their love and then worshipped at His feet; 99. just as a little girl in the home of her mother-in-law, rejoices when she sees her own mother; so these *bhaktas* became full of joy as they saw His glorious face. 100. They then bowed their heads to the two feet that were placed on the brick. They lost all sense of themselves and became absorbed in Him. 101. They said to themselves, 'Seeing Thy glorious face, we have forgotten all the sorrows of our infinite number of rebirths. Thou art the giver of all joy, and there is no other.' 102. Then one who remembered it gave to the Lord God the message that had been given to them by Kurmadas. He said, 'Kurmadas has asked You to come to Lahul to him. 103. He has neither hands nor feet, so he cannot come here rapidly. With a great desire to see You, he is waiting for You to come.' 104. As the Lord of Pandhari heard this message, He prepared Himself in a hurry to go, saying, 'When shall I see My *bhakta* Kurmadas? 105. In the meeting of saints are fulfilled My heart's longings. Aside from them I cannot see any dearest friend or close relative.' 106. God then called Namdev and Dnyandev to come close to Him, and told them of His heart's feelings. 107. 'With an intense desire Kurmadas wishes to meet Me. Let you and Me go at once to that place.' 108. The Lord of *Vaikuntha* (heaven) then took both by the hand and walked rapidly along. 109. He whom the *Vedas* and *Puranas* describe as reclining upon the serpent Shesha on the sea of milk, the Husband of Lakshmi, and the Life of the world, walked on foot. 110. He, the dust of whose feet Brahmadev and the *munis* naturally long after, the Husband of Lakshmi, whose banner is the eagle, walked along on foot. 111. He whose form does not easily come into the imagination of *Yogis* who are sitting on iron spikes, He, seeing the devotion of Kurmadas, walked on foot.

SAVATA HIDES KRISHNA IN HIS STOMACH

112. As the Lord of the world walked along the path, He noticed the village of Aranbhendi. He suddenly had a great desire to meet Savata the gardener. 113. So the Holder of the disk (Krishna) hurried to meet him, thinking, 'I must this day show a marvel to Nama.' 114. Krishna said to Nama, 'I am exceedingly thirsty.' Saying this, *Adhokshaja* (the Pervader of earth and sky) entered into the garden. 115. He left Dnyandev and Nama outside: 'I will come out quickly after drinking some water.' After saying this, Shri Hari met with Savata. 116. The latter was sitting with his eyes closed and was contemplating in his heart the form of Shri Vitthal, and singing with his lips the praises of God's name unconscious of his body. 117. When the Holder of the *Sharang* bow (Krishna) saw him thus, He placed His hand of assurance on his head, and awakening him He embraced him. 118. When he saw the Holder of the disk (Krishna), he embraced His feet. Tears of love flowed from his eyes and he felt a joy that his heart could not contain. 119. He exclaimed, 'Blessed is this day. I have seen with my eyes my mother and father. Thou beautiful, cloud-dark complexioned One, Thou hast come here walking.' 120. Then the *bhakta* Savata again placing his head at His feet spoke thus: 'O Lord of Pandhari, in caring for Thy lowly ones Thou hast greatly wearied Thyself. 121. Now sit here quietly resting, while I worship Thee.' When the Life of the world heard this, 122. the Husband of Rukmini said with an appearance of fear, 'There are two thieves following me. They will arrive here very soon. 123. Out of fear of them, I have come in here to hide myself. I think it is very strange that you should wish to worship Me. 124. When the sun is in eclipse it does not care to be given oblation (worship). When an enemy is besieging a city, the king takes no delight in his throne. 125. When

a man's mind is full of concern, he does not care for enjoyment. When Agasti was near the sea the tide would not come in. 126. You say you will worship Me, but My mind is not at ease. Now protect My life somehow or other, O chief of My *bhaktas.*' 127. Savata said to Him, 'There is no place in all the three worlds, even if searched for, that would contain Thee. 128. One cannot confine air in a cage; space cannot be confined in a jar; and how can one confine the sun in the darkness, O Govinda? 129. As the Lord of *Kailas* (heaven) among the *Yogis*, as the eagle among the birds, as Indra among the other gods, can never be hidden; 130. as musk in earth, or the sandalwood tree among other trees, or as the lion amongst other animals, cannot be hidden; 131. O God of gods, how can the *Uchchaishrava* (Indra's horse) be hidden among other ordinary horses? How can the touchstone be hidden in an iron box, O Madhav? 132. So also, O Shri Hari, Thou art supreme. In Thy womb there are infinite worlds, and on the earth Thou canst not be concealed anywhere.' 133. The Life of the world replied, 'This is no occasion for philosophic knowledge. Hide Me somewhere at this time.' 134. As *Hrishikeshi* (the Lord of the Heart) said this, Savata thought to himself, 'The Dweller in *Vaikunth* (heaven) can in His love dwell in my heart.' 135. He then took his sickle and ripped open his own stomach. The Enemy of Mura (Krishna) immediately entered into the chamber of his heart. 136. Savata thought to himself, 'The thieves may see the cloud-dark complexioned One even here.' So he wrapped his blanket around his stomach. 137. The Lord of the Universe spoke His secret thoughts to Savata from the temple of his (Savata's) heart: 'I see nothing in all this universe with which to repay you for your kindness.'

THE HUMAN HEART AS GOD'S TEMPLE

138. Hearers will remark on this strange event, 'How

can God be contained in the human heart ? We have this doubt at this time.' 139. Hearing the listeners' question, the Speaker replied giving illustrations. 'The Holder of the disk (Krishna) who assumes any form that He wishes, is able to do the seemingly impossible. 140. At the time when Krishna was an *avatar*, the beautiful Yashoda was once in her house churning. Shri Hari entered into the churning-can and ate the butter quickly. 141. A certain *gopi* said absent-mindedly in her love, " I have brought some Krishna to sell." Then in order to make her assertion true, God entered into the milk-jar. 142. The Holder of the disk (Krishna) seeing the love of Savata, made his heart contain Him. So my listeners should not harbour any doubts in their minds.'

143. That was what the Lord of the Earth said, when He told Savata of His secret thoughts, 'I see nothing in all the world with which to repay you for your kindness. 144. Now become My very form, or become everything to Me, for I do not see anything aside from this to give to you.' 145. The *bhakta* Savata replied, 'Merciful One, now I will not separate Thee from myself for eternity.' 146. After this, God and His *bhakta* became one in heart, just as the Bhagirathi and Yamuna rivers became one in their love; 147. or just as water mingles with milk; or as the life pervades the body; so the lotus-eyed One sat with great pleasure in the heart of His *bhakta*; 148. or just as an immense amount of the wonderful nectar is stored up in the moon; so the Lord of *Vaikunth* (heaven) sat in the heart of His *bhakta*, having become one with him; 149. or just as the honey lies lovingly hidden in the bud of a flower; so the Husband of Rukmini in this state of unity had hidden Himself in the heart of His *bhakta*.

NAMDEV'S ANXIETY ABOUT KRISHNA

150. In the meantime the *bhakta* Nama outside the

garden became greatly concerned. He said to himself, 'Why does not the Lord of Pandhari come outside? He is delaying a very long time. 151. I have been impatiently waiting for Him for very long. Where is it that my *Swami* has become entangled and has abandoned me in this forest? 152. Thus Pandurang is my life. I do not know now who will let me see this storehouse of every joy.' 153. With his voice filled with emotion he sobbed in his love. He could not support himself so as to hunt for the footsteps of Vithoba; 154. just as when one overcome with thirst hunts for water in the forest; or just as the child when overcome with hunger waits for the coming of its mother: 155. or just as the little deer that has missed its mother-deer hunts for her in the forest; or just as the miser, having lost his money, makes a diligent search for it with his mind full of concern; 156. so with his voice full of emotion, and tears flowing from his eyes, Nama began to beat his breast with his two hands and threw himself on the ground. 157. He exclaimed, 'O Vithoba, if Thou dost not come immediately, I shall be quite overcome with concern. Do not go away leaving me here. It would not be proper for Thee to do so.' 158. Holding on to the hem of Thy yellow robe, I will forthwith come along with Thee, O Pandurang; but O Husband of Rukmini, I have not known the intention of Thy mind. 159. While Nama was thus expressing his sorrow, he caught sight of the *bhakta* Savata who was full of joy and in his love was repeating God's names. 160. He embraced his feet and said to him, 'Where has the Lord of the World gone? I am anxiously waiting to see Him, and I am greatly troubled.'

NAMA FINDS GOD IN SAVATA

161. Then Savata came to be without bodily consciousness, and being absorbed in the form of Hari He had no

sense of distinction left to distinguish between 'me' and 'mine.' 162. As he noticed certain indications he said to himself. 'Vithoba must be with him. I see him just as I have previously experienced His form.' 163. Just as when the adulterer and an adulteress see one another, they understand the signs that they make; or when a thief sees another thief, he understands the other's mind; 164. or as a clever and wise person understands the loving heart of a speaker; or as when a treasure is invisible to others it is seen by one who is born with his feet foremost; 165. or as the *Yogi* alone understands the customary practice of the *Yogis*; so it was that Nama understood that the Lord of the Universe was within the heart of Savata. 166. He said, 'How is it, O Savata, that you have swallowed the treasure of one so helpless as myself? My soul loves that place of rest with all its joy. 167. Show Him to me only once and I will hold His form in my heart. My soul has become overcome with grief. Save me, O you merciful one. 168. Look on me with an eye of kindness and tell me something which will benefit me, and cause me to meet with the Lord of the world. I shall then accept it as an auspicious event.' 169. The Life of the world hearing Nama's pity-arousing words, said to Savata, 'Cause Me to meet Nama, My dearest friend.' 170. The Husband of Rukmini thought to Himself, 'I have got Myself caught here in Savata's heart. Now I am not able soon to get out of here. 171. Just as an insect in the cocoon makes its own bondage, and then it cannot come out, so it has now happened to Me; 172. or as the parrot sits upon a catch-perch and is not able to fly away, so it has happened to Me; I have got Myself caught in Savata's heart. 173. Because of its love for the lotus flower, the bee stops there, but when the sun sets, it gets itself caught in it; 174. so I, *Vanamali* [wearer of a garland of wild flowers] have got Myself caught in the heart of Savata. Standing outside,

Nama is overcome with concern, just like the fish when outside the water.' 175. *Hrishikeshi* (the Lord of the heart) then said, 'Nama seems as though he were helpless, so he has become overcome with grief for Me. Meet Me with him for a moment.'

WHY KRISHNA WAS CHARMED WITH NAMDEV

176. The *bhakta* Savata then said, 'O *bhakta* of Vishnu, awake. A feeling of pity has come to the Lord of Pandhari. He will now meet with you. 177. The Husband of Kamala has become impatient to meet you. He will meet you and give you peace. In His love for you, you will see Him very near to you. Let your heart sorrow no longer. 178. What heaps of good deeds you have done! It is that you have worshipped God in all things. And so *Hrishikeshi* (the Lord of the heart) who is merciful is pleased with you without effort on your part. 179. By the force of *bhakti*, you have made the Lord of Pandhari your debtor. Seeing this strange thing, I am overcome with amazement, O chief of *bhaktas*. 180. Is it that with a banner upon your shoulder, and with its design of an eagle, you went on pilgrimage to Pandhari? Or is it that you took upon your head the dust from the feet of saints, and therefore Shri Hari is pleased with you? 181. Or is it that on the tenth of the month you led a band of singers, and imitating the cowherds and taking Hari's name, you described Him in your services of praise? 182. Did Govinda become pleased with you on seeing your joy, and so the infinite ocean of compassion, the Brother of the lowly, felt gratified? 183. Or was it that you felt a sense of repentance during your infinite rebirths when you may have put your body to the saw? Or did you practise painful austerities? Or did you visit a great bathing place? 184. Or was it that you spent your life in benevolent deeds? Or when you performed services of praise on the *Ekadashi*

(the eleventh day) was the Life of the world standing there and so became pleased with you? 185. The Lord of Pandhari is the only one who understands your extraordinary good fortune.' Thus speaking, the *bhakta* Savata prostrated himself at the feet of Nama. 186. Nama replied to him, 'You are partner in my joy, O noble *Vaishnava*. Giver of my life, I see no one your equal. 187. You told me of the auspicious event (of meeting with Krishna). At once make it true. Enable me at once to meet my Vitthal. 188. Listen to me, O you God-loving chief of the *bhaktas*. I cannot hold in my impatience. Seeing my unhappy condition, why does not compassion enter into your heart?' 189. Then seizing a sickle he (Savata) ripped open his stomach. The moment Pandurang came outside, Nama grasped His feet. 190. The cloud-dark Krishna filled with compassion and emotion embraced Nama, and with the hem of His yellow robe He wiped the forehead of Nama. 191. Then the Lord of Pandhari smilingly said to Nama, 'Why have you made your heart so sorrowful? Tell Me at once.' 192. Nama grasped the feet of the god, and spoke in a sweet voice, 'Thou art my father and mother. Thou wilt be my Helper through all eternity. 193. O Thou Supreme *Brahm*, the cloud-dark complexioned One, by what allurement dost Thou preserve Thy love? I do not understand. O merciful to the lowly, O Pandurang!'

KRISHNA GOES AND MEETS KURMADAS

194. Then the Life of the world, smiling, said in soft words to Dnyandev, 'Let us hasten to meet Kurmadas. 195. If I do not meet him, My heart will not be satisfied. The day that I meet My *bhaktas*, that day is a happy one and My eyes experience a sense of peace.' 196. Then the four walking together, namely, Dnyandev, Nama, Savata and the Lord of Pandhari, they joyfully journeyed along the road. 197. Hearing all this you may feel some

doubt, because there is mention of so many names, but the King of Pandhari himself mentioned them and recorded them as they really occurred. 198. You wise *bhaktas* must not blame me. Hari proclaims Himself to be the Saviour of the sinner and Advocate of His *bhaktas*. 199. In the compound word ' Sinner-Purifier,' the word 'Sinner' comes first to the lips, and is followed by the word 'Purifier,' the Ocean of compassion. Therefore it is that in verses the names of his *Bhaktas* appear first. 200. Thus along with His *Bhaktas* the Life of the world joyfully walked.

In the meanwhile Kurmadas experienced some very good omens. 201. Just as when a cloud rains upon the earth, the lightning flashes in the East, and from the north a gentle wind blows, 202. so, because the Cloud of joy (Krishna) was coming to meet him, his right eye began to droop, and every now and then his arm twitched. Such were the omens that Kurmadas experienced. 203. Just as the mother cow with her udders full of milk rushes to her calf, so the Lord of Pandhari came to him and He could not contain his joy in His heart. 204. As Kurmadas saw the Life of the world, he reverently prostrated himself on the ground and God embraced him, holding him by His four arms. 205. After the *bhaktas* had met one another, the Husband of Rukmini said to Kurmadas, ' Whatever gifts you may ask of Me I shall give to you.' 206. Hearing Him say this, Kurmadas replied, ' I have only this to ask of You, that You give me Your blessing, and never depart from this place.' 207. The dark-complexioned One replied, ' I will do so, ' and He has remained there always. The God-loving *bhaktas* know Lahul as the sacred place equal to that of Pandhari. 208. In the months of *Ashadh* (July) and *Kartik* (November) pilgrims gather here, and sincere *bhaktas* come here to see God.

209. In the next chapter there are interesting stories. Hearers must give close attention. Just as a miser when he sees a store of wealth, lovingly becomes absorbed in it, 210. so give attention to this story and reverently listen. Mahipati, who is the dust of your feet, lovingly worships at your feet.

211. *Swasti* (Peace!) This book is the *Shri Bhaktavijaya.* As the Lord of the earth hears it He will be pleased. Listen then, you God-loving pious *bhaktas.* This is the sixteenth very delightful chapter.

CHAPTER XVII

RAKA AND GORA THE POTTERS

Obeisance to Shri Ganesh. Obeisance to Shri Krishna.

BHAKTAVIJAYA IS LIKE SPRING

1. A very extraordinary thing happened today. The *Bhaktavijaya* has come in the form of Spring, and its glories can be seen in the forest of good men. 2. The meaning of *Bhaktavijaya* is the spreading of the glory of Spring. Its enlightenment brings a flow of the cool breezes. The first thing to appear on the trees are the buds, consisting of those who desire knowledge. 3. The meaning of *Bhaktavijaya* is that new leaves and branches and flowers of knowledge have appeared. The priceless and eternal fruit of experimental knowledge has appeared. 4. The forest thus adorned seems exceedingly beautiful. Men who feel the heat of the three forms of affiction come here, and sit in the shade. 5. The royal swans (the superior *Yogis*) who are *Jivanmuktas* (free while living) come here to enjoy themselves, and satisfy themselves by the exceedingly interesting stories of the *bhaktas.* 6. There are ignorant people who look at the forest from afar and as they see the beautiful flowers and fruit their minds feel a sense of peace.

RAKA, BANKA AND VANKA

7. In the previous chapter there was the beautiful story of how the Lord of the universe met Kurmadas, protecting him with His eye of compassion. In His love He spoke to him of things that brought him joy. 8. Now among the chief of those who were indifferent to worldly things was Raka the potter, a wise *Vaishnava.* Listen, you pious hearers, to his delightful story. 9. His wife's name was Banka. She was an exceedingly pious and dutiful wife. They had a beautiful daughter named Vanka. 10. He (Raka) was a

Gujarati potter. He was living in Pandhari. He used to sell his baked clay jars and at the same time he worshipped Shri Hari. 11. Many days passed in this way and then a wonderful thing happened. He had dried the freshly made clay jars and had piled them up in the central apartment of his house. 12. In the meantime a cat had a litter of kittens and she brought her little ones and placed them in one of the jars. By day and night she used to visit the litter and feed them. 13. One day she had wandered away to catch some rats. The potter not knowing of the litter of kittens carried away the clay jars (in order to be baked). 14. Among the jars which were to be burned was the one holding the little kittens. He placed wood around the jars and set it on fire. 15. When the fire began to blaze, the cat returned from her wandering. At first she looked about in the house, but she could not find her kittens. 16. Coming outside she rushed around the furnace.

RAKA'S CONCERN OVER THE BURNING KITTENS

The potter understood what it meant, and with his hand he beat his forehead. 17. 'Alas, Alas,' he cried to his wife 'I have committed a great wrong.' She hurried to the scene and asked him what had happened. 18. Overcome with emotion-Raka said to his wife, 'There were kittens in the jars and without knowing it I have burned them. 19. The mother-cat mews loudly, and rushes back and forth to the house. What shall I do in this time of distress?' Saying this he threw himself to the ground. 20. Both Raka and Banka cried out, 'O Lord of Pandhari, rush to our help. Just as Thou didst preserve the sons of Pandu in the lacquer-house, so protect us. 21. A little frog once fell in a frying-pan and underneath was kindled a hot fire; realizing its danger the frog thought of Thee. 22. Thou, the Husband of Rukmini, didst come to its help and the water refused to be heated. In the same way, O Lord of

Pandhari, come here at this time of distress. 23. O Mother (God), we have put Thee into an extraordinary difficulty, but what is there Thou canst not do? Thou didst protect Pralhad when thrown into the fire as he remembered Thy feet. 24. The cat species has an evil propensity and it will never think of Thee. But Thou art an Ocean of mercy and a Cloud of intelligence. Preserve the life of these kittens.' 25. The wife said to her husband, 'Make some vow to God and by doing so, *Hrishikeshi* (the Lord of the heart) will quickly come to our help.' 26. Raka said in reply, 'If Thou wilt preserve these kittens from the fire, I shall never again engage myself in worldly affairs.' 27. Thus thinking in their minds, both prostrated themselves upon the ground and cried out, 'O Shri Hari, rush to our help and remove the distress of Thy lowly ones.' 28. Copious tears flowed from their eyes, all their limbs lost strength, their bodies became covered with dust, and just then a strong wind blew. 29. The fire blazed in the furnace which made both cry out. In thinking of Hari they lost all their self-consciousness. 30. (Their condition was) like a woman who is determined to immolate herself on the funeral pyre of her dead husband; she loses all bodily consciousness and accompanies her husband. 31. For two days the fire of the furnace continued. In the meantime the the potter lay lifeless on the ground. 32. With the hope that Shri Hari would come to their help because of their vow, Banka too continued weeping and crying out, 'O Vitthal, rush to our aid.'

RAKA'S PRAYER HEARD AND KITTENS SAVED

33. On the third day the fire burnt out, and when all the jars were visible, the cat, loudly mewing, walked around the furnace. 34. The Husband of Rukmini did what was seemingly impossible. Listen, you fortunate hearers. Hearing the voice of their mother,

mother, the kittens mewed from the midst of the furnace. 35. The potter and his wife looked in, and among the pile of jars in the furnace they happened to see one that had not been baked. 36. There were in this jar three little kittens which they saw alive. They exclaimed, 'The Husband of Rukmini has come to our help, the Ornament of His *bhaktas*, the merciful One.' 37. As they had taken no food for three days their faces were wan, but now they became bright with joy; 38. just as a lamp seems like a mass of light when it receives oil and a wick; or as grass grows when a great cloud rains upon the earth; 39. or as the tortoise will not feed her young, but destroys their hunger by her mere looks; or as when a miser finds some hidden wealth, his mind is full of joy; 40. or as when the sun rises in the East and the lotus-flowers lie open on the lake; so the heart of Raka rejoiced. 41. All the people of Pandhari said, 'Blessed is this loving *bhakta*. for the Husband of Rukmini has come to him in his distress. A seemingly impossible thing has taken place.' 42. Raka said to his wife, 'I had made a vow to the Lord of Pandhari, that if He saved the kittens from the fire, I would no longer engage myself in worldly pursuits. 43. The Life of the world did come to me in my distress, so why should I now think of any worldly affairs?' With contrition in his mind he called together the Brahmans of the town.

RAKA AND HIS WIFE BANKA AS FORESTERS

44. With pure feelings in his heart he had the Brahmans plunder his house. He dressed himself in a loin-cloth and gave one to his wife. 45. For his stomach's sake he gathered faggots in the forest, and with these buying their food they also gave food to uninvited guests. 46. Whatever was left over, the three, including the daughter, ate together. Continually in their love they remembered Pandurang in their heart.

47. They collected the rags from off the roads and wound these around their body. If anyone gave them any other clothing, they would not even look at it. 48. While he was gathering rags one day in front of a tailor's house the tailor said to him, 'What has brought about such indifference to worldly things ? 49. We want these rags for the purpose of making wicks.' So said that miser in his ignorance.50. Raka said to his wife, 'Pick up a rag which is uselessly lying upon the ground, and use it for covering your body.' 51. After the Brahmans had eaten they threw outside the plates of leaves on which they had eaten. These they (Raka and Banka) fastened around their hips. 52. There are very many *Vairagis*, but none has lived as these two did. Poets in trying to find illustrations, find themselves unable to do so. 53. Just as there is no balance great enough to weigh the earth, so in singing the praise of God's *bhaktas* the mind becomes crazy. 54. One may be able to hold the sun in his fist, or the wind in a cage, but the extraordinary condition of God's *bhaktas* is such that speech cannot describe it. 55. Who has given up his worldly life in order to save the life of others ? Some pray to the inferior deity for a son and for wealth; 56. 'I will distribute at least a quarter of a seer of sweetmeats, O Bhavani, if you give me so much wealth as would enable me to maintain elephants; ' another vows to give to the Brahmans sweee carrots equal to his own weight, and at the end of life h wishes to sit in a chariot of light. 57. Raka was not thus worldly-minded. He made a seemingly impossible vow which perplexed the Lord of *Vaikuntha* (heaven), yet He came to the help of His *bhakta*. 58. Their repentance was very strong, the equal of which no one has ever had. In the meantime their beautiful daughter Vanka went to bathe

DAUGHTERS OF RAKA AND OF NAMDEV QUARREL

59. Just at that moment the daughter of Nama was washing clothes on the bank of the Bhima. She was beat-

ing the clothes upon a stone slab and the sprays flew about. 60. Vanka said to her, 'Beat the clothes gently on the slab, O friend; I have just bathed, and have seated myself for mental worship (*manas-puja*).' 61. The latter replied, 'You are of the potter caste, and yet you seem very particular. You have all abandoned the happy domestic life, and now you are wandering from house to house begging. 62. Your father is a *bhakta* because of some desire in his heart. He made a vow to the Lord of Pandhari. He has placed the Husband of Rukmini in a difficult position in becoming disentangled from his domestic life.' 63. Vanka said to her, 'The sobbing Nama is well known amongst men. Although the Holder of the disk (Krishna), is in the form of Buddha [mute] he forced Him to speak by breaking his own head.' 64. Thus talking to one another they returned to their homes. Meanwhile Nama returned home after pleasing the Husband of Rukmini by his service of song. 65. The quarrel that had taken place on the bank of the Bhima, his daughter reported to Nama, saying that Vanka had blamed him. 66. She said, 'Though in the *Kali Yuga*, God has assumed the *avatar* of Buddha (mute) yet Nama the *bhakta* went to the temple and by breaking his head he forced the Husband of Rukmini to speak. 67. But *my* father (Raka) is one who truly has no desires in what *he* does. He gathers a load of dry faggots and by selling them in the bazaar he earns his living.' 68. When Namdev heard the report given by his daughter, he was very much perplexed. He went to the great door of the temple and prayed to the Holder of the disk (Krishna). 69. He said, 'O God, listen to me. Tell me whether Raka the potter, Thy *bhakta*, is with or without selfish desires.' 70. Listening to this question of His loving *bhakta*, the cloud-dark Krishna smiled and said, 'In all the world I see no one so indifferent to worldly things.' 71. Nama replied,

'O Lord of *Vaikunth* (heaven), show me the condition of his mind.' Saying that He would do so, He lovingly took the hand of the servant of Vishnu. 72. Rukmini, Nama, and the dark-complexioned One walked together. The sun was now overhead, and its twelve phases gave out intense heat. 73. They saw Raka in the jungle gathering faggots with his own hands. The Husband of Rukmini, unseen, viewed the novel sight. 74. Banka his wife, supremely pious and dutiful, took her daughter with her and the two walked in the jungle. 75. There they suddenly saw two sticks lying together. Thinking someone might have left them there they would not touch them. 76. If the wood was still connected with a tree, they would not break the branch and take it away with them; but if it fell of itself they would carefully gather it. 77. Lest he should step on an ant and kill it, Raka the potter walked very carefully. 78. Seeing this novel sight, *Hrishikeshi* (the Lord of the heart) was astonished. Motioning to Rukmini He said to Nama, 79. 'See how indifferent to all earthly things is this *bhakta* of mine, Raka the potter. He is truly without hypocrisy and worships Me without any selfish motive.' 80. Nama replied, 'O Mother Rukmini, give him something and then watch him.' Rukmini then took off her bracelet from her arm and gave it to Nama. 81. It was a bracelet that not even Brahmadev could have made, being set with priceless jewels. Even if the three worlds were given as equivalent, still they could not equal it. 82. Such was the bracelet that Rukmini took off her arm and threw in the jungle. The mother of the universe lifted up some dry sticks and placed them over it. 83. Krishna, Rukmini and His *bhakta* Nama, the noble *Vaishnava* being invisible to Raka, watched the scene as it happened. 84. Raka and his wife went on gathering faggots and accidentally lifted up the sticks which covered the gold bracelet. 85. They gazed at the bracelet with its jewel setting in gold, and as they gazed at this priceless ornament they knew of nothing in all the three worlds equal to it. 86. Raka the potter, absolutely indifferent to worldly things, pushed the sticks aside and said to his wife, 'Look at this, the root of disaster.' 87. She replied, 'This brings a hindrance in our worship of God. I wonder what *siddhi* (accomplishment personified) has come across our worship, and given us this bracelet. 88. We cast aside all worldly things and came as suppliants to the Lord of Pandhari. What do we want with a useless gold bracelet?' 89. So they not only left the bracelet but also the wood that was placed upon it; just as a Brahman will never take food that a dog has touched; 90. and as the *Chatak* bird will not drink water which is on the ground, regarding it as defiling; and as a fly will not touch the body after oil is rubbed upon it; 91. so Mother Rukmini being pleased with her *bhaktas* had given them this bracelet, but the two left both it and the stick which covered it, and went on their way. 92. Nama then said, 'O Life of the world, O Pervader of the universe, O Ornament of His *bhaktas*, Raka the potter is truly absorbed in Thy worship with feelings of love. 93. Give him a direct vision of Thyself.' The Husband of Rukmini hearing him say this smiled; 94. and said, 'You have now had experience of Raka's mental condition. It is just as I told you. If you still have any doubts let me know.' 95. Nama replied, 'Raka the God-loving *bhakta* is evidently without selfish desires. Even my mind cannot be equal to his.' 96. Nama, Hari and Rukmini then directly appeared to him. They called Raka the potter to them and gave him this direct manifestation. 97. Raka saw with his own eyes the four-armed Hari, the dark-complexioned One, beautiful in His yellow robe, with his crown and earrings, and garlands of wild flowers. 98. Raka and Banka then embraced the god, grasping tightly His feet, and bowed to the Holder of the disk (Krishna).

GORA THE POTTER TRAMPLES HIS CHILD TO DEATH

99. Among the *Vaishnavas*, those who are completely indifferent to worldfy things, was the God-loving *bhakta*, Gora the potter. You *bhaktas* listen with love to his extraordinary history. 100. His property lay in the town of Tardhoki by name [near Pandharpur]. Here he had his house, his wife and his domestic life, and at the same time he worshipped Shri Hari. 101. As he ate, as he walked about, as he rose up, as he rested, as he carried on his occupation as a potter, he was all the time repeating the names of the Lord of Pandhari. 102. While listening with his ears to the stories of ordinary life, while looking at things animate and inanimate, and while realizing the working of his ten senses, he had at the same time the thought of the Lord of the world continually. 103. Of good and evil, of joy and sorrow, of praise and criticism, he thought nothing. The prince and the pauper he regarded as equal. 104. One day while his wife had gone for water she left her child to play in the front yard. 105. Gora had raised a border of earth and within it had made the clay. With his eyes closed,Gora trod the clay in his ecstatic mood 106. Now thinking in his heart of the form of Vitthal, tears of love flowed from his eyes. He had no recollection of hsi body and became so utterly absorbed as to be identified with the Invisible. 107. While the child was playing about the yard it came creeping along near the clay, and (the ecstatic) Gora trod on it with the clay. 108. When his wife came back bringing the water, she thought of her child as her breast filled with milk. She looked about in the yard for her child but could not see it. 109. She then came near to her husband and asked him about it: 'I went to bring water, leaving the child with you. 110. I see the the child nowhere. Tell me at once, Oh lord of my heart, where is it ?' Looking about her, she suddenly discovered some blood. 111. Then she noticed in the mud

a collection of bones and flesh. Beating her breast she cried out in her agony. 112. She cried out to her husband. 'You have trodden on the child in the clay. You seem to have lost all self-consciousness. What is this awful thing you have committed? 113. You have discrarded your worldly affairs, and have devoted yourself to the finding of God. I mean to go at once from here and commit suicide.' 114. Listening to her harsh rebuke, he slightly regained consciousness and said to his wife, 'You have interrupted my contemplation without thinking what you are doing. 115. The Husband of Rukmini was sitting in my lotus-heart. You confused my mind and you drove away the Lord of Pandhari.' 116. With his heart full of anger, he seized with his hands the handle of the wheel and came near to his wife in order to beat her. 117. Full of fear she said to her husband, 'For Vithoba's sake, mind if you as much as touch me with your finger.' 118. Hearing her utter this oath, Gora sat down quietly and with peace and forgiveness in his heart he began to repeat the names of God. 119. Men and women assembled in the yard, and began to talk to one another about the event. 'The child has been trodden into the clay; we have seen this great wrong done.' 120. One said, 'He is utterly crazy. How did your husband become such?' A second one said, 'That is always the effect when one gives himself up to the worship of Hari.' 121. Thus different people reviled him in many ways with scornful words. But he would not listen to what they said and continued his worship of Hari; 122. just as when an elephant walks on the royal road, many dogs begin to bark, but he gives no attention and keeps on walking at his pleasure; 123. or just as in the assembly of *pandits*, fools make their impudent remarks, but without listening to them the *pandits* continue their discussion on the meaning of the *Shastras*; 124. or as when the ocean saw the *Rishi* Agasti it began to roar in mockery, but the *Rishi* paid no attention to it and continued his religious ceremonies; 125. or as a serpent hisses in the presence of an eagle, yet the eagle feels not the slightest fear; 126. so, although the men and women who were gathered there reviled him, Gora paid no attention to them, and steadying his mind he repeated the names of the Husband of Rukmini. 127. It did not even enter into his thought that he had trodden his child into the clay. Bringing Shri Vitthal to mind he paid no attention to the sorrows of this world.

GORA AND HIS CHILDLESS WIFE

128 After some days had passed, Gora's wife began thinking to herself, 'Though I continue refusing to speak to my husband, it will not mean the end of this affair. 129. If a king commits a wrong what can the subjects do? I have o authority to punish my husband.' 130. So one day she came near him to wash his feet. Pushing her away be said to her, 131. 'You have laid me under an oath in the name of Vitthal that I should not touch you with my fingers. Know that such an oath in the name of my Vithoba I will not break.' 132. The wife said to her husband, 'I spoke to you as I should not have done. Please forgive me. You must accept my service. 133. Busy in my daily duties, I may have said what is good or bad. But if you sit there obstinately refusing me, what will the end be? 134. When jars are placed in the furnace, they naturally touch one another, so when I am busy with my domestic life I say sometimes what I ought not.' 135. Gora said to her, 'The sun may rise in the West, but I have made a fixed determination which I shall never give up. 136. One might fasten the air in a cage, or one might confine space in a jar, but my determination will never be broken. 137. One might hide fire in a load of hay, or the wind in fear might run away from the clouds, but I will never break the oath that has been made in the name of the Husband of Rukmini. 138. A pumpkin might sink in the ocean; the

god of death might fear the ghost; but my determination is immovable, it will endure for ever.' 139. As the *Vaishnava bhakta* continued thus talking, his wife remained quiet. But as she now had no child, her mind was full of concern. 140. As she thought of this by day and night she said to herself, 'I must bring about a second marriage for him. In that way he will be pleased and my family will grow.' She then went to her own mother's house. 141. She told her mother and father all that had happened. She said, 'My husband has discarded me, and our family line will now disappear. 142. Relatives were looking for some fault, and that is just what God has done. Evil ones among our relatives are laughing at us. "His family line has ceased," they say. 143. He has already discarded me, and I must bring about a second marriage for him. But who would give him another wife, since the first one is living? 144. Now give to my husband as a wife your youngest virgin daughter.' Saying this she grasped the feet of her mother. 145. Begging this from her mother, tears flowed from her eyes. 'I am asking for only a jacket as it were, and you must meet my request.' 146. As she spoke so piteously, her father and mother replied, 'We grant your request.' Then having called a Brahman they decided upon the marriage.

GORA MARRIES HIS LIVING WIFE'S SISTER

147. Returning to her home she made all necessary garments, adornments and ornaments. 148. She sent invitations and collected all the relatives in her family line. The marriage procession then started, and the bands were playing loudly. 149. The wedding guests thought with concern amongst themselves on the way. They said, 'O gentlemen, we cannot approve of the strange fact that he should abandon his wife for the sake of God. 150. Muhammedans do not like the worship of the *Gayatri*

Mantra. Donkeys would not enjoy having the sandalwood paste put upon them. So men who are *Vaishnavas* are not liked by those who revile them. 151. A sinful man does not like good conduct. An out-caste does not like to fix his thoughts on the *Shastras.* Ghosts do not enjoy the music of the *kirtan*, nor does a fool give thought to reason. 152. The sick do not like milk. Thieves do not like the bright moonlight. Misers do not like giving away of wealth. The deaf do not enjoy hearing singing. 153. Those who eat flesh have no kindness. Those who kill are not fond of compassion. The poor through their fate do not care for the shade of the wish-tree. 154. So those who are not *bhaktas* do not like the devotion of those who are *bhaktas.*' Well in this way they went on quickly to the marriage. 155. The wedding deities were installed; all were feasted' and holding the marriage curtain the Brahmans repeated the eight verses of blessing. 156. Thinking of the Husband of Lakshmi, the (officiating) Brahman said, 'Beware, Beware.' Just as they dropped the marriage curtain, the loud music from the instruments began. 157. The marriage ceremonies continued for four days. The procession marched through the town. The mother-in-law and father-in-law then thought to themselves, 158. 'He has been given the eld st and the youngest of the daughters. He has taken a dislike to one of them, and men will now laugh at us. 159. "Just as both your eyes are alike to you; in the same way consider both of them your wives"—in this way putting our son-in-law under oath, we must make him accept her hand.' 160. They then said to Gora, 'Both these wives now belong to you. Care for them and treat them alike in your domestic life. 161. If you do not treat them kindly, Vithoba will be your witness.' Hearing them say this, he told them that he assented. 162. Said he, 'If the Lord of the world is merciful, the bondage of this life will break of itself. He will not allow His *bhaktas* to be influenced by worldly passions.'

163. Thus happy in his mind, he quickly returned to his home, and gave exactly the same garments and ornaments to his two wives. 164. Just exactly as he regarded his elder wife, so he regarded his younger wife. Seeing him so regard her, the elder wife began to feel concerned. 165. She asked Gora, 'Why does not the younger wife please you?', He replied, 'Your father placed me under an oath, 166. namely, that I would not treat you two partially. He put me under an oath to Vithoba, and this is the oath under which my father-in-law placed me. And I have his words firmly fixed in my mind.' 167. Hearing her husband say this, the younger wife began to cry. Said she, 'O sister, why did you get me entangled in this? 168. Then the elder sister said to her younger sister, 'O my dear sister, do not be troubled about this. When night comes we shall test his heart.' 169. When it was night, seeing the *bhakta* of Vishnu asleep, his two wives came near him, and slept at his side. 170. Each of them took one of his hands, and placed it on her breast. When he awoke he began to wonder. 171. Said he, 'Although my mind was not thinking of any sensual pleasure, it was my hand that broke the vow.' Thus repenting in his heart, listen to what he did. 172. He took a sword and fastened it to a post, and with a firm heart he cut both hands off. 173. As he sat there worshipping, the sun now arose. The wives seeing him now without hands, began to cry out loudly. 174. Said they, 'A great disaster has happened. Who will now carry on our domestic life? Everywhere the evil-minded will laugh at us, seeing what our conduct has been. 175. We had him perform a second marriage in order to increase our family line. But what can we do before the wrath of God?' 176. Gora then said to both his wives, 'You mourn needlessly. If the Husband of Rukmini is your Protector, why should you sorrow? 177. No one who receives the wish-cow need be troubled as to how he

is to get his livelihood. 178. If one is sitting under the wish-tree, how can there be any lack of food or ornaments to him? So if the Husband of Rukmini is bestowing His favour, why should there be bondage to things of this life? 179. If anyone gets a touchstone in his hand, what can he lack of money and property? So if one's love is given to the repeating of names of Vitthal, he cannot be injured by entanglement in worldly affairs. 180. Just as all diseases clear away when one drinks all he can of nectar, so no diseases of this earthly life can injure anyone who is repeating with his lips the names of Ram, Krishna, Hari.' 181. Thus explaining things to his wives, he continued happy in mind. He was continually repeating the names of God, and never stopped for a single moment. 182. Then came the tenth day of the month of *Ashadh* (July), and Gora with joy in his heart came to the sacred city of Pandhari together with his two wives. 183. They bathed in the Chandrabhaga river and paid their respects to Pundalik. They circumambulated the sacred town and then arrived at the great door of the temple. 184. Along with him his two wives reverently prostrated themselves on the ground. They embraced the god and with reverence worshipped His feet. 185. Nama was standing at this time by the eagle-platform. With cymbals and a band of singers and with love and joy he was performing a *kirtan*, and with enthusiasm was repeating the names of God. 186. With the sound of the *vina* and the drum, there was great enthusiasm in the *kirtan*. He danced before Pandurang, Destroyer of the earthly bondage, the merciful One. 187. Nivritti, Dnyandev, Savata, Sopan, Jagamitra the beloved sat listening to the stories related by Nama. 188. There were also present many saints, *Mahants*, and good men. Many *Vaishnavas* had gathered there. With the joy of love they worshipped, and in their love listened to the *kirtan*. 189. Then Namdev lifted up his hands and motioned them like banners, and with his lips he told everyone to raise his hands like banners in a similar manner. 190. With the joy of love clapping their hands, they shouted aloud the names of Hari. Tears now flowed from the lotus-eyes of Gora.

GORA'S HANDS AND CHILD RESTORED AGAIN

191. Gora said, 'O God, Husband of Rukmini, why hast Thou deserted me now? As I put my armless hands up, I feel ashamed. 192. O lotus-eyed One, O Husband of Kamala, Thou alone art my wealth and my property. Aside from Thee I see no one in all the three worlds. 193. I have put all my burden upon Thee, and I have no other support but Thee.' Thus Gora the potter pleaded piteously before God. 194. Hearing his piteous cry, the Husband of Rukmini came to his help. Hands like his former ones sprang from (the stumps of) his arms. 195. With great joy he now clapped his hands while repeating aloud the names of God. All the *bhaktas* cried aloud, 'Victory, victory,' as they saw the wonderful sight. 196. They said, 'Among all the *bhaktas*, the noble *Vaishnavas*, Gora the potter is the noblest *bhakta*. The Husband of Rukmini is pleased with him, and in the *kirtan* of Hari his hands sprang from (the stumps of) his arms.' 197. Seeing the wonderful sight, Gora's elder wife arose and joining her hands palm to palm before the Lord of Pandhari, 198. she said, 'Lord of the world, Thou hast looked with favour upon Thy servant. I have been very sorrowful without a child. Why dost not Thou have any pity for me? 199. Thy *bhaktas* describe Thee as the Ocean of mercy and the Life of the world. We are sorrowful without the sight of an infant child. 200. Taking Thy name, O Lord of Rukmini, my husband became unconscious of body and trod our child in the clay. Thou surely dost remember this.' 201. Hearing this piteous cry the Holder of the disk (Krishna) showed His favour. Out of the assembly a little child came creeping suddenly. 202. See-

ing the child, everyone was filled with astonishment. The mother rushing towards it in her love, held it to her heart. 203. Then the Mother Rukmini said (to Gora), 'From today you are free from the oath. Do not now abandon your wives. Our command is your authority.' 204. As the daughter of (king) Bhimak (Rukmini) thus spoke, all in the assembly of the *bhaktas* rejoiced. They clapped their hands crying 'Victory, Victory,' and wagged their heads in the *kirtan*. 205. Then repeating the hymns of praise, they waved lights over the Lord of Rukmini.

In the next chapter hearers are asked to listen with reverence to an interesting story. 206. The Husband of Rukmini will Himself relate the beautiful stories of His *bhaktas*. Mahipati is merely His servant, as he calls himself in his love.

207. *Swasti* (Peace!) This book is the *Shri Bhaktavijaya*. In listening to it the Lord of the world will be pleased. Listen to it, you God-loving, pious *bhaktas*. This is the seventeenth very delightful chapter; it is an offering to Shri Krishna.

CHAPTER XVIII
LIFE OF NAMDEV
(Continued)

Obeisance to Shri Ganesh. Obeisance to Shri Krishna.

BHAKTAVIJAYA DEPICTS NINEFOLD *BHAKTI*

1. The darkness of ignorance has disappeared. The *Bhaktavijaya* has arisen like the sun, and the clusters of stars in the form of duality are hidden because of the sun's brilliancy. 2. By the light of its knowledge the (following) nine forms of *bhakti* have become available. Those seeking salvation should therefore give due thought to the subject and (i) walk on the path provided by the hearing of the *Bhaktavijaya*. 3. (ii) Some walk along the path of *kirtans*. (iii) Some associate themselves with the God-loving *bhaktas*; in that case the dull-minded and the fools are saved, and they make *Shripati* (Krishna) subject to them. 4. (iv) Some look to the path of contemplation yet they mix with the world. (v) Some sit with concentrated mind in the cave of thinking. 5. (vi) Some prefer service at God's feet, and they walk along that path. (vii) Some observing the city of worship walk thitherward. 6. (viii) Some pick the path of supplication and walk rapidly on that. (ix) Others in their love pick out the paths of self-consecration. 7. So the seekers of salvation have made these nine possible ways exceedingly clear. Other God-loving *bhaktas* also have walked the same paths.

GORA TESTS NAMA

8. In the previous chapter there was the extraordinary story of how hands sprang from Gora's arms and how the Husband of Rukmini brought back the dead child to life and gave it back to its parents. 9. Gora then joined his hands palm to palm, and said to the saints, ' Come to my home and purify my abode. ' 10. Seeing his great desire

the saints replied that they would come and they at once set off. 11. The *Vaishnavas* walked along to the home of Gora, and were filled with joy, while with love in his heart he(Gora) bowed to them with love. 12. Gora gave them grass mats to sit upon and began to wash their feet. And as he drank the water in which their feet were washed his mind felt satisfaction. 13. Worshipping them and using the sixteen materials, he gave them all a meal of six juices, and the *tulsi* leaf for the purification of their mouths. 14. Nivritti, Dnyandev, Sopan, Nama, Savata and other *Vaishnavas*, also Muktabai the store-house of all goodness, all sat in their appointed places. 15. Dnyandev now said to Gora, 'You have placed the jars (the saints) on their seats. Now separate those that are unbaked from those that are baked, and tell me your experience.' 16. Dnyaneshwar having said this, by his own reason Gora understood what he meant. Gora then took in his hand the potter's paddle, 17. and with it he rapped the skull of all the saints who were present. All accepted it in silence. 18. But when he reached Nama, he (Nama) cried out, 'Why do you strike me needlessly ?' Gora replied, 'This vessel is as yet raw and unbaked.' 19. Muktabai said to him, 'O Gora, how did you know this ? You are good, and an expert examiner. I have without a doubt discovered that. 20. Jewellers are expert in their examination of jewels, so also a potter by a mere glance recognizes a jar (as baked or unbaked). 21. A person sick with disease is easily recognized by a doctor, so you by a mere glance know what is baked and what is not baked.' 22. Listening to what she said, all the saints broke out into a hearty laugh. But Nama was sorry at heart and was much troubled. 23. Therefore rising from the assembly, Namdev came to Pandharpur, and there meeting the Husband of Rukmini he began to tell Him the secrets of his heart. 24. His throat choked and tears flowed from his eyes and he said to the god, 'I have been greately insulted. My heart is full of ang r.' 25. The Life of the world laughed and gave Nama an embrace. Said He, 'Who insulted you? Please tell me without hesitation.' 26. Nama replied, 'O *Hrishikeshi* (the Lord of the heart), one should tell others of the praise he receives, but the criticism he receives should be kept to himself.' 27. The Husband of Rukmini replied, 'I know the feelings of your heart. But I see no one so good and dear to me, aside from you. 28. Do not be ashamed to tell your secrets to your dearest friend.' Thus spoke Adhokshaja (Krishna) to Nama in love. 29. Nama replied, 'Listen to my story, O God. Gora the potter, Thy *bhakta*, took all the saints to his house, and he did a very astonishing thing. 30. He seated them upon grass mats and lovingly worshipped them. Then Dnyandev motioning to him said something to him. 31. Gora then took his potter's paddle in his hand and rapped everyone on the head. All received it silently, and no one replied to him. 32. But when he came to rap me I was afraid, O Lord God. I said to him, after remembering Thy feet, "Go away." 33. Hearing me say this, all the saints laughed, and Dnyandev together with Muktabai began to make fun of me. 34. Gora then said about me, "He is still raw and unbaked," and all the saints still laughing I became ashamed. 35. I then arose quickly and came to tell Thee.' As Nama said this, *Hrishikeshi* (the Lord of the heart) replied.

NEED OF A *GURU*

36. The Life of the world said to Nama, 'What he has said about you is quite true. He who does not go as a suppliant to a *guru* is spoken of as one who is not ripe.' 37. As the Holder of the disk (Krishna) said this to him, Nama's spirit gave way. Just as salt dissolves in a moment when water is poured upon it; 38. or as when water is poured upon sugar it at once dissolves away; so at

the words of the cloud-dark One (Krishna), the God-loving *bhakta* became very troubled in thought. 39. When a storm comes from the South, the clouds melt away; so at the teaching of the Lord of the world Nama became sad. 40. He then replied to God, ' I came here to tell Thee my complaint, because I thought Thou wouldst take away my pain. 41. But Thou hast shown me disfavour, and hast talked to me as they did. Now O Lord of the world, I know of no place to go to. 42. If the earth feels troubled, where should the trees go? If a mother casts away her child, who will care for it? 43. If a tortoise will not look at its young, in what way will their lives be preserved? If a king does not act rightly and justly, how can his subjects be happy? 44. But Thou, O Holder of the disk (Krishna), hast made me very sad to-day. In all the three worlds I see no one aside from Thee to help me'. 45. The Lord of Pandhari then said to Nama, 'Your heart and mine are one. Just as honey is stored in a flower, there is no duality between them, 46. so you are My very life. Do not say that you are sad. Go now as a suppliant to a good *guru* and put an end to your thoughts on duality.' 47. Nama said, 'O God supreme, why do I need a *Sadguru*? When Thou, O (Krishna) Keshav, art so near to me, how can there be any bondage to my soul? 48. To engage in religious ceremonies, austerities, sacrifices and offer gifts and go as a suppliant to a *Sadguru* in order to gain Thy love, seem so unnecessary. 49. If one suddenly happens to obtain sugar, why go to the bazaar for any? If nectar should fall in one's mouth, why go to the mountain to graze? 50. If without effort one gets some tasty food, why do any cooking? If at home one has a pile of money, then why wander about for it? 51. So Thou, the *Guru* of the world, art so near to me. Then why do I need a *Sadguru*?' Listening to Nama's talk the Holder of the *Sharang* Bow (Krishna) replied, 52. ' Nama, listen to Me. When I was the *avatar* Ram, I went as a suppliant to Vashishtha in order to question him on self-knowledge. 53. When I was the Krishna *avatar*, I went with reverence to Sandipani and from him I obtained self-knowledge. 54. So if you will listen to Me, you will be acceptable to all the saints.' As the Life of the world said this, Nama grasped His feet.

GOD CHOOSES VISOBA KHECHAR AS NAMA'S *GURU*

55. Nama said to Krishna, 'To whom shall I go as suppliant ?' *Hrishikeshi* (the Lord of the heart) hearing him say this, replied to him, 56. 'Visoba Khechar is now asleep in the temple of Shiva. In all the three worlds I know of no one who is so wise or so indifferent to earthly things. 57. So go at once there and become a suppliant to that chief of *Shadgurus*.' Nama then embraced His feet, and tears flowed from his eyes. 58. Nama replied, 'O God, I cannot for a moment be without Thee. If Thou desirest any proof of this, I will swear to it by Thy name.' 59. The Holder of the *Sarang* Bow (Krishna) then said to him, 'Protect public custom. If you do not go to a *Sadguru*, how can ignorant men be saved ? 60. The Holder of the disk (Krishna) having said this, Nama arose at once, very sad in heart. How sad he was, listen. 61. Just as Shri Krishna gave knowledge to Uddhava in the eleventh chapter, when he sent him to Badrikashram and made him sad, 62. so in the *Kali Yuga* Nama the *bhakta* became his *avatar*. Therefore so using his illustration I have applied it exactly to himself. 63. It is like the eleventh day among religious observances, or like *Hrishikeshi* (the Lord of the heart) among the gods, or as there is no other river that can be compared with the Chandrabhaga. 64. Those who wander to an endless number of sacred bathing places find their pride growing. But when they see the Chandrabhaga, even at a distance, they become prideless. 65. How can I fully dis-

cribe the greatness of the Chandrabhaga? *Warkari* pilgrims who come to Pandhari recognize the greatness of the Bhimarathi, a greatness which does not belong to any other sacred bathing place. 66. Such a sacred bathing place as the Chandrabhaga, and such a sacred city as Pandhari, and such a holy *bhakta* as Nama, cannot be found in all the three worlds. 67. Though going to meet with his *Sadguru*, he could not bear separation from God. Then bringing into his heart the Lord of the world, he suddenly arose and went along. 68. Nama came quickly into the temple of Mallikarjun and looked about him. Here he saw Visoba Khechar asleep. 69. He had put on his shoes and had placed both his feet upon the emblem of Shiva. When Nama saw this, he was filled with astonishment. 70. 'How is it that the Husband of Rukmini has given me such a *Sadguru* as this one? He has arrogantly placed his feet on the emblem of Shiva, and has fallen into sleep.' 71. Coming as he (Nama) did to find a *Sadguru*, the first thing he found in him was a fault; just as when one takes the first mouthful of food and then finds a fly in it; 72. or as one setting out on a journey (to make a fortune) should come across (a woman carrying) an empty jar (of water, a bad omen); or as if at the beginning of a book, the first letter should not be written; 73. or as when one comes to look at the sun and finds it in eclipse; or as when one comes to examine the horoscope of a bride and a bridegroom and discovers that both of them were born in the same course of the star; 74. or as when looking for the moon on the second of the bright half of the month, the sky is covered with clouds; so when looking for a *guru*, he (Nama) saw at first his fault. 75. The servant of Vishnu came near and said to Visoba, 'You call yourself a *sadhu* and a saint. But what is this improper thing you are doing? 76. You have placed your feet upon the emblem of Shiva, the Husband of Parvati. Now I know what your knowledge of *Brahm* is worth.' 77. Visoba replied to Nama, 'I have indeed made a great mistake. So place my feet where Sadashiv (God) is not. 78. My body is weak and I have no strength to rise. You, a servant of Vishnu, came as a friend to meet me and to tell me what is right. 79. Place my feet where the Husband of Parvati (Shiva) is not.' Nama hearing what he said, came near to him. 80. Then as Namdev himself lifted up Visoba's feet, the whole place seemed to take the form of the emblem of Shiva. 81. Whichever way he turned his feet, there he seemed to see the emblem, he found no place empty of God whatever and his mind became perplexed. 82. The bell, the drum, all took the form of Shiva. The men and women who were there to visit God, they all seemed like (Shiva) the Husband of Parvati. 83. As he looked at his *Sadguru's* feet they also seemed to be Shiva; and after some consideration as he looked at himself he found that he himself appeared like Shiva. 84. In his love he looked all about him. The temple and all that belongsed to it seemed like Shiva the Lord of *Kailas* (Heaven). Nama was overcome with astonishment and placed his head on the *Sadguru's* feet. 85. The *Sadguru* replied to him, 'I feel very much troubled. O *bhakta* of Vishnu, quickly place my feet on the earth.' 86. Hearing this Nama replied, 'You are an ocean of knowledge, a cloud of intelligence. As I was serving your feet, O *Swami*, everything seemed to be in the form of Shiva. 87. Every where I saw (Shiva) the Lord of *Kailas* (Heaven). There seems to be no place whatever without Him. Amazed at this, I have placed my head at your feet.' 88. Visoba replied to Nama, 'Listen to the forms in which Shiva appears.' Then speaking in the *Nanda* [Kanarese] language he removed all his doubts. 89. 'His five faces, His three brilliant eyes and His ten adorable hands: I will describe to you His form. 90. As you look at His head it reaches up to heaven and His feet touch the bottom of the seventh hell. 91. The six *Shastras* in attempting to describe His power felt ashamed at their inability. The four *Vedas* in describing the full meaning, became crazy in their vain attempts. 92. The eighteen *Purans* were not able to describe Him, and so the thousand-hooded One (the Serpent *Shesha*) came to describe His qualities. And each of his tongues was divided in two. 93. Thus His limit cannot be defined.' Then he (Visoba) joined his two hands palm to palm, and said, 'I am the servant of Dnyaneshwar. I am devoted to his feet.' 94. As Nama listened to the words of his *Sadguru*, they made a deep impression on his mind; just as when God showed Himself in the form of the whole universe to Arjun, the whole scene entered into his experience. 95. Nama then said, 'O mother *Sadguru*, your feet are the means of my salvation. In bowing to your feet, all seems to me to be as but one in form.' 96. Visoba then arose and placed upon Nama's head his hand of blessing. Nama then recognized in his lotus-heart that Visoba was the Husband of Rukmini.

97. It happened on a certain day that all the saints gathered together at the eagle-platform and saw the Lord of Pandhari embracing Nama. 98. They said to Nama, 'Since you have adopted a *Sadguru* you never seem to care for us. How is it that you have hardened your heart and continually remain with him ?' 99. Nama replied to them, 'Thy form, O *Sadguru*, my Lord, is in my heart. No longer do I see a difference between Thyself and myself.' 100. Hearing the words of Nama, the Husband of Rukmini was pleased. The Life of the world then spoke to all the saints as follows:- 101. 'No longer should you call Nama raw and unbaked.' As the Life of the world said this, Dnyandev became aware of what he really meant.

PARISA BHAGAVAT THE BRAHMAN

102. Now listeners, hearken with reverence to another

most interesting story. Parisa Bhagavat in performing austerities prayed to Mother Rukmini. 103. The Primal Mother being pleased, with her eyes of compassion she showed him her full mercy, and placed over him the shadow of that mercy. 104 She met him in the visible form and held him to her heart. She said to Parisa, 'Whatever good desire you hold in your heart, tell me what it is.' 105. Parisa Bhagavat thought for a while in his heart and then replied, 'Mother, I wish my heart to be uninterruptedly steady in my worship of Thee 106. May no thought of fear come into my heart. Such is my thought. O Mother, gratify my longings.' 107. She immediately brought a *parisa* (touchstone) and placed it in his hand. She then said to him, 'O Parisa Bhagavat, never let this touchstone be separated from you. 108 Whatever pieces of iron you touch with this stone, you will have that amount of gold.' Hearing these words of the Mother he had a feeling of satisfaction. 109. Just as when one has performed a hundred sacrifices he enjoys the dignity of Indra; or a when the ten-headed One (Ravana) having performed his austerities found himself the Lord of the golden city (Lanka). 110. With a mind comforted, Parisa made an obeisance to the Primal Mother. He gave the touchstone to Kamalaja his wife. 111. She then brought some pieces of iron and applied to them the touchstone, and they immediately turned into the highest kind of gold. 112. Kamalaja was very much pleased and said, 'One cannot know the limit of Thy power, O Mother of the world. Aside from Thee who is there who will come and help us weak ones in our necessities? 113. We have often fallen into the sufferings of poverty but today Thou hast supplied all our needs.' Thus both husband and wife felt great satisfaction. 114. Parisa then took his wife aside and said to her, 'Tell no one of this. If the saints should hear of it they would laugh at me.' 115. Being of one mind in this matter they both enjoyed the very best food but in outward appearance they showed poverty. 116. They placed all their wealth in the cellar and dined every day on the daintiest food. To people, however, they showed themselves as indifferent to earthly things; 117. just as deceivers shave off their hair and then rob the unwary pilgrims on the road; or like actors who assume a variety of forms and act like the *sannyasi* Shripad; 118. or just as a gilt coin seems very brilliant on the outside; or as when an adulterer seeks to give people the impression that he is of a specially high moral standard; 119. or just as the flowers of the *Pungala* Vine(a bad smelling shrub) seem very beautiful to the eye from a distance; or as one recognizes the moral character of a miserly friend from what he shows in his outer life; 120. or as in the case of one who is not possessed by a deity, on the outside to the eye he pretends to be possessed by a god; or as a peacock which has feathers with eyes all over but has no sight; 121. so Parisa Bhagavat appeared to people as one indifferent to earthly things, but in his home he had a vast amount of wealth as any observant person could recognize. 122. Just as by looking at anyone's face, we recognise whether he has dined or fasted; and from their language we judge whether men are sincere or irritable; 123. and whether a lamp has a wick and oil in it can be recognized from the light the lamp gives; and by insight one can recognize whether a man is wise or foolish; 124. and whether a person has done a thing successfully or not is recognized by the wise from the way he acts; or as a speaker can easily recognize whether his hearer has a troubled or a quiet mind; 125. in the same way clever and wise people recognized what the indifference of earthly things of Parisa Bhagavat really was; for good qualities and bad qualities can never be completely hidden.

KAMALAJA AND RAJABAI

126. Parisa's wife Kamalaja was one day going for water. She filled her vessel from the water in the Chandrabhaga river and was returning to her home: 127. Kamalaja accidentally met on the way Rajabai the dutiful wife of Namdev. 128. Rajabai said to her, 'I am going to fill my vessel with water, and will return at once. Until then remain in this place, dear friend.' 129. Saying this she hastened and filled her vessel and returned and then the two persons again met each other. 130. As she saw Rajabai was full of concern because she (Rajabai) was without food and raiments, she said to her, 'Tell me at once your personal secrets. 131. One should never be ashamed to tell one's secrets to a friend, but should put away all thoughts of difference between them and treat each other as one.' 132 Rajabai then said to her friend, 'Listen to my secrets. The lord of my home has put away all shame and has devoted himself to the God of the eagle banner. 133. He has no idea either of the honour paid to him or of criticisms. He has not the slightest concern regarding public affairs. He brings into his mind the Husband of Rukmini and is worshipping all the time. 134. At home we have the very least of food and raiments and yet we have a very large family. Tell me at once what I am to do.' 135. After listening to her Kamalaja replied, 'Has not He Whom Namdev worships become pleased with him and given him everything? 136. If a tree does not bear flowers or fruit, why give it water? If the Lord of the heart (*Hrishikeshi*) does not give him anything to eat why does Nama give himself to His worship? 137. Why labour in vain digging when no water is reached in the well? So if the Husband of Rukmini is not pleased with one why give oneself to His worship? 138. If anyone is determined to give no gifts at a wedding, why invite such a relative there?

So, if the Husband of Rukmini is unwilling to show His favour, why be His worshipper? 139. If a medicine gives no good results, why trouble the tongue with taking it? So, if the Husband of Rukmini is not pleased, why should one worship Him? 140. Or if a field produces no crop why labour in vain there? So if the Husband of Rukmini is not pleased, why spend time in describing His good qualities?'

SECRET OF THE TOUCHSTONE DISCLOSED

141. 'Dear friend, my husband made Mother Rukmini pleased with him, and She gave us a touchstone in Her kindness to us. 142. By bringing it in contact with iron we have created an immense amount of gold at our home. Because of this, we dine every day upon the choicest food.' 143. Rajabai replied to her, 'How does a touchstone look?' Kamalaja replied, 'Come to my home and I will show it to you there.' 144. Thus after conversing with one another the two women went to their homes. It happened now one day that Rajabai came to Kamalaja's home. 145. She quickly brought the touchstone and showed it to her friend. 'Take it away for a very short time, and with your own hands apply it to pieces of iron. 146. Create a heap of gold at your home and drive away the sorrows of poverty. Then bring it back to me. 147. Do not let your husband or mine know of this matter.' Rajabai having heard this was greatly gratified. 148. She returned to her home for pieces of iron and quickly applied the touchstone to her needles, her scissors and her spinning wheel. 149. She took the gold into the bazaar and exchanged it for money which she gave to the merchants and brought home all the materials she needed. 150. She bought garments and ornaments and the best of cooking vessels, also a great quantity of food materials. Full of joy she began her cooking. 151. About noon Namdev returned and asked the news of his wife. 'Tell me,' he said, 'where did you bring all these things

from ? ' 152. She replied, ' Eat your meal. What is the use of asking me such questions ? From today your mind must have no worries about your domestic affairs. ' 153. Namdev then said to her, ' Not until you tell me will I eat.' Rajabai saw there would be trouble ahead, so she told him. 154. She said, ' A Brahman by name of Parisa Bhagavat made Rukmini pleased with him, and being so pleased She gave him a touchstone. 155. You are constantly repeating the names of Pandurang, but here at our home we have not a scrap to eat, and our children are always suffering from lack of food. 156. Kamalaja, Parisa's wife, gave me the touchstone for a short time; I touched it to iron and have stored some gold in our home. 157. As she and I are naturally friends, she lent me the touchstone. I have now accomplished what I want and now I am going to take it back and give it to her.' 158. Nama said to his wife, Show me what a touchstone is.' She went into the house and brought it and showed it to him.

NAMDEV THROWS A TOUCHSTONE INTO THE RIVER

159. Nama took the stone from her hand, took it to the Chandrabhaga river and threw it into one of its deep pools. While doing so he kept repeating the names of Vitthal. 160. Without any concern about what he had done, he sat down repeating the names of God. But Rajabai was greatly troubled and sat down weeping. 161. Just then Parisa Bhagavat returned to his home. He had kept the touchstone in his box but he did not see it there now. 162. He said to his wife, ' You have become a fool, for you have lost what it takes a whole lifetime to obtain. Though men might make the most stupendous efforts, they could never acquire such an opportunity. 163. She said to him, 'Rajabai asked for it, and took it for a moment to her home. I lent it to her because of her poverty.' 164. Parisa said to his wife, ' That is just what

I was afraid of. Hurry now to her home and bring it back here immediately.' 165. Kamalaja at once set off to the house of Namdev and said to Rajabai, 'Where have you put that thing of mine ?' 166. The other replied, 'O my friend, I have committed a great fault. My husband returned home and then took it away. 167. He will soon come back from his bath and then I will give it back to you.' But Kamalaja said to her, 'Give it to me at once.' 168. Rajabai now became greatly troubled and said, 'Let us go to where he is.' Hastening to the Bhima river, they arrived where Namdev was. 169. His eyes were shut. He was thinking of the form of the Holder of the disk (Krishna) and in his love he kept repeating the names of Vitthal. 170. Nama's wife said to him, 'Where have you put the touchstone ? Kamalaja has come to ask for it. You must give it to her.' 171. The *bhakta* of Vishnu listened and then said, 'I have thrown it into the water.' Hearing him say this, both women became furious with anger, 172. and in grief they beat their breasts. Men and women came to see what the matter was and asked what had happened. 173. Rajabai told them everything. Parisa Bhagavat learning what was taking place, and beating his breast, he also came where Nama was. 174. He told the people, 'Nama had wished for the touchstone, and now he tells us that he has thrown it away into a deep hole in the Chandrabhaga river.' 175. The different classes of people now began to revile both of them, yet the pious *bhaktas* continued to praise Nama. 176. They said, 'Gold and clay seem the same in value to this servant of Vishnu. He could never have desired to possess this touchstone.' 177. The crooked-minded, however, remarked, 'A deceiver puts on a garland made of *tulsi*. If he desired the touchstone belonging to the Brahman, how can you call him a good man ?' 178. Parisa full of emotion, said openly to Nama, 'God and His *bhakta* are both deceivers. Why have you ruined my home ? 179. You call yourself one who is indifferent to earthly things. And yet you had a longing for this touchstone. Think it over in your mind whether the saints will approve of this.' 180. To this the servant of Vishnu replied, 'Why should you want this touchstone ? Outwardly you call yourself indifferent to these worldly things. 181. So I threw the touchstone away in one of the deep holes of the Chandrabhaga river. If you regard this as untrue go into the water and look for it.' 182. Hearing Nama's words, all the people broke out into a laugh. 'We cannot think of any expert who would be able to recognize it in the sand.'

NAMDEV TURNS PEBBLES INTO TOUCHSTONES

183. Nama then leaped into the water and did a remarkable thing. He took a handful of sand in his hand and said, 'I have here many touchstones. 184. Choose the one that belongs to you.' Hearing the words of Nama, all the people began to laugh and said, 185. 'To his sight pebbles and touchstones look alike.' Others remarked, 'Let us prove what he says.' 186. Some of them therefore took a handful of needles and applied them to the pebbles, and all the pebbles turned out to be touchstones. All the people were astonished. 187. They now remarked, 'The hand of Nama, as it touched the pebbles, turned them all into touchstones.' Everyone now rejoiced and cried out, 'Blessed is Nama.' 188. In the joy of love the assembly of *bhaktas* now cried out, 'Victory, Victory.' Those crooked people who had reviled him now had to look on the ground in shame. 189. Seeing such a miracle as this, Parisa Bhagavat began to repent. He said to Nama, 'There is no one in the world who is as blessed as you. 190. I had prayed to Rukmini, and asked her for a touchstone. I was ready to give my very life for it, not knowing your power. 191. Wherever your feet touch, there all power is to be found. I

have no desire now for this touchstone. I desire only your hand of blessing.' 192. He then threw back into the water the touchstone which Namdev had brought out, and Parisa Bhagavat became a suppliant of Nama's as one attached to him. 193. In listening to the teachings of the servant of Vishnu, one acquires divine knowledge.

The interesting stories which will be related hereafter will give great joy to the listeners. 194. This special book of the *Bhaktavijaya* is really nectar. Those who drink of it with pleasure will never be harmed by the diseases of this earthly life. 195. Or you might think of the *Bhaktavijaya* as the full moon and in the mind of the *Vaishnava Chakor* there is supreme joy. 196. Revilers who are not *bhaktas*, and who are haters, have no love for its divine light. Therefore, having no trust in their hearts, they revile this book. 197. In describing them the goddess of speech in vain becomes needlessly wearied. So now, you good and noble-minded *bhaktas*, give attention in your love. 198. The Husband of Rukmini abides by the Bhima river, and pervades and overflows the three worlds. It is by His favour that Mahipati is writing this descriptive book.

199. *Swasti.* (Peace !) This book is the *Shri Bhaktavijaya.* In listening to it the Lord of the world will be pleased. Listen to it, you God-loving pious *bhaktas.* This is the eighteenth very delightful chapter; it is an offering to Shri Krishna.

CHAPTER XIX

JAGAMITRA NAGA : GOD PROTECTS HIS OWN

Obeisance to Shri Ganesh. Obeisance to Shri Radha Krishna

A DESCRIPTION OF PANDHARI

1. Today is the festival of the eleventh day in the month of *Kartik* (November). A crowd of saints has gathered at Pandhari. *Vanamali* (Krishna) Himself has also arrived in company with His *bhaktas*. 2. The Chandrabhaga and Bhimarathi rivers are, as it were, peace and forgiveness; and the Pushpavati, the river that flows by Gopalpur, is, as it were, compassion. 3. Venunad is joy itself where the Root of joy (Krishna) played. Pure devotion is in the form of Pundalik, that very well-known saint, whose deeds are beyond one's ken. 4. This book, the *Bhaktavijaya*, so interesting and delightful, is the temple of Pandurang. Having seen this beautiful spot, Krishna, the cloud-dark complexioned One, remained in it. 5. The altars of *tulsi* plants are, as it were, the noblest of good qualities. On them are raised banners proclaiming His good fame which produce a beautiful appearance. 6. Mother Rukmini is, as it were, seen in skill, wisdom and noble qualities. It is through Her favour that the mind rejoices in love. 7. Pious people come here to visit this holy sacred city, so absolutely pure. And putting aside all thoughts of honour or pride they act as *jivanmuktas* (free while living).

JAGAMITRA NAGA'S REVILERS

8. There was a Brahman at Parali Vaijanath by the name of Jagamitra Naga. He was a man of supreme piety and a *Vaishnava*. He lived there with his family. 9. He made his daily begging trips to the town and brought back to his home whatever food he collected. Thus he provided the food necessary for his family. 10. He

put aside the snares of desires and every night he performed a *kirtan* with enthusiasm. People of the town, being fond of his *kirtans*, were accustomed to attend and listen. 11. Seeing his indifference to earthly things, every one felt very kindly towards him. They remarked, 'Pandurang has in him descended as an *avatar*, so he is indifferent to earthly things.' 12. But while gaining this high reputation revilers were greatly disturbed in mind, and so they planned many things in order that he might be dishonoured. 13. They were like fireflies that are needlessly irritated when they see the sun with their eyes; or as the vessels of the laundry-man feel when they hear the roar of the Ganges; 14. or as when the *tulsi* plant is being properly worshipped the *bhang* plant seeing it becomes angry; or as the *sindi* plant becomes angry at the constant power of the wish-tree; 15. so, when the revilers listened to the praises of Jagamitra, they became very angry. They said, 'We must devise some plan which will bring about the loss of his reputation.' 16. Thus with many evil thoughts in their mind, they indulged in reviling him. Although Jagamitra heard what they said, still he had not the slightest evil thought in his mind.

HIS HOME BURNT UP

17. One day after the performance of his *kirtan*, Jagamitra Naga was asleep in his home. These evil men came suddenly and set his hut on fire. 18. All his children were asleep in the house. In the midst of this disaster he thought of the Lord of Pandhari, 19. and cried out, 'O Husband of Rukmini, rush to my help. O Brother of the lowly, O Helper of the helpless, who is there to protect us apart from Thee?' 20. The Holder of the disk (Krishna), hearing his piteous cry, quickly arrived on the spot. He had in His hand His *Sudarshan* disk and protected them. 21. The house blazed furiously and the townspeople watched

it. Pious *bhaktas* came near and wept aloud in their sorrow. 22. They said, 'O the *bhakta* of Vishnu, Jagamitra! Someone has burned up this *bhakta.* Although seeing this distress, the Lord of Pandhari has not come to help him.' 23. After all the woodwork of the house was burnt up, the fire was extinguished, and just then the sun suddenly arose in the East. 24. Rumour spread through the town that Jagamitra had been burnt up in the fire. So very early in the morning people came to see what had happened. 25. They saw that the hut had been burnt up and that the fire had now been extinguished; and yet not the slightest ashes or coal had fallen down. 26. There was Jagamitra with his family, worshipping Shri Hari. Seeing this wonder, all were greatly astonished. 27. (They said), 'When an attempt was made to burn the Pandavas in the house that was lacquered, Hari came there to protect them. So also the Enemy of Mura (Krishna) now came to protect Jagamitra; 28. just as when Prahlad was thrown into the fire he was not burnt; so the Lord of Pandhari came at this time to protect Jagamitra; 29. or as when forest fires suddenly blazed about the cows and the cowherds, Shri Krishna protected His *bhaktas* at this time.' 30. Thus remarking to one another they made their *namaskar* to Jagamitra and said to him, 'You are an *avatar* of God. Now we know this for a certainty.' 31. The people of the town now assembled together and planned among themselves, 'Let us give Jagamitra a written deed of land as a gift. 32. In this way he will be able to carry on his worldly affairs and we shall have performed a very great religious deed, and thus being pleased the Good Being will remove perplexities of our earthly life.' 33. Thus thinking of the matter they came to tell Jagamitra.

JAGAMITRA REFUSES A GIFT OF LAND

He replied to them, 'What need have I of this

bondage? 34. In my begging trips into town I am able to provide for my family. I have no need that you should give me a deed of land. 35. When the *chatak* bird is thirsty, a cloud immediately appears. So the Lord of the heart (*Hrishikeshi*) gives to His servants food and raiment. 36. When birds are hungry they find grains of food in all sorts of places. In the same way He protects His servants. 37. And so, when one is under the protection of the Life of the world, Whose family is the universe, what need have I of the gift of land? 38. If anyone has a boat to sit in, why should he have to grasp the side of a swimmer? Why leave the light of the sun and depend upon that of a light? 39. If at one's home one has a wish-cow, why have a goat there? If one has the water of the Ganges, why dig a well? 40. What need have I of your land when I would have the sacred food from begging?' 41. Hearing him say this, all the citizens pleaded with him as follows: 'The land will be deeded in your name and anyone may live on it, and whatever grain the earth will bring forth will be used in charity.' 42. They therefore wrote in the deed, 'That one acre of land is hereby given as a gift to Jagamitra of the town of Parali Vaijanath. 43. All the farmers then joined together and worked in the field and raised the crops. They brought all the grain that was produced by the land and applied it to charitable purposes.

PERSECUTED BY THE HAWALDAR

44. Many days passed in this way and then there came a hindrance to these religious acts. A new official (*Hawaldar*) was appointed to the town. 45. All the inhabitants of the town came at once to meet him because he had confiscated the land given to Jagamitra. 46. They pleaded with the official saying, 'We gave this land to him of our own free choice. You evil fellow, why have you

placed yourself in opposition to this religious deed?' 47. Although they thus pleaded with him, his mind was not moved, for Muhammadans are a very obstinate class and will not listen to anyone. 48. The official came to the house of Jagamitra and said to him, 'You call yourself a friend of the world. Now for the installation of a god I desire a tiger as divinity. 49. If you will give such a tiger to-day before the setting of the sun, your name Jagamitra (friend of the world) will have its true meaning. 50. If you are not able to do this, I shall take back that acre of land the value of which you have eaten.' Such were the words used by that evil-doer in his talk to the *bhakta* of Hari. 51. Assenting to this demand he at once went into the jungle. He brought to his imagination the Lord of Rukmini and in his love began to sing His praises. 52. He said, 'Victory, Victory, Brother of the helpless, Giver of mercy, Lover of His *bhaktas*, Ocean of compassion, Purifier of the sinner, Pervader of the universe, Saviour of the lowly, Ram, Krishna. 53. Victory to Thee, Lord of Pandhari, Husband of Rukmini, Mover of the universe, the Image of life, listen to my heart's plea. O Shripati (Krishna), hasten to my help. 54. The daughter of my friend, the Muhammadan Hawaldar, is about to be married. He truly desires the tiger deity for installation. 55. O God supreme, hasten to come for the wedding. If Thou dost not do so, I will give up my life at Thy feet.'

GOD APPEARS AS A TIGER

56. Hearing this earnest plea the Holder of the disk (Krishna) immediately arrived there. Taking the form of a great tiger, 57. He said to Jagamitra, 'Who indeed has been troubling you? Show him to me, and I shall certainly devour him.' 58. Hearing him say this, the *bhakta* replied, 'My intimate friend, the Muhammadan Hawaldar, has invited you to come at once to the marriage of his daughter. 59. So dear Keshava, be patient, and let us go

together to fulfil his purpose. You are my most intimate friend. I have no one to trust aside from you.' 60. After listening, the Holder of the disk (Krishna) replied, 'Take hold of me and let us go together to his house. Go into the village, and I shall show before your eyes something marvellous.' 61. Jagamitra then tied his upper garment around the neck of the tiger and taking hold of him there they went together into the town. 62. When they were seen by the cowherds they immediately rushed into the village. As they ran their courage gave out, and they were unable to say anything. 63. Rushing into the city, they gave the news to the people that Jagamitra, holding a tiger by the neck, was coming to the official's home. 64. Hearing what they said, everyone was astonished and asked, 'Where could he have brought a tiger from ? You are telling us what is false.' 65. One said, 'What is there to be wondered at ? God is his Debtor. Remember that when his hut was set afire, he was saved.' 66. While they were thus talking to one another, another report reached them, 'Jagamitra is bringing a large tiger into the town.' 67. All the men and women were frightened and closed the gate of the village as the people looked down from the walls of the town. 68. When men and women saw th tiger they were full of fear and every door of their dwellings they closed, they remaining inside through fear of the tiger. 69. Some of them on the roof looked at the tiger from afar, and remarked, 'How is it that Jagamitra has no fear at all ?' 70. Listening to this remark the wise one said to them, 'How is it that you do not understand matters ? 71. We see the tiger with our eyes, but he may be the Holder of the disk (Krishna) Himself. Perhaps when he heard of the distress of His *bhakta* He rushed to his help.' 72. Another one remarked, 'Your suggestion cannot be true. It looks like a real tiger. He has come to devour the Hawaldar.' 73. Still another remarked, 'That could not be so ; he may eat us all ; the Hawaldar in committing a wrong has brought death upon us all.' 74. Then calling to the wicked one, the people of the town said to him, ' By persecuting Jagamitra, you have brought destruction to our town. 75. When Sahasrarjun troubled Renuka, disaster came to all Kshatriyas. So by our association with you, death has come upon us all. 76. When Ravan kidnapped Sita all the giant monsters met with death. So by troubling this *Vaishnava* you have brought this disaster to the town. 77. When Duryodhan persecuted Draupadi, that noble woman, all the kings suffered destruction. The same is happening to us today because of our association with you. 78. Just as by association with a bee-hive a tree is set on fire, so, O evil one, through you we are all suffering disaster.' 79. Hearing what all the people said, this evil one became frightened and with all his children he hid himself in a hut ; 80. just as a scorpion after stinging hides underneath a clod of earth ; so that mine of sin became frightened in his mind. 81. Very soon Jagamitra arrived with the tiger. Seeing the gates of the town closed, he was greatly troubled. 82. He said to the tiger, ' How are we to go into the city ?' Hearing him say this, the Advocate of His *bhaktas* performed a miracle. 83. He gave one great roar and the gates of the city fell down. They entered the city and the men and women looked at them from a distance. 84. One began to cry out aloud and another began to beat his mouth. All exclaimed, ' The Lord of *Kailas* (Heaven) is angry because we have been associated with this evil man.' 85. Hearing this outcry, Jagamitra gave the people an assurance: ' Let your minds be at rest, and watch the marvel that is now to take place. 86. A man reaps according to his deeds, why then should any of you be concerned ? Let your minds be without fear, and worship the Husband of Rukmini.' 87. Hearing him say this all the people were pleased and remarked, 'He has brought the tiger in order to take the life of the Hawaldar.'

THE PANIC-STRICKEN HAWALDAR

88. Jagamitra and the tiger now quickly arrived at the house of the Hawaldar. The evil one seeing this began to tremble. 89. Seeing the big tiger he closed the door of his hut, and placing his wife and children behind him he felt fear and concern. 90. Then Jagamitra said, 'I have come bringing your deity. Why do you hide yourself in your hut? Tell me quickly. 91. Seeing the deity in person why have you closed the door in your confusion? Tell me what you intend to do further. 92. You perform various visits to the sacred bathing-places, religious ceremonies and severe austerities, still you cannot obtain the sight of God. But when actually seen, you foolish one, you close your door. 93. He who cannot be attained even by the eightfold *yoga* rites, when that deity comes to your home, why do you hide yourself away? 94. The *rishis* perform many forms of *yoga*, still He cannot be easily attained. When that very deity comes to your home why is it that you are afraid? 95. That which is very much cooler than the moon and is like nectar itself, when you see such a deity why do you let fear come into your heart?' 96. The tiger now roared and beat his tail upon the ground and when the evil one heard it he was terribly frightened. 97. The tiger forcibly sprang up and started as if to devour the reviler. Jagamitra seized hold of him just as showmen seize their monkeys. 98. In that same way the Life of the world became subservient to His *bhakta*. Failing to bring to His mind His own divinity He showed His deeds to men. 99. Showing great anger, the tiger jumped about as if saying, 'Let me devour this evil one.' The Hawaldar was in his house with his children. 100. His wife said to him, 'Go at once outside, otherwise your children will die together with you. 101. Naturally your end must soon

come through age. So go outside, and let our lives be saved.' 102. As this conversation fell upon the ears of the people, all marvelled. They clapped their hands and began to laugh. 103. The Hawaldar joined both his hands together and began to ask for mercy, 'O merciful One, have compassion on me and save me. 104. I am now receiving the fruit of my evil heart. My bad reputation is spreading all over the earth and cannot at all be described. 105. You call yourself the friend of the world (Jagamitra). My mind recognizes it now as true. And so in humility I ask your compassion and give me the gift of life.' 106. Hearing his piteous cry, Jagamitra took the tiger with him and hastened to go back into the forest. 107. When all alone, the Life of the world took His form of four arms, and with qualities He embraced Jagamitra in His love.

108. The next chapter is full of extraordinary interest. Let the hearers make their minds attentive. Just as when misers counting out their money, their minds become absorbed in it, 109. in the same way give attention and listen to the book. The Husband of Rukmini who abides by the Bhima river will be pleased with you. 110. This Being of ancient days (*purana purusha*, Vishnu), the Life of the world, is the relator of this book. Mahipati comes as a suppliant and in love worships His feet.

111. *Swasti* (Peace!) This book is the *Shri Bhaktavijaya.* In hearing it, the Lord of the world will be pleased. Listen to it you God-loving, pious *bhaktas.* This is the nineteenth deeply delightful chapter; it is an offering to Shri Krishna

---

CHAPTER XX

JOGA PARAMANAND,

NARAHARI THE GOLDSMITH AND NAMDEV

Obeisance to Shri Ganesh. Obeisance to Shri Gopal Krishna

THE STORIES OF THE SAINTS AND THEIR INFLUENCE FOR GOOD

1. Listening to the interesting stories of the saints, all sorrows automatically depart. The Pervader of the universe is pleased with the hearers and gives them the highest form of deliverance. 2. Peace and forgiveness come and live for ever in the heart. Pure moral goodness comes at once in love. 3. Lust and anger run away from the body and all sins are burnt up, if one without a sense of shame and pride describes Hari's qualities in a *kirtan*. 4. Even if *riddhi siddhi* (the accomplishments) and the place of Indra may come to him through deeds in a former birth, he does not regard these as of any value. Pure indifference to earthly things will come to his mind without effort. 5. The Good Being becomes pleased at seeing the regular worship given Him, and gives him love for his praise service and puts away the illusion of this earthly life. 6. The enemy of Tripur (Shiva) told Parvati all the supreme sweetness of these stories of the saints. So wise *bhaktas*, give attention with all your devotion.

JOGA PARAMANAND OF BARSI

7. The *bhakta* Joga Paramanand lived in the town of Barsi. He was always without concern and possessed of indifference to earthly things. 8. He was all the time worshipping Ram Krishna and Narayan. He daily made his begging trips into the town and thus provided for his family. 9. He found peace in his continual worship, paid no attention to honour or dishonour when rendered to him,

and destroyed the snares of desire by worshipping Shri Hari. 10. He would perform his baths and then worship by using the sixteen materials. He daily made to God seven hundred *namaskars.* 11. He would repeat a verse of the *Bhagavadgita,* and then bow prostrate on the ground. After completing his devotions in this way he would sit down to his meal. 12. It is said in the religious law books that anyone who eats a meal without having performed his daily devotions, that man is like a hog. 13. Birds and animals, as they wander here and there, perform neither sinful nor good deeds. There is no law given in the *Shastras* for insects, ants or animals. 14. But when one suddenly acquires a human body, one should make full use of it. Without association with the good, there is no obtaining of knowledge with this human body. 15. You may perhaps ask how can one find leisure for these regular acts of devotion while one carries on one's daily occupation ? I will tell you one way of solving the problem. Listen. 16. There is one means which is superior to all bathings in sacred waters, religious ceremonies, austerities, making of gifts, religious observances and bodily torture : it is the worship of Shri Hari. 17. In this *Kali Yuga* no means have been specially designated, aside from the repeating of God's names. Just as at the time of death, nectar can bring back life to every one, 18. so anyone who is carrying on his daily business and at the same time is constant in his thoughts of Hari, the Life of the world comes and sits beside him in his love. 19. But what is the use of saying more about this ? Every one knows the power of God's name; and no one is over impressed by that love which is outside of experience. 20. Thus Joga Paramanand indulged in his habits of worshipping Hari. Thinking of Govind in his heart, he was always full of joy.

JOGA AND THE SILK GARMENT

21. On a certain day a merchant came on business at

the great door of the temple. A cloud had rained upon the earth and the ground was exceedingly muddy. 22. But in the mud Paramanand was making his *namaskar* to Pandurang. In his heart he was thinking of the delight of Rukmini, and the destroyer of the earthly hindrances of his *bhaktas*. 23. When he saw such devotion on the part of Joga, the merchant's heart was deeply moved. He exclaimed, 'Who is this *bhakta* of Vishnu? I see in him indifference to earthly things.' 24. He then took out from among his goods a silk raiment, and giving it at once to Joga made him a *namaskar*. 25. He said, 'O *Swami*, ocean of compassion, first put on this raiment. I come to you as suppliant, a dull-minded person to plead with you.' 26. Joga replied to him, 'What need have I for a silk garment? If you have some old clothes, you may give them at once to me. 27. Putting on some old raiments, going to beg and bringing back some food, enables me to carry on my worship without hindrance. 28. You have brought a silk raiment for me, but dress the god in it instead, and by doing so, the Husband of Rukmini will show an unlimited kindness.' 29. Although he thus spoke to him, still that ignorant man would not listen. He was not able to realize what was an especially suitable gift. 30. One should give water and grain to birds. One should give grass to animals as a religious act. Those who are wise give money to those who are worthy of it. 31. If water is placed at the roots of a tree, it gives joy to the tree. Food and raiment should be given privately to one who does not ask for it. 32. But the merchant did not understand this, and used force in fitting Joga with the silk raiment. From there the merchant went to another part of the *bazaar*. 33. Joga put on the brilliant clothing and tucked up its lower part. In order that the garment might not be soiled by the mud he made his prostrate *namaskar* (*dandavat*) very carefully. 34. Before he began to wear this garment he had made his prostrate *namaskar* without any concern. But now he had lost all his aspirations and his usual practice was hindered by his desire to keep this garment unsoiled. 35. By noon time it had become exceedingly hot, and Joga had become overcome with hunger. So on that day he was unable to make the complete number of *namaskars.* 36. Seeing the drops of perspiration on his body, he became very unhappy, and said to himself, 'Why is it that I find it so hard to make my *namaskars* today ? I do not understand it.' 37. Then letting reason work in his heart, he thought. 'I see my enemy in this silk raiment. By having to look after this raiment, I have failed in my worship. 38. Just as the full moon is swallowed up by the monster Rahu, so it would seem that it is because of this silk raiment that I have lost my aspiration. 39. It is as if one should serve a plate of dainty food, and then suddenly a dog should come and lick it. So this putting on of a silk raiment has brought a great hindrance to my worship of Hari. 40. As if a *pimpal* tree planted on the bank of the Ganges should be uprooted by a great gust of wind, so it seems to me that it is this silk raiment that has become my enemy. 41. Or as if a farmer should raise a crop on his land, then suddenly there should fall upon it a swarm of locusts, so this silk raiment has become a hindrance to my good deeds. 42. Or as while a *sannyasi* is performing his austerities there is suddenly sent to him some food from the king; so this silk raiment has become an enemy to my devotion. 43. I wonder how this wrong was committed by me. What shall I do to punish my body ? I will at once go into the forest and surround myself with five fires 44. Or I will burn myself with fire. Or I will go and sit alone in the mountains. Or I will go at once and perform the eightfold *yoga.* 45. Or I will go to the junction of the three great rivers [Ganges, Jumna and Saraswati] and there put my body to the saw. By doing so, at least the Husband of Rukmini will come and meet me there. 46. Or begging for food just sufficient to cover the palm of my hand go and visit all the sacred bathing places; by doing so, at least the Life of the world will have mercy upon me. 47. Or I will hasten and go to the Himalaya mountains and there I will spend my life. By that means at least the Lord of Pandhari will surely meet me. 48. Or discarding food and drink, sit on my mat and fast; by that good deed at least the Holder of the disk (Krishna) will come at once and meet me. 49. Or getting myself devoured by fire, perform the penance of death; by that means the Lord of Pandhari will have mercy upon me.' 50. With repentance in his heart he thus thought over the matter. Then he went outside the temple and sat down.

JOGA'S SELF-INFLICTED SUFFERING

51. Just then a farmer was passing by driving two fiery oxen. There was a yoke on their necks and the farmer was taking them into the forest. 52. Joga seeing him, called him to come near him. Because of his repentance, tears were flowing from his lotus-eyes. 53. He then said to the farmer, 'Give me these two oxen. I will give you in exchange this brilliant silk robe.' 54. The farmer thought to himself, 'The silk garment will bring me twice the value of these oxen.' So he replied, 'I accept your offer.' And he gave Joga the oxen. 55. In a humble voice Joga said to the farmer, 'Take a rope and fasten my feet to the yoke. 56. Then pretending to be furious with anger lash the oxen. You go to your home and have no more concern about me.' 57. The farmer then consented and fastened Joga's feet to the yoke. As the farmer lashed the oxen with his whip the oxen began to run towards the forest. 58. Pebbles, thorns and stones hurt Joga's body in-

tensely. All his skin was torn away from him. 59. The frightened oxen ran rapidly; just as a deer runs when seeing a hunter,in the same way the oxen ran hither and thither in the great forest. 60. Joga with repentance in his heart paid no attention to his bodily sufferings. He said to himself, 'This bodily torture is a proper ending for the wrong I have committed to-day.' 61. Comforting his mind with this thought he continued repeating the names of God: 'O Shri Hari, Ram Krishna, Narayan, Purifier of the sinner, and Ocean of compassion, 62. Victory to Thee, delight of the heart of Rukmini, Dweller upon the sea of milk, Recliner on the serpent (Shesha), Advocate of Thy *bhaktas*, Treasure-house of all goodness, Life of the world, Pandurang.' 63. Taking God's names this way, his throat choked with emotion. In the meantime the oxen were running about in the forest and dragging him along. 64. All his skin was torn off; bones alone remained upon his body and his suffering went to such extremes that he was at the point of death. 65. But full of joy even at such a time, Joga continued his worship full of love. Then the Lord of Pandhari, hearing his piteous cries, rushed to his aid. 66. When (the elephant) Gajendra cried out piteously for help, Krishna rushed to his aid. When Draupadi was troubled by Dusshasan, the Holder of the disk (Krishna) rushed to her help. 67. So seeing Joga's extremities the Holder of the disk (Krishna) came rushing to help him. He took off the yoke from the oxen and let them go free. 68. Then unbinding Joga's feet with his own hands, He gave him an embrace and as He gazed at him with His look of compassion, Joga's body assumed a divine form. 69. When the sun arises no darkness is to be seen; so when the Lord of the universe shows His favour, all fear of bodily sufferings passes away. 70. The Husband of Rukmini said now to Joga, 'Why did you attempt such great sufferings? You have punished your body when you have done no wrong

71. When you eat or drink it all goes into my. mouth. When you go and come that is circumambulating *Me.* 72. If you speak to anyone that becomes *My* praise. When you lie down in peace and happiness that is a prostrate *namaskar* made to Me.* 73. That being so, My dear *bhakta*, why did you go to such extremes ?' Joga placed his head at the god's feet, and said, 'Place me in the shadow of Thy compassion.'

74. On a certain day God assembled together all his *bhaktas* in Pandhari and told them all that had happened to Joga. 75. As the Lord of *Vaikunth* (Heaven) told them in detail, all were greatly astonished. Dnyandev said to *Hrishikeshi* (the Lord of the heart), 'There is no end to Thy wonderful deeds. 76. One excelling the other Thou hast created Thy *bhaktas.* Thou alone, O cloud-dark One (Krishna), canst experience the delight arising from their love and happiness.'

NARAHARI THE GOLDSMITH

77. Now you clever hearers, listen to the story of Narahari the goldsmith, a *bhakta* of Shiva who prayed to Shiva and made the god Shiva pleased with him. 78. He would arise early in the morning and go to bathe in the Bhimarathi river. After that in his love he would worship Mallikarjun (Shiva). 79. Although he lived in the holy city of Pandhari he never went to the temple of Vithoba. He placed his trust in one deity alone and worshipped Him with joy. 80. Just as the *chatak* bird will take no water from earth, not seeing the clouds with his eyes, so Narahari would not worship any other deity but Shiva; 81. or as the lotus-flower, although it sees many clusters of stars, will not open until the sun appears to its sight, and

* In ch 20.71-72 there is described what is known as सहज भक्ति (natural devotion). See also *Eknathi Bhagwat*, Ch. 11.770-772.

then immediately becomes full of joy; 82. or just as an infant child has no liking for any other beautiful woman except its mother; or just as to a dutiful wife, no other person is her deity or object of her reverence except her husband; 83. so with body, speech and mind Narahari worshipped Mallikarjun (Shiva). He would not even look from a distance at the pinnacle of the temple of Shri Pandurang. 84. Just as men and women do not look at the moon on *Ganesh Chaturthi* (festival of Ganpati); so Narahari the goldsmith would not even look at the dome of the temple of Vitthal. 85. A certain merchant came to Pandhari and planned a vow in his mind, ' If a son is given to me of noble qualities, I will offer to God a waistband.' 86. The Husband of Rukmini had accepted his vow, and the man had come to Pandhari. After visiting and worshipping the God in love, he put the question to the priest: 87. ' Is there a clever goldsmith here who can make golden settings in a waistband and place in them diamonds and other jewels?' 88. The priest replied, 'There is a goldsmith here by name of Narahari. Go at once to him and enquire of him.' 89. The merchant carried with him some diamonds, jewels and gold and gave them to Narahari, who said, ' Measure the size you want and give it to me. 90. If it should turn out to be more or less, do not blame me.' The merchant hearing him say this was much astonished: 91. 'Although God is near to him, he does not like to look at Him. Still what does that matter to me?' So he brought and gave him the measurement. 92. Narahari with great cleverness placed the diamonds and jewels in their settings; and having prepared the waistband, he brought and gave it to the merchant. 93. The merchant bathed the eagle bannered One with a shower of water and worshipped Him with sixteen materials used for worship. He put the waistband around the idol but it was not large enough. 94. He brought it back to Narahari and he very cleverly lengthened it. When it was again brought to the god it appeared to be too large. 95. When increased in length it became too long, and when made of the exact measurement it was not long enough. The merchant became greatly concerned. 'Why has the Husband of Rukmini become angry with me ? 96. He does not regard my pure intention. Krishna will not accept this waistband.' The merchant came back to Narahari and patiently requested him, 97. saying to Narahari, ' Come to the temple yourself, look at the Holder of the disk (Krishna); and with your own hand place the waistband upon Him and then you may come back '.

THE LESSON NARAHARI LEARNED ABOUT THE ONENESS OF KRISHNA AND SHIVA

98. He (Narahari) replied, ' I am observing a vow and I have never thus far been to see Krishna in His temple. I have never as yet looked upon any deity except Shiva. ' 99. Narahari covered his eyes with a cloth and went to the temple. Seeing him blindfolded, the citizens of the place laughed and thought it exceedingly strange. 100. They said, 'It is as if a poor man should close his eyes when he sees a treasure in the ground, such we understand to be the point of view of Narahari. 101. Or he is like one who leaves his *Chintamani* (wish-stone) jewel at home and in vain wanders about to different bathing places. So is this closing of his eyes and going to look at the god. ' 102. Others remarked, ' Just as one with fever is not fond of dainty food, so the Dweller in *Vaikunth* (Heaven) does not come into the thought of Narahari. ' 103. Others remarked, ' Each one knows his own case best. What is his case to us ? ' Thus the various classes of men talked among themselves. 104. With his eyes blindfolded, the goldsmith Narahari came to the great door of the temple, and the merchant held him by the hand and guided him inside. 105. Some one laughed and said, ' Make a prostrate *namaskar*

to the god'. Another remarked, 'He does not even look at Him. How then can he worship the god's feet? 106. If one will not give a seat to one who comes to his house, will one give him daintily cooked food? If anyone will not listen to the *mantras* of the bath, will he make religious gifts? 107. Anyone who will not give water to a *tulsi* plant, will he take the trouble to circumambulate it? Anyone who will not make a bow to a good man will certainly not take him to his own home. 108. He who will not tell a traveller the way, will certainly not give him a place in his home. He who with his lips reviles god's *bhaktas* will certainly not go to listen to praise-services in honour of Hari. 109. He who will not listen to the praises of the Ganges river will not take a bath in it with all his clothes on. So, if Narahari is unwilling to look at the god, he surely will not make a *namaskar* to Him.' 110. Well, such were the remarks passed by the men and women. Narahari entered into the temple and groped for the god with his hand. 111. He groped for a form with ten arms and five faces. Around the neck He was adorned with a serpent-shaped ornaments. On the head was a beautiful mass of matted hair and hie whole body was marked with the sacred ashes. 112. He wore the skins of an elephant and a tiger. It appeared to Narahari as though it was the blue-throated Shiva who was actually standing on the brick. 113. He said to himself, 'This is the very deity whom I worship, then why have I in vain closed my eyes?' Thus full of repentance in his heart he removed the coverings from his eyes and looked at the god. 114. That dark-blue-complexioned One was standing upon a brick with a very brilliant crown upon His head. His glorious face shone with intense purity and on His neck was the garland Vaijayanti and the Kaustubha jewel. 115. In His ears were earrings shaped like crocodiles. His breast was wide. His waist was thin. Both his brilliant hands were placed upon His hips. Around His waist He was enveloped by His yellow raiment. 116. Seeing His parallel feet upon the brick, Narahari was astonished. Then again blindfolding his eyes, he found his hands touching the form of *Dhurjati* (Shiva).

NARAHARI'S REPENTANCE

117. Immediately opening his eyes again, he saw the Husband of Rukmini, and with his heart full of repentance he made the god a *namaskar* with love. 118. Said he, 'Victory, Victory to God Supreme, the Life of the whole universe! Victory, Victory to Shiva, O Keshav (Krishna), I have come as a suppliant to Thee. 119. Victory, Victory to Thee who dwellest in *Kailas* (Heaven). Victory, Victory to Thee, Lord of *Vaikunth* (Heaven). Victory, Victory to Thee, Lord of the *bhaktas*. Form without duality, O Guru of the world. 120. Victory to Thee, Enjoyer of the ocean of milk. Victory to Thee, the blue-throated One, blue-complexioned and the Dweller in the cemeteries. Victory to Thee, Lover of Thy *bhaktas*, Lord of Pandhari. Remove the illusions of Thy *bhaktas*. 121. Not recognizing Thy greatness, I thought that the two names implied two deities. Now Thou hast removed from me, O cloud-dark-complexioned One, the very thought of duality and hast increased my love for non-duality.' 122. Listening to this praise, Krishna said to Narahari, 'I want you to be My *bhakta* and that is why I have adopted this method. 123. Now do not regard Shiva and Krishna as forming two deities.' As *Hrishikeshi* (the Lord of the heart) said this, Narahari embraced His feet. 124. From that time forth Pandurang held on His head the emblem of Shiva. For *Shrirang* (Krishna) never disappoints His servants.

125. Hearing this story of Narahari, listeners may

raise the question and say, 'In the feast given by Nama, saints were invited in order to please Nama. The saints were invited to dine. 126. Among the guests we had heard with our ears the name of Narahari the goldsmith.' But Shiva had brought him along with him on that occasion. 127. Just as a father brings along his son when going to a feast, so Shiva also had brought His *bhakta* along with him.

GOD TESTS NAMA's BELIEF THAT GOD IS IN ALL CREATURES

128. On a certain day the Lord of the earth took Nama aside and said, 'Let it be a fixed thought in your mind, that I live in all creatures.' 129. The servant of Vishnu replied, 'O Lord God, why dost Thou feel any need of telling me this? Through Thy favour I have compassion upon every class of being.' 130. Then in order to test the heart of Nama, the Lord of Pandhari assumed the form of a dog. On the twelfth day the dog wandered about among the pilgrims. 131. When anyone had seated himself in order to eat, *Hrishikeshi* (the Lord of the heart) would go near to him, but no one would so much as throw him a morsel of food. Instead, they would say, 'Drive away the dog' 132. He would put his nose into the flour of some, but they would attempt to beat him then and there. But the Lord of Pandhari could not be touched by their hands and ran away. 133. When anyone was sitting at their lunch, the cloud-dark-complexioned One would come near them and if he attempted to snatch a bit of bread they would beat Him. 134. Whenever Brahmans sat to eat, there *Hrishikeshi* (the Lord of the heart) was sure to stand. No one would throw him a single morsel and he wondered at it. 135. Seeing the special purity of those who had come back from the great pilgrimage, the Holder of the disk (Krishna) would come near them and

touch them while they were eating. 136. One remarked, 'The dog has defiled you.' Another said, 'But the dog is a black one, and we have heard of a law in the religious lawbooks that black dogs do not defile anyone'. 137. While some farmers were sitting down to eat the Life of the world came near them. As He snatched up their food and tried to run away with it they took it back from Him. 138. He wandered about among all the pilgrims and tested them also. But He did not see that anyone's belief was certain, that God was in every creature. 139. Some exclaimed, 'This is a dog; drive it away from among the pilgrims.' When the Life of the world heard this remark He adopted the following method. 140. The Lord of the world came near to Nama with a leap and seized a piece of bread in His mouth and began to run away. 141. When the servant of Vishnu saw this he took in his hand a cup of melted butter and said to the dog, 'Why do you eat a piece of bread dry?' 142. Nama then went to the dog and put a morsel of bread into His mouth. The Husband of Rukmini, the dog, lovingly sat down to His meals. 143. Seeing this rather strange sight all the people laughed at Nama. They made motions to another, and said as follows. 144. Some said, 'Nama has become crazy. Look how he feeds a dog. All animals are alike to Him. He sees no superior or inferior among them. 145. Just as the earth does not regard some trees as superior and others as inferior; or just as water equally regards a cow or a tiger. 146. The full moon shines equally bright over all beings. We know that such is the heart of Nama. 147. To the royal swan and the falcon the air is the same. So it seems that the heart of Nama is the same, regarding all things as alike. 148. Or just as when the sun arises it regards kings and subjects as alike, so this servant of Vishnu puts away all thought of duality, and in that belief lives among men.' 149. The dog now laughed and said, 'How did you recognize me? Nama replied, 'It was Visoba Khechar who pointed out to me signs by which I should recognize Thee. O Lord God.' 150. After doing this marvellous deed the Husband of Rukmini became invisible. Everyone was astonished and exclaimed, 'Blessed is Nama's devotion. 151. Without any effort on our part we have met with the Life of the world in the form of a dog. We did not give it anything to eat. We were led astray by our bad deeds in our previous births.'

GOD INVITES NAMA TO EAT

152. It happened on the eleventh day of the month of *Kartik* (November) that Namdev was fasting. *Hrishikeshi* (the Lord of the heart) said to him, 'Come quickly and eat.' 153. The servant of Vishnu replied, 'One should never eat food on this day. By doing so one is able to approach Thy feet during all future rebirths. 154. Just as Thou, *Hrishikeshi* (O Lord of the heart), art superior to all gods, just as the *tulsi* plant is superior among the plants; so among all religious festivals that of the eleventh day. It is highly honoured by us *Vaishnavas*.' 155. To this the Life of the world replied, 'Nama, listen to My words. Just as Rukmangad and Ambarish observed this festival with devotion, 156. so now no one seems to have the determination to fast on the eleventh day of the month. They hypocritically show their observance of the day before men. 157. But when there is no determination in the heart to perform the religious ceremonies properly they become vain actions, just as without moisture the seed which is sown will not sprout. 158. If one should eat without feeling any hunger, how can that food be properly digested? No one can wander to different sacred bathing places if he has no feet to walk about with. 159. He whose organs of sense are not under his control cannot adopt full means to obtain spiritual life. If a man has no sense of

generosity in his heart he will not make gifts to those who are worthy of them. 160. If a man has no courage he will not be able to give his life on the battlefield. So without ability there can be no fame in the world. 161. So my dear *bhakta*, in the same way, if one has no longer belief in fasting he should not observe the festival of *Ekadahsi* (the eleventh day)'. 162. When the Holder of the *Sharang* Bow (Krishna) had said these things, Nama replied, 'If Thy favour is upon me, then there will be no lack of a fixed determination. 163. A roasted seed might sprout. An ocean might be contained in a well. But, O God, my heart will never lose its determination. 164. A fire could be hidden in the midst of grass ; the earth might be weighed; but, O Ocean of compassion, my mind will never give up its fixed determination. 165. Seed might change its character when planted in the earth; the air might be confined by a closed door; but, O Ornament of Thy *bhaktas*, my mind will never have a wrong belief. 166. A tiger might have a feeling of gentleness, and come and sit quietly in a sheepfold, but, O Pandurang, I shall never give up my purpose.' 167. Hearing Nama's words, the Life of the world laughed and said, 'Over your good deeds I must wave salt and the *nimb* leaves.' 168. Having said this the Destroyer of Madhu thought to Himself, 'I must further test Nama, and see for Myself, whether he is true to his belief.'

NAMA'S BELIEF TESTED REGARDING THE ELEVENTH OF THE MONTH

169. On the *Ekadashi* day (the eleventh dap of every fortnight) therefore *Hrishikeshi* (the Lord of the heart) assumed the form of an aged Brahman and went to the house of Nama. 170. He had a staff in his hand and old clothes on His body. He said, 'I am very hungry, and have come to ask for food. 171. You, a *bhakta* of Vishnu,

call yourself a generous man. So you must give me some food to eat.' Saying this to Nama He sat down by the door. 172. The *bhakta* of Vishnu seeing the Brahman there, bowed prostrate before Him. 'What is the wish you have which has brought you here, O *Swami*?' 173. The Lord of the world replied, 'I am in distress from lack of food. So give to some one the materials needed for cooking and get me a meal.' 174. Hearing this answer of the Brahman, the servant of Vishnu replied to Him, 'This is the *Ekadashi* day (the eleventh day.) It is not right to give cooked food. 175. If you will accept dates, fruit or roots, I will bring them at once and give them to you.' 176. Hearing him the Brahman said, 'I am not satisfied with anything other than cooked food. For this reason I have naturally come to your door for charity. 177. If you drive Me away I shall at once give up My life and the sin of having murdered a Brahman will fall upon your head.

NAMA'S RESOLVE

178. Nama replied, 'I am a *bhakta* of Vishnu. I am without good as well as sinful deeds. I have placed my heart at the feet of Pandurang, and have become a *Jivanmukta* (free while living). 179 He who cherishes in his heart no desire even for good deeds, how can sinful deeds do him harm ? He who does not love intensely, separation brings him no sorrow. 180. If anyone has discarded all love of money he will not be afraid of thieves. And if one has put away all desire to be honoured, how can he feel dishonour shown him? 181. He who feels no happiness in being praised by men, how can he feel any pain when he is reviled by men ? He who feels no pleasure in mere gain can feel no sorrow when he makes no gain. 182. When one looks upon the beautiful form of youth, and yet does not feel any pride of his own youthful appearance, how can he be troubled by the thought of old age ? 183. So, O Brahman, I

have destroyed all opportunity for sin as well as good deeds. I shall never have to go to hell because of sin.' 184. Hearing Nama say these things, the Brahman replied to him, 'You have no tenderness in your heart for others, and you go about preaching your philosophy. 185. I am a Brahman in distress from lack of food. If you do not take away my hunger, I shall immediately lose my life. Know this for certain, O *bhakta* of Vishnu.' 186. Nama said to him, 'If you give up your life, the same thing will happen to me, O Brahman.' 187. Hearing him say this, the Holder of the disk (Krishna) did a very remarkable thing. He rolled His eyes about and fainted away, falling on the ground. 188. The servant of Vishnu seeing Him thus, went close to him and looked. The Brahman was no longer breathing, he was dead.

PEOPLE REVILE NAMA

189. Hearing about this affair, men and women gathered together in the house. They said to Nama 'How is it that you have caused this murder of a Brahman at your very door? 190. The Brahman was asking some cooked food of you. You did not give it to him. And so it resulted in this great disaster. In what way can the consequence be avoided?' 191. One remarked, 'This *bhakta* of Hari preaches very verbosely his own knowledge of divine things but he never gives even a morsel of food to anyone.' 192. Thus all reviled him. But Nama's determination was unchanged. He lifted up the corpse of the Brahman and carried it to the banks of the Bhima. 193. He erected a funeral pyre and placed the corpse upon it. He laid himself by the side of the corpse and set fire to the pile. 194. Every one was astonished at what Nama did. They remarked, 'The determination of Nama is very great. We see no noble *Vaishnava* on this earth equal to him.' 195. The Brahman was not really a

Brahman. He was *Shripati* (Krishna) and, as He died, true devotion led the *Vaishnava* Nama to be immolated with Him in his fixed determination. 196. Just as the fire began to blaze, the Brahman immediately sat up and assuming a form of four arms he embraced Nama. 197. He said to him, 'If I should hunt through all the three worlds, I would not find a *bhakta* like you. Your determination to do your duty is greater than that of Ambarish and Rukmangad; 198. who took their whole city to *Vaikunth* (Heaven), but you are born as the saviour of the world.' Saying this, *Hrishikeshi* (the Lord of the heart) embracing Nama held him close to His heart. 199. He said to him, 'Ambarish observed the festival and for his faith I suffered ten rebirths. You made Me speak, although I was in my Buddha *avatar* (mute); and although I was without body you made me assume a visible form.' 200. After saying this, the Holder of the disk (Krishna) immediately became invisible. People wondered in their minds and fell at the feet of Nama.

201. O Dweller by the banks of the Bhima, the Husband of Rukmini, Thou wilt further cause me to relate the stories of the saints. Aside from Thee there is no one to illuminate the heart. 202. It is by Thy favour that words proceed out of the mouth. Mahipati comes to Thee and worships Thy feet with devotion.

203. *Swasti* (Peace !) This book is the *Shri Bhaktavijaya*. In listening to it the Lord of the world will be pleased. Listen to it, you God-loving, pious *bhaktas*. This is the twentieth very delightful chapter.

CHAPTER XXI

NAMDEV AND JANABAI

Obeisance to Shri Ganesh. Obeisance to Radha and Krishna.

GOD THE HELPER OF HIS *BHAKTAS*

1. Victory to Thee who dwellest on the ocean of milk, to Thee who reclinest upon Shesha, to Thee who assumest human body at will, Husband of Rukmini, who possessest a visible form, the Ornament of Thy *bhaktas*, a mine of goodness, Shri Vitthal. 2. Victory to Thee, who has assumed an infinite number of *avatars*. Thou who art in the form of Intelligence, Home of compassion, Protector of the gods, Lord of Pandhari, Thou who drivest away the illusions of Thy *bhaktas*. 3. Victory to Thee, Pervader of all things, Thou who art beyond all things, Saviour of the elephant Gajendra, Lord of *Vaikunth* (Heaven). Aside from Thee there is no one who can give joy to Thy *bhaktas*. 4. Victory, Victory to Thee, Mover of the heart, Cloud of intelligence, Advocate of Thy *bhaktas*, Slayer of *Daityas*, (demons), Giver of the promise to Pundalik, Husband of Rukmini, Life of the world, O Pandurang. 5. Thou who art the Father of Brahmadev, although a Doer of all things Thou art still a non-doer. There is no space even as large as an atom that is without Thee. 6. Do Thou now have compassion upon me and through me relate the stories of Thy saints. A helpless one like myself has no helper aside from Thee, O Lord of the world.

JANI THE LITTLE MAID OF NAMA

7. In the preceding chapter we had the specially interesting story of God's servant Paramanand Joga. 8. The well-known *bhakta* of Shiva, Narahari, was also made to worship Him. The Holder of the disk (Krishna) brought trouble to Nama and thereby tested his

mind. 9. It happened one day at Pandhari, when the place was filled with pilgrims, in the month of *Kartik* (November), that a little girl from amongst the pilgrims came and sat by the great door of the temple. 10. She said to her mother and father, 'I intend to remain here always. I will not come back with you to our home.' 11. Hearing the little girl say this, every one was astonished. They remarked, 'Being only seven years of age, how has she obtained such spiritual knowledge?' 12. The mother and father were greatly troubled by her resolve but she would not listen to anything. When Shri Hari casts upon anyone the eye of compassion, the love of that which is one's own does not arise in the heart. 13. Seeing her determination, however, her parents were comforted. They left their daughter at the great door of the temple, and returned to their own home. 14. When Nama saw this little girl, a feeling of compassion arose in his heart. He said to her, 'Who are you, sitting here alone in a country not your own, and without your mother and father ? 15. What town does your father belong to ? Tell me your name. What difficulties have your parents experienced, that they should have abandoned you here'? 16. The little girl replied, 'I am called Jani. The Holder of the disk (Krishna) is my mother and father. I have no one aside from Him.' 17. Hearing her words, pity arose in Nama's heart. He took the little girl by the hand, and brought her to his home. 18. Nama told Gonai of his finding the girl and how the child had been lost among the pilgrims. 'Without her mother and father she seems to look very unhappy. We must protect her. 19. At the time of Krishna's *avatarship* he had a maid by name of Kubja (the cripple). She had now appeared as an *avatar* in this *Kali Yuga*. So she has come on a pilgrimage to Pandhari, and is absorbed in the worship of Hari.' 20. Day by day she grew in stature, and men and women said to her, 'Tell us truly who you are.' 21. Jani would reply to them and say, 'I am the devoted handmaid of Nama. I have no mother nor father aside from him.' 22. While performing her domestic duties she was for ever repeating the names of Hari. When at night she listened to the praise-services of Hari she used to meditate upon them.

KRISHNA REPAIRS NAMA'S HUT

23. A very strange thing happened one day when Namdev was asleep. Five *ghatakas* of the night had passed and a dark cloud covered the sky. 24. A violent wind blew and carried Nama's hut away. When this was known to the Husband of Rukmini, He sent His *sudarshan* disk. 25. He said to it, 'Go to the home of Nama and revolve yourself for a moment around it, and I shall soon follow you.' 26. The *bhakta* of Vishnu was sleeping with his wife and children in his house. The disk of Vishnu made its visit there and revolved itself rapidly. 27. A great rainstorm raged around Nama but not a drop of water fell on Nama's hut. When one of God's servants devotes himself to His *bhakti*, He puts away from him all evil. 28. Having done this the Husband of Rukmini came quickly to that spot. With His own hand He rebuilt the walls of the hut and rethatched its roof. 29. Wise listeners may say, after hearing this story, 'If Krishna came, and in His own person thatched Nama's house, why did He not make it a more beautiful home?' 30. But Krishna does not permit His servants to become entangled in their domestic life. If He should give to them great wealth it would destory their character of indifference to earthly things. 31. Duryodhan was created as an enemy of the Pandavas. He was constantly giving them trouble, yet when they fell into trouble the Life of the world would Himself rush to their help. 32. He said to Himself, 'If I should allow them to live without fear they will not remember Me in their hearts.' Yet the Enemy of Mura (Krishna)

will not allow His servants to be drowned in the sea af worldly existence. 33. 'If I should give my *bhaktas* a very beautiful house they would fail in their worship of Me.' Therefore it was that the Lord of all things gave to Nama a thatched roof. 34. Lest the cooked food should harm a child, the mother gives it a very small morsel. So the Pervader of the universe never gives great wealth to His *bhaktas.* 35. If too much water is given to plants their leaves will turn yellow. Therefore the gardener gives the plant only as much water as it needs. 36. So the Lord of the universe gives to His *bhaktas* sufficient of food and raiment as their bodies may need. By one means or other, he keeps their minds indifferent to earthly things.

37. Returning now to the story just now told, the Life of the world came and in His love gathered straw and rethatched Nama's hut. 38. When His *bhakta* awoke he looked outside and he saw a brilliant yellow garment shining with the brilliancy of lightning. 39. He then quickly came outside and in his love grasped Krishna by His feet and said, 'O God, what art Thou doing in coming here so late at night?' 40. The Life of the world replied, 'A terrible storm was raging and your hut was carried away. I have been here and rethatched it. 41. You have abandoned all thought of worldly things and in love are devoting yourself to My worship. Therefore, I (Krishna) Husband of Shri (the goddess of wealth) re-erected the walls of your hut.

KRISHNA AND NAMA DINE TOGETHER

42. If I had not quickly come, your children would have felt the cold. Gonabai would have become very angry with Me and would have spoken to me harshly. 43. Therefore, My dear *bhakta*, I have hastened to you at night.' When Gonabai heard Him say this, she immediately fell at His feet. 44. Talking there with Nama, and telling

him His secret thoughts, the Lord of the world remained there pleased. Jani at once came and began to rub God's back. 45. She exclaimed, 'O Ocean of mercy, Delight of the mind, Home of compassion, Life of the world, by Thy effort in Thy very person Thou hast protected us in many ways.' 46. *Hrishikeshi* (the Lord of the heart) said to Nama, 'You must be hungry. Arise quickly and eat. And place Me alongside with you.' 47. Serving on a platter some daintily cooked food, Gonabai quickly brought it to them and all four at once sat down to eat. 48. Govind, Vitthal, Narayan and the fourth, Mahadev by name, were Nama's sons. The Lord of the world sat down beside them to eat. 49. Gonabai and Rajabai were seated near Nama by themselves, and Krishna, placing His *bhakta* beside Him, sat down to eat.

JANI'S GRIEVANCE

50. Seeing this going on Jani felt deeply grieved in her heart. She exclaimed, 'O Merciful to the lowly, O Holder of the disk (Krishna), why hast Thou abandoned me? 51. Thou hast placed all beside Thee and hast seated Thyself to eat. O *Hrishikeshi* (Lord of the heart), I am of very low birth, therefore Thou hast abandoned me as one without a protector. 52. Just as the cook in preparing food removes grapes from the rice, or as straw is removed from the sugarcane, 53. so without any feeling of compassion for me Thou holdest in Thy heart disfavour'. Thus the little maiden girl, Jani, became deeply grieved because the Lord of the world felt no pity for her. 54. Hearing her complaint, the Life of the world said to Nama, 'This food today gives me no pleasure. I do not understand the reason.' 55. The other replied, 'O Holder of the disk (Krishna), Jani stands outside in great grief. Hearing her cries of suffering Thy mind is overcome; 56. just as when a calf cries out loudly, the mother cow does

not enjoy her food; or as when an infant is crying in the cradle, the mother does not enjoy her food; 57. or as when a bird is collecting grain in the jungle, she remembers her little ones in the nest; or as when a doe does not see her young even for a momant, she does not enjoy her food; 58. or just as when wealth is beyond the reach of one who loves it, daintily cooked food even is not enjoyed by him; therefore, because Jani is not comforted, Thou art not able to enjoy thy food.' 59. As God put away His hand from the food, all who were sitting there stopped eating also. When Rajabai saw this she was very much astonished. 60. The Holder of the disk (Krishna) washed His hands and then sat quietly on His straw mat. Gonabai called Jani and gave her the plate on which Krishna had left some food. 61. Brahmadev and other gods, desiring the same favour, are never able to obtain it. That favour Jani at once obtained because of her association with Nama.

KRISHNA EATS THE LEAVINGS WITH JANABAI

62. Jani then quickly covered over the food that was so desired. She waited in her own hut exclaiming, 'O Lord of the world, hasten now to my help.' 63. Nama and Krishna were at that time lying upon one bed. The *bhakta* was asleep. The Saviour of the world then arose. 64. The Life of the world walked very softly and in very humble voice said to Jani, 'I am hungry and therefore I have come to you. 65. I was eating with Nama but I had not invited you there. For that reason, removing My hand, I left the food.' 66. Jani replied to the Holder of the *Sharang* Bow (Krishna), 'O Ocean of mercy, Husband of Rukmini, I have nothing to give Thee in my hut except pure faith. 67. Gonabai brought me what Thou didst leave on Thy plate and gave it to me. About giving it to Thee, O Krishna, I feel a hesitation in my heart.' 68. The Husband of Rukmini replied to her, 'Bring and give it to Me just as it is. One should not hesitate about serving to

another that which is his own. 69. A while ago I stopped eating, but I was hungry for it. Now bring Me that same food and give it to Me.' 70. Hearing these words spoken with love, you listeners will needlessly have a doubt. You will say, 'Why did the Lord of the world remain hungry, in order to eat later the food he had left on His plate?' 71. It was in order to enable Jani to carry out fully her purpose. For she had no other food with her to give to Him. Hence the life of the world asked her to let Him eat that which He had left on His own plate. 72. Then Nama's little maid seated *Hrishikeshi* (the Lord of the heart, Krishna) and at once bringing the plate with the food which had been left upon it placed it before Him. 73. Then the Holder of the disk (Krishna) seating Jani beside Him began to eat. When Mother Rukmini heard of this she became perplexed in mind. 74. He who finds His delight on the ocean of milk, He whose Banner is the eagle, He who dwells in the heaven *Vaikunth*, He, placing Himself beside the maiden, is eating that which was left on His plate. 75. He of whom the *Vedas* and *Shastras* are continually singing, and He whom the Lord of *Kailas* (Heaven) is always contemplating, He sits in the hut away from the others and lovingly eats what Nama had left on His plate. 76. Even when many sacrifices are made, He who will not accept the offering thrown into the fire, He, the Life of the world, then said to Jani, 'I have eaten and am fully satisfied.' 77. He then quickly washed His hands and laid down to sleep. Gonai came outside where Nama was and said to him, 78. 'While you were sleeping, God arose and went away. He went to the hut of Jani and there lovingly ate that which He had left on His plate.'

KRISHNA DISREGARDS CASTE

79. The servant of Vishnu said in reply, 'O Mother, the

Holder of the disk (Krishna) is a lover of His *bhaktas.* If anyone has pure heart, He comes rushing there to help him. 80. He does not enquire as to caste or family. This merciful one to the lowly, seeing a person's faith, immediately rushes to his help without wasting a moment. 81. The Bhil woman plucked the fruit from the tree and first tasted it herself. The Lord of the world, recognizing her love, lovingly ate it. 82. So seeing the *bhakti* of Jani, He ate that which He Himself had left on His plate. O Mother, what is there in this to be wondered at? How shall I explain it further?' 83. The Life of the world after listening to Nama's and Gonabai's conversation came at once beside Nama, and with love He laid down beside him on the same mat. 84. Only one *prahar* (three hours) now remained of the night. The Holder of the *Sharang* Bow (Krishna) came, and sitting upon Jani's bed told her to arise at once. 85. ' O Jani, it is getting late. Arise at once and do your grinding. I have dusted the mill and I am waiting for you.' 86. The Lord of the world placed His hand under her neck and lifted her up. The Husband of Rukmini then placed the skirt of the garment on her head.

KRISHNA HELPS JANI AT GRINDING

87. Then he plaited her hair and seated Jani near the mill and placed the basket of grain close by. 88. The Husband of Rukmini then said to her, 'I will turn the mill. Place your hand upon the handle of the mill, pretending to grind, and lovingly sing songs.' 89. While *Hrishikeshi* (the Lord of the heart) was saying this, Jani the little servant girl became awake. Full of joy in her love she began to sing verses relating to the saints. 90. ' Nivritti, Sopan, Dnyaneshwar are my dear relatives. It is through their favour that the Holder of the *Sharang* Bow (Krishna) shows His mercy to me.

91. The *Vishnudas* (Nama) is my father, Rajabai is my very dear mother, Gora the potter is my dearest uncle, and Kabir and Savata are my brothers. 92. He did seemingly impossible things. Dear friends, how can I describe them all ? They made the Holder of the disk (Krishna) subject to them, and became satisfied with the water of supreme spiritual joy. 93. Dnyaneshwar, troubled by the Brahmans at Pratishthan, also did a seemingly impossible thing. He made a young buffalo repeat with its own lips the whole of the *Vedas*. 94. Gora the potter, Thy *bhakta*, because absorbed in the thought of the Husband of Rukmini, trod his infant child into the mud and was unaware that he was doing so. 95. Because he had broken his vow made to Vithoba he cut off his hands. Thus while listening to Nama's service of song, the Life of the world came to his help. 96. As hands were being clapped, suddenly a little infant child came creeping in. That story seems impossible and one thinks of it with amazement. 97. *Vanamali* (Krishna) went to meet His *bhakta* Savata. He ripped open his abdomen and hid God in his lotus-heart. 98. Hari who has an infinite number of universes in His heart hid Himself in the heart of Savata. Nama came and drew him outside. 99. Then there is the story of brother Kabir, who lives in the far off country, Benares. *Hrishikeshi* (the Lord of the heart) sat beside him, and did his weaving. 100. On the night of the festival to Shiva, Nama performed a *kirtan* in honour of Hari. Nine hundred thousand banners suddenly came down from heaven. 101. The Dweller in the Heaven *Kailas* turned His temple to the West for him. Such extraordinary deeds are indescribable even by the *Vedas* and the *Shastras*.' 102. In this way, while continuing to grind, she sang her verses in love. The Lord of Pandhari, listening to her, wagged His head in love.

GONABAI'S REPENTANCE

103. When Gonabai heard Jani singing, she hastened

to her hut and questioned, 'Whom did you call here to help you grind ? 104. Tell me quickly whether you brought here a hired woman or a neighbour.' Jani did not reply a single word. She remained in perfect silence. 105. Then Gonabai, with great anger in her heart, took a cane and entering into Jani's hut demanded of her to whom she had been speaking. 106. 'Our domestic affairs are in a very weak condition and we have not enough flour in the house. What hired woman did you bring here ? You give her grain from the grinding, constantly stealing it from us. 107. She struck Jani, but it fell on God's head. He immediately remarked, 'My name is Vithai. I come here early in order to help Jani to grind.' 108. When Nama heard of the conversation he understood its true meaning. 'That was the Life of the world whom you struck,' Nama said to his mother; 'you do not know this.' 109. Hearing him say this, Gonabai felt ashamed. She said, 'I struck *Hrishikeshi* (the Lord of the heart).' From there she then came back to her home. 110. She said, 'The good fortune of Jani is exceedingly extraordinary. She has made the Husband of Rukmini subservient to herself. Without realizing what I was doing, I went there and did what was wrong.' 111. He who is never seen even by Brahmadev and the other gods, Him I beat with a stick. Accursed be my worldly thoughts.' Thus speaking she became very repentant. 112. The beautiful cloud-dark-complexioned supreme Brahma, the Husband of Rukmini, Whose sight cools the heart and eyes, shows pity to Jani.

113. Turning now to Jani, the handmill of indifference to earthly things was turning around the pivot of this earthly existence. She ground in love in the mill an immense amount of grain in the form of deeds done in former births. 114. All that appeared in the shape of names and forms she ground in the mill. She mixed

together the visible and the invisible and sat there unconcerned. 115. Krishna then filled a basket with the flour and placed it aside. There was still a little time left of the night and so He laid down on the easy bed. 116. As the Life of the world was speaking to Jani He fell asleep. When the dawn began to appear in the East, 117. Nama's maid came to Him and said, 'O *Hrishikeshi* (the Lord of the heart), rise quickly. Thy worshippers will come to Thy temple, and will not see Thee there. 118. If the very early morning songs of praise of wick-light-waving are not sung, there will be an outcry in the city.' The Lord of the world hearing this hastily arose.

KRISHNA USES JANABAI'S BLANKET

119. In His hasty departure the Life of the world had not thought of what He was doing. He forgot His own costly woollen garment and clothed Himself in Jani's blanket. 120. The brilliant cluster of nine jewels which was fastened to a string of pearls, the Lord of the world also forgot and hastened to His temple. 121. As the door was opened His *bhaktas* came to see and worship Him, bringing the materials for worship. There they saw the Life of the world standing on the brick clothed in Jani's blanket, 122. All who saw Him thus were astonished. They said, 'He Who is dark-blue-complexioned, like the leaves of the *tamal* tree, has done a very strange thing. Whose blanket could He have brought? We have no idea whatever.' 123. Another one remarked, 'He is a great mimic. He is very proud of His *bhaktas*. He rebukes those who trust only to deeds and sets them on the way to acquire self-knowledge.' 124. So one said to Him, 'O Life of the world, Ornament of Thy *bhaktas*, Husband of Rukmini, Dweller upon the sea of milk, Recliner upon *Shesha,* this blanket is not becoming to thee.'

JANI SUSPECTED OF THEFT

125. Another remarked, ' Reasoning over the thing, I think Jani the maid of Nama is a very clever girl. She must have deceived the Holder of of the disk (Krishna) and confused His mind. ' 126. Still another exclaimed, ' Just as the cripple servant-girl, Kubja, is described in the *Shri Bhagwat*, so are Jani's deeds. You should all know this. ' 127. Yet another remarked, ' Go and tell Nama. He will restrain his servant-girl. She has confused the mind of the Holder of the *Sharang* Bow (Krishna), and deceived Him. ' 128. Thus in different ways all the people reasoned in their minds. The priest went near to the image, and taking the blanket off, began to examine. 129. They saw that the cluster of the jewels and the pearl necklace were not to be seen upon His lotus-breast. They remarked, 'The generous *Vanamali* (Krishna) has given them away to someone. ' 130. Some made humorous remarks that Jani had done a very clever thing in offering the blanket to the god, and keeping the cluster of jewels and the garland. 131. It is as if one offered God some milk, and asking His favour brought home butter ; or as if one offered God water from an earthern jar and brought back nectar to his home ; 132. or as if one gave crystals to the jeweller and had them exchange for diamonds ; or as if one offered to the Husband of Rukmini a black garment and then took to his home His yellow robe ; 133. or as if one should offer fruit of *rui* to Maruti to please him, and take from him nectar fruit ; 134. so at this time, offering her black blanket, she pleased *Vanamali* (Krishna), and has taken for herself the cluster of jewels on the pearl garland to which the nine forms of jewels are joined. 135. The priests then exclaimed, ' What shall we do ? There is no one we can blame. All the doors being locked how did the Lord of Pandhari go away from here ? We do not understand.' 136. Another remarked, ' Let

us go at once to the house of Nama, and call the servant-girl Jani, and ask her in regard to this.'

JANI THREATENED

137. With this thought in their minds, they hastened to Nama's house and said to Jani, 'The Lord of Rukmini has taken to being with you. 138. We do not understand how you have confused Him thus. He takes no pleasure in our worship and offering. You have been guilty of some trick or other and have deceived the Life of the world. 139. The dark blue-cloud-complexioned One is in love with you. And our good deeds are all lost. Last night the Merciful one to the lowly came to you. 140. You took His cluster of jewels and pearl necklace, and in their place gave Him your blanket. Bring it at once or we shall punish you.' 141. Hearing them say this she swore by an oath, 'If I have taken the cluster of jewels, may my eyes burst.' 142. As they began to investigate, they found the garland of pearls in the raiment. They then said, 'She must immediately be impaled upon a rod of iron. 143. She has really to-day stolen the ornament of the supreme Brahm, the eagle-bannered One. All the Brahmans said, 'She must be punished.' 144. They immediately seized Jani and carried her to the bank of the Chandrabhaga river. There she brought to her remembrance the Lord of the world and pleaded for His compassion. 145. She cried, 'O Purifier of the sinner, Holder of the *Sharang* Bow (Krishna), Helper of the helpless, Husband of Rukmini, Lord of His *bhaktas*, Ocean of mercy, Saviour of the humble, Lord of the world; 146. I am without a protector, helpless and lowly. Who is there to rush to my help?' Hearing Jani's pity-arousing words, the Life of the world came to help her. 147. The iron rod (for impaling her) had been well fastened in the ground. It suddenly turned into water. Seeing this wonderful miracle all were astonished. 148. The priests were puzzled and exclaimed, 'Blessed is Jani's *bhakti*. The moment she

brought to her mind the Husband of Rukmini, He rushed to her aid in her trouble.' 149. The assembly of *bhaktas* now gathered together, and clapped their hands at the cries of 'Victory, Victory,' and said, '*Vanamali* (Krishna) rushes to the help of His servants when they fall into trouble.'

KRISHNA WRITES DOWN THE VERSES OF JANI

150. A very strange thing happened one day. The servant-girl Jani was sitting in her hut. In her mind she was composing verses in which she made mention of the Holder of the disk (Krishna.) 151. The Holder of the disk (Krishna) then took a pen and ink, and as the poetry of Jani fell upon His ears He wrote it down with His own hands. 152. You will say, 'How could words from the house of Nama reach God's ears while He was seated in His temple? This is what our minds question.' 153. But the Pervader of the universe, the Life of the world, Witnesser of the thoughts of the heart Cloud of intelligence, is the all knowing One, who knows the thoughts of His *bhaktas.* 154. Dusshasan troubled Draupadi. She pleaded with Him while she was at Hastanapur (Delhi), and how could her words reach His ears at Dwarka? Yet He at once rushed to her help. 155. When Gajendra pleaded piteously, God heard his voice in *Vaikunth* (Heaven.) The Lord of the world through His inner light of knowledge at once heard Jani's words. 156. The Lord of Pandhari alone understands the thoughts of His *bhaktas.* So the listeners must have no more doubts in their hearts.

KRISHNA ADMIRES JANI'S VERSES

157. The Lord of Rukmini then thought to Himself, I enjoy the verses of Jani.' Therefore He took a pen in His hand and sat writing them down. 158. Just then Dnyaneshwar suddenly came to the temple to make

his *namaskar* to the god. The Holder of the *Sharang* Bow (Krishna) seeing him gave thought to what he was doing. 159. He hid away His ink, pen and paper. The supreme Brahm, the Root of all joy, now manifested a most wonderful deed. 160. Dnyandev came to Him and placed his head upon the god's lotus feet. He exclaimed, 'O *Vanamali* (Krishna) sitting here by Thyself, what art Thou writing ?' 161. Hearing his question Pandurang replied, 'I am writing down the verses of Jani,' As *Shrirang* (Krishna) said this Dnyandev burst out laughing. 162. He said, 'Victory, Victory, to the Husband of Rukmini. Jani is composing verses in Thy praise. Thou art writing them down in a book. I am much surprised at this. 163. Although one has visited many sacred bathing places, and has given much wealth in charity, performed many austerities, and observed several religious vows, yet to speak of them very much with one's own lips is not proper. 164. Thy wonderful deeds, O *Vanamali* (Krishna), must be many in the world but thou shouldst never write them down on a piece of paper. 165. O Husband of Rukmini, it is Sarasvati who writes of Thy deeds. The *Vedas* and the *Shastras* proclaim Thy goodness. The *Puranas* honour Thee with song. 166. Vyas, Valmiki and other great poets have described Thee and then attained their final bliss. And now if Thou dost write down the verses of Jani the poets will laugh at Thee.' 167. Hearing him say this, the cloud-dark Krishna replied, 'The verses of Jani are full of love. I feel them today exceedingly interesting. 168. And as they fell upon My ears, I sat down to write them. But the moment I saw you I felt a hesitation in my mind. 169. And so I made haste and hid the paper and ink. But I do not understand how you understood what I was doing ?' 170. Dnyandev replied, 'O Life of the world, Ornament of Thy *bhaktas*, aside from us there is no one who knows Thy inner thoughts. 171. It is a dutiful wife alone who understands the thoughts of her husband. Only an infant can understand the love of its mother; 172. just as the delightful words of the poet are appreciated only by an expert; and as one who has knowledge understands the knowledge of philosophic books through experience. 173. O cloud-dark complexioned One, as it is the *chakor* bird who fully understands the moon, so it is the mind alone, O Krishna, that understands the objects of the sense organs. 174. So we always easily know Thy secret thoughts.' Dnyandev having said this, the god laughed.

KRISHNA AND DNYANDEV GO TO NAMA's HOUSE

175. Dnyandev then exclaimed, 'O Lord of the world, let us go to meet Nama. I will tell him how great Thy love for Jani is.' 176. The Husband of Rukmini replied, 'I agree. That was already in My mind.' Then taking one another by the hand they hastened along. 177. Dnyandev and the Holder of the disk (Krishna) came to the house of the *Vishnudas* Nama. They embraced one another and sat down upon an easy mat. 178. When *Vanamali* (Krishna) arrived at Nama's house an assembly of saints had already gathered there; just as when a king comes and sits in his assembly hall, his whole army gathers there; 179. or as when hearing that Indra is seated, He becomes surrounded by the group of gods; or as when in their love the performers of austerities surround Shiva; 180. or as whenever Indira (Lakshmi, goddess of wealth) sits there, all *siddhis* gather together; or as when God-loving *bhaktas* come rushing in their love to listen to enthusiastic *kirtans*; 181. or as wherever precious jewels are to be found, there all experts gather together; or as when bumble-bees gather around the lotus; 182. or as when their eyes discover a generous giver, beggars gather around him; or as when ants come rushing to wherever there may be a

pile of sugar. 183. So, seeing the Lord of the world (Krishna) seated in Nama's house, all the saints full of joy gathered there.

JANI INTRODUCED TO SAINTS

184. The Lord of the world, having embraced all who were there, said to Nama, 'Call Jani and bring her here, in order that she may be introduced to the saints.' 185. Gonabai remarked then to Rajai, 'Jani is out in the fields, making dung cakes. Go and tell her that the Husband of Rukmini is calling her.' 186. Hearing this request, she hastily went and told her, 'The Holder of the disk (Krishna) has come to our house and calls for you.' 187. Jani quickly washed her hands and came to Nama's home, and as she saw the Lord of Pandhari she bowed prostrate before Him on the ground. 188. Dnyandev remarked to Nama, 'I have seen a most extraordinary thing to-day. I saw the Lord of *Vaikunth* (Heaven) writing down the verses of Jani with His own hand.' 189. The Ornament of His *bhaktas* said, 'The writing down of the verses of Jani has brought Me no loss of dignity. 190. I declare by an oath, and make your feet a witness to it that you must regard the Marathi version of Jani as containing happy thoughts. 191. I, Govind, take the paper of pure goodness, and with divine knowledge and joy of a happy experience I sing her verses in love. 192. If anyone reads her verses I shall stand waiting upon him in his yard.' Such were the words that Krishna used in the house of Nama: 193. 'He who continually sings the verses of Jani, will suffer no calamities in his family life. Finally I shall certainly give him at his final end the highest form of deliverance (*Sayujyata*).' 194. When *Vanamali* (Krishna) had said this, Dnyandev burst out laughing and clapped his hands. All shouted 'Victory, Victory.' I will tell you who were there. 195. There was Kabir who

had come from Benares. There was Chokhamela the great *bhakta*, and there was Rohidas the shoemaker. The noble *Vaishnavas* were seated there. 196. There was Sajan the Pathan, God's *bhakta*. Baya the butcher who was exceedingly indifferent to earthly things. There was Kamal the gardener, a great saint and always full of joy; 197. and Mukundaraj the sifter of goldsmith's ashes, who always remained at the great door of the temple. There were Gonabai and beautiful Rajai continually crying out 'Victory, Victory.' 198. Then there was Nama, the very dear *bhakta* of God. The Husband of Rukmini sat in the midst of them, just as a king in the midst of his army outshines all in glory.

AVATARS OF NAMA AND JANABAI

199. Dnyaneshwar said to Jani, 'Namdev has assumed four *avatars*: Pralhad, Angad, and Uddhav, and made Krishna subservient to him. 200. During what birth did you especially pray to God? Tell us everything. Do not at all hesitate.' 201. When the maid of Nama heard this she became ready to speak. She said, 'When the Lord of the heart became Hayagriva [a certain *avatar* of Vishnu], I offered myself at His feet. 202. Then He as the Advocate of Ambarish assumed ten *avatars*. As the fish, the tortoise and the great boar, he came to kill the all-powerful *daityas*. 203. After becoming Narasinha, Vaman and Parashuram, He finally became Ram the son of Dashrath. Now Shri Hari, the resting place for all, has become the *avatar* of Buddha. 204. When God took the form of these various *avatars* I was with Him.' When Dnyandev heard her say this, his mind was full of astonishment. 205. Said he, 'Blessed is this servant girl Jani. By her limitless good deeds she has made *Hrishikeshi* (the Lord of the heart) favourable to her. His sight is unobtainable even to Brahmadev and other gods.'

KRISHNA APPOINTS WRITERS OF THE SAINTS' POEMS

206. The Holder of the disk (Krishna) then said to the saints, 'Now make appointments among those who are to write down the words that come from the lips of the saints. 207. Sachchidanand the Brahman will write down the jewelled words of Dnyaneshwar. Sopan who is the full *avatar* of Brahmadev will write down the words of Nivritti. 208. Dnyandev will write down the verses of Muktabai. Visoba Khechar will write down the verses of Joga Paramanand. 209. There is also the *Vaishnava bhakta*, Savata the gardener. Let his writer be Kashiba Gurav. God Supreme appointed Sudev as writer for Kurmadas. 210. Anant Bhat the Brahman should be the writer for Chokhamela. And the Husband of Rukmini will Himself write down the verses of Nama's Jani.' 211. Thus appointing a writer for each one, the Holder of the disk (Krishna) said to Dnyandev, 'Now you should have no hesitation in listening to the verses of Jani.' 212. The noble *Vaishnava* hearing Him say this replied, 'If a mighty person accepts anyone there can be no one who can blame him on the earth. 213. If the sun should take a blind man by the hand, what will he not be able to see? If Sarasvati is pleased with a dumb man, he will be able to repeat the *Vedas*. 214. Similarly, if Thou art favourable to Jani the maiden, who will call her a slave?' As the Life of the world heard him say this, He smiled. 215. Then Nama took some water and washed the feet of all. With the sixteen materials of worship he lovingly performed the worship of the Husband of Rukmini. 216. He then gave *pan-supari* to each one and made a prostrate *namaskar* to each one. Shripati (Krishna) then took leave of Gonabai and quickly hastened away. 217. *Vanamali* (Krishna) taking an assembly of *bhaktas* with Him entered into His temple. Here He told Rukmini all that had happened.

218. The Holder of the *Sharang* Bow (Krishna), the Brother of the helpless, the compassionate One, the Lover of His *bhaktas*, Ocean of mercy, and Ocean of compassion,
219. He, the lotus-eyed One, is the Speaker here and the One causing the stories of His servants to be described. Mahipati is a mere puppet. All the wise saints know this.

220. *Swasti* (Peace) ! This book is the *Shri Bhakta-vijaya.* In listening to it, the Lord of the world will be pleased. Listen, you God-loving *bhaktas.* This is the twenty-first very delightful chapter; it is an offering to Shri Krishna.

CHAPTER XXII
MATSYENDRANATH, GORAKHNATH AND CHANGDEV

Obeisance to Shri Ganesh. Obeisance to Shri Krishna.

STORIES OF SAINTS LEAD TO RIGHT FEELINGS

1. To-day you fortunate listeners have seated yourselves around the wish-tree. Therefore the longings of no heart remain unfulfilled. 2. When the touchstone touches iron, no blackness whatever remains in it. So in listening to the delightful stories of the *bhaktas* no doubt remains in the mind; 3. as when bathing in the sea it is the same as having bathed in all the sacred bathing places; or as it is by the light of the sun that all objects become visible; 4. or as when one obtains nectar, all diseases flee away; so those who listen to these stories of the saints cannot be troubled by the sorrows of this earthly existence. 5. If the moon is pleased with anyone, he will not feel any heat; so the wise one who listens to the stories of the saints will find that no lust or anger enters into his heart.

THE GURU ANCESTRY OF DNYANDEV AND NAMDEV

6. In the previous chapter we were told of God praising Jani, and that all saints expressed their astonishment and cried out, 'Victory, Victory.' 7. Having heard this statement the listeners asked this question, 'It is through association with Nama that Krishna joined Himself with Jani. 8. Now what was his guru descent? We do not know about it.' Such was the question asked by the saints. Listen now to the description of it. 9. It happened at a certain time that Shiva was sitting on the ocean of milk. He was contemplating the essential forms of Ram and repeating His name. 10. Parvati said to the Lord of *Kailas* (Heaven), 'Whose name are you

repeating ? What God is there superior to you ? This is a thing about which I have some doubt.' 11. After listening to her, the Lord of all things replied to her, 'The deity who is superior to me is Shri Ram, the Husband of Janaki. 12. O Bhavani, Brahmadev and Vishnu, develop from Him along with me. I was meditating that very form in my mind and I am constantly repeating His name.' 13. When the Destroyer of Tripur (Shiva) said this, Ambika (Parvati) was much astonished. She exclaimed, 'How is it that I being half of your own self have not been thinking rightly ? 14. Frogs are always near to the lotus-flowers, but they know nothing of the pure honey that is in the flowers. 15. Musk perfume is found in the navel of the deer. Still it wanders needlessly through the jungle. So, although Shiva has knowledge, I do not know it.' 16. Then joining both her hands palm to palm, she made a *namaskar* to the blue-throated One. Said she, 'You make your heart pure by continually repeating the name of the noble Ram, 17. Please tell me the most secret thoughts of your heart.' Hearing her say this the King of *Kailas* (Heaven) naturally in love replied to her. 18. And finding her alone, Shiva said to Parvati, 'I will truly tell you whose name I continually repeat in my heart.' 19. He (Shri Shanker) then placed His assuring hand upon her head and began to instruct her, by which Parvati became bodily unconscious and could not remember her own self.

BIRTH OF MATSYENDRA

20. While Shiva was giving her instructions the fair-complexioned One was unconscious. Just at that moment there was a foetus in the womb of a crocodile. It replied from there that it understood the instructions being given. 21. In the midst of the violent waves of the sea this foetus remained hidden in the womb of the crocodile. Hearing the instructions given by Shiva to Parvati, it held it in its

memory; 22. just as when Kayadhu was in a prison, and Narad came suddenly there and kindly gave her instructions, Pralhad still in the womb heard it; 23. so now as the Enemy of Madan (Shiva) was instructing Parvati, His words reached into the womb of the crocodile. At that moment, Matsyendranath was born, a saviour of the world. 24. He was in truth the *avatar* of Shiva. He was the very mount Meru of those indifferent to earthly things, an ocean of intelligence, descending as an *avatar* to save the world. 25. Matsyendranath was supremely wise in all divine knowledge. He was the wish-tree giver of the highest form of final deliverance, the internal Witnesser of every life, or the second Vishnu Himself, 26. the home of the qualitiless One in the form of intelligence, a moon becoming a full moon. 27. Although He came with a body, He was separate from it. He was a statue of the supreme Brahm, the essence of the highest form of happiness made manifest to this world. 28. As He came out of his mother's womb He did not forget that he was the supreme Brahm. He was not touched by the violent winds of ignorance. He at once came out of the water. 29. He began to think to Himself, 'I want to see all the sacred bathing places' From there, therefore, Matsyendra wandered about as he wished. 30. He wandered about from town to town and ate whatever was given to Him. Afterwards He was accustomed to go into the jungle and sit by Himself alone. 31. Thus indifferent to all earthly things, twelve years of his life passed away. On one occasion, however, he arrived casually at a certain town.

MATSYENDRANATH'S BEGGING TOURS

32. He begged from house to house but remained before them only for a moment. One day he happened to stand before the house of a merchant. 33. He cried out '*Alakh*' at the door of the house. He spoke very rapidly,

'If you have anything to give me, give it to me at once, O mother.' 34. Hearing His sweet voice, the wife of the merchant was astonished. She exclaimed, 'Blessed is the mother of this guest that she should have borne such a person.' 35. As she came out of the house with her offering she saw a divine form before her. There were two earrings in His ears with a shining cluster like that of the stars. 36. The beautiful brilliancy of His form was like that of gold. He had rubbed white sacred ashes all over His body. He wore a brilliant waist cord. His elongated eyes were beautiful. 37. Seeing His form she bowed to Him in her love. She exclaimed, 'O *Swami*, where have you come from? Tell me.' 38. Hearing her Matsyendranath replied, 'The country of the supreme Brahm is My country. He who understands this has a right to the happiness which comes from the union with God.' 39. The merchant's wife said to Him, 'I have no child. Although we have in our home every form of wealth, yet our house seems empty because of this; 40. just as the night without the moon, just as the earth without trees, or just as rivers when there is no water in them causing a frightful appearance; 41. just as the rainy season is fruitless without a cloud; or as fatness when there is no strength in one's body; 42. like a king without any power; like acquaintance with scriptures but failing in duty; like a lamp without oil or wick does not look well; 43. wisdom without luck; planting the garden without water; so to possess wealth but to have no child, seems to be a vain possession. 44. Give me therefore the knowledge whereby I may have an increase in my descendants.' Hearing her words on this occasion in private, Matsyendranath was pleased. 45. Then taking some of His ashes and repeating a *mantra* over them He at once gave them into her hand. He said, 'The moment you eat this, you will certainly have a son. 46. You will see in living form the *avatar* of Vishnu. Tell no one of this, and accomplish your purpose.' 47. Telling her this, Matsyendranath departed rapidly. The wife of the merchant took the ashes and placed them in the god-room. 48. She then called her friends to her and said, 'Listen to my secret, dear friends. A mendicant came into our yard, and I went out and gave him some food. 49. He was glorious and brilliant to the sight. He was unconcerned and indifferent to all earthly things and full of holiness. Seeing such a form as His, my mind felt great satisfaction. 50. I told Him that I had no child. He then looked towards me with a look of favour, and gave me ashes over which He repeated a *mantra.* 51. He said to me, 'The moment you eat this, you will conceive a child.' After telling me this He hastened away. 52. Now tell me truly whether you think the doing of this would prove true or false. I have none more intimate than you, dear friends.'

MERCHANT'S WIFE DISCARDS MATSYENDRA'S FAVOUR

53. One woman amongst these friends replied, 'What is the use of placing faith in the split-ear sect? They perform many tricks and thus deceive people. 54. If you trust to them you will lose in your domestic affairs. Wish a long life to your husband and you will prosper well in your family affairs. 55. The split-ear sect give ashes, making the one to whom they give it a dog, and make the dog run after them. At night they turn the dog into a woman and enjoy her. Such is their custom.' 56. Speaking to her in various ways they put doubts in her heart. Then they exclaimed, 'Throw these ashes at once into the fire. 57. By listening to the words of neighbours, a quarrel arises between the daughter and her mother-in-law, enmity ensues between brothers and they separate themselves and leave their mother and father. 58. It is a quarrel in the home that is the direct cause of loss to men : just

as when gruel is thrown into milk, it is at once destroyed, 59. And as when gold is covered with a metallic cement, it once appears tarnished, so, through the thoughts of others, evil character comes to one of good family.' 60. Therefore the woman at once threw into the fireplace the ashes given her by Matsyendranath; just as one might call nectar poison, and empty it on a heap of stones; 61. or as one might have found a book containing the *Vedanta*, he might think it an immoral book and throw it away; or as one might throw away pearls thinking them to be glass beads; 62. or as one might throw into the fire the seed of the wish-tree; or as the daughter of the ocean, Lakshmi (the goddess of wealth), is driven away by force; 63. or as when Kaikeyi (Ram's stepmother) obtained the remains of the (fire) sacrifice, but with doubt in her mind she threw it away; so through her fate the woman did not eat the favour given by Matsyendranath.

MATSYENDRA AGAIN AT THE MERCHANT'S DOOR

64. Twelve years passed after this event. Suddenly Matsyendranath the *Yogi* in His wanderings appeared again at her house. 65. Wandering at will from house to house in the city, He had come to the house of the merchant. There at the door He cried out '*Alakh.*' 66. Just as soon as the lady of the house heard His sweet voice she at once came out bringing her offering. The moment she looked at Him she remembered what had happened long ago. 67. Matsyendranath said to her, 'Allow Me to meet at once the son who was born to you after I had given you the ashes.' 68. The wife of the merchant having heard Him say this, her heart was filled with fear. She thought, 'If I should tell Him the very truth, He will curse me and turn me to ashes.' 69. So she remained silent, and would say nothing. Matsyendranath again repeated, 'Tell Me at once whether you ate the ashes or whether you threw

them away somewhere?' 70. To this the wife of the merchant replied, 'Listen to the exact truth. Listening to the advice of others, a doubt arose in my mind. 71. Believing that you had some deception in your mind I threw the ashes into the fireplace. Such was the writing of Brahmadev (on my forehead) when foretelling my fate.' 72. Matsyendranath said to her, 'Where did you throw the ashes (of the fireplace)? Tell Me quickly. Do not hesitate.' 73. 'I took them to that large place from where the farmers removed the manure, and have dug a ditch where for twelve years cowdung has been thrown.' 74. Then going outside with Him she showed Him the place and said, 'It is here that for many days we have thrown ashes, O *Swami*.'

THE BOY GORAKSHANATH COMES OUT OF DUNGHILL

75. Matsyendranath went to the heap of manure and stood there, and as He cried out '*Alakh*' a wonderful thing happened. 76. 'O *Guru Adesh*,' such a sound came from the ground. As every one heard it their minds were filled with astonishment. 77. Then Matsyendranath told her to have the earth removed by men. Suddenly they saw the form of a twelve-year old boy glorious in appearance. 78. As the full moon, so was this beautiful and resplendent form, a boy with thirty-two points of excellency who was the very *avatar* of Vishnu. 79. His face was beautiful and he had elongated eyes. Earrings adorned his ears and without a support he sat constantly repeating the names of God. 80. No earth had soiled his body. People seeing this were astonished. Then Matsyendranath came quickly to him and awoke him up. 81. As Matsyendranath placed his assuring hands on his head, he made Him a prostrate *namaskar*. Matsyendra tock His young boy by his hand and quickly started away. 82. Because the boy had lived in the dung and the ashes that had become mixed

during the twelve years, therefore the name lovingly given to him was Gorakshaknath.* 83. The merchant said to his wife, 'Our great treasure was almost in our hand; but the workings of fate did not allow it in the case of our fortune.' 84. Matsyendranath hearing his pity-arousing words, blessed him and said to him, 'Know this that you certainly will have another son.' 85. Saying this to the couple, he took Gorakshanath by the hand and started for a visit to sacred bathing-places.

GORAKSHANATH'S PILGRIMAGE

86. As they walked hastily along, Gorakshanath said to Matsyendra, 'Place your hand on my head and instruct me with the *mantra* that will be my saviour.' 87. His *Guru* replied to him, 'You have not yet served Me. I have therefore no authority to teach you and make you my disciple. 88. One should not tie up in his cloth coins without examining them. So wise and clever men should not give instructions even to a good disciple at once. 89. One should not sow in a land that has not been ploughed; so before I have examined you I cannot accept you as my disciple.' 90. Hearing him say this, Gorakshanath made him a prostrate *namaskar*. Joining his hands together he said, 'Your command, O *Swami*, is my authority.' 91. As they hastily walked along they suddenly came to a city. Seating themselves outside, Matsyendranath sent Gorakshanath into the town to beg for food. 92. Before each house he cried out, '*Alakh.*' As he begged for food from house to house, there was one in which Brahmans were being feasted. 93. The lady of the house came out and placed in his cloth a wheat-cake and fried hot cakes. She said to herself, 'This split-ear seems to be a very good man, he did not sit doggedly for more

* *Go*=a cow; *raksh*=protection; the story being that during the twelve years the boy had been fed by a cow with her milk at the dunghill.

food. 94. A man who is satisfied with a little food is truly an *avatar* of God.' Such were also the remarks people made to one another. 95. Then going outside the city, Gorakshanath prostrated himself before Matsyendra. He selected all the best of the food and placed it before his *sadguru.* 96. Matsyendra was pleased and said to Goraksha, 'These fried hot cakes taste very delicious, and I am satisfied with them. 97. So tomorrow going again into the city, bring me the same kind again.' He replied that he would do so and made a *namaskar.* 98. The next day very early in the morning Gorakshanath took his wallet and went into the town. 99. Thinking to himself he said, 'If I should hasten to other homes, my promise will not be fufilled. So I had better go to where the Brahmans were dining.'

GORAKH'S PERTINACITY

100. Gorakshanath then went and sat down at the door of the Brahman's house. There he called out, 'O mother, give me at once in my cloth some more fried hot cakes.' 101. The lady of the house came out and said to Gorakshanath, 'There are no fried hot cakes at all left in my house. 102. Yesterday the Brahmans dined in my house, therefore I was able to give you food. If you ask of me now the same food, tell me where I am to obtain it. 103. I can give you a pice (a small copper coin) or grain, but I have no fried hot cakes in the house.' 104. Gorakshanath said to her, 'I have no other wish. If you should give great heaps of money, they would look to me as if but clay. 105. Even if *riddhis* and *siddhis* (the accomplishments) or a royal fortune, or the dignity of Indra, should come into my hand, or indeed all the four forms of deliverance, I value none of them. 106. I ask you to fulfil the wish of my *sadguru.* Therefore I ask you for fried hot cakes. If I leave here before I obtain them, I swear by him.' 107. She

replied, 'You are using force on me, while I am doing a charitable action it is interfered with by my ill luck. You are not a guest. You are a supreme deceiver. You are asking for the daintiest of food. 108. Sometimes one throws bread to a dog and it then comes again and again to the door in the same way to get the food. So it was with you. I understand you now.' 109. Goraksha replied to her, 'We are even inferior to dogs, but unless I take these fried hot cakes, I will never leave this place.'

GORAKH GIVES AN EYE FOR HOT CAKES

110. She said, 'You obstinate fellow. You have seated yourself here with obstinacy; (but if you like to have it satisfied) take out one of your eyes and at once give it to me.' 111. Hearing her, Goraksha replied, 'I will give you one of my eyes.' She replied, 'Talking without corresponding action is useless. 112. Mendicants like you give others knowledge and themselves act unreasonably in their ignorance' 113. Hearing her say this, Goraksha putting his finger into his eye, quickly took out one of his eyeballs and placed it on her hand. 114. Seeing this the lady of the house became full of fear. Said she, 'If the officials should hear of this affair, they would take from us all we have.' 115. Then through fear she closed the door. She made a *namaskar* to Goraksha, and said, 'I spoke merely from a casual point of view. I did not know your fixed determination.' 116. The blood that flowed from his eyes she wiped away with her garment. But Goraksha said to her, 'Let there be no fear in your mind.' 117. If Goraksha had become angry, then the whole universe would have burned up with his curse. But he is a tree of peace and forgiveness. He never is angry. 118. Wherever his footsteps fall all the *siddhis* (accomplishments) come and stand before him there. But he does not care for them and continues begging from house to house. 119 A *sannyasi*

may perform many austerities, and yet be subject to lust and anger losing thereby his store of good deeds. This saying must be regarded as true. 120. Or if he should suddenly have a great desire for the *riddhis* and *siddhis* (accomplishments) he would lose the supreme spiritual riches and become entangled in great hindrances. 121. Therefore the son of Matsyendra quickly conquering his lust and pride, kicked away the *riddhis* and *siddhis* and lived a life indifferent to worldly things. 122. The lady then went into her house. She collected the materials for making hot cakes. She ground the *dal* with her own hand and added salt and cummin seeds. 123. She fried the cakes in melted butter. She then brought them outside and placed them at the feet of Goraksha, making him a prostrate *namaskar*. 124. She put the cakes in his knapsack and joining her hands together palm to palm, respectfully said, 'Let no one outside learn of this matter.' 125. 'I will not,' He replied. 'Let your mind be without any fear about this.' He covered his eye with his lotus-hand and came back to Matsyendra. 126. He bowed to Him with reverence, and said, 'I begged for food and have brought it here. So let the *Swami* show his favour to me. Let him eat it according as may suit his taste.'

GORAKH REGAINS HIS EYES

127. Matsyendra asked him, 'How did you lose your eye?' Goraksha stood with hands joined together and told him all that had happened. 128. 'While begging for the hot cakes, she asked for my eye. Then with my hand I took out one eyeball and gave it to her, O *Swami*.' 129. Matsyendra replied to him, 'Blessed is your courageous act. Now then take out your other eye, and give it to me.' 130. Goraksha replied, 'I will do so;' and at once took out his other eye. Matsyendra seeing him do this was astonished, and said, 'You truly are the *bhakta* of your *sadguru*.' 131. Then as

he waved his hands over his eyes, he immediately appeared with brilliant eyes. Matsyendra then gave instructions to Goraksha in spiritual knowledge. 132. After he had eaten with love some of the cakes he gave the remainder as a favour to Goraksha and said, 'Never have I seen such a disciple as you are.'

LINEAGE OF THE NATH SECT

133. Goraksha seeing that Shambhav was worthy of it, he gave him instructions and made him his disciple. That instruction fixed itself in his mind and through his favour all doubt flew away. 134. Advayanand came with reverence as a suppliant to Shambhav. He showed him favour and placed his hand upon his head. 135. Advayanand showed Prabhav his favour and gave him spiritual knowledge. He in turn explained the way of *yoga* to Gaininath. 136. Gaininath gave his instruction to Nivritti and he in turn gave it to Dnyandev. Visoba Khechar became the disciple of Dnyandev, giving him complete reverence. 137. The *Vaishnava bhakta* Namdev went as a suppliant to Visoba. Namdev's hand of blessing as a *Vishnudas* was placed on Jani.

138. The hearers [referred to in verses 7 and 8 above] listening to this explanation felt great satisfaction. They exclaimed, 'Our doubts have been removed, O speaker.'

DNYANDEV AND CHANGDEV SPEAK TOGETHER

139. On a certain day Dnyandev went to the temple and said to God, 'Give me leave to go to Alandi.' 140. Making his *namaskar* to the Husband of Rukmini he started from there. He arrived at Alandi and worshipped Siddheshwar. 141. Dnyaneshwar was the direct *avatar* of Vishnu. This reached the ear of Changdev. So he hastened to meet Dnyandev.

STORY OF CHANGDEV

142. You may ask who Changdev was and where he came from. Listen to the description of him. Listeners must keep their minds peaceful and listen attentively. 143. In the first watch of Brahmadev's day fourteen Indras were born. All these fell into prison. Such were the wonderful deeds of fate. 144. On a certain day the son of Brahmadev, the storehouse of all knowledge of *bhakti*, by name Narad, a noble *Vaishnava*, suddenly appeared. 145. The moment the fourteen Indras saw him they made him a *namaskar*. The celestial *rishi* with a smiling face began singing full of love. 146. Among them Changa was a noble Indra. Wearying of his many days of imprisonment he joined his hands to Narad and asked him a question. 147. He said, 'Tell me please, what means I can employ to obtain my release from this world? Tell me of that means of deliverence by which rebirths may be avoided.' 148. The son of Brahmadev, hearing him say this, replied, 'There is no such means in this world, but go into the world of mortals, and, O Changa, become an *avatar* there. 149. There is there a great sacred and holy city by name of Pandhari. You will find there a heaven on earth and the supreme Brahm will appear there to you standing on a brick. Know this to be true. 150. There you will enjoy the association of saints and the singing of *kirtans*, and all the citizens, men and women, are *jivanmuktas* (free while living). Go and become an *avatar* in the world of action and bring about your salvation. 151. Without going to the world of mortals, those who live in the city of gods and in the Heaven of Brahmadev can have no final deliverance.' 152. Hearing the words of Narad he made him a prostrate *namaskar*, and said, 'Use such methods as will free me from this body.' 153. Narad at once gave him a *mantra* with twelve syllables and he at once became free from his body.

CHANGA AND THE GOD OF DEATH

154. The *Marudgan* (Indra Changa) then became an *avatar* at Punyastamba (modern Puntamba) on the bank of the Ganga (Godavari), as the son of a Brahman. 155. Both Vithoba and Rukmini were very aged Brahmans. In having this pleasure of a son, they had supreme joy. 156. The child was glorious and brilliant. As soon as they saw it their hearts were filled with love. On their son's eighth year he was invested with the sacred thread and then he was married. 157. Whenever a thought came into his mind he would carry it out. By a mere wish he could go through the air. If he pronounced a blessing with his lips, it immediately took effect. 158. Wherever his footsteps fell, all the *siddhis* (accomplishments) were there to serve him. He knew all the fourteen kinds of learning and the sixty-four arts. 159. He knew how to hold the mind in control. When a hundred years of his life were completed the hour of death came. 160. He placed his soul at the crown of his head and deceived the god of death. He evaded the moment of death and then again brought back his life into his body. 161. Many days thus passed. Fourteen hundred years passed. Still he did not suffer the stroke of death. 162. He never became aged. His reputation in the world grew great. He was accustomed to go regularly to Pandhari to perform *kirtans* and to dance in them. 163. In joy and peace he lived in his hermitage by the banks of the Tapi river. He then used to come for his bath regularly to Puntamba on the banks of the Godavari river. 164. He accepted many disciples. They numbered fourteen hundred. He took all these together with him. He used to go with them upwards through the air. 165. Although he had this power, still he had not adopted a *sadguru*. He was accustomed to teach knowledge to his disciples and receive services at their hands. 166. Just as a physician eats whatever he

likes but prescribes a strict diet to others; or like a Brahman who without a bath tells others the *mantras* for bathing; 167. so, showing the power of *siddhis*, Changdev won a following of many disciples. But he himself never became the disciple of a *sadguru*. 168. He said, 'I have searched through all the world of mortals, but I do not see a *sadguru* worthy of me. I do not see anyone my equal in power.'

169. But indirectly he heard a rumour that Dnyandev, a direct *avatar* of Vishnu, was living in human form at Alandi. 170. Changdev then thought to himself, 'I will go as a suppliant to him. But first I will send a letter to Dnyandev and receive a reply from him.'

CHANGDEV'S LETTER TO DNYANDEV

171. He then took in his hand a pen and inkpot. After considering what to write he thought, 'I cannot address him as my younger, for I want to receive his instructions.' 172. He thought to himself, 'If I should write to him as to my elder, yet Dnyandev is younger than I am.' Therefore he sent a blank page by the hand of his disciple. 173. Dnyandev was seated as usual by the temple of Siddheshwar at Alandi. He was bringing the Husband of Rukmini to his mind and worshipping Him with love. 174. Suddenly by a path in the sky the disciple of Changdev arrived. Dnyandev understood why he came. 175. Before he told him his errand he (Dnyandev) said, 'Changdev has sent you.' He (Changdev's disciple) made a *namaskar* to him and placed the letter before him. 176. When he opened the letter, he saw that not a single word was written in it. He then said, 'Although fourteen hundred years have passed, he himself is still a blank; 177. just as if a nectar tree should grow to be great without bearing any fruit; or as if a lake were formed without any water in it; 178. or as if a wife has grown to adult age without bearing a child; or as a man without strength is useless; or as

a woman is useless who puts on adornments and yet does not possess the good fortune of having a husband; 179. or like one becoming a *sannyasi*, but without indifference to earthly things; or like a high house belonging to a miser; or like the stored wealth of a man without generosity, it deserves to be thrown into fire only; 180. or if one has no compassion in his heart, of what use is his talking of mercy to all creatures? If a cloud showers no water, it rolls through the sky in vain; 181. so, as he (Changdev) has not gone as a suppliant to a *sadguru*, his life is in vain. Although living for these fourteen hundred years, what of any value has he accomplished in them?'

DNYANDEV'S REPLY

182. Having said these things, Dnyandev wrote this reply with his own hands: 'The soul pervades all things, and is the same in all creatures. 183. There is no such thing with it as elder or younger, or of being with family or alone. And the soul is not long or short. It is never far away and never near. 184. When the sky is densely filled with clouds, space is just as it was before. Whether the size of anyone's body increases or grows small, the soul remains the same. 185. Whatever is seen in the universe, that substance is in our bodies. *Maya* or ignorance is guileful. It does not permit of a clear sight. 186. Because of ignorance, we of ourselves fall into confusion. Thinking rightly, however, we should remember all former things. 187. Whatever is the seed of the whole universe, you too have.' So Dnyandev wrote in his letter in order that Changa might understand the truth. 188. Having written the letter he quickly despatched it. The moment Changa read it he experienced its teaching.

CHANGDEV VISITS DNYANDEV

189. He thought to himself, 'I must go to meet at once one who is such an ocean of knowledge.' Then riding upon

a tiger he showed his great power. 190. Changa moved along taking with him his company of fourteen hundred disciples. At that time Dnyandev was at Alandi sitting upon a wall. 191. People came and told Dnyandev, 'A very distinguished guest has come. He is seated upon a tiger, and uses a serpent for his whip.' 192. Hearing this information Dnyandev understood its meaning. He remarked, 'I think this coming guest must be Changa.' 193. He then gave a command to the wall on which he was sitting. He remarked to it, 'Changdev, sitting upon a tiger, is coming quickly to meet me. 194. When *sadhus* or saints come to my house, you also must go forward to welcome them.' Listening to Dnyandev's words, a very extraordinary thing took place. 195. The wall on which he was sitting began to move with great speed. As men and women saw this miracle they were full of astonishment.

CHANGDEV'S PRIDE HUMBLED

196. Just as Dnyandev had come out of the village, he (Changdev) recognized him from afar. He thought to Himself, 'Blessed is the power of the *sadguru* who can make an inanimate thing walk. 197. Of what value is it, that I should sit upon a living tiger, and go to meet him?' So he dismounted from the back of the tiger and prostrated himself on the ground before Dnyandev. 198. All the pride that was in his heart at once passed away; just as when medicines see nectar they flee away ashamed; 199. or as when seeing the heroism of Bharat, Maruti was amazed in his heart; or as when Rukmini took the form of Sita, Satyabhama became ashamed; 200. or as when in Jambavati's marriage Shri Krishna made a bear sing, and hearing it sing, the pride of Narad immediately left him; 201. or as when Brahmadev stole the cows and cowherds and took them to his Heaven, Shri Krishna created others

just like them and Brahmadev felt ashamed in his heart; 202. so as Dnyandev caused the wall to move, Changdev was full of astonishment. He thought to himself: 'He is indeed Pandurang in bodily form.' He held a reverent heart towards him. 203. Then underneath a banyan tree, both of them met together. Hearing what Dnyandev had to say, Changdev was full of joy. 204. Even to this day the people call it the banyan tree of rest. Those who go there and sit even for a moment, they reach the highest state of final deliverance. 205. Dnyandev then took Changdev by the hand and brought him to his home. Muktabai happened at that time to be performing a bath. 206. When Changdev understood this he went away. Then Muktabai exclaimed, 'Confound you, you without a guru.' 207. But having heard her say this, Changa came rushing and grasped her feet. He said to her, 'Tell me, O mother, how you were able to know this?' 208. Adimaya [Muktabai: *See chap. 8. 186*] having heard him say this replied, 'From your turning back I understood it. 209. If the favour of the *guru* was upon you, such unworthy thought would not have come into your mind. There are niches in a wall. Just so, you would have taken my body and come forward. 210. Cows wander about among men and in the jungle do they put on clothes? I am just like one of these animals. Why did this not come in your experience?' 211. Hearing Muktabai's words, Changdev quickly grasped her feet and then went as a suppliant to Dnyandev. He took the *mantra* and became his disciple. 212. When the hand of him who was the supreme Brahm touched his head, Changdev became entirely indifferent to earthly things. He put aside every longing of his body. 213. All pride went away from his mind and it became spotless. Changdev embraced the feet of Dnyandev and praised him greatly. 214. Blessed is that place Alandi! It is heaven itself, situated in the world of mortals. Or it

may be called another Pandhari created in this world. 215. For the devotion of Dnyandev there came the Husband of Rukmini. This fact Mahipati always contemplates in his heart.

216. *Swasti* (Peace) ! This book is the *Shri Bhaktavijaya.* Hearing it the Lord of the world will be pleased. Listen to it, you god-loving, pious *bhaktas.* This is the twenty-second deeply delightful chapter.

CHAPTER XXIII

CHOKHAMELA, NAMDEV, JIVA AND TATVA

PLEASURE FROM THE STORIES OF THE SAINTS

Obeisance to Shri Ganesh. Obeisance to the Slayer of Kans.

1. Today good fortune comes rushing to the homes of those who listen. The wise *bhaktas* who listen to the stories of saints have realized this in their experience. 2. Just as when one eats sugar, one finds it sweeter and sweeter ; so the joy of listening to the stories of the saints fixes right thoughts in the heart. 3. Just as when one drinks freely of nectar all diseases flee away, so the moment the sweetness of the stories of the *bhaktas* is felt by anyone, ignorance no longer troubles such a man. 4. There are a great number of these stories and they are the nectar fruit of the trees of peace. God-loving *bhaktas* know how to drink it as they cast aside all wrong thoughts. 5. Those who say, ' Let us listen to the stories of the saints,' do not become subservient to *kal* (death).

CHOKHAMELA AND HIS REVILERS

6. In the previous interesting chapter there was related the instruction given to Changdev. It now happened that all the saints on the *Ekadashi* (the eleventh of the fortnight) proceeded to Pandharpur. 7. Chokhamela was a *Vaishnava bhakta* and chief among the out-castes. The dark-complexioned One showed His favour to him, seeing the loving emotion of his heart. 8. Pandhari was his birthplace and there he lived with his family. He had continually the Husband of Rukmini in his heart and was constantly repeating His name. 9. He was accustomed to bathe by the bank of the Bhima and to circumambulate the whole of the city of Pandhari. Then he would come

to the main door of the temple and prostrate himself there. 10. He had no authority to go within the temple, and meet the god; so bringing the Life of the world into his thoughts he worshipped Him from afar.

11. On one occasion he was seated at the great door of the temple and some evil-minded people saw him there. Listen to what they said to him: 12. ' If Vithoba had any love for you he would have taken you into the temple. If you do not actually see the Husband of Rukmini, why do you worship Him in vain ? 13. When the dainty food has been cooked in the house of a Brahman, dogs are not allowed to sit by the ceremonially clean plates. So outcastes have no authority to worship Pandurang. 14. How can beggars enter into the pleasure-house of kings ? Therefore Chokhamela should not go into the temple. 15. Just as an unfortunate man wanders about in the jungle, but does not see there a wish-tree, so Krishna is not seen by the eyes of Chokhamela. 16. Just as any man whose life is coming to an end, in vain licks his chops with the desire of seeing a well of nectar, so although the Lord of the world is in His temple, He will never meet with you.' 17. Hearing them say this, he prostrated himself before them, and said, ' My mother and father, why should I want in vain so great an honour ? 18. Although the sun is one hundred thousand towns [or miles] high, yet from that distance it cares for the lotus. So Krishna being in His temple, He cares for me from there. 19. The moon is two hundred thousand towns [miles] away, yet its intense love is upon the *chakor* bird; so He who is the Helper of the helpless, and the Personification of compassion, He remembers me. 20. Just as the mother-tortoise cares for her little ones from afar, so Krishna looks upon His servants with a look of compassion. 21. Though seeing one who is continually near Him, yet if that one does not love Him nothing

whatever is accomplished by a still closer contact.' 22. Saying this he hastened back to his home, but he was remembering the Husband of Rukmini in his heart, and he continued worshipping Him with love.

KRISHNA TAKES CHOKHA INTO THE INNER SHRINE

23. Now when it was night the Lord of Pandhari said to Chokhamela, 'I intend tonight to take you into My temple.' 24. The Husband of Rukmini having said this He took him by the hand and lovingly led him into the innermost shrine. 25. The eagle-bannered One then spoke to Chokhamela of His heart's secrets. He said to him, 'I cannot endure a single moment without you. 26. I might be eating with Nama, or drinking nectar with delight, but even at such times the memory of you is in my heart.' 27. Krishna having said this, Chokhamela fell at His feet and said, 'You call yourself the Helper of the helpless and fulfil the desires of your servants.' 28. The priest who was sleeping near the door heard this conversation and full of amazement he arose. 29. He called others to come and bear witness to this, and told them all that had happened, 'Some one very much like Chokha is speaking to Krishna. 30. The Dweller in *Vaikunth* (Heaven) is evidently the supreme *Brahm* and yet an out-caste has touched Him. The locks on the doors are just the same. I cannot understand how he could have entered. 31. If a man of low-caste can touch the god on whom are garments and ornaments, then our duties as Brahmans will cease. What shall we do? 32. Just as at full moon its brilliancy is at its highest, then it is that the monster Rahu comes and in love embraces it; 33. or as when the sun in the dark half of the month rolls around in the heavens, the monster *Ketu* suddenly appears and dims its light; 34. so is the Husband of Rukmini glorious in His six qualities. That He Who is described in the *Vedas* and *Shastras* should in love

be embraced by an out-caste going into the shrine at night 35. how can this be remedied? How can this hindrance be put away?' One remarked, 'Let us call him and ask him. 36. Then removing the lock of the door they questioned Chokha in reference to the whole affair. They said, 'How did you come into the temple? Tell us exactly how it happened.' 37. Hearing them say this, Chokhamela replied, 'I am your child. The dark-complexioned One took me by the hand and forcibly brought me into the temple. 38. Forgive me of wrongdoing and let your eye of favour rest upon me.' Saying this he at once started to depart.

PRIESTS ORDER CHOKHA OUT OF PANDHARI

39. The priests said to him, 'You should remain no longer in Pandhari. For if you are here the Lord of Pandhari brings you into His temple. 40. So you must dwell on the other side of the Chandrabhaga river a short distance away. If you do not do so we shall certainly punish you. 41. You have done a very great wrong. You have defiled the supreme God and because of all this sin you will have to experience hell.' 42. To these words of the Brahmans, Chokha replied, 'That I have defiled the Husband of Rukmini is a false charge. 43. If an out-caste and a Brahman both bathe in the Ganges, one should not blame the Ganges. 44. The earth is regarded as pure and on it all castes walk. How is it defiled? And in what *Shastra* is it written that it can be defiled? 45. If the wind strikes an evil man, his evil qualities will not attach themselves to the wind. It is a wrong thought to blame the wind. 46. If space fills the washerman's vessel and an earthen jar, still it is quite detached from the two. It is not entangled in them. 47. So to God supreme, the Lord of Rukmini, all castes are alike. How can you think that He is defiled? 48. The Lord of *Vaikunth*

(heaven) fills all the universe but is unattached to it. You therefore have wrong thoughts in your mind and have become worthy of blame.'

INSULTED BRAHMANS EXCOMMUNICATE CHOKHAMELA

49. While he was thus speaking and giving illustrations, the Brahmans became full of rage and said, 'He is from a low and dirty caste and yet he teaches us knowledge. 50. A locust proud of itself, tries to teach an eagle how to fly. A shepherd comes and gives knowledge to Brihaspati (the *guru* of the gods). 51. Or it is like a thin coating of tin showing its bright qualities to the gold. It is like common serpents showing their jewels before the great serpent Shesha; 52. or as when other elephants show off their gait before the elephant Airavat (Indra's elephant); or as if before Shiva His servants should perform the *tandav* (dance) to show Him how it should be done; 53. or seeing the sun, the firefly shows off its brightness; or as if the ocean, on seeing the *muni* Agasti, should begin to roar. 54. We are Brahmans of high caste. We are expert in every *Shastra*, but you are of low caste, and though an out-caste you are attempting to give us knowledge. 55. So now go to the other side of the Bhima river and live there. If on the morrow you are seen here we shall give you a good punishment.' 56. Hearing these words of the Brahmans, Chokhamela replied. He said, 'Mother, father, I am your servant and truly call myself your sweeper. 57. You have taken care of me for many days but now you drive me off.' Having said this his eyes became full of tears. 58. He then exclaimed, 'O merciful Mother Vitthal, from today I am separated from Thy feet. My fate is very powerful. What am I to do?' 59. Saying this he hastened as fast as he could to his home, at the same time remembering the form of Hari in his heart and in love repeating His name. 60. He told his wife all that had

happened and said, 'The Lord of Pandhari has neglected us. Let us now go to the other side of the river and there we shall live.'

CHOKHA IN EXILE

61. Then looking for a spot straight in front of the temple, on the other side of the river, he built there a pillar for lights. There it was that Chokhamela lived contemplating the cloud-complexioned Krishna in his heart. 62. Even today, when anyone goes on a pilgrimage to Pandharpur he sees there the pillar for lights. At that place then the chief of *bhaktas* lived indifferent to all earthly things. 63. Bringing the Husband of Rukmini to mind he continued to worship Him with love, saying 'God has abandoned me and cast off His love; so it seems.' 64. On a certain day this God-loving *bhakta* Chokhamela was eating his meal when suddenly the cloud-dark One (Krishna) appeared and sat down beside him. 65. Underneath the *nimb* tree there was a dense shade. Sitting in this shade *Vanamali* (Krishna) ate along with Chokha. 66. Just then a priest suddenly came on some business or other and for a moment stood looking at the astonishing sight. 67. At that moment his wife was serving curds to the god and the food rose up and fell down. Chokha said to his wife, 'A great fault has been committed by you. 68. The Husband of Rukmini is dining with us and you have soiled His yellow robe.' Hearing this conversation the Brahman was full of amazement. 69. Chokha turned to a crow in the tree eating the fruit of the *nimb* tree and throwing it down and said, *Vanamali* (Krishna) is sitting here and it is falling on His body. 70. Go at once from here and sit on another branch.' While the *bhakta* of Vishnu was saying these things the priest became very angry. 71. Said he, 'Seeing me here, he is talking at random. For how can the Lord of the world have dined with one who is an out-caste?'

CHOKHA RESTORED TO THE TEMPLE

72. The Brahman hastened to come near Chokha and slapping him over the mouth he immediately went away. 73. Then after bathing by the bank of the Bhima, the Brahman went into the temple of the god and there saw a most wonderful sight which astonished him. 74. There was Krishna standing on the brick but His yellow robe was all soiled with curds. Seeing this the Brahman looked straight at the god's face. 75. He saw that the cheek of the god was swollen. His eyes being closed by the swelling, the Brahman was full of astonishment as he came to understand the meaning of it. 76. Said he, 'I have persecuted Chokha and God has made me realize this. Just as when an evil man troubles an infant and this troubles the mother, 77. so when anyone persecutes a *bhakta* the Life of the world becomes sorrowful. Then punishing the ones who are not *bhaktas* He increases the glory of His servants.' 78. Thinking thus in his mind the priest came back to the bank of the Bhima and there said to Chokha, 'Come with me into the temple. 79. I did not know the glory of *bhakti.* I have persecuted you needlessly, just as if one should hammer a diamond on an anvil and only weary himself. 80. I punished you but the Lord of Pandhari felt the force of it in His temple. When I saw that His cheek was swollen, I became full of fear. 81. Therefore O dear *bhakta* of His, come at once with me. Perform some means or other and reconcile the Lord of Pandhari to me. 82. Then taking Chokha by the hand the priest came into the temple and there seeing the Lord of Pandhari, his (Chokha's) mind became filled with peace. 83. When he embraced the god, his heart felt great comfort. The face of Hari that was swollen now lost its swelling 84. The Lord of *Vaikunth* (heaven) had become weary. through the strain of separation from His *bhakta* but just

as soon as He met him again, His joy was unlimited. 85. From that time Chokhamela began to go into the temple always, just as when the Ganges accepts a streamlet, it becomes holy. 86. All the saints, *sadhus* and *Vaishnavas* became full of joy and said, 'The Life of the world takes pride in His saints.'

HOW GOD HELPS HIS *BHAKTAS*

87. Now listen to another story. The Lord of *Vaikunth* said to Rukmini, 'I am very weary today. Massage Me for a moment.' 88. Krishna having said this, Rukmini laughingly replied, 'What exploit have You performed and come back so soon to our house? 89. Have you been weeding the garden of Savata, and therefore are wearied, O Lover of *bhaktas*? Or were you weaving a gold bordered scarf at the loom of Kabir, showing your love and compassion? 90. Or was it because you were thatching Nama's house? Or because You have hastened back here from Lahul? Or were You wearied by drawing the wall on which Dnyandev was sitting? 91. Did you draw the dead cattle for Chokha and thereby your hands and feet are wearied? Or is it that you rushed to the help of Joga and have turned back?' 92. Hearing these words of Rukmini, the Life of the world replied, 'It has taken Me from early morning to finish the grinding for Jani. 93. A great many *sadhus* and saints had come to the house of Nama as his guests. And so I hastened to perform whatever was necessary. 94. Because of the abundance of work to be done, Jani had to make great haste, so I took her water jar and carried a great amount of water for her. 95. As the maiden Jani swept, I filled a basket with the refuse and threw it outside. I washad the clothes with My four hands and pounded rice for her.' 96. As *Vanamali* (Krishna) thus replied, Rukmini was astonished. She placed her head at His lotus-feet and looked with love into His face. 97. On a soft bed of flowers

Shri Hari lay, while Rukmini sat by His side and massaged His feet with her hands.

KRISHNA LEADS IN NAMA'S CHORUS

98. Now listen to another story. On a certain day Namdev stood by the eagle platform performing a *kirtan*. 99 As there was no one to stand behind him and help him, Shri Krishna at once appeared on the scene. He took the cymbals in His own hands and stood there sounding them. 100. Seeing this the *Vaishnava bhaktas* were astonished in their hearts. Indra and other gods came and showered flowers upon Him. 101. Krishna also took another form and danced on the *kirtan* stage. Accidentally His yellow robe slipped off and fell to the ground. 102. The Life of the world was overcome by His love, and He was lost to all consciousness of body, while all the *Vaishnavas* were overcome with astonishment yet no one spoke a word. 103. Dnyandev then took the god with his arm and stood Him up. He laughed at the god and listen to what he said, O clever and devoted ones: 104. 'You call Yourself all wise and clever and yet You dropped Your yellow robe in the *kirtan*. Now wake up and put on Your garment, O Lord God.'

BHAKTI MAKES KRISHNA FORGET HIMSELF

105. Hearing these words the Life of the world said, I know nothing of honour or of dishonour. 106. Dropping shame and the idea of " I " and "Thou, " dropping all consciousness of body, dropping all pride of being God, I dance on this *kirtan* stage. 107. Whatever form the love of Nama takes, I Krishna become that form, just as in a mirror the face appears as it is. 108. The sky appears according to the three seasons and in the same way, I, the Lord of *Vaikunth* (heaven) become like My *bhaktas*.' 109. While this conversation was going on, suddenly the *bhakta* Kabir appeared. The noble *Vaishnavas* all stood up and embraced him. 110. The saint Kabir in Benares and the *bhakta* Nama in

Pandharpur were both intensely loved by God as He saw the purity of their trust. 111. Blessed is Pandhari the city of *Vaikunth* (heaven) where Nama performs his enthusiastic *kirtans*, where all the men and women are *jivanmuktas* (free while living) in their love. 112. Here in Pandhari banners with eagle emblem wave, kettle drums are sounded, *vinas* are played with their sweet music, and men clap their hands and wag their heads with joy. 113. Then lighting the five wicked platter of lights as if they were the five vital airs, Rukmini came and performed the service of praise. Namdev waved the lights over Shri Krishna and lovingly prostrated himself before Him. 114. Krishna then said to His *bhaktas*, 'There was great enthusiasm in today's *kirtan*.'

GOD'S PRESENCE CREATES ENTHUSIASM

Dnyandev hearing him say this, replied to Him, 115. 'It was because You Pandurang took the cymbals and standing behind Nama helped him in the chorus. Therefore the whole *kirtan* became one of enthusiasm, seeing the love of the heart of the *bhaktas*. 116. If the sun should hold a torch in its hand, what lack would there be of light ? If the moon should use a fan, what opportunity would there be for heat ? 117. If the ocean were to pour water into a jar there would be no lack of water. Where there is a heavy fall of rain no place remains dry. 118. Where Lakshmi performs cooking, all tastes are to be found there. If the wish-cow should perform the churning, there would be enough cream for the three worlds. 119. So when you, the Husband of Rukmini stood behind Nama and led the chorus, then why wonder at the enthusiasm that was aroused ?' 120. Hearing these words of Dnyandev, the Life of the world began to laugh and said, ' You now understand the secrets of My heart.' 121. Then the Husband of Rukmini, after distributing sweetmeats to all who were present, re-entered His temple. Here the *bhakta* Kabir came privately and in his love prostrated himself before the god. 122. Taking leave of the Husband of Rukmini, Kabir started for Rameshwar and as he walked along the road he was bringing Shri Ram into his mind.

JIVA AND TATVA DEFY ORTHODOX CUSTOM

123. As he (Kabir) walked along the road he saw a certain city and here the noble *Vaishnava* lodged. By night he performed an enthusiastic *kirtan* with his heart full of joy. 124. Many people came to listen to him and all who listened became absorbed in his performance. Among them were Brahmans, one by name Jiva and another by the name of Tatva who were supremely wise. 125. They exclaimed, 'Blessed is Kabir the *Vaishnava* servant. He is especially wise in all philosophic knowledge. So with reverence let us go to him and let us both receive his instructions.' 126. Jiva and Tatva both came to Kabir and with reverence prostrated themselves before him. They said to him, 'Save us.' 127. Seeing that their purpose was pure he had compassion on them and placed his hand on their heads, and immediately made them his disciples. 128. The *bhakta* Kabir after seeing Rameshwar and the other Southern bathing-places returned to Benares with a feeling of repentance. 129. Now all the Brahmans began to revile the two brothers, Jiva and Tatva, and would not go to see them. 130. They were thrown out of caste. The Brahmans said to one another, 'Those who form connubial relations with them will be considered as belonging to the Muhammadan caste. 131. Kabir himself may be wise, though evidently he is a Muhammadan. But the moment these became his disciples they began to revile the religious deeds of Brahmans and have become possessed of spiritual knowledge.' 132. Thus spoke all the evil-minded, but these (Jiva and Tatva) would not listen to their words.

They said, 'If one prays at the feet of the *sadguru*, what is the need of different castes?' 133. In the meantime the son of one of them and the daughter of the other became of marriageable age. They therefore became deeply concerned and could not think what to do. 134. Seeing that they could not find a husband for their daughter, nor find a bride for their son, they went to Benares and told Kabir. 135. The father of Kamal (Kabir) through his power of inner sight understood what had happened without their telling him. Thought he to himself, 'They have received my instructions and have been turned out of caste.'

KABIR'S ADVICE TO DISREGARD CASTE

136. The *bhakta* Kabir then said to Jiva and Tatva, 'Listen to my advice. You two become the relatives of one another. 137. Lose all fear of such a deed and make one another your relatives.' To those words of their *sadguru* the Brahmans replied, 'We will do so.' 138. Kabir said to them, 'If you will trust my word all your trouble will at once vanish and you will reach final deliverance.' 139. Worshipping the feet of their *sadguru*, the Brahmans at once started back. Returning to their country they decided to perform the marriage. 140. Appointing the day for the marriage they at once began to collect the needed materials. When this news was heard in the city all were astonished. 141. The parents repeated the *mantras* with their own lips, invested the son with the sacred thread, and the marriage of the two was decided upon for the next day. 142. Then all the Brahmans came together and asked them for information. They said, 'Whom have you appointed as your relatives that you have determined on the marriage for tomorrow?' 143. To these words of the Brahmans they replied, 'We have a bride and a bridegroom at the house. 144. Just as in the case of animals and birds

such is the custom of our caste.' Hearing them say this, all the Brahmans were astonished. 145. They said, 'If we turn them out of caste, then there will be a mixture of castes. The blame will fall on us, and God will surely be angry with us. 146. Trusting to the feet of their *sadguru* they have cast aside all orthodox customs. Thus by testing their minds we have discovered the full facts.' 147. All the Brahmans then called Jiva and Tatva, and said to them, 'We will provide relatives for you gladly.' 148. So choosing a bridegroom for the daughter and a bride for the son, all the Brahmans helped and the marriages were performed. 149. Both of them went to Benares and told the whole story to Kabir. Hearing their words the *sadguru* was well satisfied in his mind.

150. In the next chapter, there is a story with deep meaning containing the very purifying history of Padmanabh. Mahipati says, 'Let the fortunate and wise *bhaktas* give attention to it.'

151. *Swasti* (Peace)! This book is the *Bhaktavijaya*. In hearing it the Lord of the world will be pleased. Listen, you God-loving, pious *bhaktas*. This is the twenty-third very delightful chapter ; it is an offering to Shri Krishna.

CHAPTER XXIV

PADMANABH AND KABIR

Obeisance to Shri Ganesh. Obeisance to Gopal Krishna.

THE IMAGE OF KRISHNA DESCRIBED

1. Victory to the Husband of Rukmini, Dweller upon the banks of the Bhima, Protector of His *bhaktas*, O Narayan, Saviour of the ignorant, Purifier of the sinful, Life of the world, and the Primal Being. 2. Thou, O Lord of the earth, hast remained standing with both hands upon Thy hips, Thy eyes directed to the tip of Thy nose. And thus dost Thou wait for Thy *bhaktas*. 3. In order to be the Advocate of Ambarish, Thou didst assume the form of ten *avatars*. Thou didst perform limitless deeds, according to Thine own pleasure. 4. But now, O Krishna, Thou, art standing with Thy hands placed on Thy hips revealing the glory of Thy *bhaktas*. Thou hast turned the minds of the ignorant to Thy contemplation. 5. Thou dost not look to caste or family. Thou didst dine with Nama. Thou didst drag the dead cattle for Chokha. Thou didst weave a scarf for Kabir. 6. It is Thou who didst cause their most wonderful lives to be recorded. So now, hearers, give attention and listen with love.

KABIR'S *BHAKTI*

7. In the preceding chapter there was related the story of two Brahmans, Jiva and Tatva, how they went to Benares, and there told their affair to Kabir. 8. Kabir was a *bhakta* with intense love for God. He was always unconcerned, and indifferent about worldly things. He put away all the troubles of his mind and devoted himself constantly to the worship of Ram. 9. He had no snare of desire in his heart. Cow-dung and gold were alike to him, as were also diamonds, jewels and pebbles, they all

seemed alike to Kabir. 10. Brahmadev and an ant, Mount Meru and a fly, all seemed to him alike. A speaker like Brihaspâti (the *guru* of the gods) and a dumb idiot were alike to Kabir. 11. Day and night when awake, when dreaming, and in dreamless sleep, he was worshipping Shri Ram. There never was a moment without his worshipping Ram.

THE HOPELESS LEPER

12. There was a certain merchant, supremely pious and extremely generous. He had five sons grown up and every kind of wealth in his home. 13. His money and grain were without limit. His wife was beautiful and of noble family. He was honoured by all his relatives, friends and family connections. 14. Although this was so, and everything was favourable, yet he was attacked by leprosy. His whole body became filled with worms. This was the result of deeds in some former births. 15. A person who has in his house wealth, health of body, sons, and an excellent wife, and has compassion on all creatures alike, is seldom found. 16. One learned in the *Shastras*, expert as a speaker, and yet without pride and of a high caste, and who does not find fault with others, is seldom found. 17. He who is not obsequious, to whom a prince and a pauper are alike, and to whom all other women are as his mother, is seldom found. 18. One who always performs acts of benevolence, whose mind puts aside all concern, and is always worshipping Shri Hari, such an one is seldom found. 19. He who has property and wealth and yet to whom all is as clay, and who in time of famine gives food, such an one is seldom found. 20. But according to the life one has lived in his former births he reaps fruit in conformity to it; and so the body of the merchant had become very diseased. 21. His whole body was filled with worms and the stench from him spread everywhere. No one

could even look at him, every one became disgusted. 22. Those for whom he had cared and whom he had fed during his life, now when he was about to die, put him off at a distance. He had not remembered in his heart Shri Hari, the Lord of heaven.

FAILURE OF REMEDIES

23. Physicians called it a very serious disease. They gave him all kinds of medicines, but Pandurang did not show him favour and his disease only grew worse. 24. Astrologers told of adverse planets and how they were all disturbed, therefore to recover his health they told him to propitiate these by repeating their *mantras.* 25. The sorcerers said, 'The goddess must have become angry,' so if you will go and beg in her name, you will certainly be restored to health.' 26. He heard all these various remedies and yet became worse and worse. If one has not the feet of Shri Hari in his mind, in his case even nectar becomes poison. 27. A Brahman came to his house and told him to repeat the name of Malhari. Another said, 'Divide all your wealth today among the Brahmans.' 28. Another said, 'Read the *Saptashati* and the goddess will then make you well.' His sons did for him according to the various remedies suggested. 29. One said, 'You must worship the sun by ablutions of water. You must repeat the *Gayatri mantra* regularly.' 30. Another said, 'You must propitiate Shiva by a shower-bath of *maharudra*,' Another said, 'You must circumambulate Hareshwar.' 31. Another said, 'You must make the elephant-faced god (Ganpati) favourable to you. You must observe the *Sankashti chaturthi* (the trouble-removing festival of the fourth day) and offer to Him sweetmeats.' 32. Another said, 'You must quickly try the remedy of a *mantra*-understanding person.' Still another said, 'You must worship Kal Bhairav that he may advocate your cause.'

THE LEPER THINKS OF SUICIDE

33. Others said, 'Call Brahmans and give them the gifts of elephants.' Another said, 'You must have yourself weighed and according to your weight give money to the Brahmans.' 34. He listened to every one, and at once used the remedy each one suggested. He spent all his money in order to regain his health. 35. But day by day the merchant became worse and the stench spread far and wide and no one came near. 36. His whole body became full of worms. He was in great misery. Finally he thought to himself, 'I must offer my body to the Bhagirathi.' 37. The merchant called his sons, his wife, his relatives and his neighbours and said to them, 'Take my body and throw it into the river Bhagirathi. 38. You have suggested many remedies, but my *karma* (fate) is opposed. Now I will perform a penance by drowning in the Bhagirathi '. 39. Hearing him say this they mourned because of their love for him. They then lifted up the merchant and took him to the banks of the Ganges. 40. An innumerable crowd of people assemble to see the marvellous act, saying, ' The merchant is about to give up his life because his disease is so terrible.' 41. On the banks of the Bhagirathi there was an unimaginably dense crowd; men and women viewed the scene and greatly wondered. 42. One remarked, ' He never thought to commit suicide '. Another said, ' How is it that his sons and wife have become indifferent to him ?' 43. One replied to the other, 'Our end might become like that. One should now therefore give attention to the worship of Shri Hari.' 44. Hearing what the people said, the merchant replied to them, ' Now push me at once into the Bhagirathi river. 45. I cannot endure this intolerable disease.' All agreed to his request. They brought four water jars and fastened them to his hands and feet.

PADMANABH'S ARRIVAL AT THE CRISIS

46. Just then the Brahman Padmanabh came there in order to bathe. With his lips he was repeating the names of God, 'Rama, Krishna, Govind.' 47. He was a disciple of Kabir and with real love for God he was repeating His names. The *bhakta* of Vishnu came there with a garland of *tulsi* beads around his neck. 48. Here by the banks of the Bhagirathi a crowd of men and women more dense than would seem possible was viewing the sight. and because of their love all were full of sympathy. 49. Padmanabh asked them, What is the unusual thing which you are looking at ?' They then told him all about the affair. 50. Hearing what the people said he at once came near the merchant and said to him, 'You should not commit suicide. 51. You have passed through eight million four hundred thousand rebirths. And now at last you have a human body. If with it you commit suicide you will never get free from your rebirths. 52. As men are born in this world of action, it is only by the worship of Hari that births and deaths can be certainly ended.' 53. The merchant replied to Padmanabh, '*Karma* (fate) is very powerful and utterly impossible to withstand. I have made use of very many remedies in order to regain my health. 54. But all my body is full of worms. The stench from my body extends everywhere. All my relatives are in trouble about me. All means that have been devised have failed.'

RAMA'S NAME HEALS THE LEPER

55. Padmanabh then said to him, 'One remedy remains to be tried. If you repeat the name 'Rama, Rama, ' three times, your disease will entirely depart from you. 56. If anyone should listen to the *Vedas* and *Shastras* or the *Puranas* or pronounce *mantras* or perform austerities, and yet if the name of Rama does not come into his speech, everything will be in vain. 57. One might worship the various

deities, perform sacrifices and give the offerings, and yet if the name of Hari does not come into one's speech, everything done will be in vain. 58. One may make himself thoroughly wearied in going to sacred bathing-places, one may have performed all the religious ceremonies, but if the name of Rama does not come into his speech, then all these acts are in vain. 59. One might sit on iron spikes, might give away cows, land, jewels, and food, but if Rama is not remembered in the heart, all goes for naught. 60. At the beginning of an act the name of Keshav and Narayan are repeated, and at the end the name of Vishnu is repeated, and all one's acts are brought to full completion. 61. Now repeat the name 'Rama, Rama' and all your pain will at once depart.' So said the disciple of Kabir to the merchant. 62. To the great crowd that had gathered, Padmanabh said, 'If you will repeat the name of Rama three times, all the diseases of this earthly life will at once depart.' 63. Hearing these words of the *bhaktas* of Vishnu, every one began to repeat the name of Rama. As they repeated His name three times an extraordinary thing took place. 64. As the sound of repeating arose, the merchant's body became divine. That is due to the great glory of the *bhaktas*. Even the chief of the gods do not understand it.

RAMA'S NAME HEALS THE WHOLE CROWD

65. People who assembled there to see the great sight, as they repeated the name of Rama, all their troubles at once disappeared. 66. Of all the people there with diseases not a single person remained with a disease. Every kind of trouble at once disappeared. 67. Some had chills and fever, some were suffering from tuberculosis, but as they repeated with their lips the name 'Rama, Rama' their bodies became free from disease. 68. Some were suffering from ear-aches, some had a swollen jaw, but as they repeated with their lips 'Rama, Rama' they were freed from this

condition. 69. Some were suffering from guinea-worm and some were footsore, but as they remembered the Husband of Janaki their disease disappeared. 70. Some had pain in their abdomen and some had weak knees, but as they repeated the name of 'Rama' their bodies became healed. 71. Some had the skin disease, the itch, and others had white leprosy, but as they repeated the name of 'Rama, Rama' their diseases fled away. 72. Some were not able to see and some were deaf, but as they repeated the name 'Rama, Rama' (the Holder of the bow) they at once became free from their troubles. 73. Those who were afflicted with coughs, colds, leprosy, and diseases of the spine, they also in remembering the Lord of Ayodhya were at once without their troubles. 74. Some who were troubled by being possessed of devils and had to resort to many kinds of *mantras* and remedies, they also in remembering Rama became at once healed. 75. Well, enough of such long descriptions. The one hundred and eight severe diseases fled away at the sight of Padmanabh. 76. The merchant now healed, quickly arose and made a prostrate *namaskar* to Padmanabh. He exclaimed, 'Blessed are you, O noble *Vaishnava.* You have been born to be the saviour of the world.' 77. All the people of Benares now worshipped the feet of Padmanabh, and in their joy they worshipped Rama continually. 78. In their working moments, in their dreams and in their dreamless sleep, they continually worshipped Shri Rama.

PADMANABH GAVE THE WHOLE OF BENARES THE FORM OF SHRI RAMA

79. All the people came and told Kabir what had happened. They said, 'The Brahman Padmanabh is your disciple. 80. He caused the people to repeat the name of Rama three times with their lips and thereby made every one well. Such a marvellous thing has never been seen

before in this world of mortals.' 81. Kabir then said to Padmanabh, 'Why did you have the people repeat the name of Rama three times? All the healing could have been done at once by repeating the two syllables *Ra-ma.* 82. Evidently you have not understood the supreme power of Rama's name. In explaining this in detail, I will tell you a story of what happened long ago. 83. Valha the fisherman was a very great sinner. By the preaching of Narad and by repeating the names of Rama, he became the *rishi* Valmiki. 84. It was before Rama had become an *avatar* that the *Ramayan* foretold His story. Through his own inner knowledge Valmiki wrote down the ten billion, verses. 85. The Lord of *Kailas*, the Husband of Parvati took the *Ramayan* and made a distribution. The inhabitants of heaven, the world of mortals and the region below came to receive their portion. 86. Shiva then distributed among the three worlds the one hundred thousand million verses.' All this with his own lips Kabir told to Padmanabh. 87. 'In this way he gave thirty-three crores of verses (330,000,000) to the world of mortals. He gave just as much to the inhabitants of *Vaikunth* (heaven) and the same number to the inhabitants of the lower regions. 88. There still remained one hundred million which the Lord of *Kailas* distributed. Thirty-three hundred thousand He gave to the inhabitants of Heaven, and the same to the inhabitants of this mortal world and to the regions below. 89. The one hundred thousand verses that remained the Lord of *Kailas* (Shiva) distributed, just as a father distributes to his sons by his own hand. 90. *Chandramauli* (Shiva, with moon-crest on his head) distributed thirty three thousand to the region below, the same amount to those in this world and the same number to the inhabitants of heaven. 91. One thousand verses still remained. He gave to each of the inhabitants of the three worlds three hundred each. There remained now one hundred which he also divided. 92. Thirty-three verses He gave to this world, the same to heaven, and to the regions below. In making this division there remained now but one verse. 93. Its thirty-two syllables He divided equally among the three worlds. The two syllables that remained, the Husband of Uma (Shiva) kept to Himself. 94. When Hari assumed the *avatar* of the tortoise form it was then that the ocean was churned, and the great and virulent poison came out of the sea. 95. That poison started to burn up the three worlds, and the gods were greatly troubled. But at that time the Husband of Uma repeated the two syllables "Rama." 96. The moment He repeated "Rama," Sadashiv (Shiva) became cool. And now Padmanabh, why did you make the people repeat the name of Rama *three* times?' 97. At this question of the *bhakta* Kabir, Padmanabh prostrated himself before him.

TEN THOUSAND *VAISHNAVAS* AS KABIR'S GUESTS

You pious *bhaktas*, now listen to an extraordinarily delightful story. 98. Although Kabir had a wife and sons yet his mind was indifferent to earthly things; just as the sun is reflected in the jar, but does not become wet with its water; 99. or just as the lotus-leaf, although in the water, is not made wet by it; or as when the pleasure-seeking man looks at his face in a mirror, he does not become entangled in it; 100. in the same way the *bhakta* Kabir did not become entangled in the affairs of his life. Free from care and indifferent to all earthly things, and intensely pious, he worshipped God. 101. Now it happened on a certain day that ten thousand *Vaishnavas*, with three upright marks upon their foreheads and adorned with *tulsi* garlands, arrived at Benares. 102. With caps on their heads, and with marks of white clay made upon their bodies they worshipped God in their love. Such were the *Vaishnava bairagis* (ascetics) who arrived suddenly in the city. 103. Shouting out the names 'Sita Rama' they asked the people of the town, 'What *Vaishnava* is there in this town who is the devoted worshipper of Shri Rama? 104. What extremely pious man is there, who will give food to the *Vaishnavas* and satisfy their appetites? Tell us at once the name of such a giver in this place.'

105. Hearing what these *bairagis* had to say the inhabitants of the town replied, 'At this sacred place, the wealthy Kabir of a Muhammadan caste lives. 106. He is able to satisfy the need of ten thousand *Vaishnavas*.' Thus the crooked-minded people told the *vairagis* in order to enjoy the fun. 107. One who has money and grain in his home, and yet will not give to the hungry to eat and points out the house of another, he truly is a poor man. 108. He who builds a house of many storeys and yet will not give a lodging-place to the traveller, that house should not be called a house but a cemetery. 109. He who has the gift of poesy and yet does not describe the goodness of God, and one who foolishly mutters heretical opinions, his power of speech should be called devilish 110. Anyone who has great strength of body and yet will not perform works of benevolence, he is not a man but a village hog. 111. And so while the *vairagis* were asking for food, the very miserly people of the town got rid of their nuisance by pointing to them the house of Kabir. 112. Then all the *sadhus* who dwelt at the various sacred bathing-places went to the house of Kabir. At the door of the house they shouted out 'Sita Rama.' 113. As the father of Kamal heard their shouts he came outside. With reverence he made them a prostrate *namaskar* and embraced them in love. 114. The *sadhus* replied to him, 'We are ten thousand noble *Vaishnavas*. We have been wandering all over the earth to sacred bathing-places. Now we have come here. 115. The people of this sacred bathing-place have

told us the fact that the father of Kamal is a giver of food.' Listening to what was in the minds of the *sadhus*, Kabir replied, 'I certainly will do as you wish.' 116. In the *bazaar* there was a grocer by name of Tulsidas and Kabir went to his shop. He said to him, 'Some saints have come to my house as guests. Select the materials needed for cooking and give them to me.'

[Verses 117 to 165 are not translated, because these are similar to chapter XI 16-98. The two stories may be summarised as follows :—

In Ch. XI 16-98 The wife brings the provisions. To obtain these she promises the grocer to come back and pass the night in his company. She keeps her promise with the consent of her husband. The grocer on seeing her at his place repents, and takes her back to her husband.

In Ch. XXIV 116-166 Kabir brings provisions from a grocer on condition that his (Kabir's) wife goes to fulfil the evil desire of the grocer that night. The promise is kept. Kabir's wife goes to the grocer in company with her husband. God protects her in the form of the city *Kotwal* (police officer), and takes her back to her husband. Kabir goes to the real *Kotwal* and takes him to task for his interference. The *Kotwal* ignores the charge. Then Kabir becomes aware that it was God who went to the grocer as the *Kotwal*. The grocer had the sight of God as the *Kotwal* and is saved.]

166. *Swasti* (Peace) This book is the *Shri Bhaktavijaya*. In listening to it the Lord of the world will be pleased. Listen, you God-loving, pious *bhaktas*. This is the twenty-fourth deeply delightful chapter.

CHAPTER XXV

ROHIDAS THE SHOEMAKER

Obeisance to Shri Ganesh. Obeisance to Radha Krishna.

A HUMBLE TRADE NOT BLAMEWORTHY

1. Listeners, give close attention. Rohidas was a *Vaishnava* of the highest type. He was accustomed to worship Hari with feelings of love. 2. He had put aside every wrong desire. With reverence he sang the praise of Hari. He regularly bathed and then performed the worship of Vishnu. 3. Although he was entangled in domestic affairs he planned acts of benevolence. To any *Vaishnava* who came to his house he gave a pair of shoes. 4. The occupation of a worker in leather appears to be a low one but there is not the least fault to be found with it. If such a one performs acts of benevolence the Pervader of the universe will certainly be attained. 5. Carpenters and potters who perform their accustomed tasks do so without blame, and in doing acts of benevolence the Pervader of the universe is attained by them. 6. Masons and workers in stone as they perform their tasks are without blame, and in performing acts of benevolence the Pervader of the universe is attained by them. 7. Weavers and fishermen in performing their usual tasks are without blame and in performing acts of benevolence the Pervader of the universe will be attained through their devotion. 8. Washermen and dyers in performing their tasks are without blame and in worshipping through acts of benevolence, while in the body, the purpose of life can be attained. 9. If there is no hypocrisy in the performers of austerities, and the acts of the Brahmans, then on account of their benevolent acts the Husbard of Rukmini will certainly show His favour

to them. 10. Well, enough of all these general statements. If I should describe the characteristics of the eighteen castes my story will increase too much in length. So let my hearers give attention.

DAILY LIFE OF ROHIDAS

11. Through acts of benevolence Rohidas served the servants of Vishnu. He used to repair the worn shoes of the pilgrims. 12. Hari is more fond of benevolent *bhaktas* than He is of His own life. At the home of the benevolent the Life of the world abides day and night. 13. Some preach to the people and demand their services but never oblige others by giving even a little water; 14. such a person though a learned man is a fool and ignorant. Rohidas understood this and worshipped the servants of Vishnu with reverence, realizing that earthly things are illusory. 15. He was accustomed to rise at dawn and to take breakfast before doing other things. He first performed his bath and then worshipped Vishnu. 16. My listeners may think this a wrong way of doing; but Rohidas thought that if he sat down to contemplate while hungry, his mind would not be undisturbed. 17. In this *Kali Yuga*, life is made up of food, so wise men say. When two watches of the day have passed the body becomes exhausted. 18. If one is hungry when sitting down to contemplate, the mind will at once wander. Rohidas understood this, and therefore he first ate; 19. just as when one is attacked by a thief, he should first abandon the money he has and run away; or in order that a person may not suffer injury from the possession of devils, the exerciser first makes an offering to them; 20. or when digging for a treasure, lest ghosts should persecute him a man first offers an offering as a preventive; or that the *Hawaldars* (village officials) may not swear at them, men give them bribes; 21. and so Rohidas in the same way was accustomed to make first an

offering of food to his life [i. e. to sustain himself]. Then he would hasten to his bath and worship God in private.

22. Now it happened on a certain day that this *bhakta* of Vishnu was sitting performing his worship of God. He had withdrawn to be alone with materials of worship, and he held his fickle mind in restraint. 23. He brought a bottle of leather and placed it there filled with water. His mat and his sacred bag and casket were also made of leather.

LEATHER (OR SKIN) ALL OVER CREATION

24. Rohidas was sitting down with all his vessels made of leather and just then a Brahman came to his house to explain to him the Calendar. 25. The Brahman sat down by the holy and beautiful *tulsi* altar. Rohidas at once arose and with reverence made him a *namaskar*. 26. The Brahman said to Rohidas, 'You are worshipping God while sitting upon a leather seat. What do you expect from that? 27. We Brahmans worship *Shaligram*, the idol of Vishnu. How is it you have placed Him in a leather bag? 28. How is it you have placed in a leather bag Him who dwells in *Vaikunth* (heaven), the Life of the world whom *Yogis* contemplate? How is it you have placed Him in a leather bag? 29. He Who dwells upon the sea of milk, the Recliner upon Shesha, and who cannot be described adequately by the *Shastras* though you might search there for Him, you have made a leather bag and placed Him within it. 30. *Shri Rang* (Vishnu) who cannot be attained by ceremonial acts, by bathing at sacred places, by austerities or by sacrifices, this Dweller in *Vaikunth* (heaven), Terminator of the earthly existence of His *bhaktas*, how is it you have enclosed Him in that leather bag?' 31. Hearing what the Brahman said, Rohidas replied, ' What object have you ever seen which has not leather connected with it? 32. Musical instruments and

drums are used in the praise-service of Hari. One has never seen any of them without their being connected with leather. 33. The black cow has a leather skin, yet her milk is holy. And in the *Panchamrit* bath (in milk, curds, ghee, sugar and honey) it is used in the bathing of the god. 34. Animate things that are born, those hatched from eggs, and those produced from seed, all three are covered with skin, and *Atmaram* (God) is in them all alike. 35. Shudras, Vaishyas, Kshatriyas and Brahmans are covered with skin. They make drums with skin,and play them with hands covered with skin. 36. A pleasing sound comes from them that is heard by the ear which is of skin. The tongue is covered with skin and repeats the *Vedas.* 37. With hands covered with skin one eats food and drinks water. And from a leather shrine (the human body) *Atmaram* (God) speaks with His gentle voice.' 38. The Brahman now replied to to Rohidas, ' You are talking philosophy, but while life is in the body the body is never defiled.' 39. To this Rohidas answered, 'If the Pervader of the universe, the Life of the world is in a leather bag, how can you regard Him as defiled by the leather ? 40. You considered the body of one who is conceiving or bearing a child as defiling.* 41. One just born and one dead you regard as defiling. What good object do you see in them ? 42. The skin might be filthy and yet the good God *Atmaram* may be in it. Krishna who is without spot is alike in everything.' 43. The Brahman now replied, 'The emblem of Vishnu (*Shaligram*) is a holy pebble and so if a shoemaker worships Him, He is defiled thereby.' 44. Hearing the Brahman say this, Rohidas continued, 'Who should worship the *Shaligram* (the emblem of Vishnu)? Tell me, O *Swami.*' 45. The Brahman replied, 'You hundred times a fool. We alone should worship the Lord of

* This verse is merely paraphrased, not translated.

Vaikunth (heaven). Among the four races we Brahmans are the highest. 46. Shri Hari is chief among the gods. The Brahmans are the highest among the four races. They alone have authority to invest themselves with the sacred thread and they alone can worship Vishnu.'

THE BRAHMAN'S PRIDE HUMBLED

47. Hearing this remark, Rohidas replied, 'O *Swami*, I will show you my sacred thread.' 48. Then with his sharp tool he ripped open his stomach, and showed the sacred thread within it. 49. The Brahman then exclaimed, 'You are indeed a *bhakta* of Vishnu, I was thoughtless and persecuted you. 50. Gold is cast into the furnace, and thereby its value is increased. In persecuting you I have but advanced your glory. 51. Or just as experts bore a hole in a coin in order to test it, thus in persecuting you I have only increased your glory. 52. If sandalwood is rubbed on the flat stone, its full fragrance is at once known, so in persecuting you I have but increased your glory. 53. When iron comes in contact with a touchstone it at once turns into gold, so in persecuting you I have only increased your glory. 54. Or as stone is shaped by a chisel and then the idol of God is firmly placed, so in persecuting you I have done what I did ignorantly. 55. You are a supreme *bhakta* of Vishnu. Worship the *Shaligram* at your pleasure.' Thus speaking, the good Brahman went back to his home.

56 In the next chapter, there will be a description of a very purifying story of the life of Pipaji. And Mahipati says, 'Let the good people listen with attentive minds, and with love.'

57. *Swasti* (Peace)! This book is the *Shri Bhaktavijaya*. In listening to it the Lord of the world will be pleased. Listen, you God-loving, pious *bhaktas*. This is the twenty-fifth very delightful chapter; it is an offering to Shri Krishna.

CHAPTER XXVI

KING PIPAJI OF GADEMANDAL

Obeisance to Shri Ganesh. Obeisance to the Husband of Rukmini.

SUPERIORITY OF VAISHNAVA SAINTS

1. Listen now with attention, my hearers. This story is of special importance. As the story falls upon the ear all faults at once flee away. 2. In the country of Gademandal there was a very holy king. In his home, duty made its home. 3. When an assembly of *sadhus* came to his place he used to go out and meet them. He gave them lodgings in his place. He gave them to eat according to what they desired. 4. He was brave, exceedingly powerful, generous, wise, religious and a worshipper of Bhavani (the wife of Shiva). 5. Bhavani was favourable to him. He had a son, a wife and an abundance of wealth. With reverence the king was accustomed to worship Bhavani. 6. He used to rise early in the morning and perform his worship, using the sixteen materials. He offered Her garments, ornaments and flowers of perfume. 7. He brought incense and lights and made an offering of them. Seeing his reverence Bhavani accepted his offering. 8. With reverence he offered to Her fruit and *pansupari*' and then circumambulating Her, made Her a *namaskar* after which the king returned to his own palace and sit down to his meals. 9. Now it happened on a certain occasion that a great assembly of *Vaishnava* saints, going to different bathing places, came to Gademandal to the king's city. 10. They were without desires and were indifferent to all worldly things. Undefiled by anything they lived in this world. Such were these *Vaishnava bairagis* (ascetics) who came unexpectedly to that place. 11. Men who in their former births have wandered

from place to place and have performed sacrifices, only to the house of such do the saints suddenly come. 12. If one has observed *Ekadashi* (the eleventh day of every fortnight) and served his parents, only to the house of such do *Vaishnavas* come suddenly. 13. If one has dug a well or a tank, and made a garden, then only because of his good deeds do the *Vaishnavas* come to his house. 14. Only to the house of one who has made gifts of a cow and food and offered them to Krishna, do the *Vaishnavas* suddenly come. 15. He who in an infinite number of rebirths may have performed in this world extraordinary austerities, to his house the assembly of saints will come because of his good fortune. 16. The infinite number of the king's rebirths had at this time come to their fruitage, hence it was that the assembly of *Vaishnava bhaktas* came to the home of Pipaji. 17. Servants told the king that the *Vaishnavas* had come to his city. He honoured them and gave them the materials for their food. 18. After performing his bath he went to the temple of Bhavani as usual. He performed his worship there and presented Her with his offerings. 19 He was continually worshipping Bhavani, and Bhavani ate the offerings he made. Then after making Her his *namaskar* the king would sit down himself to eat.

VISHNU'S SUPERIORITY

20. *Bhadrakali* (Shiva's wife Parvati or Bhavani) then said to the king, 'An assembly of saints has come to your city. I cannot, however, eat your offerings until the saints have eaten. 21. The loved ones of the Lord of the universe, Who dwells in *Vaikunth* (heaven), Whose slaves are the infinite heavenly powers, they have come to your house, your good fortune has no limit.' 22. The king now joined his hands palm to palm and made a request of Her. 'What God is superior to you?' Hear-

ing his question, mother Bhavani replied, 23. 'He Whose limits are unknown even to Brahma, Indra and Shiva, He who dwells on the sea of milk, the Husband of Kamala (Vishnu), is superior to all. 24. It was He who gave light to the sun and the moon, and by His power they act. So He, the Husband of Rukmini, the Primal Being, is superior to all gods. 25. He who assumed the *avatar* of a fish and killed the monster Shankha by dashing him upon the stone, He, the Lord of the universe, the Life of the world, is superior to all other gods. 26. He assumed the *avatars* of a tortoise, a wild boar, a half man and half lion (Narhari), Vaman and Parashuram, and made the cows and Brahmans happy. This Slayer of Madhu is superior to all gods. 27. Indra and all other gods were imprisoned by Ravana. Rama assumed an *avatar* and by His power He delivered them all.' 28. The king replied to the Mother of the universe, 'Cause me to meet Him Who is the Chief among the gods.' Saying this he fell at her feet. 29. Hearing his request, the Primal Mother said to him, 'You must go as a suppliant to the saints. If you, O king, worship them, they will cause you to meet the chief of the *Raghus* (Rama). 30. If you asked of Me *riddhis* and *siddhis* (the accomplishments), a kingdom, or wealth, I could give them to you, but to cause you to see Shri Rama is not in My power. 31. It is the *Vaivhnava* saints who are glorious, generous, wise, wholly indifferent to earthly things, and possess the glory of six qualities. 32. Such *Vaishnava* saints to whom the supreme and eternal God has become subject, even these have arrived at your city.'

ADVISED TO OBTAIN RAMANAND'S FAVOUR

33. Bhadrakali (Shiva's wife) having said this, the king arose and came to where the assembly of the saints was gathered. 34. The king came there and made them a *namaskar*. He supplied them with the needed materials

and gave them to eat. 35. With reverence he gave them *pansupari*, and put garlands of flowers around their necks. He then prostrated himself before the saints and made to them a request. 36. Standing before them the king joined his hands palm to palm and made his request. He said, 'I want you to cause me to meet Shri Rama.' 37. The saints replied to him, 'Go as a suppliant to Ramanand, receive his instruction and become his disciple. The purpose of your life will be a success. 38. If you worship an inferior deity, you can never acquire spiritual knowledge. So at least now, O king, give attention to His worship. 39. To worship an inferior deity is like that of serving a feeble king. An ignorant talker never gives happiness to his listeners. 40. A praise-service in honour of Hari but without love, an ignorant *guru*, a miserly disciple, and a sterile husband, never give happiness. 41. A speaker who is in bondage because of desires, a listener who is not a *bhakta*, one given to constant disputes, one who proclaims spiritual knowledge but is without experience of it, can never give happiness. 42. Becoming a *sannyasi* without proper knowledge, an idiotic son, a poor citizen, and an ugly looking wife, can never give happiness through association with them.'

GURU ALONE CAN MEET A *BHAKTA* WITH GOD

43. So the saints said to the king, 'Now give attention and go quickly as a suppliant to Ramanand.' 44. Hearing these words of the saints, the king realized his faults. Then calling his ministers he put the burden of the kingdom upon them. 45. He brought out from his treasure-house garments, adornments and ornaments. He then called the Brahmans, and had himself robbed by them. 46. In the name of Krishna he gave gifts of horses, elephants, chariots, and cows. Then he went as a suppliant to Ramanand and arrived at the Joy Forest (Benares). 47. The faithful wife

of the king also left behind those she loved and cared for, and distributed among the Brahman women her garments and ornaments. 48. Both of them came to Ramanand and placed their heads at his feet with reverence. 49. They offered to this *guru* their wealth, their minds and bodies. Supplicating themselves before Ramanand they became his disciples. 50. He gave them the *mantra*, 'Rama, Krishna, Narayan.' They then began to listen to the words that fell from the lips of their *sadguru*, to meditate upon them, and to study and experience them. 51. If a *guru* is wise and a disciple is repentant there will be found the light of spiritual knowledge. Studies without this are false and hypocritical. 52. It is like an excellent touchstone being applied to a piece of pottery. So what can a *sadguru* do with a disciple who is not a *bhakta* and who is filthy in his ways? 53. A saint is compassionate to all, to him a prince and a pauper are the same. But one gets the fruit according to his own devotion. 54. When the sun is fully arisen it gives light alike to every one. All doers of evil are punished and the wise receive honour. 55. The moon shines alike for the *chakor* bird and for the burglar. The burglar, seeing the moon, thinks it a nuisance, but the *chakor* bird thinks it to be nectar. 56. So *sadhus* and saints act continually with the idea of all things being alike but the fruit is obtained according to devotion.

57. Well, let this long statement suffice. Having visited and worshipped Ramanand *Swami* the king received the full spiritual knowledge through his look of mercy. 58. The king now listened to *kirtans* and performed them in honour of Hari. Night and day he was engaged with the worship of Hari and in repeating the *mantra* 'Rama, Krishna, Govind.'

PIPAJI GOES TO DWARKA WITH HIS QUEEN

59. Now it happened on a certain day that the king

took leave of his *Swami*. 'Give me now leave to go to Dwaravati.' 60. After worshipping the feet of his *guru* the two started for Dwarka. They bathed in the Gomati river. The king and queen went to see and worship Krishna in His temple. 61. Having come to the great door of the temple, there they made a prostrate *namaskar*. Then the two joining their hands palm to palm gave praise to Shri Hari. 62. 'Victory, Victory, to Mukund, Murari, the Primal Being, Shri Hari, have mercy upon us lowly ones. We have come as suppliants to Thy feet. 63. I was ignorant of the supreme God, the eternal one, and not knowing Thee I worshipped *Shakti* [another name for Shiva's wife Parvati, Bhavani, etc.]. 64. It was like rejecting nectar and drinking the water in which rice has been washed. It was like rejecting the touchstone and taking in its stead a common pebble. So because I did not know Thee, I worshipped *Shakti*. 65. It was as if I neglected the *ashvattha* tree and gave water to the *shundi* tree. So not knowing Thee I worshipped Bhavani. 66. So long as the sun has not risen I might consider the firefly as a special light. So, because I did not know Thee, O Krishna, I worshipped Bhavani. 67. So long as the *Vedanta* had not fallen upon my ears, I looked upon the treatise of the art of love with a special interest. So, not knowing Thee, the Holder of the disk (Krishna), I worshipped Bhavani. 68. Rejecting the wish-tree which was near me, I gave honour to the *babhul* tree. So, not knowing Thee, *Vanamali* (Krishna) I worshipped Bhavani. 69. But now the good deeds done in my infinite number of rebirths, most surely have come to their fruitage. Therefore it is that *sadhus* and saints have come unexpectedly to my home. 70. They told me of Thy glory above all comparison.' Having said this, he made a prostrate namaskar, and then again made another. 71. Hearing his pity-arousing plea, God gave him an embrace. Pipaji the king then had a direct vision of Krishna.

72. He was in His form of four arms, with qualities, and dressed in His yellow robe. The Life of the world had on His head a resplendent crown. Pipaji thus saw the eternal God. 73. They performed a praise service at the great door of the temple. In their enthusiasm, shouting loudly the names of God they danced. They remained in Dwarka for four months, performing their enthusiastic *kirtans* in honour of Krishna's name,

A TIGER SUBMITS TO PIPAJI

74. Then taking leave of the Lord of *Vaikunth* (heaven), both of them, husband and wife, started to return. Further on as they were walking through a forest they saw a great tiger. 75. The tiger had a fearful appearance and he came forward with a roar. The wife of the king, seeing the tiger, became full of fear. 76. This supremely beautiful wife, a very mine of loveliness, turned and looked at her husband who was following her. She said to her husband, 'Did you notice a tiger over there?' 77. The king's wife trembled violently with fear. As the tiger came near to them, Pipaji the king said to her, 'Have no fear whatever. 78. It appears to you as a tiger but Shri Rama is in it. Not the least space can be seen anywhere that is without Him. 79. The sun's reflection is the same in all jars of water. Just as in all liquids there is water, so the Lord of Yadavas is the same everywhere. 80. Just as the reflection of the sky is the same in every jar and in every house, so the Lord of the world pervades everything alike. 81. The air is alike both to a locust and to the king of birds (the eagle). So, *Hrishikeshi* (the Lord of the heart) is the same in all creatures. 82. There is no difference between cloth and thread, and gold in another form is called ornaments. So, not knowing the form of Him as *Vishwambhar* (who fills the universe), the ignorant call Him the universe itself.'

KRISHNA PERVADES THE UNIVERSE

83. 'The Life of the world fills the whole of the infinite universe and extends beyond it. This is not a tiger but the Husband of Rukmini. Know this for a certainty. 84. Krishna fills all waters and all rocks and extends beyond them. There is not the least space anywhere that is without Him.' 85. King Pipaji having said this to his wife she stood there amazed. The tiger came near and stood very close to them. 86. Pipaji said to the tiger, 'Worship Rama day and night.' The tiger then with reverence embraced the feet of Pipaji. 87. Having looked at the saint he at once received divine knowledge. Pipaji said to him, 'Cease all acts of killing.' 88. Pipaji then took off the garland of *tulsi* beads from his own neck and placed it on the neck of the tiger. He gave him the *mantra* of 'Rama, Krishna.' 89. He said, 'There is no *mantra* more important than that of, "Rama, Krishna, Narayan." The ignorant animal gajendra was saved by his worshipping Ram. 90. The fisherman Valmiki, who was a wayside robber when Narad gave him instructions and made him his disciple, began to repeat the name of Rama and became the *rishi* Valmiki. 91. Ajamil was a very sinful Brahman, wholly absorbed in his evil deeds, but by repeating the name of Narayan he was taken to *Vaikunth* (heaven). 92. Lust, anger, and pride, envy, hypcrisy, evil desires and arrogance, at once flee away by repeating the name of Rama.'

93. The tiger then joined his paws together and making a prostrate *namaskar* to Pipaji, he said to him, 'By your favour I have begun to worship Shri Rama. 94. Formerly my evil deeds were many, but now by the name of Shri Rama I am purified from them.' Then again he made a prostrate *namaskar* to Pipaji. 95. Having thus given to the tiger the chief of all *mantras*, Pipaji departed from there and went to the Joy Forest (Benares). 96. The

tiger was wholly repentant. He ceased from all acts of killing, discarded the eating of meat and ate only fallen leaves. 97. After wandering over the forest for seven days for the purpose of worshipping Shri Hari, he died. 98. Tigers, scorpions, lions, dogs, serpents, snakes, falcons, fierce elephants, all these have evil characteristics in their nature. None of them have good characteristics. 99. But through the power of association with a saint, the tiger received spiritual knowledge. Keeping in his mind the worship of Hari he offered his body to Krishna.

THE TIGER BECOMES NARSI MEHETA

100. He who is in this world may be entangled in the net of desire, but he who remembers Krishna at the time of death, he becomes delivered from rebirths. Have no doubt about this. 101. Putting his desires into the worship of Hari, the tiger left his body. But it was in order that he might take birth as a Nāgar Brahman in the city of Junagad [in Kathiawad, Gujerat]. 102. The tiger was reborn in the form of the noble *Vaishnava* Narsi Meheta.

Hearers must listen with reverenee to this most pleasing history. 103. The lives of the saints may be regarded as the Ganges river or the Bhagirathi or Chandrabhaga rivers. One should bathe in them and then with reverence go as a suppliant to Pandurang. 104. Taking *tulsi* leaves and flowers as pure mind and pure devotion ih his hand, Mahipati places his head at the feet of Pandurang.

105. *Swasti* (Peace)! This book is the *Shri Bhaktavijaya*. In listening to it, the Lord of the world is pleased. Listen then, you God-loving, pious *bhaktas*. This is the twenty-sixth deeply delightful chapter; it is an offering to Shri Krishna.

CHAPTER XXVII

NARSI MEHETA

Obeisance to Shri Ganesh. Obeisance to Shri Krishna.

GOD'S FAME INDESCRIBABLE

1. Victory to Thee, Merciful to the lowly, Husband of Rukmini. Thou pervadest the three worlds and extendest beyond them. The *Vedas* and *Shastras* attempt to describe Thee but are not able to describe Thy wonderful deeds.
2. In their attempt to describe Thee the eighteen *Puranas* become wearied. The six *Shastras* in attempting to discuss Thy character find that they do not understand Thee.
3. The serpent who supports the earth when attempting to describe Thy infinite qualities became wearied, and because Thy qualities have no limit his tongue became divided into fangs. 4. Becoming ashamed, therefore, he made of his body a place for Thee to recline upon, and with his thousand hoods made a shadow over Thee, O Lord God.
5. Saraswati made a resolution that she would not describe Thy power. She made the ocean of milk into ink and began to describe Thy qualities. 6. Taking pens that were made from eighteen *bhars* (a bhar=8,000 tolas) of reeds, and taking the earth itself as paper, she in her love tried to describe Thy qualities. 7. In her attempt to describe Thy qualities the ocean full of ink was exhausted. The earth as paper was insufficient. Seeing thus Thy wonderful nature, Saraswati fell at Thy feet. 8. In describing Thy wonderful qualities great writers have had to become silent. Thou art the Lord of an infinite number of universes.
9. Thus Thou art the infinite Pervader of every place. Thy power fills the universe and extends beyond it, O Lord of the universe, Lord of the earth. 10. I am fond of the lives of Thy *bhaktas*, O Husband of Rukmini, therefore en-

lighten my mind and cause me to compose this book properly. 11. And you, my hearers and saints, give me your attention.

BIRTH AND BOYHOOD OF NARSI

In the previous chapter the description given was heard by you all. 12. While coming from Dwarka, Pipaji gave instructions to a tiger. It then gave up its habit of killing and began to eat fallen leaves. 13. He was not in reality a tiger but was the Husband of Parvati. In becoming an *avatar*, however, it was the skin of a tiger that he beheld. 14. Because evil qualities entered into his thoughts he became a tiger. Just as in dreams one sees that which has been noticed in one's waking condition; 15. so when Shiva became an *avatar* it was his tiger-skin that was seen. Therefore it was that he was born an *avatar* from the tiger. 16. After seven days were passed he died. But then again in the city of Junagad [in Kathiawad, Gujerat] he was born to a Nāgar Brahman. 17. Day by day he grew in stature and he was invested with the sacred thread. When he was seven years of age his mother and father died. 18. His cousins (paternal uncle's sons) now cared for him. As the children of the village played, he also played amongst them. 19. They played at *itidandu*, *lingurchya* kissing games, hide-and-seek, *hamama*, *humari* and diving. 20. *Vaghodi*, *atyapatya*, *jhijya*, *bokat*, *agalgotya*, *pheravatya*, *bhoware*, *chakre* and caught each other in the square. 21. Thus he played many childish games. After some time had passed, a most extraordinary thing happened.

NARSI'S SISTER-IN-LAW REBUKES HIM

22. In playing these childish games, his whole life was now being spent, but he did not remember the cloud-dark Krishna. 23. Now on one occasion after playing various kinds of games, Narsi Meheta hastened to his home. 24. He

said to his sister-in-law, 'I am very thirsty. Please give me some water.' The other replied. 'What hard work have you been doing that you have come here wearied? 25. This very childish and disobedient boy has driven his parents to death. He plays day and night and eats like a glutton. 26. You do not study and you spend your life in vain. Your wife will hereafter cry, you useless and impudent boy.' 27. Such were the harsh words spoken to him by the wife of his eldest brother. This brought him to repentance and Narsi Meheta then started to go away. 28. He went a long way off towards a forest, and thought to himself, 'My fate is a very unhappy one. But it is very powerful and hard to resist. 29. To lose a mother in childhood, to lose a wife in youth, and to lose a son in adult age must be called the anger of God. 30. I am now receiving the fruit of the deeds I committed in former births.'

NARSI WORSHIPS SHIVA

As he was thus speaking to himself, he saw a forest further on. 31. Coming about four miles from his village, he saw the beginning of a very great forest. After Narsi Meheta had noticed it, he began to look about him on all sides. 32. Suddenly just before him he saw a temple to Shiva. Narsi Meheta entered it and there saw the Lord of *Kailas* (heaven). 33. It was a deserted forest and there was no passing by of men. Taking courage he worshipped the feet of Shiva. 34. It was Upamanyu, the son of a Brahman, who asked his mother for a cup of milk, and because she did not give it to him he sulkily sat down. 35. It was the King Uttanpad whose son was the child Dhruva; he also sulked and prayed to the Lord of *Vaikunth* (heaven).

NARSI PLEADS WITH GOD

36. In the same way Narsi Meheta felt dis-

satisfied and cried, 'O Filler of the universe, Lord of the universe, care for me, Thy helpless one. 37. He lay himself on the body of the Holder of the *Pinak* bow, the Husband of Parvati. He discarded all food including fruit, nor did he drink water. 38. After seven days had passed, the Lord of *Kailas* (heaven) with a perplexed mind thought to himself, 'In his devotion Narsi has offered to Me all his body. 39. People offer to me perfume, sacred rice, flowers, sandalwood paste, all kinds of brilliant jewels, strings of pearls, and golden ornaments. 40. By spending an immense sum of money, some build temples of Shiva and with great delight offer to me the water of the Bhagirathi. 41. Some come and offer to me a *lac* of leaves of the *bel* tree, but no one has ever offered to me his whole body. 42. Caring for their body they make use of many other means. All their knowledge has, however, gone in vain. The Life of the world does not meet them.'

SHIVA PLEASED WITH NARSI'S DEVOTION

43. Now seeing the unwavering devotion of Narsi Meheta, (Sadashiv) was pleased. He now revealed Himself in His form as Mahadev with qualities. 44. He who has ten arms and five faces, and has a serpent around His neck as an ornament, He who has yellow-coloured matted hair on his head and ashes rubbed all over His body, 45. manifesting Himself in this form as the Holder of the *Pinak* bow (Shiva), then raised up Narsi Meheta and gave him, His assurance not to fear. 46. He said to him, 'My child, My *bhakta*, I am now pleased with you. Tell Me everything which your heart desires.'

THE BOON ASKED FOR BY NARSI

47. Narsi Meheta having heard these words embraced the feet of the Lord of *Kailas* (heaven) and said, Thou hast become pleased with me, and hast given me the

word of assurance. 48. I am but an ignorant child. I do not know the best things to ask for. Give me, O blue-throated One, that which thou art more fond of than Thou art of Thine own life. 49. Just as the infant ignorant of its mother does not know the proper time, but is at all times pleasing to its mother and in her love she adorns him with ornaments, 50. so, O Lord of the universe, art Thou pleased with me to-day and art ready to give me a boon with Thine own lips. So give me, a helpless one, whatever pleases Thee.' 51. The Holder of the *Pinak* bow (Shiva) with a smiling face was perplexed in mind, and said to Himself, 'Never have I seen such a clever *bhakta*.' 52. In reply Shiva next said to Narsi Mehta, 'I am more fond of Shri Krishna Who is the object of the worship of all other gods. 53. Without telling Ganga or Parvati, I repeat the name of the Lord Shri Krishna, but I am more fond of the stories of the saints. 54. You say to Me, "Show me the secrets of your heart." But if a beggar asked the king for his kingdom, it would be of no use whatever. 55. If a beggar asks a miser for his wealth, he is not made happy by him. If one asks for the gift of his wife from a libertine, the one asking for this receives no honour.' 56. The other replied, 'Holder of the *Pinak* bow (Shiva), Thou givest me illustrations and dost try to make me understand, but still I have a doubt in my mind. 57. Seeing that king Bali was a very generous man, Shri Vaman (Vishnu in His fifth *avatar*) went to him in the form of a beggar. He at once gave Him his kingdom and also made an offering of Himself to him. 58. King Harischandra was a very good king. Vishvamitra in the form of a beggar having asked for a gift, he (Harischandra) gave to him his kingdom, his wife, and his son, and thus he preserved his goodness. 59. So Thou, O generous Lord of *Kailas* (heaven), if Thou art pleased with me show me Him who is dear to Thee.

SHIVA'S FONDNESS FOR KRISHNA'S *RAS* DANCE

60. Having heard these words, the Destroyer of Tripur (Shiva) replied, 'I am especially fond of the Krishna-*lila* (the popular stories of the deeds of Shri Krishna). 61. The Krishna-*lila* (sports or deeds of Krishna) among men are extraordinary. He amused Himself in Gokul by *Ras* dancing [a special dance] which I am more fond of than I am of My very life. 62. On the bank of the Jumna river, the Lord of the world amuses Himself with the *Gopis* [cowherdesses]. I love that dancing greatly and go often to see it. 63. He arranges dancing, and dances with them. I myself sit beating the time on the drum.' 64. Saying that He would show it to him, He placed his assuring hand upon him and the blue-throated god (Shiva) gave to him the dress of the *Gopis*. 65. The Holder of the *Finak* bow (Shiva) then took Narsi with Him into the dancing and worshipped the Holder of the disk (Krishna). 66. Hearing such a statement, the wise will have a doubt in their minds. You will say that it was in the *Dwapar Yuga* that Krishna amused Himself in the dance. 67. Now in this *Kali Yuga* in relating the story of the *bhakta* Narsi Mehta, why was the story of Krishna introduced? You may hold this doubt but you should not say the verses composed about it are useless. 68. Even today the Holder of the disk (Krishna) is amusing Himself at Mathura, Gokul and Vrindavan. Those who are pious *bhaktas* are able to see the Hari-*lila* (or deeds of Hari) with their eyes.

STORIES OF *BHAKTAS* NOT IMAGINARY

69. This story is found in the *Bhavishyottar Purana* written by Shri Vyas himself. He has also described the stories of the chief of *bhaktas* of the *Kali Yuga*. 70. Just as the water of the ocean does not pass over the shore and cover the land, so the lips of the chief of poets will not describe a thing unless it exists. 71. Unless one's life-

time has come to an end, death will not punish any being; so the chief of the poets will not describe deeds unless they have really happened. 72. The sun does not set until the full measure of the day and the proper hour of the setting of the day has arrived; so unless deeds have been done, poets do not write regarding them. 73. Just as a dutiful wife will not act unless she receives the opinion of her husband, so the voice of the chief poet will never relate a useless or an untrue story. 74. When a neighbour is asked to come and help in the cooking she never brings her own materials to help in the cooking. 75. If the cook is a clever one, she will make very tasty food; and the poet with a few appropriate illustrations will give his description. 76. But the poet will never describe the original verses by inventing the story himself; so I beseech the *pandits* not to hold wrong thoughts in their minds in regard to this. 77. The Husband of Rukmini, who dwells on the bank of the Bhima and is pure intelligence, is the giver of inspiration to the mind. He is the One that causes this book to be written ; otherwise I, Mahipati, am too ignorant to write.

SHIVA TAKES NARSI TO KRISHNA'S DANCE

78. Now listen, you pious people, and give your attention to the story as formerly told. The Husband of Parvati (Shiva) has taken Narsi to the Hari-*lila* (the dance of Hari). 79. On the banks of the *Kalindi* (Jumna) there were intensely high trees, that kissed the very sky ; they were such as the *davana*, the *ketaki*, and the *parijat* trees, and doves cooed in their branches while watching the Hari-*lila* (the deeds of Hari). 80. Mango trees, the *jambhul*, the *avali*, the *nimboni*, the *raikayli*, the *bakuli*, the *Rama-Sita-phali* and the *padli*, moved to and fro with their fragrance. 81. The *bilva* tree, the *banyan*, the *gondhani*, the *ashvattha*, the *rudraksha*, the *saramani*, the *champak*, the pomegranate, with their many flowers waved on the dancing stage of

Krishna. 82. The *pimpari*, the *sherga*, the *maharukha*, the *pasarani*, and the *selataka*, the *phanas* and *moha* waved their branches in the sky while beholding the Lord of the Yadavas. 83. There was a row of trees around them, and inside it was a flower-garden. In it there were the *mogra*, the *jai*, and the *sevantika* that beheld the Lord Krishna. 84. The *sahasrapadi*, the yellow *sevanti*, the *bhuyachampha*, the *jasundi*, the *sevanti*, the *kapurveli* and the rose beautified the place and watched the acts of Krishna. 85. The *sarante*, *shyam*, *hansarashi*, the *batmogra*, the *suhasi*, the rose, the red *gulchhani*, and the *tulsi* were planted in the *Kunjavan* (garden). 86. The spring coming there had adorned *Kunjavan*. In such a place the Son of Yashoda (Krishna) joyfully danced. 87. The very look of Krishna has the greatest power. The *sarante* (thorn bushes) become wish-trees. Even nectar is not able to equal the water of the streamlet in the garden. 88. There *Shrirang* (Krishna, the Holder of the *Sharang* bow) amused himself. Pebbles of no value became precious stones and ordinary stones became touchstones for ever. 89. Pigeons, parrots, swans, *chash*, *chatak*, all beautiful birds, doves, sparrows, *salonki* and the *vamana*, wagged their heads and performed a *kirtan* in honour of Krishna.

KRISHNA IN THE *KUNJAVAN*

90. Well, this long description is quite sufficient. In this exceedingly beautiful garden by the bank of the *Kalindi* (Jumna) Shri Krishna amused Himself. 91. Narsi Meheta and the Husband of Uma (Shiva) going there, quickly with reverence bowed to Krishna and lovingly gave him an embrace. 92. Shri Krishna was the visible image of the supreme *Brahm*. The *Gopis* (cowherdesses) were *avatars* of the *Vedas*, and when Krishna played on the pipe all the *Gopis* out of love assembled together. 93. The *Gopis* stood together in a circle, and in the midst of them was the

cloud-dark Krishna, the Lord of *Vaikunth* (heaven). The *Gopis* seeing this attractive One rushed and embraced His feet. 94. The feet of Shri Krishna were exceedingly tender. There were marks of *Vajrankush* and the *todar* ornament on His feet. Even Brahmadev, His own son, was not able to have a sight of those feet. 95. As to holiness, the Ganges flows from His feet. Therefore, the Husband of Uma (Shiva) held it gladly in His head. 96. Ornaments such as the *Vanki* and the *Nepura* shouted out on His feet, 'Blessed are we in the three worlds. The Husband of Kamala (Krishna) being pleased with us has fastened us upon His feet.' 97. The moon looking at Krishna's nails became extremely ashamed at heart. The *todar* loudly proclaimed, 'At the feet of Hari, sins are destroyed.' 98 The calves of His legs and His thighs were beautifully shaped. A yellow robe enveloped His thighs. A million brilliant lightning flashes shone from His body. 99. Shri Krishna's hands reached down to His knees. Both His arms were like clubs. Although Brahmadev was born from His naval, he did not know his limit. 100. His abdomen was of vast expanse. His body was of a dark complexion. On His breast were the beautiful three folds. The colour of His hair was without comparison. The *Shri Vatsa* jewel, how can I describe it? 101. In His face all joy seemed to be gathered. The happiness arising from the enjoyment of the nectar of His lower lip was understood by Lakshmi alone. 102. Krishna's eyes were like the petals of the lotus. His straight nose appeared glorious, as though the spring had come and settled there. 103. In His ears were wonderfully lustrous earrings. His eyebrows were well formed. His brows were wide. His curly hair was very attractive. It was surrounded by peacock feathers. 104. When the sun looked upon the crown of Krishna it became ashamed of itself. The sun on seeing the *Kaustubh* jewel around the neck of Krishna was at heart frozen through shame. 105. Just as in the clear sky the clusters of stars shine, so the great diamonds surrounding the *Kaustubh* jewel looked brilliant with the ornaments of Krishna. 106. Around His neck was a necklace of pearls. The *Vaijayanti* garland waved back and forth down to His feet. His *bhaktas* had placed garlands of many flowers around His neck. 107. His whole body had been rubbed with sandalwood perfume. On His forehead was the beautiful mark of *kasturi* (musk). The Lord of the Yadavas lovingly wore the *tulsi* garland.

KRISHNA'S *RAS* DANCE

108. So appeared in visible form the supreme *Brahm* itself. As he sounded His flute the eyes of the *Gopis* (cowherdesses) became fixed upon Him (Krishna), gazing on His form. 109. Krishna sounded the flute very sweetly. The *Gopis* danced all around Him. They sang many songs to Govind (Krishna), the Attracter of the heart. 110. Stringed instruments, the flute, the pipe and cymbals were the attractive instruments that were played, and songs were sung in accompaniment. 111. The Husband of Parvati played on the drum and the *Gopis* danced to it. The Lord of *Vaikunth* (heaven) manifested His inner feeling by the beating of time. 112. The *Gopis* said to Krishna, 'You pervade everything. With our heart's desire fixed upon You, O Krishna, we have hastened here. 113. We are many *Gopis*, but You, O Holder of the *Sharang* bow (Krishna), seem as one person. Seeing Your form, cupid became excited. 114. We look at your face, O Krishna, and we feel as though our lips wish to be kissed by Your mouth, and placing heart to heart give you an embrace.' 115. As the *Gopis* said this, Hari took many forms. According to each one's fancy the Enemy of Mura (Krishna) becomes. 116. Krishna took as many forms as there were *Gopis*. They took the Life of the world by the

hand and danced. 117. Taking the dark-complexioned One by the hand, the *Gopis* hung upon His neck. As their eyes fell upon His *sagun* form, they (the women) hastily gave Him kisses. 118. A Krishna's form and a cowherdess took each other's hand, dancing in pairs; such was the arrangement in the *Ras* dance in which they enjoyed Krishna. 119. Krishna's body was extremely tender. His chest was broad. His waist was slim. Seeing the hair on His chest, the *Gopis* became love-sick. 120. Taking Krishna's hand the *Gopis* placed it upon their hearts. Again and again they kissed His face. From His mouth they took into their own mouths the *tambul* (*pansupari*) chewed by Him. 121. Just as each one desires, the dark-complexioned One supplies. Krishna becomes next to every one. The blue-throated God (Shiva) repeated His name. 122. Arranging the platform for dancing, He and the *Gopis* sang and danced.

KRISHNA INQUIRES ABOUT NARSI

At that moment Krishna recognized Narsi Meheta. 123. Just as among the eighteen *bhars* (a *bhar*=8,000 tolas) of herbs, the *tulsi* plant becomes specially recognizable, so with His eyes He recognized Narsi Meheta. 124. Just as when the sky is filled with clusters of stars, one recognizes among them the polar star (*Dhruva*), so Krishna recognized Narsi Meheta. 125. Or as among the nine planets one prominently discovers the sun, so seeing Narsi Meheta, Krishna was surprised. 126. Just as among the assembly of the great adepts and seekers of spiritual knowledge the son of Anasuya is distinguished, so the Holder of the *Sharang* bow (Krishna) recognized at sight Narsi Meheta. 127. He who was the ornament of Vraja said to Shiva, 'Who is this new *Gopi* whom you have brought here today ? O blue-throated One, You have betrayed our friendship, 128. for it is only because of the close love between You and

Me that I invite You to the dance.' As *Vanamali* (Krishna) said this, the moon-headed One (Shiva) laughed. 129. The Husband of Parvati (Shiva) by the movement of his eyes made a sign to Narsi Meheta. He then came forward at once and worshipped the feet of Krishna. 130. Shiva said, O Lord Krishna, I will tell you in detail the ancient story regarding your servant Narsi Meheta. 131. In a former birth he was a great ti er of evil disposition While he was in the forest Pipaji told him to repeat Your name. 132. And as he repeated Your name all his sins departed. Thus in the city of Junagad he was born as a Nāgar Brahman. 133. In his childhood his father and mother died. He then offered his whole body to me, O Lord Krishna. 134. For seven days he refused food and water. Being pleased, I became favourable to him. 135. He then said to me, "I do not know the best thing to ask of You. Whatever You are fond of give it to me, O blue-throated One (Shiva)." 136. O Life of the world, I am fond of You. Therefore I have come here bringing him. So now place Your hand upon his head, O Husband of Kamala (Krishna), and give him Your blessing.'

KRISHNA COMMANDS NARSI TO DESCRIBE HIS SPORTS

137. As he heard this, the Husband of Kamala (Krishna) took Narsi Meheta by the hand and this Image of compassion gave him His assurance and embraced him with love. 138. The Holder of the disk (Krishna) then said to him, 'You have seen the *Ras* dance with your eyes. Compose poetry on the subject and so cause every one to hear it. 139. My character and *lila* (voluntary acts) you will always see.' Such was the blessing of the cloud-dark One (Krishna). 140. Krishna now said to Shiva, 'Depart, taking him with you.' Hearing this the Husband of Uma (Shiva) made His *namaskar*. 141. Giving him his assurance He brought him and by the

action of His wish He seated him in His temple and then He retired to *Kailas.* 142. Staying in Shiva's temple, Narsi Meheta performed *kirtans.* Night and day he lovingly repeated the names of God. 143. He sang of the *lila* and nectar deeds of Krishna in his love and danced. He threw aside all shame and sang of the character of Shri Hari. 144. Just as Shri Krishna had performed in this dancing game, so Narsi Meheta wrote of it in his books. Even to-day the people in that part of the country sing it. The language in which it is written is Gujarati.

NARSI MARRIES A BRAHMAN'S DAUGHTER

145. In the preceding description we found that Narsi Meheta had left his home and had gone sulking into a forest. His relations had seen him do this. 146. Now in the forest there were cows feeding. Along with them were cowherds. They were always delighted to hear the *kirtan* of Narsi Meheta. 147. Returning to his home he told his brothers of the event that had occurred. They replied, that Narsi Meheta was describing the qualities of Hari in the temple of Shiva. 148. Hearing of this affair they were well pleased and persuading Narsi Meheta brought him to their home. 149. Some of the pious men in the town, experts in the *Vedanta* and scriptures, said, 'Narayan is delighted with him; you can see this by the changed signs. 150. The little streamlet that joins with the Ganges receives the qualities of holiness. So, as the Life of the world has shown him mercy, the mark of goodnees has come to him.' 151. There was a Brahman in the town who was a *Vaishnava* of supreme piety. He gave to Narsi Meheta his daughter and had the marriage performed. 152. Just as when the touchstone touches iron it immediately turns into gold, so when Narayan shows His compassion what lack can be there to anyone ? 153. He never asked anything of anyone. A prince and a pauper were alike to him. He

regarded the poor and the rich as of equal rank. 154. After becoming a householder he became an adult. He had two issues, a daughter and a son.

155. Now hearers, give attention to a very interesting story to be hereafter related. The marriage of Narsi Meheta's son will be performed by Himself. 156. All these stories of the saints are indeed priceless. They are like a garden of fragrant flowers. Here Shri Krishna who dwells in Dwarka is like the friendly spring to them. 157. The verses in Marathi may be regarded as flowers. Mahipati as gardener strings them into garlands and takes them into the assembly of the *Vaishnavas.*

158. *Swasti* (Peace) ! This book is the *Shri Bhaktavijaya.* In listening to it the Lord of the world will be pleased. Listen then, you God-loving, pious *bhaktas*. This is the twenty-seventh deeply delightful chapter ; it is an offering to *Sri Krishna.*

CHAPTER XXVIII

MARRIAGE OF NARSI MEHETA'S SON

Obeisance to Shri Ganesh. Obeisance to the Husband of Rukmini.

PURANIC STORIES OF GOD'S DEEDS

1. O Giver of the promise to Pundalik, Pandurang, Father of Madana, Delight of Rukmini, Thou, O Krishna, didst dance with the *Gopis* (cowherdesses) on the dancing floor. 2. Those *bhaktas* who have a longing for Thee in their hearts are always desireless. Thou art the resting-place of all beings, O God, O Rama. 3. Thou art the Mover of the heart, the Sun of all intelligence, extending beyond qualities and at the same time Quality-less. Thou dost give a gift of final deliverance even to Thy enemies. Thou art the Sun of all joy. 4. Thou art God supreme and eternal. Ambarish came as a suppliant to Thee. With affection and delight he performed the regular ceremonies belonging to the *Ekadashi* (the eleventh day of the fortnight). 5. The *rishi* Durvas, a performer of innumerable austerities, came in order to persecute Ambarish. That cruel-hearted *rishi* having cursed him, he pleaded with Thee, O Ocean of compassion. 6. Hearing the pity arousing cries of Ambarish, Thy heart overflowed with love. At once Thou didst come to his help, O Life of the world, O Delight of the heart, O Shri Krishna. 7. Thou didst send Thy disk after the *rishi* Durvas who had become dispirited, but Thou, O Lord of the world, didst look with the eye of mercy upon Ambarish. 8. Thou didst give assurance to Thy *bhaktas*, Thou didst suffer births ten times from the womb.

VISHNU'S AVATARS

Thou didst assume the *avatar* of the fish, the tortoise, the wild boar, and supported the earth on the tusks. 9. When

Hiranyakashipu began to trouble Thy *bhakta* Pralhad, Thou didst hurry to his aid Thou didst roar from the midst of the pillar and quickly made Thy appearance. 10. In Thine anger Thou didst destroy the *Daitya*, and didst protect Thy servant Pralhad. When the Kshatriyas prevailed over the earth, Thou didst become Parashuram. 11. Thou wast then born as an *avatar* from the womb of Jamadagni and Renuka. And Thou alone, O Shri Hari, didst destroy the Kshatriyas. 12. So, having overcome the Kshatriyas, Thou didst give the kingdom to the Brahmans. Such wast Thou, O Ocean of mercy, O Saviour of the universe, O Rama Krishna. 13. When Shiva gave His blessing to Ravan, that monster became exceedingly intoxicated with power. He conquered all the gods and put them into prison. 14. That ten-faced one (Ravana) used the nine planets as his stairway and carried on his kingdom. The wind used to come and sweep his yard and the rain watered it. 15. The sun became his barber and shaved him. The elephant-faced One (Ganesh) kept his cows without feeling any shame at doing so. 16. The goddess *Adimaya* (Primal Mother) constantly shampooed the feet of Ravana. The goddess Satavi washed the clothes of his wife who was lying-in and felt no shame in her heart for doing so. 17. All the gods worked for him. He imprisoned even the Lord Indra and so all the gods in their trouble appealed to Thee. 18. Thou didst listen to their pity-arousing cries. Thou didst feel compassion for them. Thou didst become an *avatar* in the form of Rama and Thou didst destroy Ravana. 19. Thou didst deliver all the gods and didst establish the duties of life. And when Kans and Chanur grew powerful, Thou didst become the *avatar* of Krishna. 20. Thou didst destroy all doers of evil. In various ways Thou didst protect Thy *bhaktas*. Thou, Enemy of Mura, Shri Hari, didst clothe Draupadi with garments.'

21. 'And now in this *Kali Yuga*, Thy chief *bhaktas* have with reverence followed Thee, and Thou hast made their cause Thine own, and hast given them final deliverance. 22. Because of the *bhakti* of Ramdas, Thou, O Lord of the world, didst go to Dakur. He sold Thee in the market for a *val* in gold. 23. At the house of Thy loving *bhakta* Jayadev, Thou didst raise to life a corpse. Thou didst place upon him Thy hand of assurance and didst increase his glory in the world. 24. Thou didst show to Narsi Meheta, Thy loving *bhakta*, Thy dance with the *Gopis* (cowherdesses).' And now, all hearers, listen to the story that is interesting beyond all comparison.

KRISHNA'S POPULARITY EXPLAINED

25. I have already stated that Shiva showed to Narsi Mehta the dancing of Krishna with the *Gopis*. That exceedingly beautiful *lila* (sports or act) of Shri Krishna's therefore continually came to his sight. 26. And just as it appeared to him in its beautiful form, he composed verses to describe it. And Shri Krishna, the Destroyer of His *bhaktas'* desires for worldly existence, gave him His blessing. 27. In many forms of poetic composition he described the qualities of Hari. Taking the cymbals and *vina* in his hand, he danced in the midst of the *kirtan*. 28. He did not count on anyone's favour. He was always repeating the names of God. To his view a king and his lowly citizens were alike. 29. The wish-tree and the *babhul* tree, a *pandit* and a herdsman, a *sadhu* and a wicked reviler appeared alike to him. 30. Having adopted the principle of asking no one for anything; he accepted whatever garments or food were given to him. Being satisfied with that he carried on his duties of providing for his family.

A MERCHANT'S DAUGHTER MARRIED TO NARSI'S SON

31. Near to Junagad there is a village by name of

Shampur. The merchant Tripurantak of that village was a follower of the same *Vedic* branch. 32. His daughter had reached the marriageable age, and the merchant was considering the question of her marriage. He sent his priest here and there to make propositions. 33. He (the priest) was a Brahman by name of Krishna Bhat and of supreme piety, who came to the house of Narsi Mehets and spoke to him as follows. 34. Krishna Bhat said, ' My patron has sent me to say that he would offer his daughter in marriage to your son. ' 35. In examining the horoscopes he found that they reached the point of thirty-six. After an agreement for the marriage was made the priest returned home. 36. This relationship which was agreed to by the priest was acceptable to all, for it was the custom in that country for all to accept the decision of the priest. 37. If the patron did not accept the promise made by the priest, then the priest would cut off a finger and give it to the one he had chosen as a bridegroom. 38. Such being the rule in that country, the Brahman announced his decision and said to his patron that he had fixed the marriage of his daughter. 39. He said, ' There is a Nāgar Brahman at Junagad, supremely pious and a *Vaishnava*. I have made an agreement with him to offer your daughter to his son. ' 40. Listening to the words of the priest, every one began to laugh exclaiming, ' The fate of the girl seems to be a very unhappy one.'

THE MERCHANT DISLIKES THE PROPOSAL

41. The merchant exclaimed, ' He is a *Vaishnava* indifferent to worldly things. He is constantly dancing in his *kirtans*. How is it you offered my daughter to him ? Do not accept him as our relation. 42. We are not agreeable to a relationship to the house of one where *sadhus* and saints listen to the *Shri Bhagwat*, and one always unconcerned and indifferent to worldly things. 43. We do

not want any relationship with one who does not recognize similarity or dissimilarity, that which is his and that which belongs to another, and one who looks with the same reverence on all creatures. 44. How is it that you agreed to give my daughter in marriage to one who is without anger, a doer of good deeds, and one who has friendship for every creature, and one in whose house is the very least food and raiment?' 45. The priest replied, 'Listen to my words. I have returned having made an agreement. If you reject the agreement, I will cut off one of my fingers and give it to him.'

MERCHANT'S SEVERE CONDITIONS

46. Hearing him say this, the merchant Tripurantak said, 'Tomorrow is the appointed day for the marriage. Let the would-be bridegroom come to the marriage, bringing all the materials necessary. 47. I am a noted merchant and my relationship will now be with a very weak *bhakta* of Vishnu. The evil-minded will laugh at me and therefore such a thing must not happen. 48. Bring to the marriage five hundred elephants, horses, palanquins and chariots. Let there be innumerable players of instruments to accompany the procession. 49. Let the bridegroom come bringing garments and ornaments for the bride, and let him give to the inhabitants of our town a banquet of dainty food. 50. If the bridegroom does not come tomorrow bringing these materials then the engagement is broken off. Know this for a certainty, you noble *guru*.' 51. The priest understood the meaning of such a proposition, and he gave Tripurantak several illustrations. 52. He said, 'The daughter of King Bhimak was offered as a bride to Krishna. Rukmini insulted Him and you have done just the same. 53. Parvati was the daughter of the Himalaya mountains and the Destroyer of Tripur (Shiva) was fixed as the bridegroom. His wives insulted Him and

you have done the same. 54. All that your mind wishes will take place.' Saying this, the Brahman went back to give information. 55. He said to Narsi Meheta, 'Tomorrow is the most auspicious time for the wedding. You must all come bringing the needed materials, taking Shri Krishna as your helper.' 56. Krishna Bhat, a supremely pious *Vaishnava*, told him concerning the things that would bring about the marriage.

IMPORTANCE OF GOOD MEDIATORS

57. He thought to himself, 'If I should tell him of the things that had happened there all the arrangements would be destroyed. Narsi Meheta is supremely indifferent to worldly things. He has no desire for anything.' 58. Speaking in a very humble way as to how the marriage would be accomplished, the priest made the remaining arrangements and returned to his home. 59. Where a needle, borax and a good man act as mediators, there is no duality seen there. They bring two together. 60. Where a bad man, scissors and an axe act as mediators there an instant destruction is certain. These are at the root of all evils. 61. At the wedding there should not be a vilifier. In a battle there should not be a coward. In a *kirtan* there should be no noise or confusion. Among *tulsi*-plants she-goats should not be allowed. 62. While a *Purana* is being read, there should not be a garrulous person. Among pious men there should not be wicked revilers. In travelling there should not be anyone who is always excessively hungry. When worship is going on there should not be anxiety. 63. A relative should not be a neighbour. In the rainy season there should not be a southern wind. When receiving the *mantra* of the *shri guru*, there should be no doubt regarding it. Those who are indifferent to worldly things should not have a store of wealth. 64. The weak should not be haughty. There

should be no thorn in a narrow path. A learned man should not be proud. 65. A person who is worthy of receiving a gift should not have the desire for it. Maintenance of sacred fire should not be practised in a miserable village. A physician should not give medicine to one who needs to be put upon a diet. 66. A friend should not be a trouble-maker or a miser. One should not lend with interest to a relative. For a seeker of spiritual things to eat royal food is a way to destroy his good deeds. 67. Well now, this long discussion is quite sufficient.

MERCHANT'S RELUCTANCE

After the priest had made the agreement he returned to his village. 68. He told his patron that the bridegroom would surely come on the morrow for the wedding. 'Go and make all necessary preparations and be on the watch.' 69. Tripurantak laughingly replied, 'Narsi Meheta is all alone. How can he come tomorrow, since he has no materials of his own ? 70. I announced that the marriage would be tomorrow in order to break off the possibility of any relationship with him.' He then explained his action and illustrated it. 71. 'The two-faced earthworm went in the month of *Shravan* (August) to ask for the daughter of the serpent Shesha. The serpent replied to him that the marriage would take place in the month of *Vaishakh* (May). 72. When the hot season was near, the two-faced *davane* had died. Just so, I have announced that the marriage would take place on the morrow.' 73. The priest replied to him, 'You are an unfaithful man. You are not thoughtful. Your heart is full of pride. You will be very soon dishonoured. 74. Duryodhan was dishonoured because he persecuted the good Draupadi. The same thing will happen to you today I think.'

NARSI STARTS FOR HIS SON'S MARRIAGE

75. On the next day Narsi Meheta at the rising of

the sun performed his bath and worshipped Shri Krishna. 76. He drew twelve marks on his forehead and person. He hung the *tulsi* garland around his neck. He took along with him *Vaishnavas*, all the time repeating the names of God. 77. Taking his son and wife with him this *bhakta* of Vishnu started for the marriage. With music of cymbals, the drums and the *vina* the goodness of Hari was described. 78. 'Victory, Victory to Thee, Mukunda, Enemy of Mura, Helper of the helpless, Advocate of Thy *bhaktas*. Ancient of days, Slayer of the *Daityas*, Madhu and Kaitabh, Dweller in the hearts of Thy *bhaktas*. 79. Victory to Thee, Dweller at Dwarka, Lord of the earth, Husband of Rukmini, Father of Brahmadev, Slayer of Kans. Thou art the One dear friend of Thy *bhaktas*. 80. Victory to Thee, God supreme, Lord eternal, Protector of Thy *bhaktas*, Slayer of Madhu, Pervader of the universe, Life of the World, Delight of the heart, Govind. 81. Victory to Thee, Ancient of Days, Possessor of names without end, Whose name is the Being of qualities, dark-complexioned One, the Wish-tree of Thy *bhaktas*, Delight of the heart, Shri Hari.' 82. Describing the qualities of Shri Hari in this way, they sang and danced in their love. Narsi Meheta walked along at that time full of joy. 83. At that time Shri Hari was seated on His throne in Dwarka, and went into the private room and sent for Rukmini. 84. He said to her, 'The great *bhakta* Narsi Meheta has with reverent spirit followed Me. The marriage of his son takes place today. But he is singing of My qualities without any sense of shame.'

KRISHNA AS MARRIAGE GUEST

85. 'We should now go there before him and ourselves bring the ceremony to a successful consummation.' Thus speaking that Store-house of compassion gathered together an assembly of *bhaktas*. 86. Uddhav, Akrur, Narad, Tumbar,

Shuka, Valmiki, Pralhad, the great Bhishma, Bibhishan, Vidur and Maruti were quickly invited. 87. Sudama, Penda, Vankada, Vadaja, Kana, also a set of cowherds, one who was dumb and lisping another with one eye, one who was a dwarf, another who was lame and had mucus eyes, one with a running nose. 88. Such were the *bhaktas* small and great that He collected. Krishna said to them, 'Come at once to the marriage'. 89. Saying this to them Shripati Himself invited Jambavanti, Satyabhama and Kalindi the good. 90. Shri Krishna taking with Him Mitravinda, Yadnyajiti, Lakshamana and Bhadravati walked along for the wedding. 91. Mother Rukmini sat in a palanquin bringing the *Gopis* (cowherdesses) along with her as the marriage-party of the bridegroom. The kettle drums were sounded. 92. Taking with Him eight *siddhis* (accomplishments) and all female slaves, the Lord of the heart (Krishna) hurried along to the marriage of Narsi Meheta's son. 93. As Narsi Meheta walked along the path, he danced and sang in his fulness of love. In front of him the Lord of the world moved rapidly along.

KRISHNA'S ARRIVAL

94. As Krishna approached the city and was in sight of it, he sent word of their approach. Tripurantak hearing this report, was overwhelmed with amazement. 95. The townspeople also reported that an innumerable company had come to the marriage. They would not be able to find sufficient room in the village for them. What was to be done ? 96. Some people climbed up their roofs to gaze at the people coming, and as they listened to the playing of the sweet instrument they felt the air was reverberating with sound. 97. Tripurantak taking the citizens of the village with him, started to meet the procession. He took with him one band of players and started out, 98. just as when the sun is ris-

ing, the moon disappears, and as when a mere pool of water finding itself near the ocean is ashamed of itself. 99. What is the flying of a grasshopper before an eagle's flight ? And the lustre of a piece of glass is dimmed before a priceless jewel. 100. It was just as when a poor fellow proud of his knowledge is lost sight of before a really learned man in philosophy, or just as a poor fool is ashamed before a wise *pandit*; 101. so, seeing the procession of the bridegroom, all the bride's party felt very insignificant. The priest exclaimed, 'O Life of the world, Thou hast come to my help.' 102. The Creator of the world has come Himself and made all the necessary preparations. He prepared a great, beautiful pavilion with seats. 103. Pillows, cushions, mats and wooden seats of many kinds were placed there. Rambha and Tilottama came and danced there, while all the gods were looking on. 104. There were many kinds of gifts, and perfumes of *keshar* (saffron), musk and sandalwood. God Himself, coming with the procession of the bridegroom, sat down with them. 105. Mother Rukmini sat in the midst of the female party of the bridegroom, which made a delightful circle. The wife of Narsi Meheta came and sat down near her. 106. There were many kinds of garlands of flowers around their necks and in the midst of the assembly of *bhaktas* the Holder of the *Sharang* bow (Krishna) sat full of joy.

NARSI'S RECEPTION

107. Taking the people of the town with him Tripurantak started out to meet Narsi. As he came near to them the Lord of *Vaikunth* (heaven) arose. 108. Hari with all the *bhaktas* around Him embraced those who were to become their relatives. Krishna spoke in a gentle voice to Tripurantak. 109. He said, 'When a river is in flood a pumpkin raft takes one to the other side;

in the same way, Narsi Meheta is to be united to you in relationship true and close. 110. Just as when the life of anyone is coming to an end, nectar prevents him from death, so this God-loving *bhakta* Narsi Meheta is to be in a relation to you of that kind. 111. You were about to fall into lust, anger, pride, and the other diseases of this life, and in order that all these may be put away from you, you have gained a *Vaishnava* relative. 112. When the touchstone touches iron, rich people make ornaments of it. so through him we have the opportunity of meeting you. ; 113. Hearing Him say this Tripurantak replied, ' Tell me please your name. I had never met you before. Where have you come from ? ' 114. Hearing him, God Supreme answered, ' My name is Savalasa. I am the one who buys and sells for Narsi Meheta. 115. I live in Dwarka and act as his agent. I am the only one who understands his personality. ' 116. Thus spoke the Life of the world and no one recognized who He was. No one understands the glory of this Delighter of the mind, and skilful in acts of illusions.

BRIDE'S FATHER FEELS HIS INFERIORITY

117. The clothes with which the bridegroom was to be honoured on the outskirt of the town were of small worth and so Tripurantak felt ashamed in his mind. 118. Understanding this the Lord of *Vaikunth* (heaven) said to Tripurantak, ' An innumerable number of people have come to the wedding. I see that your mind is perplexed by this. 119. Now, when preparing the banquet of tasty things, one shonld not put much salt into the food. One should not form any relationship with one who is greater than oneself. 120. One should not give money at interest to the king of one's own town. So one should not give one's daughter to form a relationship with one greater than oneself. 121. Who is able to discuss the verses of a chief poet ? So, one should not form a relationship with one

of higher rank than oneself. 122. Just as when the sun arises the moon appears to fail, so, seeing the wealth of Narsi Meheta, you feel hesitant in your mind. 123. The preparations made by you can only be for a very few, and yet innumerable people have arrived for the wedding. After saying this to him, the Lord of *Vaikunth* (heaven). advised him as follows. 124. Krishna said to Tripurantak, 'Whatever materials are possible for you bring them here, and carry to completion the marriage arrangement. 125. All *Siddhis* (accomplishments) are favourable here. Put what little you have into it. Do not keep in your mind any sense of duality through doubt. 126. The knots of relationship are as strong as those of silken threads. Consider the question from the point of view of knowledge and hold in your mind no sense of duality.' 127. Seeing that he agreed, he returned to the city and brought the materials for the wedding together with the bride. 128. King Bhimak whose *bhakti* was perfect, having agreed to offer his daughter in marriage to Shri Krishna, lovingly came to Mulmadhav for the wedding. 129. In the same way Tripurantak, putting aside all mental opposition, came there with the bride and all the materials for the wedding. 130. When a little streamlet joins the Ganges, who is there who would call it unholy ? So when the Life of the world accepts anyone, no pious person lacks anything.

MARRIAGE DESCRIBED

131. The marriage was performed with great eclat and the band played sweet music. Termeric powder was applied to the bride and bridegroom. The wedding was carried on in the most elaborate way. 132. The gods were installed and Brahmans were feasted with many forms of dainty food, and God Himself offered gifts of money to the Brahmans. 133. Shri Krishna offered clothes with love to

Narsi Meheta. At the setting of the sun the Brahmans repeated the eight auspicious verses of the marriage ceremony 134. 'When Durvas persecuted Ambarish, God supreme Dweller in *Vaikunth* (heaven), suffered ten births; may He protect the bride and bridegroom. 135. He, at the repeating of Whose name all sins are burnt up, Dweller at Dwarka, the Delight of the heart, may He protect this bride and bridegroom. 136. He whom Brahmadev and the other gods, including Shiva, continually contemplate in their hearts, He, the Lover of His *bhaktas*, Lord of the heart, may He protect this bride and bridegroom. 137. Thou, O God supreme and eternal One, who reclinest on *Shesha* (the serpent) in the ocean of milk, Husband of Lakshmi, Life of the world, protect this bride and bridegroom.' 138. With these eight verses the Brahmans performed the marriage, instruments gave out their sweet music, and the drums were beaten. 139. Because the Lord of *Vaikunth* (heaven) was present, there appeared no lack of anything. And in this offering of the daughter, gifts without limit were made t. the Brahmans. 140. To all the citizens of the village a banquet was given as they desired, and to the bride and bridegroom were given beautiful ornaments, garments and adornments.

COMPLETION OF THE MARRIAGE

141. Blessed, blessed are the people who were assembled there, for they saw Narayan. It was the Life of the world who completed all arrangements for both parties. 142. With great eclat the procession of the bridegroom walked the streets, the sound of the instruments was heard, and the four deliverances came and fell at their feet. 143. Rockets of all kinds were let off and guns were fired. Eight dancing women sang and danced and the *Vaishnavas* repeated aloud the names of Hari. 144. After many festivities, Mother Rukmini per-

formed the ceremony of looking at the face of the daughter-in-law. At this the wife of Narsi Meheta was amazed. 145. For five days the marriage ceremony continued and the Life of the world, Shri Krishna, gave gifts to the party of the bride, offering them garments and ornaments. 146. The Lord of *Vaikunth* (heaven) then said to Tripurantak, 'You have now become a relative of a *bhakta* of Vishnu and in the midst of your domestic affairs you have also seen what the supreme spiritual riches are.' 147. After the marriage the bridegroom party returned to Junagad and Narsi Meheta continued joyfully to sing of the greatness of Shri Krishna. 148. The Lord of the world whispered to Narsi Meheta, 'Whenever any distress comes to you, think of Me.' 149. Having said this the Husband of Rukmini returned to Dwarka.

BHAKTAVIJAYA LIKENED TO *TULSI* PLANTS

And now let the hearers lovingly give attention. 150. This book of the *Bhaktavijaya* is like a forest of tender *tulsi* plants. The Husband of Rukmini, who dwells on the banks of the Bhima, dwells here. 151. Clouds of joy gladly and with love rain upon it and the *Vaishnavas* who are pious and fortunate are made happy by hearing it.

152. In the next interesting chapter Narsi Mehta will write a cheque for God to cash. Mahipati says, 'You fortunate listeners, be prepared to listen with reverence.'

153. *Swasti* (Peace) ! This book is the *Shri Bhaktavijaya*. In listening to it the Lord of the world will be pleased. Listen, you God-loving, pious *bhaktas*. This is the twenty-eighth very delightful chapter; it is an offering to Shri Krishna.

CHAPTER XXIX

NARSI MEHETA'S CHEQUE IN GOD'S NAME

Obeisance to Shri Ganesh. Obeisance to the Lord of Pandhari.

GOD'S NAMES AND EPITHETS REPEATED

1. Victory to Thee whose face is auspicious, Lord of all blessings. One who extends beyond the three qualities, Lord of the heart, Pervader of the universe, Lord of all, Lord of Pandhari, Shri Vitthal. 2. Victory to Thee, Ancient of Days, Whose name is Infinite, the Wish-tree of His *bhaktas*. Thou who takest the form of One with qualities, One with the complexion of a dark cloud, the Object of love of Thy *bhaktas*, 3. Victory to Thee who didst prevent the dishonour of Draupadi, Deliverer of Gajendra, Recliner upon *Shesha*, Dweller in the sea of milk, lotus-eyed One, Ornament of Thy *bhaktas*, Pandurang. 4. Thou art God above all gods. In repeating Thy name, Shiva became cooled. All the gods including Indra praise Thee. 5. Thou art the internal Witnesser, Cloud of intelligence, Object of contemplation by the *yogis*, Thou who givest the highest form of deliverance even to Thine enemies, Cloud of joy, merciful One. 6. Thou who art the Father of Brahmadev, although Thou doest everything, Thou art a non-doer, Lover of Thy *bhaktas*, Husband of Rukmini. Even the *Vedas* do not know Thy limit. 7. The fourteen sciences and the sixty-four crafts praise Thee, Lover of the *bhaktas*, O Gopal. Thou goest from these to be near Thy loving *bhaktas*. 8. Leaving Thy heaven of *Vaikunth*, leaving the ocean of milk, leaving the drinking of nectar, Thou huntest with love for Thy *bhaktas*. 9. Leaving the city of Dwarka, Thou didst come to the home of Pundalik. Thou didst place Thy hands upon Thy sides, and there Thou standest upright, O Shri Hari. 10. And so Thou art fond of the love of Thy

bhaktas, O Being of goodness. O Thou whose home is in the heart of Thy loving *bhaktas*, Thou art the rest of the soul. 11. Therefore again and again I bow to Thee, Thou, O Shripati (Krishna), inspire me to write this book.

KESHAV BHAT CALLS ON NARSI

12. Now listen, you hearers. In the preceding chapter it was related how after completing the wedding the Life of, the world left. 13. And Narsi Meheta, God's loving *bhakta* continually repeating the names of Krishna in his heart, danced continually in his *kirtans*. 14. Putting aside all pride of knowledge, putting aside bondage through the snare of desires, putting aside his desire for public honour, he continued to think of Shri Krishna. 15. Putting aside all sensual things, breaking the chains that would bind him to things of his own, putting aside all wrong thoughts, he put on the beautiful garment of peace. 16. Putting aside all ideas of equality and inequality, he considered a citizen and a king of the same value; He regarded the beings of the infinite universe and Indra and the other gods as on an equality. 17. He did not consider the evil qualities of tigers, scorpions, lions, and dogs. A herder of goats and a Brahman seemed alike in his sight. 18. The wish-tree and the *babhul* tree, the *hingan* and the *malayagar* he regarded as the same in value. In his sight he regarded discourteous and courteous language as the same. 19. If he saw before him a heap of money fallen on the ground, to his sight it was of the same value as dirt. The most priceless of jewels he regarded like common pebbles.

STORY OF KESHAV BHAT

20. Now on a certain day a procession of pilgrims was on its way to Dwarka. They came and stayed one day at Junagad. 21. Among them there was a supremely pious Brahman by name of Keshav Bhat. Coming into the city he made enquiries of the people there. 22. In the public

square of the town there were many revilers and evil men. Coming near to them, and standing before them, he spoke as follows. 23. He spoke to the people in a very courteous way, 'I am a Brahman making a pilgrimage. I am on my way to Dwarka to see and worship the feet of Shri Hari 24. What merchant is there in your town who can write a cheque for me? Tell me quickly, according to what may be true.' 25. Hearing what he said, these revilers and evil men began to laugh. They said, 'Narsi Meheta *bhakta* lives in the midst of all luxuries. 26. He is a most fortunate one and wealthy, but he lives as if indifferent to all earthly things. Go to where he is, and your purpose will be fulfilled. 27. O Brahman, you will recognize the house of Narsi Meheta by the banners, altar of *tulsi* plants, the banners with eagle-picture, and the praise-service of Hari.' 28. Hearing them say this, and placing confidence in what they said, he hurried at once to the house of Narsi Meheta. 29. You hearers may say to me, 'Since Shri Hari is in all hearts, how is it that there can be persecution of His *bhaktas*. Tell us truly.'

GOODNESS IS VALUED BECAUSE OF BADNESS

30. God Himself has created *bhaktas* and those who are not *bhaktas*. For His servants receive honour because of those who are not *bhaktas*. 31. If the crocodile had not seized the Gajendra, then why would the Dweller in *Vaikunth* (heaven) have had to rush to his aid? If Dusshasan had not persecuted Draupadi, then why would Hari have given her raiment? 32. If the *Daitya* Hiranyakashipu had not troubled the *bhakta* Pralhad, then how would the Lord of the universe have revealed Himself from within the pillar? 33. If iron had not been created, then who would have placed any value upon the touchstone? So by means of those who are not *bhaktas*, the servants of God receive honour. 34. If a beggar had no desire

for anything, he would not ask anything of the wish-tree. If the darkness did not fall at night, who would ever light a lamp? 35. If there are no false statements, then who would have considered truth as a good deed? If subjects were not created, then who would have honoured the king? 36. If the stars were not so very small, who would have regarded the moon as being superior in size to them? If there were no iron hammers to test a diamond, who then could have become expert in testing them? 37. If the city of Yama had not been created, then who would have had a desire for heaven? If there were no eighty-four hundred thousand rebirths, then who would have paid attention to the final deliverance? 38. So having created in the world those who are not *bhaktas*, God looks with an eye of compassion upon those who are His *bhaktas*. When the Lord of the world sees His *bhaktas* in distress He rushes to their help.

KESHAV BHAT MEETS NARSI

39. Turning now to the preceding description, the pious Brahman, Keshav Bhat, arrived quickly at the house of Narsi Meheta. 40. That Vishnu *bhakta* was seated by a a pure *tulsi* altar. Remembering the Lord of *Vaikunth* (heaven) in his heart, he was lovingly repeating His name. 41. Having put aside all thoughts of bodily needs he enjoyed deep meditation. Putting aside disturbances of his life, he lived in peace because of his knowledge of non-duality. 42. Suddenly seeing the Brahman coming into the house before him, Narsi Meheta lovingly bowed to him. 43. He spread a mat for the Brahman and seated him upon it. He said to him, 'Where are you from, and where are you going?' 44. The Brahman replied, 'I am going to the city of Dwarka. The road from here is through a very difficult country and there are robbers in the way. 45 I have brought here with me money to the value of seven hundred rupees

as travelling expenses. Write a cheque for the same and give it to me. 46. When darkness had settled upon the town I enquired of the people, " What merchant is there here who would write a cheque for me ? " 47. They gave me your name.' When Narsi Meheta heard these words of the Brahman, he was much troubled in his mind and said to himself, ' Truly the people have deceived him. 48. But the Helper of the helpess, the Advocate of His *bhaktas*, my Protector, He has assumed many forms of *avatars* for the sake of His *bhaktas*. ' 49. Thus determining in his mind, he said to the Brahman, ' The money which you brought from your home, place it here. ' 50. The Brahman hearing him replied, ' Who is your agent at Dwarka ? Tell me his name.'

GOD AS TRADER

51. Hearing him say this, the *Vaishnava bhakta* replied, ' His name is Savalasa. Indra and all the gods worship Him. 52. The four *Vedas* breaking out into song continually praise His good deeds. The Lord of *Kailas* (heaven), the Husband of Uma, continually repeats His name. 53. His chief shop is on the sea of milk. Another shop is in *Vaikunth* (heaven). He has lived at Gokul, Brindavan, Mathura, and in the home of *Vaishnavas*. 54. In Mandesh on the banks of the Bhima He has placed a great shop at Pandhari. And he still stands there near to His *bhakta*, *Shet* Pundalik. 55. He it is who is at Dwarka and who is carrying on His merchant's business from there. Vyas and Valmki carry on business in such things as are connected with *kirtans*. 56. One of His customers is Nama, and another the pious *bhakta* Kabir. Buying the articles they sell, the dull-minded have been saved through their devotion to Him. ' 57. Hearing him say this, the Brahman was satisfied. He placed the seven hundred rupees on the *tulsi* altar.

NARSI'S CHEQUE TO KESHAV BHAT

58. At the same time Narsi Meheta wrote a letter in pleading terms. He said, 'O Krishna, Dweller at Dwarka, hear the plea of Thy servant. 59. Thou art generous, O Ocean of compassion. When Upamanyu as a child asked for milk, Thou didst listen to him and gave him the ocean of milk. 60. Brahmadev has become weary in describing Thy qualities, O Husband of Rukmini. When the Brahman Sudama came to visit Thee Thou didst give him a city of gold. 61. Thou didst perform a very wonderful thing. Thou didst place the child Dhruva in his immovable position. Such Thou art, Husband of Ramā [Ramā is another name for Lakshmi, Krishna's wife], Thou art the Protector of Thy *bhaktas.* 62. Do Thou, chief among the generous ones and the brave, listen to the reading of my letter, and by giving money to the Brahman, O Holder of the disk (Krishna), satisfy him. 63. It is because I trusted to Thee that I took the money from him. After hearing these pity-arousing words, do Thou, O Cloud of joy, rain down upon him. 64. Thou mayest say that I have written the cheque on Thee, although Thou art the unmanifested and the unconquered. But do not do that which will cause people to laugh at me.' 65. He wrote the following cheque, 'Savalasa, Dweller in Dwarka, pay seven hundred rupees to the bearer.' Thus writing the cheque he gave it to the Brahman.

KESHAV BHAT'S DOUBT ABOUT THE CHEQUE

66. Then immediately he invited the saints and *sadhus*, all the *Vaishnavas* and all the Brahmans of the village and distributed all the money at once to them. 67. Becoming free from disturbances he (Narsi Meheta) sat repeating the names of God. The Brahman made his obeisance to Narsi Meheta and started on his way. 68. But as he walked along the path he was wondering in his mind. He thought,

'I have never seen before a merchant so generous. 69. In every way he seems generous and one indifferent to earthly things. He has in his house the very least food and raiment. With love and peace in his heart, he lovingly performs his *kirtans.* 70. It is with such an one that I have carried on this business. How did I make such a mistake ?' Becoming deeply concerned he thought to himself as follows :—71. 'Just as when one throws salt into the sea and it can never return, so my money is offered to Krishna, as it were, and will never come back. 72. If one makes a sound into the air no echo returns, just as I have now done by carrying on this business with Narsi Meheta. 73. If you throw butter into the fire it will never return, do what you may. So what I have given to that *Vaishnava* has really been made an offering to *Brahm*, as it were. 74. When giving water to the *tulsi* plant one should not desire any fruit from it. So I do not now see that anything will come back to me from that cheque. 75. If water is mixed with the sea water it never will return; so my money has truly gone into the storehouse of Kuber. 76. It is as if I placed flowers in the sky and they gave honey to the wind; so the god's *bhakta* has distributed the money to the Brahmans.' 77. He now said finally to himself, 'Why mourn in vain for it ? The Lord Shri Krishna, the Pervader of the universe, cares for every one.'

KESHAV BHAT AT DWARKA

78. Comforting himself in that way the Brahman came to Dwarka. After bathing in the Gomati he went to see and worship Shri Krishna. 79. Worshipping the feet of Shri Krishna he stood with hands joined palm to palm, and with love and complete reverence he praised Hari. 80. He said, 'Victory, Victory to the Husband of Rukmini, Brother of the lowly, Lord Ranchhod !

Helper of the helpless, merciful One, remove my concern.' 81. Having spoken these pity-arousing words, he prostrated himself before God. The Brahman then sought information from the priest. 82. He said, 'Show me the house of the merchant Savalasa. That name is written upon the cheque which I hold.' 83. Hearing him say this, all the people replied, 'We have never heard of a merchant by the name Savalasa, nor have we seen anyone of that name. Nor could we do so, if we hunted throughout the city of Dwarka.'

REVILERS CALL NARSI'S CHEQUE VALUELESS

84. 'Narsi Meheta has given you a cheque that is valueless. In giving your money to him you did not properly consider the question. 85. One should carry on business looking to profit, and one should give only to those worthy of it. One should go as a suppliant to one's *guru* and ask him for the needs of one's soul. 86. When one sees a *Vaishnava*, one should with reverence make a prostrate *namaskar* to him; but one should not transact worldly business with him. 87. One should give food and garments with reverence to God's *bhaktas*, but one should never carry on the business of buying and selling with them. 88. They make like themselves anyone who associates with them. When a river meets with the ocean it becomes a part of the ocean without effort. 89. When iron touches the touchstone, all its darkness flies away. So when one associates with a saint worldly business comes to naught. 90. When a little streamlet joins the Ganges, it takes but a moment to change its name and form. So by one's association with a *Sadhu*, business abilities no longer remain with him. 91. Such being our custom from the elders, *you* have carried on business with a *Vaishnava*. So now, O noble Brahman, where will you hunt for the merchant Savalasa?' 92. Hearing these words of the priest, the

Brahman became deeply concerned. Then bowing to God the Brahman departed. 93. Returning to his lodging the mind of the Brahman continued greatly disturbed. He said to himself, 'Narsi Meheta distributed the money at once. 94. Abandoning all illusion regarding money, let me go as a suppliant to the King of *Vaikunth* (heaven).' Thus remarking, the Brahman sat down in the square.

KRISHNA AS A BANKER

95. Just then God supreme, the Husband of Rukmini assumed the form of a merchant. Bringing Uddhav and Akrur, He drove along in His chariot. 96. The Life of the world, sitting in His chariot, said to Daruk (His charioteer), 'Narsi Meheta has sent a cheque with our name written upon it. 97. In order that I may accomplish his purpose I have become to-day Savalasa the merchant. I have changed My four-armed form, and am going, instead in the form of a man.' 98. Uddhav then said to Him, 'O Life of the world, even the *Vedas* do not know the limits of Thy power. Thou, O Narayan, dost assume an infinite number of forms in order to carry out the purposes of Thy *bhaktas.*' 99. Narad said to Him, 'Thou actest like a skilled actor in a drama. Thou puttest hindrances in the way of Thy *bhaktas*. Then assuming a form with qualities, Thou, O Hari, dost rush to their help; 100. just as a mother tells a child about a goblin when one is not really there, and when the child cries out with fear she comforts it in love.' 101. Conversing in this way with His *bhaktas*, Govind came along. Such is the Advocate of the *bhaktas*, One praised in the universe and Whose unfathomable *lila* (deeds) cannot be understood. 102. With His divine ornaments, garments and adornments, beautiful in form, He appeared with qualities. The Life of the world hastily drove along the royal highway. 103. As the chariot was moving steadily along, He said to His (charioteer)

Daruka, 'A Brahman is seated in the square who is full of concern. Take Me at once to where he is.' 104. Having given this order, the Husband of Rukmini and His chariot moved swiftly along. And as the people lovingly saw this form with qualities, all wondered.

KRISHNA SEES KESHAV BHAT

105. As the Lord of the world approached, He saw there the Brahman. The Husband of Rukmini asked him, 'Why are you thus concerned?' 106. At the question of the Dweller in *Vaikunth* (heaven) the Brahman felt astonished, with reverence he bowed to Him, and gave Him the reasons for his concern. 107. 'There is a *Vaishnava bhakta* at Junagad by name of Narsi Meheta. His agent Savalasa is here at Dwarka. 108. Because I cannot find him, I am very much troubled.' Hearing him say this, the Lord of the world spoke to the Brahman. 109. At this the Husband of Rukmini laughed and said, 'They call Me here Savalasa. What is the order which Narsi Meheta has given to me?'

KESHAV BHAT COMFORTED

110. As the Life of the world said these things the Brahman was much comforted; just as when during a drought a cloud pours down rain, the grass on the mountain side is made happy; 111. or as God-loving *bhaktas*, hearing at a *kirtan* the praising of Hari, are comforted thereby; or when a person repentant of his sins, sees a sacred bathing-place, then his mind experiences comfort; 112. or as when listening to the reading of the *Bhagwat*, *Vaishnava bhaktas* become full of joy; or as when suffering from thirst, one sees water and he feels a sense of joy; 113. or as when a seeker after spiritual things finds himself in association with a saint and through connection with him he feels satisfaction; or when one who has a request to make and sees a generous giver, he is

delighted in his heart; 114. in that same way the Brahman hearing what the merchant said was greatly pleased. He at once took out the letter and placed it in Krishna's hand. 115. After looking over the letter, He lovingly bowed to it with His hand. He Whom the *Vedas* and *Shastras* praise, but Whose extraordinary deeds they are unable to describe, 116. this God supreme, Husband of Rukmini, became thus subservient to His *bhakta.* As the Life of the world read the letter he spoke with a smile on His face. 117. The Lord of *Vaikunth* said to Uddhav, 'Narsi Meheta the God-loving *bhakta*, although living in the midst of domestic matters, is one indifferent to all earthly things. He has sent Me a small cheque to be cashed.' 118. Saying this He took out seven hundred rupees. The Husband of Rukmini gave this to the Brahman.

HOW CAN A SERVANT BE GREATER THAN HIS MASTER ?

119. As the Brahman saw the money, he was much comforted. Astonished however in his mind, he answered in a humble voice, 120. 'You seem to be a wealthy merchant, but Narsi Meheta seems a very poor person. A rich servant with a helpless lord seems to me to be very strange. 121. I have never seen the charioteer of the sun more brilliant than the sun itself. The *Puranas* never speak of a streamlet running through a village as superior to the Ganges. 122. I have never seen in the world a minister greater than the king. I have never heard that any monkey was greater than Shri Ram Himself. 123. Who is there greater than the Lord of *Kailas* (heaven), the Husband of Parvati ? One has never seen or heard of a river of greater importance than the ocean. 124. I have never heard of a *siddhi* (accomplishment) greater than Lakshmi. There are no stars more brilliant than the moon. 125. I have never seen a little diamond more brilliant than a large diamond. I have never heard of any-

one learned in the *Vedanta* (philosophical knowledge) who was greater than one in the *siddhanta* (established facts). 126. Now today I see with my eyes what seems topsyturvy, Therefore I ask you to explain it.' Hearing what the Brahman said, Krishna began to speak.

KRISHNA DISPELS KESHAV BHAT'S SCRUPLES

127. The Husband of Rukmini said to the Brahman, 'A *Vaishnava bhakta* is continually indifferent to all earthly things. Although he is in worldly surroundings he is without illusion and without desires. 128. As the sea has no desire that the cloud should continually rain upon it, so a *Vaishnava* does not allow his mind to be entangled in the snare of desire; 129. just as the sun has no desire to light a lamp in the house, so a *Vaishnava* does not allow his mind to be entangled in the snare of desire. 130. Those who have nectar to drink will make no effort for medicine. A *Vaishnava bhakta* despises money and wealth. 131. As the Lord of Lakshmi does not willingly accept the *bakul* or *shevanti* flowers as more important than the *tulsi*, so a *Vaishnava* does not consider in his mind that money or wealth is more important than worship. 132. Those who have the knowledge of *siddhanta* will not listen to the reading of an immoral book, so a *Vaishnava bhakta* remains absorbed in the worship of Hari. 133. Narsi Meheta, supremely indifferent to earthly things, does not care for money or property. How are we to help this character? 134. It is a mother's characteristic that she desires to put ornaments upon her child. So Narsi Meheta has showed his favour towards Me without limit. 135. A father does not steal from his property and wealth, and so Narsi Meheta has placed great confidence in Me.' 136. The compassionate One to the lowly having said this, all the *Vaishnavas* were astonished. They exclaimed, 'Narsi

Meheta the God-loving *bhakta* has made the cloud-dark Krishna subservient to him.' 137. Hari, after having performed this miraculous act, became invisible. The Brahman felt it very strange, and his mind was astonished. 138. Then he counted the money to see how much it was. He found it to be an immeasurable quantity. This made him exclaim to himself, 'The Lord of Dwarka quickly met me.' 139. Comforting himself in this way the pious *Vaishnava bhakta* satisfied the Brahmans with a feast.

KESHAV MEETS NARSI

140. While waiting at that beautiful city of Dwarka, the Brahman distributed all the money to those worthy of receiving it. He offered it to those learned in the *Shastras*, to Brahmans and to priests who were pure and worthy of it. 141. Then going to the great door of the temple, with reverence he bowed to the Lord of Dwarka. Taking leave of the god, the Brahman started on his way home. 142. Returning to Junagad he went to see Narsi Meheta. He told him everything about the event that had taken place. 143. He said to him, 'You are a God-loving *Vaishnava bhakta*. You have made the Lord of Dwarka a debtor to you. Savalassa came quickly and met me. 144. I placed your letter in His hand. In His love He bowed His head to it. Having read it, His mind showed His love. 145. He at once took out seven hundred rupees, and placed them in my hand. When I counted it out it was beyond my power of reckoning the amount. 146. When I looked back to him at that moment He became invisible.' Hearing these words of the Brahman, tears filled Narsi Meheta's eyes. 147. He exclaimed, 'O Dweller at Dwarka, Husband of Rukmini, Brother of the helpless, Delighter of the mind, Filler of the universe, Cloud of mercy, Thou dist weary Thyself for my sake. 148. Thou art the Brother of the lowly, Ocean of mercy, even the *Vedas* and the *Shastras*

do not know the limits of Thy power. Thou art the indescribable, even by the four forms of speech. Thou alone art the Saviour of the world. 149. O Lord of the helpless, Lover of Thy *bhaktas*, Thou dost carry out the wishes of Thy servants.' Saying these things, tears flowed from his eyes. 150. At once he steadied his mind and began to repeat the names of God.

BHAKTAVIJAYA AS OCEAN OF MILK

In the next chapter will be described the puberty ceremony (of Narsi Meheta's daughter). Let the saints listen to me. 151. This book containing the lives of the saints, may be considered as the ocean of milk. The Recliner upon the *Shesha*, the Husband of Lakshmi, continually dwells upon it. 152. There I, a lowly and helpless one, have been able to drink the supreme nectar. Here the Lord of *Vaikunth* (heaven) in His love gives the water of affection. 153. In the rows of the *Vaishnava bhaktas*, pious *bhaktas* have seated themselves. With love and pleasure Mahipati eats what they have left on their plates.

154. *Swasti* (Peace)! This book is the *Shri Bhaktavijaya*. In listening to it the Lord of the world will be pleased. Listen, you God-loving, pious *bhaktas*. This is the twenty-ninth deeply delightful chapter; it is an offering to Shri Krishna, an offering also to Jagadishwar (the Lord of the world).

CHAPTER XXX

MATURITY CEREMONY OF NARSI'S DAUGHTER

Obeisance to Shri Ganesh. Obeisance to the Slayer of Putana

NARSI MEHETA INDIFFERENT TO ALL EARTHLY THINGS

1. Listen, O hearers, with a reverent mind. Narsi Meheta the *Vaishnava bhakta*, full of love, living at Junagad, was continually in the worship of Shri Hari. 2. He in whom forgiveness and peace continually dwell in personified form, is one whose characteristic is that he does not ask for anything and is always satisfied with a little. 3. With complete *bhakti*, knowledge and indifference to earthly things he worshipped Hari in his love. Although he had a family and a wife he was unattached to anything; 4. just as when a lotus plant is growing in a lake, the water does not touch it; or as when the sun is seen reflected in a jar of water, it does not become wet with it; 5. just as the wind, being everywhere, the stormy wind cannot be confined; so a good man, although in the midst of domestic life, is untouched by the evil effects of it. 6. Ignorant men say that the *bhaktas* of Hari are affected by domestic affairs, but such great revilers are a burden to the earth. 7. Those who seek to stain the sky find that their own hands are stained. So he who reviles a *Vaishnava bhakta* is guilty of a wrong.

GOD PROVIDES NARSI MEHTA WITH GIFTS TO BE GIVEN AWAY

8. Narsi Meheta was indifferent to earthly things. His daughter had reached maturity and to celebrate it he had an invitation from his new relative. 9. At his own home he had neither raiments nor food. His wife said to him, 'What have you planned to take as gifts?' 10. He

replied to her, 'I have the name of Hari to take as gifts.' Saying this to his wife he hastened to where his daughter was. 11. Everybody there began to laugh, when they saw Narsi Meheta, and exclaimed, 'What is the purpose of his having come here? 12. As a matter of conventional formality we sent him an invitation, but he has come with a *tulsi* garland around his neck and cymbals in his hand.' 13. Musical instruments sounded loudly and his chief relatives assembled together, remarking, 'Having no presents to give his new relatives, why has he come here?' 14. The daughter full of doubts in her heart said privately to Narsi Meheta, 'Bringing nothing you are losing in reputation, and I feel ashamed.' 15. Hearing what all said Narsi Meheta replied, 'Let each one tell what gifts he would like. 16. Let each one write down what he wishes, and give the list to me.' Hearing him say this, all the people broke out into a hearty laugh.

A LIST OF GIFTS

17. Then there came a mischievous fellow bringing a piece of paper, and exclaiming, 'I will write down what all of us want.' Such were the words of this evil fellow. 18. Then the father-in-law, and the son-in-law and the evil minded relatives, all of them said what gifts they desired, and the daughter said, 'I want ornaments.' 19. Whatever each one desired he wrote down. Narsi Meheta then said to him who had written down what was desired, 20. 'Whatever *you* desire, write down upon this paper.' The unbeliever, because he did not believe him, replied to him, 21. 'I want a stone.' He wrote it down at once, and all the people laughed at him. 22. He remarked before all the people, 'I cannot believe that the gifts he tells me to write down will ever come.' 23. Someone has said that he who will not trust the words of the saints, and

is a hater of his father, is a very bad man. Having fallen into the whirlpool of worldly existence he cannot be freed even to the very end of the time 24. A learned fool, who is a hater of Brahmans, and a reviler of sacred bathing places and sacred cities, such an one cannot attain to Hari. 25. One running after women, and a hater of his mother, are sure to fall into the whirlpool of death. Such cannot attain to Hari. 26. Those who do not know what is permitted and what is not permitted by law, those who have a desire for the wives of others, never attain to Hari, no, never. 27. Such being that wicked person, he exclaimed, 'I want a stone.'

NARSI'S PLEA

Narsi Meheta hearing this, bowed to Hari. 28. He exclaimed, 'O Merciful to the lowly, Lover of Thy *bhaktas*, Lotus-eyed One, Dweller in *Vaikunth* (heaven), the Moon to the *Chakor*, Heart of Rukmini, come quickly this time to my help. 29. Thou callest Thyself the Helper of the helpless. Thou suppliest the desire of Thy *bhaktas*. Now do not throw aside Narsi Meheta, O merciful One.' 30. When Krishna heard these pity-arousing words he was pleased. He came with a bale full of garments. 31. Hari took the form of a Brahman and stood at the door and requested the men there to tell Narsi Meheta that he had brought a whole bale of cloth. 32. The relatives questioned Him, 'Who are you and where are you from? The Life of the world hearing them say this answered: listen to what He said:- 33. 'I am one of the agents of Narsi Meheta in his shop at Dwarka. I have hastened here today bringing the gifts for you, his relatives.

KRISHNA'S DISTRIBUTION OF GIFTS

34. So spoke the Ornament of His *bhaktas*. No one, however, recognized who He was. People were deceived by

their love of things and closed their eyes of knowledge through illusions. 35. Hari having brought a box full of ornaments, stood there. Narsi Meheta then said to his new relatives, 36. 'All of you ask for whatever you desire. Putting aside the idea of duality, hold no doubt in your mind.' 37. The Husband of Rukmini asked for the paper with the list of gifts wanted and took it in His own hand. He then undid the bale of cloth and with His own hand distributed the garments, 38. The Lord of the heart gave a shawl woven with golden threads to the son-in-law of Narsi Meheta. A jacket and a silk *sari* He gave to the mother-in-law. 39. To some He gave short *saris*, to some long *saris*, and to some jackets, to some a neck ornament, to some garments with coloured spots. To some He gave turbans woven at Mungi Paithan. 40. To some He gave some very finely woven crimson cloth and to some a yellow-cloured garment. The Life of the world gave to some a green thin cloth woven with golden threads. 41. To some He gave turbans and *Parakala.* Some who had asked for a shawl with coloured borders received it. To some Hari gave a pair of silk *dhotars.* 42. To some He gave black cloth with gold borders. Some asked for a yellow raiment, and the Holder of the *Sharang* bow (Krishna) immediately took it out of the bale of gifts and gave it to them. 43. Narayan gave one a garment with beautiful borders. The enemy of Madhu (Krishna) had brought a bale full and it continued to remain full. 44. Men came to see this strange thing, and he gave to them beautiful garments. Krishna distributed limitless beautiful shawls to them. 45. Women of the town assembled to receive saffron and yellow-coloured paste for their foreheads. The Lord of the heart (Krishna) gave them garments with His own hands rapidly.

KRISHNA'S GIFTS TO ALL THE GUESTS

46. *Vanamali* (Krishna) distributed to them different

sorts of *saris.* He divided among them the white thin shawls worn in royal palaces. 47. Blessed, blessed were those people to whom Narayan distributed the garments. What illustrations can I use to compare them ? 48. When that wicked man at Hastinapur started to remove the cloth of that pure one Draupadi, Hari rushed there with garments for her, and so He did now. 49. After distributing the garments, he gave them ornaments. To some He gave head ornaments of crescent shape, to others head ornaments of various shapes. 50. To some the Husband of Rukmini gave pearl earrings, to others clusters of ear-ornaments of the shape of fishes, to others the neck ornaments. 51. To some He gave garlands of pearls, to others necklaces and others neck ornaments with pendants. Krishna gave them with His own hand. 52. Govind distributed with His own hands the bracelets according as each one had desired and to others gold bracelets. 53. The enemy of Mura (Krishna) gave to some waist-cords, woven with golden threads, and others ankle-jewels, chains and many ornaments. There were toe-rings for the feet and earrings which Shri Krishna Himself put on some people. 54. The Holder of the disk (Krishna) fastened their neck-ornaments, fastened their waist-cords and distributed to them these jewels. 55. As the Holder of the *Sharang* bow (Shri Krishna) did this marvellous deed, men and women were all pleased. He was infinitely generous in His benevolent acts for His *bhaktas.* 56. Just what they wanted, Narayan gave to them in full. The Saviour of the world brought a stone to the man who had done the writing and who had asked for it. 57. The Life of the world lifted up the stone with His own hands and placed it upon the man's head. The people who had assembled there all laughed as they saw this remarkable *lila* (sport, or deed). 58. All the people said to him, 'Your fate has broken down. You are as one sitting under a wish-tree, and yet begging. 59. When the *daitya* Bhasma pleased the Husband of Girija (Shiva) he asked Him for a wrong blessing, so you have done.' 60. All having said this to him, that evil-minded person became ashamed, just as when a clod of earth is put into water, it melts away.

PEOPLE RECOGNIZE KRISHNA AS NARSI'S HELPER

61. All again and again made their *namaskar* to Narsi Meheta, They said to him, 'Shri Krishna has come to your aid, now we truly understand this.' 62. In this way having celebrated his daughter's puberty-ceremony, this *bhakta* of Vishnu started from there to Junagad, there to see and worship the image of Krishna. 63. He said to Him, 'O Husband of Rukmini, Shri Hari, Thou hast today wearied Thyself greatly for me. O Enemy of Mura, Thou hast brought for me the presents to be given to my relatives.' 64. The Lord of *Vaikunth* (heaven) thought to Himself, 'I distributed garments to the people, but I did nothing to honour Narsi Meheta.' 65. Being pleased therefore, the dark-blue-complexioned One took off from Himself His flower garland mixed with *tulsi* leaves and placed it around the neck of His *bhakta*. 66. He became invisible at the same place, where in the form of a Brahman He had brought gifts for the new relatives so that all the people worshipped the feet of Narsi Meheta. 67. And whenever he made a *kirtan* in praise of Hari, that garland appeared about his neck.

NARSI PERSECUTED

Someone conveyed the news of this to King Manduk. 68. The king came to see him and worshipped the idol, but he had a doubt in his mind, thinking there had been some crooked dealings. 69. He therefore took a needle and thread and fastened the garland to His coat. Showing anger, he said to Narsi Meheta, 70. 'By means of your knowledge of tricks you have deceived many pious people. If your garland does not appear around your neck to-day,

I shall punish you.' 71. Narsi at once taking his cymbals and his *vina* in his hands, danced full of love in his loud shouting of the names of Hari. 72. In many ways he described the good qualities of Hari, but the garland did not appear around his neck. Then joining his hands together palm to palm, he pleaded with God:—73. 'Thou didst at once take the form of a fish, and in a moment's time didst destroy the *daitya* Shankha. Now why art Thou delaying to give me the garland? 74. Thou, Lord of *Vaikunth* (heaven) didst take the form of a tortoise and didst skilfully take out the fourteen jewels. Now why art Thou at all delaying to give me the garland? 75. Thou, O Krishna, taking the form of a wild boar, didst kill Hiranyaksha, and why, O Govind, art Thou delaying to give me the garland? 76. When Pralhad was persecuted Thou didst break out from the pillar. Why dost Thou not yet take pity on me and give me the garland? 77. Taking the form of Vaman, with one step Thou didst measure the whole three worlds; then why dost Thou not feel pity today, on hearing my piteous request? 78. Because the Kshatriyas troubled the wish-cow Thou didst come with an axe and didst kill them. But now Thou dost not have pity on me, though hearing my cries. 79. Because the gods were thrown into prison, Thou didst kill Ravana and Kumbhakarna; so I do not understand why my distress is unheard by Thee. 80. When Draupadi was insulted, Thou, Husband of Rukmini, at once camest to her help. Why dost Thou not now feel pity when Thou hearest my cry of distress? 81. O Krishna, although hearing my piteous words, Thou art yet not pleased.'

KRISHNA FOND OF ABUSIVE WORDS FROM HIS *BHAKTAS*

Krishna replied, 'Speak to Me with abusive words, and I will take off My garland and give it to you.' 82. The king in the meantime said to Narsi Meheta, 'Now I understand the purpose of your tricks.' Saying this, the king came forward to punish him. 83. Seeing his own distress Narsi Meheta cried out, and by it the Life of the world was pleased. Let good and pious people listen. 84. He said, ' What does it matter to Thee or Thy father about giving me the garland ? ' The Lord of Dwarka having heard him give this abuse was pleased. 85. When he had in countless words pleaded piteously, it did not come to God's mind to give it, but the moment he used abusive language the garland came upon his neck. 86. The king looked and the garland was still there with the stitches, which made him exclaim, 'Blessed is this *Vaishnava.* He is the complete *avatar* of Shiva.' 87. The king then with reverence lovingly embraced the feet of Narsi Meheta and said, ' Do not further consider in your mind my transgression. 88. You are a noble *Vaishnava* and God's *bhakta.* Sinner as I am, I surely did not understand this. I heard what people said and came here to trouble you. 89. Just as when Duryodhan was persecuting the Pandavas, that evil one was defeated, so in persecuting you the same thing has happened to me.' 90. The king then made Narsi a prostrate *namaskar* and returned to his city. And Narsi Meheta full of love continued his worship of Shri Hari.

91. In the next chapter we shall read of how the Husband of Rukmini came from Dwarka to Dakur. Mahipati pleads with his hearers to listen with love and joy.

92. *Swasti* (Peace) ! This book is the *Shri Bhaktavijaya.* In listening to it the Lord of the world will be pleased. Listen then, you God-loving, pious *bhaktas.* This is the thirtieth deeply delightful chapter; it is an offering to Shri Krishna.

End of Volume I of the English

Translation of Mahipati's Marathi BHAKTAVIJAYA

Appendix

103 Extra Verses

There are four printed texts of Mahipati's **Bhaktavijaya***. In addition there is an unpublished manuscript of this work in the possession of Martand Chintaman Taharabadkar, Esq., Retired Mamlatdar, 828 Sadashiv Peth, Poona, who is the sixth descendant of Mahipati's brother. This manuscript was written by the brother of his grandfather and the writing was finished on the bright 11th of Vaishakh (May), Virodhkrit Sanvatsar in 1773 of the Shaka Era, i. e. A. D. 1851. Mr. Taharabadkar has very kindly loaned this manuscript for the present book and it has proved to be of immense use. The manuscript has 103 extra verses which we give below. Our numbering of the verses is taken from the manuscript. This is the first occasion on which these verses have been published. In each case the English rendering is printed on the left hand page and the Marathi original on the right hand.*

Chapter 2

251. If one listens with devotion [to the reading of the *Bhaktavijaya*] the Life of the world is pleased with him, and frees him from his earthly bondage in a moment's time. 252. Earthly enjoyments and salvation become his slaves, and the eight *siddhis* (accomplishments) wait upon him. *Hrishikeshi* (the Lord of the heart) always remains with him. 253. *Shri Hari* always abides at his home together with *Lakshmi* [Vishnu's wife, the goddess of wealth], and fully satisfies whatever wish he has in his heart. 254. God Supreme, honoured by other gods, lets him lack for nothing. All his pains, poverty and calamities at once disappear. 255. The Son of the sun (*Yama* the god of death) stands before him with both his hands joined palm to palm, and even the Creator (Brahma) and Hara (Shiva) always bow down to him. 256. Even Shiva and Brahmadev are not able to describe his glory. *Purushottam* (the good Being) takes him finally to *Vaikuntha* (His heavenly home). 257. The fruit of listening with devotion cannot be described completely. The cloud-complexioned One (Krishna) is found through devotion, and there is no other means of finding Him. 258. Devotion itself is God. Everything else is of no value without devotion. If one listens with devotion, *Madhav* (Vishnu) becomes subject to him.

भावें करितां श्रवण ॥ तयासी पावे जगजीवन
त्याचें निवारी भवबंधन ॥ अर्धक्षण न लगतां ॥ २५१ ॥
भुक्तीमुक्ती दासी ॥ सिद्धी तिष्ठती सेवेसी
तया जवळी हृषीकेशी ॥ सर्वकाळ वसतसे ॥ २५२ ॥
लक्ष्मीसहित श्रीहरी ॥ सर्वकाळ राहे त्याचे घरीं
जे इच्छा असेल त्याचे अंतरीं ॥ ते परिपूर्ण करीतसे ॥ २५३ ॥
तयाचें कांहीं न्यून ॥ घडो नेदी देवमान्य
दुःखदारिद्र्यदैन्य ॥ निरसोनि जाय तत्काळ ॥ २५४ ॥
तयापुढें सूर्यकुमर ॥ उभा जोडोनि दोन्ही कर
विधी आणि हर ॥ सर्व काळ वंदिती ॥ २५५ ॥
तयाचा महिमा ॥ वर्णू न शके शिवब्रह्मा
तो आवडे पुरुषोत्तमां ॥ वैकुंठधामा नेतसे ॥ २५६ ॥
सद्भावें श्रवणाचें फळ ॥ न वर्णवेची सकळ
सद्भावें सापडे घननीळ ॥ उपाय दुसरा नसेची ॥ २५७ ॥
भाव तोचि देव ॥ भावार्थेंवीण सकळ वाव
भावें श्रवण करितां माधव ॥ वश होय तयासी ॥ २५८ ॥

Chapter 4

259. By listening to the lives of saints, bad qualities disappear. Good qualities arise, and one loves devotion to perfection. 260. Those who love the stories of the *bhaktas* of Hari become more attentive to the supreme spiritual riches. The Lord of Pandhari loves them more than his own life. 261. *Vanamali* (Krishna) comes near him to protect him, and constantly lives with him, and does not go away from him. 262. Such is the great glory of listening which cannot be expressed by speech. May the hearers listen with reverence to the reading of this book. 263. In fact Shripati (Vishnu the Husband of *Shri* the goddess of wealth) is the author of this book. It is He who causes me to speak out with love the tales of His *bhaktas*. It is only a marvel that Mahipati's name appears in the verses.

Chapter 5

157. By your favour surely I have had poetic inspiration. I describe the deeds and fame of *Hari* by the favour of saints. 158. By Thy kindness an ignorant man becomes knowing. Even the blind are able to test a brilliant diamond. Such is Thy greatness. 159. By Thy favour a lame person is able to climb the top of Mount Meru, then what wonder is there that Thou shouldst enable me to compose a book ?

अध्याय ४ था

संतचरित्रें करितां श्रवण ॥ हरपोनि जाय तमो गुण ॥
आंगीं प्रगटे सत्वगुण ॥ भक्तीपूर्ण आवडे ॥ २५९ ॥
आवडे हरि भक्तकथा ॥ दक्ष होती परमार्था ॥
ते आवडती पंढरीनाथा ॥ प्राणाहूनी पैलीकडे ॥ २६० ॥
त्यासी येवोनि वनमाळी ॥ क्षणक्षणा सांभाळी ॥
अखंड राहे त्याचे जवळी ॥ कोठें दूरी नव जाय ॥ २६१ ॥
ऐसा श्रवण महिमा थोर ॥ बोलतां वाचेसि अगोचर ॥
श्रोतीं धरोनि आदर ॥ ग्रंथ सादर परिसावा ॥ २६२ ॥
ग्रंथकर्ता श्रीपती ॥ भक्तकथा वदवी प्रीती ॥
अभंग नाव महिपति ॥ नवल किती हें केलें ॥ २६३ ॥

अध्याय ५ वा

तुमचे कृपेनें निश्चितीं ॥ मी लाधलों कवित्वस्फूर्ती ॥
हरिगुण वर्णितों किर्ती ॥ हा प्रसाद संतांचा ॥ १५७ ॥
तुमचे कृपाळूपणें ॥ अज्ञानासी होय ज्ञान ॥
अंध परिक्षिती महारत्न ॥ ऐसें महिमान तुमचें ॥ १५८ ॥
तुमचे कृपेनें एकाएकीं ॥ पांगुळ चढे मेरुमस्तकीं ॥
ग्रंथ वदवाल माझे मुखीं ॥ याचें नवल कायसे ॥ १५९ ॥

Chapter 7

155. For revilers, heretics and the evil-minded this food is not obtainable. It is obtainable by him who is in the possession of unlimited good deeds done in his former births. 156. When this food is obtained the Husband of Rukmini becomes subservient. *Riddhi* and *siddhi* (eight accomplishments personified) cling to such a person, and (the four kinds of) salvation become his slaves. 157. When the loving God becomes subservient, Brahmadev and Shiva and the great gods like Indra and Chandra (the moon) prostrate themselves before him without doubt. 158. Such is the importance of listening to the *Bhaktavijaya.* This is thrice true, and can never be otherwise. 159. Should anyone consider this as untrue in his mind, he cannot escape hell, and deliverance from the servants of Death is certainly impossible.

Chapter 8

187. In the same way it is the Lord of Pandhari who causes me to compose this book. Know this for certain. Good people who listen to it with devotion meet with God. 188. They who listen with faith, the Husband of Rukmini is pleased with them, and whatever wish they may entertain He fulfils it. 189. If one wishes to have a son, the Lord of the universe will grant him one. To those who are sad on account of the pain of poverty, He will give wealth and fortune. 190. If one listens who is afflicted with disease, his disease will be destroyed. If one has a desire for marriage, Narayan (God) will bring it about. 191. One wishing to have a daughter will have a daughter. A soldier will obtain victory on a battlefield. A Brahman will obtain wealth of learning. 192. A man who is troubled by debt will surely be free from it. Such boons the Husband of Rukmini has granted for listening to this book. 193. He Himself has declared this fact. It cannot be otherwise. The loving *bhaktas* know that the Lord of Pandhari is the author of this book.

अध्याय ७ वा

निंदक पाखांडी दुर्जन ॥ तयासी प्राप्त नसे हें अन्न
अगाध पाहिजे पूर्व पुण्य ॥ तरीच प्राप्ती होय याची ॥ १५५ ॥
या रसाची जालिया प्राप्ती ॥ वश होय रुक्मिणीपति
ऋद्धीसिद्धी वोळंगती ॥ दासी होती मुक्ती पैं ॥ १५६ ॥
विरंचि आणि हर ॥ इंद्रचंद्रादि थोर थोर
तयासि वंदिति साचार ॥ सखा श्रीधर वश होतां ॥ १५७ ॥
ऐसा महिमा श्रवणाचा ॥ असे पैं भक्तविजयाचा
सत्य सत्य हे त्रिवाचा ॥ अन्यथा नोहे सर्वथा ॥ १५८ ॥
कोणी असत्य मानील चित्तीं ॥ तयासि न चुके अधोगति
सुटका नव्हे कल्पांतीं ॥ यमदूता पासोनी ॥ १५९ ॥

अध्याय ८ वा

तेवि ग्रंथ वदविता पंढरीनाथ ॥ हें जाणावें निश्चित ॥
भावें ऐकती जे संत ॥ तयासि भगवंत भेटे पैं ॥ १८७ ॥
जे श्रद्धायुक्त करिती श्रवण ॥ तयासि प्रसन्न रुक्मिणीरमण ॥
जे जे इच्छा धरील मनें ॥ ते परिपूर्ण करील ॥ १८८ ॥
पुत्र इच्छा धरितां पोटीं ॥ पुत्र देईल जगजेठी ॥
दरिद्र दुखें होतां कष्टी ॥ धनसंपत्ती देईल ॥ १८९ ॥
व्याधिस्त करितां श्रवण ॥ होय व्याधीचें निरसन ॥
लग्नार्थियाचें लग्न ॥ नारायण कर्ता पैं ॥ १९० ॥
कन्यार्थियासी कन्या होय ॥ क्षेत्रीं पावे रणी जय ॥
ब्राह्मणासी पाहे ॥ विद्याधन लाधे पैं ॥ १९१ ॥
जो रिणें पिडिला गृहस्थ ॥ तो ऋणमुक्त होय निश्चित ॥
ऐसा वर रुक्मिणीकांतें ॥ ग्रंथश्रवणीं दिधला ॥ १९२ ॥
तोचि वदला यथार्थ ॥ अन्यथा नसे निश्चित ॥
ग्रंथकर्ता पंढरीनाथ ॥ प्रेमळ भक्त जाणती ॥ १९३ ॥

Chapter 9

46. Then asked the Brahmans, 'What are your names'? Then Sopan told them in reply: 47. 'My eldest brother is Nivritti, and the wise Dnyandev comes after him. I, Sopan, am their younger brother, and sister Mukta is the youngest of all.'

* * * *

206. If one listens to the reading (of the *Bhaktavijaya*) the Life of the world lives with him. He Himself destroys his hindrances. 207. Whatever desire he has in his mind is fulfilled. He lets him lack nothing. He in person provides everything. 208. *Shri Hari*, who is merciful to His *bhaktas*, what will He not do? One who loves to listen is honoured by the gods with bowed heads. 209. One who is loved by *Shri Hari* is highly honoured by all. *Riddhi* and *Siddhi* (eight accomplishments personified) perforce enter his house. 210. The friend of Shri Hari is revered in the three worlds. Such is the power of listening. Even the Lord of the *Yadavas* (Krishna) becomes subservient to the listener. 211. Therefore, listen day and night. Make the Husband of Ramā (Krishna) your friend, and thus increase His reputation in the world. 212. The importance of the reputation is great. It takes place in every age. Mahipati tells this to the saints with hands joined palm to palm.

मग म्हणती ब्राह्मण ॥ तुमचीं काय नामाभिधानें ॥
मग सांगतसे सोपान ॥ तयांलागुन ते काळीं ॥ ४६ ॥
वडील बंधू निवृत्ती जाण ॥ त्याचे पाठिचे ज्ञानदेव सुजाण ॥
त्या कनिष्ठ मी सोपान॥ मुक्ता बहीण धाकुटी ॥ ४७ ॥

* * * *

प्रीतीनें करितां श्रवण ॥ तयाजवळी राहे जगजीवन ॥
तयाचीं विघ्नें निवारून ॥ स्वयें आपण टाकिता ॥ २०६ ॥
तों जें जें मनीं कल्पित ॥ त्याचे पुरवी सर्व आर्त ॥
कोठें उणे पडो नेदित ॥ स्वयें पुरवीत निजांगें ॥ २०७ ॥
जो भक्तवत्सल श्रीहरी ॥ तो काय एक न करी ॥
श्रवणाची आवडी धरी ॥ तयासि देव शिरीं वंदिती ॥ २०८ ॥
जो श्रीहरीचा प्रियकर ॥ तो सर्वांसि मान्य थोर ॥
ऋद्धी सिद्धी तयाचें घर ॥ दाटोनिया रिघती ॥ २०९ ॥
जो श्रीहरीचा सखा ॥ तो वंद्य तिही लोकां ॥
ऐसा श्रवणाचा महिमा देखा ॥ जो यदुनायक वश करी ॥ २१० ॥
यालागी धरोनि प्रीती ॥ श्रवण करिजे अहोराती ॥
सखा जोडा रमापति ॥ जगीं कीर्ती वाढवा ॥ २११ ॥
थोर कीर्तीचें महिमान ॥ युगायुगीं होय जाण ॥
हेचि महिपति म्हणे ॥ कर जोडोनि संतांसी ॥ २१२ ॥

Chapter 12

169. At this the heart of Nama became full of delight and said, ' The Merciful Husband of Rukmini fulfils my longings. '

* * * *

191. The moon should not be compared with the stars, nor Indra (the Lord of the gods) with other gods. A king should never be called an ordinary man. 192. A touchstone should not be called an ordinary pebble. Gold should never be called a common metal. 193. A wish-tree should not be called an ordinary tree. A diamond should never be called an ordinary stone. 194. The sandalwood should never be called ordinary wood. Rice should not be called an ordinary grain, nor *tulsi* plant be called an ordinary vegetable. 195. The silk yellow divine garment (of Vishnu) should not be called ordinary cloth. Not every dark-complexioned person can be divine (like Vishnu) The Son of the wind (Maruti) should not be called an ordinary monkey. 196. The vehicle of Shiva (the bull *Nandi*) should not be called an ordinary bull; and the eagle (the vehicle of Vishnu) should not be called a common bird. 197. Mount *Meru* should not be called an ordinary mountain, and soul-knowledge should not be called ordinary knowledge.

हें देखोनि नामयाचें चित्त ॥ तेव्हां जालें स्वानंदभरित
म्हणे माझे लळे पुरवितो बहुत ॥ रुक्मिणीकांत कृपाळू ॥ १६९ ॥

* * * *

नक्षत्रासमान नव्हे चंद्र ॥ सुरासमान नव्हे इंद्र
नरासमान राजेंद्र ॥ सहसाही म्हणों नये ॥ १९१ ॥
पाषाणासम परीस ॥ म्हणों नये तयास
धातुसम सुवर्णास ॥ म्हणों नये सर्वथा ॥ १९२ ॥
इतर वृक्षासमान ॥ कल्पतरु न म्हणावा पूर्ण
खड्या सारिखें रत्न ॥ म्हणों नये सर्वथा ॥ १९३ ॥
काष्ठासमान चंदन ॥ सर्वथा म्हणों नये जाण
तंदुळ म्हणों नये कण ॥ तुलसी भाजी न म्हणावी ॥ १९४ ॥
पीतांबर न म्हणावें वस्त्र ॥ दैवत नोहे नीळगात्र
वानरासमान वायुपुत्र ॥ सर्वथाही न म्हणावा ॥ १९५ ॥
इतर वृषभासमान ॥ म्हणो नये शिववाहन
पक्षी न म्हणावा सुपर्ण ॥ इतर पक्ष्यासारिखा ॥ १९६ ॥
इतर पर्वतासमान ॥ मेरु न म्हणावा पूर्ण
कीं इतर ज्ञानासमान ॥ अध्यात्मज्ञान न म्हणावें ॥ १९७ ॥

Chapter 13

204. One who hungers after listening, he alone will understand its taste, and as he enjoys it his heart is for ever satisfied. 205. Blessed, blessed are they in the world who have devotion for God at heart. The Lord of the universe comes to their help, and will give them refuge in *Vaikunth* (Vishnu's heaven.). 206. ' Even they will dwell in *Vaikunth*, and will obtain without effort the *Sarupata* salvation: ' such a promise is made by *Hrishikeshi* (the Lord of the heart) Himself in the *Bhaktavijaya*. 207. The listener should consider it as true and revere it, and should listen to all the lives of the *bhaktas*. 208. God has a great liking for the lives of His *bhaktas*, by listening to which the hearers will reach the other side of the worldly ocean.

Chapter 14

219. In the twelfth chapter of the *Bhagavadgita* the Lord Shri Krishna has propounded devotion. So the Lord of Pandhari spoke to Rukmini in the fourteenth chapter (of the *Bhaktavijaya*).

Chapter 16

207. Just as the deer is tempted by a song; or the bee by the fragrance of a lotus flower; or as a *chakor* bird is attracted by the moon; 208. or as the *chatak* eagerly awaits the cloud; or as the thoughts of a love-stricken husband are for his beloved.

अध्याय १३ वा

ज्यासी क्षुधा श्रवणाची ॥ त्यासीच लागे हे रुची
सेवितां मनें तयाचीं ॥ तृप्त होती सर्वदा ॥ २०४ ॥
ज्यासी श्रद्धा आहे पोटीं ॥ तेचि धन्य धन्य सृष्टीं
तयासीच पावे जगजेठी ॥ ठाव वैकुंठीं देईल ॥ २०५ ॥
तेचि होतील वैकुंठवासी ॥ स्वरूपता पावती अनायासी
ऐसें वचन हृषीकेशी ॥ भक्तविजयीं बोलिला ॥ २०६ ॥
ते मानोनि साचार ॥ श्रोतीं धरावा आदर
भक्तचरित्रें सार ॥ श्रवण केलीं पाहिजे ॥ २०७ ॥
भक्त चरित्राची आवडी ॥ देवासी फार याची गोडी
श्रवण करितां पैलथडी ॥ भवसागराची पावती ॥ २०८ ॥

अध्याय १४ वा

कीं गतिमाजी द्वादशांत ॥ भक्ती सांगे श्रीकृष्णनाथ
तैसें रुक्मिणीस पंढरीनाथ ॥ चतुर्दशाध्यायीं बोलिला ॥ २११ ॥

अध्याय १६ वा

कीं गायनीं वेधे हरिण ॥ का कमळीं मिलिंद जाण ॥
कीं चकोरही जाण ॥ चंद्रीं वेधे ज्यापरि ॥ २०७ ॥
की चातकाचें मन ॥ अखंड मेघाजवळीं जाण ॥
की कामुकाचा प्राण ॥ कांतेजवळीं सर्वदा ॥ २०८ ॥

Chapter 17

206. These most sanctifying stories of the *bhaktas* of God, if attentively listened to, will always result in the Life of the world (Vishnu) being well pleased with the listener. 207. One who longs for a son should repeat the wish, and he will obtain a son as precious as a jewel by the grace of the Husband of Rukmini. 208. That son will be virtuous, handsome and dutiful to his father. He will be diligent in offering prayers day and night to Shri Hari. 209. This son will live a full term of life. He will be fortunate, glorious, famous and bright by the grace of Shri Pandurang. 210. A pauper will be a wealthy man, a sick person's trouble will vanish, and the sins of a sinner will all burn up in half a moment. 211. He who wishes to have a daughter will have one. He will always obtain victory on the battlefield. The ignorant will have knowledge by listening to this book. 212. An aspirant of *moksha* (liberation of soul) if be hears this book read will obtain *Sayujyata* (salvation as absorption into the deity): *bhukti* (earthly enjoyments), *mukti* (salvation) and *kalyan* (beatitude) will be within his easy reach. 213. If one with love in his heart receives with his ears the sweetness of this, he alone will surely see the other bank of this worldly ocean. 214. Even while conducting a family life he becomes a *videhi* (unconscious of bodily pains and pleasures), and is free from the fear of this dreadful world.

अध्याय १७ वा

भक्तकथा परम पावन ॥ श्रद्धायुत करितां श्रवण ॥
तयालागी जगजीवन ॥ सुप्रसन्न सर्वदा ॥ २०६ ॥
पुत्र इच्छा धरोनि मन ॥ कोणी करील आवर्तन ॥
तयालागी पुत्ररत्न ॥ रुक्मिणीरमण देईल ॥ २०७ ॥
पुत्र सुलक्षणी सुंदर ॥ पितृभक्त अति उदार ॥
श्रीहरिभजनीं तत्पर ॥ अहोरात्र सर्वदा ॥ २०८ ॥
पूर्णायुषी भाग्यवंत ॥ प्रतापवंत कीर्तिवंत ॥
ऐसा होय दिव्यसुत ॥ श्रीपांडुरंग कृपेनें ॥ २०९ ॥
दरिद्रियासी होय धन ॥ व्याधिस्थाची पीडा हरण ॥
पापियाचे दोष दहन ॥ अर्धक्षणीं होतील ॥ २१० ॥
कन्यार्थियासि कन्या होय ॥ क्षेत्रीं पावे सदा जय ॥
अज्ञानासी ज्ञान होय ॥ ग्रंथश्रवणें करोनी ॥ २११ ॥
मोक्षार्थी करील श्रवण ॥ तयासि प्राप्त सायुज्यसदन ॥
भुक्तिमुक्तीकल्याण ॥ सर्व तोच होय पैं ॥ २१२ ॥
परंतु चित्तीं धरोनि आवडी ॥ श्रवणीं घेइजे येथिची गोडी ॥
भवसागराची पैलथडी ॥ तेचि रोकडी देखती ॥ २१३ ॥
संसारीं असतां पाहीं ॥ तो होय विदेही ॥
तयालागी नाहीं ॥ चिंता भवभयाची ॥ २१४ ॥

Chapter 19

109. His fate will be marvellous and with him God will be pleased. The goddess of prosperity and success will roll at his feet. Brahmadev and other gods will bow before him.

Chapter 21

216. He Who is extraordinarily liberal, Whose merits the serpent Shesha praises, Whom Shiva contemplates, know ye that He is the Life of the world. 217. He Who is the Father of the god Brahma, Who is the Creator of the movable and the immovable, Who is the Regulator of *Maya* (the primal force of the universe), know ye that He is this Pandurang. 218. He Who is the Regulator of infinite time, Who is the Redeemer of the world-wearied, proud of His *bhaktas*, He is this Pandurang, the Life of the world. 219. He Whose praises the *Puranas* sing, (in describing Whom) the *Vedas* remain silent, Whom Sanak and others contemplate, He is this *Shri Hari*, the Feeder of the universe. 220. He Who is the Espouser of the cause of His worshippers, Supporter of the Pandavas, Who sportively holds the strings of the universe, even He is standing at Pandharpur.

अध्याय १९ वा

ज्यावरि तुष्टेल भगवंत ॥ तयाचें भाग्य अद्भुत ॥
ऋद्धी सिद्धी वोळंगती तेथ ॥ ब्रह्मादिक वंदिती ॥ १०९ ॥

अध्याय २१ वा

जो परम उदार जाण ॥ जयाचे शेष वर्णी गुण ॥
सदाशिव करितो ध्यान ॥ तो जगजीवन जाणिजे ॥ २१६ ॥
जो विधीचा पिता ॥ जो चराचर निर्मिता ॥
जो मायेचा नियंता ॥ तो हा पांडुरंग जाणिजे ॥ २१७ ॥
जो काळासी शासनकर्ता ॥ जो भवभ्रमहर्ता ॥
भक्ताभिमान धरिता ॥ तो हा पांडुरंग जगदात्मा ॥ २१८ ॥
जयासी गाती पुराणें ॥ वेद राहिले धरोनि मौन ॥
सनकादिक करिती ध्यान ॥ तो हा जगजीवन श्रीहरी ॥ २१९ ॥
जो भक्तकाज कैवारि ॥ जो पांडवाचा साहकारि ॥
जो लीलासूत्रधारी ॥ तो पंढरपुरीं उभा असे ॥ २२० ॥

Chapter 22

214. Where the *bhaktas* of Hari dwell, that place is evidently to be called *Vaikunth* (heaven). That place is holy beyond description. 215. Where the *bhaktas* of Hari dwell, that place is ever highly purifying. The glory of it Indra, Brahma and other gods have described. 216. The country in which the saints live is very holy; such is the wonderful glory of the saints that even the serpent Shesha cannot comprehend it. 217. The village in which the merciful saints live, even the cesspool of that village is as holy and clear as the Ganges. 218. The town in which the saints live is sacred. The road on which the saints walk, that road is highly purifying. 219. Conversing upon the mode of life of the saints, the speaker and the hearer both attain holiness. By listening to stories of saints, salvation is at once obtained. 220. The lives of saints, are highly purifying. They are the highest. Hearing the sketch of the saints' lives, *Vaikunth* (heaven) is obtained. 221. He Who by his ears hears the lives of saints, with him *Chakrapani* (the Holder of the disk, Vishnu) is pleased, and coming with *Lakshmi* (Vishnu's wife the goddess of wealth), He stays at his house. 222. Wherever he goes, Hari goes before and after him. He will allow no difficulty to befall him.

जेथें राहती हरिभक्त ॥ तेचि वैकुंट साक्षात ॥
तें स्थान पुनीत ॥ कोठवरि वर्णावें ॥ २१४ ॥
जेथें हरिभक्त राहती अखंड ॥ तें स्थळ पावन प्रचंड ॥
तयाचे वर्णिती पवाडे ॥ शक्रादिक विरंची ॥ २१५ ॥
ज्या देशी वसती संत ॥ तो देश पावन बहुत ॥
ऐसा संतमहिमा अद्भुत ॥ सहस्त्रवदना कळेना ॥ २१६ ॥
जेथें वसती संत दयाळ ॥ त्या गाविंचा वोहळ ॥
तो पवित्र निर्मळ ॥ गंगेसमान जाणिजे ॥ २१७ ॥
जया नगरीं राहती संत ॥ तें स्थान पुण्यवंत ॥
ज्या मार्गी चालती भक्त ॥ तो मार्ग परम पावन ॥ २१८ ॥
संतांची लीला वर्णितां ॥ पावन होय श्रोता वक्ता ॥
संतकथा परिसतां ॥ मोक्ष जोडे तात्काळ ॥ २१९ ॥
संतचरित्र पावन श्रेष्ठ ॥ संतचरित्रें वरिष्ठ ॥
संतांची ऐकतां गोष्ट ॥ वैकुंठपीठ जोडे पैं ॥ २२० ॥
संतचरित्रें ऐकतां श्रवणीं ॥ संतुष्ट होय चक्रपाणी ॥
लक्ष्मीसहित येउनि ॥ त्याचें सदनीं राहतसे ॥ २२१ ॥
तो जाय जिकडे तिकडे ॥ हरी तयाच्या मागेंपुढें ॥
कांहीं तयासी सांकडे ॥ पडो नेदि सर्वथा ॥ २२२ ॥

Chapter 23

149. Kabir felt satisfied, and pronounced the blessing: 'May the bride and the bridegroom be happy, and the Husband of Ramā protect them.' 150. One whose heart is at the feet of his *sadguru*, his troubles disappear. To him there is no hindrance. 151. One who has faith in the word of his spiritual *guru*, to him there can never be destruction. The *Parama Purusha* (Supreme Spirit Vishnu) comes in person, and makes provision for him. 152. One who has a liking for his *guru's* advice, his millions of troubles will disappear, and of a certainty he will reach the other shore of the worldly ocean. 153. One who is entirely his *guru's* slave, he obtains with ease all pleasures. Him the Pervader of the universe never neglects. 154. The *bhakta* of a *Shri Guru* is the highest of all. A *bhakta* of a *guru* never sees a calamity. 155. The glory of a *guru's bhakta* cannot be described even by Shiva or Brahmadev. Even Vishnu, who is the Supreme Spirit, bows down to him. 156. God likes a *guru's bhakta*. He is God's rest. Through the service of a *guru*, one surely attains the Husband of Ramā. 157. A *guru's bhakta* certainly fears neither *Kali* (the *Kali-Yuga*) nor *Kala* (death). *Kala* himself bows down to him, then what of others ? 158. Blessed, blessed are the *guru's bhaktas* in the world. They are honoured by all the gods. By their sight men are saved. 159. I have sung the praise of *guru's bhaktas* according to my ability. Therefore the listeners should not entertain a doubt in their minds.

संतोष पावोनि कबीर ॥ आशीर्वाद देती सत्वर ॥
म्हणे सुखी असो वधुवर ॥ रमावर सांभाळो ॥ १४९ ॥
सद्गुरुचरणीं ज्याचें मन ॥ तयाचीं निवारती विघ्नें ॥
तयालागी जाण ॥ कांहीं संकट पडेना ॥ १५० ॥
ज्यासि गुरुवचनी विश्वास ॥ त्याचा कदा न होय नाश ॥
आंगें येउन परमपुरुष ॥ साहित्य त्याचें करीतसे ॥ १५१ ॥
गुरुवचनीं ज्यासि आवडी ॥ त्याच्या नासती विघ्नकोडी ॥
भवसागराची पैलथडी ॥ ते पावती निर्धारें ॥ १५२ ॥
जो अनन्य श्रीगुरूचादास ॥ तो सर्व सुख पात्रे अनायासें ॥
तयालागी जगन्निवास ॥ कदाकाळीं नुपेक्षी ॥ १५३ ॥
श्रीगुरुभक्त सर्वांत श्रेष्ठ ॥ गुरुभक्त वरिष्ठ ॥
गुरुभक्तासि संकट ॥ कांहींच न पडे सर्वथा ॥ १५४ ॥
गुरुभक्ताचा महिमा ॥ वर्णू न शके शिवब्रह्मा ॥
विष्णु जो का परमात्मां ॥ तो ही तयासी वंदित ॥ १५५ ॥
गुरुभक्त आवडे देवा ॥ तो देवाचा विसावा ॥
गुरुभक्तीनें रमाधवा ॥ पाविजेती निर्धारें ॥ १५६ ॥
जो गुरुभक्त निश्चयेंसी ॥ तो न भी कळिकाळासी ॥
स्वयें काळ वंदी त्यासी ॥ मा इतरासी कोण गणी ॥ १५७ ॥
गुरुभक्त जे असती जाण ॥ तेचि जगीं धन्य धन्य ॥
सर्व देवासि होती मान्य ॥ दर्शनें जन उद्धरती ॥ १५८ ॥
असो गुरुभक्ताची स्तुती ॥ वर्णिली म्यां यथामती ॥
म्हणोनिया श्रोतीं ॥ विकल्प चित्तीं न धरावा ॥ १५९ ॥

Chapter 25

56. Such is the life of Rohidas, highly purifying and pure, which if listened to both day and night, not a particle of bad deeds will remain. 57. If one listens to this with devotion, the Husband of Rukmini is pleased with him, and destroys the snares of his worldly life without a moment's delay. 58. In one's worldly life He never lets calamity approach him; but gives him wealth and fortune, and after death will elevate him to his own position. 59. He is God's great darling, and *Sharangdhar* (the Holder of the *Sharang* bow, Vishnu) is his helper. He (God) accepts him as His own, and greatly increases his reputation. 60. *Shripati* (Vishnu) is pleased with him who has a liking for His saints' lives. He stays by him day and night, and hindrances never trouble him. 61. One who is dear to Shri Hari, to him all gods bow down their heads. He dominates over *Kali* and *Kala* (death); and is revered by all.

ऐसें रोहिदासाचें चरित्र ॥ परम पावन पवित्र
श्रवण करितां अहोरात्र ॥ दोष अणु मात्र उरेना ॥ ५६ ॥
श्रद्धायुक्त करितां श्रवण ॥ तयासी पावे रुक्मिणीरमण
तोडी त्याचें भवबंधन ॥ अर्ध क्षण न लगता ॥ ५७ ॥
आणि संसारीं असता सदा ॥ कांहीं होऊं नेदी आपदा
पुरवी सकळ धनसंपदा ॥ अंतीं निजपदा नेईल ॥ ५८ ॥
तो देवाचा परम प्रियकर ॥ तयाचा साहकारी सारंगधर
करोनि त्याचा अंगिकार ॥ सत्कीर्ति थोर वाढवी ॥ ५९ ॥
भक्तचरित्रीं ज्याची प्रीती ॥ तयास प्रसन्न श्रीपति
जवळी असे अहोरातीं ॥ विघ्न कल्पांतीं न बाधी ॥ ६० ॥
जो श्रीहरीचा आवडता ॥ तयासी देव वंदिती माथा
चाले कळिकाळावरि सत्ता ॥ तो समस्ता वंद्य होय ॥ ६१ ॥

Chapter 26

102. The loved ones of God are the only fortunate persons. Their fortune is without limit. Blessed are their former births. 103. Blessed and fruitful is their birth, blessed are their family and caste, and blessed is their worldly life. 104. Blessed is their knowledge and blessed is their birth, who have made themselves subservient to Shri Hari alone. 105. Blessed are they who have become the suppliants of God alone. They have saved their ancestors and other men without number. 106. The *bhaktas* of God have in their possession many good deeds. Those who see them are free from the worldly ocean. 107. 'To the *bhaktas* of God the worldly ocean is like a mirage:' such a statement is made in the *Vedas* and *Shastras*. 108. The glory of God's *bhaktas* cannot be described even by Indra and Brahmadev. They become the loved ones of the Supreme Being, and go to *Vaikunth* (Vishnu's heaven). 109. They become the dwellers of *Vaikunth*, and are for ever near *Hrishikeshi* (the Lord of the heart). Their fortune has no limit, indeed. 110. Mahipati places his head at the feet of the saints, both present and future.

जे भगवंताचे प्रियकर ॥ तेचि परम सभाग्य नर
त्यांचिया भाग्या नाहीं पार ॥ धन्य जन्मांतर तयांचें ॥ १०२ ॥
धन्य तयांचें जन्म सफळ ॥ धन्य तयांचें यातिकुळ
धन्य तयांचा सकळ ॥ संसार होय जाण पा ॥ १०३ ॥
धन्य तयांचें ज्ञान ॥ धन्य तयांचें जनन
जे श्रीहरीस गेले शरण ॥ अनन्य भावें करोनी ॥ १०४ ॥
जे अनन्य शरण गेले ॥ ते प्राणी धन्य जाले
तयांनीं पूर्वज उद्धरिले ॥ जन तारिले असंख्य ॥ १०५ ॥
जे भगवंताचे भक्त ॥ ते महा पुण्यवंत
त्यांचें दर्शन जयासी होत ॥ ते भवाब्धी तरती हो ॥ १०६ ॥
भगवद्भक्तासी भवसागर ॥ मृगजळवत् साचार
ऐसें हें उत्तर ॥ वेदशास्त्रीं बोलिले ॥ १०७ ॥
भगवद्भक्ताचा महिमा ॥ वर्णू न शके बिडौजब्रह्मा
ते प्रिय जाले पुरुषोत्तमा ॥ वैकुंठधामा ते जाती ॥ १०८ ॥
ते वैकुंठींचे रहिवासी ॥ अखंड जवळी हृषीकेशी
ऐसा तयाच्या भाग्यासी ॥ पार नाहीं पाहतां ॥ १०९ ॥
ऐसे जे भक्त असती ॥ अथवा जे का पुढें होती
तयांच्या चरणावर महिपती ॥ मस्तक भावें ठेवित ॥ ११० ॥

INDEX OF TECHNICAL WORDS, NAMES OF PLACES AND PERSONS

A

B

C

E

F

G

I

J

L

M

N

P

S

U

V

W

Y

PART II

CONTENTS

FOREWORD

BY

J. F. Edwards

The Late Pundit N. R. Godbole

This is the tenth volume in the 'Poet Saints of Maharashtra' series begun by the late Dr. Justin Edwards Abbott in 1926. Since the publication of the ninth volume last December the cause of Marathi literature has suffered a serious blow by the death from pneumonia on Friday morning, February 16, after a brief illness, of Pundit Narhar Ramchandra Godbole. This able and unassuming Marathi scholar had collaborated in the preparation of this series of English translations, first with the late Dr. Abbott through Dr. Nicol Macnicol and latterly with the present editor of the series. On September 1933 the Pundit whose passing has left such a sad gap in the ranks of Western India entered on his sixtieth year. We can never forget the occasion of our last visit with him. Little did we dream it was to be our last, and the mellowing light of that closing fellowship seems to throw itself back over the years that preceded. We had called to see him on the Tuesday evening previous to the end and found him doubled up with asthmatic pain. Instead of discussing with him the various points we had taken for his customary elucidation, we found ourselves commending him in prayer to our common Father-God. For though this learned Brahman held a different faith from ours, there was in him a deep strain of devotion which manifested itself at all times and never so impressively as in this hour of need. Pundit Narhar Ramchandra Godbole was one of the humblest and most patient of scholars, to work with whom one came to regard as a high privilege.

That the fellowship was also prized by the departed Pundit appears from a sacred document which we shall treasure, a document he had handed over to us for the purpose of a Preface, but from which to quote here would be scarcely fitting because of its over-generous terminology and characteristic oriental charity in relation to ourselves. In the same document Pundit Godbole expressed great surprise at Dr. Abbott's desire that he (the Pundit)' should be recognized on the title-page as joint-author of this and the preceding volume, the Pundit adding characteristically: 'Among us Hindus there is a saying that if a great man coats a stone with red paint it is deified and then worshipped by the public; that saying is now verified in my own case, for my master has put on me the coat of editorship.' We are happy to be able to add that although the good Pundit who worked for several years on this series of translations of the Poet Saints has not seen the completion of the task, he has left enough of solid preparation in manuscript form to ensure that his capable hand will be seen in the volumes still remaining.

Corrections

In our Foreword to the earlier volume on the *Bhaktavijaya* dated December 7, 1933, we find we were in error in stating that the late Dr. Justin E. Abbott was 'born at Rahuri.' We are indebted for this correction to Dr Abbott's brother in America who kindly acknowledges a copy of the volume by writing us on February 2, 1934 as follows:—'My brother was born in Portsmouth, New Hampshire, United States, and went out to India with our parents in 1857 when Justin was four years old, and father was assigned to Rahuri.' We are deeply grateful for this correction, and we request all those readers who may detect errors of date, of translation, of opinion, etc. kindly to communicate the same to us.

Usefulness of Dr. Abbott's Benefactions

The Annual Report of the Deccan Sabha presented to the annual meeting on February 26 this year refers to the completion of Gokhale Hall, Poona, toward which Dr. Abbott bequeathed 5,000 dollars, following a previous donation of Rs. 15,000 in 1930. The Report speaks of the need for a special library in the Gokhale Hall, and then adds :

'We never intended to rest content merely with the construction of these buildings. Our aim has always been that this memorial to one who was never tired of emphasising the importance of a careful study of public questions on the part of public workers should provide facilities for such study by means of a suitable library specialising in politics and economics—the two subjects in which the great patriot was deeply interested. The provision of a well equipped library of this character will involve expenditure on scale which is out of the question, at any rate for some time to come, owing to the economic depression. But a decent beginning in that direction can be made with the amount due to us for this purpose under the will of the late Dr. Justin E. Abbott. He left to the Deccan Sabha a bequest of five thousand dollars earmarked for the purchase of books. It is difficult at the moment to say precisely how much money will accrue to us but during the year we have received about Rs. 6,500 from his executors which apparently represent a substantial portion of the amount that may ultimately fall to our share.'

Expressions of profound gratitude are also placed on record in the annual Marathi Report of the *Bharata Itihasa Sanshodhaka Mandala* whose headquarters are at 314 Sadashiv Peth, Poona, to which Dr Abbott bequeathed thirty thousand dollars 'for a building or an addition to a building to house properly Marathi manuscripts and other historic documents.' After quoting the words of the Abbott bequest, the Report of this Society for Indian Historical Research expresses in terminology of deepest religious devotion the Society's greatful appreciation of the noble-minded donor and of the inspiration from above that led to such a gift.

With reference to Dr. Abbott's munificent benefactions, our late Pundit Mr. Godbole wrote : 'Dr. Abbott's last will and testament fell into the hands of his legatees in India on Friday, 12th August, 1932. His munificence supplied food for thought to the English and vernacular journalistic world of India and especially that of Maharashtra. The whole atmosphere was as it were ringing with the fame of his bounty.' We would like to take this opportunity of gratefully acknowledging the many tributes paid by the Indian press to the large-hearted generosity of this former editor and missionary among the people of Maharashtra whom he came to love so deeply.

The Best Edition of Mahipati's *Bhaktavijaya*

In the preparation of these two volumes containing the English translation of Mahipati's *Bhaktavijaya*, the three workers (the late Dr Abbott, the late Pundit and ourselves) are indebted to one particular publication above all others, and that is the edition of this great Marathi classic entitled अभिनव भक्तविजय (*Abhinava Bhaktavijaya*). Other editions are in the *pothi* form inconvenient for holding, and while they are attractive because the chief scene in each chapter is given as a sample of Indian art, yet the ordinary book form adopted in this later edition makes the reading of the Marathi original a real pleasure, no minor consideration when the original extends to forty thousand lines of Marathi poetry. Published in June 1930, its editor's name is given as दिनदास (Dindās); its publishers the Paramartha Sādhanālaya Sansthā at Shivdav, P. O. Phonda Ghat, Savantavadi State, Ratnagiri District; its printer D. A. Savant at the Shri Ram Tattva Printing Press, Belgaum ; its price only Rs. 4–8. At the the foot of each page there appear useful explanatory notes on difficult words in the text (of course in Marathi), and each chapter in this excellent seven hundred-page Marathi work has a brief sketch of the teaching at the beginning and a brief summary of contents, with questions arising, at the close. The Marathi text alone takes up 651 pages and at the end of the book are two valuable appendices; one consisting of Notes based on the chief Pauranic Names mentioned in the *Bhaktavijaya*, the other consisting of instructive sections amplifying the Pauranic Narratives in the text. Both these were translated by Pundit Godbole and they appear in the present volume as the first two of the five invaluable appendices he prepared, our own additions being indicated by our initials (*J. F. E.*) at the end of the few paragraphs we have added. Those who desire to compare the Marathi original text with the English translation in these two volumes should without fail obtain this Marathi edition of Mahipati, the details given above being adequate guidance how to obtain the volume from any bookseller. In the introduction to the *Abhinava Bhaktavijaya* the following approximately complete list of Mahipati's published works is given :—

Name of book	*Chapters*	*No. of verses*	*Year of Composition* 'Shake' Era	A.D. Era
1. *Bhaktavijaya*	57	9916	1684	1762
2. *Sant Lilamrita*	35	5259	1689	1767
3. *Bhaktalilamrita*	51	10,794	1696	1774
4. *Santavijaya*	26 (incomplete)	4628	1696	1774
5. *Kathāsaramrita*	36	7200	1687	1765
6. *Pandhari Mahatmya*	12			
7. *Anantavratakatha*		186		
8. *Dattatreya Janma*		112		
9. *Tulsi Mahatmya*	5	763		
10. *Ganesh Purana*	4 (incomplete)	304		
11. *Pandurang Stotra*		108		
12. *Muktabharanavrata*		101		
13. *Rishipanchamivrata*		142		
14. *Apradha nivedana stotra* (verses on confession of sin)		101		
15. *Saransha Dnyaneshwari* (abridged *Dnyaneshwari*)		2431		

LIVES IN VERSE BY MAHIPATI

1.	Life of Shri Nāmdev	62	verses
2.	„ „ Haripal	58	...
3.	„ „ Kamāl	67	...
4.	„ „ Narasinha Mehta	52	...
5.	„ Raka Kumbhar	47	...
6.	„ Jagamitra Nāgā	63	...
7.	„ Mankoji Bodhale	67	...
8.	„ Santoba Pawar	102	...
9.	„ Chokha Mela	47	...
10.	„ Shri Tukaram		

In addition there are many unpublished works of Mahipati.

The Idea of Sin in India

It is worthy of note that one of Mahipati's works in the foregoing list (No. 14) consists of 101 verses of confession of sin. Now although it is outside the purpose and plan of this book to discuss the religious or theological implications of the entrancing stories handed down by Mahipati, yet these stories of Indian saints in Mahipati's *Bhaktavijaya*, even in an English translation, make an important contribution towards dispelling from the minds of their readers the error very widely held that the Indian saints evince little or no sense of personal sinfulness. Scores of pages both in this volume and in the preceding volumes of the Poet Saints series supply sufficient answer. On this interesting subject a German scholar of international repute, at a Conference held in Berlin in the closing days of January this year for the purpose of exploring the primitive and pre-historic memorials of the German race, applied the term 'heathen' to a Western race. Said Professor Witte of Berlin: 'We have now a self-conscious German heathenism,' referring in particular to a certain German racial 'conception of a Nordic God, a Viking of the skies.' After pointing out that the idea of sin and of the need of redemption was abhorrent to 'the German pagans,' the learned Dr. Witte went on to emphasize that the Sages of India have pondered deeply over the problem of sin and evil. His words on this subject are worth quoting:

'They (the Indian sages) have taken it indeed so seriously that they have discovered no remedy except in setting up the doctrine of reincarnation, according to which man is forced to pass through innumerable lives on earth–a fearful prospect! And these many reincarnations are necessary because it is impossible to wipe out evil. It must be paid for in the tortures of ever-new existence. And in many other ways India has striven, like all other peoples, to devise means for the removal of guilt. By sacrifices, by asceticism, by prayers, by offerings. Yet never was peace attained. It was in India that the idea arose that sin might be atoned for in the cleansing fires of purgatory; but neither there could peace be found. The longing for a Redeemer is found in these Eastern faiths, and with it went the hope of a Divine incarnation.'

Or as the noble-minded Bahinabai says in volume 5 of this series on the Poet Saints (page 99): 'Wherever we ask, we find our doubts are not solved.... No one who really understands the heart tells me. On whose words then shall I rely to give my mind rest? They tell you very many rules and methods, various forms of worship and various *mantras*. Some prescribe repeating of *mantras* sitting in the five different postures, such being the importance ascribed to how one sits. Others tell you of sacred waters, of austerities and rites. Others again tell you an infinite number of ceremonials in worship. Says Bahinabai, "My mind is not at rest. The battlefield of ignorance I see everywhere."' On the other hand, according to Dr. Witte, German secularism is adopting a new guise in the 'pantheistic mysticism' of European 'neo-pagans,' for 'it is the self-worshipping man who revolts against God and refuses to hear the truth.'

'The Empire of the Spirit' in India's Religious Quest

Enough has been said in the foregoing to establish the truthfulness of the observation made recently by a western writer who said we need to remember in all our religious study of the Orient that the religious history of a country 'does not commence with the moment of a missionary's arrival in it, nor are the movements of the Spirit of God most faithfully delineated by the recital of all that has happened to him and his wife.' That the Divine Spirit Himself is at work in man's agelong quest after God is a conclusion long since accepted by all reverent scholars, and the forty thousand Marathi lines in Mahipati's *Bhaktavijaya* are themselves sufficient to establish the conclusion set forth recently by Dr. S. Radhakrishnan, India's most popular philosopher, that beneath the bewildering variety in Hinduism there is 'a common quest' (*The Hindu View of Life*, p. 58). Though it is true that a few years ago a symposium on 'What Makes a Man a Hindu' yielded sixty different definitions out of which only three agreed and these only in saying that a Hindu was one who was born such and who had not renounced the Hindu faith; and though the term 'Hindu' is so comprehensive that a man may be a pantheist, a polytheist, a theist, even a monotheist and yet be a Hindu, the term 'Hindu' so defying definition or a complete analysis, and the Hindu creed being so intangible; though, as we say, these things are true, it is also true to say with Radhakrishnan that 'the Hindu spirit is that attitude towards life which regards the endless variety of the visible and temporal world as sustained and supported by the invisible and external spirit' (*Ibid* 124). And though the facts of Hinduism compel the acceptance of another verdict of Radhakrishnan's, viz., that in orthodox Hinduism as set forth in the Upanishads 'the pursuit of truth is more negative than positive, more an escape to incomplete conceptions than the attainment of perfect truth' (*The Reign of Religion in Contemporary Philosophy*, pp. 413-414), yet a just verdict shows also that it is equally true that in the loftier reaches of the *Bhakti* Hinduism which we see in the 57 chapters of Mahipati's *Bhaktavijaya* we are introduced to what Professor Muirhead has finely described in a recent issue of *The Hibbert Journal* (October 1932) as 'the empire of the spirit.' And it is because Mahipati provides such an entrancing introduction to that 'empire of the spirit' that he has a real message today to so many in both East and West who are like so much drifting sand in the arid desert of agnosticism and materialism. For the same reason we can say that Mahipati has built a golden bridge of understanding contact between those who live in India and those who live in other lands.

India's 'Incorrigible Religiousness'

Granted that there is much in great Indian religious classics like Mahipati's *Bhaktabijaya* which we find difficult to square with the needs of religious life in these strenuous modern times, nevertheless there remains much ground for Dr. Rabindranath Tagore's observation that 'India's chief fault is that she is incorrigibly religious.' How religious, India really is, may be dimly realized when we think of her two millions of so-called 'holy men' some of whom Mahipati has sympathetically pilloried in his pages; yet men who, notwithstanding their perversion of true religion as seen in these 'stories,' were all the time sincerely dedicated to the ideal of poverty and self-denial. Think of the hundreds of thousands of *sannyasis* living in solitary places that they may be 'alone with God' in the astonishing fashion Mahipati has described. Think of the religious festivals he paints so vividly, still held all over India, one of them attended according to one estimate by no less than three million people, many of whom tramp hundreds of miles on foot, some of them two thousand miles and more, with the sole object (as Mahipati shows) of having their sins washed away. And yet some people doubt the existence of a sense of sin in India!! Sir Leonard Rogers once ascertained by careful investigation that the average number of Indians who go on pilgrimage each year cannot be less than twenty millions: half the population of England! Surely no one can read such a work as the *Bhaktavijaya* without feeling that in its religious devotion India, holds the pre-eminence, though so much of it is so sadly misdirected and perverted. And though India is changing at a rapid rate, with thousands of her noblest sons and daughters going over to secularism, who will dare to say that in an India of such unfathomable religious emotion and such astonishing powers of renunciation, if only her religious ideas can become purified and worthily dedicated—who will dare to say that, in a renovated India, secularism and agnosticism may not encounter their Himalayan barrier? Such a situation would but fulfil the anticipation of those who have held that in the order of Providence India is destined to provide the arena for the final Armageddon of religion.

Religion the Backbone of India

Ideas akin to these were finely expanded in a speech given by Swami Vivekananda some years ago in reply to an address presented to him by the Hindus of Kumbhakonam, the theme being that religion is the backbone of Hindu society. Said the Swami:

'For good or for evil, the religious ideal has been flowing into India for thousands of years; for good or evil the Indian atmosphere has been filled with ideals of religion for shining scores of centuries; for good or evil we have been born and brought up in the very midst of these ideals of religion, till it has entered into our very blood, and tingles with every drop of it in our veins and has become one with our constitution, become the very vitality of our lives. Can you give such religion up without the rousing of the same energy in reaction, without filling the channel which that mighty river has cut out for itself in the course of thousands of years? Do you want that the Ganges should go back to its icy bed and begin a new course? Even

if *that* were possible, it would be impossible for this country to give up her characteristic course of religious life and take up a new career of politics or something else for herself. You cau only work under the law of least resistance, and this religious line is the line of least resistance in India. This is the line of life, this is the line of growth, and this is the line of well-being in India, to follow the track of religion.'

The Maratha Epic Fight For Religious Liberty

There is a great deal in Mahipati's *Bhaktavijaya* to show that the Marathi saints of the seventeenth and eighteenth centuries regarded themselves as Providentially designated to preserve for their fellow-countrymen the worthiest ideals of Hindu *bhakti*. This is one of the chief themes in that brilliant historical fragment by Mahadev Govind Ranade, *The Rise Of The Maratha Power*. It is also a recurring theme in many of the poems of those saints of whom Mahipati has handed down to posterity such a living picture. One example will suffice here, where Ramdas sets forth the plight of *Dharma* under Muslim domination in the 17th century. Ramdas exclaims: *' *Tirthas* (i. e., places of holy waters) and *Kshetras* (i. e., holy places) have been destroyed, sacred places of *Brahmans* have been defiled; the whole world has grown sick (of these things) and *Dharma* has disappeared....

*** These 14 lines of an English translation and the version of the original 8 lines of Marathi are both taken from *The Mahratta* of May 22, 1927. The Marathi text reads:**

तीर्थे क्षेत्रें मोडिलीं । ब्राह्मण-स्थानें भ्रष्ट झालीं ।
सकल पृथ्वी आंदोळली । धर्म गेला ॥ . . .
देव-ब्राह्मण गोब्राह्मण । करावया संरक्षण ।
हृदयस्थ जाला नारायण । प्रेरणा केली ॥
उदंड पंडित पुराणिक । कवीश्वर याज्ञिक वैदिक ।
धूर्त तार्किक सभानायक । तुमच्या ठायीं ॥
या भूमंडळाचे ठायीं । धर्म रक्षी ऐसा नाहीं ।
महाराष्ट्रधर्म राहिला कांहीं । तुम्हाकारणें ॥

God Narayan residing in the heart has inspired you to protect the images of gods, *Dharma*, cows and Brahmans. You are the patron of many *pundits* (men learned in the *Shastras*), *Purāniks* (reciters of *Purānas*), *Kavīshwaras* (poets), *Yājniks* (men versed in sacrificial ceremonial), *Vaidikas* (men who have learned the Vedas by heart), and *Dhurta Tarkika Sabhā Nāyaks* (members of assemblies wise and versed in logic). On this earth there is no one able to protect *Dharma*. It is because of you (Shivaji) that *Dharma* in Maharashtra (or Maharashtra-*Dharma*) is getting protection.' How rich is this word *Dharma* in all the Marathi *bhakti* literature will be clear from the following:—

'In the introductory passage of the *Yadynavalkya Smriti* the meaning of the word *Dharma* is very briefly and lucidly stated and illustrated as follows :—" Here the word *Dharma* is used to denote six kinds of *Smarta Dharmas*, viz., (1) *Varna Dharma* (the duties, prescribed for the people of different *Varnas* or castes; (2) *Ashrama Dharma* (the duties prescribed for people belonging to the four orders, viz., *Brahmacharya* (student), *Grihastha* (householder), *Vanaprastha* (one who has retired to a forest), and a *Sanyasi* (one who has given up the world); (3) *Varnashrama Dharma* (duties prescribed for a man of a particular caste and particular order); (4) *Guna Dharma* (duties relating to one holding a particular status); (5) *Nimitya Dharma* (occasional duties); (6) *Sadharan Dharma* (duties common to all)." That a Brahman should never drink wine is an instance of *Varna Dharma* (i. e., a duty belonging to a man of a particular *Varna* or caste). That a *Brahmachari* should perform morning and evening *Homa* is *Ashrama Dharma* (duty prescribed for a man belonging to the *Brahmacharya* order). That a Brahman *Brahmachari* should use the staff of a Palasha tree is *Varnashrama Dharma* (duty prescribed for a man of a particular *Varna* or caste and a particular *Ashrama*, i. e., order). That a king who has been crowned and who possesses qualities prescribed by *Shastras* should protect his subjects is *Guna Dharma* (duty prescribed for a man holding a particular status). Undergoing penance with a view to cleanse a man of the blame arising from not doing what the *Shastra* has prescribed to be done and from doing what the *Shastra* has prohibited is *Nimitya Dharma* (duty arising by reason of the occasional lapses of duty or breaches of injunctions of the *Shastras*). The duty of not killing (*Ahimsa*), of speaking the truth etc, etc., which duties are to be practised by all men from a Brahman to a Chandala, is *Sadharan Dharma* (duties common to all beings). (From *The Mahratta*, May 22, 1927).

Maratha Pre-eminence in Indian History

To these admirable definitions of what *Dharma* really means, we only need to add that the 850 pages of English translation in these two volumes of *Stories of Indian Saints* provide a veritable gold mine of illustrations taken from actual life. These were the religious ideals to which Ramdas appealed in his famous couplet :

मराठा तितुका मेळवावा । महाराष्ट्रधर्म वाढवावा ॥
येविषयीं न करितां तकवा । पूर्वज हांसती ॥

This means: 'Unite all the Marathas and spread everywhere Maharashtra *Dharma.* If you do not exert yourself for accomplishing this, your ancestors will look upon you with derision.' The response to that appeal has given us one of the greatest epic stories in Indian history and hence the historian can say that 'the Marathas alone of all the various nationalities of India crushed the growing Moghul power' (see G. S. Sardesai, *Main Currents of Maratha History*), the Marathas being the only *Indian* nation that has ever ruled so great a part of India. The explanation lies in the fact that the people of the time 'looked upon the Maratha leaders as the liberators and defenders of their faith,' and the result of this fight for religious liberty, extending over more than three centuries, gave to the people of Maharashtra the famous epithet of *Jayishnu* or 'conquering' while those of other provinces are described as *sahishnu* or 'passively suffering,' to quote the apt distinction made by Mr. Rajwade. When Mahipati was engaged on his *Bhaktavijaya*, the Maratha Power was at the zenith of its influence, but as he wrote his closing chapters the historic Maratha Confederacy was being shattered on the fatal battlefield of Panipat (1761). In the *Bhaktavijaya* stories we see at work in the daily life of peasant, priest and poet alike those religious ideals which gave to Maharashtra its well-deserved pre-eminence over all the other people of India. Alas ! that so many in Maharashtra have lost the pristine glory of their *bhakti* patriots and poets and have made patriotism itself their sole religion.

When Religion Is Perverted

Mahipati lived in such a different climate from the atheism and agnosticism of modern India that a Foreword to such a book as this is no place to deal adequately with the growing revulsion in India against that corruption of religion which has been responsible for the toleration and perpetuation of those monstrous evils of Indian society such as infanticide, child-marriage, untouchability, etc. These have so long masqueraded under the guise of religion as to alienate thousands of India's educated minds from religion as such. Even the mild and tolerant Mahipati makes one of his heroes in this volume, Ganeshnath the mendicant, tell some high-caste Brahmans who were boasting that they 'belonged to the highest class, (page 336), ' The palm tree is very tall but its shade is of no use to anyone. ' And in another place (page 323) Mahipati puts into the mouth even of Krishna the words, ' We must not give the mystic *mantra* to a man of the low caste, ' to whom Krishna gives the offensive name of 'Unmentionable,' the whole story that follows showing how a Mahar was disgraced before the people. How terribly a corrupt form of religion can mislead the people has been illustrated for India anew while this Foreword was being written. We refer to the tragic outbreak of violence arising out of the protest by the villagers of Tiruvadi in the Tanjore District of South India against the attempt of the police, acting under definite orders from Government, to stop the brutalising practice of self-torture in the form of hook-swinging and hook-dragging as acts of propitiation of the local deity ; so fierce was the popular resentment against interference by the law that one official was battered to death inside the temple and two others were murdered outside. Similarly tragic corruptions of religion are also being seen (as we write) in the recurrence of animal sacrifices in widely separated Indian centres, accompanied by terribly cruel methods that have evoked many noble protests, e. g., from the All-Indian Humanitarian League. In such incidents one is equally amazed at the passionate quest after God and at man's perversion of this quest.

Why Indian Religious Literature Is Unattractive

These biographical fragments from Mahipati offer to Western students a new method of studying Indian religion. With the best will in the world to understand Hinduism at its noblest, even the most diligent students in Western lands find India's traditional literature to be forbidding and unattractive in the highest degree. This point has been put so well and so recently by a British writer of high standing that we will quote his words. In the book which has a misleadingly militant title, *Counter Attack From The East*, Mr. C. E. M. Joad, after stating that ' Radhakrishnan is definitely critical of the sterile dogmatism in which Hindu thought has apparently come to rest,' continues :

'The vital flow of religious inspiration has trickled away into the sands of scholarship and formalism, and there apparently it has lost itself. It is, indeed, difficult to read Indian philosophy with its endless commentaries upon the semi-sacred texts of its various systems without deriving the impression that one is being presented with a testimony, one of the most striking, to the perverted ingenuity of the human mind. . . . The ideas are unacknowledged in the West, the philosophy almost entirely unread. The reason is, I think, the unfamiliar, the perverse form which Indian philosophers have chosen to adopt. . . . Contemplating this curious *corpus* of dogma, piety and learning the Western reader is doubly repelled. So far as the past is concerned, he finds the ideas, the undoubtedly valuable ideas, of Indian philosophy clothed in the unfamiliar and forbidding garb of a commentary upon sacred texts ; so far as the present is concerned, he is led to suppose that philosophy has reached a dead end.'

The Biographical Method of Studying Indian Religion

This extract, though from one declaring himself 'an avowed agnostic,' illustrates the need of an entirely new method of presentation if Indian religious literature is to capture the imagination of the world. Mahipati's entrancing stories of Indian saints, of which the *Bhaktavijaya* is full from end to end, supply the needed change in method, for they provide us with hundreds of examples of the religious life of the *individual* in Hinduism. We venture to suggest this biographical method is not only more interesting but that it also supplies a more reliable test of the value, or otherwise, of Hinduism in the everyday life of India's people. Systems of thought, agelong institutions and extensive movements we have had in plenty in the study of Hinduism. Mahipati offers us a new method of understanding this vast and all-pervasive influence on India's people. By his biographical method Mahipati presents us with many varying types of those individuals who have prevailed in every period of Hinduism and who never abounded as they do today all over the land, people by the thousand who feel that the philosophical tenets and the priestly systems of orthodox Hinduism are alien from the daily needs of the common people. Craving as they do some other form of religion, they have created in India a type of 'religious outsider' who feel they can no longer accept many things for which the traditional religion stands. Though most people of this type have not definitely broken with the accepted system, and though many of them seldom if ever attend the Hindu temple, yet their number is increasing immensely, especially among the ever growing student population of India. Mahipati's biographical stories offer an almost ideal method of learning how to understand these people, many of whom occupy positions of great influence in Indian society. Since these people to-day are the true religious descendants of many of those whom Mahipati has so skilfully portrayed in the *Bhaktavijaya*, this eighteenth century biographer can help us to establish invaluable points of contact with many of the Indian citizens in our own day.

Religious Value of Mahipati's Biographies

Concerning the question whether Mahipati's characters are drawn from actual life or are examples of eighteenth century Indian religious fiction, we cannot do better than quote what we have found in one of Dr Abbott's manuscripts handed over to us. Says our late friend: 'Whether the stories of the different saints are real or legendary matters little, but from them we learn what was popularly considered their conception of God, and their way of approach to Him. That they considered an image of an *avatar* like Rama or Krishna a way of approach cannot be doubted. Tukaram's enthusiasm before the image at Pandharpur and the devotion of Ramdas to images of Rama give abundant evidence. But it should also be remembered that the approach by way of the idol was not their only way. They practised and taught what is called *manas puja*, that is, worship in their inmost mind. It was their way of going as it were into their inner chamber and of closing the mind's door as they prayed in secret to God, Whom they called Mother and Father. If Hindus of the present day were to follow the ideas of these their own *bhakti* saints, they need never seek approach to God through an idol but could always use the method of *manas puja* (mental worship). Of course not all the *bhaktas* in these stories held to the *high* ideal of *bhakti* (devotion) and *vairagya* (self-denial) as did Tukaram and Ramdas. Many were sincere *bhaktas* while carrying on their worldly business, but they had the *spirit* of *vairagya*, that is, their indifference to worldly things (their *vairagya*) was one of mind and spirit. It meant that they did not look upon their riches as acquired for their own happiness, but to help the needy. They understood that they should not lay up the temporal riches of this world but should aim at the supreme spiritual riches. Saints like Eknath, Tukaram and Ramdas tried to live the life of *complete* indifference to worldly things. But they did not press this highest ideal upon others, unless others themselves so chose it. Others were to continue in the business of life, doing their respective duties, but always with the unselfish spirit of *vairagya*, or of indifference to worldly things. *Bhakti* saints like Eknath, Tukaram and Ramdas tried to obey *literally* the precepts, " Give to him who asketh of thee," 'Take no thought for the morrow, what ye shall eat or drink, nor yet for your body, what ye shall put on." They trusted God for everything. '

' India's Religion Of Grace '

Careful readers of Mahipati's biographical stories of the *bhakti* saints of Maharashtra will note many personal confessions, prayers and records of the most intimate religious experience which illustrate most strikingly the conclusions of that reverent investigator of the Science of Religion at the University of Marburg, Professor Rudolf Otto, who is rightly acknowledged as ' one of the very first theologians of Germany, ' and who sees in Indian *bhakti* ' the working of the Spirit of God among all men ' as ' an actual preparation ' for ' the coming of the day when all the world will be united in one faith and on communion, which will be the Kingdom of God.' The words are those of Dr Frank Hugh Foster of Oberlin, Ohio, U. S. A., in his 'Translator's Preface' to the English edition of Dr Otto's remarkable book entitled *India's Religion of Grace* published in 1930. The attitude of this book to India's religious aspirations is indicated by the one and only reference to Marathi religious literature where Dr Otto speaks (p. 63) of 'the wonderful, delicate and spiritual songs of the Mahārāshtra saints.' To show what Dr Otto means by his conception of *India's Religion Of Grace* it is impossible to give more than the following selections from his rich 141 pages :—

Indian thinkers have not engaged in speculation for the sake of mere metaphysics or to gain a theoretical view of the universe, but the purpose has been to give a doctrine of salvation, that is to set forth the "Way" to a good above the world and infinite, which is at the same time fundamentally different from all mere happiness and cannot be estimated in worldly values, not even in "moral" values, but has a purely religious value. Involvement in the boundless misery of "being lost;" longing for "redemption" from the chains of such misery, a misery arising directly from the mere fact that man and the world are what they are; the way through redemption to an eternal, imperishable good which cannot be compared with anything of earth, or either found or appropriated by one's own reason or power, but is an "altogether different" good; these are in India as well as with us the impelling interests, awakened by the text and the meaning of the *Sruti*, the Holy Scriptures of the old Upanishads. And, consequently, the Indian systems of doctrine, too, are not properly "philosophy," but doctrine founded upon "faith," not interesting metaphysics, but theology' (Otto p. 13). 'The religion of India is, in its last and highest form, the religion of acosmistic mysticism, a mysticism denying the reality of world, things, personality' (p. 16).

India's Battle Against Pantheism

Dr Otto proceeds to show that in contrast with 'a particular form of the Vedānta,' 'in India itself there has been waged the hottest battle *against* this "monistic" mysticism of an impersonal Absolute, and there has arisen there, moved by original impulses and drawn from original sources, that which I call its "religion of grace" ' (p. 17).

'Beginning in the profound verses of the pre-Christian *Bhagavad-gita*, the book most loved and honoured by millions of Hindus, passing through times of obscuration and reformation, as with us, this doctrine of grace rises till it gains at last positions which dumbfound us Protestants by their analogy to our fundamental ideas....*Bhakti*-religion and the strange perplexities of its " doctrine of grace " have in the East not only seized upon Hinduism, but have also penetrated and shaped certain peculiar forms of doctrine and communions in Buddhism' (p. 18). 'In this Indian *bhakti*-religion there is presented, without doubt, a real, saving God, believed, received, and-can we doubt it ?-experienced' (p. 21). 'Great and wide circles of the pious people of India recognize with glowing enthusiasm the way of *bhakti* as the *only* way, and reject that of Shankara as damnable heresy and soul-destructive error'(p. 22).

India's Struggle For God

In a spirit which combines appreciation with discrimination the Marburg theologian goes on to say :

' Long before the *bhakti*-religion had assumed a settled form, men had sought in India for God, had questioned, struggled and known about Him, and not merely about a God of metaphysical speculation, but a real and living God' (p. 25). 'It was a struggle for God, a real God, not such a God as philosophical speculation gives us, but such as the heart and the soul need and seek, a God to inspire personal trust, love, reverence and loyal self-surrender' (p. 29). 'Here we are dealing with a *genuine religion* and *religion of experience*. Religion is here no mere fringe of sentiment furnishing a border to the rest of our life, but is conceived as the true meaning of life itself. With this is connected a trait which is characteristic of the later theology of this religious communion; the properly speculative questions recede more and more, and the direct questions of practical religion come forward, questions regarding salvation, what is connected with it and how it is attained' (p. 44).

This is not the place to follow Dr Otto in the remainder of his fascinating study as he contrasts the spirit of Indian *bhakti* as seen in the *Gita* and in the *bhakti* poets with the *bhakti* of the Bible, and as he sets forth 'the incomparably more piercing and vigorous spirit of Palestine,' witnessed in a quickened conscience for sin through communion with the *Holy* God and in the heart's cry for, and heart's assurance of, forgiveness. Enough has been said, we would hope, to lead non-Indian readers in East and West to search in the gold mine of Mahipati's biographical narratives of the religious history of Maharastra for numerous illustrations of the correctness of Dr Otto's position concerning both the excellencies and shortcomings of Indian *bhakti*. How grave some of those shortcomings are have been noted already by readers of the previous volume, e. g., such moving stories as that of Gora the Potter (see chapter xvii, verses 99–127) whose *bhakti* led him to 'become so utterly absorbed as to be identified with the Invisible' and to trample his own child to death as he danced in his 'ecstatic mood' in 'worship of Hari.' On the principle of avoiding 'that irritating method, as unscientific as it is ungenerous, which selects the worst in one religion and contrasts it with the best in another,' we have allowed Dr Otto to speak for himself in the extensive quotation given above. It speaks volumes for the scholarship and sympathy, the insight and the tolerance of Dr Otto and the late Dr Abbott that they succeeded in distilling from the *bhakti* literature two such expositions of *bhakti* aspirations and experience as those in the foregoing paragraphs.

Pauranic Atmosphere of Much *Bhakti* Literature

One grave defect of this *bhakti* literature is what may be called the Pauranic stamp which mars so many pages. How deeply that Pauranic stamp affects almost the whole of Mahipati's narrative can be seen at a glance, for well-nigh every one of his moving stories makes frequent reference to those Pauranic Names and Narratives set forth in the first two Appendices at the close of the present volume. The case of Krishna (see pp. 396-7 and 424-8) is alone sufficient to indicate what must be the influence of many of the *Puranas* so popular still all over India, with the account of his 16,108 wives and of his dalliance with the female cowherds. The growing disquiet among India's educated people regarding these aspects of their sacred literature is one of the most striking indications of India's slow but sure acceptance of 'new standards of historical truth and ethical holiness.' Under the influence of these 'new standards' an increasing number of Hindu scholars are retaining these Pauranic narratives only as emblem, imagery and allegory, this allegorical principle of interpretation being more and more applied also to certain difficult aspects of the great and wonderful *Bhagavadgita*. On this interesting point one of the most sympathetic and understanding of scholars on Indian history, Edgar W. Thompson, M. A., himself twenty-five years in India and author of the excellent *History of India* for Indian High Schools and Colleges, writes in his latest book :

'Indeed, it would be highly inconvenient and repugnant to the feelings of many modern Hindus, if the *Gita* were to be regarded as a narrative of fact....It would follow inevitably from an acceptance of the *Gita* as history, that Krishna had inculcated, in the most literal sense, the necessity for and the righteousness of killing....but there may be room for doubt, if its history is not assumed. If, however, we believe that a living Krishna, in bodily form, on the particular occasion described by the poem, actually spoke the words attributed to him, then there is no escape from the conclusion that Krishna sanctioned warfare of the most wanton and ruthless type. The teaching of the poem would be in flagrant contradiction of any doctrine of *Ahimsā* or *Satyāgraha* (soul-force). Mr. Gandhi, to whom the *Gita* has been as the staff of his life, seeks to turn the point of this objection by declaring that the setting of the poem is unhistorical-that it is an allegory.'

Bhakti and Pantheism Often Found Together

It is, on the other hand, a tribute to the growing conscientiousness of Indian, particularly of Hindu, scholarship that a growing number of Hindu writers frankly recognize that emblem, imagery and allegory may too often be treated as a convenient hiding-place for both 'bad history and bad morality' and that the doctrines of the *Advaita Vedānta* have helped to blur the ineffaceable distinction between fact and fiction. No more eloquent protest has ever been made, and certainly none by greater authority, against the inadequate historical sense and defective historical methods of Indian students, than was made some years ago by that greatest of all Eastern savants, the late Dr Sir Ramkrishna Gopal Bhandarkar on the occasion of the opening of the Bhandarkar Research Institute in Poona. These things in no way imply any lack of appreciation of India's marvellous *Gita*, still less of the *bhakti* literature which the *Gita* inspired; they simply recognize that only an 'indolent and shallow syncretism' can overlook the fact that the doctrines and practices of opposing sects and schools of Hindu thought are strangely blended in the greatest of India's religious classics, and that the Hindu Pantheists and Dualists, the followers of Shankara's Monistic philosophy of the Absolute and the *bhakti* believers in a Personal God, alike claim the *Gita* as their authoritative book of devotion. Hence it is that it is true to say on the one hand with Dr Barnett in his book on *The Lord's Song* that the *Gita* has for its *aim* the setting forth of 'a consecration of life's every work to the selfless service of God, and an Infinite Love that at every place and every time pours forth its illimitable grace to all that seek after it;' and that it is equally true to say that the *Gita*'s testimony to a Personal God is marred by so often 'veering away from this God to the bare and inconceivable Absolute of the *Advaita*;' about which the great Kabir cried out of the depths of his soul's need that 'the Impersonal' did 'not satisfy' his soul.

An *Advaitic* Strain In Much Marathi *Bhakti*

Such facts as the foregoing help to explain the remarkable mingling all over Maharashtra of Vaishnavite (*Hari* = हरि) and Shaivite (*Hara*=हर) elements in the popular worship, and may throw light on an opinion widely held that over ninety per cent of Hindus still hold to the *Advaitist*, Monistic, Pantheistic view of an Impersonal Deity. They are also in line with the statements made by Professor R. D. Ranade, M. A., on pages 178-9 of his notable work published last year entitled *Indian Mysticism : Mysticism In Maharashtra*, being the seventh volume in the great work *History of Indian Philosophy* projected by S. K. Belvalkar, M. A., Ph. D., of Poona and Professor Ranade of Allahabad. Though Professor Ranade agrees that 'Farquhar fitly calls Dnyandeva the "Coryphaeus" of the whole *Bhakti* movement in the Maratha country,' nevertheless he (Ranade) is able to say that 'the philosophical grounding of Dnyandeva, as evidenced in the *Dnyaneshwari*, is more or less of the *Advaitic* kind, though occasionally here and there some concession is made to the other schools of the *Vedānta*. Sir Ramkrishna Bhandarkar once expressed his great inability to understand how the Maratha Saints could reconcile *Advaitism* with *Bhakti*.' On this R. D. Ranade makes the comment :

'It is exactly this reconciliation which is made in Mysticism generally, and more particularly in the Mysticism of the Maharashtra school which is worth while noting. The philosophical foundation of the *Amritanubhava* is somewhat in a different line. There we see how Dnyandeva is under the influence of the philosophy of the *Shiva-Sutras* when he refers to such terms as *Pinda, Pada Shiva* and *Shakti*.' And again later ; 'Dnyandeva's spiritual Mysticism reconciles both Monism and Pluralism. "Not in the

Monism of Shankaracharya, nor in the Dualism that is quite satisfied to remain two, but in the spiritual experience that transcends and includes them both, is peace to be found" (Macnicol). It is not our busniess here to enter into a philosophical discussion of the nature of Mysticism. But we may say that it does not regard the duality of devotion and the unity of mystical experience as contradictory of each other.'

Pioneers of Indian Religious Reform

If we are disposed to pass severe judgments on the *bhakti* saints in Mahipati's biographical and autobiographical pages for their habitual references to the Pauranic stories which are often marred by such easy-going morality, let us remember on the one hand that such stories provided the chief, if not the only, quarry in that age for religious vocabulary and meditation in the peoples' vernacular ; and on the other hand that these same *bhakti* saints, by their experience and message of a Personal God, raised against themselves the cry of Hindu conservatism, 'Our religion in danger!' How fierce the persecution they incurred is clear from many of Mahipati's stories, some of which are epic in character; for example, the opposition Eknath encountered from the orthodox Hindus at Paithan on the Godavari and the monumental patience and charity with which he confronted it. When we remember how novelty of all kinds, religious novelty in particular, is ever an affront to love of ease, and how the followers of Hindu *bhakti* were regarded as endangering all that was counted dear and best in immemorial Hinduism, we shall not be slow to give the meed of praise due to those intrepid religious reformers represented by the pioneers of the *bhakti* school, even though we today now see that there were still clinging to their message some of the defects of the teaching which they were slowly outgrowing. Considerations such as these compel the conclusion that the followers of the *bhakti* school, both in their noble protest against the unsatisfying conception of a Monistic, Pantheistic, Impersonal God, and in their fearlessness as religious pioneers in those dark and stormy times, are to be regarded as the heralds of the nobler and purer India for which we all still labour and aspire.

Political India's Need of Religion

We are convinced that in these intense days when India's political future is trembling in the balance, there is more need than ever that India's people should imitate the pioneers of the *bhakti* school by keeping the spiritual vision fixed on the high destiny of the individual soul. Only so can individual leaders be inspired for the vast tasks of reconstruction that await the Indian nation. Of course, if we are to follow to their strict logical issue the tenets laid down by the ancient Sages of India's *Advaita Vedānta*, no rational being should concern himself with politics, for 'there is a rift, an irreconcilable opposition, between India's present occupation with politics, and the ancient philosophy of the *Advaita Vedānta.*' Much the same may be said of those who lose themselves in the 'ecstatic' extremes of *bhakti* moods, for though little children are not trodden to death as in the case of Gora the Potter, it yet remains a sad blot on the *bhakti* pilgrim centre of Pandharpur that its appalling infant death rate has sometimes figured among the very highest in India. Modern India, however, is very painfully realizing that it is not by solitary contemplation of the Deity, either by the *Dnyana Marga* of pantheistic philosophy or by the *Bhakti Marga* of devotional ecstasy, that her needy millions will rise to their destined greatness. Indeed, India is today in danger of swinging to an extreme in the other direction as seen in the tendency (not unnatural in view of many facts) of many of her most earnest sons and daughters to make politics their religion. But even the politically-minded will never be inwardly satisfied either by political activity or by social service.

Helping 'Things Human' By 'Things Divine'

In his interesting book, *East And West In Religion* published a few months ago, Dr Sir S. Radhakrishnan relates a story told by Aristoxenes of the third century B. C. about the visit of an Indian philosopher to Socrates. 'Socrates told the Indian stranger that his work consisted in enquiring about the life of men and the Indian smiled and said that *none could understand things human who did not understand things divine.*' The words we have italicized have a very real message to India at this momentous hour in her history, and Dr. Radhakrishnan makes the double comment: 'It is a common temptation, to which Indian thinkers have fallen more than once victims, that spirit is all that counts while life is an indifferent illusion, and all efforts directed to improvement of man's outer life and society are sheer folly;' but on the other hand, 'Rabindranath Tagore uses the visible world as a means of shadowing forth the invisible,' for 'he touches the temporal with the light of the eternal.' Happy the nation that has two sons such as Rabindranath and Gandhiji who, despite their contrasts and (may be) their defects, so constantly amid all the national struggle 'touch the temporal with the light of the eternal.' Our own deep conviction is that if, in the social, moral and religious revolution that is convulsing India far more deeply than are politics or economics, her people will but follow the light that comes from two such sons and from all other sources, then, however revolutionary the changes, religious or political, that may sweep over the land, 'nothing which is beautiful and good in India's heritage need be lost.' It is because we believe Mahipati's stories help to build a bridge of passage from ancient India to

the new India that is to be that we send them forth as a preparation for the fuller light that is dawning everywhere in wonderful Hindustan.

Request, Acknowledgment, Recognition

We would fain crave the indulgence of our readers for the defects that must of necessity mar the pioneer translation of so extensive and difficult a piece of work as is the *Bhaktavijaya*, and prepared for the press under such difficult conditions as these two volumes have had to be. With the chief author gone from this mortal sphere before printing had begun, followed by his companion in authorship when the second volume was only half printed, it has sometimes appeared as if the task could not be completed.

A special word of gratitude is due to the cooperation of the entire staff at the Aryabhushan Press, Poona; their uniform patience, courtesy and help have alone made possible the publication of this work. In this as in so much else besides they have shown themselves worthy to be called 'Servants of India.'

Finally, it gives us pleasure to inform our readers that the first nine volumes in this Poet Saints of Maharashtra series have received the recognition of the Director of Public Instruction, Bombay Government, by his sanction of their use in teachers' libraries. This was signified in his Office Notification No. 86 (*a*) -I-C of 15th May, 1934, and published in Part II of *The Bombay Government Gazette* dated May 24, 1934.

June, 1934,
United Theclogical College of Western India,
7 Sholapur Road,
Poona Camp:
Office of the Poet Saints of Maharashtra Series

J. F. Edwards

BHAKTAVIJAYA

BY

MAHIPATI

VOLUME II

CHAPTER XXXI

RAMDAS OF DAKUR

Obeisance to Shri Ganesh. Obeisance to Shri Krishna.

STORIES OF THE SAINTS BURN UP SIN

1. Victory to Thee, the Husband of Rukmini, Dweller at Dwarka. Mover of the heart, Cloud of intelligence, Father of Brahmadev, Ornament of Thy *bhaktas*, Slayer of the monsters, Shri Krishna. 2. Victory to Thee, Pervader of the universe, Lord of all, Giver of the gift of final deliverance, infinitely generous, Purifier of the sinful, Saviour of the world, Husband of Radhika, Govinda. 3. Victory to Thee, who hast taken forms with qualities, O cloud-dark One, the most beneficent Being, Dweller in the universe, *Atmaram* (Divine Spirit). May I have love of Thee in my worship. 4. Victory to Thee, Dweller on the banks of the Gomati, *Guru* of the world, Lord Ranchhod. Let the shadow of Thy mercy fall upon me so that my heart may remain steady at Thy feet. 5. Victory to Thee, the Bee on the lotus-heart of Thy *bhaktas*. Thou who dost exist and art intelligence and joy, Root of joy, place my heart at Thy lotus-feet. Do this for me, O Govinda. 6. Being my Helper, assist me to describe the wonderful stories of Thy *bhaktas*, by which the ears of Thy hearers in their love are delighted.

RAMDAS OF DAKUR AS PILGRIM TO DWARKA

7. And now listen, you pious people, to the interesting

story, infinitely pure. As this story falls upon the ear, all one's sins are burnt away in a moment's time. 8. Seeing he *bhakti* of Ramdas, the antique idol (of Krishna) at Dwarka came to Dakur; Dwarka is three hundred miles beyond Dakur. 9. There was a Brahman there by name of Ramdas, supremely pious and wise. He used to beg for uncooked food and with it he supported his family. 10. He was always desireless and contented. All mental unrest was put aside. Day and night he continually repeated God's name. 11. On the *Ekadashi* (the eleventh day) of every fortnight he was accustomed to go to Dwarka. Ramdas in devotion held to this regular rule. 12. In a piece of *Saya* wood he scooped out a place, and in it he planted the *tulsi*. Holding this in his hand he used to go to Dwarka. 13. As he walked along the road full of love, he continued describing with joy the goodness of Hari. He had abandoned all interest in his body and was full of *vairagya* (the idea of indifference to worldly things). 14. Whenever Dwarka came into sight his heart was full of supreme joy, just as when a miser suddenly comes upon some money as he walks along a road; 15. or as when a young bride has been roughly treated at the house of her mother-in-law and sees her own home she is full of joy; or just as men rejoice when after a season of drought, clouds moisten the earth. 16. Repentant in heart, he would bathe at the bank of the Gomati, and then after *manas-puja* (worshipping God in his heart) he would go to the great door of the temple. 17. Making there a prostrate *namaskar* with reverence and putting aside all pride of body he was accustomed to say, 'O God, I am a devoted suppliant of Thine. End my rebirths and redeaths.' 18. He carried the *tulsi* plant along with him. With reverence he used to pluck off a flower and give it to God and after worshipping the Lord of *Vaikunth* (heaven), he would plead pitifully in devotion. 19. He used to say, 'O Purifier of the sinner,

One with the eagle banner, this is my worship as a helpless one.' Then making a *namaskar* to God he was accustomed to return to Dakur. 20. He used to remain one day in his house, and then start again on his journey. For twenty-five years he had made these trips to Dwarka.

KRISHNA'S REQUEST TO BE TAKEN FROM DWARKA

21. His body had now become weak. Old age had come upon him. On one occasion therefore he came to Dwarka and thus pleaded with God: 22. 'My body has become weak. I have now no more strength to come here. Love me still, dear Lord.' With this he placed his head at the god's feet. 23. Tears flowed from his eyes and he was not able to continue his praise. He then said, 'This is the last time I shall see Thee. I shall not be able to come again.' 24. As Ramdas said this the Dweller in the universe was stirred with emotion. With His four arms He held his *bhakta* in tight embrace. 25. God said to Ramdas, 'You have suffered much for my sake. I owe you much for your service. I can never repay you. 26. Your service has been great. Now take Me to your town.' Ramdas said to Him, 'O Krishna, how am I to take Thee?' 27. God said to him, 'I will give My chariot. Harness the horses and place Me in the chariot at night and start. I will come to you.' 28. Ramdas then brought the chariot and seated in it the dark-blue complexioned One, and with love in his heart the Lover of His *bhaktas* came to Dakur. 29. Ramdas now said, 'O Bhagwant, where shall I hide Thee? When the priests hasten from Dwarka here, they will punish me.' 30. At dawn at Dwarka the priests came at the hour of the wave offering, and to their amazement the idol was not in the temple.

RAMDAS, ACCUSED BY DWARKA PRIESTS OF THEFT, TELLS A LIE

31. As they thought about the matter one of them said 'Ramdas was here, and he must have taken the god away.

I see the tracks of the chariot on the road.' 32. The priests having seen the chariot-tracks, all of them came to Dakur. But Ramdas had taken the idol and had thrown it into the pond. 33. The priests said to Ramdas, 'You have brought the idol from Dwarka. Show us where it is.' Such was their request. 34. Ramdas told them a lie: 'I did not bring the Life of the world here. Search in my house for Him, that Ornament of His *bhaktas*, that supreme Spirit.' 35. The priests then went into the town and searched from house to house. They examined every tank and well. 36. Then they began to investigate a pool of water outside the village. The idol of Krishna was struck with a dagger in the chest and blood gushed out from it. 37. Reasoning in their minds on this, they said, 'We have found Lord Ranchhod.' They then dived into the water and drew out the Husband of Rukmini. 38. Then bringing a chariot there they quickly placed the idol in it. Ramdas became greatly concerned and spoke to God. 39. He said, 'O Lover of Thy *bhaktas*, Helper of the lowly, art Thou going to abandon me and go away? For Thy sake, O Husband of Rukmini, I told a lie.' 40. The Life of the world came into his meditation and said to His *bhakta*, 'Let your mind be at rest, and continue your worship of me. 41. Placing my hands upon my side I remain at the door of Pundalik. So I shall for ever remain with you at Dakur.'

HIS OFFER TO GIVE GOLD IN WEIGHT EQUAL TO THE IMAGE

42. Ramdas then replied, 'The priests will take Thee away and how shall I prevent this? I do not know.' 43. The merciful One then said to him, 'Go to the priests and promise them gold equal to my weight. 44. Your wife's nose-ring weighs a grain, I will become of that weight and will stay with you here.' 45. Ramdas, happy in heart, went to the priests and said, 'Since I have brought

the idol from Dwarka, let it remain here. 46. I will give gold of the same weight as the idol.' This promise was agreeable to all, for Narayan is the giver of reason. They said, 'Bring the god here. 47. Going to where the towns-people were seated, he said to them 'I am going to give gold to the priests equal to the weight of the idol. 48. In that case the idol will become mine. All of you be witnesses of this.' The crooked-minded laughed as they heard these words. 49. They said, 'You are weak, poor, and without anything. You have not even food enough to eat. How can you give gold? We are surprised.'

HARI'S MIGHT IS ABLE TO REMOVE HIS *BHAKTAS'* WEAKNESS

50. Ramdas exclaimed, 'The mighty Hari has come to my house and yet you call me poor; yo seem to feel no shame in your heart at this. 51. The Daughter of the Ocean (Lakshmi) came suddenly to the house of a poor person to give a gift. To call such a person poor shows your foolishness. 52. If in a box of iron a touchstone is suddenly found, it is useless to speak of the former value of the box. Why should one weary his tongue by such talk? 53. If the Ganges water flowed into the sewerage of a town, then anyone who might find fault with it would bring blame on himself. 54. When Sarasvati is pleased with a dumb person and teaches him to study, then anyone who calls him a fool will bring blame on himself. 55. So even when the Husband of Lakshmi, Lord of *Vaikunth* (heaven), is pleased with me, they do not hesitate to call me weak.' 56. Some people remarked, 'Let us watch this fun and we shall bear witness.' The scales were fixed and the Husband of Ramā (Krishna) was put in one. 57. The priest said to him, 'Go and bring your gold.' Ramdas at once went to his house. Holding the nose-ring in his fist, he at once returned. 58. People said to him, 'Show us the gold; though you went to your house you have

come back empty-handed.' 59. Opening his fist, the people began to scoff, saying, 'We think this will make a great quantity of gold!' 60. Then Ramdas, joining his hands palm to palm, prayed to the Husband of Rukmini, and said, 'O Helper of the helpless, Holder of the *Sharang* bow, Saviour of the lowly, Shri Krishna. 61. Satyabhama gave to Narad a gift of Krishna but in return he accepted from Rukmini a *tulsi* leaf and gave her the victory of securing Him. 62. I am poorer than she. Let Thy pride in me remain.' Saying thus he placed the gold that weighed a a grain in the scale. 63. As the nose-ring was placed in the scale, He in Whom is the Infinite universe rose to its level. The *bhakta* cried out 'Victory, Victory' and the gods threw down flowers. 64. They exclaimed, 'Blessed blessed are you, Ramdas, for you have bought God. You gave a nose-ring, and acquired for yourself the Lord of Dwarka.' 65. They said 'Blessed, blessed is your *bhakti*. Blessed, blessed are your good deeds.' The priests then returned to Dwarka.

A NEW IMAGE INSTALLED

66. There they made a new idol, and installed it in the town of Dwarka. The idol of Krishna remains at Dakur because of Ramdas. 67. Today people still go to Dwarka, but first they come to Dakur to see and worship Krishna and then they go on to Dwarka.

68. The next chapter will arouse interest. It is about the ancient idol at Mathura. Seeing the *bhakti* of a celibate, the ancient idol of Mathura will come to Hardwar. 69. God records many lives and increases the glory of His *bhaktas*. Mahipati in his love describes His goodness.

70. *Swasti* (Peace)! This book is the *Shri Bhaktavijaya*. In listening to it the Lord of the world will be pleased. Listen then, you God-loving, pious *bhaktas*. This is the thirty-first deeply delightful chapter: it is an offering to Shri Krishna.

CHAPTER XXXII

KALYAN AND NIRADHAR THE CELIBATE

Obeisance to Shri Ganesh. Obeisance to the Lord of Dwarka.

KALYAN AND NIRADHAR AS PILGRIMS

1. Let the hearers listen with reverence to the infinitely holy story of how the ancient idol at Mathura went to Hardwar. 2. A pilgrimage had gathered at Rameshwar at the night-festival in honour of Shiva. Two Brahmans from the Northern country had at that time arrived there. 3. Both of them lived at sacred bathing-places. Both were holy Brahmans and indifferent to worldly things. By day and by night they worshipped Hari in their love. 4. Asking one another about their domestic affairs, one of the Brahmans said to the other, 'All my family live at Hardwar.' 5. The other replied, 'My birthplace is the country of Gaud. But I have here no mother, father, brother, or any close friends aside from Hari. 6. Visiting sacred places, and the seven salvation-giving cities, I have now come to Rameshwar. I am as a *brahmachari* (a chaste unmarried man) and Niradhar is my name.' 7. Kalyan the Brahman hearing these words was pleased. Both of them then joined together and visited the sacred bathing-places and sacred cities. 8. Day and night they sang the description of the good deeds of Shri Hari, and they discussed among themselves publicly what was soul and what was not soul. 9. Afterwards visiting together many sacred bathing places, the two finally came to Mathura. They bathed at the banks of the Jumna and then went to worship Krishna. 10. They remained there three nights but suddenly Kalyan had a chill. Although he used the best remedies, the chills and fever would not leave him. His body became very thin. 11. According

to one's former deeds suffering never leaves the body, just as the moon experiences consumption (waning of its phases), and as Indra has a thousand holes (in his body). 12. Ill luck unceasingly persecuted Shiva which made Him exceedingly sad; he then took deadly *Halahal* poison and thereby His throat became blue.

NIRADHAR NURSES SICK KALYAN

13. Well, to continue the story. The two remained at Mathura. The *Brahmachari*, just with the intention of obliging others, continued his kind service of caring for Kalyan. 14. Those who are called saints in this world but who have in their hearts no compassion for creatures can·never attain Shri Hari even to the end of time. 15. But this *Brahmachari* was not like that. He was the very embodiment of speaking the truth, of kindness to others, and of compassion towards all creatures. 16. The *Brahmachari* sat near him day and night and gave him medicine and a wholesome diet. For six months Kalyan lay there in his bodily suffering. 17. During all this time the *Brahmachari* remained near him and cared for him day and night. He was continually praying, 'O merciful One, O *Vanamali* (Krishna), make him better.' 18. Finally the time of suffering ended and Kalyan regained his health.

NIRADHAR'S KINDNESS REPAID BY A MARRIAGE OFFER

Kalyan said to the *Brahmachari*, 'From now you are my dear relative and close friend, my all-in-all (*or* my very god), 19. Your name is rightly 'The supporter of the supportless.' I can never repay your kindness, even during all my rebirths. 20. My wife, sons and daughters, all remain at my home. In this foreign land you, a *bhakta* of Vishnu, came to help me. 21. My daughter is unmarried at my home, a would-be-bride of eight years of age. If you will come to my home I will give her to you.' 22. The *Brahmachari* hearing him, said in reply, ' I shall never live the life of a householder. Why do you want to put me into the sorrowful domestic life?' 23. Kalyan said to him, 'How can there be any harm from the domestic life? Krishna Himself will undertake the burden of it. 24. I vow this in this holy purifying sacred city of Mathura. Accept the gift of my daughter, O *bhakta* of Hari, indifferent to worldly things.' 25. The *Brahmachari* said to him, 'You are now an old man, dwelling at sacred bathing places. When you go home you will find that your wife will not accept this proposition. 26. If I now accept your proposition, and later on if the marriage does not take place, then I shall feel that my life has gone in vain. 27. I shall be one without the life of a *Brahmachari* and at the same time without the home of a householder.' Kalyan said to him, 'I call Krishna as a witness to my proposition.' 28. Both then went to the great door of the temple and there worshipped the feet of Shri Krishna. He (Kalyan) seated the *Brahmachari* and poured water on his hands, 29. saying, 'I have given my daughter to you. Come to my house and there be married. Madhavrao (Krishna) of Mathura, Life of the world, is witness to this.' 30. After worshipping the feet of Shri Krishna, both hastened from there and after journeying for three weeks they arrived at Hardwar. 31. Kalyan went to his home but no one would speak to him. He had been living at sacred bathing places and was now aged in body. 32. All become your friends in times of prosperity but finally they abandon you. Therefore the mind should always be watchful.

KALYAN'S UNFILIAL SON AND CRITICAL WIFE

33. His son said to him, 'You have wandered a great deal but the end of your life has not yet come. We do not understand who this *Brahmachari* is whom you have brought here.' 34. When Kalyan was resting in his home, he said to his wife, 'When I was

at the sacred bathing place at Mathura, I suffered from chills and fever.' 35. She said to him, ' You have not laid up for yourself good deeds sufficient to enable you to die at the sacred bathing place. Now you have returned home to show your face here.' 36. Kalyan said to her, ' Listen to what I have to say. When life is given to one there is no death. In the company of this *Brahmachari* I have experienced much joy. 37. In a foreign country he gave me proper food and medicines.' She replied to her husband, 'What is there strange in that? 38. When anyone is in the company of others they always care for one another. You are now wearied, lie quietly and go to sleep.' 39. The *Brhmachari* who was sleeping near the door heard this conversation.

KALYAN'S WIFE RAISES OBJECTIONS

Kalyan then said to his wife, 40. ' When I was at the sacred city of Mathura I went to the great door of the temple, and there I agreed definitely to offer my daughter to this *Brahmachari*.' 41. His wife said to him, ' Make another marriage, and the daughter who may be born give *her* to him.' 42. Kalyan said to her, ' If you offer your daughter to a *bhakta* of Hari there is no end to your holy deeds. Do not break my promise to him.' 43. She replied, ' I would rather at once push my daughter into a well, or else keep her at home unmarried. 44. But I will never put my daughter into the home of a *bhakta* of Hari.' Kalyan asked his son but he too would not accept the proposition 45. On the next day both went to the door of the king's palace. There they related what had taken place at Mathura. 46. The Brahman said, ' O king, my promise has gone for naught. I feel that I shall have to go on the road to the city of death. 47. In my love I made a promise. Here at home my wife and son will not listen to it. O king, speak to them, and cause them to give my daughter to him.' 48. The king said to the Brahman, 'I do not feel that your words are true. When you made this agreement at Mathura, whom did you place as a witness?' 49. Nirashraya (the unsheltered) *Brahmachari* said to the king, 'The Lord of *Vaikunth* (heaven), the Enemy of Mura, the Dweller at Mathura, Shri Krishna, is the witness. 50. I place as witness Him by whose mere wish infinite universes are created and destroyed. He is the Ancient of Days, the Lord of Rukmini.' 51. Hearing him the king replied, 'You say you have placed the Husband of Rukmini as your witness. Let Him come here quickly, if He will, and bear the witness before us. 52. In that case I will cause your daughter to be given to this *Brahmachari*.'

NIRADHAR BRINGS KRISHNA AS WITNESS

Hearing these words the *Brahmachari* said, 'I will bring the Life of the world here to bear witness.' 53. He immediately departed and for three weeks he travelled. Arriving at Mathura he saw and worshipped the beautiful dark-complexioned One. 54. He said to Him, 'O God infinite and supreme, come now with me in order to bear witness. If Thou dost not come, my life as *Brahmachari* will have been in vain.' 55. God said to him, 'How can a stone idol walk?' The other replied, 'It will walk just as it can talk. 56. I am *Niradhar* (one without a supporter); Thou, O Hari, art my shelter. Now merciful One, Lord of the world, come with me as far as there.' 57. Hearing him say this, Shri Krishna quickly followed him to carry out the purpose of His *bhakta*. But He said to the *Brahmachari*, 'Do not look back at Me. 58. If you do look back, I shall stop in that very place.' Saying this the Life of the world walked along behind him. 59. This glorious and brilliant idol, with lustrous ornaments, spread light. On His feet the *Nepur* and the anklets tinkled. Walking all night they arrived at Hardwar. 60. The Pervader of the universe, having approached the city, was only a mile from it now. Here the Lord of the heart (Krishna) stood still. 61. The Brahman looked back and there he saw Krishna remaining standing. His brilliancy could not be contained in the very sky. He said to the Brahman, 62. 'I told you before that if you looked back I should remain there. Now go to the king and ask him to come here to meet me.' 63. The *Brahmachari* named *Nirashraya* (one without shelter) at once started. He entered the royal assembly and said:

KRISHNA'S IMAGE AS WITNESS

64. 'He who took the side of Ambarish and who showed contempt for the *Muni* Durvas, He, the Dweller upon the sea of milk, Giver of final deliverance, I have brought *Him* to give evidence. 65. He who killed Ravana, Kumbhakarna and Indrajit, and delivered the gods from prison, Raghav the Dweller in Ayodhya, Him I have brought to give evidence. 66. When He was at Gokul He went from house to house stealing butter. His mother fastened Him to the handle of her churn. The Lord of *Vaikunth* (heaven), the Enemy of Mura, I have brought here to give witness. 67. Having killed Kans and Chanur, He installed Ugrasen over the kingdom. The Life of the world I have brought to Hardwar to give evidence. 68. When pure Draupadi was insulted by Dusshasan, the hand of the Infinite One clothed her with raiment. The Advocate of His *bhaktas*, Husband of Rukmini, I have brought here to give His testimony.' 69. Hearing the *Brahmachari* say this, all the people were greatly astonished. The king rushed forward to worship the Brahman's feet. 70. The king started to welcome Krishna. There were eagle banners. Drums and musical instruments sounded loudly. The king went to receive the Brahman, and the *Vaishnavas* shouted out the names of God. 71. There took place at once a united cry of 'Victory, Victory.' The gods showered

down innumerable flowers. The noble Yadava (Krishna) had come from Mathura to give His evidence. 72. While the saints and good people were singing the God's praise, the king came and prostrated himself before it. He saw the idol in its brilliancy and with its beautiful four arms. 73. Ornaments glistened in its crown. Around its waist was the yellow robe. Seeing the noble Yadava thus, all rejoiced. 74. The king then asked the *bairagis*, saints and *bhaktas*, 'You are accustomed to go to Mathura. Is this the very idol from there?' 75. The saints said to the king, 'This is Shri Krishna Who dwells at Mathura, the Life of the world, Who has now rushed to carry out the purpose of His *bhaktas*.'

NIRADHAR'S MARRIAGE

76. The king said to the rich citizens, 'Prepare at once whatever is needed for the bride. 77. I shall perform the duties on the side of the bridegroom.' Hearing this, arrangements for the wedding were made and a great pavilion was erected, *Panch Kos* (ten miles) in circumference. 78. Hearing the news that Narayan Himself had come to the wedding, an innumerable number of learned people assembled for the glory of the *bhakta*. 79. The Husband of Lakshmi having come there, no lack of anything was felt. Innumerable instruments were played and the gods came to look on. 80. When the marriage curtain was held up the Brahman said, 'May Bhagwan the Dweller at *Vaikunth* (heaven) protect this bride and bridegroom. 81. He who took the form of a fish, and killed the *Daitya* Shankha by dashing him on a stone, may He, Dweller on the sea of milk, Holder of the disk (Krishna), protect this bride and bridegroom. 82. When Pralhad was persecuted, God came out from the pillar, so may Bhagwan in the form of a half-man and half-lion protect this bride and bridegroom. 83. Eating dirt at the house of Nand. He opened His mouth to His mother and showed in it the

whole universe; may He, the Son of Yashoda, the Enemy of Mura, protect this bride and bridegroom. 84. He who removed the used-up plates at the house of Dharma and in many ways protected the Pandavas, may He, the Lover of His *bhaktas*, Shri Hari, protect this bride and bridegroom. 85. And now, in the *Kali Yuga*, the Life of the world has come walking from Mathura. May He, Shri Krishna, Dweller at Mathura, protect this bride and bridegroom.' 86. Hoving repeated this eight-verse formula, the Brahmans completed the marriage. The festival continued for four days, and then people saw the wedding parties on their way.

GOD THE CREATOR OF HIS *BHAKTA'S* FAITH

87. The idol has remained at Hardwar, and a new idol was installed at Mathura. Proud of His *bhaktas*, Shri Hari has performed many wonderful deeds. 88. Seated at many sacred places He has saved His *bhaktas*. Just as anyone conceives of God in reverence, God becomes like that to him. 89. In this Southern country at Shri Pandhari, in the Western country in the city of Dwarka, and in the North at Hardwar, He waits for His *bhaktas*. 90. In the East is Jagannath (Lord of the world); His four-armed idol is glorious. And now may the hearers with quiet attentive minds listen to the further stories of the *bhaktas*.

91. In the next chapter we shall have the interesting story of the *avatar* of Akrur by name of Surdas. The narrative about him is exceedingly delightful. Let the hearers listen with reverence. 92. Shri Pandurang may be called a lake of joy. The stories of the *bhaktas* may be called great lotus flowers. Mahipati as a bumble bee comes there and drinks of their honey.

93. *Swasti* (Peace) ! This book is the *Shri Bhaktavijaya*. In listening to it the Lord of the world will be pleased. Listen then, you God-loving, pious *bhaktas*. This is the thirty-second very delightful chapter; it is an offering to Shri Krishna.

14

CHAPTER XXXIII

SURDAS THE BLIND SAINT

Obeisance to Shri Ganesh. Obeisance to Shri Gopal Krishna.

KRISHNA'S WIFE SATYABHAMA, AKRUR AND KRISHNA'S CURSE

1. In the *Kali Yuga* the story of the *bhakta* Surdas is a very special one. Let the saints and all good people listen to it with attention. 2. During the Krishna avatarship at Dwarka, Satyabhama was His specially loved wife. Suddenly at her house the *bhakta* Akrur arrived. 3. Satyabhama gave him a seat and Akrur sat down after paying her his respects. Without any hesitation she told him her affairs:—4. 'Shri Krishna does not come to my house as He formerly did. Now, Akrur, explain things to him, and bring us together. 5. Shri Hari is subservient to you. I know this in my heart. Akrur, beseech the Enemy of Mura, and cause me to meet Him. 6. This fire of separation has severely burnt me. Again and again I beseech you, O Akrur, to cause me to meet the Son of Vasudev. 7. To whom shall I tell this secret matter, and who will look upon me with an eye of compassion? Now go at once, and cause me to meet Him, the Lord of the world. 8. Although He has sixteen thousand homes for His wives, still He sits at the home of Rukmini. Cause me now to meet with this Pervader of the Universe, the Enemy of Mura.' 9. Akrur thought to himself, 'If Shri Hari does not come at once, this beautiful one will give up her life. 10. Then Shri Krishna will be angry with me.' Realizing this fact, the *bhakta* Akrur himself took the form of Krishna. 11. He said to her, 'O mother, regain consciousness. I will bring Hari at once.' So Krishna Himself appeared at once to her sight and stood before her.

AKRUR CURSED BY KRISHNA

12. Shri Hari then said to Akrur, ' What was the thought in your mind, that when I was not at home, you took a false guise? 13. Therefore, Akrur, in the *Kali Yuga* amongst the mortals you will become blind. ' And turning to Satyabhama He said, ' In the *Kali Yuga* you will be a maidservant.' 14. The *bhakta* Akrur hearing these words joined his hands together palm to palm and thus pleaded: ' O *Atmaram* (O God), Thou knowest perfectly the thoughts of my mind. 15. If Thou should not come at once, Satyabhama would give up her life. In order to give her courage, O Life of the world, I took Thy form. ' 16. Hari replied, ' I know, O Akrur, the effort you are making. In the *Kali Yuga* you will become an *avatar* for the salvation of men. 17. Outwardly I have cursed you but there is no hatred in my heart.' Akrur replied, 'Thou art Mother and Father. In the *Kali Yuga* give me the vision of Thee.' 18. Hari replied, 'When you are blind, you will meet with the maidservant Satyabhama and I will manifest Myself at that time, and unite you with My essential form.'

BLIND SURDAS AS AKRUR'S *AVATAR*

19. In the country where Mathura is situated, a great saint Surdas appeared as an *avatar* of Akrur. Although blind from his birth, day and night he repeated the names of the Lord of the universe. 20. When sitting down, when sleeping, when eating, he was constantly thinking of Hari. And in the privacy of his heart he remembered the former events of his having been a *yogabhrashta* (one whose austerities have not been completed). 21. With love he performed his *kirtans*, and sang the names of God in verses he composed. Continually composing poetry, he called upon the Good Being. 22. Now it happened on a certain day, that a pilgrimage took place at Mathura and

Surdas himself went there to see the idol of Shri Krishna.
23. At the great door of the temple he lovingly made a prostrate *namaskar.* Joining his hands together palm to palm he brought the form of God into his heart. 24. He exclaimed, 'O Shri Krishna, Purifier of the sinner, Ocean of compassion, Delight of the heart, I had committed no fault. O Life of the world, why didst Thou curse me? 25. At the time of the *avatarship* of Krishna I was Akrur and I committed only one fault. Such is the witness that my heart gives me, O Govinda. 26. Kans sent me to Gokul to fetch Thee. When I went there Yashoda felt so sad. 27. When I was taking Thee away, Yashoda wept. Her anger then, O Gopal, is troubling me now. 28. The dissatisfaction of the people of Gokul, as I took Thee from them, has been visited upon me I think. 29. The *Gopis* (cowherdesses) loudly wept. They called out, "Give us back Shri Krishna as a gift in charity." I did not listen to them and therefore I am suffering this blindness. 30. Some let down their hair and wept aloud and some threw themselves before the chariot. Because of their anger, O Lord of the world, Thou must have cursed me. 31. Even if I did take the form of Krishna at the house of Satyabhama, it was no fault of mine, O Shri Hari. Thou art witness to this, O Enemy of Mura, Thou knowest the secrets of the heart. 32. Yet my heart bears witness that at Gokul I did commit a fault.' Tears now flowed from the eyes of Surdas.

SURDAS' SIGHT RESTORED

33. Listening to these pity-arousing words. Narayan was pleased and Surdas at once received his sight. 34. The *bhakta* saw before him with his own eyes the beautiful image of God with conch, shell, the disk and the club in His hands; four-armed in form, with His dark complexion and 35. His crown; His garland

reaching down to the feet and His *Kaustubh* jewel; His brilliant yellow robe wound around His waist; with his four *nepurs* and anklets jingling loudly; and dimming the light of millions of suns. 36. Seeing this form before him, Surdas prostrated himself on the ground. God said to him, 'I am pleased. Ask of Me any blessing.' 37. Embracing Him in love, Surdas said, 'I have this request only. I ask you to make my eyes as they were at first. 38. All through my life I never saw any object. Now I have stored up Thy form in my heart, O Govinda. 39. Though now Thou takest away my sight, I shall always have Thy form in my heart.' Hearing the words of Surdas the Lord of the heart (Krishna) smiled. 40. Bringing to His mind the form of Hari, this *bhakta* of His remained at Mathura. Now, you good people, listen to the story of what occurred further on.

TANSEN AND THE KING OF UJJAIN

41. In the city of Avanti (Ujjain) there was a pious, holy king. He had collected together five hundred singers. 42. The greatest among them was Tansen, an expert in music and exceedingly learned. At his singing, extinguished lamps became lighted. 43. The king said to Tansen at that time, 'I have hunted all over the world but I do not see any other singer better than you.' 44. Hearing this Tansen said, 'Do not say that. It is God who has made one better than the other. 45. "I am the Creator of the World," so said He who sits upon the lotus (Brahmadev). Then God created Vishvamitra and had him make all material things. 46. "My bed is the most majestic," thus said the ocean. God by the hands of Agasti caused him to sip its water. 47. Narad became proud, saying, "My singing is very beautiful," and Krishna then invited a bear and caused him to perform a *kirtan*. 48. When Maruti thought there was no monkey mightier than himself in the

world, Bharat subdued his pride. 49. Therefore no one should be called great or small.' Hearing these words of Tansen, the king was pleased. 50. The king said, 'If there are any singers now greater than you are, tell me of them quickly.'

SURDAS EXPERT IN SINGING

51. Tansen said to the king, 'The greatest expert in singing is Surdas at Mathura, the *avatar* of Akrur.' 52. The king said further to him, 'How many *ragas* (modes of songs) does Surdas sing ?' Tansen brought a handful of sand from the Bhagirathi river, 53. and said, 'He knows as many as there are grains of sand.' The king hearing this was surprised. He sent a palanquin to Mathura and brought Surdas from there. 54. Honouring him in many ways the king prostrated himself before him. Because Surdas was a *Vaishnava* he worshipped him, making him sit upon the golden throne. 55. All the singers then assembled and sat down in the assembly hall, and Tansen then pleaded with Surdas. 56. He said, 'Cause all to listen to a *Kirtan* sung by your lips. The king has invited you to come here with that purpose in mind.' 57. Surdas said to Tansen, 'I am a dweller in *Vaikunth* (heaven). From there I have come to this world of mortals. There I sing the qualities of Hari. 58. If you have a liking for the same, I will describe for you in brief the qualities of Hari.' Then taking the *vina* in his hand he properly tuned it with the seven musical notes. 59. As Surdas was singing, Ganesh sounded the cymbals, and Sarasvati taking the *vina* helped him in his sweet tone. 60. All the *Gandharvas* (heavenly singers) became absorbed in the music. So also Rambha, Urvashi and Menaka, and the Husband of *Ramā* (Vishnu) while he was performing the *kirtan* came there and danced in joy. 61. Even He whom the *yogis* when sitting on iron spikes are unable to bring into their contemplation, even

He danced in Surdas' *kirtan*. It was wonderful. 62. Although the *munis* perform austerities, they cannot attain Him by their ceremonial rites. Yet at the *kirtan* of Surdas He danced. This is novel indeed. 63. He whose limits are unknown by Indra, Chandra (the moon), Brahmadev and Shiva, even He in joy danced in front of Surdas. 64. Thus singing, he (Surdas) performed his *kirtan* with the loud acclaim of God's name. He described the good deeds performed in the *avatarship* of Krishna. 65. For one month Surdas remained at Avanti (Ujjain) city. He set all the men and women of the city to worshipping God. Full of love, they wagged their heads.

KRISHNA UNITES SURDAS AND THE HANDMAID IN HIS ESSENTIAL FORM

66. Now it happened on a certain day that the king went to his palace and his wives pleaded with him, joining hands palm to palm. 67. They said, 'The *Vaishnava bhakta* Surdas is continually singing of the good deeds of Hari. Our desire is that we should listen to his *kirtan*.' 68. Hearing this the king replied, ' Surdas is without sight, therefore you need not hesitate about bringing him here.' 69. The king's five hundred wives and all concubines sat together with modesty and undivided attention and they invited Surdas to come. 70. Seating him upon the golden throne they lovingly worshipped him. Surdas then took the *vina* and began to sing. 71. All these beautiful women became absorbed in listening to him. Now listen to what had happened then. In the avatarship of Krishna, the Lord Shri Krishna had cursed Satyabhama. 72. That beautiful daughter of Satrajit had now become a slave in the palace. Now as Surdas performed his *kirtan* she came rushing into the place. 73. Hearing his beautiful song she forgot all bodily consciousness, just as a deer when hearing the sound of music becomes lovingly absorbed in it. 74. As

she walked along at that time, she did not consider either land or water, and at that moment Surdas regained his sight. 75. Surdas said to her, 'The tank yonder is filled with water.' Then becoming at once ashamed, the women drew the curtain. 76. 'He has sight', they said to one another. Then being ashamed they sat hiding themselves. 77. Seeing them all alone, Shri Krishna manifested Himself there and He united in his own essential form Surdas and the maidservant (Satyabhama).

78. In the next chapter will come the wonderful story of the *Vaishnava bhakta*, Sena the barber. Let all the God-loving, wise and pious *bhaktas* listen with love to his story. 79. The Life of the world is pleased with those who listen with love to the stories of the *bhaktas*. So Mahipati joining hands palm to palm pleads with the pious *bhaktas*.

80. *Swasti* (Peace)! This book is the *Shri Bhaktavijaya*. In listening to it the Lord of the world will be pleased. Listen then, you God-loving pious *bhaktas*. This is the thirty-third deeply delightful chapter; it is an offering to Shri Gopal Krishna.

CHAPTER XXXIV
SENA THE BARBER

Obeisance to Shri Ganesh. Obeisance to Radha and Krishna.

A MEAN CALLING DOES NOT HINDER DEVOTION

1. Sena the barber was a great saint. He was intensely devoted to the worship of Hari. His story pleases the ear. Listen with reverence, you pious people. 2. Knowing that the things of this world are perishable, in his unconcern Sena was indifferent to all earthly things. Day and night he devoted himself to the worship of Hari. 3. The idol of the beautiful dark complexioned One, the four-armed One, clad in yellow garment, was in his house, and was beautiful in its brilliancy. 4. Bathing early in the morning, he worshipped Vishnu first. Having completed his regular performances, he would turn to his occupation in his domestic affairs. 5. The occupation of a barber is considered low and lower than that is slavery. Because of his bad deeds in his former birth, Narayan gave him his birth in this caste. 6. A goldsmith is much lower than the astrologer of the town. They are born in these castes on account of deeds in their former births. 7. The watchmen of the town and the scribes are higher than are the outcastes. God gave them births as these for bad deeds in their previous births. 8. The town police punishes the Mangs and the fisherman, yet it is God Who gives them birth as such, because of their bad deeds in their former births. 9. Butchers and the like, and sellers of cloth, are always merciless, yet it is God who gives them these births for their bad deeds in their previous births. 10. Listening to the list of caste-duties, the hearers must not cherish any anger. In the *shastras* the blame is laid upon the doers of evil but the fault is not yours.

SUPPLICATION DESTROYS SINS

11. If you accept any of these occupations in life, any fault which occurs through you will be unwittingly so. Therefore, good people, in listening to this moral law, you need not feel any repentance of heart. 12. He who is born in any of these particular castes and does not worship Shri Hari, he may be said to have fallen into the whirlpool of this worldly existence and he can never be freed from it. 13. Knowing this to be true, Sena the barber went as a suppliant to Shri Hari and at once his faults were destroyed. 14. A streamlet of the town, as soon as it offers itself to the Ganges (it becomes Ganges itself); so in going as a suppliant to Shri Hari, all faults are destroyed; 15. just as by contact with the touchstone, iron at once becomes gold, so in going as a suppliant to Shri Hari, all faults are destroyed; 16. just as when many sticks of wood are put in the fire they assume one colour; in the same way if one surrenders to Shri Hari all his sins are destroyed. 17. Though born into any low caste, if with a repentant heart one goes as a suppliant to Hari, the Saviour of the world makes him as Himself.

THE KING'S RAGE AT SENA

18. On a certain day Sena the barber with reverence sat worshipping. Just then the officer of the king came and called him to come out at once. 19. His (Sena's) wife told him as he sat worshipping God, that the royal messenger was calling him. 20. He said in reply, 'Go and tell the officer that I am not at home.' The call was repeated four times. 21. To each one who came to call Sena, she said, 'Sena is not at home.' Some evil-minded neighbour saw in this lie an opportunity and he went and informed the king. 22. He said to the king, 'Sena is sitting worshipping God.' Hearing what this evil-minded person said, the king grew very angry. 23. To begin

with, the king was an evil Muhammadan and when he told of this fault in Sena, it was as if liquor had been given to a monkey and had in addition the bite of a scorpion. 24. Remember that an onion has a very disagreeable odour and if to that some garlick is added, the odour is worse than before; similarly evil-minded men are of the same species. 25. The king said to his officer, 'Bind Sena and bring him here. Fasten him into a bundle and throw him into the river.'

KRISHNA SERVES AS BARBER

26. Knowing what was the king's intention, Narayan the Advocate of His *bhaktas* took the form of Sena, and came to the door of the King's palace. 27. He who is the very first being, Narayan the Dweller on the sea of milk, Recliner upon Shesha, He, Shri Hari, bringing His bag of barber's instruments, came to the door of the king. 28. He whom Brahmadev and other gods and the *rishis* contempate day and night, He, becoming Sena the barber, approached the king. 29. He whom *yogis* continually bring to their contemplation, sitting on the beds of spikes, He, seeing the distress in which Sena was, became a barber and went to the king. 30. He through whom the ten senses, the intellect and the mind all function, He the Pervader of the universe, the Cloud of intelligence, never gave consideration to His guise, whether it was high or low. 31. Krishna took off His crown, His earrings, His *Kaustubh* jewel, and taking on His shoulder the bag containing the barber's instruments, hurriedly started. 32. He for Whose knowledge they search the *Vedas* and the *Shastras* and humiliate themselves, He, Shripati, stood before the king and made him an obeisance. 33. The moment the king saw this form of a barber taken by Hari his anger at once disappeared. 34. Seating the king before him he shaved him, and then this clever Life of the world

shampooed his head. 35. The king said to him, 'You must remain here with me. Amongst all barbers I think you are the cleverest.' 36. 'But,' said the barber (incarnation of) the Life of the world, 'I pervaded the whole of the universe. There is no place empty of Me, no, not a single atom. 37. So it is not in My power to come and go, to do or to remain. Although I do, I am not a doer. Pervading all things, I am separate from all things. 38. In order to carry out this errand for my *bhakta*, I have for the moment taken this form with qualities. But I can never put aside My condition of being unmanifested.' 39. As the Holder of the *Sharang* bow (Shri Krishna) said this, the king was made very happy, and to be rubbed over his body he ordered fragrant oil. 40. Placing a square seat made of sandalwood from the mountains of Maila he came and sat upon it, and Sena rubbed the oil upon him. 41. In the beautiful cup set with jewels there was the *Mogra* oil. In it was reflected the beautiful four-armed One in a visible form. 42. His glorious crown was shining with lustre. Clothed in His yellow robe He appeared in His complexion of a dark black cloud. When the king saw this form he was filled with amazement. 43. Turning his eyes upwards he saw Sena who was rubbing him, and turning to the cup he saw reflected in it the form of Krishna. 44. His eyes were fastened on this form. The king lost all consciousness of body. He did not realize that he should say that the rubbing might cease. 45. His ten organs of sense, his intellect and his mind all became inactive and were absorbed in this essential form of God. The men in the king's assembly laughed at the king and said, 'He has become possessed.' 46. His servants then said to him, 'You must get up now and go to your bath, it is now midday, waken yourself, O king.' 47. The king said to Sena, 'Sit a while beside me. If you go back to your house I will give up my life.' 48. Shri Hari replied to him, 'I shall return quickly. O king, do not confine me in your heart.' 49. The king then brought a handful of golden coins, and placed them in the cloth of Sena the barber. 50. Hari went to Sena's house and putting his bag of barber's instruments on a peg, and throwing the golden coins into the bag, He became at once invisible.

THE KING'S UNEASINESS

51. The king after having performed his bath gave his command to his servants, 'You must at once go and invite Sena. 52. I do not need these things such as garments, ornaments and adornments; cause me to meet Sena the barber. 53. I do not care for dainty food, nor for fragrant powders, garments or fragrant flowers; invite Sena to come and cause me to meet him. 54. If he does not come at once, I shall lose my life. Cause me to meet at once that king of *bhaktas.* 55. The moment that I see him I shall be free from rebirths and deaths. Bring that *Vaishnava* Sena the barber and cause me to meet him.' 56. The king was entirely overcome and his servants were frightened. They then went to the house of Sena and requested him to come. 57. Sena replied, 'The king is angry with me.'

SENA AT THE PALACE

Still taking his bag of instruments on his shoulder he arrived at the door of the king. 58. The moment the king saw Sena he stood up to greet him and all the people of the king's assembly laughed to see this most extraordinary sight. 59. The king said to him, 'You were here early this morning and showed yourself in your essential form, being four-armed. 60. Show me the same form again.' So saying, he tightly embraced Sena's feet. Hearing the king say this, Sena the barber was full of astonishment. 61. Bringing the cup with the oil, the king made Sena look into it. There the four-armed One was not to be seen. He thought this a most wonderful miracle.

62. He exclaimed, 'Brother of the lowly, Purifier of the sinner, Dweller in *Vaikunth* (heaven), O Narayan, Delighter of the heart, for my sake Thou hast engaged Thyself in this lowly work. 63. Helper of the helpless, Husband of Rukmini, Father of cupid, beautiful with Thy dark complexion, Saviour of the world, generous Giver of the final deliverance, for my sake Thou didst perform this lowly work. 64. The *Vedas* and *Shastras* describe Thy good deeds, but they do not know the limit of Thy power. O merciful One, for my sake Thou didst accept this low occupation. 65. Brahmadev, Indra and Shiva do not know of Thy limits. Why didst Thou today for my sake take a bag of barber's implements upon Thy shoulder ?' 66. He then broke out into weeping and loud crying and was moved to great sobs. The king rushed up to Sena and held him by his feet.

ASSOCIATION WITH SAINTS

67. He said to him, 'By association with you, I have been able to see Krishna. How can I describe the power of association with the saints ? 68. It was by having met with Narad that the fisherman (Valmiki) wrote the *Ramayana.* Such is a *Vaishnava*, merciful and saviour of the dull and ignorant. 69. Through the favour of Vyas, Sanjaya had the privilege of listening to the *Bhagavadgita.* So through you I have had the sight of Shri Krishna. 70. Sena saw the coins which (God had thrown) into the bag of implements. He then distributed them among the Brahmans in the presence of every one. 71. The king became repentant and gave himself to the worship of Hari. Sena the barber was pleased, because Hari was pleased.

72. In the next chapter there will be the unusually interesting story about King Satvika at Jagannath. Listening to these stories wise men are made happy. 73. The Husband of Rukmini has caused me to compose

them according to His description. Mahipati beseeches his hearers to listen to them with love.

74. *Swasti* (Peace)! This book is the *Shri Bhaktavijaya.* In listening to it the Lord of the world will be pleased. Listen then, you God-loving, pious *bhaktas.* This is the thirty-fourth very delightful chapter.

CHAPTER XXXV

KING SATVIK AND KARMABAI

Obeisance to Shri Ganesh. Obeisance to the Lifter of the Mountain Govardhan.

1. Listen now, you hearers, to a most extraordinary story. As one drinks the supreme nectar of the story of the *bhaktas* he will at once experience their value. Diseases of this earthly experience will immediately disappear.

SATVIK'S LEFT HAND

2. At Jagannath there was a King by name of Satvik. Nothing aside from God was pleasing to his heart. 3. This sacred city of Jagannath Vadaya is truly a heavenly city amongst mortals. There the Life of the world lives in the *avatarship* of Buddha and there He performs all His *lila* (voluntary deeds). 4. That king living by the Eastern sea was rightly called *Satvik* (truthful). The eagle-bannered One was always very favourable to him. 5. Three times a day at the time of worship the king came and seated himself at the temple. Receiving as his favour a *tulsi* leaf he afterwards would sit down to eat. 6. Garments, ornaments, adornments and daily food he offered to God. If uninvited guests should come, the king himself gave them food, 7. He kept a light burning night and day in the temple. He provided a place for free food and gave to those he thought were worthy. Food and water he gave to every creature. 8. Now it happened on a certain day that the king sat by the great door of the temple. In order to pass the time, he began to play some gambling game. 9. Laughingly he threw down the dice and had no consciousness of what he was doing. Just then at the great door of the temple a priest came to distribute favours. 10. In order to receive a favour the king put forward his left hand. The

priest felt that this was a very strange act. 11. Because he presented his left hand the priest went back again in the temple. When the king had finished his playing dice he asked the people regarding the favours which the priest had been distributing. 12. They replied, 'When he distributed them around you put out your left hand. Therefore the priest went back again into the temple.'

THE KING'S REPENTANCE

Hearing this the king was startled. 13. 'My former deeds were wrong I know. Later they have appeared in the form of a dice. Discarding nectar, I have drunk intoxicating liquor, so I think. 14. Or it is as if I had allowed the wish-tree to wither away and gave water to the *sindi* tree; in playing with dice the same thing happened to me, I think. 15. Just as if in picking up charcoal a treasure of money should be lost, so the same has happened to me, I think, in playing with the dice; 16. or as if someone should take a handful of ashes and the *kasturi* (musk) paste should disappear; I think the same has happened to me in playing with the dice. 17. Driving away the royal swan, I kept a crow; I cut down the sandalwood tree, and planted a *hingan*; so I think the same has happened to me while playing with the dice. 18. Or just as when a Brahman gets up and goes away when he sees a Mang; so it had happened to me in playing with the dice.' 19. The king was very repentant and did not go again into the temple. As one who listens surreptiously to the service, the king sat quietly at the door of the temple.

THE CULPRIT PUNISHED

20. He said, 'My hand has committed a great wrong and I must punish it.' Saying this he devised a plan. 21. He called his minister, and told him his thought. 'When sleeping at night in my palace I am visited by a

ghost; 22. he puts his hand in through the window and I become greatly frightened; so you remain by my bed and cut off his hand.' 23. The minister replied, 'Your wish is my command. When the ghost appears I will cut off his hand.' He then took a sharp instrument and at night he sat hiding himself. 24. The lights were burning in the palace and the minister remained awake, waiting for the ghost. He proposed as soon as the ghost appeared that he would cut off his hand. 25. At that moment the king put out *his own* hand through a window and the minister took his instrument and immediately cut off the hand. 26. The moment the hand fell down the minister recognized it. He was overwhelmed with sobs and threw himself down upon the ground. 27. He mourned aloud. Just then the king came inside and said, 'My hand was my enemy, therefore I had it cut off. 28. Let your mind be at rest.' He then placed his hand in a palanquin, and sent it by the hand of messengers to the great door of the temple. 29. The king said to them, 'Go now to the great door of the temple and say to Jagannath, "Thou, O Husband of Rukmini, listen to the list of my many transgressions. 30. With an evil heart I played with dice, therefore I did not receive Thy favour; that which has transgressed Thy command I have sent to Thee in the form of my hand. 31. I find that among my organs of action my hand was the transgressor. I have therefore punished it, and sent it to Thee. 32. It may have killed some and they were innocent. It may have stolen some time from Thee. Therefore I immediately punished my hand and have sent it to Thee. 33. Intoxicated with pride, it may have hunted in the forest. That transgressor I send to Thee. 34. It had not worshipped Thee. It has been a great killer, an evil-doer and evil-minded. O Being of goodness, Thou knowest how great an evildoer it is. 35. It has not served the saints. It has not worshipped Thee, O Keshav. So I have sent this evil hand to Thee.

36. O Jagannath, punish it as it may seem right to Thee."'

THE WRONGDOER BEFORE GOD FOR DECISION

Giving this message to the messengers he sent them to the door of the temple. 37. They took the hand to the great door of the temple and told God in reference to it. There were cries of 'Victory, Victory', and the *Vaishnavas* showered upon it flowers and fragrant powder. 38. They exclaimed, 'Blessed is the king. Although engaged in domestic affairs he is indifferent to all worldly things. Putting the responsibility upon God he cut off his own hand. 39. Innumerable men and women receive their perishable bodies, but they do not complete the full purpose of life, because not holding in their hearts the Husband of Janaki (Rama). 40. Many men wander from country to country in order to gain their livelihood. They spend their lives in all kinds of ways but they do not die worshipping God. 41. The moment they are afflicted with a nine days' fever, they go through fourteen different fasts; but these unfortunate ones do not perform good deeds in this world by observing the *ekadashi* (eleventh day of the fortnight). 42. Even those friends quarrel if in their business a shell's worth is lost; but the shameless ones who have no good in them from their former births do not sing of the good qualities of Hari. 43. If robbers rob them of their wealth they wring their hands, and take no action; but the evil-minded do not make their lives at all valuable by spending their wealth on those who are worthy of it. 44. Such is the condition seen in the practices of this *Kali Yuga*. Many are desirous of these illusory things, but we know that King Satvik is a man of great devotion.' 45. Thus spoke the *Vaishnava* saints to one another. Suddenly an extraordinary thing took place. Let good people listen to it with love.

46. The hand which the king had cut off turned suddenly into a *davana* plant. It was taken at once and planted in a garden. 47. Priests then in their love brought the favours of Hari. The king had lost all concern for his body and he put out just the stump of the hand he had cut off. 48. But as soon as he put it out, it became just as it was before. The *bhaktas* therefore shouted, 'Victory, Victory,' and were greatly astonished.

THE STORY OF KARMABAI

49. Again listen, you pious people, to the recital of a most delightful story. The moment you listen to it the three kinds of affliction and all doubts will be destroyed. 50. Because Bhagwan is in the city of Jagannath in the form of Buddha, His *bhaktas* continually live there as it is a great sacred city. 51. There was a Brahman woman by name of Karmabai whose mind was ever at the feet of Hari. While she was with child her husband died. 52. She mourned bitterly. She was in great distress and at the end of nine months a son was born to her. 53. She exclaimed, 'O God Supreme, Jagannath, let this *bhakta* of Thine live.' The son grew from day to day. Then she had him married. 54. When his wife became with child Karmabai was greatly pleased. Just when her grandson was born, however, her son died. 55. She mourned for him day and night, but she controlled her mind and said, 'If this child but lives he will be of use to me.' 56. Karmabai took special care of him day and night. She never neglected her grandson even when she was sitting or when she was lying down or when she was eating. 57. Many days passed in this way, but the god of death took away the child, and Karmabai's heart felt no peace anywhere. 58. Mourning day and night she would exclaim, 'O merciful One, Shri Hari, why hast Thou placed me in this sad world?'

KARMABAI AND THE SAINTS

59. Just then some *sadhus* and saints who were on a pilgrimage to Jagannath arrived and took lodgings in the house of Karmabai. 60. Seeing her mental distress, they asked her for the reason of it and Karmabai told them just what had happened. 61. The *Vaishnavas* said to her, 'This world is of a sorrowful nature. Know for certain that there is not the least happiness here. 62. If one should sleep upon a bed infested with bugs, then it would only be as in a dream that he could see any happiness in this world. 63. If one is distressed with thirst, then he can only find happiness in this world by the satisfaction derived from seeing in a mirage floods of water. 64.. If one can live after ending life by drinking poison, only then can he find the happiness dreamed of in this world. 65. If a reader of *Puranas* can receive happiness by explaining *Puranic* stories to a deaf man, then only as in a dream can he find everlasting happiness in this world. 66. So now, Karmabai, give attention. All worldly things are perishable.' As the *Vaishnava bhaktas* said this, her heart melted. 67. Karmabai exclaimed to those *sadhus* and saints, 'I will do as you tell me.' They said to her, 'Day and night you must worship Jagannath.' 68. The *sadhus* preach according to one's worth. They have come as *avatars* into this mortal world in order to save sinners. 69. They have come into this mortal world as *avatars* in order to help men to listen to the praise of the good qualities of Shri Hari, and to give to them the happiness of love. 70. It is to teach knowledge to the ignorant and the dull-minded. They have come into this mortal world to sweep away the pride of evil men. 71. Lest the path of *bhakti* should become fouled and all men sink into worldly things, therefore *Vaishnavas* in the *Kali Yuga* have descended as *avatars* to this mortal world.

BEREAVED KARMABAI FONDLES GOPAL'S IMAGE

72. Well, Karmabai devoted herself to the feet of the saints. They took out of their things an image of Gopal and gave it to her. 73. The *Vaishnavas* said to her, 'Continue to worship it. Give to it the same love that you had given to your son.' 74. Saying this the *sadhus* went to live at the sacred bathing-places. and Karmabai's heart felt great joy. 75. Just as she used to play with her grandson, so now she acted crazily over the idol. The moment she saw it she would take away from it the effect of an evil eye and caress it in her love. 76. She would take warm water and bathe the idol as she used to do with her little child on her feet. Then placing the god in a cradle, with love she would swing it. 77. In her love she used to dress it in garments and adornments. Nothing else pleased her aside from the idol of Krishna. 78. Placing buttermilk and rice in a plate, she would present it to this image of Gopal and tell it stories. She would exclaim, 'Eat this, eat this, O Lord of the world; You are hungry.' 79. Seeing her feelings of devotion, Hari began to eat at her house. Just then a Brahman who had maintained a perpetual fire came to lodge there. 80. She had arisen early one morning and was feeding the god. The Brahman asked her in reference to it and she told him her story. 81. The Brahman said to her, 'Listen to my words, Karmabai, give attention. Perform your bath and then worship Shri Krishna. 82. If you make your food offerings to God with unclean clothes, He will not pay respect to them.' Hearing what he said, she replied, 'I will do as you say.' 83. The next morning arising early she cleaned the floor and the yard, and then she brought holy water and prepared to cook. 84. In performing her domestic affairs she was delayed and therefore Jagannath became hungry.

KRISHNA BEYOND EARTHLY RULES

Privately He went into the dream of the priest and told him what had happened. 85. 'At the house of Karmabai, a very orthodox Brahman was staying. He placed a doubt in her mind, and then hastened on his way. 86. He advised her to observe a very strict cleanliness and the offering of food is therefore delayed. Go to her at once and inform her. 87. The *Paramatma* (Supreme Spirit), the Pure Intelligence, One beyond all illusions, the *Atmaram* (Divine Soul) is never harmed by any bondage to religious deeds. 88. Although a Doer, He is still a Non-doer, and yet Witnesser of the hearts, of all creatures. He Who for the sake of His *bhaktas* has become an *avatar* can never be harmed by any bondage to religious deeds. 89. The Pervader of the universe, the Life of the world, in preaching knowledge of divine things, can never be harmed by any bondage to religious rites.' 90. The priest went and gave the information to Karmabai. She then brought the offering, and Hari in the presence of all ate from her hand. 91. Cries of 'Victory, Victory' followed the clapping of hands. All the assembly of *bhaktas* rejoiced. All the holy Brahmans were astonished. 92. They exclaimed, 'Where the sacrifices and *yoga* practices are, there Shri Hari does not come, but He is eating here from the hand of Karmabai. This indeed is a novel sight. 93. He Whom Brahmadev and other gods and Shiva continually contemplate in their hearts, He eats from the hand of Karmabai. This is novel indeed. 94. He Whom the various forms of *yoga* and various opinions continually search for, He eats from the hand of Karmabai. It is novel indeed.' 95. One said, 'Even Brahmadev is unable to describe the power of a *bhakta*.' All the people then worshipped the feet of Karmabai. 96. Even today at the sacred place of Jagannath, the god Jagannath gives the evidence of this. After the food of Karmabai arrives. then the offerings are presented.

97. In the next chapter there is the delightful story of the *bhakta*, Janajaswant. Mahipati says, 'Let all good people in love give their attention.'

98. *Swasti* (Peace)! This book is the *Shri Bhakta-vijaya.* In listening to it the Lord of the world will be pleased. Listen then, you God-loving, pious *bhaktas.* This is the thirty-fifth deeply delightful chapter.

CHAPTER XXXVI

JANAJASWANT AND SURDAS MADANMOHAN

Obeisance to Shri Ganesh. Obeisance to Shri Gopal Krishna.

I. JANAJASWANT THE MERCHANT SAINT

1. This is an auspicious day. The wise, God-loving hearers who have assembled here, having had all desires fulfilled, are here where the delightful stories are being related. 2. The merchant Janajaswant was a great *bhakta*, devoted to the worship of Rama. Listen, you wise and pious hearers, to his exceedingly delightful story. 3. He had five sons. He was a millionaire. His house was filled with every form of wealth. Still day and night he worshipped Shri Rama with love. 4. If uninvited guests appeared he gave them food. He gave respect to all *sadhus*. Those who asked alms of him were made happy. He sent no one away empty-handed. 5. His desire to give away money for charitable objects was great.

In the meantime his sons grew up but they were miserable evildoers. They turned away from the worship of Hari. 6. Just as the hater of Vishnu, Ravana, was born in the family of Pulastya, or as Duryodhan who was in the family line of the moon was a man with exceedingly many faults, 7. so from Janajaswant these *non-bhaktas* and evildoers were born. They did not know what right or wrong was. They were wicked rascals, most contemptible. 8. They had no love for giving charity. They would exclaim, 'The old man is crazy, what shall we do with him?' Such was their constant thought. 9. All men come to befriend one in prosperity, but finally they abandon him. Therefore one should always have a wakeful mind. 10. While the tongue is active, one should be relating the good deeds of Shri Hari.

While one possesses hands, one should worship Vishnu with devotion. 11. While one has feet he should without any shame dance whenever Hari's good deeds are described. While one has ears he should listen with fondness to the stories of the saints. 12. While one is in good health he should constantly go on pilgrimage; and while one has eyes he should look with love on the Husband of Rukmini.

JANAJASWANT'S SONS AND THE KING CONSPIRE AGAINST HIM

13. Janajaswant was alive to his duties to all men, but his sons and his wife did not like his deeds of charity. 14. They exclaimed, 'He is our enemy. He has ruined our business.' So they stole some of his money and hid it away. 15. Evil men do not like good men. Thieves do not like the moon to shine. An adulteress becomes irritated if she hears a faithful wife praised. 16. When the sun rises, owls think the time to die has come. Seeing a wise *pandit* fools are unhappy. 17. Seeing *sadhus*, revilers become supremely displeased. A man of physical weakness has no liking for a powerful and courageous man. 18. Seeing a Brahman devoted to good deeds, the wicked become very much disgusted. And so the wicked sons of Janajaswant raged in many ways against their father. 19. Therefore they said, 'Let us go to the door of the king, and tell him our complaint.'

PARRICIDAL SONS

They decided that they would kill their father. 20. The four men went to the king's door and told him their complaint. They said, 'Our father is a complete fool. He scatters his money according to his own wish. 21. While we possess money we consider it as yours, O king. Should you fall into any distress, it would certainly be of use to you. 22. So call him and punish him, O king.' Listening to the evil thoughts of these wicked persons the low-minded king became angry. 23. That exceedingly thoughtless king, having listened to their words and without giving the matter any further thought, sent word to Janajaswant to come to him.

PLACES FIT TO BE AVOIDED

24. Where a king is thoughtless, and his ministers wicked, where the water of a river is not seen, and where pious God-loving men do not live, one should immediately leave such a place. 25. The place where there are no good people and *sadhus* and where there is no praise of Hari, where there is no thought about the soul, where there is no listening to the *Puranas*, one should leave such a place. 26. Where there is no love for good deeds, where the king pays no attention to justice and morals, where unrighteous customs are prevalent, one should not seat himself in any company at such a place. 27. Where there are neither rich men, nor gardens, and where men are thoughtless, good men should not remain there a single moment.

JANAJASWANT TO BE DROWNED

28. The king said to Janajaswant, 'Why are you so obstinate ? You distribute your money to beggars without the knowledge of your sons.' 29. Janajaswant gave reply, 'That is my nature to be obstinate. With love for the worship of Shri Rama, I pay respect to *sadhus* and saints.' 30. Hearing him say this the king became full of rage; just as when a parrot speaks from within his cage, a falcon becomes angry. 31. Then the evil-minded king said to the sons of Janajaswant, 'With your consent I will kill your father.' 32. The sons then said, 'He is not our father; he is our enemy. Fasten him in a bundle, and throw him into the water.' 33. Janajaswant was then fastened in a bundle with stones in it and thrown into a pond in front full of water.

GOD SAVES JANAJASWANT

34. As soon as the Husband of Janaki (Rama) saw this He appeared for the sake of His *bhakta*. The Husband of Ramā took the form of a tortoise and held him on its back. 35. Janajaswant said to the king, 'The Lord of the heart is protecting me, just as He upholds the heaven without a pillar. 36. He who gives light to the sun and the moon, and by Whose light they revolve, He, the Pervader of the universe and the Lord of the world, protects His *bhaktas*. 37. During the *avatarship* of Rama, He made the stones float on the water. That Life of Janaki, the Son of Raghu, is my Protector. 38. In the form of a tortoise He has lifted Janajaswant up and is holding me in the air. Come and see this for yourself.'

THE KING'S PENITENCE

39. Hearing these words the king became repentant. He leaped into the water and drew Janajaswant out. 40. He untied the bundle with his own hands. He grasped the feet of Janajaswant and exclaimed, 'I have done wrong. Forgive me, O king of *bhaktas*.' 41. Having punished the sons he told them to go as suppliants to their father. They also accepted the command and prostrated themselves before him. 42. Having abandoned all evil thoughts, with reverence they worshipped their father. Seeing the miracle in the case of their father, God's *bhakta*, they now devoted themselves to the worship of Shri Rama.

II. SURDAS MADANMOHAN

SURDAS AS ROYAL OFFICIAL

43. Hearers, listen to another story. The story of Surdas Madanmohan is an extremely purifying one. Listen to this delightful story with its deep meaning. 44. King Akbar was ruling in Hastinapur (Delhi), and Surdas was an official under him. The king soon appointed

him to be an official in the district of Mathura. 45. It was here at Mathura, Gokul and Vrindavan, ancient sacred cities, that Shri Krishna, becoming an *avatar*, manifested all His *lila* (voluntary deeds). 46. Therefore many *Vaishnava bhaktas*, holy men, and many *Vairagis* (ascetics) live here. Although engaged in worldly affairs they are indifferent to worldly things and devote themselves to worship. 47. When giving garments and food to *Vaishnavas*, the Life of the world feels that He Himself has been supplied. Just as when the wishes of one about to be a mother are carried out, the child to be bornfeels satisfied; 48. and as a father rejoices, when he hears of the success of his son; so Krishna feels the same happiness when anyone reverences his *bhaktas*; 49. or as when water is lovingly given to the roots of a tree, all the branches are refreshed; so the Lord of Vaikunth rejoices when His *bhaktas* are reverenced in love, 50. or as a mother feels great pride when she adorns her infant child with ornamant; so Krishna rejoices at the constant reverence for *Vaishnavas*. 51. With this idea in his mind Surdas began to serve the *Vaishnavas*; he used to prepare dainty foods and lovingly feed the saints. 52. He used to fill carts with sweetmeats and milk-cakes, and send them to the saints. 53. In thus spending his money for worthy objects the Husband of Rukmini was greatly pleased. He said to Himself, 'Although Surdas is engaged in worldly business, still he lovingly worships My *bhaktas*.'

SURDAS SPENDS ALL MONEY IN CHARITY

54. Possessing this feeling towards the *Vaishnavas* he spent on them all the money he possessed. That threw the mind of Surdas into an ocean of anxiety. 55. He exclaimed, ' Now my own money has been spent. And my service of the saints will fall short. And if I do not provide dainty food for the *Vaishnavas*, then what is the use of my living this earthly life ?' 56. Then he thought to himself, 'I am in

charge of the king's revenue. I can spend that with a solemn purpose and feed the saints. 57. Although the king may become angry with me, he may even put me to death, still this earthly life of mine will have served its purpose.' He therefore decided definitely to do so. 58. For He said, 'Although I should give away my life, it would be in the service of *Vaishnavas*, and it would at once remove the terribly hard diseases of this earthly life.' 59. Thus thinking he broke into the treasury containing the money of the King. He had the noble idea of at once being of service to the *Vaishnavas*. 60. He had all kinds of dainty food prepared and began to feed the saints. He supplied the needs of the saints in Mathura, Gokul and Vrindavan. 61. After making an offering to God of garments and ornaments, he gave them to the saints. He built many free lodging-houses and gave them to all. 62. Thus he gave away more than eight million and ten thousand rupees on this occasion.

ACCUSED OF MISAPPROPRIATION

His assistant was an evil man and seeing what Surdas did he became very angry. 63. He went to Hastinapur and told the facts to the king. He said, 'You have appointed Surdas Madanmohan over the district of Mathura. 64. He has spent all your money in a wrong way.' When King Akbar heard this he became very angry; 65. just as when melted butter falls into a sacrificial fire, the ignorant say it has been wasted in vain; or as when one gives water to the *tulsi* plant, fools think of it as a waste; 66. or as when one has given food to one who asks for it, misers feel as though they had been robbed; or when *yogis* wander from bathing place to bathing place, those who live for enjoyment regard it as a crazy act; 67. or when Brahmans continually read the *Pavaman* [in the *Rig Veda*], the Muhammadans think that they are merely babbling; or when one lovingly reverences the saints, revilers think it a foolish thing to do; 68, so when Surdas spent money for the *Vaishnavas*, his evil-minded assistant thought that it was spent in vain. So when the king was told of what Surdas had done, his heart was convulsed with anger.

SUMMONED BEFORE THE KING

69. The king then sent his officers to go and call Surdas. He said to them, 'Tell Surdas to bring here at once all the money belonging to the district of Mathura.' 70. Having written such a letter he sent it by the hands of his messengers. He said to them, 'You must ask of him eight million and ten thousand rupees.' 71. The messengers of the king suddenly appeared at the house of Surdas. They surrounded his house and spoke with great anger. 72. They said, 'Two years have now passed, yet you have not given account. Akbar is therefore angry, and has called you to his presence. 73. Take all the money that has been entrusted to you from the district in your charge. If you do not bring all the money, we shall bind you and take you in accordance with the king's command.' 74. Surdas said in reply, 'The king has become angry needlessly. Out of the money I have purchased priceless jewels. 75. I think if these jewels are shown to the king, he will be satisfied. When an expert examines their value it will come to twice the value of the money.'

SURDAS' LETTER TO AKBAR

76. Saying this to them, Surdas went into his private apartment and by the hand of his wife brought out two boxes. 77. He filled them with crystals and wrote a letter to the king. He said, 'It is true, O king, that I have spent all the money for *sadhus* and saints. 78. I have spent in worthy objects more than eight million and ten thousand rupees, and Surdas absconded at midnight.' Such were the contents of the letter. 79. He put the letter

into one of the boxes and carefully locked them and placed his stamp upon them with his name. 80. He brought out the boxes and gave them to the messengers of the king who were sitting at the door. He said to them, 'I have purchased priceless things and kept them in my house. 81. It was already in my mind to come at once to see the king.' Hearing Surdas say this, the messengers were pleased. 82. They said, 'You are a wise man, and exceedingly alert for the work of your master. This being so, the king has certainly become angry with you neeedlessly.' 83. Surdas had dainty food of various kinds prepared and fed these messengers. He gave garments and ornaments to all and made them delighted. 84. He caused them to lie down and sleep and then at midnight he ran away and went into the jungle, lovingly to worship God.

SURDAS AS VAGABOND

85. When the whole night had passed and the sun arose, the messengers of the king arose and looked for Surdas. 86. They did not find him in his house. They hunted for him in the town with great earnestness and they hunted for him in the region around the town and in the jungle. 87. They said to themselves, 'From fear of the king, Surdas must have run away and is wandering to sacred bathing-places. When the king hears of this he will punish us.' 88. Having this fear in their minds, they sought ways of comforting themselves. They said, 'Surdas filled these two boxes with jewels and has placed them with us. 89. When we show these boxes to the king, he will never be angry with us.' Saying this they started on their way to Hastinapur (Delhi). 90. They told Akbar their story and taking out the boxes they gave them to the king. 91. They said to him, 'Listen to our words, O king. Surdas is a supremely clever man. He had already put aside priceless jewels in his house. 92. But believing the complaint of

the evil-minded assistant, you hastened in your demand of money. He was free of any fear and intended to come and see you. 93. But when we went and sat close to the door fear arose in his mind. After showing us the jewel-box he finally ran away.' 94. Hearing these words of the messengers, Akbar became much astonished. Then calling his minister Birbal, he told him all the news. 95. He took the boxes and unlocking them looked inside. He looked for jewels but found merely crystals. The messengers then began to tremble violently from fear. 96. Just then they discovered inside it the letter. As it was read, all the people listened. The king with respect and with love listened to it. 97. He said, 'Surdas has spent the sum of eight million and ten thousand rupees for *sadhus* and saints. But feeling fear in his mind at midnight he ran away.'

THE BACKBITER PUNISHED

98. As the king read the letter he was very much astonished. He called the slanderer to him and said, 'You have spoken an untruth. 99. Surdas has spent this money in worthy causes. You told us that he had wasted it. I see now that you are a hater of *Vaishnavas*. I must punish you.' 100. After punishing him, Akbar read the letter. He recognized the handwriting of Surdas. 101. Tears filled his eyes. He spoke kindly of Surdas to his ministers: 'Although I were to hunt through the three worlds, I should not find a servant as faithful as Surdas. 102. Though I have been intoxicated by my royal position, he has caused me to seek for the supreme spiritual riches. So give him an assurance not to be afraid, and go and bring him here. 103. Send letters from district to district to bring Surdas here quickly.' Hearing this command of the king every one felt great joy. 104. They sent letters to the officials in the Western districts immediately saying that if they should see Surdas they should send him at

once to meet the king, 105. 'Fearing me, he has started to wander with penitence to sacred bathing-places. If anyone should suddenly see him, give him an assurance not to fear and send him here.'

RETURN OF SURḌAS

106. The writing and sending of letters spread the news from district to district. Surdas was at that time at Mathura and there heard of the king's order. 107. He was astonished. He said, 'Mercy has arisen in the mind of the king. I do not understand the doings of God, the merciful Shri Krishna. 108. The Pervader of the universe, Shri Hari, is in the hearts of every one. It is through this mercy that the king is now pleased in his heart.' 109. With his mind comforted, he went at once to Hastinapur (Delhi). The moment he was in the presence of the king he received great honour. 110. King Akbar arose and gave Surdas an embrace. He said to him, 'If I should hunt through all the three worlds, I could not find a servant such as you. 111. I did not know that you had spent my money in such worthy objects. I persecuted you because of the report of the evil-minded one. 112. Now be free from fear and continue with your former authority.' The King having said this to him, Surdas replied, 113. 'Listen, O king. I have put aside all desires for earthly things. Why put me again into the snare of these worldly things ?' 114. Akbar replied, 'I see that you have become *virakta* (a *Vairagi*, one indifferent to earthly things). You have cast aside all illusory thoughts. 115. Still carry on your former authority and spend the money for the saints. I see no one, apart from you, wise enough to be of service to the *Vaishnavas*. 116. On your own authority spend eight million and ten thousand rupees and feed the *Vaishnava bhaktas* in the sacred district of Mathura. 117. Feeling

repentant in your heart, you decided to abandon the service of the king. But according to my command, receive my authority to be of service to the saints.' 118. Listening to these humble words of the king, Surdas thought over the matter in his heart. 'If I can attain the supreme spiritual riches while still engaged in worldly things, I should not turn away from doing so.' 119. Then he said to the king, 'Your command is my authority. Give me the work of serving the saints.' King Akbar honouring him gave him a written permission. 120. Surdas Madanmohan then returned to the sacred city of Mathura and there gave many forms of delicious food to the saints. 121. Formerly he feared that the king would be angry with him, but by Shri Hari's favour, that fear was no more there. His joy could not be contained in his heart. 122. Holding his love for the service of the saints, he brought often into his imagination the idol of Krishna. Day and night he would repeat God's name and lovingly describe His good deeds. 123. He composed and sang with his own lips many songs. By these Surdas pleaded with the Husband of Rukmini, with feelings of great reverence for Him.

WORDS WITHOUT ACTIONS WORTHLESS

124. One day when performing a *kirtan*, he was praising the saints and in the joy of love composed a poem. Listen what he said. 125. 'Surdas is the holder of the shoes of the saints. It is so written in the *abhangs*.' Hearing him say this the noble *Vaishnavas* felt great surprise. 126. One said, 'It is an untrue statement which Surdas has written in his poetic composition, for if it is not seen by men in his actions, then what is the good of his describing it in words? 127. If a cloud does not rain down upon the earth, then the sky-thunder is in vain. When there is no life in the body, it is the Lingayats who

adorn the corpse. 128. As if one should sit in the *bazaar* to sell musk which has no fragrance; so of what use is poetic ability without action? 129. Putting on different disguises an actor acts, but because his action is not real, his colour does not remain. 130. If one has made a picture of the sun, he cannot give it light. So this poetic composition of Surdas' seems to us.' 131. The three kinds of people variously put blame upon him. Some were pious and wise and they were well satisfied. 132. Those given to talk and of curious minds said, 'This poetry is merely modern. His composition is useless as it is not realized in his action. 133. Even if a coin is new, a fool rejects it. So without good reason some blame modern poetry. 134. After many days have passed, however, people will accept it. *Maya* has given a wrong idea to men. 135. Last season was a good one for crops, but this season is one of famine. A dead man is fortunate.' These are common sayings. 136. When a wise man is before them, the ignorant call him a fool. After he has died, they loudly praise him. 137. First there is a mistake, and then the remembrance of it. That is the custom of man. But wise men understand it from experience.

SURDAS PASSES HIS TEST

138. Well, it is needless to speak any more of this. God's *Maya* is irresistible and puts men into the snare of wrong ideas, or sinks them into the mire of doubt. 139. The *bhakta* and noble *Vaishnava* Surdas continued constantly in the service of the saints. Those who reviled his poetry did so without proper thought. 140. They said, 'He possesses no action, and he is speaking in a hypocritical way.' As Surdas was going one day to see and worship God, a *bairagi* (ascetic) approached him. 141. He said to himself, 'I want to test Surdas and see how his poetic statement is true.' So thinking to himself he spoke to Surdas.

Listen to what he said. 142. He said to Surdas, 'I am hurrying to see and worship at the temple. Keep my shoes in your hand and for the moment take good care of them.' 143. Hearing what the *bairagi* said, Surdas was quite pleased. He said, 'For many days that was the purpose which I was holding in my mind. 144. That longing in my heart has come to good fruitage. I have lost my mental perplexities.' He then descended at once from his palanquin. 145. He asked the man for the shoes, and took them in his hand. He then stood by the great door of the temple and folding the shoes in his garment held them close to his heart in his love. 146. Giving command to his servants he sent the palanquin home. Seeing the devotion of Surdas, the *bairagi* was astonished. 147. Then hastening to the great door of the temple, he thought to himself, 'I will delay here and I shall then have a good chance to see whether Surdas' mind will be troubled thereby.' 148. So going into the assembly hall he then sat down singing the praise of Hari, remaining there from early morning till the setting of the sun. 149. After two hours of the night had passed the *bairagi* came outside to look for Surdas. There Surdas stood holding his shoes.

KRISHNA'S MANIFESTATION TO SURDAS

150. Seeing the *bairagi*, Surdas was greatly pleased. Then springing forward he took the shoes and held them close to his feet. 151. He placed his hand on Surdas' head and said, 'You are a devoted noble *Vaishnava*. In order to test your mind, I made this long delay. 152. You speak of yourself as a servant of the saints. And you do as you say. Coming here with this idea in my mind I have tested you. 153. In calling yourself the holder of the shoes of the saints you have spoken the truth.' Hearing him say this the heart of Surdas melted. 154. Then feeling repentance in his mind he had himself robbed of all he possessed, and free from all things he then gave himself up to

the worship of God with love. 155. He gave great service to the saints and thereby the Husband of Rukmini was pleased, so that He gave to Surdas a visible manifestation of Himself.

156. In these stories are described one greater than the other supremely pious *Vaishnava bhaktas*. In the next chapter there is a most delightful and unusual story, which if listened to will give happiness to the hearers. 157. The Husband of Rukmini, Dweller upon the banks of the Bhima, is causing me to relate the stories in the form of this book. It is by His favour that Mahipati is relating them to the hearers.

158. *Swasti* (Peace)! This book is the *Shri Bhakta-vijaya*. In listening to it the Lord of the world will be pleased. Listen then, you God-loving, pious *bhaktas*. This is the thirty-sixth very delightful chapter ; it is an offering to Shri Krishna.

CHAPTER XXXVII

RASIK MURAR

Obeisance to Shri Ganesh. Obeisance to the Loved One of Rukmini.

GOD'S ASSISTANCE IN WRITING THESE STORIES

1. O Husband of Rukmini, Dweller on the banks of the Bhima, Thou art the Enlightener of the heart. Aside from Thee, O infinite One, there is no other relator, nor any other one to cause these stories to be written. 2. Just as it is the roots that cause the tree to live; or as it is water that is necessary to ripen the grain; so do Thou, O Krishna, cause me to write these most delightful stories. 3. The sea is the refuge of the animals and the sky is the refuge of stars; so Thou, O Ocean of mercy, art the Enlightener of my intensely dull mind. 4. As the holder of the strings causes the dolls to dance in the presence of the crowd, so entering into the temple of my heart Thou art enabling me to describe the noble stories of Thy *bhaktas.* 5. Instead of describing Thy good qualities, to compose extensive poetry is to weary the tongue for nothing, so it appears to me. 6. Therefore, O Krishna, I pray Thee again and again to confer on me a loving gift to compose this book.

A SHIRKER DETECTED

7. In the previous chapter there was the description of the *bhakta* Surdas Madanmohan, whose story all of you have listened to with its deep meaning. 8. And now hear the story of the great *bhakta* Rasik Murar, who was exceedingly alert in the service of the saints. He continually lived in the district of Mathura in the town of Saya. 9. He was accustomed to bathe in the Jumna and then worship Shri Krishna. He used the sixteen materials for worship and offered God flowers and *tulsi* leaves. 10. Then calling the *Vaishnavas* together he would wash their feet

with his own hands. Drinking the water in which their feet were washed he then worshipped the saints. 11. Preparing many kinds of dainty food he used to feed the saints. In his love he regarded these saints as the same as Vishnu. 12. This brought him a great many disciples who helped him. Sitting quietly by himself he lovingly worshipped God. 13. It happened on a certain day that *Vaishnavas* came to his house. He gave to everyone a grass mat to sit upon. 14. He then said to one of his disciples, 'Worship the saints and bring the sacred water at once with which their feet are washed and give it to me.' 15. When this command was given, the worship of the saints began. With laziness and wrong thoughts, one immediately began to wash their feet. 16. There was there a Brahman, a foul smelling leper. His feet were covered with sores and intensely filthy. His clothes were torn and exceedingly old and he was dressed filthily. 17. Looking at him the disciple felt disgust. He said to himself, 'If I should wash his feet, it will make me vomit.' 18. So he washed with love the feet of those who were wise and clean. And having worshipped the saints according to custom, he waved lights over them. 19. Collecting the water in which the feet of the saints were washed he gave it to the *sadguru*. Murar immediately drank it.

SECRET OF THE HOLY WATER

20. He called all his company of disciples together and told them the secret of his heart. He said, 'I drank the water today in which the feet of the saints were washed, but it did not taste properly. 21. I think the sacred water was brought to me with a doubt in the mind. I understand this from my very feeling.' Then he added, 22. 'Now you all think over the matter and tell me why it is that this nectar waterin which their feet were washed tasted so unpleasant.' 23. Hearing what their *sadguru* said they all gave

themselves to thinking. He who had been engaged in the worship of the saints was much astonished by that question. 24. Then coming before Murar, he stood still, joined his hands together, and told him all that had happened. 25. He said, 'Listen O *Swami*, to my true words. I was worshipping the saints, and seeing there a filthy Brahman leper I felt disgust. 26. I felt a great sense of repugnance. Then excepting him I worshipped all the other noble *Vaishnavas* and hastened back, O *Swami*.' 27. Murar *Swami* then went up to the Brahman leper, and made him a postrate *namaskar* on the ground and washed his feet with his own hands, 28. wiped his feet also with his own hands and held them lovingly to his heart. He pressed the toe of his foot to his eyes and drank with pleasure the water in which his feet were washed. 29. Then he exclaimed, 'Now the water in which his feet were washed tastes good.' Hearing this all the *Vaishnavas* wondered and said, 'No one can understand the reverential feelings of Murar *Swami*. 30. Such is the power of a *guru's* favour. Only a good disciple understands its secrets. Just as the *chakor* bird only fully knows the nectar of the moon; 31. or as the faithful wife alone understands the mind of her husband; or as only one indifferent to worldly things can indentify himself with the experience of the God-loving *bhaktas* while listening to their stories; 32. or as it is the bee alone that has experience of the sweet taste of the lotus-flower; or as it was Vishvamitra who alone understood the extraordinary power of the *gayatri-mantra*; 33. or as it is the Lord of Kailas (Shiva) alone who has the deep experience of the name of Shri Ram; or as it is the *bhaktas* of Vishnu who realize the extraordinary power of the religious teachings of the *Bhagwat*; 34. thus it was that the sweet taste of the water in which the saints' feet were washed was realized by Murar *Swami*. Nothing equal to it in sweetness could he find anywhere.'

35. Saying this, the *Vaishnava bhaktas* placed their hands of blessing on his head. They said to him, 'The Lord Krishna will be your helper because of your devotion.' 36. Because Murar felt this reverence for the feet of the saints he understood the sweetness of the water in which their feet were washed and from that time they gave him the name of Rasik Murar.

DAYARNAVA'S VILLAGES CONFISCATED

37. Murar's *guru* was Dayarnava. He was an exceedingly learned man in divine knowledge. He very lovingly and according to the prescribed rules worshipped God. 38. With the sixteen materials needed in worship he used to worship the beautiful idol (*Shaligram*) made from the *gandaki* stone, and in his reverence used to have it clothed in raiments, ornaments and adornments. 39. There was a king who came to the same temple to see and worship God. With great pleasure he noticed the worship of Dayarnava, and then gave him the written deeds for the revenue of four villages. 40. The king said to Dayarnava, 'These villages have been given to you for the sake of helping you in your worship. Let all the revenue from these villages be used for the worship of *sadhus* and saints.' 41. Saying this the king returned to his city and Dayarnava was greatly surprised. 42. He said to himself, 'Shri Krishna has supplied me with all the means I have wished for.' He was very happy over it, and continued his worship of Hari.

43. These rites lasted for many days, but suddenly a hindrance came in the way. A very wicked and sinful man came suddenly to the town. 44. By giving money to the king's treasury he got himself appointed as the leaseholder of all that country, and bringing a written document to that effect he came to live in the city where the *Vaishnava* was. 45. Hearing of Dayarnava's right to the revenue

from these towns, that evil man confiscated them; just as the wicked man Duryodhana took away the kingdom from Dharma. 46. People told him fully of the laws and the moral side of the case but that evil-minded man would not listen to anyone. He had fallen into the error of being envious for illusory things and was falling into hell. 47. Misers do not like to hear of the giving of charity. Those who are not *bhaktas* do not enjoy the stories of Hari. An adulteress on seeing her husband feels troubled. 48. But that evil man would not listen to anything. He said, 'Who was it that gave this useless deed to this *bairagi* ?' 49. Hearing what this non-*bhakta* said, Dayarnava considered it carefully in his mind and then immediately wrote thus to Rasik Murar:—50. 'Although you might be eating at the time you receive this letter, get up and come here immediately.' Having written this, the *sadguru* sat waiting for him. 51. Now it happened that Rasik Murar was sitting in his house eating when suddenly a man bringing a letter hurried to him. 52. On seeing this man from his *sadguru* he felt supreme happiness ; just as when upon a withering tree a cloud bursts and causes a heavy downfall of rain; 53. or as when a mother sends an invitation to her daughter, who is living at her mother-in-law's, to come and visit her own home. It was in such a joyful manner that he asked the news of this man. 54. He said to him,' What is the command of the *sadguru* with which he sent you here?' The man then immediately took out the letter and placed it before him. 55. Murar took the letter in his left hand and read it. Bowing to the command of his *sadguru* he quickly arose, although he was in the midst of eating, 56. and without speaking to anyone he started at once. He said to himself, 'I will do at once what I am told to do.' His heart rejoiced in doing so. 57. Going to the city of his *sadguru* he entered into his house. The moment he saw him, he made him a prostrate *namaskar*. 58. His *sadguru* seeing that his hands were already soiled by the food he had taken, enquired of him, 'Tell me the reason why your mouth is soiled with food.' 59. The other replied to his *sadguru*, 'Your command is my authority. Receiving your letter, although I was eating at the time I immediately started.' 60. Hearing him say this every one was astonished. They exclaimed, 'No one aside from you understands the characteristic of the *bhakti* given to a *sadguru*.' 61. The *guru* then told Murar the whole affair. He said, 'This evil man has confiscated the revenue of the towns given to me for the worship of God. 62. Although he was fully told about the laws and ethics of the matter, still that evil-minded man would not listen. Go to him at once and preach to him his duty. 63. Freeing my towns from his grasp, come back quickly with your errand accomplished. Take the name of Shri Krishna and start immediately.'

RASIK MURAR AT THE CONFISCATOR'S TOWN

64. Bowing his head to the command of his *sadguru*, he hurried along and going into the city he took lodgings. 65. There were some pious people there when he told all the news. He said, 'The official in your town has confiscated Dayarnava's land. 66. Therefore, my *sadguru* has given me a command and sent me at once. So let us go just now and accomplish this errand' 67. The people replied, 'Our official is a supreme rascal, a hater of *Vaishnavas* and an exceedingly low-minded man. Therefore you should not go there hastily. 68. You are merely a true *bhakta* and he will not listen to your preaching. Why needlessly throw a golden lance into a well? 69. If one has no iron near him, what is the use of rubbing it upon a piece of pottery? A common cow cannot be compared with the wish-cow. 70. If *rishi* Agasti is thirsty, he should not go to a mere pond (instead of the ocean); instead of the

wish-tree, one should not place his desire upon a mere *babhul* tree; 71. although the infant child of someone else is hungry, a barren woman's breast will not fill with milk; likewise evil-minded men will not listen to the words of a true *bhakta.* 72. So do not go personally to see him. We shall quietly accomplish your purpose by some other plan.' 73. When the leading men in the town had said this, Rasik Murar replied saying, 'My *guru* gave me the command to accomplish this purpose immediately. 74. His command is my authority. I am going to that man's house. If he will not give what I ask, there will be no help for it.' 75. In the meantime, someone told that evil man the news, saying,' Rasik Murar is coming in order to reclaim the towns from you. 76. The moment an evil man sees *him*, he falls into deep confusion of mind.' Hearing this the evil man was astonished.

RASIK IN A PREDICAMENT

77. Then planning a scheme this evil-minded man did as follows. He had a fierce elephant brought and in private he spoke to a wrestler. 78. He said, 'Rasik Murar is coming at once to meet me. Make the elephant stand in the square and kill him. 79. If you accomplish this, I will give you some money.' Hearing this the wrestler said, 'I will do so.' 80. Then he gave the elephant a great deal of intoxicating liquor and had him stand in the king's highway. Just then Rasik Murar came with a procession singing and praising God. 81. He came with a great number of his disciples who brought with them cymbals and drums and with great fondness were singing the names of God. 82. 'Victory, Victory to Thee, the Husband of Rukmini, Pervader of the universe, Father of Brahmadev, Killer of Kans, aside from Thee, O Lord of *Vaikunth*, Thy *bhaktas* have no intimate friend. 83. There is no place anywhere without Thee. The space pervades everything

but is not soiled. 84. Just as when sandalwood and *hingan* wood are set on fire, one gives out fragrance and the other a vile odour, but the fire is alike in both; 85. so the Life of the world is the same in both evil and good men. With love I bow to Thee, O Thou whose form is that of the universe.' 86. Murar was thus filled with joy and was praising the good qualities of Hari. All the people of the city watched the novel proceeding. 87. Just then the intoxicated elephant came hastening along the royal road. When the townspeople saw this tbey surmised what it meant. 88. They came quietly to Rasik Murar and told him, 'That evil-minded man holds against you an evil purpose, and he has sent this elephant to kill you.' 89. Although they told him this he felt no fear in his mind, but he said, 'Although I should protect this perishable body, yet at the end *Kal* (the god of death) will seize it. 90. But if it is used for the sake of the *sadguru*, all hindrances at once flee away.' Thus speaking he continued to walk forward. 91. Just then he saw the intoxicated elephant from a distance coming towards him, and his company of disciples addressed him. Listen to what they said.

RASIK'S DISCIPLES DESERT HIM

This company of disciples said to him, 92. 'The elephant is coming towards us. Let us run away from here. If we do not we shall be killed.' 93. Rasik Murar answered them saying, 'You have loyally and lovingly accepted the teaching of your *sadguru*. 94. Now loving your own bodies, you say: "Let us go away from here." If you wanted to do so, why did you at all put the *tulsi* garlands around your necks and entangle yourself in this?' 95. Hearing what he said, all took off their garlands. The *sadguru* said to them, 'I am now free from you'. 96. As they heard him say this, they all forsook him and fled and Rasik Murar alone remained on the spot; 97. just as when the hot season has arrived, clouds leave the sky;

or just as when the cold season arrives, rivers run down; 98. or as when an enemy besieges a king, his followers out of concern for themselves run away; or as when a time of distress comes, hypocrites abandon their proper duties; 99. or as when old age arrives, the organs of sense drop the object of sense; or as when a man falls into poverty, evil men forsake him; 100. or as when Shankaracharya asked for alms, he received in his hands a fused mass of hot glass and the disciples ran away; 101. so now all the people of the town looked at the strange scene from a distance. They exclaimed, 'The official of the town, intoxicated with pride, is going to kill Murar, but without any reason.' 102. In the meantime Rasik Murar with love continued to worship Shri Hari. Standing at a distance from him the disciples looked upon the scene.

THE CONFISCATOR'S PRIDE HUMBLED

103. The intoxicated and evil-minded wrestler of the elephant drove his intoxicated animal forward, but his (Murar's) confidence was that Shripati (Krishna) pervaded all beings; 104. and those whose mental condition is such, never receive any harm. The elephant came near him and humbled itself at his feet. 105. Although the elephant was intoxicated, and was of a bad disposition, still it made Murar a prostrate *namaskar*. Seeing this strange sight every one wondered. 106. They said, 'This elephant is exceedingly intoxicated. He has killed very many. Now here he is making a prostrate *namaskar* to Murar *Swami*. This is a most extraordinarily novel thing. 107. All the garlands which the disciples had taken from around their necks, Murar collected together and placed around the elephant's neck. 108. He gave him the mystic *mantra* 'Ram, Krishna, Narayan' and said, 'Leave your intoxicated condition and serve the saints. 109. In becoming a suppliant to the saints with one's whole body, speech and

mind, even if one loses one's life, the command of one's *guru* shoud not be disobeyed' 110. The elephant now changed to one of good disposition and the servants of the leaseholder hastened to tell him of the strange event. 111. They said to him, 'You sent an elephant in order to kill Murar, but instead of doing that he has made him a prostrate *namaskar.*' Hearing their story he was full of astonishment. 112. Suddenly he felt repentant and he walked to the place where Murar was, saying, 'I did not know of your extraordinary glory and I needlessly persecuted you. 113. You are truly a *bhakta* of Vishnu; now command me to do whatever you please.' Saying this he prostrated himself before Murar. 114. Rasik Murar replied to him, 'I have no other wish in my heart than that of bowing my head to the command of my *sadguru* and asking you to free the revenue from the villages intended for worship. 115. I have given instructions to the elephant (and he is now my disciple), so I desire that you should give him up to me.' The official replied, 'I will do so.' Then he again made Murar a prostrate *namaskar.* 116. Receiving a written document he took the elephant away with him. Singing the praise of God he returned to his *sadguru* having accomplished his errand. 117. Among beasts an elephant is most fierce but even he became wise. Seeing this all the people felt astonished.

AN ELEPHANT SERVES THE SAINTS

118. The elephant finally received full knowledge. At night he listened to the praise of Hari. In the daytime, going into the jungle, he used to return with faggots, 119. When all the *Vaishnavas* dine they need leaves on which to eat, so the elephant used to go into the jungle and bring back leaves. 120. Leaves with food left upon them were thrown away but the elephant lovingly ate them. Aside from them the elephant would eat nothing.

121. *Vaishnava bhaktas* continually read the *Shri Bhagwat* at the door of the *Thakurdwar* (Krishna's temple.) * The elephant listened constantly to its reading and his mind became extraordinarily indifferent to all worldly things. 122. The elephant said to himself, 'Among beasts I was born with the exceedingly fierce body of an elephant. And now by the mercy of the *sadguru* I have found association with saints. 123. In a former birth I must have done good deeds and they are now coming to fruitage.' Thus the elephant with pleasure used to think in his mind.

124. After many days had passed, Rasik Murar started to go to sacred bathing places. The *Vaishnava bhaktas* felt great joy in their minds. 125. Taking the elephant along with them the chief *Vaishnava* walked to bathing-places and the burden of all the garments and vessels they placed upon the elephant. 126. If on the way they met thieves and they began to harm the *bhaktas* of Vishnu then the elephant becoming angry would kill them. 127. He would let no one come near him, aside from one who repeated the names of Rama and who had around his neck a *tulsi* garland. 128. Thus repentant in spirit he visited many sacred bathing-places. Then many of them felt a strong desire to go to the sacred place of the Kurus. 129. As they hastened along the road they reached Arunavati. There the saints stopped the elephant and lodged there. 130. They held to their plan of remaining there three nights.

THE KING DEMANDS THE ELEPHANT

Now there was here a Muhammadan king exceedingly insolent who learned of their story. 131. A messenger had hastened to tell him that some *bairagis* (ascetics) had taken lodgings in the city and that they had brought with them a very fierce elephant. 132. 'Such an elephant of a

* See Note on Chap. 38. 14, p. 67.

beautiful appearance would certainly be an ornament to our kingdom. So you should go to Murar and forcibly demand it of him.' 133. The messenger having said this, the king felt a desire for the elephant. He said, 'Why does that beggar needlessly desire what is an ornament for a king?' 134. He then at once gave command to his officers and told them to take away the elephant by force, and if the *bairagis* did not deliver the elephant to them then they should punish them. 135. Hearing the commands of the wicked one the soldiers hastened to fulfil the order. The elephant was seated with a quiet mind in the midst of the *Vaishnavas.* 136. The king's servants said to the saints, 'The king has sent us to you. His desire has fallen upon the elephant which is with you. 137. So give it to us at once, or we shall take it away from you by force.' Hearing these words of the evil-minded men, the noble *Vaishnavas* became concerned. 138. They said to one another, 'This insolent king is an evil-minded Muhammadan and even if he is told of law and ethics he will never listen. 139. If a crow is put in a cage and an attempt is made to teach it to talk, yet it can never repeat the name of Krishna. If one should ask money of a miser, it will be in vain. 140. You might give water to the *sher* tree but it will never bear nectar fruit. If a cow should lick a butcher, will he therefore protect her from being killed? 141. A he-goat may listen to the glorification of the *tulsi* plant but he will feel no compassion for the plant (but will eat it). A drunkard when seeing a man wise in divine things feels disgust. 142. If a falcon should see a speaking parrot, will he therefore protect it? A fish might be flapping about out of the water but the crane will not feel any mercy for it. 143. So although one might preach law and ethics to those who are non-*bhaktas*, yet it will never be to their taste.' Thus thinking, the saints gave reply to the messengers. 144. They said, 'Aside from Vishnu's *bhaktas* the elephant will permit no one to touch it. If you should touch it, it will in a moment kill you.' 145. Although the *bhaktas* of Vishnu said this, the king's messengers tried to seize the elephant, but they were not able to do so; for in its anger it attempted to kill them. 146. They then went back to the king and told him all the news. They said, 'No one aside from the *bhaktas* of Vishnu can master the elephant.' 147. The king hearing what they said suggested a plan to the driver of the elephant (the *mahant*): 'Dress in the guise of a *Vaishnava* and then go to the elephant.'

THE ELEPHANT CAPTURED BY DECEIT

148. Saying he would do so he placed a *tulsi* garland around his neck, marked his forehead with the paste of white clay, and went repeating the names 'Krishna, Gopal.' 149. In order to rob pilgrims on the road, robbers dress as ascetics; and although hunters sit to listen to a *kirtan* they will not fail to set a snare for deers; 150. as when to secure a livelihood an actor disguises himself as a *sannyasi*; or a crane seems to sit in meditation, but it is for the purpose of catching a fish; 151. likewise that very proud man deceitfully became Vishnu's *bhakta*, and he approached the elephant while repeating the name of Krishna. 152. Then coming near to the elephant he tried to catch it. In its mind it understood that through deceit the driver had changed the appearance of his body. 153. But as he came repeating the names of God, it felt that there was no remedy. The elephant therefore becoming quiet he was quickly overcome by the deceitful man. 154. As the elephant was being driven to the door of the king, its mind was very disturbed and it said to itself, 'From now on, the service of the saints comes to an end.' 155. When he was bound in his stall he would eat no grain or grass. After

seven days had passed he went to the heaven *Vaikunth*, 156. for as he was taken to the Ganges to drink water he drowned himself in it. Desiring to be in the essential form of Hari he attained final deliverance. 157. Having been associated with saints, the animal was saved without a moment's delay. What is there novel then in a man's acquiring goodness? 158. On and around the mountain of Maila the *bor* and the *babhul* trees grow. Although they look different from one another in appearance they do not lack in fragrance. 159. So an evil man might be of a low caste and his mind might be very evil, still if he finds himself in the neighbourhood of saints he will be saved. 160. So, fortunate hearers, listen to the delightful stories of the saints.

In the next chapter there is the story of how Krishna came to help Mirabai when she was in distress. 161. As the fortunate listeners seat themselves in line I shall serve them with this delightful story. Mahipati requests the listeners to feel happy through their own joy.

162. *Swasti* (Peace)! This book is the *Shri Bhaktavijaya*. In listening to it the Lord of the world will be pleased. Listen then, you God-loving, pious *bhaktas*. This is the thirty-seventh deeply delightful chapter.

CHAPTER XXXVIII

MIRABAI

Obeisance to Shri Ganesh. Obeisance to Shri Krishna.

BHAKTAVIJAYA AS THE FULL MOON

1. Listen, O hearers, with an attentive mind. Faith may be said to be a full-moon festival. There the *Bhaktavijaya* is the moon that has suddenly become visible. 2. And when revealing itself in the sky of the heart the darkness of ignorance is driven far away. The wise *chakor* bird, seeing the moon, feels great happiness in its mind. 3. Looking with faith and fondness one receives a nectar rain of love, therefore he feels in his heart a limitless happiness. 4. Others who are lovers of interesting stories receive a blessing from these stories. Feeling great satisfaction thereby they partake of the happiness of final deliverance. 5. When the moon is seen, the hesitating thieves grumble, for they cannot continue their evil course and they flee away. 6. A tree though entirely ignorant yet feels the beams of the moon on it, and when the month of *Chaītra* (April) comes, it becomes densely covered with flowers and fruit. 7. Therefore with attentive minds listen with reverence. In the previous chapter the audience listened with love to the story of Rasik Murar.

MIRABAI'S BIRTH AND CHILDHOOD

8. In the great country of Hindusthan there is a holy city by name of Udaipur. The king of that region was a reverent *bhakta* of Vishnu. 9. If any uninvited guests arrived the king provided them with garments and food. If *Vaishnavas* suddenly appeared he used to worship them. 10. In his house the king used to worship the idol of Krishna with the sixteen materials used in worship.

With love he was accustomed to dress it in garments and ornaments and sing its praises. 11. Then after receiving the favour of Hari he was accustomed to eat. At this time a jewel of a daughter descended through him, a treasure-house of devotion. 12. After twelve days had passed they gave her the name of Mirabai. The mother lifted her up and placed her at the feet of Krishna. 13. She had a charming form and was extremely beautiful. When the king saw her it was a great pleasure to him. She grew up day by day and her mother and father were made happy. 14. It was at that time the custom of the king to take his daughter and go to *Thakurdwar* (Krishna's temple) * where with reverence he used to worship the eagle-bannered One (Krishna) with the sixteen materials used in worship. 15. He used to put ornaments on the extremely beautiful idol of Shri Krishna. In his love the king used to dress it in priceless jewels and pearl-garlands. 16. The idol of the cloud-dark Krishna looked beautiful with His brilliant crown, and His beautiful waistband. Around His waist was the gorgeous yellow robe and around His neck was the *Vaijayanti* garland. 17. In His ears were earrings set with jewels and on His breast was the exceedingly beautiful *Kaustubh* jewel. His glorious face was most pleasing with His broad smile.

HER RESOLVE TO MARRY KRISHNA

18. As she regularly looked at this form, Mirabai's heart was impressed by it and she said to herself, 'I am not going to marry any one except God alone.' 19. Having this determination in her mind the daughter of the king held to it in her love for God. Now it happened on a certain day that the king came and conversed with his wife. 20. The king said to the queen, 'I see that

---

*टाकुर = *Thakur*, which in North India is one of Krishna's names; द्वार = *door* (of temple).

Mirabai appears to be grown up. We should now look for a worthy bridegroom and have her married at once.' 21. Mirabai was listening to her father's words and spoke in a sweet voice, ' I have already chosen a husband for myself. 22. If you should ask me who he is, I will tell you how you may recognize him. Shri Krishna whom you are regularly worshipping is the one I love. 23. You, mother and father, are my elders. Both of you think over the matter and offer me to the Lord Shri Krishna without making any objection.' 24. The king replied to the daughter, 'That stone idol is lifeless. You are a mere child and therefore do not understand and in consequence your love has been given to it. 25. In the *Kali Yuga* Krishna has taken the form of Buddha and has remained silent. No one can see Him in His visible form. 26. Your childish mind does not comprehend this, therefore you desire to marry this idol of Krishna. This is a foolish notion. Marry some distinguished prince.' 27. Mirabai replied, 'Hunt where I may, there is no God superior to God-supreme, the Husband of Rukmini. 28. He is the Father of Brahmadev. Although He does all things, He is still a non-doer. Shiva's burning pain left Him when He repeated Krishna's name. Do you not know this, father? 29. In the three worlds there is no God, man, or king who is superior to Him, therefore my intense love is for Him. 30. You say that this is a lifeless stone. But you should not say so. Pralhad believed God, and God manifested Himself out of the wooden pillar. 31. You might say that these are old fables, and doubts about them may come into your mind, but still in the *Kali Yuga* the Lord of the world walked from Dwarka to Dakur. 32. On a certain night the antique idol of Mathura went to Hardwar. He saw the perfect *bhakti* of Nama and dined with him. 33. Know that the pure devotion of God's *bhaktas* is God Himself, and wherever His praise is sung with love there he dwells. 34. When a bee feels love for a lotus-flower, it buzzes around it. So the Husband of Rukmini hastens to the place where there is a *kirtan.* 35. In the *Kali Yuga* the Life of the world is silent with one who is not a *bhakta*, but with a God-loving, pious *bhakta* God speaks. 36. So hold no hesitation and listen to my request, O king. Offer me to the idol of Krishna and let me worship Him with love.' 37. Hearing his daughter say this, the king was astonished. He said, 'I understand now. I now truly understand what her life means. 38. She is but an ignorant child who has not listened to the *Puranas*, and where has she gained this extraordinary knowledge? I do not understand.' 39. So he said to his daughter, 'I give to you an image of Krishna. Take it into your room, and there worship Krishna with love.' 40. Listening to her father's acquiescence, Mirabai's heart rejoiced.

HER WORSHIP OF KRISHNA

She at once took the idol of Krishna and went to her room. 41. She installed the eagle-bannered One in her room and worshipped it with the sixteen materials for worship. The king supplied her with all materials she needed for the worship, believing his daughter was a wise girl. 42. In the early morning, having bathed, she repeated the names of God. Then taking a *vina* in her hand she sang hymns in her love. 43. Then waving the lighted wicks over Krishna she sang His praise and worshipped Him. She rubbed Him over with fragrant oil and bathed Him in warm water. 44. She then washed the idol with milk, curds, butter, honey and sugar mixed with crude sugar. After bathing Him in the five nectars she would wash Him in pure water. 45. After wiping it with her own garment she dressed Him, placed a crown on His head and adorned Him with brilliant ornaments. 46. On his forehead and person she made the three upright and other twelve marks, and with these she made Krishna look beautiful. He looked charming in the intensely lustrous earrings and the *Vaijayanti* garland. 47. She adorned Him with the *Kaustubh* jewel and made him look lovely with a garland of pearls and a waist-cord and *radhavali*. 48. On His wrist were ornaments of *pohochya* and hero's bracelets, and on His fingers were rings set with jewels. On His feet were the ornaments of *nepur* and *vale*. These she put on Him in her intense love. 49. Around His neck was a garland of tender *tulsi* leaves and over it was sprinkled the fragrant black powder. The dark-complexioned One looked beautiful and in visible form showed His beauty. 50. She used to wave over Him incense made of ten materials and the platter light. In her love she offered Him dainty food and with a final hymn of praise she prostrated herself before Him in her love. 51. She would exclaim, 'O Purifier of the sinful, the eagle-bannered One, the adornment of Thy *bhaktas*, and One who is not known by the senses, O King of kings, Shri Krishna, You honour my crude faith in You.' 52. Worshipping Him in this way, she would invite *Vaishnava bhaktas*. She would worship them reverently and bow to them in her love. 53. If any food remained she ate it as the favour of Hari. Then after the third watch of the day she would listen to the reading of the *Bhagwat Purana*. 54. In order to listen to the stories of Krishna, Vishnu *bhaktas* used to come to her room, especially those who had knowledge of philosophy, who were examples of goodness and whose minds were indifferent to worldly things; 55. those who were indifferent and always contented, who loved the devotion to the visible God, whose touch made the sacred water clean, were merciful to the lowly, and compassionate, 56. who regarded a common citizen as on equality with a king, to whom dung and gold seemed the same and who had the same feelings for the heavenly singer Urvashi as for a she-wolf.

57. *Sadhus* and saints who were thus filled with the spirit of indifference to earthly things came to listen to her. At night full of love she used to perform *kirtans* describing the goodness of Hari. 58. Mirabai composed many poems. Putting them to use in the worship of Krishna she lovingly described His good deeds.

MIRABAI'S REVILERS

59. There were some crooked-minded men in the town who reviled her day and night, saying, 'That king's daughter has ruined the reputation of the king. 60. She collects *bairagis* (ascetics) and in the *kirtans* dances before them without shame. Although beautiful in form, a very treasure-house of beauty, she has brought a stain upon good manners. 61. When outsiders turn aside from the right road the king punishes them, but he does not know of the evil done in his own house, as his mind is always intoxicated and blind with pride. 62. Although the sun appears brilliant, yet he has for his children the ominous *Vyatipat* and *Kalyani*; likewise the king is the chief jewel among the powerful, yet this daughter is lacking in good manners.' 63. Revilers laughed and clapped their hands in ridicule and they said, 'She is like a broom which is associated with dirt though made of *mol* [holy] grass. In this way they conversed among themselves with sinful hearts. 64. A crow sits upon a tree and watches the cattle with sores upon them ; so a reviler not being a witness of goodness naturally talks of one's imagined bad qualities.' 65. Thus they spoke to one another.

HER FIRM RESOLVE

The king finally understood this and full of anger he went to his wife privately and said to her, 66. 'You do not yet understand the rumours that are afloat. Our family reputation is being stained. Evil people revile the God-loving *bhakta* Mirabai. 67. They say, "She gathers together *Vaishnavas* and without any shame she sings in their company ; she has bad manners for one of good family." 68. Now hasten and tell our daughter, "Until now you were a child and had not sufficient understanding. 69. Now the king will find out a bridegroom for you and marry you to him." Come back soon to tell me her intention.' 70. According to her husband's advice she went and advised her daughter, saying, 'Men are constantly reviling you, because you are unwilling to marry. 71. Until now you were but a child, and now the king is going to have you married to a prince. He has sent me to tell you at once of his decision.' 72. Her daughter listened and then replied, 'Tell my father that aside from Krishna every other person, O king, is the same to me as you are. 73. My decision being what it is, why do you frequently come and needlessly request me? Whatever harm there might be in people reviling me I am responsible for it. My heart has no fear. 74. When one buys anything in the market without weighing it he should never say that it is expensive. So, mother, as you do not know my heart, why blame me? 75. With cymbals and drums I perform *kirtans* in the assembly of *Vaishnavas* Just because I do this, evil men revile me. 76. But those who are pious and wise say, "She has brought a bright light into her family line." It is only those who are not *bhaktas* who revile me and say that I have chosen for myself the path to hell. 77. Some say of me, "She has conceived a great fondness for worship." Others say, "Mirabai has become crazy." But those ignorant people do not know my pure heart. 78. With a weapon of knowledge in my hand I am determined to walk the path of *bhakti*. Evil-minded people try to blacken my pure action by blaming me, but thereby they only clean it without being paid for it. 79. Tell my father that I have become absorbed in the name of Rama.' Hearing her daughter thus express her opinion the mother quickly left her.

MIRABAI POISONED

80. Coming to the king in private she told him all the conversation. 'I spoke to her a great deal regarding her moral duty but our daughter did not pay respect to what I said.' 81. Hearing this the king then became very angry and said to his wife, 'I am going to give her the most virulent poison. Now go and with your own hands make our daughter drink it. 82. "One should either hear of his daughter as dead or that she is living peacefully at her husband's house." Such is the public saying. Think well of this.' 83. Thus speaking to his wife, the king at once brought some poison. He poured it into a cup, and sent it to his daughter by the hand of his wife. 84. She was not able to go against her husband's wish but felt supremely unhappy over her errand. The mother went along crying bitterly, for she deeply loved her daughter in her heart. 85. She went to the temple where Mirabai was and said to her, 'The king has sent some virulent poison to you.' 86. As she said this, tears filled her eyes. She exclaimed, 'O my beautiful lovely child, the god of death has now come here for you.' 87. Seeing the great love of her mother, Mirabai replied, 'Man's body is extremely perishable. It is certain that it will perish at the end of life. 88. If I have to depart because of my worshipping Krishna, why, O mother, should you needlessly mourn? If the water of a mirage should go dry, why be troubled by it? 89. If the match of a son of a barren woman is broken, why mourn over it? To say on a new moon night that the moon has disappeared from the sky is of course a false statement. 90. Because the sky flowers are withered, the bees are unhappy. As that would be absurd to say, why needlessly mourn, O mother? 91. A fruit loses its hold of the stem and falls somewhere So now my love is fixed upon the feet of Shri Krishna and I have no relation with you. 92. Pearls are developed in

water and the rich make ornaments of them. So I, born of you, have given my love to Shri Krishna. 93. Or as men in order to make ornaments beautiful set jewels in them, so the Lord of the Yadavas (Krishna) has accepted me. 94. Therefore now put aside all love for things of this worldly life and mourn no longer needlessly over me.' Thus speaking to her mother she fell at the feet of Shri Krishna. 95. Placing her heart on the god's feet she said to Him, 'My father has sent poison for me, O Krishna. 96. So now by your favour I shall reach my home in heaven. But who will there be then to give You the worship that I do? This is my great concern. 97. Revilers will say, "Because Mirabai showed her *bhakti*, poison was finally given to her to cause her death, according to the determination of the king." 98. If the non-*bhaktas* speak in this way, then who will worship You as I do? O God Supreme, I am very anxious about that. 99. Who will dress You in garments, ornaments and adornments, and weave garlands of many kinds of flowers for You and who will put these upon You? That is what makes me deeply concerned. 100. The king used to make offerings to You, now he also has become angry. Calling me the cause (of the revilers' rumours) he has turned aside from Thy service. 101. O beautiful dark-complexioned One, and lotus-eyed, evil men will continue to give me such blame as this. They will say, "Mirabai died for that reason." 102. Still however, O Husband of Rukmini, why should I worry over this blame? There is no other but Thee who brings about the past and the future. 103. When the lacquered house was on fire, Thou didst protect the Pandavas. Even the *Vedas* and the *Shastras* do not know the limits of Thy power, O Ocean of mercy, Helper of the helpless. 104. When poison was given to Pralhad, Thou, O Lord of the heart, didst protect him. If Thy name is on one's lips the god of death cannot harm him. 105. The poison that Shiva took lost its virulence when Thy name was taken. So now why should I be troubled, since Thou art One merciful to the lowly?' 106. Then taking the cup of poison she presented it to God as an offering saying, 'Shri Hari is the Enjoyer of this.' Then she at once drank it.

COLOUR OF KRISHNA'S IMAGE CHANGES

107. Immediately a most wonderful thing happened. Listen to it, you pious people. The poison which Mirabai drank became like nectar. 108. The idol, made of stone from the Gandaki river, immediately changed its colour. It became green all over and every one saw this. 109. Because the king did not believe his wife he immediately came there. Seeing the change right before him, his throat choked with emotion. 110. He then exclaimed, 'I am a sinner, and an extremely wicked person. I have made God drink this poison.' Thus repentant in his heart, he grasped the feet of his daughter. 111. She lifted up the head of her father and made him a prostrate *namaskar*, exclaiming, 'O father, it is because of you that I have been united to Shri Krishna.' 112. Mirabai's father then said to her, 'When I made you drink the poison, the colour of the idol changed, therefore I am much concerned. 113. Go now and pray to the Husband of Rukmini that He will make the idol as it first was. By doing so I shall be made happy, and your reputation will spread in the world.' 114. Mirabai then joining her hands palm to palm, said to the idol of Shri Krishna, 'The moment You drank just a little of the poison, Your form changed. 115. At the time of the Krishna *avatar*, You killed the serpent Kaliya in the Jumna river. Now how comes it today, after taking a little poison, You have changed colour ? 116. When your *bhaktas* repeat Your name poison becomes nectar, so the *Puranas* say. To-day I had experience of it. 117. When Shiva repeated Your name, His burning pain at once became quiet. But now I see that the moment You took this poison, O Lord of the

world, You became troubled. 118. If Agasti abandons his austerities out of fear of the ocean, then only, O God, will the poison be harmful to You. 119. If the burning fire begins violently to tremble at the sight of grass, then only, O Husband of Rukmini, will the poison harm You. 120. If repeating the name of Rama continually would harm *bhaktas*, then only would poison harm You suddenly. 121. But to say that in drinking nectar, O Govinda, mankind would be afflicted with disease, then only would harm come to You. 122. In order to show miracles to men, You perform many deeds of various kinds, so now, O Lord of the heart, become as You formerly were.'

IMAGE RESTORED TO FORMER COLOUR

123. Hearing Mirabai's plea, Krishna was joyful and immediately the Husband of Rukmini became as He was before. 124. In order that the world might have evidence of this He left His throat green. Thus the merciful One, destroying the evils of this life, continued uninterrupted to increase the glory of His servants. 125. The king at once arose and made a *namaskar* to the god. Then he said to Mirabai, 'You have brought salvation to your family line.' 126. Hearing what the King said, all the slanderers looked down with shame, saying, 'In persecuting this *bhakta* we have become disgraced.' 127. Cries of 'Victory, victory' and clapping of hands then took place. All the assembly of *bhaktas* rejoiced and said, 'Krishna has become favourable at this time to Mirabai.' 128. Mirabai continued to worship Shri Hari with a mind filled with satisfaction, thus manifesting the power of a *bhakta* who has attained spiritual knowledge. 129. Even today in that country in the palaces of kings there is placed in their idol-rooms the intensely beautiful idol of Shri Krishna.

130. In the next chapter there will be the beautiful story of the great *bhakta* Kanhopatra. You reverent and

pious people, listen with intense love to her delightful story. 131. He Who is the Lord of the primal *maya* and Who is the Father of Brahmadev, naturally living in my heart, causes me to relate the incomparable story. 132. Holding this determination in my mind, and that it is the Husband of Rukmini who is the Relator, Mahipati speaks of His words of compassion and blessing.

133. *Swasti* (Peace) ! This book is the *Shri Bhaktavijaya.* In listening to it the Lord of the world will be pleased. Listen then, you God loving, pious *bhaktas.* This is the thirty-eighth very delightful chapter; it is an offering to Shri Krishna.

CHAPTER XXXIX

KANHOPATRA

Obeisance to Shri Ganesh. Obeisance to Shri Krishna.

HER MOTHER'S SUGGESTION ABOUT MARRIAGE

1. You pious hearers, now listen attentively. In the southern country there is the sacred city of Pandhari Fourteen miles from there is the town of Mangalvedhe. 2. The name of the prostitute of that place was Shyama. Kanhopatra was born of her, a divine jewel. 3. In looking at her beauty the heavenly maidens became ashamed of their looks. Among mortals Brahmadev never created anyone the equal of her in beauty. 4. While she was young she learned the art of singing and dancing. When looking at her, Rambha, Tilottama, and Menaka felt ashamed of their own skill. 5. Shyama said to her daughter, 'Let us go to the king's palace and when he sees your beauty he will give you ornaments.' 6. Kanhopatra replied, 'O mother, realize that however much one may make search, no one my equal in beauty can be found. 7. If any man can be found a million times more beautiful than I am, I am willing to marry him.' Kanhopatra had decided in her mind, 8. 'All men in this mortal world seem to me now like fire-flies before the sun.'

9. Now on a certain day there was a pilgrimage going to Pandhari. The pilgrims carried banners with the design of eagles upon them and with drums the *Vaishnavas* were shouting loudly. 10. When Kanhopatra saw them she made them a prostrate *namaskar*. She asked them, 'Where are you *Vaishnavas* going? Please tell me.' 11. They replied, 'We are going on a pilgrimage to Pandhari where at Pundalik's request the Dweller in *Vaikunth* (heaven) remained.' 12. Kanhopatra further questioned the saints,

'Describe the Dweller in *Vaikunth* (heaven).' They answered, 'Even Brahmadev and the other gods are unable to describe His glory. 13. He is generous, wise, beautiful and perfect. His beauty exceeds that of Lakshmi a billion fold. It is by His light that the moon and the sun revolve.' 14. Kanhopatra further questioned them, 'If I go as a suppliant to the Lord of the heart, will He accept me?' 15. They replied, 'The dwarf, the slave of Kans who was at Mathura, was accepted by Krishna and He turned her into his own likeness. 16. He at once accepted Ajamil and Chokhamela, and He, the blue-complexioned One, calls Himself the Purifier of the sinful and the merciful One to the lowly.' 17. On hearing what the saints said to her, Kanhopatra hastened to her home and there she bowed to her mother and said, 'I am going to Pandhari.' 18. Then taking a *vina* in her hand the beautiful one sang with love. Kanhopatra then went to Pandhari singing the good qualities of Hari as she went along. 19. At the great temple door Kanhopatra prostrated herself with love. She said to God, 'Hearing of Your name, I have come as a suppliant to You, O Shri Vitthal. 20. Because You are generous, brave, beautiful and perfect, and possessing the glory of the six noble characteristics, therefore I have come as a suppliant to You, O Shri Vitthal. 21. When Ajamil and Ganika came as suppliants to You, You saved them. Because the saints told me of this, I have come to You as a suppliant, O Shri Vitthal. 22. I first desired sensual things, and pride of body existed in me. But now I have abandoned them and have come as a suppliant to You, O Shri Vitthal. 23. Now accept me. I have supplicated myself to Thee, O Shri Hari.' Thus pleading, Kanhopatra placed her head at His feet. 24. Contemplating the form of Hari in her heart, Kanhopatra remained at Pandhari and at the great door of the temple with reverence she sang describing the goodness of Shri Hari.

KANHOPATRA'S BEAUTY

25. Now it happened on one occasion that there was an evil man who went to Bedar and said to the king, 26. 'In Pandharpur at the main door (of the temple) there is a beautiful prostitute and in this mortal world there is no woman her equal.' 27. A fisherman kills fish though they have committed no wrong; just so, evil men continue their enmity against good men. 28. A hunter kills wild animals although they have committed no wrong; in the same way the wicked treat the good with constant enmity. 29. When a tiger sees a man it looks with anger at him, and seeks to devour him; so also evil men always carry enmity in their hearts against good men. 30. Bed-bugs bite men when they are asleep though men are without fault; and evil men always carry enmity against the good. 31. Likewise, although Kanhopatra had done no wrong the evil man went and told the king about her. When he heard this he sent his officers at once to Pandhari. 32. Kanhopatra was at that time in the temple singing God's praise with love and reverence. Just then the officers of the king came and said to her, 33. 'Come at once to Bedar. If you refuse, we shall take you there by force.' She replied, 'I will make a *namaskar* to the god and then start at once with you.' 34. The king's messengers stood outside the assembly-hall while Kanhopatra went into the temple. Here she joined her hands palm to palm and with very humble heart 35. she prayed, 'O Giver of Blessing to Pundalik, O Pandurang, I call myself Yours, O Shri Krishna. If You should now abandon me, O Destroyer of existence in this world, who will be blamed for it? 36. When I say I belong to you, and if the king should carry me off to Bedar, then O Dweller in Pandhari, Shri-Hari, who will be blamed for it? 37. When You heard the pleading voice of the elephant Gajendra, You immediately came to his help, O Life of the world. Now if You,

O Cloud of mercy, abandon me, who will be to blame for it ? 38. When a pigeon fell into distress You removed its troubles, and now if You should reject me, on whom will the blame fall ? 39. When a doe fell into a snare, the moment she remembered You, O Lord of the heart, You came to her help; so now, O Lord of Pandhari, if You abandon me, on whom will the blame fall ? 40. When Ambarish was persecuted by Durvas, You suffered the agony of being born, and now if I am taken to Bedar, on whom will the blame fall ? 41. You accepted Ajamil and Chokha the Mahar (outcaste); now if You should reject me, on whom will the blame fall ? 42. A young toad was put into a frying pan and it at once remembered You and You came to its help ; now if You should abandon me, on whom will the blame fall ? 43. My heart has been united to Your essential form. If those evil men touch me, O God, all saints and good people will laugh at You.'

HER DEATH AT PANDHARPUR

44. As she pleaded so piteously, Narayan melted with compassion. Removing her soul from her body, He united it with His essential form. 45. Saints and priests near there observed the scene and the merciful One took Kanhopatra and concealed her in His lap. 46. Kanhopatra died on His lap and the evidence of this still continues. Those who go to Pandhari with reverence see this with delight. 47. The corpse was taken at that time and buried by the southern door and a *tarati* tree immediately sprang up at that spot.

48. In the meantime the messengers of the king from Bedar stood in the assembly-hall. They now asked the priests what had become of Kanhopatra ? 49. The priests answered them, 'Her soul has become absorbed into the essential form of Hari.' The messengers said, 'Bring the

corpse and show it to us.' 50. The priests said to the messengers of the king, 'Her body has turned into a tree.' They replied, 'It is because you yourselves wished to possess her. 51. You dug into the ground in front of the door of the temple and through an underground passage you made her escape; and now you say, she has become a tree. You are telling us a falsehood.' 52. Without any further thought the king's messengers seized the priests and taking them to Bedar told the king all the news. 53. The Muhammadan king was a very thoughtless man, therefore the priests trembled with fear, but they placed a cocoanut and black powder as God's favour before the king. 54. As he took the favour they offered, a hair appeared in it. The Muhammadan king became angry and asked the priests the meaning of it.

MIRACLE OF THE HAIR

55. The priests felt great fear and wondered what to do. They decided to say to the king that the hair belonged to the god. 56. So they said, 'The hair truly belongs to the Dweller in *Vaikunth* (heaven) Who stands upon the brick on the banks of the Bhima and is the Advocate of Kanhopatra. 57. Come to Pandhari and see if the god has no hair on His head and then you may punish us.' They gave this in writing. 58. The king asked the Brahmans how it was that Kanhopatra was absorbed into God. The priests replied, 'She united with Him just as salt unites with sea-water.' 59. In order to obtain evidence for himself the king started for Pandhari and the Brahmans feeling great concern they said, 'What shall we do now? 60. If the king does not find any hair upon the god he will kill us. The Dweller in the world will either (help us and) spare us shame or He will disregard us. We do not know.' 61. When the Brahmans approached near to Pandhari they pleaded with God in piteous tones, saying, 'O merciful One, Madhav, You are our

Protector. 62. When the lacquered house was aflame, You Infinite One did rush to help the Pandavas, so apart from You there is no one to protect us. 63. When serving food to evil ones, You turned the good Draupadi into the four-armed one. So now, O Husband of Rukmini, You are our Protector. What concern do you feel for us in our distress? 64. When in a forest a fire raged and was burning the cows You swallowed its flames and protected the cows and cowherds. What difficulty can you have in protecting us at this time? 65. When a terrible rain was falling You held up the mountain of Govardhan on the tip of Your nail, therefore what difficulty can You have now in sparing our lives? 66. Knowing Your power we stated in writing to the king that the curly hair belonged to the four-armed One, the dark-complexioned One.'

KING GOES TO PANDHARPUR TO VERIFY HER DEATH

67. The king arrived at the great door of the temple and saw the Brahmans prostrating before God near the eagle-platform. 68. They said, 'O Infinite, O Giver of blessing to Pundalik, You are our Saviour at this time of trouble. Apart from You, O Lord of the world, we see no one to help us.' 69. Then the king went into the god's bedchamber, and looked at the god. Suddenly he saw the god's very brilliant crown. 70. His most beautiful curly hair, His large lotus-eyes, His divine earrings of the shape of crocodiles, and around His neck the garland of the *Kaustubh* jewel. 71. On His breast was an extremely beautiful ornament and both His hands were placed upon His hips. Around His waist was the yellow robe and around His neck appeared the delightful *Vaijayanti* garland. 72. He Who is the object of contemplation for the *yogis* and Whom all gods worship, He was at that moment seen by the king. 73. The moment the king saw Him he became

repentant and said to the Brahmans, 'I have seen the idol of God just as you told me He would appear.' 74. With entire reverence the king prostrated himself before God and giving an embrace to the god he said to the priests, 75. 'Kanhopatra's fortune is supreme in becoming united with the essential form of Hari. I am an unfortunate one and ignorant of knowledge, and because of that I have persecuted her.' 76. He then said to the priests, 'You say that Kanhopatra turned into a tree. How is that?' They then took the king to the southern door of the temple and showed him there the *tarati* tree. 77. The Brahmans told the king that the sacred city of Pandhari was a very ancient one and that all the gods became trees and remained here.' 78. That *tarati* tree is still at the southern door of the temple and pious *bhaktas* coming to Pandhari see it.

79. In the next chapter we shall have a most wonderful story of the *bhakta* Damaji. Mahipati going as a suppliant to him reverently describes his good qualities.

80. *Swasti* (Peace) ! This book is the *Shri Bhaktavijaya.* In listening to it the Lord of the world will be pleased. Listen then, you God-loving; pious *bhaktas.* This is the thirty-ninth deeply delightful chapter; it is an offering to Shri Krishna.

CHAPTER XL

DAMAJIPANT OF MANGALVEDHE

Obeisance to Shri Ganesh. Obeisance to the Lord of the millions of universes.

GOD'S READINESS TO HELP HIS SAINTS

1. Victory, victory to thee, Lover of *bhaktas*, the Husband of Rukmini, Brother of the lowly, Helper of the helpless, Giver of joy to His *bhaktas* who have no one but Thee. 2. Victory, victory to Thee, Who assumed an infinite number of *avatars*, Ocean of mercy, Home of compassion, Ocean of goodness, King of the Yadavas, and who destroys the illusions of Thy *bhaktas*. 3. Victory to Thee, Lord of the universe, Thou exceedingly generous one in giving final deliverance, the Ornament of His *bhaktas*, the Saviour of the world, Dweller in the hearts of Thy *bhaktas*. 4. Victory to the Husband of Kamala, of imperishable form, lotus-eyed, Cloud of intelligence, Creator of the universes, beautiful-eyed and Saviour of the lowly, and *Guru* of the world. 5. When Thy *bhaktas* fall into distress, Thou, O Lord of the world, dost rush to their help. Thou dost accomplish their desire without being ashamed to do so. 6. It is Thou, O beautiful-eyed One, Who art causing me to write. I am merely Thy instrument for I have no independent understanding otherwise.

GOD PLEASED WHEN SAINTS ARE SERVED

7. In the preceding chapter hearers listened with love to the description of how the Life of the world gave to Kanhopatra in His mercy a visible manifestation of Himself. 8. And now listen to the stories of His *bhakta* Damajipant who was most generous, wise and brave. Although living in the midst of earthly affairs he was

most indifferent to all earthly things. 9. In the city of Bedar there was a Muhammadan king. Damaji served him with single devotion and knowing in his heart that the things of this world were illusory, he used to worship Shri Hari. 10. The sacred city of Pandhari was about sixteen miles from Mangalvedhe where the king placed Damaji in charge of the revenue of the district. 11. The king seeing that he was a faithful man placed his store-houses also in his keeping, and there together with his family Damaji lived. 12. At noon-time he used to give food to the uninvited guests who came to him and he always placed his reverent heart at the feet of Shri Pandurang. 13. Many days had passed when suddenly a famine fell on the country and because of this even animals died from hunger. 14. Many people reached the abode of death with gold coins in their mouths (i. e. in their possession). but nowhere could they obtain food. Such were those difficult times. 15. Deserting their own country many went away but weak people had to remain there. They were not able to obtain food at Pandhari, for there were no plantations of vegetables or cornfields there. 16. Now one day a very hungry Brahman came to Mangalvedhe and His wish was great to have some food that day. 17. He came therefore to the house of Damajipant and as soon as he saw the Brahman he made him a reverent *namaskar*. 18. Damaji said to him, 'Bathe and come back quickly to receive God's favour.' Such great respect gave the twice-born (the Brahman) great joy of heart. 19. The Life of the world is always pleased when one speaks kindly to a person who asks of Him, just as a mother feels happy to see her child loved by another person; 20 or when a father sees his son respected he is greatly pleased. So the Holder of the *Sharang* bow rejoices when a man reverently pays respect to anyone who makes a request of him. 21. If any householder in the time of difficulty has no garments or food to give, still he should speak kindly to the one asking for them and bow to him with reverence. 22. Although he may have nothing to give him he should restrain himself from speaking rough, doggish words towards him. If he scolds him and attacks him he will fall into a terrible hell. 23. So say the *Shastras* and the ethical laws. Damajipant knew this and was therefore very courteous to the twice-born, showing him his love. 24. The Brahman performed his bath and Damaji seated him by his side to dine. Many kinds of choice food were served to him. 25. Then lastly ghee was served and the priest made the offerings to the gods and asked the Brahmin to sip the water, when suddenly he saw a strange scene.

A BRAHMAN'S GRIEF

26. The man who came from Pandhari began to weep aloud and tears flowed from his eyes. All wondered at it. 27. The master of the house questioned him, 'What is the occasion and what the pain that have caused you grief?' 28. The twice-born hearing him say this replied, 'Four days have passed in which my wife and children are remaining starving at Pandhari. 29. I am a harsh, thoughtless man. I am here eating at your house but hereafter what is going to happen? That is what makes me grieve.' 30. Damajipant hearing this said to the twice-born, 'I will provide you all with food for a whole year. 31. Now quiet your heart and dine. In the evening I shall send grain to your house.' 32. Listening to this assuring promise the twice-born felt great satisfaction; just as Indra might give nectar as drink to a man at the point of death. 33. Then the twice-born ate with satisfaction and Damajipant gave him *pansupari* and gifts of money with love. Then he gave him his blessing with a feeling of pleasure. 34. Calling his servants

to himself Damajipant said to them, 'Take two loads of grain to Pandhari and give them to this twice-born.' 35. The moment this command was given the Brahman felt great joy and exclaimed, 'The Husband of Rukmini has come to my aid.' As he said this he felt great joy in his heart. 36. Then placing the bags of grain on the oxen he had them sent to Pandharpur and as the men and women there saw the bags of grain they fell on them in their hunger. 37. They tore the bags open and looted all the grain. No one's resistance was of any avail because all were without food. 38. The Brahman to whom the grain had been given began to cry saying, 'Who are you to rob me of the grain?' 39. Just as when a farmer's crop has ripened, there falls upon it a great cloud of locusts and he feels sorely troubled, so it happened to this Brahman.

STARVING BRAHMANS GO TO DAMAJI FOR FOOD

40. All the Brahmans at Pandhari then asked him for his news. 'From whence did you bring this grain? You must please tell us.' 41. He replied, 'It was Damajipant the generous, wise and brave who had mercy upon me, and gave me food. 42. God gave, but my *karma* (fate) has taken it away. Such is what has happened to me. My family's good fortune has broken down, and all the people stole the grain.' 43. Hearing the man's story all the Brahmans hastened and came to the house of Damajipant. 44. Seeing the Brahmans, he made a reverent *namaskar*. The Brahmans then blessed him saying, 'May a blessing rest upon you. 45. A severe famine has fallen upon us. You have given food to a Brahman and we have heard of your act. We have all therefore hastened here. 46. You are brave and exceedingly generous. In giving food you have no idea in your mind whether one is small or great; you have no thought of whether the person is worthy of it

or not. 47. When the sun is risen in the sky, it shines alike on every man, so when you give food you never think of great or small. 48. We are Brahmans dwelling at the sacred city and we are dying for want of food. We have heard of your fame and have therefore hastened here.' 49. Hearing the Brahmans' story pity arose in Damajipant's heart. Then giving his assurance that they should not fear he seated all the Brahmans. 50. Going into his house he said to his wife, 'Those Brahmans who dwell at Pandhari are dying for want of food. 51. They have come together and have arrived at our house. If we say "No" to them our character for goodness will suffer loss. 52. To make them happy by supplying their needs we have not sufficient grain. Therefore I feel very great concern. What shall I do? 53. The grain which I gave to a Brahman has all been taken away from him. The people are in distress from the famine and some have deserted their country and gone away.' 54. His wife said to him, 'Carry out any plan that may suggest itself to you and satisfy the Brahmans.'

ROYAL GRANARIES PLUNDERED

55. Damaji said, 'The king has two storehouses of grain which are in our charge. Those storehouses of grain I should let the Brahmans loot and thus save all their lives. 56. As soon as the king hears of this he will take my life, but by the loss of one life the Brahmans of the holy city will live. 57. If I alone love my body then death will come to all of them.' He thought this to himself and immediately came outside. 58. He at once opened the storehouses and said to the Brahmans, 'Take back to your homes just as much grain as you need.' 59. Hearing these generous words the Brahmans all blessed him and remarked, 'May the Husband of Rukmini bless you and always give you His blessing.' 60. Then all the Brahmans

looted the unlimited supply of grain and when the people of Pandhari heard of this they all hastened to Damaji's house. 61. The Brahmans, *Kshatriyas*, *Vaishyas*, *Shudras*, grocers, *Gondhalis*, the helpless and the poor all came to Mangalvedhe, took grain and then went back. 62. The carpenters, labourers and others of of various castes, potters, barbers, and those without much understanding, hearing of Damajipant's fame came to carry away grain. 63. Masons, milkmen, workers in stone, fishermen, workers in copper and gardeners all hastened to Mangalvedhe and took away grain as much as they desired.. 64. People from Gujarat, dyers, salt manufacturers, *yogis*, saints and *mahants* exclaimed, 'The Husband of Rukmini is pleased with us and has entered into Damaji's heart.' 65. Tailors, washermen, workers in stone and an endless number of castes and out-castes came and took an unlimited amount of grain. 66. Hearers may have a doubt and say, 'Why was it necessary to bring there all castes? Why did he not attempt to select those who were worthy?' 67. But all who lived at the sacred city of Pandhari should be considered alike, so the ancient verses composed by the saints say, therefore you should not have any doubts in your mind. 68. There are ninety hundred thousand water animals in the midst of the sea, but the sea looks alike on all of them, so the Lord of the world looks with mercy upon all castes. 69. One million kinds of birds fly about in the air, and to the Husband of Rukmini all are alike. 70. There are two million kinds of trees and to the earth they are all the same; likewise the Purifier of sinners and the Saviour of the lowly considers all beings alike. 71. Those who have full knowledge of the soul, they are the ones who understand the doctrines connected with it. Seeing that this is so, they do not speak of any of the different castes as superior or inferior. 72. Damajipant quite understood this fact regarding the state of superior *bhaktas.* Therefore in his kind heart he distributed food to all creatures. 73. During this famine he saved the lives of the helpless, the weak and those desperately poor but he never thought that he was the giver of grain.

A CHARGE AGAINST DAMAJI

74. When this fact was told at Pandhari, Damaji's praiseworthy deeds were noised abroad all through that country. But the mean worldly minded men burned in their hearts out of jealousy. 75. Sneeringly they said, 'He has distributed the grain belonging to the king. What has he given of his own ? He has not distributed what he gathered together by hard labour.' 76. Others however remarked, 'Why do you abandon your daily avocation ? Why do you needlessly revile him ? If the king hears of this he will be filled with anger and will treat him very roughly. 77. One should distribute the wealth which he himself has gained by hard labour, but he has done more than that. When the Muhammadan king hears of the news, he will take his life.' 78. Thus people spoke to one another in their homes, but Damajipant full of happiness was not affected by either joy or sorrow. 79. For a whole month those who came to ask for grain took it away. Then occurred a very great hardship for him. Listen to what it was, you good and pious people.

80. A Moozumdar (tax-collector), a Kanarese Brahman, was an evil man and a hater of Vishnu. He wrote a letter to Bedar sending the following information to the king. 81. He said, 'O great king, superior lord of the city, listen to the request of your servant. Damajipant has looted your grain by the hands of Brahmans. 82. I call myself your servant and I have devoted myself to your service. Therefore I have submitted this information.' This was the substance of what he wrote in a letter which he hastened to send to Bedar. 83. As soon as the letter

was read to him the Muhammadan king became full of rage ; just as when melted butter is sprinkled over a fire it blazes up to heaven ; 84. or as when an elephant is made to drink intoxicating liquor, he seeks to destroy any buildings that he may come across ; likewise the king hearing this news would not even investigate the affair. 85. He said, 'Damaji did not first receive my permission. How is it he distributed the grain of my storehouses ?' Thus the king expressed his anger and sent his soldiers to demand money.

DAMAJI SUMMONED BY THE KING

86. The king held an evil wish in his heart to summon Damajipant into his presence and he was determined to punish him by instant decapitation. 87. The king's officers came to Mangalvedhe and showed Damajipant the royal mandate at which all the people of the town became deeply concerned. 88. They exclaimed, 'The king thinks Damaji has done a very great wrong in having his storehouses looted, therefore the king's officers have come to take Damaji to Bedar.' 89. When Damajipant read the letter from the king he understood it all. He said, 'I have done a great wrong. Whyshould I now sorrow over it ?' 90. To the officers sent by the king to take him to Bedar, Damajipant said, 'As you go along on the road to Bedar allow me to meet the Husband of Rukmini at Pandhari.' 91. Saying this he set off for Pandharpur. After bathing on the banks of the Bhima he went to the great door of the temple. 92. He made a prostrate *namaskar* before the eagle-platform and going a little further into the inner chamber he there made a prostrate *namaskar* to the god. 93. Looking up he saw the supreme *Brahma* standing upon a brick, the Helper of the helpless, the Advocate of *bhaktas*, the Saviour of the world, the *Guru* of the world. 94. His face was exceedingly beautiful. Brilliant earrings in the form of crocodiles hung from His ears. Around His

neck were the *Kaustubh* jewel and garlands of flowers. Around His waist was the yellow robe. 95. His feet were parallel on the brick. His hands were on His hips and His sight was directed to the tip of His nose. Seeing the Lord of the world in this form he felt great joy. 96. He gave him a loving embrace and then with reverence grasped both of His feet. Gazing at His form he joined his hands together and made a request. 97. He said, 'O God supreme, Husband of Rukmini, this is my last visit to You. Never leave off Your love for me.' With this Damaji placed his head on the god's feet. 98. 'I committed a wrong known to all. The king feels great anger towards me and now he has sent his soldiears to take me to Bedar, there to behead me. 99. Still I think I have accomplished a worthy deed at the very end of life, and I have seen Your feet.' Saying this Damaji was filled with emotion, 100. and his throat was filled with sobs. Tears flowed from both eyes, and again gazing at the god's form he asked his leave to go. 101. When they heard his prayers to the god the soldiers said to him, 'Come along quickly in order that we may not delay. It is necessary for us to go at once.' 102. Damaji then made a prostrate *namaskar* to Satyabhama, Radha and Rukmini, worshipped the eagle and Hanumant and quickly started. 103. The dwellers at the sacred city said to one another, 'What the Lord of Pandhari will do, no one of us can understand.'

KRISHNA'S DISGUISE AS A MAHAR AT ROYAL COURT

104. Going around Pandharpur, keeping it at his left, Damajipant walked along quickly. And now the Husband of Rukmini, seeing Damaji's distress, did as follows. 105. He said to Himself, 'Damaji has placed his burden upon me and caused the king's storehouse of grain to be looted. Now the king is exceedingly angry and is calling him in order to kill him. 106. But I am the Advocate of

bhaktas, so say the *Shastras* and the *Puranas*. If I do not rush to his help now, I shall lose My reputation.' 107. Having thus thought over the matter, the Giver of final deliverance calculated the value of the grain and took the money along with Him. 108. The Lord of Pandhari assumed the form of an out-caste, for on account of His *bhaktas*, the Pervader of the world feels great joy in His heart. 109. He wrote a request to the king in Damajipant's handwriting, and becoming Damaji's messenger He hastened to Bedar. 110. The Husband of Rukmini fastened on His head tattered garments, placed around His neck a black cord and in His ears the *pagar* earrings (the ornaments worn in the ears of Mahars). 111. Around his waist was a loin cloth and He had a staff in His hand. Rukmini remarked to Him, 'What is it that the Lord of the world is planning to do?' 112. The Lord of *Vaikunth* replied, 'My *bhakta* Damaji has been carried to Bedar in order to be put to death. 113. For his sake I have become an un-namable (or out-caste). When My *bhak as* fall into distress I am never ashamed to help them.' 114. Taking a bag of money he sealed it with the king's seal and immediately the Holder of the *Sharang* bow appeared at the city of Bedar. 115. To the doorkeeper the Life of the world related His story saying, 'I have come from Mangalvedhe. Let your master know of this.' 116. At the king's command the doorkeeper took him into the palace. The Lord of Pandhari then saluted him with the word *Johar* (the Mahar word used in salutation). This may seem very strange to us. 117. He whose glory is not understood by even the *Vedas* and *Shastras* which describe Him, He bowed His head low and saluted the king with the word *Johar*. 118. He, to attain whom the eighty-eight thousand *rishis* perform austerities, He addressed the Muhammadan king with the words, 'You are My mother and father,' for His *bhakta* who was accused of wrong.

119. The minister of the king said to Him, 'Whence have You come?' Hearing him, the Delighter of the heart answered; listen to it. 120. 'I am the Mahar servant of Damaji of Mangalvedhe. I call Myself his hereditary slave.' 121. You will perhaps ask, 'Would He who lives on the sea of milk and reclines on the serpent Shesha use such obsequious words?' But you should not keep in your mind any question or doubt about this; 122. for when He, Krishna, was protecting the cows at the house of Nanda He openly called Himself a cowherd, and when He was at the house of Dharma, the King of the Yadavas (Krishna) gladly removed the used-up dining plates; 123. when He was Arjuna's charioteer He washed his horses with His four hands; therefore the Husband of Rukmini without any hesitation called Himself the hereditary slave of Damajipant. 124. When the king's minister asked the Mahar his name He said, 'My name is Vithonaik, an adopted child of Damaji.' Thus speaking, the dark complexioned One threw down before him a letter. 125. He recognized the handwriting of Damaji and all believed it to be genuine. He (the minister) then read the petition to the king. 126. Seeing the letter the king listened to it with curiosity and said, 'Damaji has committed a wrong and what has he now to say in the letter?' 127. The contents of the letter were as follows:—'King of kings, Lord of the world, your servant Damajipant makes to you a humble request. 128. A famine prevailed in this country and food became very scarce; I therefore sold seven hundred *Khandis* (Lbs. 1600 = a *Khandi*) of grain, for your advantage. 129. The rate of every *payali* (lbs. 8)was a rupee. I have filled a bag with this money and have sent it in your service. 130. Vithonaik is our servant and he does every form of work at our house. He will give an account of this money. Kindly send back by him a receipt.' 131. Hearing this letter read every one thought it to be untrue. For seeing

that the bag was small they felt great doubt about its contents 132. Having examined the account they went and said to the king: 'We need one hundred and thirty-eight thousnd rupees as the amount.'

DAMAJI'S VINDICATION

133. When the bag was broken open it was filled with so much money that they were not able to count it and their hands became wearied in counting it. The king was amazed; 134. just as when water is taken from a ditch made in the sand and it does not fall short; just so the Life of the world, performed a miracle which He showed to them. 135. Yet no one could uuderstand it. They were deluded by God's *maya* and they congratulated the king and called him fortunate. 136. This immense amount of money could not be finished in its counting, so they threw the bag into the king's treasury as it was and said, 'The blessed Damajipant understands what is to his own good.' 137. The king said, 'In listening to my *Moozumdar's* (deputy revenue collector's) accusation I needlessly demanded money. It was as if one should believe the braying of a laundryman's donkey and drive away a wish-cow.' 138. Krishna then spoke from outside, 'Please give me the receipt quickly. Mangalvedhe is very far from here and it will take me a long time to go there.'

ROYAL MANDATE

139. A letter was written and sent by him to Damaji saying, 'All the money has been received and I have ordered the deputy revenue collector to be put into jail. 140. The moment you read this letter, at once confiscate all his rights. I wish you to live at Mangalvedhe always.' 141. The king gave garments to Vithonaik and honoured him. Seeing this the Life of the world [who was in the form of the servant Vithonaik] gave His blessing to the king: 142. 'May you enjoy a long life and may the

whole wealth of the world come to you.' Then making a low bow He took with Him the letter. 143. The king gave to Damaji garments and ornaments with great satisfaction of mind, and by the hands of his servants sent to Damajipant a palanquin, elephants and a chariot. 144. With them the Life of the world started for Mangalvedhe. This was not known to Damajipant. 145. Coming to Bedar they missed one another on the road. The Lord of *Vaikunth* (heaven) thus shows to His *bhaktas* an illusory *līlā* (miracle).

DAMAJI AT ROYAL COURT

146. The king's messengers brought Damajipant to Bedar. When the king heard the news he went forward to meet him. 147. The king gave him an embrace saying, 'Vitho the Mahar came and gave me the full amount of money. 148. We affectionately sent to you garments and ornaments by his hand. We listened to the evil report of the Kanarese tax-collector and were angry. 149. After having sent for you, Vithonaik came yesterday. He told us of what you had done. 150. He brought us your letter in your handwriting and having given us an immense amount of money he returned.' 151. When he heard this, Damajipant was most astonished and said to himself, 'The Lord of Pandhari has wearied Himself in order that I might escape any hardship. 152. He Who is qualityless, formless, desireless, and Who can never be compared with anyone else, He took the form of an out-caste and brought on His head a load of money. 153. Seeing the lustre of His crown, a billion suns see their lights fade away. He, the Ancient of Days, the Husband of Lakshmi, fastened a rag upon His head. 154. He cast aside His crocodile-shaped earrings and put into His ears such earrings as are worn by the out-castes. Putting aside His beautiful *Kaustubh* jewel He wore in its place a mere string. 155. The Lord of the world cast

aside His conch-shell and disk and took a staff in His hand. He must have removed His yellow robe and for my sake dressed in a loin cloth. 156. He must have removed from His feet His ankle-ornaments and put on torn sandals. Cursed be my life that I have wearied the Life of the world.' 157. So thinking these things, Damajipant was moved to emotion and in his love tears flowed from his eyes. I cannot describe his joy. 158. Together with the king everybody was astonished. They acknowledged, 'He was not a real out-caste, but the Husband of Rukmini. Through experience we have learned to recognize that fact. 159. If he were a mere man how could he have carried so heavy a load? When counted out the money was one hundred and thirty-eignt thousand rupees. 160. And still there was nothing lacking in the bag (i. e., the money in the bag did not diminish). The hands of those who were counting became wearied, so they had to throw it into the king's treasury as it was.' 161. When all spoke in that way Damaji showed great sorrow of heart saying, 'I will not again repeat that act which wearied the Husband of Rukmini. 162. In putting earrings in, if the ear drops down, then what is the need of the gold? I shall not again do that by which the Life of the world is wearied.'

DAMAJI GOES TO LIVE AT PANDHARPUR

163. He then said to the king, 'I no longer wish to work in your service. Give me permission to live in Pandharpur. 164. The king said to him, 'God has become your debtor, and through you I have met with the Holder of the disk (Krishna).'

165. To return now to the Holder of the *Sharang* bow (Krishna). He hastened to Mangalvedhe and there informed those at Damaji's home of his welfare and then at once became invisible. 166. Damajipant then gave up the king's service and came to Pandhari to live. Filled with emotion he embraced the god. 167. He exclaimed, 'O

Purifier of the sinner, Husband of Rukmini, Brother of the lowly, Lord of Pandhari, no one can ever count the number of my transgressions. 168. Thou art worthy of the worship of Sanak, Shiva, and the other gods. They sing the praise of Thy feet. Thou didst become an un-namable (or out-caste) and didst save my life. 169. Thou art the Father of Brahmadev and the father of the holy Ganges river. O Lord of the world, for my sake Thou didst needlessly become an out-caste man. 170. Who was there to call Thee by the name of Vithonaik brought up as a child at Damaji's house? Still Thou didst so report to the king.' 171. Having exclaimed thus, tears flowed from his eyes because of his love, and gazing at His form he placed his head at the god's feet. 172. Together with his family, Damajipant went to live at Pandhari, and filled with love he performed *kirtans* and described the goodness of Hari. 173. Citizens of that holy city exclaimed, 'Blessed, blessed is his *bhakti.* He has made the Husband of Rukmini his debtor and has increased his reputation immensely.' 174. Because he has performed a wonderful deed, the Holder of the disk (Krishna) is pleased with him.' So said the people to one another in their homes.

175. In the next chapter is the extraordinary story of the life of Mrityunjaya. Listen to it, you pious people, with pleasure. It is one that will give joy to all. 176. Some one may not have any specially reverent feeling for the story, still it purifies by the mere hearing of the words. When the *chakor* bird receives the nectar of the moonlight, the light is seen everywhere. 177. Therefore Mahipati beseeches all, old and young, to bring love into their hearts and worship the Husband of Rukmini.

178. *Swasti* (peace)! This book is the *Shri Bhaktavijaya.* In listening to it the Lord of the world will be pleased. Listen then, you God-loving, pious *bhaktas.* This is the fortieth very delightful chapter; it is an offering to Shri Krishna.

CHAPTER XLI

MRITYUNJAYA SWAMI

Obeisance to Shri Ganesh. Obeisance to Shri Krishnn.

KRISHNA DWELLS IN THE HEART

1. Victory, victory to Thee, Lord of Pandhari, Performer of *līlā* (voluntary deeds), Pervader of the world, Thou Whose form is that of the universe, Lord of the heart, eternal Lord of all, Pandurang. 2. Victory, victory to Thee, Lord of Kamala, Soul of the universe, the Light of the heart, even the *Vedas* find it impossible to describe the state of Thy essential form. 3. Victory, victory to Thee, Hari and Shiva without a limit, supremely generous. Thou Saviour of the world that dwellest in the temple of the hearts of Thy *bhaktas*. 4. Victory, victory to the essential form, made visible, O dark-complexioned like a cloud, Treasure-house of goodness, Delighter of the heart, God supreme, the highest of beings, let love exist in our worship of Thee. 5. Now reveal Thyself in the words I use and cause me to write properly the stories of Thy *bhaktas* by which the hearts of my hearers may be filled with waves of love.

THE MUHAMMADAN KING SHANTA BRAHMANI

6. In the preceding chapter there was the extraordinary story of the God-loving *bhakta* Damajipant. In his distress the Husband of Rukmini came to his help at once. 7. At Bedar there was a king by name of Shanta Brahmani. After ruling many days, he came to the knowledge of the value of indifference to earthly things. 8. If you ask me how this was brought about then listen carefully to the following story. Taking his wife upstairs he held a conversation with her.

9. Both had on them garlands of many kinds of flowers and sandalwood paste. They wore brilliant garments, ornaments and adornments. Being without any fear both lived enjoying themselves. 10. Around them they had placed servants to guard the palace. While sitting at the window they had sugar and bananas brought which they ate with pleasure. 11. As they peeled the bananas they threw the skins down on the path. Suddenly a crazy, weak beggar came there and began to eat the peelings. 12. The queen seeing the beggar there pointed him out to her lord with her hand saying, 'I do not understand how he could come there when entrance was forbidden.' 13. Hearing these words of his wife king Shanta Brahmani became very angry. Calling the doorkeepers he said to them, 14. 'I have placed you at the entrance door in order that you may not allow anyone to come into the palace grounds. How is it that this crazy beggar has come inside ?' 15. Thus speaking he began to beat the doorkeepers, all of whom came to the beggar and attacked him with kicks and blows.

THE KING ASKS THE BEGGAR WHY HE LAUGHED

16. The beggar paid no attention to his pain but began to laugh. Shanta Brahmani seeing it simply wondered in his mind. 17. The king said to his messengers, 'Do not strike him.' King Shanta Brahmani was moved to emotion by the beggar's pain and he began to cry. 18. The king then questioned the beggar and said, 'As the doorkeeper was beating you, how is it you began to laugh? Tell me quickly.' 19. To this question of the king the beggar replied, 'I laughed at my *karma* (fate), seeing how strangely odd it was. 20. If I was punished so severely for taking merely such a small bit of banana peel what will be *your* future ? And therefore I was wondering. 21. By coming into the palace grounds I was punished so

severely, then I am deeply concerned about *you* who regularly sleep in the palace. 22. If by tasting the banana peelings with my tongue, my *karma* (fate) causes me to be kicked, I cannot think what punishment *you* will have who eat the inside pulp. 23. If a fish in swallowing a bait of lifeless flour meets its death, then who can measure the consequence to the man who takes life and makes his livelihood upon it. 24. The thought of your future pain made me laugh.' Hearing what this beggar said the king's heart changed at once.

THE KING IN PENITENCE RETIRES TO A FOREST

25. Feeling repentant he discarded all his kingdom and wealth and without anyone knowing of it he went into the great forest. 26. There king Shanta Brahmani sitting alone became exceedingly sorrowful. 'I am living by myself like an unfortunate person without the support of saints. 27. I do not know how to worship God. I do not know what means to adopt for attaining union with Him, nor do I know what punishment to give to my body. 28. What are the teachings regarding indifference to worldly things? How may I repent? How will Shri Hari look upon me with the eyes of pity when I am in any distress? 29. I do not understand how to perform *manas puja* (mental worship). I do not know how to make offerings to the eagle bannered One. How can my life be made fruitful? I do not know. 30. In what way should I live among men? When shall I meet with saints?' Such were the thoughts which came into the mind of King Shanta Brahmani.

KING AND PILGRIMS

31. It now happened that in the month of *Ashadh* (July) at Pandharpur a pilgrimage passed by with its loud shouting of God's names. 32. Cymbals, drums and *vinas* were being played, *Vaishnavas* in their joy were singing, dancing, bowing to one another and embracing one another in

love. 33. Many brilliant banners were fluttering in the air, and before them were waved banners with the design of eagles and other ensigns of greatness. Many *Vaishnavas* walked along. 34. Looking at such a gathering the king, Shanta Brahmani, felt great joy in his heart. In love he went towards them, making prostrate *namaskars* to the *Vaishnavas*. 35. He exclaimed to himself, 'Blessed is this day in which I have had contact with saints. The good deeds which I have committed in a former birth have truly begun to bear fruit. 36. That which I was wishing for in my heart I have obtained this day.' Regarding this with great satisfaction he at once started to go with them.

THE KING AT PANDHARPUR

37. When he arrived at the sacred city of Pandhari he bathed in the Chandrabhaga river. Then worshipping at Pundalik's tomb he bowed to the saints and good people. 38. After circumambulating the sacred city, Shanta Brahmani came to the temple. Hearing people shout loudly in their *kirtans* he felt great joy. 39. One may have seen and heard of the great numbers of sacred bathing-places and their deities, but so extaordinary a sacred city as Pandhari is not to be seen in the three worlds 40. When one looks anywhere to find anything with which to compare it no such place can be found. It matters little how evil the heart of a wicked man might be, he cannot help loving Pandhari. 41. When men bathe in any other sacred bathing-place they immediately become proud of their deed, but the moment they see the Chandrabhaga river they make prostrate *namaskars* to one another. 42. In seeing such a sacred bathing-place Shanta Brahmani felt great joy in his heart. Then prostrating before the eagle-platform, with love in his heart he moved from there to another place. 43. Bowing to all the *Vaishnavas* he gave them embraces in his love and went into the inner chamber

to see and worship God. 44. There he saw the supreme *Brahma* standing upon a brick. He reverently embraced His breast and made a *namaskar* at His feet. 45. He exclaimed, 'Victory, victory! Ancient of days, Thou with a visible form, Lord of the heart, Performer of *līlā* (voluntary deeds), Lord of all, Lord of Pandhari, Shri Vitthal. 46. Hearing of Thy good deeds, I have come as a suppliant to Thee, O Krishna. But I have not met any *sadguru* in order that I may know Thy essential form. 47. O fulfil the longing of my heart.' Thus exclaiming he sat persistently at the door of the temple and would take no fruit, vegetables or even water. Because of his repentance he refused all food.

MRITYUNJAYA AS SAHAJANAND'S DISCIPLE

48. After three days had passed the Husband of Rukmini showed His pleasure to him and in a dream brought direct to him the book called the *Vivekasindhu* (by Mukundraj). 49. The Lord of Pandhari told him in a dream to receive the mystic *mantra* of *Swami* Sahajanand at Kalyan, and after He had told him about it he awoke. 50. He did not see the Lord of Pandhari now, but the book alone was there. Seeing this wonderful miracle he felt great astonishment. 51. He said to himself, 'The *Guru* of the world has given me a revelation of Himself and by that means I have become purified.' Then reading the *Vivekasindhu* book he began to contemplate by himself its teaching. 52. He remembered also that in his dream he was asked to make Sahajanand his *guru*. Then asking leave of the god to go he made his bow to Him. 53. He went at once to Kalyan but the *sadguru* was not there. So afterwards in the month of *Kartik* (November) he came again to the sacred city of Pandhari. 54. While he was there the *Swami* Sahajanand suddenly appeared. He also had come on a pilgrimage. Shanta Brahmani met him at once and told him about his

dream. 55. *Swami* Sahajanand gave him instruction and gave him the name of Mrityunjaya. King Shanta Brahmani then hastened to go back to the city of Narayanpur to live. 56. Here listening to the teaching of his *sadguru*, and contemplating what he said, he acquired a love for study. Then coming to understand exactly the truth he experienced the facts about the soul.

A JANGAM LOSES HIS CASTE

57. At the place there was a **Jangam* by name of Bhavaraya who was supremely pious and learned. He came as a suppliant to Mrityunjaya and lovingly took instruction from him. 58. There was another *Jangam* there by the name of Samuchchaya who was considered the superior of all *Jangams.* He reviled Bhavaraya and had him excommunicated. 59. He said, 'Mrityunjaya belongs to the Muhammadan caste and he has the very least of knowledge. How is it that Bhavaraya was ignorant of this and took instruction from him ? 60. Will a Brahman when he sees dainty food in the house of a *Shudra* partake of it? Even if the water of the Ganges is brought in a cup with intoxicating liquor one should not drink of it. 61. Although one may have new sandals they should not be placed upon the head when walking. Should one worship the steps of the temple in the shrine of God ? 62. Though one's anklets were made of gold one should not wear them as nose-rings. Will the castor oil tree seek to be on the same level as a great tree ? 63. Even if brass is polished highly it does not become equal to gold. Although *Vrindavan* (a bitter fruit) is mixed with sugar, still it will remain bitter. 64. The king's prostitute may be beautiful and clever, still will she sit by the king during the " Blessing the day ceremony ? " So one should never pay respect to

* (1) The name of an individual who follows Shiva, worships the *lingam* and hates the Brahman; (2) the title of a *guru* among this sect.

one of the Muhammadan caste in place of a *Sadguru.*' 65. With such opposing thoughts Samuchchaya continued to revile him. Bhavaraya hearing him then became very sorrowful. 66. He therefore went to Mrityunjaya at his hermitage and told him his story. The *Sadguru* hearing him gave him an assurance. 67. He said to him, 'Hold steadily in your faith and in a quiet mind worship God. Never listen to the words of one whose hatred comes from wrong thoughts.'

KING KASHIPATI

68. There was also there a king named Kashipati. He was a supremely generous man, a veritable statue of knowledge and exceedingly devoted to the *bhakti* of Shiva. 69. He used to invite every day to his house ten thousand *Jangams.* With the sixteen materials for worship he used to worship them and gave them dainty food to eat. 70. Now it happened on a certain day that Kashipati seated the *Jangams* in a line for a feast, lovingly performed worship and was serving food on their plates. 71. The king served to all melted butter and sugar with his own hands, and then gave the command that the offering should be given to Shiva. 72. When they unrolled the cloth they found it empty of the emblem of the god. Saying that a strange thing had happened, they felt ashamed. 73. Just as a Brahman learned in six *Shastras* who loses his sacred thread will feel ashamed, so it happened to these people. 74. How could they now worship and how could they have dinner ? They had to perform a penance of death. When Shiva has gone they should not seek to prolong their lives. 75. When they first put the *linga* (emblem of Shiva) around their necks, their *gurus* tell them they must never remove it to the end of their lives; they make them promise to that effect. 76. The question of who should be excommunicated confused them because the condition of each was the same. There were

ten thousand men who sat at the feast and all wondered what they should do. 77. One remarked, 'Let us give up our lives.' Another said, 'Why live any longer?' A third said, 'What is the use of a feast? A great hindrance has suddenly appeared.' 78. Still another remarked, 'We have eaten the food of a king and that has been our fault. So Shiva has deserted us all.' 79. Another said, 'Food is not to be blamed. It is because we have no pure faith. That is why Shiva has openly left us and showed us this wonderful *līlā* (miracle).' 80. Thus they spoke to one another but no one saw any remedy. The opinion of every one was confused and all looked down in shame. 81. Kashipati of Kalyan then said to the *Jangams*, 'It would seem to me that some one of you has persecuted a saint. 82. For this reason the Lord of the universe has become angry with you all and has gone away.' Having listened to the words of the king (Kashipati) they consulted with one another.

TWO DOGS VOMIT SHAIVITE EMBLEMS

83. Then Samuchchaya the *Jangam* confessed saying, 'The fault has occurred through me. I reviled Bhavaraya calling him the disciple of a Muhammadan. 84. This terrible fault is mine. My conscience bears witness to this. We do not know what is the remedy for this.' 85. The king then said to them, 'Let all of you pray to Mrityunjaya and then you will certainly be freed from your troubles.' 86. This word of the king was acceptable to all and the whole line of diners started to go. 87. They all went to the hermitage of Mrityunjaya and prostrated themselves before him. They told him what had occurred and stood before him with hands joined together palm to palm. 88. They said, 'We have truly spoken roughly to Bhavaraya. For this reason it appears that Shri Shankar has disappeared from us.' 89. Hearing their words, Mrityunjaya seated them and shouted out to them all. 90. He said to them,

At my home I have two dogs. One by the name of *Vedanta* (philosophy) and the other by the name of *Siddhanta* (facts). It is they who stole your *lingas* (emblems of Shiva) and have taken them away I think.' 91. He then called *Vedanta* which at once appeared. He said to the dog, 'Why have you needlessly stolen the *lingas* (emblems of Shiva) belonging to the *Jangams* ? 92. Throw them all down here.' Listening to Mrityunjaya's words the dog vomited up five thousand *lingas* (emblems of Shiva). 93. He then called *Siddhanta* and the other dog appeared. He also vomited up five thousand *lingas* (emblems of Shiva) and threw them down. 94. Seeing this astonishing sight all the people there were amazed. They said, 'We do not understand the power of the *bhaktas* of Vishnu.' 95. No one was able to recognize and pick out his own (emblem of Shiva). So they again prostrated themselves with reverence before Mrityunjaya and said, 96. 'Just as the Husband of Parvati showed to Shriyal one hundred and eight Chiliyas but he could not recognize his own Chiliya, so it has happened to us. 97. Then the Dweller in *Kailas* (Shiva) being favourable to him, He gave His own son to him. So do for us.' Saying this they fell at his feet. 98. After these piteous words, each (emblem) went to the one to whom it belonged. All then shouted, 'Victory, victory,' 'Hara, Hara' (Shiva, Shiva). 99. They then called Mrityunjaya *Dnyansagar Ayya* (an ocean of knowledge). They then went into the king's palace and sat down to a feast. 100. In this way the *Vaishnava bhaktas* show their marvellous deeds. Mahipati comes to them as a suppliant to describe their good deeds with love.

101. *Swasti* (Peace) ! This book is the *Shri Bhaktavijaya*. In listening to it the Lord of the world will be pleased. Listen then, you God-loving, pious *bhaktas*. This is the forty-first very delightful chapter; it is an offering to Shri Krishna.

CHAPTER XLII

BHANUDAS*

Obeisance to Shri Ganesh. Obeisance to Shri Khrishna

INVOCATION

1. Victory! victory to Thee! Vasudev, Lord of the Earth, lotus-eyed One, Husband of Rukmini, Giver of happiness to His *bhaktas*, without whom there is no happiness. 2. Victory, victory to Thee of the lotus-navel whose form is the Universe, Father of Brahmadev, Lord of heaven, Radiant of form, dwarf-shaped, indescribable by *Vedas* or *Shastras*. 3. Victory to Thee, unlimited universal Arm, the all-seeing Eye, He who fills universal space, Thou who hast spoken in the words of the *Vedas*. 4. O Thou, whose form is universal radiance, Lord of the heart; because Thy *bhaktas* cannot fully know Thee, Thou didst take a *saguna* form and set them to worshipping Thee. 5. O Lord of Lakshmi, Thou becomest to them whatever they desire, just as a mother of graceful carriage leads her child along, holding it by the hand, 6. her heart rejoicing in the sweet prattle of the little lisper. She speaks back to it in the same prattling way, kissing it in her love. 7. The same thing happens to Thy *bhaktas* who lacking knowledge praise Thee in foolish babbling words, and Thou, Life of the world, in Thy loving mercy makest Thyself as simple to them.

THE BIRTH AND BOYHOOD OF BHANUDAS

8. In the previous chapter there was recorded the deeply delightful story of the life of Mrityunjaya, in which you hearers became absorbed as you listened. Such is the infinite glory of the saints. 9. Now it happened that the

---

*For further information regarding Bhanudas see the first volume of this series.

sun appeared as an *avatar* at Pratishthan. And I would that you good people would listen with loving attention to the interesting story. 10. To a wise, holy and pious Brahman, a worshipper of the sun, there was born the treasure of a son to the great delight of his heart. 11. Day by day the boy grew and in due time the ceremony of the sacred thread was performed. His father and mother bestowed on him boundless love.

12. It happened one day that in assigning him the task of studying the *Vedas* the father showed anger. Out of fear of that anger the boy sulked. 13. He left the house. He made great efforts to find a place in which to conceal himself. At first he failed, but suddenly in his wandering his eye fell on a temple. 14. This temple lay underground. People did not visit it, so the boy at once entered and remained there in hiding. 15. There was an antique image of the sun in that temple and the boy at once prostrated himself lovingly at its feet. 16. Seeing the boy's devotion the sun was pleased and said to himself, 'Although this child is ignorant his heart has firm trust in me.' 17. The sun then assumed human form and approached him. He gave the boy milk as much as he could drink and gave him the assurance of his protection from all fear. 18. He said to him, 'Let your heart be without fear, keep Shri Pandurang in your remembrance. If you should ever fall into any distress at your call I will immediately be present with you.'

19. Turning now to the father and mother, who with sad hearts were searching for their son, it happened that seven days passed and yet they had not found him. 20. But one day the Brahman's son stepped outside the temple. There happened to be there one of the twice-born and he spied the lad. 21. He called out to him but the boy at once ran back into the temple. The Brahman then came

into the town and related the event to the father. 22. The father and mother rejoiced to think that their son had been found, and taking some of their townspeople with them, started to find him. 23. There in the forest they discovered to their surprise a deserted temple. They lighted torches and bravely descended into it. 24. As they entered they all saw the image of Narayan (sun) and the Brahman's son sleeping with his head on the feet of the image. 25. The father and mother bent over their son and drew him to their lotus-hearts exclaiming, 'How has it happened that you have survived in this place all alone ?' Tears flowed from their eyes. 26. The people then asked him, 'How have you kept yourself alive here ? For your hunger and thirst you surely could not obtain food here.' 27. He replied, 'A supremely glorious, radiant Brahman has appeared to me here. He has fed me with milk and thus saved my life.' 28. Hearing these words of the child, all marvelled, exclaiming, 'Evidently seeing the child's trust and devotion, Suryanarayan (the sun) has manifested himself to him.' 29. And it was because the sun had manifested this delight in the boy, that he was given the name of Bhanudas (slave of the sun). The parents carrying him on the hip returned to the town. 30. They remarked to one another, 'It is God who has saved his life. Let us forbear speaking to him in harsh words. Narayan (God) in His mercy has given us this gift of a son. 31. Whatever events are fated to occur they will take place in time. Why should we needlessly distress his heart ?' 32. Thus comforted in mind, the parents let affection govern them. 'We will not assign him the task of acquiring knowledge,' they said, 'lest he should again sulk and leave us.' 33. They now made search for a bride, and had Bhanudas married. But in the intervening days Bhanudas devoted himself entirely to the worship of Sri Hari.

HONEST BHANUDAS BECOMES AN UNWILLING PEDDLER OF CLOTH

34. When the allotted life of Bhanudas' parents had come to an end they passed away. Bhanudas, however, without concern for consequences was unwilling to engage in any worldly occupation. 35. He would serve no one for remuneration; he would engage in no trade or commercial dealings; he would have no borrowing or lending of money; he refused ever to enter the king's service. He wished only to be occupied with the worship of Pandurang. 36. There was need, however, in his home for food and clothing. His wife moreover was distressed in mind. And although he had children, yet he lived indifferent to all worldly needs. 37. A few men of influence therefore came together to speak to Bhanudas on his affairs: 'Your wife needs food and clothing,' they urged, 'but you seem unable to comprehend this. 38. While your father and mother were living they bore on their own heads the burden of your worldly necessities. But what is going to happen in the future, if your mind continues indifferent to these things? 39. It is also true that you have not acquired much learning. Hence we make you a certain proposal. Let your ear listen to it with respect. 40. We will supply you with a hundred rupees as working capital. Buy cloth and peddle it. 41. From the profit you gain, you will be able to provide your family with food and clothing. Carefully preserve the principal and return it to us gradually as you may find it convenient.'

42. These men then went to the market, purchased cloth and handed it over to Bhanudas. These men had other peddlers under them, and Bhanudas was committed to their care. 43. 'When you go to the market-place take him along with you,' they told them. 'Seat him at your side, and put him in the way of gaining his livelihood.

44. The pedlars listened to the words of the men and consented. They took Bhanudas with them and seated him beside them. 45. They taught him their secret numerical code: *mulu* (five), *udanu* (three), *angolu* (ten), *kevala* (one), *kathi* (twenty), *pavitru* (seven), 46. *selu* (six) *poku* (four), *dhakar* (one thousand), *avaru* (two), and other numerals. They explained to him about the cloth and how to sell it; 47. how one should carefully protect the principal, and what pains should be taken to sell at a price that would yield a profit; how also if one should tell the exact truth, one would certainly meet with loss 48. To this last advice Bhanudas replied, 'I will never, so long as time lasts, speak an untruth. I will speak only the absolute truth.' 49. At this all the pedlars laughed. 'It is evidently written on his forehead that he must live by begging,' they exclaimed. 'This explains why it is that he will not listen to anything we say. His name should rather be *Poor man.*' 50. One remarked, 'Let him once get the taste for gain, then he will utter falsehoods in plenty. One has never seen anyone favoured by Fortune who speaks the truth in his business relations.' 51. How true it is that one who is born blind thinks that all men are blind. Even savoury food seems bitter to one bodily sick. 52. So it is that the man who is false in heart sees no one true. As a man's heart is, so others seem to him.

53. But Bhanudas showed great courage. He refused to utter any falsehood in his business. The result was that every one marvelled at it and people flocked to his stall. 54. If a customer asked him about the cloth he would tell him the exact cost price to him and the profit he was asking on the principal. He gave them but one answer 55. 'If you approve of it take it. If not, pass to another stall.' This is all he would say to them and then con-

tinued his repeating of the names of God. 56. And all came to recognize the truth that Janardan (God) does fill man. 'Bhanudas will never even to the end of time speak an untruth,' they declared. 57. Customers appreciating his truthfulness all came to him. The other pedlars, dishonest in their dealings, had to watch the marvel from where they were. 58. They began to murmur, 'That we have given him a place beside us has been to our injury.' And hatred now arose in the heart of these evil-doers. 59. 'He sits beside us and draws away to himself our customers,' they cried. '(Hypocritically) we look him boldly in the face, but within we burn with rage to no avail.' 60. Another remarked, 'He throws a spell on people. That is why they have become bewitched. They pay down whatever price he asks, and no one even haggles over it.' 61. Still another observed, 'People have come to believe in him and that is why they patronize him. We are untruthful. We are the slaves of worldly desires. And God does not approve of this.' 62. Finally one said, 'Let us now speak the truth.' To this another objected saying, 'Though we should do so, no one would regard us now as really worthy of confidence. 63. Once character is fixed it continues the same through life. This we see exemplified in Bhanudas before our very eyes. 64. A dog may be siting quietly in the house. Thieves may come and steal away the bread. The accusation, however, will fall on the dog, for no one could know by intuition who really took it. 65. A tiger may be lying down peacefully but it will be said he is crouching to spring and kill. A miser may become an ascetic, but it will be said that he has started out on a course to deceive.. 66. An adulterer may indeed visit sacred watering places, but it will be said that he is in search of others' wives. A cat may be lying perfectly quiet, but people will remark that it is looking for a rat. 67. So it is with us. Our whole life has been spent openly in the sight of others, speaking untruths. And now, though we should act with honesty, people will say, "This is useless hypocrisy." 68. Bhanudas began before our very eyes with a very small business in cloth, and now he has become a prosperous man. God has been his Helper. 69. We make great effort, but we are unable to obtain sufficient bread to satisfy our appetites. Our creditors come and sit at our doors. What are we to do? 70. Ever since we gave Bhanudas a place beside us we have become bankrupt. He has drawn away all our customers and we are now in distress.'

BHANUDAS TURNS AWAY FROM WORLDLY AFFAIRS

71. One day all those pedlars started on their way to a distant market-place. Their journey ending, they put up in a temple precinct. 72. Bhanudas the *Vaishnava bhakta* had also come along with them to that market-place, and as usual had placed his stall next to theirs. 73. Now it happened that a *Haridas* had come to that same town, and had arranged for a *kirtan* that very evening. An invitation had been passed round the town that all should come to the recital. 74. When Bhanudas heard of this he was filled with great delight. 'To-day is an auspicious day, the *Ekadashi* (the eleventh of the moon),' he exclaimed, 'I must go and listen to this *kirtan.*' 75. Bhanudas invited the pedlars to go with him to the *kirtan.* (As they refused) he said to them, 'If because of laziness you are unwilling to come with me, you will at least be sleeping beside our wares. 76. So protect my stall and care for my goods with yours.' This request of Bhanudas made them very angry. 77. 'You have become God-crazy' they sneered. 'You are for ever telling the truth. Now go to this Hari recital and take your goods along with yourself. 78. We are all wearied and are going to sleep. Seek some other place for your stall where you can display your wares.

79. There are thieves around here and we wish for no words of blame from you. We cannot understand what gain is going to fall into your lap from going to this *kirtan*.' 80. Bhanudas replied, 'Well, let my goods remain here or be stolen (I care not). My heart is fixed on Pandurang. I will never desert Him.' 81. Thus remarking, Bhanudas the *Vaishnava bhakta* left his goods as they were and hastened away, soon reaching the place where *sadhus* and saints were gathered to listen to the *kirtan*. 82. With his heart full of joy he made a *namaskar* to the *Haridas*, 'Happy is this occasion' he said, 'the *Ekadashi*' (the eleventh of the moon). He then embraced the saints. 83. The *Vaishnavas* sang lovingly the Rama and Krishna stories that bring salvation to mankind, and Bhanudas listened with great delight, for he had a great love for them.

MALICIOUS PEDLARS

84. In the meantime the evil-minded pedlars sat beside their wares and planned as follows. 'Bhanudas has left his wares here and has gone to the *kirtan*. 85. Let us therefore play a trick on him. Unknown to him we will let his packhorse go loose, and throw his bundle of cloth into a ditch. 86. When he comes back to ask us about it, we will say, "Thieves came while we were in deep slumber and stole it without our knowing of it." 87. He will then go back to his own home, and we can then divide the cloth here among ourselves.' Having thus planned, these evil men let his packhorse go loose. 88. There was a deep pit near by and into it they threw the bundle of cloth. Then clapping their hands over the deed, they said to one another, 89. 'Since Bhanudas has been with us he has acquired wealth while we have become poor. All customers go to him. 90. Now all our anxiety is gone. Without the use of medicine the itch has disappeared.' In this manner these evil men talked the matter over among themselves.

91. Just as Duryodhan rejoiced in his heart when he robbed Dharma of his wealth, so these evil-minded pedlars rejoiced in their hearts.

GOD'S CARE FOR BHANUDAS

92. But when the Husband of Rukmini saw the calamity which had befallen Bhanudas, He immediately arrived on the scene, saying to Himself, 'Bhanudas is sitting listening in the *kirtan* in fixed contemplation. 93. These evil-minded men have conspired together and thrown his wares into the pit. What plan shall I follow?' said the Life of the world to Himself. 94. 'His packhorse will wander away somewhere. Where will he then look for it? He has put aside fondness for worldly things and gone mad after my worship.' 95. Thus thinking to Himself, Pandharinath assumed the form of a Brahman. Finding the packhorse near the market-place he sat down holding it. 96. He who reclines on the serpent Shesha in the ocean of milk, He on whose feet Lakshmi meditates, He who espouses the cause of his *bhaktas*, Captivator of the heart, He sat holding the horse. 97. He who does not come quickly even into the mental conception of the *Yogis* as they sit in meditation; He, the espouser of the cause of his *bhaktas*, Lord of the organs of sense, He sat holding the horse. 98. He, *Sri Ranga*, who cannot be attained by religious rites, by sacred places, by austerities, or by *yoga*, He, Pandurang who gave his promise to Pundalik, He sat holding the horse! 99. He, the father of Brahmadev, the Creator of the limitless universe, caught the horse of Bhanudas as it was wandering about, and sat holding it in the public square!

PEDLARS' DISASTER

100. In the meantime the pedlars were sitting in the temple precincts reviling Bhanudas: 'He will soon come back to look after his wares' they said. 101. 'When he hears all we tell him that has happened here, he will be-

come greatly agitated.' As these villains were thus talking among themselves the dark-complexioned One became very angry. 102. And while the Life of the world was expressing his anger, suddenly thieves approached. They robbed the pedlars of their goods and gave all a severe beating. 103. They loosened all their packhorses and took them all away. And now the pedlars sat weeping. 'We persecuted Bhanudas,' they said, 'and Pandurang has made us experience the result.' 104. One remarked, 'According to our *karma*, so are our minds. We certainly lack knowledge. We have not used forethought.' 105. Still another remarked, 'Fortune has played us false. Therefore we performed this loathsome act. Bhanudas is a single-minded *bhakta*. With no gain to ourselves we have troubled him.' 106. They now made a loud outcry but no one came running to them from the town. The Husband of Rukmini, skilled in the use of *maya*, had cast a spell upon all.

GOOD FOR EVIL

107. Turning now our attention to the *kirtan*, there were heard shouts of joy. The drum and the *vina* gave out their sweet sounds. The air was filled with the music, while the names of God were being acclaimed aloud. 108. The night was lacking only four *ghatikas* when the *Vaishnavas* sang the final hymn of praise, waving incense reverently before the Husband of Rukmini. Sweetmeats were then distributed. 109. Bhanudas made his obeisance to the *Haridas* and started back to his lodgings. Suddenly he saw a Brahman sitting by the wayside holding a horse. 110. As he was passing by, the horse neighed. 'How happens it that my horse is here?' he said to himself; 'I cannot understand it.' 111. Just then the Brahman who had thrown his scarf around the neck of the horse and was sitting by it, holding it, saw Bhanudas and suddenly vanished from sight.

112. As Bhanudas saw this marvel he was overwhelmed within with wonder, but leading the horse along he arrived at his lodgings. 113. Here he found the pedlars weeping aloud. Asking them what the trouble was about, they made full confession to him. 114. 'We evil-minded wretches sought to do you harm. We threw your bundle of cloth into yonder pit and let your horse loose. 115. When it was the second watch of the night thieves appeared and robbed us of our all. Now to whom shall we go and complain of the ways of destiny? 116. All our horses and bundles of cloth are stolen. We have also received a severe beating. And now it looks as though our business has come to an end. 117. We have lost all our capital. God has protected yours. We threw your bundle of cloth in yonder pit. Let us all now go and take it out.' 118. When Bhanudas heard their story his heart melted. 'I think,' he said, 'it must have been the Husband of Rukmini who was sitting holding my horse. 119. Botheration! All this worldly business is without real value. It is no storehouse for the happiness of the soul. Worthless wretch that I am! I have been seduced. 120. Think of it! That He, fair of complexion, delicate with the eyes of a lover, clothed in the yellow silk robe, Life of the world, in the form of a Brahman should be sitting holding my horse! 121. No longer will I engage in a business that brought weariness to Pandharinath.' With this repentance in heart he then addressed the pedlars. 122. 'Let your minds be at rest. Thieves have beaten you, but let not your hearts sorrow.' 123. Then drawing the bundle of cloth out of the pit he distributed the pieces of cloth among them. Bhanudas further offered to them his horse and his money and then left them.

BHANUDAS BECOMES AN ASCETIC

124. He returned to his home and there devoted himself entirely to the worship of Hari. He put aside all

thought of whether he was being honoured or dishonoured He spent his life singing in *kirtans* the attributes of God. 125. He refused to enter anyone's service. He would not let his mind be involved in the anxieties of worldly affairs. Though he had a wife and children, yet he acted with perfect indifference to worldly things. 126. It became his custom in the months of *Ashadh* (July) and *Kartik* (November) to lead bands of pilgrims to Pandhari. On the sands of its river he would perform *kirtans* accompanied by cymbals, drums and loud acclamations. 127. He would compose verses in different metres and would plead earnestly with the dark-complexioned One. His heart was full of intense love. In his *kirtans* his voice would choke with emotion. 128. When Bhanudas stood up to perform his *kirtans*, tears of joy filled all eyes. And the Husband of Rukmini, seeing this love of theirs, would himself come there and dance. 129. Wicked men, evil-minded and the ignorant, even they as they listened became filled with love and would exclaim, 'We could listen for ever to these enlightening *kirtans* sung by his lips. 130. How false indeed are the illusions of this worldly existence! How perishable are these bodies of ours!' And as these listeners gained in knowledge they began to love all creatures.

131. Adopting the non-begging method of the ascetic life, Bhanudas accepted such food and clothing as were voluntarily offered to him. His own lips asked nothing of anyone. 132. The idea of 'mine' and 'thine' had now no meaning to him. He realized the unity of all creatures. He had put aside all thought of differences. 133. Thus Bhanudas' mind was characterized by utter indifference to worldly things. He spent his days and nights in the joy of his heart, in the worship of Shri Hari.

134. In the next chapter we shall listen to the story of the taking of the Saviour of the world by King Ramraja to Vidyanagar. The intelligent listener to this story will feel joy within his heart. 135. You saints and good people in this divine assembly, Mahipati stands in your presence with a handful of flowers, in the form of Marathi verses.

136. *Swasti* (Peace) ! As the Lord of the earth listens to this book, the *Shri Bhaktavijaya*, He also will be pleased. Loving, devoted *bhaktas*, listen then to it. This is the forty-second delightful chapter; it is an offering to Shri Krishna.

CHAPTER XLIII

BHANUDAS

(*CONTINUED*)

Obeisance to Shri Ganesh. Obeisance to the Son of Vasudev.

GOOD DEEDS SECURE AN ETERNITY WITH GOD

1. Listen, you hearers, good and loving people. To-day the Wish-tree has come to fruitage. These intensely interesting stories of the saints are now revealed to you as enlightening and incomparable. 2. I would have you know the indescribable glory of Vishnu, the limits of which even Brahmadev does not know,and of which the *Vedas* also are ignorant, a glory which is love beyond compare. 3. Those to whom good deeds are the supreme thought, they finally attain the abode of Brahma. Those who perform sacrifices go to Indra's heaven. 4. Those who have confidence in ancestral worship will finally live and move in the abode of those ancestors. Whatever God men worship they finally reach His abode. 5. Those who worship the evil demons become like them after death. So those who give ear to the stories of the saints will finally attain *Vaikuntha* (the heaven of Vishnu). 6. The moment *Chakrapani* (Holder of the disk, Krishna) sees his *bhaktas* in distress He comes to drive it from them, and finally giving them his own four-armed form provides them a place in the home of full union with God. 7. Such a promise Pandharinath has given in connection with this book. Therefore, O hearers, listen with a reverent and loving heart.

8. At the close of the preceding chapter we saw how the Husband of Rukmini revealed Himself to Bhanudas, and how deciding to become free from all worldly desires Bhanudas gave up his commercial affairs.

THE KING OF VIDYANAGAR HEARS OF THE GLORY OF VITHOBA

9. Now listen to the following tale. There was a Brahman living in the sacred city of Pandhari. Feeling the desire in his heart for money he started on a begging trip from country to country. 10. Visiting many towns and cities in his journey he arrived finally at Vidyanagar. Entering the city he thought to himself, 'I must meet the king.' 11. So the Brahman took his bath, performed his devotions and then attempted to enter the palace. The doorkeeper would not let him go inside, however. He said to him, 'Just wait here a little while. 12. I will go and get the king's permission ; then sir, you may enter within the palace.' The servant returned after informing the king, and the Brahman then entered within. 13. Ram Raja, when he saw the Brahman, bowed and worshipped him. The Brahman felt exceeding joy and exclaimed, 'Blessed are you, great king, the very image of charity.' 14. The king then enquired, 'Whence have you come, sir ? With what desire in your heart have you come ? Please tell me.' 15. To this enquiry of the king the Brahman replied with joy thus : 'The sacred city of Pandhari is a most wonderful city. It is there that I dwell. 16. I have heard of your generosity and have hastened here begging from country to country on my way.' The king listened to his story and felt keen pleasure. 17. The king replied to the Brahman, 'Let your mind be at ease. I am going now first to my bath, and then to the worship of the goddess. 18. Come with me and see her temple. The temple glitters with gold. I shall make to her the various offerings, and present her with the *tulsi* leaf.' 19. The Brahman was delighted at this conversation with the king and accompanied him as he went to worship the goddess. 20. The king had planted costly flower gardens around the temple. In the inner

temple he had placed the image of *Ambika* (mother, goddess). Here he now performed the appropriate ceremonies of worship. 21. These were accompanied by the loud noise of many musical instruments. While the king performed his part of the worship the Brahmans repeated *mantras*. The loud noise was a joyful one. 22. In worshipping the goddess they used the sixteen rites; they clothed her with garments, and adorned her with jewels. Thus adorned with these various divine jewels the goddess looked beautiful. 23. They perfumed her with sandal oil and other scents. Around her neck was placed a garland of flowers. With incense and lights the king made his offerings. 24. Lighting the five lamps he waved them before *Mahamaya* and fell at her feet making a postrate *namaskar*. 25. After distributing gifts to all, the king sat for a while in quiet contemplation. He then entered into conversation with the Brahman from Pandhari.

RAM RAJA'S BOAST

26. 'You see,' said he, 'you may hunt throughout the three worlds, and yet you will not find a divinity the equal of Rajai. I have never seen or heard of her equal. Blessed is her boundless marvellousness! 27. You also see with your own eyes this beautiful temple. It is plated with silver. Around it I have planted this flower garden, that I may worship the Mother of the world with flowers. 28. All the people of Vidyanagar come here to worship her. I have commissioned my ministers to her service. The special rites of worship I perform myself. 29. You live at Pandhari, but its glory cannot be equal to that here. It is hardly possible that Pandurang can be worshipped with such pomp as Rajai is worshipped here. 30. When it is poor Brahmans who have to do the worshipping, how can they provide such garments and adornments as those I provide?' The Brahman listened to these words of the king and his heart became filled with anger.

THE BRAHMAN EXTOLS THE GLORY OF VITHOBA OF PANDHARPUR

31. 'King of kings,' said he, 'you in your vain pride, without even having seen Pandhari, boast of your own divinity as alone great. 32. You have plated the temple with silver and you proclaim to men that ornamentation. But our sacred city was built by *Vishvakarma* (the Creator of the world) and plated with gold. 33. There are forests there of the wish-tree. Touchstones and wish-stones lie about like common pebbles. Divine floating banners flash everywhere like lightning. 34. There are herds of wish-cows there. The *Vrindavana* (*tulsi* altars) are set with jewels. And here loving *Vaishnavas* joyfully perform *kirtans*. 35. The river Chandrabhaga is there flowing with nectar. She is the mistress of all sacred waters. By the mere sight of her, men become freed from this worldly existence and attain heaven. 36. The beautiful Rambha and Tilottama come and dance on the eagle-platform. *Gandharvas* (the heavenly choir) sing by the door of the temple, and space itself resounds with their music. 37. The God supreme, the Husband of Rukmini, who was living blissfully in the ocean of milk when He saw his *bhakta* Pundalik there, He came at once to that spot. 38. And *Chakrapani* (Holder of the disk, Krishna) placing His hands on His hips has remained standing there. If He sees any of His *bhaktas* in distress, He immediately comes in person to their relief. 39. Lakshmi even becomes ashamed of herself as her eyes behold His glorious form. Ten millions of suns hide themselves away before the glory of His crown. 40. Fair of complexion, delicate in form, holding the *Sharang* bow. His yellow garment tucked tightly about Him, His glorious bewitching face is adorned with the divine earrings of crocodile shape. 41. In order to see this form of His with their own eyes, Indra and the three hundred and thirty million gods stand constantly before Him with hands palm to palm, and reverently and lovingly praise Him. 42. He

whose name the Dweller in *Kailas* repeats to Himself day and night, He whom the *Vedas* and *Shastras* describe. He whose limits Brahmadev even does not know, 43. He whom the serpent Shesha praised with his thousand mouths, each tongue splitting into two, and then settled into quietude, 44. such an one is the divinity Pandurang. Such is the holy city of Pandhari. Such is the purifying water of the Chandrabhaga. Where else are such to be seen in the three worlds? 45. Without first paying attention to all this you vainly praise your own works of ornamentation. Rajai is your family goddess, but I care nothing for her. 46. Why, she comes regularly to Pandhari and there she performs the service of sweeping the temple and smearing it with cow-dung.' As the Brahman thus spoke the king became furious with rage.

THE ENRAGED KING THREATENS THE BRAHMAN

47. 'Before my very face he has insulted the deity whom I worship,' the king exclaimed. 'Heedless of what he is doing, he sings the praise of his own deity. 48. I ought to put him to death, but being a ruler I would be blamed. So I will punish the Brahman and drive him away to regions out of the city.' 49. The king therefore said to the Brahman, 'You have spoken falsely. I certainly have never heard of this golden Pandharpur. 50. And this goddess Rajai, who continually remains here where she first revealed herself, you with your own mouth have called her a slave of Pandurang. I am going to punish you and drive you away into the jungle.' 51. The Brahman replied, 'Hear, O king, I have told you the exact truth. You should come at once to Pandhari, and see the Husband of Rukmini for yourself. 52. His glory is ten million times as great as I have described it. If (after coming to Pandhari) you do not see it to be so, then you may rightly punish me. 53. So long as you have

not seen God supreme, this Rajai seems to you to be great as a lamplight seems bright only so long as the sun has not arisen. 54. So long as one has not seen the elephant of Indra, other elephants seem great. The stars seem bright only so long as the full moon has not arisen. 55. One praises other juices only so long as one has not obtained nectar. So long as one has not seen the ocean, a river seems extraordinarily great. 56. Until one has seen a forest of wish-trees, one delights in a mango grove. Until one has listened to the wisdom of the *Vedanta*, one is pleased with heretical doctrines. 57. So long as one has not seen the mountain of gold, so long does brass glitter. So until one has seen Pandharinath one is satisfied with other deities.' 58. The king listened and responded, 'I will at once hasten to Pandhari, and if I see there things just as you have described them to me, then only will it be well with you, O twice-born. 59. But if you have told me untruths, then I shall immediately punish you.' The king then commanded his ministers to prepare the equipment for the journey.

RAM RAJA GOES TO PANDHARPUR

60. Accompanied by horses, elephants, chariots, palanquins and a small army, the king started on his journey that he might see Pandurang. 61. They marched along to the sound of many musical instruments. Behind them all walked the Brahman thinking to himself, 'The Husband of Rukmini will either protect me from humiliation in my need or He will disregard me. 62. If the king does not see things as I have described them to him he will undoubtedly punish me.' 63. So bringing the image of Pandurang to his mind he praised him from his heart and prayed, 'O Thou who tenderly carest for *bhaktas*, Husband of Rukmini, come to my rescue in this hour of my need. 64. I your Brahman, helpless and poor, went on my begging

journey from country to country. Through the proclaiming of Thy name I have gained support for my family. 65. O God, the saints of old have proclaimed Thy wondrous renown. And I have but described the same renown to the king, but he is unable to regard it as true. 66. The king has become angry at what he calls an insult to his family goddess, and he is now on his way to witness for himself, O Pandharinath. 67. I have related to the king what Pandhari really is. It is only in this *Kali Yuga* that it seems to men to be built of earthen walls, for there is no essential difference (between gold and earth). 68. Just as coins buried by some ancestor appear to the luckless man as mere charcoal, so Pandhari, though really golden, seems otherwise through a wrong conception. 69. As the saints of old have described Pandhari, in those same words I have described it. But now if the king does not see *Chakrapani* (Holder of the disk, Krishna) as I have portrayed Him, he will punish me. 70. Then I shall commit suicide, and the words of the saints will be proved false. Moreover, when good people will hereafter read about the glory of Pandhari they will not believe it. 71. O Protector of the helpless, Husband of Rukmini, in this my present distress come quickly to my rescue.'

BRAHMAN'S WORD VERIFIED

This appeal of the Brahman for mercy made the Saviour of the world aware of his need. 72. He thought to Himself, 'Because the Brahman has extolled my profound renown he is being dishonoured, so I shall have to make things seem as he has described them' 73. And with this the Holder of the *Sharang* bow said to Rukmini, 'The king of Vidyanagar is hastening here on his way to see us. 74. Pandhari in reality excels all that the city of Dwarka was. We must show this to the king in the twinkling of an eye and thus remove his doubts. 75. If we do not do this, the Brahman will be punished. He will then take his own life. Our reputation will suffer loss and the saints and good people will laugh at us.' 76. The Mother of the world after listening to these words made at once a *namaskar* at His feet and said, 'I shall bring here at once the buildings of *Vaikunth* (Vishnu's heaven) and show them to the king.' 77. No sooner did she think this than in less than a moment it all took place, and by so doing, the Life of the world, expert in the use of *Maya*, magnified the glory of his *bhakta*.

THE KING HAS A GLORIOUS VISION

78. Now let us turn to Ram Raja as he was hastening along and arriving near Pandharpur, and while the Brahman in great fright was imploring the aid of the Husband of Rukmini. 79. Ram Raja called the Brahman into his presence and said, 'If you do not now satisfy my doubts I shall bring you to dishonour.' 80. He called for an elephant to be brought to him, and seated himself on its canopied seat. (From this height) he gazed at the city of Pandhari and saw a strange and marvellous sight. 81. Just as the constellations appear about the full moon, so around about the pinnacle of the temple lustrous buildings seemed to glitter. 82. As the king saw this wonder he was overwhelmed with amazement and exclaimed, 'Pandhari looks exactly as the Brahman has described it to me.' 83. Repentant in heart, the king descended from the elephant and making a prostrate *namaskar* to the Bradhman, said. 84 'I see before me exactly what you described to me. It was my ignorance that made me proud and led me to wrong thoughts.' 85. With these words the king again made the Brahman a *namaskar*, and freeing his mind of all ill feeling he sat at his feet. 86. The Brahman himself was also amazed and exclaimed, 'The Husband of Rukmini has indeed come to my rescue.' The three worlds could not

contain his joy, and with love he sang His praise. 87. 'Chief among *bhaktas* and their head-jewel was Pundalik,' he sang, 'and *Chakrapani* (Holder of the disk, Krishna) came from Dwarka to see him. 88. Of all the sacred waters the Ganges is considered the chief and yet the Chandrabhaga surpasses her. By the mere sight of her the world is purified. She permits no place for pride. 89. It is true that the Life of the world dwells in such places as Mathura, Gokul, and Vrindavan. Shri Krishna resides also in Dwarka for the sake of his *bhaktas*. 90. But to me the glory of this sacred place seems incomparable.' Thus with utter abandonment the Brahman in his love sang of the glories of Pandhari. 91. The king now had cymbals and drums brought and made a celebration. He gathered together the *Vaishnava bhaktas* and loud was the joyful noise they made. 92. As the king continued gazing he saw before him a forest of wish-trees and touchstones and wish-stones lying about like pebbles.

WONDERS OF PANDHARPUR

He approached the open lands around Pandhari. 93. Here there were innumerable wish-cows all round. The king amazed, ejaculated, 'Blessed are these infinite wonders.' 94. Holding the Brahman's hand the king continued gazing. He saw the resplendent city of Pandhari and his eyes were dazzled by it. 95. He saw various birds sitting on the trees singing in their delight. Swans and peacocks danced strutting about in their joy. 96. Ascetics were performing their austerities. Brahmans were studying the *Vedas*. The *bhaktas* of Vishnu with drum and *vina* were singing His praise. 97. Heavenly damsels, collected here and there in groups, were dancing, thereby compelling eyes to stare at them and infatuating sensually-minded men. 98. Here and there saints were sitting discussing the supreme Soul, and as they experienced absorption into that Soul they embraced one another. 99. One hundred and eight sacred rivers, taking a bodily form, came and bathed in the Chandrabhaga and were purified, and this took place while the king was looking on. 100. A golden *tulsi* altar had been erected studded with gems, and the *tulsi* adorned with garments and jewels was being worshipped by men and women. 101. The king having first bathed in the Bhimarathi then went to see and worship the god, and behold! Indra and all the other gods were also there, beholding the Lord of Pandhari.

RAJAI AS A SLAVE

102. All the eight supernatural powers, as slaves, were personally serving about the god. Suddenly the king recognized Rajai amongst them. 103. 'She is our family goddess whom we adore in our worship in Vidyanagar,' he exclaimed, 'and she is sweeping the dooryard here at Pandhari!' The king was amazed. 104. '*Udo*!'* The king called out to her and began immediately to question her. 'Mother,' he asked, 'why are you here? You are here sweeping with your own hands!' 105. Bhavani (the wife of Bhava, Shiva) replied, 'You hold vain pride in your heart. Endless female slaves like myself come here to Pandhari to serve. 106. Here to this d oryard of Pundalik all sacred waters come, and prostrating themselves on the gronnd, thereby becoming immediately pure, let their waters flow.' 107. Still amazed, the king looked further and saw to his surprise Narad (the *rishi*) and Tumbara, singing the god's praise. 108. Males and females with four arms were seen as actual beings. The king threw himself prostrate before them in the fulness of his joy. 109. Both the gods, Victory (*Jaya*) and Conquest

* See *Bharata Itihas Samshodhak Mandal Pustak* 11, p. 271, and 18, p. 79.

(*Vijaya*) holding weapons such as the shell, disk and others, stood before the temple door. Divine banners flashed like lightning in the heavens.

KRISHNA'S HALO DAZZLES RAM RAJA

110. After prostrating himself on the ground the king entered the temple. As he saw the light from the god he had to close his eyes and hold on to the hand of the Brahman. 111. Then there met his gaze the *sagun* form of the fair-complexioned, delicate One, lotus-eyed, clothed in the yellow silk robe, smiling faced, Life of the world; 112. that form which is the object of the *yogi's* meditation; that form which the five-faced (god Shiva) contemplates in His heart; that form which when one attempts to describe, all descriptions are seen to fall short of reality. 113. When describing the taste of nectar, what other sweet juice is there with which it can be compared ? So God supreme, the Husband of Rukmini, though He can be seen, cannot be compared. 114. Those who are His *bhaktas* can see Him with their eyes. They alone, through actual experience, know the marks by which He is to be recognized. The mere wise, who undertake to praise Him, become as dumb as the *Vedas.* 115. The king then with love embraced the incomparable image of the Supreme *Brahma.* And gazing intently on His form, tightly clasped His feet. 116. The king now said to the Brahman, 'You are my dear friend, my *sadguru*, my close companion. How can I thank you enough for your kindness! You have enabled me to meet the eagle bannered One. 117. I have here seen things ten million times as wonderful as you described them. I have seen the Lord of heaven with my own eyes and have felt its exceeding joy. 118. I also saw my family goddess Rajai sweeping the threshold of the temple and Indra also, accompanied by other gods, standing there with their hands palm to palm. 119. I now

see nowhere in the three worlds a sacred city as wonderful as Pandhari, a deity as supreme as Pandurang and a purifying stream like the Chandrabhaga.' 120. An insect inside of a fig thinks to itself, 'This is my vast universe.' When the fig is broken open and it looks round about, its mind is lost in wonder. 121. So it happened to the king and clasping the Brahman's feet he cried out, 'I was enveloped by ignorance, but through you I have been freed from it.' 122. But now suddenly all the marvellous vision which had been shown to the king vanished, and lo! his eyes now saw only the earthen walls, to his great astonishment. 123. The sacred city of Pandhari is in reality what was shown to the king, but because of the effects of a man's *karma* it seems to him to be of earthen walls. 124. The king with amazed mind now saw the city just as it appears to us to-day, and he exclaimed, 'I have seen a great miracle.'

THE KING TAKES THE IMAGE OF VITHOBA TO VIDYANAGAR

125. The king now thought to himself 'Why should I now in vain worship Bhavani? If the ocean of milk is near at hand, why should I leave that to bathe in river-water? 126. If I see a lake of nectar, why should I take even heaven-made medicines? When a wish-tree is close by, one should not sit in the shade of a *babhul* tree. 127. Why throw away the touchstone already in one's hand, and become an alchemist? If a wish-cow comes to one's house, why worship a goat? 128. When the sun is shining into the house, why bring in a lamp? So having had a vision of Pandurang, why now worship a goddess?' 129. Thus reasoning with himself Ram Raja besought the eagle bannered One thus, 'God supreme, King of heaven, fulfil the desire of my heart. 130. I have the desire in my heart to take You to Vidyanagar. So giving

to me, Your suppliant, the assurance of Your blessing, come along quickly with me, O God, my King.' 131. The god replied, '(I agree to come) but if you during the journey should rest me on the ground I shall certainly remain at that very spot. Or if in your kingdom you are guilty of any injustice I shall come back to Pandhari.' 132. As *Chakrapani* (Holder of the disk, Krishna) thus replied, the king was overjoyed in heart. 'I shall place relays of men at intervals along the route and thus take the god with me,' he said to himself. 133. And with this idea he stationed men at intervals from the sacred city of Pandhari as far as Vidyanagar, and taking the idol (out of the temple) started to carry it away. 134. The officiating Brahmans did not resist. They knew their power could not prevail against that of the king. The idol was lifted up and carried along from hand to hand. 135. Thus Pandurang was carried along swiftly to Vidyanagar and there installed. The king in his own person performed the installation rites and the ceremonies of worship.

PANDHARPUR WITHOUT VITHOBA

136. Now let us turn to Pandharpur where in the month of *Ashadh* (July) *Vaishnavas* arrived on their pilgrimage. Here they learned the fact that the god had gone to Vidyanagar. 137. Pandharpur now seemed desolate like a body without life, or like a river without water. The city was oppressed with fears. 138. It was like an army without a king, like constellations without the moon or as a virtuous, devoted wife, deprived of her husband, seems unprotected among men. 139. So with Hari gone to Vidyanagar, the whole of Pandhari seemed desolate. Dejected, the saints and *mahants* sat down by the eagle-platform. 140. 'Whose praises can we now sing?' they said among themselves; 'the Life of the world has deserted us. The promise he gave to Pundalik (to remain

here always) has become a broken promise.' 141. Pious *bhaktas* arrived and all exclaimed, 'What has happened to the King of Pandhari?' And all learned the news that the god had gone to Vidyanagar. 142. The saints, *sadhus* and other *Vaishnavas* said to one another, 'Some one should go to Vidyanagar and bring back the Husband of Rukmini.' 143. They discussed this proposal among themselves but no one gave any assurance that he would go on such an errand. Some indeed remarked, 'Pandurang has paid no regard to his promise to Pundalik. He will not come back by any effort of ours.' 144. Another added, 'We have no entry into the king's palace. If the king should learn the purpose of our coming he would punish us well. 145. One brought forward an excuse from the point of view of the attributelessness of God, 'God is within us,' he argued; 'if we have no experience of this the philosophers (knowers of self) will have misled us.' 146. Still another added, 'Whatever and however anything takes place, it is by the will of God. We should watch it, but let no one be troubled thereby.'

BHANUDAS OFFERS TO GO AND BRING VITHOBA BACK

147. In this group of saints was Bhanudas the *Vaishnava bhakta*. He gave them a solemn assurance saying 'I will go and bring back the Husband of Rukmini, or give up my life in the attempt.' 148. And with these words he started at once. Arriving at Vidyanagar at night time he began to question the people. 149. 'The king has brought here from Pandhari the image of Pandurang. Tell me quickly where he has installed it.' 150. From fear of the king no one was willing to tell him the facts and they replied, 'We do not know.' 151. Bhanudas then asked someone privately and was told by a *Vaishnava bhakta* that the king had installed the Husband of Rukmini in the palace temple and that he worshipped

Him in private; 152. that after the king had worshipped Him no one was allowed to see Him; that the king had put padlocks on the doors of the temple; and had stationed a guard for His protection. 153. When Bhanudas heard this he became full of joy. Midnight arrived and all the guards were asleep. 154. When Bhanudas approached the door of the temple at that moment the padlock dropped. He entered within and prostrated himself before the god. 155. He gazed for a moment on the god's form and then lovingly embraced him. With a voice choked with emotion he thus pleaded with him :—

BHANUDAS CHIDES THE GOD AND PLEADS

156. 'Husband of Rukmini, Dweller in *Vaikunth* (Vishnu's heaven), Giver of the promise to Pundalik, King of the Yadavas, have You dropped Your affection for us and become subject to the king ? 157. You gave a promise to Pundalik that You would never go away from Pandhari. And now this promise is seen to be false. 158. It is evident You do not care for our lowly worship. The king here worships You with the sixteen rites. Regarding that as happiness, You, *Adhokshaja* (Vishnu), eagle bannered One, choose to remain here. 159. Because of these heavenly garments and adornments and these offerings of various dainty foods you have lost recollection of us, poor people ! 160. O *Purushottama* (Good Being), You have left Rukmini, Radha and Satyabhama. O dark as a cloud, the king by his professions of love has caused You to leave us. 161. You have left Pandharpur and made Vidyanagar Your abode. But great *rishis* and noble *bhaktas* are waiting there for You. 162. Rambha, Tillottama, Urvashi, Menaka and the eight chief wives of Yours came there to serve You, but leaving them, O Father of Brahmadev, You have comfortably settled Yourself here ! 163. Or is it because of some awful fault of ours, the fear of which has caused you to run away from us ? Or may it

be because we have asked of You tokens of Your love that You have run away? 164. Can it be that it is the noise and confusion in the *kirtans* whereby You are unable to sleep? And so You have selected for Yourself this quiet spot? I now understand what the facts are. 165. Or could it be the countless pilgrims who gather there, in meeting whom You become weary, that has made You to come here to Vidyanagar for a quiet rest?'

VITHOBA'S REPLY

166. The Life of the world listened to these chidings of Bhanudas and replied, 'You are speaking without due thought these disconsolate words. 167. I am not enjoying these many kinds of rites with which I am worshipped, nor these garments, adornments and ornaments. My soul is really pining away for a sight of the banks of the Bhima river. 168. It is the king who has brought Me here and imprisoned Me. And you have also hardened your hearts in that no one has come here to take me back. 169. I used to give you *riddhi* (prosperity), *siddhi* (supernatural powers) and the four forms of deliverance, but you used to worship Me out of love alone, disregarding those benefits. 170. Aside from those benefits I had nothing I could give you. So that My debt to you, incurred by your service of love, I was unable to repay, hence I deserted you.' 171. As the Husband of Rukmini uttered these words (of explanation), He became choked with emotion. But tears of joy flowed from His eyes and moved by mutual love both sobbed together. 172. The Life of the world then embraced Bhanudas and said, 'Tomorrow in the early morning, as you worship I shall reveal Myself to you' 173. The Holder of the *Sharang* bow then removed his necklace of nine jewels and placed it on Bhanudas, adding, 'Hasten now to your lodgings, for the king will soon be coming to worship Me.' 174. As soon as Bhanudas had stepped outside, the padlock

returned again to its place on the door. Thus the god had met His *bhakta* without anyone having the least knowledge of it.

BHANUDAS CHARGED WITH THEFT

175. The king arose early, performed immediately his bath, and lovingly bowing to the god, waved before Him the burning wick-lights. 176. Suddenly he missed the string of jewels on the god's neck. The king enquired at once of the officiating priests. 'What thief has been here?' he demanded, and he flew into a rage. 177. He gave them a severe beating and cried out, 'Bring back at once the string of jewels. If you cannot produce those priceless jewels you must search for them the whole world over.' 178. No sooner was this order given than a house to house search was made but nowhere could the string of jewels be found. Then they began to look for thieves outside the city. 179. And lo! there sat Bhanudas on the bank of the Ganga river. He had had his bath and was repeating the names of God. The king's officers looked attentively at him and spied from afar the string of jewels on his neck. 180. 'We have found the thief,' they shouted, 'let us seize him.' The king's servants at once bound the noble *Vaishnava* and carried him along. 181. As he was brought into the city every one laughed as they saw him, and mocking him said, 'This fellow is wandering about in the guise of a saint in order to deceive the people. 182. Look! He has placed violent hands on a god. Is he likely to have any fear of man? If a butcher met even the cow *Kapila* (a cow with a black skin supposed to be very sacred), would he so much as think of worshipping her?'

DERISION OF BHANUDAS

183. Thus many kinds and classes of men derided Bhanudas as they saw him being carried along. But

Bhanudas showed no sign of being troubled thereby and continued repeating the names of God. 184. One observer reminded the crowd of a proverb, 'A garland of the sacred *tulsi* around the neck of a highway robber,' adding, 'our eyes have seen the truth of this proverb to-day. This man is evidently the one who stole the string of jewels.' 185. The officers now took the string of nine jewels and brought it to the king exclaiming, 'We have bound the thief and brought him to you. What punishment is to be given him?' 186. In a great rage the king cried out, 'Impale him at once!' But in so ordering he did it without taking thought that he ought to find out who the man was and what kind of a thief he was. 187. Bhanudas said to the officers, 'My death is at hand. Allow me therefore in these my last moments to see and worship Pandurang.' 188. There were some good men among these officers and they paid respect to Bhanudas' request. Obtaining the king's permission they took Bhanudas to the temple. 189. Bhanudas said to the god, 'Evidently it is because I came to take You away secretly that You have devised this plan to have me punished by the king. So be it! 190. Deprive of life whoever comes here to take You away, and enjoying wanton pleasures in this place of the king, remain happily here! 191. Was it with this thought in mind, O dark-complexioned One, that You put the string of jewels around my neck? And yet as You talked with me tears flowed from Your eyes. 192. Be it so, and yet to the end of my hundred thousand births I will never leave you, O Husband of Rukmini.' And with these words he lovingly made an obeisance to the god. 193. The officers now cried, 'Get up! Hustle! If to begin with, you had not committed this theft, nothing of this kind would have taken place.' 194. With these words the officers dragged Bhanudas outside the temple. They placed the impaling stake on his shoulder and applied *shendur* to his forehead. 195. Numberless men and women assembled to see the unusual spectacle. They led Bhanudas outside the city and hastened to fasten the sharp stake in the ground.

BHANUDAS VINDICATED

196. As they were about to lift him up on to it to impale him Bhanudas thus supplicated God, 'Let the very heavens fall crashing upon me, yet will I remember Thee. 197. Though the seven oceans should unite and overwhelm me, still I will not leave Thee, O God, my King. I wave as an offering before Thee this destructible body of mine. 198. Though the whole earth should go to destruction, and the five elements be dissolved, yet aside from Thee, O Husband of Rukmini, I need no one at my side. 199. When the submarine fire shall devour the three worlds, Thou wilt be my beloved still.' The Life of the world seeing the determination of Bhanudas came to his rescue. 200. A most wonderful, a most strange marvel, now took place. Listen ye *bhaktas*, with reverence, to what now happened. The impaling stake, fastened in the ground, suddenly burst into leaf. 201. It blossomed into flower and fruit. The officers of the king went and told him what had taken place, adding, 'He is a *Vaishnava bhakta*. Pandharinath has come to his rescue. 202. The impaling stake has turned into a green tree.' The king listened to the story told by his servants of what had taken place, and expressed his great astonishment. 203. He hastened to the scene and saw the tree with his own eyes, Remorse now seized his heart and he cried out, 'I have committed a great wrong.' 204. The king then made Bhanudas an obeisance in love and reverence and said. 'From lack of thought I have done you this wrong.' 205. Without any delay the king took Bhanudas to the temple, and as he saw the image of Pandurang he became choked with emotion. 206. As Bhanudas embraced His feet the Life of the world raised him up and embraced him.

VITHOBA REINSTALLED AT PANDHARPUR

The Husband of Rukmini said to Bhanudas, 'You have suffered much because of me. 207. Take me up now on your shoulder and carry me to Pandharpur. There at the door of Pundalik's shrine I will dwell for ever.' 208. Ram Raja now clasped the feet of the god and cried, 'Are You leaving me, and going away ?' The god replied, 'You have committed a wrong, though unintentionally it is true. 209. You had performed some good deeds (in your former births) and therefore I remained here with you for these many days. But I must go now. Henceforth keep My form in remembrance in your heart with love. ' 210. Bhanudas now said to the Husband of Rukmini, 'How am I able to lift and carry You ? Moreover I have not the kingly power to collect many men to bear You.' 211. The Merciful to the humble replied, 'I am entirely at your service. All My powers are now yours, My *bhakta*.' 212. With this the Life of the world assumed a diminutive form and said to Bhanudas, 'Put me in your deer-skin bag, and take me along.' 213. Bhanudas went at once for his bag and placed *Chakrapani* (Holder of the disk, Krishna) inside.

BHANUDAS CARRIES VITHOBA TO PANDHARPUR

Now, let no one who hears this story have doubts about it. 214. For example, space is of infinite expanse, yet as you look into a jar the space there is only as large as the jar. So the Lord of *Vaikunth* (Vishnu's heaven) in love to please His *bhakta* became small in size. 215. Or again, there are many great currents of air, but if one uses a fan one makes a current of air of the same nature as the others. So the Husband of Rukmini of His own free will became subject to His *bhakta*. 216. Back in the time when Krishna was an *avatar*, as Yashoda was churning, her hand grasped him in the vessel, the same who now entered the little bag of Bhanudas. Why then should one doubt this story? 217. To one who looks with the eye of knowledge, He appears to pervade infinite spaces great and small, even smaller than an atom. 218. So the Lord of the world, out of affection for Bhanudas, fitted Himself to the space of the deer-skin bag, and Bhanudas carrying it on his shoulder hastened on his return journey. 219. From out of this bag the Life of the world spoke sweet words to his *bhakta*: 'Blessed is this day, for in it we shall meet the saints and the other good people.'

BHANUDAS AT LAKE PADMALAYA

220. When Bhanudas arrived at the Padmalaya lake (near Pandharpur) he placed the Pervader of the world on the ground, and with joy in his heart began his bath. 221. Suddenly the Husband of Rukmini in the skin-bag became great in size, the upper part was on His head and the lower part was smashed to pieces. 222. When Bhanudas returned (from his bath) and saw what had happened he exclaimed, 'God supreme! What is this that You have done! You have become big again. How shall I now be able to lift You?' 223. The Husband of Rukmini replied, 'Go on at once and inform the saints and *sadhus*. They will come to welcome me back with loud music of many instruments. 224. And let them place me on My throne in an auspicious hour this very day.' In accordance with these words of *Chakrapani* (Holder of the disk, Krishna), Bhanudas started on his way.

VITHOBA'S PROCESSION

225. Now by the eagle-platform all the *Vaishnava bhaktas* were sitting, oppressed with concern. 'Bhanudas has been gone for many days,' they exclaimed, 'but the Husband of Rukmini has not come back.' 226. Just then suddenly they saw coming the victorious *bhakta*, with his smiling face, calling out, 'I have brought back the Recliner on the Serpent Shesha (Vithoba)'. 227. Bhanudas embraced

the saints and said to them, 'The Husband of Rukmini has come as far as the Padmalaya lake.' Hearing this joyful news all were delighted. 228. Then with banners and flags the noble *Vaishnavas* went out (to welcome back the god) accompanied by the music of countless cymbals and drums. 229. Priests, leaders, men and women, joined the procession (to welcome the god back). Arriving at the Padmalaya lake they beheld the dark-complexioned One. 230. All prostrated themselves on the ground and then after embracing the god they put Him, the Husband of Rukmini, on a chariot and carried Him along in an enthusiastic procession. 231. The saints loudly proclaimed His praise. Dancers danced wildly before Him. Drums and other musical instruments sounded aloud and all felt joy. 232. In describing that occasion there are no comparisons that are sufficient, and yet in that month of *Kartik* (November) the *Warkaris* (pilgrims) saw that sight with their own eyes. 233. When at full moon a chariot procession takes place, that procession is the nearest comparison that can be made. It was then that Pandharinath thus passed along in pompous procession. 234. When the procession arrived at the bank of the Chandrabhaga, the leaders among them came forward, bathed the god and then all started on their way to the great door of the temple. 235. They took the dark coloured idol from off the chariot and passing it from hand to hand placed it in a palanquin. They carried it along to the temple and there anointed it with the special ceremonies for a welcome back. 236. Brahmans repeated *mantras* aloud. *Vaishnavas* sang lustily His praises. The Pervader of the universe sat now on His throne. Blessed was this happy day! 237. With garments, ornaments, adornments and the sixteen rites they worshipped Him. Offering Him dainty food and other offerings they invoked His blessing. 238. Priests made offerings of handfuls of flowers to the god, with loud repetitions of *mantras*. Saints, *Vaishnavas* and the pilgrims, all felt the joy of the occasion.

BHANUDAS APPLAUDED

239. And now the assembled crowd of men and women praised Bhanudas saying that it was through Him that the Lord of *Vaikunth* (heaven) had come back to Pandhari. 240. Some distributed sweetmeats throughout the city. Others gave feasts of daintily cooked food to Brahmans. Thus all the dwellers of that sacred city rejoiced in heart. 241. Just as when Raghunandan (Rama) came back to Ayodhya after enduring fourteen years of exile the people of the city rejoiced, so the people rejoiced in the same way. 242. As when a mountain becomes dry in a time of drought, and rejoices when a cloud pours abundant rain upon it, so all the people of Pandhari rejoiced. 243. It was as when the clouds rejoiced that they saw the ocean issuing from the stomach of *Rishi* Agasti. 244. It was as when the Spring comes and all vegetation appears beautiful. So was it at the return of the Protector of the helpless to Pandhari. All the inhabitants were happy. 245. It was as when life returns to the body and all the senses are quickened and begin to perform their functions. So it happened to all the people of Pandhari.

246. As one listens to the interesting story in the next chapter he will gain faultless victory. Therefore, O *bhaktas*, peacefully gain it for yourselves. 247. As the glorious Husband of Rukmini increases the glory of His good saints, so His slave, Mahipati, sings of their noble qualities.

248. *Swasti* (Peace)! This book is the *Shri Bhaktavijaya*. The Lord of the world will be pleased in listening to it. Listen, then, you God-loving pious *bhaktas*. This is the forty-third very delightful chapter.

CHAPTER XLIV

THE STORY OF BAHIRAMBHAT

Obeisance to Shri Ganesh. Obeisance to the Slayer of the Kaliya.

MORAL EFFECTS OF THE STORIES OF THE SAINTS

1. Today among all the sense organs the tongue appears to be holy on account of good deeds performed by it. For in describing the good deeds and character of the *bhaktas* of Vishnu all sins flee away. 2. Bringing into one's imagination the appearance of the saints the very eyes are purified. By merely listening to the saints, the ears are purified without any further strenuous effort. 3. By going to listen to the stories of the saints the feet become holy. And thus in resisting laziness, and sitting listening, the whole body becomes purified. 4. In making a *namaskar* to this book the hands become purified. Touching it with the head, egotism quickly leaves one. 5. Bowing to the stories of the saints, the thought of one's self is lost, and the mind, coming to the state of quietness, enjoys peace. 6. Therefore fortunate hearers should hold in their hearts intense desire to listen.

BAHIRAMBHAT REPENTS AT HIS WIFE'S TAUNT

In the previous chapter you listened to an intensely interesting story, 7. how Bhanudas went to Vidyanagar in his state of love and by pleading with the god he brought back the idol of Pandurang and reinstalled it at Pandhari. 8. Listen to another most interesting story. Bahirambhat lived at Pratishthan (modern Paithan). He was a learned *pandit* in the six systems of philosophy, and skilled in the knowledge of *Vedanta*. 9. Brahmans who read the *Vedas* called themselves his pupils. A number of Brahmans associated themselves with him and studied the stories of the *Puranas.* 10. Although he was so great a personage, he would never go to visit the king. At his own home he maintained a perpetual sacred fire, performed many holy deeds, and had no sorrow in his heart. 11. Without any desire to ask anything of anyone, the Brahman carried on the occupation of an ordinary Brahman. Bathing on the banks of the Godavari river he performed there his austerities. 12. Then arising in the middle of the day Bahirambhat was accustomed to return to his home. After making his offering to fire and the gods he used to invite noble Brahmans to dine with him. 13. After the dinner was over at the third watch of the day he would read aloud the *Puranas.* Wise people who were learned in the philosophy of the *Vedanta* would come there to listen. 14. One day while sitting eating he playfully referred to his wife saying that she had served vegetables without salt. His wife heard him say this 15. and replied to him, 'You are now sixty years of age. Why do you wish for a keen sense of taste on your tongue?' 16. Hearing these words of his wife he felt repentant. He said to himself, 'Why should I pass my life in vain? I must make it fruitful.' 17. Bahirambhat at once arose and made a *namaskar* to his wife. He said to her, 'Mother you have given me a valuable instruction in your love. 18. All the good deeds which I performed in a former birth have surely now come to their fruitage. Therefore through the instrument of words I have become possessed of strenuous indifference to worldly things.' 19. Bahirambhat thought to himself, 'If now I go straight away into the forest, they will bring me back through the influence of others. 20. Still I must plan that my relations with my own caste should suddenly break so that no one should question me.' Such were his thoughts. 21. 'If I should now become a *Sannyasi,* all the Brahmans will worship me. If I enter into the highest stage of the order they will still pay honour to me as one absorbed in the eternal *Brahma.* 22. Those who are in the highest positions, however, seeing me thus, will spit upon me. Evil men will seek to dishonour me. This is what ought to follow on such an occasion. 23. By this happening to me, my body will become pure.' Holding such repentance in his heart, he went away from his home.

HE BECOMES A MUHAMMADAN

24. Bahirambhat then went to the house of a *Kazi* (Muhammadan priest) and he spoke very humbly to him saying, 'Take me into your caste. 25. Your *Shastras* speak of making a Hindu into a Muhammadan as a holy thing to do. Therefore do not hesitate and make me like yourself.' 26. The *Kazi* (Muhammadan priest) replied, 'Why have you become indifferent to-day? Why have you a sudden change of mind? I will help you out of difficulty. 27. You are a learned *pandit.* Why do you wish to come into our caste? If you have any desire in your heart, I will supply it.' 28. Bahirambhat replied, 'I have not become one indifferent to desire, but your way seems to be to concentrate on acquiring God.' 29. Seeing his determination, he defiled Bahirambhat (i. e., received him into his caste). When Brahmans heard of this, all were full of sorrow. 30. Seeing there was no remedy for it, however, they finally settled down quietly. There were some evil thinkers at Paithan who reviled him when seeing him. 31. Some said, 'There is an evil thought in his indifference.' Some said, 'He is possessed of demons' Others said, 'If we so much as take his name all our good deeds will vanish.' 32. Still another said, 'His wife ought not to have spoken to him in the way she did.' Others said, 'Her luck appears to be unfavourable.' 33. Some said, 'He has a cruel heart. Our wives too speak to us in the same way, and a great deal

too, but the idea of indifference to worldly things does not come into our mind.' 34. Some exclaimed, 'When he had acquired wealth to secure the welfare of his family; it was easy for him to think of indifference to worldly things.' Thus people spoke to one another. 35. Others said, 'He was learned in the *Shastras* and he ought to have become a *Sannyasi*. Yet he has entered into the low caste and become a Muhammadan.' 36. Others said, 'In performing his religious acts he may have made a slip in his repetition of *mantras*.' Others rebukingly said, without thinking, 'Why are you needlessly reviling him? 37. If one has knowledge, adult age, good family line, abundance of wealth and property, a son and wife, it is impossible for him to become indifferent to worldly things.' 38. In this way some of the people of Paithan reviled and some praised him. But Bahirambhat, repentant, always lived without fear.

BAHIRAMBHAT A BRAHMAN AGAIN

39. On a certain day, however, the Brahmans were seated on the banks of the Godavari river. He went to them and in repentance began to cry. 40. His throat choked with emotion and tears of joy flowed from his eyes. Seeing him thus, the Brahmans questioned him. 41. They said to Bahirambhat, 'For what purpose did you become a Muhammadan? What good qualities did you find amongst them, that you should cast us aside?' 42. When the Brahmans said this to him, he replied, 'My *karma* (fate) was very powerful, therefore I fell into this thoughtless action. 43. In order to attain God, I of my own will became a Muhammadan. But I do not see there any way of obtaining knowledge of the soul.' 44. The Brahmans replied to him, 'One's deliverance is in one's good deeds.' Saying this to him, they consulted among themselves. 45. He was a wise and good man. He became

defiled because of his *karma* (fate). So now giving him a penance according to prescribed rules, let us again bring Brahmanhood to him. 46. The inhabitants of other cities come here to question us regarding the laws of the *shastras*. And now why should we hesitate regarding the decision to make him pure? 47. After the sewage of villages has united with the Ganges, it becomes pure. Then if the water of the Ganges itself spreads outside, will it be called filthy? 48. If one belonging to another town has been defiled in another caste, he becomes pure by coming to Pratishthan (nodern Paithan), then why drive away any good man belonging to this place? If we do so, we shall be reproached.' 49. Examining the *shastras*, they at once gave him penance. Spending an enormous amount of money, the Brahmans made him pure. 50. Now all the Brahmans assembled and said to Bahirambhat, 'Because of your good deeds in a former birth, you will have a sight of Shri Hari.'

BAHIRAMBHAT'S ARGUMENTS

51. Then all the Muhammadans assembled and said to the Brahmans, 'You have turned a Muhammadan into a Brahman. Come and tell the king how you did it.' 52. Bahirambhat said to them, 'How is it you made me a Muhammadan? See now the marks of piercing still appear in my ears. I am doubtful about your assertions. 53. If a man sees, how can anyone call him blind? When a man has the strength to walk, no one should call him a cripple. 54. If one has pride, it is of no use to describe him as having been delivered from earthly bondage. When one can listen by his ears, he should not be called a deaf man. 55. When sugar is mixed with intoxicating liquor, its sweetness does not go, so though you may have defiled me, still marks of piercing by earrings remain. 56. I have these marks in my ear and

while so, you still call me one without marks (a Muhammadan). And you are not ashamed of this.' In this way he discussed the matter with the Muhammadans. As the talk was going on all became wearied. 57. He then said to the Brahmans, 'Listen to my words; you gave me a penance and made me a Brahman again. What your law books on this subject are I do not know. 58. As the foreskin which they cut (or circumcised) has not come back through the penance I have taken, how is it I have become pure by applying to it cowdung and holy ashes? 59. If the nose is cut off, who will respect that person? So these Muhammedans having defiled me, my Brahmanhood no longer remains. 60. The full moon makes the moon bright but the dark spots on it still remain. So although you have purified me by penance, still the stain of defilement remains. 61. If the barber lets the tuft of hair remain it will grow; but the (circumcised) foreskin does not come back again. This doubt in my mind is always present with me. 62. Therefore, I am not altogether a Brahman, and you cannot call me a Muhammedan. I cannot be regarded as of either caste. 63. As the potter places on his wheel a lump of mud, it is not a jar or mere earth. So it has happened to me.'

BRAHMANS SILENCED

64. Having listened to his words, the Brahmans remained silent. They remarked, 'How shall we be able to remove his doubts?' 65. If he met any wise man anywhere, he asked him to tell him who he was, and having put to him that question he went on. 66. If people said he was a Muhammadan he would become angry and would say to them, 'You do not know the facts, and in vain you try to delude me. 67. If I were truly a Muhammadan then why are my ears still pierced? Without knowing anything you try to delude me. You speak out of your foolish-

ness.' 68. If anyone said that Bahirambhat was a great Brahman of Pratishthan (modern Paithan) he scolded him saying, 69. 'You call me a Brahman. If so, why is the sign of circumcision still there ?' He showed it to them and all wondered. 70. As he thus questioned every one he met, he got the name of 'Crazy Bahira.' He said to himself, 'When shall I meet with a *sadguru* who will remove the impression of my doubt ?' 71. Thus wandering about for many days, he came to the town of Vadaval. Here Nagnath the spiritual expert lived in the hermitage of his *sadguru*. 72. He was building a great tomb for his *Swami*. He used in the work some carts made of *Sharakand* wood, and placing on them stones as big as mountains he hitched monkeys to them in order to draw them.

NAGNATH REMOVES CRAZY BAHIRA'S DOUBTS

73. When Crazy Bahira saw this with his eyes, he was astonished and said to himself, 'I am sure he will remove my doubt, and bring steadiness to my mind.' Bahirambhat now said to Nagnath, 74. 'Tell me plainly Am I a Hindu or a Muhammadan ?' Hearing this seemingly impudent speech, the *Sadguru* grew angry. 75. He had his staff in his hand and he at once struck him on his head. Bahirambhat immediately fainted and fell on to the ground. 76. He could remember nothing. His very life seemed to have disappeared. He had no consciousness of who he was. There was no more life in his body. 77. Nagnath having done this he said to himself, 'I must entirely remove his misunderstanding. I must remove his doubt and put him on the way of understanding himself.' 78. He had a pestle brought by the hands of his disciples, and had his body pounded by them. Then having thus pounded his bones and flesh together, he made a lump of them with his hands. 79. He then made

of it an image and with his own hands cremated it. All who looked at the strange doing were full of astonishment. 80. When the fire was out, Nagnath did a seemingly impossible thing. He looked upon it with an eye of compassion. A living force entered into it. 81. It was a divine body with all good qualities, such as *Yogis* enjoy and then sit contemplating the divine essence. Such a form Nagnath now saw. He felt great joy at heart. 82. The *Sadguru* then asked him who he was. 'Bahirambhat, listen to my words. Tell me quickly who you are.' 83. Hearing this question, he thought for a while and then said, 'Doubts have now disappeared.' Saying this he remained silent. 84. 'If I call myself a Muhammadan, yet my foreskin is already there; if I say I am a Brahman my ears look as if already pierced.' 85. *Sadgurus* teach the knowledge of philosophy, but who can change the body? Nagnath did that which was seemingly impossible and removed his great doubt.

BAHIRAMBHAT OBTAINS SOUL KNOWLEDGE

86. Nagnath placed his hand upon Bahirambhat's head and gave him the instruction needed to make him his disciple. He became at once a knower of soul and set himself to the worship of *Hari*. 87. Bahirambhat full of joy exclaimed, 'Blessed is the *sadguru* Nagnath. He has given me another birth without a moment's delay. 88. There are a great many *gurus* with the knowledge of the soul who can remove births and deaths; but they certainly cannot change the body, for the action of *karma* cannot be resisted. 89. Bringing the image of Pandurang into their minds, a great number of *bhaktas* worship him. Namdev caused the stone idol to eat and this seems most strange. 90. Everywhere the people speak of the illusory nature of *Maya*, and in distress they show themselves very brave. But Kabir killed his son and this seems most

strange. 91. Old men can teach young men knowledge in many forms of the *Vedas* and the *Shastras*, but in causing a buffalo to repeat the *Vedas* Dnyandev did a most wonderful thing. 92. Blessed is Savata the noble *bhakta* who when Pandharinath came to him to be hidden, with his own hand he ripped himself open and hid Him in his heart. 93. Thus the God-loving *bhaktas* of Vishnu seemed to be greater one after the other. No one understands properly their glory by which Krishna, who is dark as a cloud, is made subservient to them.'

94. Going now back to the story. Nagnath manifested his mercy and Bahirambhat arrived at an understanding of his soul. 95. Then going at once to Pandhari he looked upon the *sagun* form of Krishna. Full of love he danced with love in the *kirtans*. 96. It was the same Bahirambhat who made a Marathi commentary on the tenth *Skandh* of the *Shri Bhagavata*, and pious men listening to those loving and priceless verses become happy. 97. Bahirambhat finally composed many *padas* and other poems and the moment one listens to them, sins flee away. 98. Listening to the fame of God's *bhaktas*, all the dull-minded become purified. Mahipati therefore pleads with his hearers to listen with love.

99. *Swasti* (Peace)! This book is the *Shri Bhaktavijaya*. In listening to it the Lord of the world will be pleased. Listen then, you God-loving, pious *bhaktas*. This is the forty-fourth very delightful chapter; it is an offering to Shri Krishna.

CHAPTER XLV

EKNATH

Obeisance to Shri Ganesh. Obeisance to the Son of Devaki.

SALVATION THROUGH LISTENING TO THESE STORIES

1. Listen now, O hearers, to the following delightful story. As one listens all the sorrows of this earthly life disappear, full reason is impressed on one's heart, and peace and joy are within one's reach. 2. Without performing any of the means of the *Yogis*. without having to go wandering to bathing-places, if anyone gives his mind to listening to the stories of the saints, he can obtain *Vaikunth* (heaven). 3. Although one may not have much knowledge of the *Shastras*, and though the condition of being indifferent to worldly things does not come to his body, still in giving his love to the singing of the praises of Hari, he is purified immediately. 4. Those who cannot perform the regular religious duties, those who cannot keep in restraint the tongue's desire, even they, remembering and repeating the name of Rama, become as God Himself. 5. Those who are naturally misers and whose affection for their families has especially increased, even those, if they listen to these stories of the saints, turn to repentance. 6. Just as a bar of iron that has become rusty changes the moment it touches the *paris* (touchstone), so the moment there is a taste for the stories of the *bhaktas* the ignorant are visited with sound reason. 7. If one has a store of former good deeds, then only will he have a delight in these stories. But other poor fellows, who are without good deeds laid up in former births, they are hindered in every way by wrong thoughts. 8. Therefore you God-loving, pious people, you seem to me to be immensely fortunate. Like royal swans you enjoy the delightful stories (of the saints).

THE BIRTH OF EKNATH

9. In a previous chapter (43) hearers have listened to the supremely purifying and beautiful story of how Bhanudas brought back to Pandhari the image of Pandurang. 10. The son of Bhanudas of noble qualities was named Chakrapani. He was a supremely pious and wise *Vaishnava*, always engaged in the worship of Hari. 11. His son was Suryanarayan who shone by the glorious light of his knowledge. His beautiful wife was named Rukmini. 12. She gave birth to a son and his name was Eknath. He was in fact a world-*guru*. Listen to his history. 13. Day by day he grew and was soon invested with the sacred thread. His mother and father were exceedingly devoted to him.

EKNATH VISITS JANARDAN

14. There was one there by name of Janardanpant, an exceedingly wise man. He was accustomed to have a manifestation of the god Dattatreya. It happened on a certain day that Eknath went to visit him. 15. Placing his garments on his head, he went and with reverence bowed to him. When Janardanpant saw him at that time he was much astonished. 16. He said to Eknath, 'To whom do you belong ? Why have you come here ?' So Janardan addressed him and asked him for his history. 17. 'You have evidently sulked and leaving your mother and father have come here to me. You must tell me the truth without any hesitation of mind.' 18. Then joining his hands together palm to palm, Eknath replied very humbly. He said, 'I am a *Rigvedi* Brahman's son. I have come here to see you. 19. I am not irritated against my mother or father, but I felt a sense of repentance in my heart. But the love of this earthly life has become part of me. My mind is in trouble by lust and anger. 20. I constantly see in me the love of things, desires, hypocricy and pride. Therefore I have come to see you with a sense of love. 21. Now my

only desire is that I may always remain with you, and that I may serve you day and night with reverence and delight. 22. I am a sinner and have come to you as a suppliant. O mother *Sadguru*, receive me.' Thus speaking he grasped Janardan's feet with reverence. 23. Listening to these words of Eknath, Janardan was much astonished. He said to himself, 'He seems to be small of age, but his great knowledge seems beyond comparison.'

EKNATH'S SERVICE OF JANARDAN

24. Janardan then gave him his assurance that he should not fear. He said to him, 'You may remain with me with great pleasure.' Hearing these words of Janardan, Eknath felt great joy in his heart. 25. Just as Vyas, when he fell in deep doubt, felt happy at the sight of Narad Muni, so by the assurance of Janardan, Eknath's mind was pleased; 26. or as when Brahmadev met God in the form of a swan he felt a sense of peace, so by the assurance of Janardan the heart of Eknath rejoiced. 27. He continued constantly in the service of his *Swami*. He was alert for his service day and night. He left nothing lacking. He held his *guru* in high reverence. 28. When Janardan at night went to retire, with his own hands Eknath sat massaging his feet. And when he fell into sleep he would not arise from his place. 29. Collecting together all the materials for the *pansupari* and with his own hands putting them into shape, he would make the request to Janardan and with love put it into his mouth. 30. In order to rinse out his mouth he would bring and place a spittoon before him. With his own hands he would help him to bathe and give him the materials for worship. 31. Whenever Janardan asked for perfume, rice, flowers, and sandalwood paste, light and incense, he would immediately bring them to him. 32. Whatever Janardan left on his plate Eknath ate with great love. Thus he

served him for many days, always doing it with love 33. At night Janardan had a cough and bile and he spat into the spittoon. Eknath used to take it away and privately drink it with love. 34. With his own hand he used to make clean the place to which Janardan used to retire. So Eknath gave himself up always to the *bhakti* of his *guru*.

JANARDAN'S ESTIMATION OF EKNATH

35. Janardan seeing this was much astonished. He said, One should not call Eknath a man. He is superior to all the *bhaktas* who follow a *guru*.' 36. Seeing him sitting by himself one day Janardan graciously asked him, 'You are serving me here without your father and mother knowing of it. 37. You seem as one indifferent to all earthly things. At your home, however, they are in need of garments and food. Both your parents are aged and both are deeply concerned for you.' 38. Knowing this Janardan used to send to their house garments and food. When the parents heard the news of their son they were comforted.

EKNATH AS A BOOK-KEEPER

39. Janardan then thought to himself, 'I must give him some special service.' He then requested Eknath to keep his accounts in the account book. 40. If you are efficient in this you will learn all kinds of knowledge.' Assenting to this he made his bow and said, '*Swami*, your command is my authority.' 41. So without any failure in his service he always kept his accounts. Janardan said to himself, 'He is an exceedingly clever boy. I understand him now. 42. So by some means I must turn his mind to divine knowledge.' So he called Eknath to him and said to him, 'Show me your accounts. 43. Look over your day-book and ledger and then show me the account.' Saying that he would do

so he embraced his feet. 44. After having completed his regular service, at night he filled the lamp with oil. He then found that he had made an error of one pice and he sat and attempted to find it. 45. But he could not find the error. The account would not balance. Then concentrating his mind upon it, he sat hunting through and through the account. 46. He did not sleep even for a moment, nor even consider the weariness of his body. Although he was extremely thirsty, he would not drink any water. 47. He said to himself, 'If I should partake of some food and drink water, then I shall feel sleepy and feel lazy. Then what shall I say to my *guru* ?' Thus he thought to himself. 48. When Janardan awoke and looked all round, he did not see Eknath and was much astonished thereby. 49. He hunted for him, and in another room Eknath sat looking over the account to find out the missing one pice and was constantly adding oil to his lamp.

JOY AT MISTAKE FOUND OUT

50. Just then the account balanced and Eknath was full of joy. He clapped his hands together without anyone being near him. 51. Janardan stood there looking at the amusing sight. He then came up in front of him and asked him. 52. The *sadguru* said to Eknath, 'What is the wonderful thing which makes you rejoice and laugh ?' 53. As he heard these words he looked up and then immediately standing he bowed to him with reverence. 54. He said, 'As I was looking over the account I found an error of one pice, and having just now balanced the account I am very happy in my mind and 55. I laughed.' Hearing these words Janardan was full of astonishment. 56. The *sadguru* then said to Eknath, 'Just as your mind was fastened on the pice, so if it is absorbed in the feet of Shri Krishna then you will arrive at your own good.' 57. Hearing these words of his *guru* he immediately felt repentant

at heart. He replied, 'This was the very desire I have had· give me your command, O *Swami*.'

EKNATH'S BLESSED DAY

58. 'Blessed is this day. I have received your instructions through your graciousness. You have separated me from the evils of *maya* and wiped away my desires for this earthly existence.' 59. Then taking his pen he placed it at the feet of his *sadguru*. He then explained the way in which he had written his account. Let good people listen to it in love. 60. 'This human body is as it were the principal of the current year. During the last year was the result of a former act. The page of love is in one's heart. A great deal was expended in performing one's duty. 61. Having rejected all idea of fruit as a reward, I am brought near to my *Swami*, and without my knowing it will be offered to God. 62. I have submitted this interesting account of my regular service. It bears the signature of the *sadguru* and that shows the account is rightly balanced. 63. And now bringing forth for clearance this human body its balance as ignorance is acquired, and have devoted myself to your feet gladly turning from all business relations. 64. You are the *Swami* of the three worlds. My business relations have been with you. I am now delighted with the name of Krishna through your grace. 65. *Soham* (I am He) has been given me by you and I bow to it with my head. I have received an unlimited amount of garments of love. 66. I have received the *pansupari* of *mukti*. With it all the distress of the diseases of this earthly existence have been turned away. Then going to the city of final absorption I occupied the bastion of the supreme Spirit. 67. I have submitted at last to my *Swami* the revenue in the form of my experience. By the association of the good I have been able to

collect the revenue in arrears, and so I have received the receipt of *bhakti*. 68. I must have done some good deeds in a former birth, when I started in with this business of the name of Rama.' Saying these things to Janardan he bowed prostrate at his feet.

EKNATH AS JANARDAN'S DISCIPLE

69. Janardan hearing him say this was astonished. He said to himself, 'I see that he has the authority to receive instruction for making him my disciple.' 70. Then raising Eknath up, Janardan embraced him with graciousness. He taught him the saving *mantra* of 'Rama Krishna.' 71. Placing all his faith in this he obtained the sacred means for the supreme spiritual riches. Then in his love in the *kirtans* he sang of the good deeds of Hari. 72. After the gracious deeds of his *sadguru* there was no lack in his service to him. Day by day he became more and more devoted. 73. Seeing his determination Janardan said to himself, 'Who can call him a man? In order to save the universe he is the complete *avatar* of Vishnu.'

JANARDAN THINKS TO MEET EKNATH WITH DATTATREYA

74. After this Janardan looking with an eye of compassion, thought of giving Eknath a sight of Shri Dattatreya and communicated his secret thought to Eknath. 75. Janardan said to Eknath, 'I will cause you to meet the god Shri Dattatreya. But let your mind be without fear when you see Him. You need not fear at all. 76. He appears in all sorts of forms. He now and then changes His form. He assumes just the very form at which the ignorant people revile. 77. But embrace the feet of the person with whom I shall talk. Then having embraced Him, hold the *Sadguru* to your heart. 78. If He gives any favour, eat it then and there with love.' As Janardan gave Eknath these instructions he grasped him by his feet 79. Eknath replied to him, 'This has been my wish

for a long time. It has been in my mind but I did not wish to overstep the limit my *Swami* had set by speaking to him about it. 80. Now, however, with your own lips you have given me the assurance. So fulfil today my heart's desire and give me a manifestation of Dattatreya.' 81. Recognizing thus Eknath's earnest wish he took him into the jungle. Suddenly there the Son of Anusaya (the god Dattatreya) appeared to meet them. 82. Janardan then said to Eknath, 'Recognize now my *Swami.*'

DATTATREYA AS A MUHAMMADAN FAKIR

Suddenly a Muhammadan sitting upon a horse came there. 83. At such a form Eknath became frightened. He said, 'He seems to me to be a real Muhammadan. What you say to me seems to be untrue.' 84. He had a broad forehead and bloodshot eyes. In His hands were weapons. Riding upon a horse he came near to them and dismounted. Janardan then bowed to him. 85. In the language of the Muhammadans the son of Anusaya began to speak with Janardan. Eknath seeing this was full of astonishment. 86. The *sadguru* then said to Janardan, 'I am hungry; let us eat.' He then prepared various kinds of dainty foods and exhibited a wonderful sight. 87. In a jewelled golden plate six sweet juices were served. Janardan sat close to Him and the two dined together. 88. The *sadguru* then said to Janardan, 'I see a boy over there; call him here to eat with us, if you are so pleased.'

EKNATH DOUBTFUL

89. At this Eknath had a doubt in his mind and he said to himself, 'How can I eat the food of a Muhammadan?' So he ran away a good distance. 90. Just then Dattatreya became invisible and Eknath was astonished. Placing his head at the feet of his *sadguru* he questioned him with love. 91. He said to him, 'Who was that Muhammadan who came here in our midst?'

JANARDAN REMOVES EKNATH'S DOUBT

The other replied, 'You did not recognize Him by His characteristics. He was the Son of Atri (Dattatreya). 92. Although many means are devised, still no one is able to have a manifestation of Him. You met Him here without effort, and wrong thoughts came into your heart. 93. As an unfortunate man was going along the road he suddenly came upon a wish-tree, but he ran away from it, and so you have thought about Him. 94. Or as when a pearl should suddenly fall upon one's hand, and having no good fortune he should close his eyes, so it has happened to you. 95. If the ocean of nectar appeared, one could even strike the god of Death with a stick, but the Son of Anusaya cannot be seen by any common person. 96. Although sitting upon spikes is a difficult task, still even that can be easily accomplished, but a manifestation of Dattatreya does not occur to men, yet you had the opportunity without effort. 97. Secrets of human beings can be known even without their telling them, but the seemingly impossible thing is the sight of the Son of Atri, O Eknath. 98. By special effort you may be able to bathe in the seven oceans, but the sight of the *sadguru* can only happen through good fortune. 99. One does not know the future, yet for once one may know it; but it is not *any* one that Dattatreya comes to meet. 100. You had the opportunity of meeting Him without any effort and you needlessly had the doubt; but in the future there may be another opportunity of seeing Him, so be on your guard.'

EKNATH'S ARGUMENT

101. To this Eknath replied, 'I call myself your disciple, but if I try to fasten my mind on any other object, wrong thoughts arise in it. 102. Know that an infant is in the heart of its father; therefore a grandfather naturally loves his grandson; so if I hold my head at your feet,

Dattatreya will be pleased with me. 103. So long as a flower clings to the stem it will naturally receive the sap from the roots, so if I give my attention to you, Dattatreya will without effort on my part meet with me.' 104. Thus talking with his *sadguru* both hastened home.

MANIFESTATION OF DATTATREYA

On a certain day Janardan said to Eknath, 105. 'Let us go into the jungle today for your sake. Then I will cause Dattatreya to appear to you, though I do not know in what form He will appear.' 106. Saying this to him they went quickly into the jungle. There Dattatreya suddenly appeared in the form of a Muhammadan *Fakir*. 107. *Maya* (the primal force of the universe) had taken the form of his wife. The wish-cow appeared as a she-dog. Seeing this form Janardan rejoiced. 108. Going forward he made a *namaskar* and embracing him they talked to one another. 109. In the Muhammadan language the Son of Anusaya said to Janardan, 'I am very hungry, let us eat together at once.' 110. On producing an earthen vessel with His own hands he himself milked the she-dog. Crumbling the bread in the milk, the two sat together to eat. 111. The *sadguru* said to Janardan, 'Who is that whom I see over there? Invite him and bring him here to sit and eat with us.'

EKNATH'S HESITATION

112. Hearing these words Eknath felt hesitation. 'Why he seems clearly to be a *fakir*. How shall I do that which is not lawful?' 113. Janardan made signs to him, 'Now by the instructions I formerly gave you, you have now met that *sadguru*. Take His favour and go.' 114. But Eknath still hesitated in his mind. He came near to the *fakir* with fear. He said, 'I will not stay close to you, but give me at once the favour.' 115. Then Janardan in his love

gave him a mouthful of what was left. He (Eknath) bound it in his garment and then sat by himself. 116. As soon as the dining was over Dattatreya said to Janardan ' Who is that boy over there ? Tell me. '

DATTATREYA'S BLESSING

117. Janardan then called Eknath and placed him at His *Swami's* feet. He gave him His blessing and spoke to him in words of promise. 118. ' This boy will explain clearly in Marathi the deep, secret meaning of the *Shri Bhagwat* which Vyas has written as the substance of the *Vedas* and the *Shastras.* 119. He will compose a delightful book as the *Bhavartha Ramayana.* In hearing it, all men will be saved. 120. He will also sing with love in his *kirtans* of the supremely wonderful deeds of the life of Shri Hari composed in many *padas.* These will save the sinner by merely being listened to.' 121. Giving him this promise he placed his hands of assurance upon his head. Then without a moment's delay He became invisible. 122. Janardan said to Eknath, 'You will now be satisfied with what has occurred today. Tell me where you have placed the favour which He gave you ? ' 123. Eknath said in reply, ' I threw away that morsel. ' Janardan then took the *pansupari* out of his mouth and with his own hand put it into Eknath's mouth. 124. Then taking Eknath by the hand they came home quickly. They did not forget each other, just as the mother does not forget her child. 125. A mother does not forget her infant ; the hearts of both bore witness to this. In that way both Eknath and Janardan were truly of one heart. 126. A lamp and its light, gold and its brilliancy, fluidity and water are without distinction. 127. The sun and its rays, moon and coolness, the wind and motion, between these there are no distinctions. 128. The ocean and its waves although different in appearance are but one, just as nectar and its sweet

juice live together. 129. Just as attentiveness and listening, or the earth and its solidity, spiritual philosophy and the quality of goodness are different in name only; 130. so Janardan and Eknath, though two different names still, did not forget one another. Like dear and near relatives they felt distressed at each other's absence.

JANARDAN SENDS EKNATH BACK HOME

131. It now happened on a certain day that Janardan after thinking over the matter said to himself, 'It does not seem right that I should now accept his service.' 132. Janardan then said to him,'My command is your authority. Now go to Pratishthan (modern Paithan) and live there as a householder. 133. Show to the people by example the way of bathing, devotions, worship of God, worship of fire and so forth, how to worship uninvited guests and how to perform the regular and the occasional religious practices. 134. Though you may become skilled in the knowledge of the soul, never leave the doing of good deeds. After you have crossed over a river, why destroy the ferry boat on which you came? 135. Even if you feel in your mind that some duty of yours is not correct, still you must carry it out as a popular custom, then having done it according to prescribed rules, leave it to God.136. If you accept these words as an authority you will make the Husband of Rukmini pleased with you.' Janardan then placed his hands upon Eknath's head and Eknath started quickly for Pratishthan. 137. The *sadguru's* words are full of authority and there is no superior means to that. Knowing that this is the secret of *guru*-worship he did what others could not have done.

EKNATH AS A HOUSEHOLDER

138. Then going to his home he bowed to his aged parents, who seeing their son felt great comfort. 139. Here he bathed and performed his devotions, his worship of God and the service of his mother and father. According to

the prescribed rules he began to live with his wife at the personal spring-time. 140. He made no request of anyone. He did not regard anyone as great or small. Whatever of animate or inanimate things he saw they all seemed to him to be Janardan. 141. There was an old idol of Pandurang at his home which he worshipped with love. As he was told to do in the scriptures so he worshipped it. 142. With reverence he offered to it many kinds of flowers, sandalwood paste and many fragrant substances, incense, light, the platter of lights and food. 143. With a handful of flowers and hymns of praise he used to go around the god. making to it a prostrate *namaskar*, and with repentance in his heart would plead for God's mercy. 144. 'Victory, victory to Thee, Purifier of the sinner, Saviour of the world, Dweller at Dwarka, Husband of Rukmini, Helper of the helpless, compassionate One, Lord of all, Pandurang. 145. I come as a suppliant to Thee with exclusive devotion. Therefore I bow before Thee.' Then taking with him a favour of *tulsi* leaves he drank the water in which the idol had been bathed. 146. Taking Brahmans into his dining line he used to dine with them in love. At the third watch he used to listen with reverence and good devotion to the reading of *Puranas*. 147. At night he started a *Harikirtan*. Pious people assembled to listen to it. Hearing the words of Eknath men and women became absorbed. 148. Through Janardan's favour he composed verses in a happy language. As saints and good people listened to them their minds felt great joy.

RAMA'S COMMAND TO COMPOSE MARATHI *RAMAYANA*

149. As Eknath was asleep one night Shri Raghunath (Rama) came to him in a dream and said to him, 150. 'The *Ramayana* composed by Valmiki is in Sanskrit and its deep meaning is not understood by people. Therefore make a commentary in Marathi and give its contents to

men.' 151. As soon as he saw this in his dream he became at once awake. Regarding that command as his authority he began the Marathi version of the *Ramayana*. 152. Choosing a favourable day he began to search the seven chapters. As he brought the meaning of it into his mind he became absorbed in it. 153. He thought to himself, 'The meaning of this is deep. How can I put it into Marathi? Still by the mercy of Janardan I will compose the book as best as I can.' 154. He began the *Bālkūnd* [the chapter dealing with Rama's birth and childhood] and composed verses of praise in the first chapter. Worshipping the feet of Ganpati and Sarasvati he then praised the *sadguru*. 155. Praying to the saints and good people Eknath began his book. With good devotion he did the composition, therefore it was called the *Bhavartha Ramayana*. 156. Shri Raghunath (Rama) sitting upon his lips caused him rightly to compose the book. Eknath became a mere instrument which all His holy *bhaktas* know.

A REVILING NEIGHBOUR

157. There was, however, in the city a certain citizen who was always reviling him. He would remark, 'Why has Eknath made a Marathi commentary on the Sanskrit?' 158. There were other pious ones, lovers of God who called his poetry delightful. As soon as they listened to it all troubles of their hearts disappeared. 159. Now it happened one night when Eknath fell asleep that the Husband of Janaki (Rama) came to him in a dream and said to him, 160. 'Put aside your drowsiness and sit writing the *Ramayana*. I am fond of the delightful language spoken by your lips.' 161. The Lord of Ayodhya got for him pen and paper. When he awoke he did not see Shri Rama. 162. Repeating the names of Raghunath (Rama) he sat writing the *Ramayana*. Just then a seem-

ingly impossible thing occurred. Listen to it with love, O good people. 163. While writing of Maruti going in search of Sita, Eknath lost all consciousness of body and he had no thought whatever of himself. 164. As he was writing the passage where Hanuman flew from the mountain Mahendra he experienced the same thing as Maruti. 165. With love in his heart Eknath started to fly. It was the middle of the night and he fell into tho yard of a neighbour. 166. The citizen becoming awake looked into his yard and there he saw Eknath lying in a fainting condition. Seeing him thus he was full of astonishment. 167. Taking the page in his hand and reading it he understood what it all meant. He said to himself, 'It was with love that he began to fly.' 168. The citizen questioned him, 'How did you come here and fall to the ground?' He had no consciousness of body, therefore he did not speak. 169. Seeing this condition of Eknath his mind felt repentance. He said to himself, 'In vain I have reviled this *avatar* Eknath.' 170. Then taking Eknath on his back he placed him in his house. Eknath became awake in a moment and then continued writing.

REVILER INTENDS TO BECOME EKNATH'S DISCIPLE

171. The citizen made a *namaskar* to him and then went back home. There he determined that he would take instruction from Eknath and become his disciple. 172. When one sees an exceedingly wonderful miracle which creates reverence, that is not pure devotion; it is rightly called hypocrisy. 173. One knowingly makes a god of the *parīs* (touchstone) and worships it in the shrine with the sixteen materials for worship; still such reverence on the part of a *bhakta* can only be called hypocrisy. 174. If one circumambulates the wish-cow after seeing the wonders performed by her, the pious and the God-loving *bhaktas* understand

the secret of this devotion. 175. After the wish-tree is recognized, those with desire give it water. If anyone calls them obliging, good men should not consider it as true. 176. So having first reviled the saints, and then having seen a miracle, reverence is aroused; still he must be called a hypocrite. There is nothing else that can be said. 177. When relatives have acquired wealth the evil-minded pay them respect. But remembering their past dishonour they do not feel well. 178. So this citizen, having first reviled and then having seen a miracle, came as a suppliant. Eknath remembering his past history, saw that it was hypocrisy.

EKNATH AND THE REVILER

179. One day Eknath was sitting in his house and that citizen came to him and made a request. 180. He said to him, ' O *Swami*, I did not know your power and therefore in vain did I revile you. And now with reverence in my heart I have come to your greatness. 181. Place now your hand upon my head and give me the instruction that will make me your disciple. ' Eknath hearing what he said remained silent. 182. ' Not seeing in him authority to become a disciple, how can I make him a disciple? In a ground that can never bear fruit one should never sow seed. 183. One should not give his daughter in marriage to one whose family line has no place in the world. Seeing a broken jar, one should not fill it with water.' 184. Speaking thus to himself, Eknath gave the man the reply, 'After searching out some one worthy of you, have reverence for him.' 185. As he said this to him he would not listen at all. He said, 'I will take no instruction from anyone except from you.' With that he fell at his feet. 186. On account of his importunate urging Eknath outwardly said to him, 'Tomorrow is an auspicious day. Bathe first and then come to me.' 187. As the citizen arose and went home Eknath sat thinking over

the matter. He said to himself, 'I should not give instruction to a lazy man or a miser.' 188. The next day after having bathed Eknath came to the temple. He said to the people at his home, 'Do not place any water here for worship. 189. Although I might call for some one, let no one give me an answer.' Then making this resolve of his own he sat worshipping mentally.

THE REVILER TESTED

190. Just then the citizen having bathed came into the god-room. Here he saw Eknath sitting in contemplation, repeating the names of Krishna with his lips. 191. Eknath thought to himself, 'I must put him to a test. If he is really a hypocrite, I should not give him the instruction.' 192. Calling aloud to the people in his house he said, 'You have not placed here any water for worship. What is the reason for it today?' 193. Then he called out to them to bring it quickly. Still no one in the house gave him a reply. Then Eknath suddenly arose. 194. Taking a vessel in his hand he said, 'There is no one here to give me water.' So he went himself into the house and brought the water. 195. Thus testing the man, Eknath again sat worshipping the god. He said to himself, 'He is still a reviling and a lazy person, so I must not give him instruction to make him a disciple. 196. He who will not give God water that costs nothing, how will he later on do Him service? He who will not make a *namaskar* to an earth-god (Brahman), will not give him a meal of dainty food. 197. He who will not tell anyone the way, how can he give him a lodging in his house? He who will not give a seat to a guest, he will not bind a turban on his head. 198. So one who will not bring water that costs nothing, of what use will he be in the future?' With this thought in his mind he continued worshipping Shri Hari.

THE REVILER PROVED A HYPOCRITE

199. The citizen then said to him, 'Place your hand on my head.' Eknath said, 'The auspicious time has passed, and I do not see any time after that.' 200. Listening to what Eknath had to say, the citizen returned to his home and Eknath felt very satisfied in his heart. 201. He said to himself, 'Why do I want a disciple who is a hypocrite? It is necessary to discard all hindrances and worship the King of Pandhari. 202. What need has the infant son of Janardan for a band of disciples? I fear it will only make me proud.' 203. Thus filled with the spirit of indifference to earthly things Eknath continued to worship.

In the next chapter we shall hear of how the god Shri Krishna came from Dwarka and entered into Eknath's service personally. 204. The hearers who listen to that story will find it sweeter and sweeter. Then all the discomforts of the diseases of this earthly existence will at once flee away. 205. Mahipati again and again pleads with his hearers to give their ears to the story with love, and let their mind be attentive.

206. *Swasti* (Peace)! This book is the *Shri Bhaktavijaya*. In listening to it the Lord of the world will be pleased. Listen then, you God-loving, pious *bhaktas*. This is the forty-fifth deeply delightful chapter.

CHAPTER XLVI

SHRI KHANDYA THE BRAHMAN

Obeisance to Shri Ganesh. Obeisance to the Slayer of demon Dhenuka.

THE STORY OF SHRI KHANDYA GIVES PEACE AND SALVATION

1. The sea of nectar has come with full tide today. One might speak of a treasure of divine knowledge as having been opened, or as the beaatiful light of the sun having appeared in the heart of the hearers. 2. Or we may speak of the secret things of pure knowledge suddenly falling upon the ear, or of having obtained today through good fortune the seed that produces the highest form of salvation. 3. Or we might think of this as a chief *mantra*, a storehouse of blessing, as having come today by means of good fortune, or we may regard it as the thought of indifference to earthly things received in listening to the story of the *bhaktas* of God. 4. Or we may think of it as the happiness from peace, or as if there has sprung up a sprout of the vine of right thought, or as the joy of happiness appearing upon this round earth. 5. Or we may view this story of a saint as the desireless state of being indifferent to earthly things, or as creating love for all creatures, or as creating love and affection. 6. Or it may be called the home of final deliverance, or again the love of happiness from *kirtans*, or we might think of it as the appearance of a pure wish-tree, or it can be called an accomplishment without a desire.

* SHRI KRISHNA COMES IN THE FORM OF A BRAHMAN TO EKNATH

7. In the preceding chapter Eknath tested the citizen

* For a version of the same story from the *Bhaktalilamrit* see No.2 of the Poet-Saints of the Maharashtra Series, page 156.

and sent him home. He appeared black like brass does when placed in a furnace. 8. When gold is tested on the touchstone the lacquered one appears as inferior. The expert then discards it as unacceptable to him. 9. The singing of a prostitute may be exceedingly beautiful, but those indifferent to earthly things do not give their minds to it. Holy men will not accept the yearly royal gifts. 10. A skilled housekeeper picks only one kernel and thus tests the whole boiling rice. So when Eknath asked the citizen for some water he recognized his laziness.

11. With the sixteen materials for worship Eknath continued to offer his offerings to God with feelings of reverence. He had nothing else to give, this the eagle-bannered One understood. 12. He thought to Himself, 'Eknath loves dearly to worship Me. His love for Me is great. So I will at once go to him and help him to accomplish his purpose.'

13. Thus speaking to Himself, the Lord of Dwarka took the form of a Brahman. This infinite One came to Pratishthan and questioned the people. 14. He who is the internal Witnesser, He who is a cloud of intelligence, Dweller in the universe and the Life of the world, He asked where the home of Eknath was, although in his own heart He knew where it was. 15. He said to the people, 'Show me the house of that noble *Vaishnava* who devotes himself with exceeding reverence to the worship of Shri Krishna and who continually gives feasts to Brahmans.' 16. The dark complexioned One having thus spoken, men and women pointed out to him Eknath's house into which He then entered and made him a *namaskar*.

KRISHNA A MENIAL

17. The Life of the world said to Eknath, 'I am a Brahman from another country and without protection.

Having heard that you are constantly giving food to Brahmans I have come here. 18. So give me garments and satisfy my hunger with food and I will then remain here constantly and do what you ask me to do without giving way to any laziness in my mind.' 19. Eknath then asked Him, 'Where is Your home? And who are You? Who is depending upon You? What is Your name?' 20. The Husband of Rukmini having listened to him said, 'I am entirely alone. I have no son, no wife, no property at all. 21. Having determined in my heart to serve you here devotedly and receive your favour, I have come here. 22. I have looked about me in many places, but I can find no place that pleases me.' As Eknath heard His words he was astonished. 23. He said to Him, 'If such is your wish, You may remain here in my home.' With this Shri Hari was pleased.

KRISHNA'S DAILY SERVICE

24. He who is worthy of the worship of Brahmadev and the other gods, He whom Shiva and others contemplate, this Actor as if in a play, this Life of the world became a Brahman menial. 25. In describing rightly His deeds of fame, the *Vedas* and the *Puranas* became crazy; He fetched the water of the Godavari on a sling. 26. In the sea of milk there is an island by name of Prabhakar. The Recliner upon *Shesha*, the Dweller in *Vaikunth* (heaven), rose as soon as it was early dawn, regardless of weariness to His body. 27. Of whom *Yogis* weary themselves in performing the eight forms of *Yoga* practice, He rising early had the vessels polished bright that were used in the worship of God. 28. The beautiful dark complexioned Husband of Rukmini who is all over the world known as Giver of final deliverance, the Lord of the world, He swept the yard and sprinkled it with water and then smeared with cowdung the god-room

Himself. 29. He from whose feet the river Bhagirathi sprang, He, Shripati, lovingly filled the vessels needed in the worship of God and placed them there. 30. He whom the eighty-eight thousand *rishis* reverently worship, He, the Life of the world, becoming a Brahman menial, lovingly prepared the sandalwood paste. 31. He at whose feet the eight *Siddhis* (accomplishments personified) day and night cling, He, the Lord of the heart, making garlands placed them for the worship of God. 32. He by whose power the moon, the sun, and the bright stars look bright, He (*Adhokshaja*) trimmed the light used in the worship and was not ashamed of doing so. 33. He whose command the hosts of the gods including Indra obey, He gave to Eknath the various materials needed in the worship of God. 34. Whenever Eknath called out to Him 'Krishna,' He came at once up before him reverently, He never allowed anything to be lacking in his service. He was always attentive.

PROPLE CALL KRISHNA SHRI KHANDYA

35. People called Him 'Shri Khandya the Brahman' because He prepared the sandalwood paste for Eknath. All the citizens of the town mardelled at it. 36. They said among themselves, 'There is a Brahman who is serving at the house of Eknath, who does not accept any wages and who does all his work.' 37. Without Eknath knowing it the Lord of Dwarka used to go into the other part of the house helping Eknath's wife in her duties lovingly and full of joy. 38. He swept the yard, sprinkled it with water and cleaned the household pots. He churned the curds. He said, 'Do not hesitate to ask me to perform any errand for you.' 39. At times when work was behind, the dark complexioned One would sweep the kitchen with His own hands. Taking with Him the materials for cooking He went into the kitchen to do the cooking. 40. If there was any necessity for hurrying, He

used personally to serve food to the Brahmans. The food had a strange kind of sweet new taste. 41. The Life of the world served water to the Brahmans who as they drank it said, ' It has a new sweetness to it. ' And this astonished their minds. 42. He the god was very fond of removing their used plates. He readily tucked up His *dhotar*, removed the food left on the plates and ate it with infinite delight. 43. Then taking the leaf-plates He would throw them outside and washing His hands He would also wash the dining ground.

44. The mother and the father of Eknath had already died and a very strange thing now happened. Let the pious listen to it.

EKNATH INVITES BRAHMANS

45. The day for the worship of ancestors came and Eknath invited the Brahmans saying, ' Tomorrow is my ancestors' day. Please come to the feast. ' 46. Arising early in the morning He had the cooking prepared in his house. Just as soon as one and a half watches of the day had passed he asked the Brahmans to go and bathe. 47. Where Krishna serves in the form of a Brahman menial. how can there be the lack of anything ? Garments and gifts of gold were there ready to give to the Brahmans. 48. After bathing, Eknath came back to his home. Going to the roof of his house he dried there the garments. 49. Just then an *unnameable* (out-caste) and his wife were both sweeping the alley below and suddenly the fragrance of the dainty food came to them. 50. The wife said to her out-caste husband, ' I receive delightful fragrance from food, such food as is not obtainable to *us*, but the fortunate Brahmans will eat it. ' 51. The out-caste then said to his wife, ' Why do you lick your chops in vain ? Such dainty food *we* can *never* have in all our lives. 52. There is the worship of ancestors in his (Eknath's) house to-day and so

they will bury even that which is left on the plates. So not recognizing this you have foolishly cherished such a useless desire. 53. An ox goes to a wedding and even rich men give it fodder to eat; but, my wife, how can there be in *our* fate that pleasure of dining upon such dainty food ?'

EKNATH FEASTS OUT-CASTES FIRST

54. As they were thus talking to one another their conversation fell upon Eknath's ears. He then descended from the roof and said to his wife, 55. 'Two out-castes are sweeping. They desire to eat of the dainty food. Come now and give to them a feast of the food already prepared at our house.' 56. The wife said to him, 'A great amount of food has been cooked. Invite all the out-castes together with their children. 57. If we give a feast to two only, the others will remain unsatisfied. These two will go and invite the others and they will all come rushing here. 58. So let us invite them all and give them all to eat. *Janardan* (God) is in all creatures, and so we should make these out-castes happy.' 59. Eknath then went outside and invited all the out-castes. Seeing them in the alley he felt intense compassion for them. 60. He served perfumes, rice, flowers that had been prepared to use in the worship of the Brahmans, and Eknath made an offering of them to the out-castes. 61. Placing the leaf-plates before each by the hand of *Shudras* he served them with the dainty food. He placed before them melted butter, sugar, vegetables and salt.

OUT-CASTES MADE HAPPY

62. Knowing certainly that *Janardhan* (God) is in all men, Eknath made the offering to God and said, 'Krishna is the enjoyer of this food.' 63. Eknath said to them, 'Start now to eat; and all the out-castes great and small, including children, then partook of the dainty food. All ate to their fill. 64. They received such delicious

food as they had never seen or heard of. They exclaimed, 'Blessed is your action, O Eknath. You have indeed made us feel happy. 65. We belong to the most inferior out-castes. We never had seen such food before. We shall remember you all our lifetime, as the merciful *Vaishnava.* 66. Eknath served them with whatever dish they desired. All were fully satisfied and to all he gave *pansupari.* 67. Every bit of food remaining in the house he gave to them. Then he had his house and pots cleaned. 68. Giving out new materials for cooking he engaged many female cooks and the dainty food which resulted was ten times more than before.

BRAHMANS ANGRY AT EKNATH FEEDING OUT-CASTES

69. The Brahmans who were asked to bathe learned the news that Eknath had feasted the out-castes before them. 70. They said to one another, 'Eknath has done a very strange thing. He invited us to the feast of the anniversary of his ancestors, but instead he gave a feast to the unnameables.' 71. The Brahmans angrily consulted among themselves and said, 'Let no one from to-day take food from this defiled person.' 72. All who were learned in the *Shastras* went to Eknath's house and angrily belaboured him with harsh words. 73. Some said, 'You evildoer, you have violently insulted us. Without having feasted the Brahmans, you wicked man, you honoured the out-castes. 74. Were *your* ancestors unmentionable that you honoured these lowest of the out-castes, namely, those reviled by the *Vedas* and the *Shastras*? 75. You are seeking to bring about at once a mixture of castes. You have set about establishing an evil custom, thereby doing away with the duties of Brahmans.' 76. Hearing these words of the Brahmans, Eknath joined his hands and humbly pleaded with them, 'I have already had prepared another cooking in the house. 77. The fragrance of the

first cooking was smelt by the out-castes. How could I have given you that which remained after the feast? 78. So having given to them a feast I immediately had another feast prepared. Forgive me, you compassionate ones, and purify this memorial day.' 79. The Brahmans replied, 'You have insulted us to-day. The food which is to be offered to fire in great sacrifice, you have thrown it before the crows. 80. You have, as it were, thrown a bottle full of the sacred Bhagirathi water into a latrine; or it has been like taking the jewel ornament of a queen and giving it to a slave; 81. or as if you tóok the paste of sandalwood of the Maila mountain and rubbed it on a donkey; or as if you had taken the *tulsi* leaf used in the worship of Vishnu and offered it to a mosque; 82. or as if you took nectar and wholly wasted it by throwing it on ashes; 83. so without giving us a feast, you have gladly honoured the out-castes; thus you have done what is wrong and placed a stain upon yourself.' 84. Having spoken thus the Brahmans excommunicated Eknath and somewhat concerned he sat in silence.

ANCESTORS ATTEND THE FEAST

85. Krishna, who was in the house as a menial Brahman and who was also known by another name of Shri Khandya, said to Eknath, 'Why are you sad? 86. Your ancestral ceremonies are to be performed here to-day. Therefore do not be concerned in reference to it. Your ancestors will come speedily to eat the prepared feast. 87. After the feast has been prepared let the leaf-plates be placed for the feast.' Eknath now became full of joy, yet was very much astonished. 88. He served many kinds of dainty food, melted butter and sugar. The moment his lips uttered the word 'Come,' his ancestors came and sat down. 89. After they had been honoured and their feet washed, and after the *pansupari*, the

sandalwood paste and the sacred thread, he gave them golden gifts. 90. The moment Eknath made an offering of food to the supreme *Brahma*, the ancestors began to eat. Whatever food they had a desire for, they took it and gladly ate. 91. The confidence he placed at the feet of Janardan was seen in the form of ancestors. Eknath was indeed happy when he saw his ancestors. 92. After his ancestors were satisfied with the feast, he gave them water to wash their hands, and after having given the *pansupari* and the gifts of money he said to them, 93. 'What shall I do with the food that still remains?' They replied, 'Dine on it together with your friends.' 94. The Brahmans who were standing by the door heard these words, and opened the door and came inside to see. 95. There they actually saw the ancestors completing their feast. The moment they were seen they became invisible. All the Brahmans were astonished at what they saw. 96. The Brahmans then went outside and said amongst one another, 'Eknath is not an ordinary man, but a direct *avatar* of Vishnu. 97. We have been proud of our rights and have tried to nullify his purpose. But Shri Krishna is helping him and is favourable to him because of his devotion. 98. The moment he falls into any distress the eagle-bannered One comes to his help. He has today caused his ancestors actually to dine with him thereby bringing shame on us.' 99. Some said, 'We have lost the various kinds of dainty food; as one cannot understand the future, it is fate which is to be blamed. 100. Now let us all go tomorrow and humbly tell Eknath that he should now take penance and remain in his caste. 101. If we say he is already purified, our pride will have gone for naught. By putting a penalty upon Eknath we shall turn him again to a right course of action.'

THE BRAHMANS ASSIGN TO EKNATH A PENANCE

102. The next day all the Brahmans assembled together

on the sandy bank of the river and invited Eknath to come to them. 103. When Eknath came he made these Brahmans a *namaskar*. He said to them, 'For what purpose have you, my lords, invited me here?' 104. They replied to him, 'Without knowing what you were doing, you have committed a fault. Now take penance and give honour to these rules of the *Vedas*.' 105. Hearing what the Brahmans said Eknath replied, 'I absolutely refuse to perform a penance. So long as Shri Krishna is my mother and father, how can I do what is wrong?' 106. The Brahmans replied, 'Act with reason and give honour to our request. Your body will not be purified unless you receive a penance.' 107. Then having bathed him in the Godavari they gave Eknath a penance. They placed ashes and cowdung on him and repeated the *mantras* given in the *Vedas*.

A BRAHMAN LEPER ARRIVES AT PAITHAN

108. Just then a Brahman suddenly arrived from Trimbakeshwar. He said to the people, 'Which one i Eknath? Tell me.' 109. This man's whole body was covered with leprosy sores and no part of his body was clean. Seeing such a form as this the Brahmans said clearly to him, 110. 'That one over there, who is taking a penance in the water, is called Eknath. Why do you ask for him? Tell us quickly.' 111. To this the Brahman leper replied, 'While performing austerities at Trimbak, Shiva appeared to me in a dream and sent me here. 112. This Husband of Uma said to me, "At Paithan there is the *bhakta* of Vishnu, Eknath. He has feasted a great many of the unmentionables on the day of the ancestor ceremony. 113. This is a holy deed of his. If you go at once to him and if he will give you a part of his holy deeds, your leprosy will go away at once." 114. The moment I had this dream I started to come.' Hearing these words, all the twice-born were astonished. 115. 'In what

Shastra', they said, 'is it written as a holy thing to cast Brahmans aside and dine the out-castes?' Some said, 'This is all false. Shankar (Shiva) got rid of this fasting Brahman.' 116. Another one said, 'Sit quietly. Does one need a mirror to see the bracelets on one's hand? Let us see how Eknath's trust turns out.'

EKNATH CURES THE LEPER

117. The leper then went into the water of the Godavari and said to Eknath, 'Shiva causes you to repeat for me the good deed you did for the unmentionables.' 118. Eknath said, 'I will give you what you desire', and he poured water upon his hand. All the Brahmans stood amazed at seeing the strange sight. 119. Suddenly in the twinkling of an eye his skin had a lustre. Seeing this very wonderful thing the Brahmans were astonished in their minds. 120. They said to one another, 'We have been proud of our clinging to our usual duties and that is what has hindered us. To give a penance to a Vishnu *bhakta* has only brought a stain upon ourselves.' 121. The twice-born then said to Eknath, 'You are indeed the *avatar* of Vishnu. You are not an ordinary man, we now truly understand this. 122. The Himalaya mountains do not need a breeze from a fan; the sky does not need a garment; fire does not need a bath; so you, a noble *Vaishnava*, are pure. 123. Nectar does not require cooking; the ocean does not need to go to sacred bathing places; so you do not need a penance. We now understand it. 124. You have shown us a seemingly impossible thing. You have brought and feasted your ancestors. No one has ever seen or heard such a thing before. Now we have seen it personally with our eyes.' 125. Then taking Eknath by the hand they immediately proceeded to his house. They said to him, 'The Husband of Rukmini is your helper. We know it now for a

certainty.' 126. There Eknath gave the Brahmans gifts, and bowed his head to the water in which their feet were washed. They then returned to their homes and their minds were full of astonishment. 127. They exclaimed, 'Blessed is this *bhakta* of Vishnu. He is constantly interested in the service of Brahmans. With loving feelings he worships God according to prescribed rules.' 128. So it was in connection with all the people of Paithan. Some reviled Eknath, some praised him, but Eknath was always full of joy. He did not allow himself to fall into any excess either of joy or sorrow.

IDENTITY OF SHRI KHANDYA DISCLOSED

129. There was a Brahman who went to Dwarka. Having a repentant heart he performed austerities with a desire to meet the Husband of Rukmini. 130. Just then Radha and Rukmini appeared to him in a dream. They said to him, 'The Holder of the disk (Vishnu) is not here at Dwarka, so depart from here. 131. On the banks of the Godavari at Pratishthan (Paithan) there is the *Vaishnava bhakta* Eknath who constantly feasts the Brahmans. Go to that place. 132. Krishna, or Shri Khandya, as a Brahman menial has lived there for twelve years. He is truly Narayan the supreme *Brahma*. So you should have a sight of Him. 133. The Lord of *Vaikunth* (heaven) is remaining there serving His *bhakta*. He does not care anything for us, so go at once and bring Him here.' 134. Listening to what was said to him in the dream, the Brahman was delighted. He then came to Pratishthan and inquired of the people, 135. 'There is here a *bhakta* of Vishnu by name of Eknath. He is very interested in the service of Brahmans. Show me his house at once.' Saying this he proceeded. 136. Asking again and again he finally reached Eknath's house. When Eknath saw this performer of austerities he bowed to him. 137. Eknath

gave him a seat and said to him, ' From whence have you come? What are the various bathing-places you have visited, and from which have you come to this place?' 138. The performer of austerities replied, ' I have come here to meet Krishna or Shri Khandya, the Brahman menial. I have come hurrying here.' 139. Eknath said to him, ' He has gone to the Godavari river for water. Remain a moment quietly. He will soon return.' 140. Just then Krishna with vessels full of water on a sling on His shoulder came into Eknath's yard. Seeing the performer of austerities there He felt a hesitation. 141. He said to Himself, ' I have been here for twelve years full of joy. I wonder what this creditor of mine has come for whom I suddenly see here.' 142. Thus the Lord of *Vaikunth* (heaven) thinking to Himself became concerned.

KRISHNA AS A BRAHMAN MENIAL

Just then a very remarkable thing happened. Listen to it, you *bhaktas* of His, and pious ones. 143. Eknath said to the performer of austerities, ' Look, here is Krishna the Brahman menial.' The man then suddenly arose and embraced Krishna's feet. 144. The lord of the earth carrying the sling of water then went into the god-room. Putting down the water jars, He became invisible. 145. The performer of austerities stood outside waiting for Him, but the Husband of Rukmini did not return. When he looked into the god-room he saw no one there. 146. So mourning over the matter he threw himself down on the ground and exclaimed, ' On seeing me, the Holder of the disk (Krishna) ran away.' 147. When Eknath saw this he asked an explanation of the performer of austerities. He said to him, ' Why have you become so sorrowful ? Tell me quickly.' 148. The man told him everything. He fell at Eknath's feet, and both full of emotion embraced one another. 149. Eknath said to the performer of austerities. ' Blessed is your special fortune. You recognized at sight the Pervader of the world and worshipped His feet at leisure. 150. I have not recognized God and I gave Him many things to do.' Thus with repentance in his heart Eknath now praised Keshava (Krishna). 151. He said, 'O Lover of Thy *bhaktas*, Helper of the lowly, You have borne heavy burdens here. Your story not being known, a great wrong has been done here to You. 152. You, the Holder of the disk (Krishna), supremely tender One. used to carry the load of water barefooted. Pebbles must have hurt Your feet. You have done a most remarkable thing. 153. You have been here twelve years and it did not come to my understanding who You were. Seeing You in the guise of a (menial) Brahman, I asked You to do many things for me. 154. You are worthy of the worship of Brahmadev and other gods; Your feet Shiva contemplates; with Your own hands You prepared the sandalwood paste and gave it to me for performing worship. 155. The performers of austerities go through many different kinds of practices and would look at You with extreme delight. Some are constantly visiting sacred bathing-places, but You do not become visible to them. 156. You, O Lord of the heart, are difficult to approach. No one understands Your miraculous deeds. Having been born to Yashoda, she considered You as her son, 157. but when You were leaving Gokul, You went to Mathura and then she recognized You. In the same way twelve years have passed and I did not recognize You, the Infinite One.' 158. With this repentance in his heart Eknath mourned in many ways. Now if I in love should go into details, this book would increase overmuch.

159. Eknath's wife was a supremely pious and dutiful wife. She said, ' O God supreme, Husband of Rukmini, we needlessly caused You weariness. 160. You, the supremely tender Govinda, arose to perform Your service

in the early morning. O Mukund (Krishna), without knowing You, we acted very disrespectfully towards You. 161. You, who are worshipped by all the gods, used to eat after we had done so. You paid no attention to hunger or thirst. So evil a person am I, O Shri Krishna.' 162. Thus for twelve years Shri Krishna had remained with them. If we make mention of the constant good deeds He performed during that time, great will be this book in its details.

DNYANDEVA APPEARS TO EKNATH IN A DREAM

163. It happened one night that Eknath was asleep when Dnyandeva came to him in a dream and said to him, 164. 'Come to Alandi, open my tomb and look inside. There the roots of the *ajan* tree have come near me and hurt me. 165. Push these roots aside and then again close my tomb.' Eknath having this dream, immediately awoke. 166. He then came to Alandi and bathed in the Indrayani river. He worshipped Siddheshwar and opening the tomb, looked inside. 167. There on his hard couch Dnyanraj was sitting. His divine form was a mass of light. There was nothing to be compared to it. 168. Eknath made his *namaskar* to Dnyandeva and kept gazing into the tomb. He there saw the root of the *ajan* tree that reached Dnyandeva. 169. With his own hand he pushed the roots aside and then closed the door of the tomb. With mortar he closed the tomb and arranged the slabs of stones as they were before.

170. Alandi at that time was quite deserted and he was unable to obtain materials for cooking. His band of disciples became hungry. Just then the Lord of Pandhari came to his help. 171. The Lord of the world personally provided for the hunger and thirst of His *bhaktas*. Taking the form of a grocer He erected a small tent and sat there. 172. Eknath seeing this rejoiced in his heart and said, 'A merchant has come here in this bazar. Let us

purchase of him whatever we need.' 173. He then sent two Brahmans and they brought back all the materials necessary in their garments. They remarked, 'Be calm in your mind. We shall bring you the money.' 174. The Lord of Pandhari then said, 'I am here for today. Let all of you perform the cooking and eat at your lodging. 175. I am acquainted with Eknath. But he does not recognize Me. Hearing that he has come on a pilgrimage here, I have brought all the materials needed for cooking.' 176. The moment the Brahmans had turned their backs on *Hrishikeshi* (the Lord of the heart, Krishna) He became invisible. They all felt this very strange, and they reported the matter to Eknath. 177. They said to him, 'The grocer gave to us all the materials that we needed and then at once he became invisible. He did this without our giving any money to Him. A most extraordinary thing has taken place.' 178. Eknath hearing what they had to say was moved with emotion. He exclaimed, 'The Lord of Pandhari has laboured hard on our behalf.' 179. When the cooking was ready he dined along with the Brahmans and remained there that night and lovingly performed a *kirtan*.

EKNATH AND HIS GURU JANARDAN

180. The next day making his *namaskar* to Dnyandeva's tomb he immediately started for home. Returning to Pratishthan he there worshipped with love. 181. Such was the condition of the mind of Eknath. All the three worlds appeared to him in the form of his *guru* Janardan (i.e., God) Who is present in every creature.* I have no doubt of this in my mind. 182. Thus contemplating Janardan he himself became Janardan; no difference could be seen there; just like the water of a river in the sea; 183. or like a lamp and its light, are of different names but are the same thing,

Or, There appeared to him in all the three worlds the form of his *guru* Janardan (i. e., God) Who is present in every creature.

so there was no difference whatever between Eknath and Janardan. 184. Camphor and its fragrance are one; there is no difference between water and fluidity; a flower and its honey live together in love; 185. likewise Eknath and Janardan became one in essence. Mahipati comes to them as a devoted suppliant and with reverence worships their feet.

186. *Swasti* (Peace)! This book is the *Shri Bhaktavijaya*. In listening to it the Lord of the world will be pleased. Listen then, you God-loving, pious *bhaktas*. This is the forty-sixth very delightful chapter.

CHAPTER XLVII

RAMDAS *

Obeisance to Shri Ganesh. Obeisance to the Lord of Dwarka.

STORIES OF SAINTS BRING PEACE AND LOVE

1. Listen, O hearers, to the following beautiful story. By it there will be created a love for the supreme spiritual riches. 2. And the moment one listens to it the snare of desire and the wrong thoughts of doubt are thereby destroyed; the very idea of diversity entirely ceases; peace and joy come without effort into one's hands. 3. Free from action and non-action one should be impressed with the love of worship. The good Being has proclaimed the incomparable glory of the stories of the saints. 4. Why need explain this at length ? Fortunate ones understand this secret by experience, namely, those whose hearts are possessed by indifference to earthly things, who have turned to the path of *bhakti*, 5. who have also discarded popular praise, and who dance enthusiastically in the *kirtans*. Others than these do not know the sweetness of these stories. 6. But you fortunate hearers are already rich in good deeds, therefore with the earnest longing to listen to these stories you are seated with love to listen.

PARENTAGE OF RAMDAS

7. In the previous chapter we listened to the extraordinary story of the God-loving Vishnu *bhakta* Eknath who was the embodiment of the *avatar* of Vishnu. 8. There is upon the banks of the Godavari the town of Jamb. There was here a noble Brahman who was a worshipper of Rama. He was supremely pious, wise and clever, and

*For a detailed life of this saint, see the volume entitled *Ramdas*, the 8th volume of the *Poet Saints of Maharashtra*.

generous in everything. 9. Both husband and wife were of one mind. Night and day with love they worshipped Shri Rama. 10. He carried on the occupation of *kulkarni* (the town scribe). They always lived at Jamb and used to feed those who came to ask for food, feeling in their hearts a compassion for all creatures. 11. When the birth-festival of Rama arrived he invited *Sadhus* and *Vaishnavas*; erecting a pavilion they celebrated the festival in joy. 12. Lovingly preparing all the materials needed they feasted the twice-born with dainty food. During the nine days they performed *kirtans* at night with joy and the watch-night service. 13. They had in their house antique images of Shri Rama, Sita and Lakshman. Chairs of state were erected for them and they were worshipped with the sixteen materials. 14. In the pavilion musical instruments were played and they celebrated this festival every year enthusiastically. 15. On the tenth night they performed the *lalit* ceremony and all *sadhus* and saints were honoured. Feeling for them intense love, with reverence they bowed to them.

RAMDAS AS MARUTI'S 'AVATAR'

16. But they had no son and therefore the wife was troubled. But one night as they were soundly sleeping the Brahman had a dream. 17. In the dream Shri Raghunath (Rama) said to the Brahman, 'An embodiment of the *avatar* of Maruti will be born to you. 18. Complete *bhakti* and indifference to earthly things will live in him. So you will see a treasure of a son, the *avatar* of the son of Anjani (Maruti).'

BIRTH AND BOYHOOD OF RAMDAS

19. When the Brahman had this dream he at once awoke astonished in his mind and told his wife of the dream. 20. Hearing what her husband had to say she experienced peace of mind and after nine months she gave birth

to the treasure of a son. 21. In their house was every form of wealth and happiness. Then on the top of that they looked upon the face of a son. The Brahman felt supreme happiness and exclaimed, 'The Husband of Janaki (Rama) has come to our help. 22. The Lord of Ayodhya (Rama) being pleased has given us a son.' It was a matter of great joy and the name of Ramdas was given to him after twelve days had passed. 23. Day by day he grew and at five years of age he was invested with the sacred thread. They kept in the house a Brahman who knew the *Vedas*, and Ramdas was kept under his tuition.

MARRIAGE OF RAMDAS

24. The wife now said to her husband, 'We must have our son married.' The priest then went immediately and chose a bride. 25. Then they prepared the materials for the wedding and selected a great number of ornaments, garments and adornments, and taking with them male and female relatives they set off. 26. The father of the bride received the party of the bridegroom and worshipped him. A place was given them to lodge and instruments were played with intense joy. They installed the gods and made offerings to the Brahmans. 27. The deities of the ceremony were installed and Brahmans were feasted, and as the fixed time for the wedding drew near the ceremony of the offering of honey to the bridegroom was performed. 28. The Brahman priests who held the curtain then began to repeat the eight-verse blessing. At last all of them finally began to repeat the words *Savadhan* ('Beware' or 'Be attentive!') 29. Ramdas asked a priest who was near him, 'To whom are you saying *Beware*? Tell me.' 30. He replied, 'It is for *you* to *beware*. From today the bondage of domestic life falls upon you. 31. One's domestic life is full of supreme sadness. There is not the slightest happiness there. Those who have entered this domestic life suffer

hindrances to the utmost. 32. Therefore all the priests are telling you *to beware*.' When Ramdas heard this he trembled violently. 33. With a feeling of indifference to worldly things he immediately ran off into the woods.

RAMDAS RUNS AWAY INTO A FOREST

His mother and father ran out to catch him, but he had no love now for his home. 34. If the diner understands that the cooked food is mixed with poison, he at once puts away his plate and turns away from every formality; 35. likewise disgusted with the happiness of sensual things, Ramdas suddenly ran away. People tried hard to pacify him but he would listen to no one. 36. His mother and father went into the forest in search of him. They thought they might create a love in their son but he would not return. 37. Ramdas said to his father, 'Why do you in vain seek to entangle me in earthly things? Life in earthly things is a heap of suffering. I understand all this now. 38. In order to provide for one's desire one may marry a beautiful wife and in caring for her he may exhaust his body. 39. By serving a wealthy person one may obtain wealth, but suddenly a thief will come and take his life. 40. When a fish understands that there is a hook in the bait he will run away in the water. So it has happened to me. 41. A parrot, seeing with his eyes an instrument made to catch him, flies away into the sky. In that way I understand not to fall into the snare of worldly things. 42. So drop your concern for me and return to your home.' Saying this to them he quickly walked away into the forest. 43. The father, understanding in his heart that this Brahmachari (an unmarried, chaste youth), the *avatar* of Maruti, would never agree to be drowned in the flood of worldly things, returned to his home. 44. He then reminded his wife of the vision which he had had. He exclaimed, 'Blessed is our family, for a son has proceeded from us indifferent to worldly things.' 45. Thus comforted in mind they returned to their home, put aside affection for their son, and in their hearts contemplated Shri Raghunath (Rama).

MARUTI REVEALS HIMSELF TO RAMDAS

46. Ramdas then went and sat alone in the forest. Full of indifference to worldly things he thought thus: 47. 'In this *Kali Yuga*, austerities and bathing in different sacred places are not the means (to salvation). The proper means is to go as a suppliant to Shri Rama and contemplate Him. 48. When Pingala the prostitute took the name of Rama she was immediately taken up to heaven. Dhurjati (Shiva) by repeating God's name was cooled in heart.' 49. With this belief he sat repeating the names of Rama and partook neither of fruit, root or water but started on a very severe course of austerities in his complete devotion. 50. He exclaimed, 'Victory to the Dweller in Ayodhya, Son of Dashrath, the Son of Kausalya, the Husband of Janaki, Slayer of Ravan, Saviour of the world, and generous in His gifts of final deliverance, Shri Rama. 51. I am Thy helpless, lowly one. I am sitting here in the forest in a very pitiful condition. Thou who art the Advocate of *bhaktas*, Purifier of sinners, give me a manifestation of Thyself.' 52. Thus while he was pleading for compassion, Maruti immediately revealed himself. He appeared in a terrible form, but Ramdas was not afraid. 53. It was just like a blazing fire endeavouring to burn out another fire. But he had no fear whatever because the two were one. 54. If the sun (the day-maker) goes to the house of the sun (the possessor of brilliant rays) he does not feel the heat, so although Maruti met him with a very terrible form, Ramdas was not at all disturbed. 55. The full moon brings high tide to the ocean; it might attempt to hide

its waves but they will not sink in the water because they and the water are one. 56. If space full of anger suddenly wished to swallow the sky, would it be able to swallow it ? This would be a vain attempt, like that of frightening Ramdas. 57. So the Son of Anjani tried to make Ramdas afraid, but he was without fear because he considered himself as one with him. 58. Seeing the determination of Ramdas, Maruti felt comforted and assuming a very mild form he lovingly manifested Himself to him. 59. Ramdas embraced and worshipped Maruti's feet. He exclaimed, 'Now tell me some means by which I will have a vision of Rama.' 60. As soon as Maruti had assured him that he should not fear he became invisible. Ramdas then went into the town to beg for food on his open palm. 61. Having eaten a small amount of that food he then went into the forest and there began to meditate on God. Because of his feelings of repentance he felt no drowsiness or laziness. 62. There his own mind was his audience and his own mind was the speaker. There is no giver of knowledge or *sadguru* of more importance than the mind. 63. He instructed his own mind and he composed two hundred and five verses. Those who with love sing those verses and read them, indifference to earthly things becomes their slave. 64. Keeping the form of Rama in his mind, he danced in the *kirtan* with love. His throat choked with emotion and tears of joy flowed down from his eyes. 65. He had the firm conviction that bushes, trees, stones, birds, animals, and wild beasts were all his dear friends. 66. At midday he would go into the town and remain there long enough to beg. With that he quieted his hunger and then continued sitting in the forest. 67. Men who were engaged in domestic life would come to him and he would run away from them. He said to himself, 'They will get me entangled in the net of illusion.' 68. He who seeks the supreme spiritual riches is indifferent to earthly things, knowing and courageous; if such an one associates himself with worldly-minded men they surely will lead him to disaster. 69. If a bag of musk is placed even for a moment with *Hing* its value will be lessened, for even by a moment's contract it contracts evil qualities. 70. If tobacco and betelnut are placed together the betelnut will take the vile smell; of this there is no doubt. 71. So all those who are ignorant and engaged in worldly things are entirely surrounded by illusions. If good people indifferent to earthly things associate with them they are hindered in their purposes. 72. Therefore Ramdas, who was of ascetic temperament, ran away the moment he saw men, and as a God-loving man unconscious of his own body was all the time repeating God's name.

RAMDAS GOES TO PANDHARI

73. It now happened on a day in the month of *Ashadh* (July) that Ramdas as a pilgrim was on his way to Pandhari. Maruti said to him, 'Shri Rama will meet with you there.' 74. Seeing this vision he felt supreme happiness. Ramdas then with love and enthusiastic singing proceeded rapidly to Pandhari. 75. There he found *Vaishnavas* singing and dancing with joy, sounding the cymbals and the drums. He saw before him the Bhimarathi and a doubt came into his mind. 76. He said to himself, 'He whom I contemplate is not here at all.' Still despite this doubt, he continued in the worship of Shri Rama. 77. He sang with his lips the deeds of Shri Rama and coming to the great door of the temple he suddenly saw before him the Eagle and Hanumant. 78. Bowing to Maruti as he began to gaze onward he saw the *Vaishnava* saints and *sadhus* continually praising God with joy. 79. They danced with music and with banners having on them the designs of eagles, as if *Vaikunth* (heaven) had descended to the earth. Ramdas felt joy with love as he saw

all this. 80. He then bowed to the *Haridas* and proceeded to obtain a vision of God. Suddenly from a distance he saw the Life of the world standing on a brick. 81. His feet were parallel, His hands were on His waist and he was looking at the point of His nose. Seeing such a form as this, Ramdas would not embrace him. 82. He said to himself, 'I continually perform *manas-puja* (mental worship) in which I see the form of Shri Rama which I do not see here.' Then standing before the god he said, 83. 'What have You done with the bow and the arrow, and why have you placed Your hands upon Your hips? Why have You changed your form? Tell me at once, O Shri Rama. 84. O Lord of the world, have you determined not to speak? You say nothing to us. What fault do You hold against me? Tell me at once. 85. Have You left Sharayu Ganga? For here I see flowing the Bhimarathi river in its stead. Why has this sudden change happened? Tell me, O Raghunath (Rama). 86. Has Ayodhya City been wiped out that the sacred city of Pandhari is founded here? What has become of beautiful Sita? And why have Your four wives been brought here? 87. I do not see here at all the army of innummerable monkeys. Now to whom shall I bow? Tell me at once, O Shri Rama. 88. I see Hanumant alone here. Why has he broken away from the army of monkeys? What *bhakta* was he who by deceiving You has stood You up in this place? 89. Now whom shall I embrace, so that my heart may feel comfort? To whom shall I bow prostrate? I do not know.' 90. His throat choked with emotion, tears flowed down from his eyes and he said, 'O Dweller in Ayodhya, O Husband of Janaki, meet with me at once. 91. I am Your helpless and lowly one. I see myself here in a piteous condition. Now look towards me with compassion, and give me a vision of Yourself, O Shri Rama.'

VITHOBA APPEARS AS RAMA

92. Seeing Ramdas' determination the Husband of Rukmini was pleased. He exclaimed, 'Blessed is the *bhakti* of Ramdas. His worship is worthy of that name.' 93. The Life of the world then said to Rukmini, 'My *bhakta* the worshipper of Rama has come here to see us. So become Sita.' 94. Speaking thus, the Lord of Pandhari changed His form. Taking the form of Shri Rama He was now ready to embrace Ramdas. 95. He wore His crown and brilliant earrings and assumed His beautiful clear complexion, dark as a cloud. He held his bow and arrow in his hand and stood in an upright posture. 96. Mother Rukmini stood by Him, having at that moment taken the beautiful form of Sita. The *bhakta* seeing this, felt great joy of heart. 97. Ramdas then came near to the god and gave Shri Rama an embrace. As he gazed upon His form he felt comfort. 98. His throat choked whih emotion and tears of joy flowed from his eyes. He embraced His feet and placed his head there with reverence. 99. It had been a long time since he had met Him and so now he felt comfort as the Lord of the world looked with the eye of compassion upon him. 100. He said to Ramdas, 'Because of My love for you I have assumed the form of Rama. Now bring into your contemplation this very form and destroy all thoughts of duality. 101. Collect a band of disciples and continue to perform *kirtans* reverently, whereby the dull-minded and the ignorant will turn to worship me.' 102. The Husband of Janaki having told him this He placed upon his head the hand of assurance' Then placing His hands upon His hips He again changed His form. 103. The Life of the world at that moment took the form of Pandurang. He, the Performer through the power of *maya* (illusion), and Enchanter of the Heart, does not allow His wonderful deeds completely to be under-

stood. 104. Blessed is the loving *bhakti* of Ramdas whereby He has made the Lord of the world subservient to him; and Shripati (Krishna) took the form that he (Ramdas) had desired. 105. Then having embraced the image of Vitthal with reverence he grasped His feet. Ramdas then began to perform a *kirtan* in honour of Hari with love and joy. 106. He had a doubt that these were two different forms such as Rama and Krishna but God removed it and set him to worship with a sense of non-duality.

RAMDAS VISITS JEJURI

107. After the festival of the *Gopalkala* he took leave of the god and started home. As he was going homeward along the road he came to Jejuri. 108. When Ramdas came into the city the Husband of Mhalsa (Khandoba) was pleased at heart and exclaimed, 'Blessed is this *aishnava bhakta* who knows no other deity but Rama. 109. He does not bow to the image of Pandurang, then how can he accept the sight of myself ? Still I will take the form of a man and go to meet him.' 110. So the Husband of Mhalsa became exactly like King Shivaji. He rode upon a horse and on his brow he rubbed the turmeric powder. 111. In this form the Slayer of Mani and Malla came towards him without a moment's delay. Seeing Ramdas at a distance he dismounted from his horse. 112. He exclaimed, 'Blessed is this happy day that I have had a sudden sight of you, my *Swami*.' He then seized the feet of Ramdas and lovingly gave him an embrace. 113. He who was truly the *avatar* of Shiva, He worshipped the feet of Ramdas. Joining His hands together he said to Ramdas, 114. 'Whenever you go to Pandhari, give me the opportunity of seeing you. I have lived here in this fort for many days and have wish to meet you.' 115. The Husband of Mhalsa (Khandoba), having thus spoken to Ramdas, added. 'Those who worship Shri Rama are pleasing to me

as good men. 116. As Ramdas was about to reply to him, he became invisible. Neither the horse nor the king was now there. He exclaimed, 'This is an astonishing and novel thing.' 117. When he looked at the matter from the point of reason he said to himself, 'The Husband of Mhalsa, the real *avatar* of Shiva had really come here, He who continually worships Rama. 118. So let me go and look at His place of abode.' Thus thinking he started forward. 119. This beloved of Shri Rama, the true *avatar* of Maruti, hastened to the fort and looked upon the Husband of Mhalsa. 120. Bringing to his mind the form of Shri Rama he made there a *namaskar* and in the assembly hall performing a *kirtan* he composed and sang there a hymn of praise. 121. The hymn of praise which Ramdas composed started: '*Panchanan* (five faced), *Hayawahan* (riding on a horse).' Then making Him a *namaskar* he started homewards.

SHIVAJI BECOMES DISCIPLE OF RAMDAS

122. As Ramdas returned to Jamb, Shivaji received the news that Martand (Khandoba) had taken his own (Shivaji's) form and had met Ramdas. 123. Having heard this praiseworthy report of Ramdas he came to him as a suppliant with feelings of reverence. Then Ramdas seeing that Shivaji had the authority of being his disciple he gave him instruction.

RAMDAS COMPOSES THE *DASBODH*

124. Ramdas caused other ascetic disciples to worship God as God-loving *bhaktas.* Ramdas, always indifferent to earthly things, was never disturbed in mind. 125. To him honour or dishonour were the same. He sat by himself in the forest. If he thought that he would be entangled by any popular movements he would finally run away from that place. 126. To his sight a king and a pauper and one of humble birth were the same. He was well-intentioned

towards all creatures. This knowledge of the soul had been revealed to him. 127. In select words drawn from his personal experience he composed the book entitled *Dasbodh*. Even if the dull-minded should read it with reverence they would become like those with deep knowledge. 128. The knowledge of Ramdas was extraordinary and he composed a book on philosophy. Those *Vaishnava bhaktas* who listen to it become *Jivanmuktas* (delivered though still living). 129. This noble *Vaishnava* became an *avatar* here upon this earth in order to save the world, a learned man in philosophy, extremely generous and compassionate to the humble. 130. Ramdas in his extraordinary state of mind saw everything with the same value as cowdung or dust. If he had received the wealth of Indra he would in no way have given any value to it. 131. He gave himself up to the listening of the praise of Shri Rama, to the repeating of His name and to bringing *Atmaram* into his contemplation. He regarded equally all creatures.

132. In the next chapter there is a most delightful story of incomparable interest of the Vishnu-*bhakta* Tukaram. It will show how the Good Being was pleased with him (Tukaram). 133. It is the Husband of Rukmini who is causing the interest of this story to be created. So Mahipati beseeches his hearers to give close attention.

134. *Swasti* (Peace) ! This book is the *Shri Bhaktavijaya*. In listening to it the Lord of the World will be pleased. Listen then, you God-loving, pious *bhaktas*. This is the forty seventh deeply delightful chapter; it is an offering to Shri Krishna.

CHAPTER XLVIII

TUKARAM

Obeisance to Shri Ganesh. Obeisance to the Lord of Pandhari

GOD'S MOTHER-LOVE

1. Victory, Victory to Thee, O Ocean of mercy, the Cloud of joy, Merciful to Thy *bhaktas*, lotus-eyed One, the Father of Brahmadev, the Destroyer of the demons, the Life of the world, and the Lord of the world. 2. Victory, victory to Thee, the Pervader of the universe, the Husband of Kamala, the Life of the good, and the Image of joy; O thou, the Lord of the universe with Form and without Form, Whose ways are unimaginable to the *Vedas* and *Shastras*. 3. Victory, victory to Thee, Who hast hands without number, and Who art without limit. Thou seest with Thy universal eye and walkest with the universal feet, so the *Vedas* have described Thee. 4. Victory, victory to Thee, pure Intelligence, delighting in the contemplation of one's own soul, O Mine of virtues, the Best of the best, resplendent with one's own joy, O *Purushottam* (Vishnu); Thy glory is incomparable. 5. Thinking of Thee, the *Vedas* were defeated, and said, ' Not so, not so.' The *Puranas* have been wearied and the *Shastras* have been put to shame. 6. Thou art not obtainable by austerities, and by visiting the sacred places. Thou dost rush to listen to the praise-services of Thy *bhaktas*. 7. The ascetics practise all postures of *yoga*, including the *vajrasan* (bed of spikes). But O *Chakrapani* (Krishna), Thou dost ignore them and dost go in search of the pious. 8. Thou art the crest-jewel of all the gods, Thou art revered by Sanak and others and art higher than they, and Thou in person dost labour at the houses of the pious. 9. In working for Thy *bhaktas* Thou art not ashamed. Thou dost not care

for honour or dishonour, O Lord of Pandhari. 10. Such is the devotion of Thy *bhaktas* that they never put Thee to trouble. Thou dost make them to experience the miseries of the earthly life, and then dost grant them the highest indifference to worldly things. 11. Through the force of that indifference to worldly things they always sing Thy praises with love and abandon the uneasiness of their hearts. 12. Thou dost enter the hearts of the impious and dost make them persecute Thy *bhaktas*; then in person Thou dost rush to their help and dost keep their honour intact. 13. By doing something extraordinary Thou dost increase their reputation in the three worlds. In this way, O *Chakrapani* (Krishna), O Govinda, Thou art the debtor of Thy *bhaktas*. 14. Thou dost make someone as Thy instrument to describe their lives as men. As for me I am a plain dullard. Thou, O lotus-eyed One, art the enlightener. 15. O Lord of the helpless and the Husband of Rukmini, I bow to Thee again and again. Even in speaking in this way, my talent becomes wearied. 16. Without Thy favour, even an obeisance to Thee is not easy. Whatever will take place will not be without Thy power. 17. My mind is fickle and undergoes changes every moment. Good and bad thoughts will arise in my mind. O Shripati, Thou dost witness them. Need I speak of them with my own lips? 18. But O Husband of Rukmini, if I do not express them, Thou will not have mercy on me. For if the child does not cry the mother keeps it at a distance. 19. In the same manner, O Chakrapani, Thy *bhaktas* plead with Thee in words of compassion. Then Thou lookest on them with a merciful eye, and grantest them the boon of singing Thy praises full of love. 20. Such is the rule of Thy house. Ancient and fortunate saints have described it as such. Then, O Shripati (God), cause me to relate the astonishing fame of Thy *bhaktas*.

21. In the preceding chapter the wonderful story of Ramdas is related as to how the Lord of Pandhari, seeing his firm resolve, personally became the Lord Rama.

TUKARAM'S DISTRESSES

22. Now may the loving people with reverence listen to the following interesting narrative. At a distance of twelve from Alakapuri (Alandi), there is on the earth the sacred town of Dehu. 23. The god's *bhakta* of that place was Tukaram, whose surname was Ambale, and who carried on the business of a grocer, but in this business with the people he never told a lie. 24. He had two wives and a large fortune in his house. But he was always without pride for his body. All alone he was always thinking of God. 25. After the death of his parents his family life was full of misery. There was a dreadful famine in the land and whatever fortune he had was all spent. 26. Whatever grain and money he had before, nothing remained; just as the tidal flow of the ocean is dissolved in the ocean itself, 27. or as the clouds in the rainy season are dispersed in the cold season, or at the rise of the sun the stars disappear; 28. or just when old age comes, youth passes away or as grass is scorched at the advent of summer; 29. in the same way, when there was famine in the land, all the grain and money had gone; adults and children struggled for food, but they could not get it. 30. The elder wife had two sons, and the younger one had no issue. All of them boiled vegetables, and ate them; but they could not obtain a kernel of grain. 31. But what is destined cannot be avoided. The elder wife starved to death for lack of food. On this account shame overcame (Tukaram), and he could not have love for the family life. 32. Along with his fortune his honour passed away also. The relatives of Tukaram laughed at him as they saw him and then he was overcome with shame. 33. Those who former

ly respected him now reviled him. He was always in calamity for want of food and raiment, and his business was not at all in a good condition. 34. When men lose a fortune, no one cares for them; just as when the leaves of a tree are withered, a sensualist will not find it interesting; 35. or as when a king dies on the battlefield, those who love their bodies desert the field; in the same manner when poverty overtakes a person the evil-minded disrespect him. 36. When that hard time came, Tuka became full of shame. He could not see any friend in his family life Then a thought arose in his mind. 37. If he intended to improve his business he could see nothing but loss. At such a calamitous time when he found himself in trouble, repentance arose in his mind. 38. He thought, 'This earthly life is unreal. It is the outcome of *maya* (illusion). The human body is perishable, I have spent my life for nothing, and I have forgotten the Lord of Pandhari. 39. If one sleeps on a cot full of bugs, how can he happily sleep there ? If food is cooked with poison, it cannot be called good. 40. So those who say that there is happiness in the earthly life are the biggest fools. It is like the feeling of joy at the birth of a son to a barren woman.'

TUKARAM'S ASCETICISM

41. As he began to think in this way, *vairagya* (the ascetic spirit) came to Tuka. Then he considered joy and sorrow alike, and continually sang the praises of God. 42. There was an old temple of Pandurang in a dilapidated condition. He plastered it with mud himself, and then coated it clean with cowdung. 43. Among all the religious means of salvation, *Ekadashi* (the 11th day in each fortnight) is the highest of all rules. He began to observe it with entire devotion. 44. He wanted to perform a *kirtan* himself but he had not previously studied it, therefore if a saint sang he stood behind him as his companion. 45. He learnt

by heart the sayings of great old saints. He could see no better way, and so had a firm belief in them. 46. As he looked at people, compassion arose in his mind. He put himself to trouble to oblige them. If they were hungry, he quenched their hunger. 47. You might ask how he did it. Then I will tell you that in short. Listen to it. If a traveller wanted a lodging he would take him into the temple. 48. If anyone was hungry he gave him food. If he had none he would procure it with trouble. 49. If anyone was thirsty in a forest he gave him water. If anyone had travelled a long way he massaged him to his satisfaction. 50. If he saw a load on anyone's head, he took it on his own shoulders and gave the man some rest. 51. If he saw anyone sick on a journey and without any of his relatives by him, he very kindly gave him medicine and digestive food. 52. When cows and bullocks became feeble their masters left them with cruelty: he used to stroke them with his hands and gave them fodder and water. 53. If any *bhaktas* of Vishnu came to him he prostrated himself before them, reverently washed their feet, and drank the sacred water. 54. On account of this bodily penance, he gained poetic inspiration. He expressed in Marathi whatever is laid down in the *Vedas* and *Shastras*.

NAMDEV'S VOW TO WRITE POETRY

55. By way of illustration for the context, let us go back to a most interesting story. May the listeners listen quietly to it. 56. Once upon a time the *Vaishnava bhakta* Nama was saying to Pandurang, 'I will sing Thy praise in Marathi in a hundred million verses.' 57. At this the Husband of Rukmini said, 'In vain have you made this vow, O Nama. In this *Kali Yuga* one has only a hundred years of life, and it is full of accidents. 58. But you have made a vow and expressed it in words, but it will not be fulfilled.' Then Nama placed his head on the

feet of the Husband of Rukmini and thus implored Him: 59. 'My vow depends on thy help, O God. Therefore do Thou fulfil it in person. What is there that Thou art not able to do? Of what value am I?' 60. Hearing this entreaty of Nama, the Holder of the bow (God) was pleased. He placed His assuring hand on his head and ordered Sarasvati (the goddess of learning), 61. 'You sit on the tip of his tongue, and enable him to express poetically the secrets of the *Vedas* in the Marathi language.' 62. Then the daughter of Brahmadev (Sarasvati) humbly said, 'Namdev will speak out of inspiration; but O Chakrapani, employ someone to write quickly his utterances. 63. He must write the words as soon as they come from his mouth, but if asked to repeat the same words they will not come.' 64. On this He who is dark as a Cloud replied, 'I myself will write it always. Just now I do not see any quick writer.' 65. Then Chakrapani set aside all his games and enjoyments and taking an inkpot and pen in hand, began to write continuously the verses of Namdev. 66. I very much wonder over the fact that He whom the Vedas and *Shastras* praise, and Whom the poets like Vyas and Valmiki describe, became the writer of Nama's poetry. 67. The Life of the world gave up His home in *Vaikunth* and abandoned His reclining on the serpent Shesha in the ocean of milk, and waited upon Namdev with pen and inkstand in his hands. 68. Chakrapani was all attention to what came out from his lips. He shook off sleep and sloth, and was attentive day and night. 69. In this way Shripati sat in the company of Nama for several days. Listen to the vast amount of the poetry. 70. The verses amounted to ninety-four millions and forty-hundred thousand, and in the end there was the *lalit* containing nine hundred thousand. Seeing such a large amount the Lord of the world was wonder-struck. 71. He said, 'Blessed is Nama's love. He has sung My glory in a wonderful way, the limit of which is not even understood by the *Vedas*. He has made Me *Purushottam* (Vishnu), his own. 72. Saying this, the Lord of the world patted Nama on the back, and then said, ' Still some of My love remains to be described. 73. Now think of My form at heart and look at Me with love and with eyes wide open. ' As Chakrapani thus spoke, Nama fell at His feet. 74. ' You have made a vow to compose a hundred million verses, and to fulfil it, I, the Life of the world, will do the remaining verses Myself and thus carry it to completion. '

TUKARAM'S POETIC WORK A DIVINE COMMAND

75. Then God held Nama by the hand, and went to Tuka in a dream and said, 'Do not say anything senseless. By My order, now compose verses. 76. The limit of them is a hundred million. You carry it to completion.' Having said this the Lord of the world stroked his back. 77. As he woke up he could see neither the Husband of Rukmini nor Nama. It was a great wonder to him. 78. With bowed head he accepted the dream as an order and started with the art of poetry, contrary to which he did not utter anything meaninglessly. 79. In his *kirtan* he uttered words full of pathos and love. The pious *bhaktas* with love and devotion listened to it. 80. There were amongst the listeners some who were scrupulous and critical. They said, ' These poems are quite new and we do not consider them as an authority at all. We will not listen to them. 81. Why do you give up the words of the ancient saints, and try to show your greatness ? When we obtain dainty foods without trouble, why should we put ourselves to the trouble of cooking and burn our hands ?' 82. Now listeners are likely to ask, ' If the Husband of Rukmini ordered it, why should people call in question the poetry ?' But it is an old story that behind devoted people there are always many reviiers. 83. When in the *Treta* age Valmiki composed his *Ramayana* containing

his prophecies, even at that time there were impious men who did not consider it as an authority. 84. Then when the Husband of Janaki (Rama) became an *avatar* and acted exactly according to prophecy, and when the people saw it with their own eyes, they believed it. 85. In the *Dwapar*-age the poet Vyas gave out his prophecy but the Kauravas had no faith in it. But when it came true in its natural course, Dhritarashtra bowed to Sanjaya. 86. In this way for a long time past, men have persecuted the pious ones. This was why the low-minded reviled the verses of Tukaram; 87. just as at the sunlight the owl censures it, or like a thief does not like the coming of the moon in the east. 88. Hearing the reputation of a donor, the miserly despise him for nothing. At the sight of divine herbs shining at night diseases feel uneasy in mind. 89. The oration of a learned person is supposed as nonsensical prattle by a cowherd. Where there is the singing of a *gandharva*, the donkey is sure to bray. 90. Will the *pungal*-creeper like the odour of the *bakul* flower? Will the Muhammadans worship a cow, even if it is of a dark colour? 91. The Brahmans worship images but the Muhammadans smash them. In the same manner the pious listened to the praise services of Tuka while the revilers derided them. 92. But he considered both alike and continued his worship of Hari (God). If a *Haridas* performed a *kirtan*, he used to listen to it with reverence. 93. Day by day his love for God grew and along with it grew his devotion also. As he sang the praises of Hari (God) all alone at night, sleep did not overpower him at all. 94. In the months of *Ashadh* (July) and *Kartik* (November) he used to go as a pilgrim to Pandhari. Then on every fortnightly eleventh day he went to visit the god devotedly.

SHIVAJI VISITS TUKARAM

95. His freedom from desires was extraordinary.

One day King Shivaji hearing the reputation of Tukoba came to visit him. 96. In those days the Muhammadans were in power. King Shivaji was at Sinhagad. Without the knowledge of anyone he entered Poona. 97. There at a grocer's house the Vaishnava Tuka was performing a *kirtan*. As the king knew of it he was greatly pleased. 98. Then at night without anybody's knowledge he stealthily came into the town. He was very much afraid of the Muhammadans, for they might apprehend him and take him away. 99. The king came secretly with a view to visit Tukoba and go back to the fort. 100. He put some gold and silver coins in a shining plate of silver and placing it before Tuka, prostrated himself before him. 101. As the *bhakta* of Vishnu saw the money of the king he began to tremble all over. O pious good people, listen to what he said to Shivaji then: 102. 'We do not need a store of money. We need Vitthal only. Aside from Him we have no liking for anyone in the world. 103. As one should honour a jeweller with pebbles, in the same way is the offer of gold to us. 104. We had heard of your great reputation and today we have witnessed your generosity. But what we *Vaishnavas* do not like, you have with love laid before us. 105. The money which you have brought to offer us, is to us like beef.' At these determined words the king felt abashed. 106. Tukaram further addressed the king and said, 'If you wish to do something which would satisfy us, then we will tell you a secret. 107. Think only of Vitthal's name and thereby only we shall be happy. Any other fortune to us is like earth, O king. 108. Put a rosary of *tulsi* beads around your neck, and observe the *ekadashi* (every 11th day). We shall be satisfied by that only and not by heaps of money. 109. With love and joy at heart, call yourself the slave of Vithoba. This is our only desire; fulfil it to our satisfaction.' 110. Seeing such freedom from desires, the king wondered in his mind and then with sole devotion he prostrated himself before Tukaram over and over again.

SHIVAJI PROTECTED BY KRISHNA

111. That was the day of Hari [*Ekadashi*] and the king was listening to the *kirtan* with love. In the meantime two thousand Pathans were sent by the Muhammadan General (to apprehend Shivaji). 112. The spies of the Muhammadan General told him of the king's arrival into Poona to visit Tuka at night. 113. Then that bad man sent (two thousand) horsemen to arrest him at once. They equipped themselves with various weapons and came running at midnight. 114. They beseiged the house in which the *kirtan* was being performed and did not let out anyone from the house. 115. They had orders that they should discover Shivaji and arrest him and bring him out. The king had this intelligence that the army of the enemy had beseiged the house. 116. Some advised the king to get up and run away at once. His mind was full of fear and in great perplexity. 117. Seeing the sorrowful commotion of the listeners, Tuka understood the whole thing and he asked them, 'What are you whispering to yourselves? Tell me at once.' 118. On hearing the question of Tukaram, the people who knew replied to him in a low voice, 'A fearful army of the enemy has arrived to arrest the king. 119. Therefore the king must be removed from this place at once. If you permit us to do it, then only will his life be saved.' 120. Thereupon Tuka replied, 'None should go away from the *kirtan*. Such is the rule of religion. Don't you know this? 121. At this the king sat there determinedly and said to himself, 'Aside from the Husband of Rukmini, there is no one in the three worlds who can save or destroy. 122. To-day is the *Ekadashi* festival, an auspicious day. Near me are the *Vaishnava* saints. If I die in the *kirtan*

my fortune will be great.' 123. Outside the army was thinking of apprehending the king without delay. Many spies went into the house but none of them recognized (Shivaji) the king. 124. The spies went to the General and told him that there were many men sitting in the *kirtan* but they did not know which of them was King Shivaji. 125. On hearing his soldiers' message the evil-minded person became hot with anger and said, 'Kill as many men as there are in the *kirtan*. 126. Amongst them the king will naturally be included.' Such was his firm resolve, but Tuka who could understand the hearts of others knew this. 127. Then he brought into his mind the Lord of Pandhari and pleaded with Him in a plaintive manner, 'Victory, Victory to Thee; the Lord of the help-less, the merciful One. Now rush at once to my help. 128. These people here have come to listen to Thy praise-service. They are all fallen into a sudden calamity. Who else aside from Thee will destroy it? 129. Disturbances run away from the place where Thy praise-service is being performed, so the saints have said, but it is about to be falsified. 130. O Life of the world, if Thou art testing my mind, then let me tell Thee that I am not afraid of my death. But the saints and other good people will be full of sorrow and I cannot bear that sight. 131. This (fear) is hereditary with us. Dost Thou not know it, O Husband of Rukmini? An interruption to my service is nothing short of death to me.' 132. Hearing this compassionate pleading, the Life of the world at once arrived there and embraced Tuka and said, 'Continue your praise-service. 133. I will disperse the mighty disturbance of the enemy's army myself. With a quiet heart you continue with love your *kirtan*.'

KRISHNA DISGUISED AS SHIVAJI

134. Saying this, the One beautiful as a cloud, Himself

took the form of King Shivaji, and riding a horse at once came out of the house. 135. The men who sat to listen to the *kirtan* did not know of this event. O pious ones, the *bhaktas* of God, listen to the extraordinarily wonderful story. 136. The Life of the world suddenly appeared near the house in which the *kirtan* was being performed and Himself shouted loudly, ' O the king is running away!' 137. Two thousand Pathan soldiers had besieged the house. They looked before and behind them, and plainly saw the king. 138. For a moment he came within their ken and at once hurried on. The Lord of the world with the army at His back worked a great wonder. 139. The citizens left their beds pell-mell, stood on the terraces of their houses, and talked between themselves: 140. 'The king is running ahead and the Muhammadan soldiers are pursuing him. Now his life cannot be safe. We can clearly see future disaster.' 141. To the spies who were on the look-out in the enemy's army the Life of the world appeared as King Shivaji. 142. Some shouted, ' Here the king is running away; catch him.' The soldiers were in a state of consternation and began to run pell-mell. 143. He was seen near one man but as he attempted to catch hold of him he could see no one. Some thought of killing him instead of running after him. 144. Some cried, ' What are you looking here and there for ? Surround him.' Others cried 'Cowards that you are, you cannot take hold of a single brave man. 145. We are two thousand brave soldiers, and that he should escape from amongst us is shameful to us Why do you carry weapons in your hands ? Why not cut your own throats with them ? ' 146. Some exclaimed, ' We shall catch the king at our leisure when it is day. We cannot see now, then why struggle for nothing ?' 147. *Sharangadhar* (God) remained steady for a while in one place, and worked a wonder. He showed Himself at once and shouted ' He is found. Catch him.' 148. The soldiers went in pursuit of him, but the Lord of the world could not be caught by them. Sometimes He appeared near them but as they tried to catch Him He escaped far away. 149. It was a bright fortnight and so there was moonlight. With the help of that light the Muhammadans began to run. In the course of three hours they were taken forty miles far away into a dreadful jungle. 150. The Life of the world took the army into a mountainous, very frightful and barren jungle full of prickly shrubs and then returned. 151. All the soldiers looked about them but they could nowhere see King Shivaji. They said, 'We were labouring under a wrong idea, and rushed about at night for nothing.' 152. Some said, 'Our eyes were wandering wildly and glaringly and thereby we were put to trouble for nothing.' Others said, 'We clearly saw him near us.' 153. As they began to return, the moon had set. In the darkness of the night they could see nothing and they could not find their way. 154. They rode one after the other and stumbled. They began to say to one another, 'The prospect is not good.' 155. The brambles rubbed against their persons and their clothes were torn. Some loudly lamented saying their lives were in peril. 156. It was intensely cold and the army was therefore in a perilous condition. They struggled in the barren jungle and their horses ran away. 157. The Life of the world performed a wonder and did not take the life of anyone. The Muhammadans wandered here and there in a naked state and were all overtaken by a great disaster. 158. Their weapons fell from their hands and their horses had already run away in the forest. Their clothes were snatched from them by the thorny bushes and all were in a beggarly condition. 159. In this way, having punished the evil-minded, Chakrapani (Krishna) returned, went to the *kirtan* of Tuka and danced full of love. 160. None of the listeners knew what had happened. The Lord of Pandhari had warded off disaster and had performed a great *maya* (illusion). 161. The Life of the world came near Tuka and whispered in his ear all the news, and told him to continue his *kirtan* with love and without any fear in his mind. 162. Then all the audience shouted 'Victory! victory!' and clapped their hands and loudly sang the names of God. The *Vaishnavas* danced in the *kirtan*, and *Vanmali* (Vishnu) was pleased. 163. All the people told the king of the coming of the enemy's army and how it ran away without being opposed. 164. The king wondered and said that the Husband of Rukmini was pleased with him, for an irresistible disaster had come on all. 165. He felt satisfied in this way and continued listening to the *kirtan*. The audience were awake for four watches (12 hours) and it was dawn. 166. Auspicious lamps were waved over the Husband of Rukmini, and the people shouted Hari's names and fell prostrate on the ground full of love. 167. As the king was returning home the men and women in the town accosted him saying, 'Last night we saw one like you running through the town quickly. 168. As the Muhammadans saw him they ran after him ; but how you escaped the disaster we very much wonder.' 169. The king wondered at heart and said, 'God's deeds are unfathomable. The merciful Chakrapani (Krishna) has saved me from calamity.'

SHIVAJI OFFERS GRAIN TO TUKARAM

170. One day King Shivaji was thinking to himself, 'If I offer a fortune to Tukoba he does not accept it. 171. Therefore I shall present myself as a humble person and take grain to his house. Otherwise he will not accept my offer of royal food.' 172. With this plan he wore torn clothes, and loading two maunds of grain on a bullock, started to go. 173. As the night had advanced two *ghatikas* (48 minutes) he arrived at Tukoba's house. Tukoba was sitting near the *tulsi* altar with a rosary in

his hand. 174. Just then the king quickly arrived and threw down the sack of grain at the door and said, 'Swami, I have acquired this grain by labour. 175. With devotion I have brought a little to your feet. I am very humble and lowly. Please store this up in your house.' 176. Then the king bowed to him and quickly went away. Tuka knew in his heart the plan the king had adopted. 177. He thought, 'If I tell the king that I have made him out, his love will receive a blow.' Therefore he silently went on repeating the names of God.

TUKARAM'S ADVICE TO HIS WIFE

178. Then he told his wife, 'If we keep the whole of the grain which the king has brought, our good deeds will suffer. 179. Therefore keep only one day's provisons for ourselves and distribute the rest among the Brahmans.' 180. Hearing this, his wife flew into a rage and began to beat her forehead with her hands and said, 'I am unfortunate. 181. A sack of grain came to our house without anyone's asking for it. But he won't let the children eat it. If it is distributed to the Brahmans, what am I to do? How shall I conduct the family affairs? 182. To this he replied, 'How can we have a bigger share than what is stored up for us in our fate?'

A DEAD CHILD COMES TO LIFE IN TUKARAM'S *KIRTAN*

183. One day Tukoba was performing a *kirtan* with joy in a temple when a very wonderful event took place. Listen to it, O pious ones. 184. The loud sound coming from the beating of the cymbals, the drums, etc., filled the sky. Men and women sat listening to the *lila* (life) of Hari attentively and with respect. 185. A pious man who was a coppersmith came there to listen to the *kirtan*; his son was dangerously sick and he was very uneasy. 186. His wife said to him, 'Don't go to the *kirtan* tonight.' But he did not listen to her and went. 187. After he had

gone the child died and the mother wept bitterly. Then she lifted up the dead body of the child on her shoulders and going to the place where Tukoba was performing a *kirtan* she left it there. 188. Then she addressed Tukaram, 'You have been persecuting us. You have made my husband crazy and made him discard affection and desire. 189. Because he came to listen to your *kirtan* my child died. In our house for a long time past the name of Hari (God) has not been profitable.' 190. Saying this, she rudely placed the child on the floor during the *kirtan*. Thereby the minds of the audience were upset but all sat quiet; 191. just as if a beggar should begin to eat dainty food and some earth should fall upon it, so in the same way when the dead body was brought there the pleasure of the service was dissipated. 192. The people said, 'Hear, O wife of the coppersmith, you have brought the dead body here; but Tukaram does not possess an elixir which would bring the dead to life. Then how is it possible that he can make your child live?' 193. While all the people thus spoke, Tuka replied to them, 'Even divine nectar is nothing before the name of God. It is not obtainable even to Indra and others. 194. If your hearts waver in believing this statement, you will at this very moment experience the truth of it.' Having said this, the *Vaishnava bhakta* worked a miracle. 195. He asked his audience to repeat 'Vitthal, Vitthal' with their lips and told them that it was the real elixir that would bring the dead to life and that they should entertain no doubt about it. 196. As he thus spoke, loud acclamations of the name of Vitthal were heard. It appeared as if the sound of *Brahma* came there and reverberated through the sky. 197. Even the canopy, the pillows and the carpets shouted the name of Vitthal and the pebbles and stones on the earth began to utter the name of Hari. 198. From the musical instruments such as cymbals and banners there emanated the sound of the name of Vitthal. Gods came in the sky and looked on the scene with eyes full of delight. 199. The knowing and the ignorant, the great and the small, all lovingly cried 'Vitthal.' And all the simple-minded people began to rock themselves with love to and fro. 200. As the people looked at one another they saw in each one the image of Vitthal. They did not notice the presence of different castes. Such was the wonderful state the audience was enjoying. 201. Just then a wonderful event took place there. The dead body sat up alive and just then the people cried, 'Beware.' All of them were wonder-struck. 202. The child's mother was near; feeling satisfied she said, 'I reviled Tuka through ignorance.' 203. All the people saw the wonder and it filled their hearts with faith. They exclaimed, 'There is no mightier nectar than the name of Hari.' 204. In the next chapter the Husband of Rukmini will make me relate a beautiful story. He has placed His assuring hand on the head of Mahipati and in His mercy has housed Himself in Mahipati's heart.

205. *Swasti* (peace) ! This book is the *Shri Bhaktavijaya*, listening to which the Lord of the world will be pleased. Therefore listen, O pious ones, to the deeply delightful forty-eighth chapter; it is an offering to Shri Krishna.

CHAPTER XLIX
TUKARAM
(Continued)

Obeisance to Shri Ganesh. Obeisance to the Husband of Shri Lakshmi.

GOD PLEASED WITH ASCETICS

1. Victory to Thee, the Ocean of mercy, the Lord of the world. When Thy worshippers fall into disaster Thou of Thy own accord dost act for them in Thy visible *sagun* form. 2. Thou dost look beautiful all over as a cloud looks. Around Thy waist is the yellow, silk divine garment. On Thy chest is the yellow medal from which shine rays of jems studded on it. 3. Thy yellow crown is of shining gold at whose sight the moon is abashed. In Thy ears shine the yellow crocodile earrings of beautiful form. 4. Around Thy neck is the yellow *mohanmal* (necklace) in the midst of which is the lustrous Kaustubh jewel, at the sight of which Thy loving *bhaktas* have become dazed. 5. On Thy forehead is the yellow saffron spot. On Thy body is the yellow daub of sandalwood paste. Around Thy waist are tiny yellow bells which rivet the eyes. 6. Thy upper garment is yellow. On Thy wrist is the hero's bracelet of yellow colour. Thou art very beautiful with Thy yellow ornaments. 7. On Thy ankles and feet yellow *vaki*, *todar*, *wale*, and *nepur* look very beautiful. Thy *bhaktas* for ever see the lustre of Thy nails. 8. Thy feet which are not obtainable even to Brahmadev and others, are accessible to Thy servants who forget their family life and sing of Thy virtues. 9. An idea of public honour or dishonour never comes in their minds. They have abandoned the public way of behaviour. They who sing without a sense of shame in Thy praise-

service have attained Thee, O Shripati. 10. Those who have heartily forsaken bad desires and equally regard cowdung or gold, and who cherish a dislike for even heavenly happiness, become Thy dear ones; 11. who have given up affection for their bodies and have kicked away the four kinds of salvation; they whose freedom from desires is of this kind they have attained Thee, O Husband of Rukmini. 12. When Thy loving *bhaktas* are in difficulty Thou dost at once assume a *sagun* form. Thou, Merciful to the lowly, dost come to their help without thinking of the favourable or unfavourable time. 13. The *Shastras* and *Puranas* say Thou art in Thy Buddha *avatar* in the *Kali Yuga*; but in opposition to their saying Thou dost become *sagun* at Thy will. 14. Just as a child without heed to time goes to its mother (to be fed), and she out of affection nurses it and is never cruel; 15. in the same way, although it is not time for Thee to assume an *avatar*, Thy loving *bhaktas* call on Thee, and heeding their ardent desire Thou dost at once whisper Thy secrets. 16. My mind takes delight in describing the good qualities of those *Vaishnavas* who are solely devoted to thee and who have made Thee their own. 17. O *Vanamali* (Vishnu), Merciful to the lowly, I have formed an unreasonable longing that Thou wilt sit in my lotus-heart and cause me to describe new and delightful stories. 18. As a father teaches his child the alphabet by holding his hand and by placing pebbles on the ground; in the same way, O Thou, the Husband of Rukmini, Thou dost cause my hand to write this book. 19. Thou didst lift the Govardhan mountain and didst give the glory to the cowherds. In the same way, in order to satisfy my desire Thou dost inspire me to compose this book. 20. I am dull of intellect, O Lord of Pandhari; I am not even able to deliver a message. That through the mouth of such as I am Thou dost describe the stories of Thy *bhaktas* is indeed wonderful. 21. I have not witnessed with my eyes when and what happened. But if I am in difficulty, Thou comest to help my remembrance. 22. O Holder of the *Sharang* bow (Krishna), Thou art the Enlightener of intellect. I have put all my burden on Thee. Thou dost defeat the pride of self, enabling me to compose the book.

TUKARAM'S FOREST LIFE

23. In the end of the preceding chapter the listeners have heard the story as to how a dead body was brought to life by the names of Vitthal being lovingly repeated. 24. At the sight of that miracle by Tukaram, people began to respect him more and more. Then Tukoba went into the forest and sat contemplating Hari (God) with a complete abandonment of devotion. 25. He considered any hypocritical public honour as dog's dung. He discarded all ideas about honour and sat singing the praises of Hari (God) with concentrated devotion. 26. He went and sat in a secluded place in an unconscious bodily state for which the crooked minded reviled him and called him a devil. 27. He ran away from any place where he heard his praise, and went to sit where he was being censured and listened to it. 28. If anyone offered him dainty food with respect he did not like it, for he had thoughtfully curbed his tongue. 29. But if any poor and humble person offered a simple vegetable food, he ate with love just as much as would sustain his body. 30. He went and sat in the forest of Ballal in seclusion during the day and at night he would come into the town and in love perform *kirtans.* 31. Although he was in his town for two months he did not go home and his wife went from house to house publicly complaining about him.

TUKARAM RETURNS HOME

32. She said, 'Hear, O my friends, my fate is adverse. My husband does not care for me but goes and sits in the forest. 33. He has given up his business and dances in

the *kirtan* with love. He constantly thinks of Purushottam (Vishnu) and as a rule sings His praises. 34. He has been in the town for the last two months but all that time he has never come home. O friends, I am worn out by anxiety day and night. 35. If you ever see him, teach him the morals of religion. He has abandoned his wife, and therefore his life has become disreputable among the people.' 36. She repeatedly complained about him to her neighbours and one day she took a pot and went to fetch water. 37. She filled the pot with water and was going back home when she met Tukoba on his way to the temple after bathing. 38. His wife at once went to him and caught him by the end of his *dhotar*. Listen to what she said to him without any sense of respect: 39. 'You are without any sense of shame and scruple and you dance day and night in the praise services of God. You never come home and on that account I feel so uneasy. 40. On account of public shame I weep bitterly at home. Tell me at once what you mean to do with us.' 41. On this he replied to his wife, 'Your parents married you without any thought of my circumstances; then why should I provide you with food and clothing?' 42. Then his wife said to Tuka, 'Whose circumstances, then, did they consider?' He said, 'Of my parents, and they have given you into *their* care.' 43. On this the wife replied, 'Your parents are dead. Where can I go, to find them? You yourself have cremated them in the funeral ground.' 44. On this the *bhakta* of God said, 'Pandurang is my father, and the Mother of the universe, Rukmini, is my mother. Both of them are for ever imperishable and immovable. 45. They do not grow with the growth of creation and are not destroyed with the destruction of the world. 46. If the sky reflects in a pot of water, and the pot is broken, it cannot be said that the sky is broken. 47. In the same way are my parents. Contemplate their feet in your heart

They will provide you with food and clothes. Have no doubt about it.' 48. The wife then said, 'O lord of my life, now please come home. The revilers will be put to shame thereby. And by your presence our family life will look well. 49. I will worship the feet of Shri Hari (God). Even they will provide food and clothes for me. You sit quietly at home and continue your worship of Shri Hari.' 50. The husband then said, 'If you listen to my advice, and if you give me your word for it, then I will now come home at once.' 51. The wife gave her promise and brought home the *Vaishnava* Tuka. The people wondered very much and began to talk between themselves: 52. 'He made an exhibition of his *vairagya* (asceticism) for a few days, and let his reputation spread, but again he has yielded himself to *maya* (illusion) and has returned to his family affairs.' 53. Some said, 'It is as it ought to be; for spiritual riches are to be truly gained in family life. That Tuka has accepted his wife is a matter of satisfaction to us. 54. Many go and sit in the caves of mountains, but which of them has attained *Vaikunth* (Vishnu's heaven).' In this way the people gossiped without any consideration. 55. Some derided Tuka while some praised him. Some called him the best while others called him the worst. But he disregarded both praise and blame and he was ever full of joy.

TUKA'S ADVICE TO HIS WIFE

56. That day was the day of Hari (*ekadashi*). Tukoba was sitting near the *tulsi* altar. He called his wife near to him and said, 'Listen to the story of Hari (God)' 57. Saying this, he seated her in front of him and took cymbals and *vina* in his hands, and gave her a piece of advice in eleven *abhangs* which the good have already heard. 58. I will bring to my mind the purport of it, and describe it in my uncouth language. But it is as if showing the sun with

the help of a light. 59. Where there is the need of nectar, some physicians give ordinary herds; and in the same way, dull as I am, I am endeavouring to explain the meaning of Tuka's *abhangs.* 60. When dirty rivulets meet with the waters of the Ganges they can no more be described as unsacred. The rust of iron remains no more as soon as it has come into contact with the *paris* (touchstone). 61. For after all, the incomparable expression of saints has a meaning which is very profound; and through their favour I will try and explain a little. Listen to it, O ye good people, with love. 62. Then he (Tuka) seated his wife by his side, and said, ' Consider this human body as a field. If there we remember Hari (God) then by our good fortune the crop will be tremendous. 63. Those who have not ensured the spiritual riches are entirely lost. They have laboured in their family life for nothing, and have merely worn out their bones. 64. Eighty per cent of this we have to pay as revenue to the government, otherwise the officer *Kaloji* (death) will greatly terrify us. 65. Through his fear ten per cent have been paid off, but he does not see the remaining seventy per cent. 66. You are likely to ask what the ten per cent means. If you have a doubt about it, know that they are the ten organs which have been at present worn out. 67. To my ears any sweet praise or bad words are alike; and I look without any sense of difference at gold or earth. 68. To my tongue, sugar or the bitter fruit of *vrindavan* are just the same; and I smell as equal the stinking *pungal* creeper or the fragrant flower of *bakul.* 69. There in the heart is the fickle mind, but it has been steadied at the feet of Vitthal. In the same way are the organs of action which have lost the power of action. 70. In this way the ten have been shaken off as they have become incapable of understanding their own functions. Now I shall give you an account of the remaining seventy which I have.

71. Pandurang (God) is the officer of this place. He sits in the heart's public square and says, "Pay off the remaining revenue. 72. Sell off your pots and your cattle, and with their cost pay off the remaining revenue and bear this thought in your mind and become clean." 73. My darling wife, if we do not pay Him His due, where have we a place to hide in ? Without Him there is no other place. Thoughtfully consider this. 74. He is the Lord of the World. He is the Pervader of the Universe. If we run away from Him through fear, there is no one who can give us shelter. 75. When His servants are behind me, where shall I wander for refuge ? Had I but refused to undertake the cultivation right at the beginning He would not have troubled me like this. 76. Therefore let us pay off the remainder and stay here for ever. Whatever He is pleased to give us as our wages we shall eat. 77. There is no limit to those who have been plundered by Him. They have not come back to enjoy the family life. For fear of Him, nobody is willing to undergo births. 78. The *sadguru* has deprived one of his bodily consciousness and he is totally destroyed. People laugh at him for his disregard to honour and dishonour. 79. He takes those who have passed the test to *Vaikunth* (Vishnu's heaven). He was much after me also and then I had to pay for it with my life. 80. I have understood this already, but I ignore the knowledge. I have been found in the hands of Him who has harassed so many with cruelty. 81. Now think well in your mind and be indifferent to worldly things. My life is in peril, then why should you hesitate ? 82. If you have clearly seen this without trouble, then why do you not like it ? Tell me. I have actually to starve, then why cling to any sense of shame ? 83. If I love my own body then I cannot say what will happen to your life. I will adopt a plan which will never separate us. 84. We will live together with all our children. If you will listen to

this advice of mine, there cannot be a talk of separation. 85. Now you might ask what the children will eat. But do not think of that at all. They are destined to get as much food and clothing as is fixed by the Creator. 86. You cut asunder the noose which is around your neck and avoid the eighty-four millions of births and deaths and free yourself from the trouble of living in the womb. I will tell you how to effect it. 87. I will forsake you and run away, then seeing you as my property they will impose it on me. Why, your very hands will come to oppose and attack me. 88. At the sight of the beating of the servants of the god of death I tremble through fear. If you care at all for me, then be generous. 89. What shall I do to my fate? My life and fortune are at stake. But this is not my doing, it is the Lord of Pandhari who likes it. 90. I have been reduced to the state of a beggar but He does not leave me. He has no mercy and I see destruction as sure and certain. 91. We shall drink water out of a dry gourd, and as for food, there are leaves created by God. Therefore with a large heart give away everything. 92. If you form this resolve, then the good people will honour you. Your reputation will spread in the two worlds. Listen how it will be. 93. Think of the cattle as dead through disease. Imagine that the pots have been stolen by thieves. And make your heart so hard as to think that you have no children at all. 94. Overcome all desires and harden your heart. As a simile, I will tell you to make it as hard as adamant and to brace up courage. 95. There is little happiness in the family life. Throw it away. When you experience the supreme joy to satiety, you will have it in a large quantity which even sages like Sanak and others longed for. 96. These mighty disturbances will pass away. The snares of the worldly life will be torn asunder. And eventually we shall enjoy glorious festivals as we walk along the path of *Vaikunth* (Vishnu's heaven). 97. The celestial sages will perform the festivals and we shall both be happy. The servants of Vishnu will seat us in a chariot of light studded with gems. 98. Many saints and *Mahants* and *Kinnars* and *Siddhas* will come forward to receive us. They will seat us in the chariot of light, and make a loud clamour by the repetition of God's names. 99. As we shall see our parents there we shall cling to their feet tightly, and there we shall pass our time in telling tales of joy, and will remain with them. 100. If you like to see that wonder of happiness, you must make your heart large; give up the troubles of the family life, and accomplish the acquisition of the supreme spiritual riches. 101. You should make every effort to see God and don't run after what is perishable. Get up early morning and bathe with repentance. 102. Tomorrow is Monday and the twelfth of the fortnight and a festival. Therefore with a pure heart send for the Brahmans. 103. Make the *sankalpa* (resolve) according to religious rites and have the house plundered by the Brahmans. Do not entertain an anxiety as to how you will obtain it in the future. 104. Pandurang is at our head as our father, mother, friend and a dear and near relative. He Himself will provide everything for us. He will not let us fall into calamity. 105. He is near me. My lengthy description makes Him out to be very far away. You are not blind. You have seen Him and you know all His signs. 106. Pandurang has manifested Himself in my heart and therefore I do not like such happiness as arises from sensual objects. As I see His *sagun* form, all the struggle of my heart is quieted. 107. Worldly people like only two things more than even their own life, viz., gold and woman. As to us, they are worse than pebbles. Do you not know it? 108. My hunger and thirst are satisfied. My friends and relatives, and this forest and the trees in it, are alike to me. 109. I consider joy and sorrow as equal, because the

Husband of Rukmini is near me. The illusion that the sensual objects are imperishable should be cut off and we should only sing the praises of God. 110. Through the favour of the *sadguru*, God made me to utter this. You too with reverence have listened to it;then act now accordingly. 111. The Husband of Rukmini is pleased with me and has accepted me as His own. Now know for certain that there is no other consideration before me. 112. Believe these words and brace up your loins with courage. Without any effort on your part you had the mystic *mantra*. 113. Now sweep the ground clean and sprinkle it with water. Decorate the *tulsi* altar, and worship the casual guests and the Brahmans with devotion. 114. In body, speech, and mind become the slave of the *Vaishnavas* with sole devotion and in love take the names of Vitthal day and night.'

115. The good people know that in the course of my narrative I have taken advantage of the advice of Tuka to his wife as a piece of advice to women in general. 116. *Vaishnava* Tuka uttered only eleven *abhangs*. I have commented upon them in *ovi* verses and have explained them clearly. 117. May the Saints see the original and bring the meaning to their minds. If they behave accordingly they will surely cross over (the ocean of this worldly life). 118. Tuka in fact has advised the seekers after spiritual riches, making his wife as an example. Thereby the snares of earthly life will be severed, and happiness arising from peace will be within one's easy reach; 119. just as seeing the longing of the *chatak* bird, the Husband of Rohini (the moon) rises in the sky. But no one is deprived of its light, for it is equally given to all. 120. Although he has advised his wife, still no one is deprived of its meaning. It is there and will be his who accepts it.

TUKA'S WIFE HAS HER HOUSE PLUNDERED BY THE BRAHMANS

121. As the advice fell upon her ears, her heart

melted; then lovingly she listened to the story of God in the *kirtan*. 122. The praise-service continued, and deeds of Hari (God) were described. In this way they kept awake for four watches of the night, and then when it was dawn auspicious lamps were waved over the Husband of Rukmini. 123. She went to the Indrayani river to bathe and after coming home she sent for the Brahmans. 124. With a pure heart she made the *sankalpa* (resolve), and with her mind free from desires she had her house plundered by the Brahmans. 125. The Brahmans carried away pots, cattle, clothes and grain. Then a *sannyasi* with long matted hair came there, and searched for something in the house. 126. But he could find nothing, therefore he took the ashes from the oven, and smeared his whole body with it; at which all the people laughed heartily. 127. They said, 'At the time of the distribution of the fourteen jems coming out of the ocean, God Shankar (Shiva) got only the deadly poison. In the same way we have seen what sort of luck an unfortunate man has.' 128. After this Tukoba went out. Here in the house his wife was in great concern; for there was not a kernel of grain. 129. The day before she had a fast on account of the *ekadashi* (the 11th day of the fortnight). The children were troubled by hunger. She was worn out by anxiety and did not know what to do.

RUKMINI APPEARS AS A FEMALE MAHAR TO TEST TUKA

130. There was a poor female Mahar of that village. Mother Rukmini assumed her form, and thought of asking for a cloth from Tuka in order to test his devotion. 131. So thinking, the Mother of the universe started out and as she saw Tuka she addressed him thus: 132. 'You have had your house plundered by the Brahmans. I am a female Mahar, and serve you, therefore, O father and mother, if there is anything remaining please give it me.'

133. He saw a female garment drying in the rear of the house. Tuka pulled it down, and gave it to her. 134. The people of the town wondered greatly when they saw this and said, 'He has acted quite unseemingly and has destroyed his family.'

TUKARAM'S WIFE'S COMPLAINT

135. As they reported the matter to his wife she flew into a rage. She said, 'My luck is not in my favour. I have become notorious in the public eye.' 136. In her house her female neighbours assembled she complained to them: 'O my friends, I do not know to whom I should go and tell of my sorrow. I only struggle mentally. 137. For two months past my husband has forsaken me. O dear friends, he does not come to the house even if he is in the town. 138. Three kinds of people ridicule us behind our back or in the face. Therefore yesterday I appealed to him and brought him home. 139. Last night he performed a *kirtan* and allured me. He gave many illustrations; listen to what he said: 140. "Vitthal and Rakhumai are our mother and father. Think of their feet. They will give you food and clothing when you need them, without an effort on your part." 141. I believed his words and had all my money, grain, pots and cattle plundered. And now I am sitting sorrowfully. 142. O friends, I washed my garment and spread it to dry in the rear and you saw that he gave it to the female Mahar. 143. I fed the children by my own labour. As for him, he has good luck, and everything goes on well with him. 144. In this way as I was passing my days I made a mistake in bringing my husband home and have lost everything. 145. I believed his words that if I think of the feet (of Vitthal and Rakhumai) they will give me food and clothing. 146. I thought of them twice or thrice and as a result I saw instant poverty. For lack of food the children are in

trouble. 147. The feet have betrayed me in this way; therefore my mind is on fire. Now I shall go to the temple, hear what I shall do.

TUKARAM'S WIFE GOES TO SMASH VITHOBA'S FEET

148. My husband describes the glory of those feet. Now I will go and break them. So saying she lifted up a stone and started towards the temple. 149-150. She said: 'I will at once smash with a stone the feet of the Husband of Rukmini which Brahmadev and others contemplate and of which Narad and others sing and describe their glory.' With this determination she started towards the main door.

KRISHNA'S ANXIETY

151. Knowing this, the Lord of Pandhari began to tremble all over in the temple. The Merciful to His *bhaktas*, and the Lord of the lowly, showed His *līlā* (deeds) to His servants. 152. He who became a fish and killed the demon Shankhasur in the waters of the ocean, *that* Chakrapani (Krishna) was afraid of the wife of Tuka and therefore trembled. 153. The One who is dark as a cloud became a tortoise, and sustained Mount Mandar on His back. He, seeing the strength of loving devotion, trembled in every limb of His. 154. He who became a boar and suspended the earth on His tusks; that Actor, as in a play and in *Vaikuntha* (Vishnu's heaven), was afraid of His own *bhaktas*! 155. He Who forcefully entered a pillar and tore the demon Hiranyakashipu, He cherished a fear in His heart from His *bhaktas*. 156. King Bali was proud of his giving; then *Vanamali* (Vishnu) became Trivikrama and forced him into the nether world and He trembled all over. 157. He Who was born of Renuka and extirpated the Kshatriyas (the warrior race) from the earth; *that* Chakrapani (Krishna) out of fear from His *bhakta* was trembling. 158. He Who killed the ten-faced demon (Ravana) who had captured all the gods; that

powerful One, the Ornament of His *bhaktas*, trembled through fear. 159. Even Lord Shri Krishna, Who Himself had killed the most powerful demons Kans and Chanur, He was afraid greatly of the wife of Tuka. 160. Chakrapani was covered all over with perspiration at which Rukmini wondered greatly and asked, "Tell me the concern of Thy mind please.' 161. On this Chakrapani replied, 'The perplexity which has arisen in My mind is that Tuka's wife is coming here full of wrath and with a stone in her hand. 162. She has resolved to break My feet; I do not know what remedy I should adopt to avoid the calamity.' 163. Rukmini said, 'To avert the calamity it is well for Thee to run away from here and come back when the crisis is passed.' 164. On this the Life of the world replied, 'It is not in My power to run away, for I am in the power of My *bhaktas*, and I behave as they command. 165. If a child catches a father by his *dhotar* (cloth), the father cannot get rid of it by force; he stands still out of affection; it is just so with Me. 166. A bee bores a hole in a wood, but it cannot break through a lotus-flower; of its own affection it is shut up in it; such is My condition at present. 167. If we leave this place Tuka's mind will be wounded. He will give away his very life if he does not see My image in a *sagun* form. 168. If I stay here out of regard for him, his wife will come and destroy My feet with a stone and this is My concern.' 169. Tuka's wife was burning with anger and she hastened to the temple. When Tuka saw her he asked her where she was going. 170. His wife said in reply, 'Your father, the Husband of Rukmini, has ruined me as in my heart I thought of His feet. 171. You advised me to think of His feet and that He would provide for me food and clothing, and I obeyed you. 172. I believed your advice and then our house was plundered by the Brahmans. But now my children look so pitiful and helpless, for they get no food or clothes.

173. Such is the disaster which these feet have worked; therefore I am going into the temple to crush them with this stone, to be sure.' 174. As Tuka heard his wife's resolve, his heart melted through affection and he cried, 'You are doing something unseeming and extraordinary;' and he began to weep copiously. 175. He decided to go along with her and to speak to her in a humble and gentle way that if she was unable to check her wrath, she should dash the stone at him instead. 176. With this thought in his mind he followed her at a quick pace. Knowing this the Lord of *Vaikunth* (Krishna) was perplexed. 177. A little while ago He was trembling, but now He was quiet. At this Rukmini felt greatly astonished and jestingly asked Him, 178. 'O God of gods, the Lord of Pandhari, Thou wast trembling with fear a little while ago. Has anyone come to Thy rescue ? I have my doubts. 179. Who is this Thy heart's friend who has come to shield Thee, and therefore Thou, the Lord of *Vaikunth* art now quiet ?' 180. Then the Merciful to the lowly said in reply, 'Now there is another more powerful calamity. Pity for Me arose in the heart of our loving *bhakta* Tuka. 181. Knowing that his wife is coming to crush My feet he is following her to request her to throw the stone on himself. 182. Therefore this makes Me forget My own sorrow, and now I feel concerned about him. I am at a loss to know what remedy can be devised to avoid this accident. 183. Hers is an opposing devotion. There is no room for thought or consideration in her mind. She might accidentally strike Tuka. This is My concern. 184. If she strikes his feet and they are hurt, how will he dance in his praise-service? This is My heart's concern.' 185. On this Rukmini replied, 'I do not know why Thou shouldst be so concerned. Even *Kali* (Kali age) and *Kāl* (death) tremble at his sight who is favoured with the least of Thy mercy. 186. He with whom the sun is pleased can never be in the

dark; and he who gets a lodging in the ocean of milk is no more hungry. 187. If one is in possession of a life-giving herb, then he is not affected by diseases. So also, when Thy name is on the lips of Tuka, what fear can he have, O Chakrapani ?' 188. No sooner had the Mother of the world said this than the wife of Tuka arrived there They could see the stone she had on her head as she came to the main door.

RUKMINI SAVES TUKARAM

189. As soon as she went inside the temple, Rukmini closed the door and shut out Tuka. Know why she did so. 190. His wife might strike him out of anger, therefore as soon as she entered the temple Tuka was put outside. 191. In this way the Lord of Pandhari saves His *bhaktas* and wards off their disasters, just as a mother saves her child that is going to touch a burning coal.

RUKMINI PACIFIES THE ANGER OF TUKARAM'S WIFE

192. Tuka thought that the Lord of Pandhari was pleased with his wife and the Husband of Rukmini was displeased with him, and therefore the door was closed. 193. 'The one who is beautiful as a cloud was awake all through my *kirtan* and intended to sleep in order to rest Himself. Because I was going there, and might make a noise. I was shut outside. 194. Is it with the purpose that I should now go home and not disturb His sleep? Or is it because the Husband of Rukmini is displeased with me that the door was shut? 195. Or is my wife's devotion superior to that of mine, and therefore the Life of the world has given her refuge and shut me out?' So thinking he began to weep. 196. If I try to describe the love (of Tuka) at that time the book will be too large. As she (Tuka's wife) lifted up the stone to dash it against the feet (of Vitthal), Mother Rukmini interrupted her by saying, 197. 'What wrong has the Life of the world done, that you have come to

crush His feet? Tell me that without any reserve.' 198. The latter replied, 'Hear, O Mother, once or twice I thought of the feet. But in my house there is no provision even for a single person. All our family life has been ruined. 199. There is not a kernel of grain in the house. The children weep and weep, and therefore my mind is in anger, and I have come to break the feet. 200. Those feet have ruined us, and therefore my mind is in a rage.' As Rukmini heard her story she replied to her, 201. 'I will make good that which might he lacking in your family.' Saying this she gave her a garment, a jacket, and a handful of *hons* (silver coins). 202. The gift satisfied her and she threw down the stone and wore the garment and held the feet of Rukmini. 203. She took the handful of *hons* and came out at once. This most interesting story is continued in the next chapter. May the listeners listen to it with reverence. 204. The Husband of Rukmini sits in my heart, and causes me to speak correctly. Mahipati is His badge-bearer and the slave of His slaves.

205. *Swasti* (Peace)! This book is the *Shri Bhaktavijaya.* The Lord of the world will be pleased if it is listened to. Therefore, O loving and pious *bhaktas*, listen to this most interesting forty-ninth chapter; it is an offering to Shri Krishna.

CHAPTER L

TUKARAM

(Continued)

Obeisance to Shri Ganesh. Obeisance to the Slayer of the demon Pralamba.

INVOCATION.

1. Victory, Victory to Thee, O Chakrapani, Ocean of mercy, Destroyer of the earthly existence, and Giver of the fourth stage of salvation. Look at me with eyes full of mercy, and free me from the law of works. 2. O Shripati (Vishnu), sever the snares of my desires, make me desireless and indifferent to worldly things, and grant me love for Thy worship. 3. The six enemies of man, viz., anger, pride, malice and others, become irresistibly powerful in me. O Holder of the *Sharang* bow (Krishna), the heart will be cleansed only through Thy mercy. 4. Before me there are great hindrances arising from public etiquette and the sense of honour and dishonour. My mind clings to these and therefore I cannot contemplate Thee. 5. I am full of such bad qualities; still I describe myself in public as belonging to Thee. But be proud of this (false assertion of mine), and save me, sinful as I am, O Shri Hari. 6. The mind is very fickle and I only wish that it should be steadied at Thy feet for ever, O Pandurang, Thou knowest my heart. 7. My hands wish to worship Thee in the sixteen ways. So satisfy them and fulfil their wish. 8. O Lord of *Vaikunth* (Vishnu's heaven), I should see Thee alone in the moveable and immoveable creation. O Shripati, make me so that doubts and hatred will never arise in my heart. 9. The use of the feet will only be accomplished when they go on a pilgrimage of Thine and dance (in Thy praise-service)

without a sense of shame and bodily pride. 10. I should describe the fame of Thy *bhaktas* only, O Husband of Rukmini. This is my heart's desire, and therefore I implore Thee, O merciful One. 11. I have formed a seemingly impossible wish that Thou wouldst cause me to compose the delightful narrative, so that as soon as it falls on the ears of the loving listeners they may be satisfied.

12. At the end of the previous chapter it is related that Tuka's wife went to the temple and that Mother Rukmini was pleased with her and, as good fortune would have it, spoke to her. 13. As Tuka's wife received a garment, a jacket and a handful of *hons* (silver coins) she was satisfied. She was wonder-struck to see that the image of stone spoke. 14. She wore the garment and bowed to Rukmini. Tuka knew of the event as she came out.

TUKARAM'S ADVICE TO HIS WIFE

15. Tuka said to his wife, 'You were very impatient and thereby you lost the benefit of the spiritual riches' Listen to my explanation. 16. If we use the crop as it grows, the grain will eventually fall short. If we eat the cream on the milk, where can we get butter from ? 17. If we suck up all the sugarcane, how shall we get sugar ? Advize your mind in this way and give away the *hons* (silver coins) to the Brahmans. 18. Though we give away a bead of glass we obtain a pearl. Therefore encourage your heart and be indifferent to worldly things. 19. Though we heartily let go the firefly the sun comes to our house. Though we neglect a pond of water the ocean come up to us. 20. Though we do not use lovingly the garlands of red and black berries we shall in future obtain precious jems. Though we disregard drugs we shall in future obtain the sweet divine nectar. 21. Though we disregard the *siddhis* (accomplishments personified), we come across a wish-tree. By leaving the company of bad

men we meet with a *sadguru*, then why not give these *hons* away? 22. In the same way, if you drive away from your heart *riddhi* (prosperity), *siddhi* (accomplishments), wealth, and fortune. then you will be absorbed into Brahm (the home of salvation) which even the gods wish for in their minds.' 23. Hearing these illustrations the wife of Tuka was satisfied. She at once sent for the Brahmans and gave them the *hons*. 24. Discard avarice and affection and remember the Lord of Pandhari.

DEV OF CHINCHWAD AND TUKARAM

Now, O listeners, listen with attention to the extraordinarily wonderful story which took place after the above event. 25. Tuka's reputation spread very widely. The great honoured him and the people began to say among themselves that the Husband of Rukmini dined with him. 26. Dev of Chinchwad heard of this and it became unbearable to him. He said, 'I am a Brahman, the highest of all castes. and I have propitiated Ganpati. 27. Tuka is by caste a Shudra, and has the business of a grocer. That Chakrapani (Krishna) dines with him is clearly an unprecedented wonder. 28. Therefore let me cal him here and witness some evidence of this rumour.' So he thought in his mind and Tuka knew it. 29. Said he, 'The great Brahman of Chinchwad has thought of me. So let me go that far and pay reverence to him.' 30. With this intention he at once started. He visited the god whose vehicle is the mouse (Ganpati) and sat near Dev (the Brahman). 31. As he saw Tuka he thought to himself, 'What I intended has easily come to pass. So let me see the wonder with my own eyes.' 32. It was midday and all the Brahmans sat in a row to dine. He also gave a plate to Tuka. 33. The worshipper of Vishnu (Tuka) said to Dev, 'The Lord of Pandhari is my Companion. He will come to dine here, therefore lay one more plate. 34. You also request *Gajavadan* (the elephant-faced-God, Ganpati) to come and dine here.' As Dev heard these words he was surprised. 35. Said he (to himself), 'This is very well, indeed. My own trick has come home to me.' Then he went to the god-room, and joined his lotus-hands palm to palm before Him (Ganpati), 36. and praised Him in various ways, but Ganpati would not come to dine. In the absence of devotion, of what use is the skill of the *Shastras*? 37. Outward worship with a bad and a wandering heart will not please any god. 38. The Lord of *Vaikunth* was pleased with the Gajendra (elephant). Did *he* know any *Shastras*? God saved cowherdesses without number just on account of their loving devotion. 39. The feet of Shri Krishna were far from them, who followed the law of works according to religious rites. The wives of *Rishis* carried food to Shri Krishna and the Life of the world met them. 40. The Merciful to the lowly yielded to these *bhaktas*, who were simple in heart full of devotion and loving. The One dark as a cloud at once listened to the call of the cowherds for play. 41. Well, what is the good of talking at length? The noble *Vaishnavas* know the secret. With their pure heart they made the Holder of the *Sharang* bow (Krishna) their own. 42. Then the Brahmans said to Tuka, 'How will an image of stone dine? As we offer food to the elephant-faced god (Ganpati) the smell of it goes to Him.'

GANPATI RESCUES A MAN FROM DROWNING

43. On this the noble *Vaishnava* replied, 'The Destroyer of disasters (Ganpati) is not among the other images. If you doubt this, lend me your ear for explanation. 44. A worshipper of His was on the point of being drowned as he was bathing in the waters of the sea. He prayed to *Ekadant* (the one-tusked god, Ganpati) to rush to his rescue. 45. To

pull him out, *Vinayak* (Ganpati) has gone there. If you want an evidence of what I say, then wait a while. 46. When Gajavadan (Ganpati) was not in the shrine, to whom did you offer the food ?' Dev (the Brahman) was surprised to hear Tuka say this. 47. Presently they witnessed a wonder with their own eyes. The image of Ganpati on the throne was dripping with water. 48. As they wrung the yellow silk garment, the water of the sea tasted salt. That miracle was simply marvellous and at that sight all began to wonder. 49. The Brahman (Dev) asked Tuka, 'Why is the silk garment wet ?' On this the noble *Vaishnava* replied, 'The Destroyer of hindrances (Ganpati) has now returned here. 50. He had rushed to the rescue of His *bhakta* as he was being drowned. He was safely put on the shore and then Ganpati returned.' 51. As Dev heard Tuka's words, he greatly wondered at heart and said, 'The procedure of the *Vaishnavas* is simply wonderful and beyond our knowing.' 52. Further the Brahman said, 'How did you know that the Son of Parvati (Ganpati) had gone to the sea ? And how were you able to give evidence of it ?' 53. But he himself (Dev) answered this question: 'He has worshipped the Husband of Rukmini, and therefore he knows the ways of all other gods. 54. When the sun favours one, what will he not see ? When one sees a garden of wish-trees, one's desires do not remain unfulfilled. 55. If one inhabits the ocean of milk, he will no more be troubled by hunger and thirst. If a seeker after spiritual riches obtains nectar, he is not in need of drugs. 56. In the same way if the Lord of Pandhari favours one, then all other gods cling to him, just as in looking at the moon, one sees all the stars.'

GANPATI DINES WITH TUKARAM

57. In this way Dev spoke indirectly. On this the *Vaishnava* Tuka said, 'Seeing my pure devotion the

Lord of Pandhari has come to dine. 58. Now you call Ganpati and let us clearly see Him dine.' As Dev heard these words he was silent. 59. The noble Brahman then said to Tuka, 'You have implored the Husband of Rukmini to come to dine! Then feed with love the Destroyer of hindrances (Ganpati) in His row.' 60. 'Very well.' Having said this, he had a plate served with food by him. Then he approached Ganpati and joining his hands palm to palm prayed to Him: 61. 'Victory, victory to Thee, O *Lambodara* (Thou with the big belly, Ganpati), the Ocean of the fourteen sciences (see note on p. 145, Vol. I), seeing Thy *tandava* dance, the delight of the Husband of Uma (Shiva) could not contain His heart. 62. At Thy very sight, hindrances at once take to their heels. If one lovingly experiences this with his own eyes, the meshes of the earthly existence are cut asunder. 63. Now I pray Thee to eat the offering of food with love.' Ganpati consented to his prayer and began to dine. 64. Near one plate was the Husband of Rukmini and near Him was Ganpati. Both of them came for the love of Tuka. 65. But they were not visible to anyone while the food on the plates was being consumed. Dev (the Brahman) felt surprised at this wonderful sight. 66. He said, 'We worshipped Ganpati, but he never before has dined in our presence. But Tuka has worked out this *lilā* (a great wonder), and all of us are surprised. 67. As for the dining of Ganpati, it cannot be called unprecedentedly wonderful, for the Lord of Pandhari Himself has come to dine, which is impossible to a mere seeker of spiritual riches. 68. When the ocean is in one's possession who will care for the rivers? In the same way if the Husband of Rukmini favours one, then all other gods are pleased. 69. As the wish-cow comes to one's house, all other ordinary cows naturally come there. In the same manner, at the sight of the moon all stars are seen.

70. That Lord of the world who is difficult to be seen by the *Yogis*, even by those who sit in the *vajrasan* posture, (on spiked beds), He in His *sagun* or human form comes to the help of His *bhaktas* in difficulties.' 71. In this way the Brahman (Dev) praised Tuka and said, 'Tuka is a loving *Vaishnava bhakta*. He has made the Lord of *Vaikunth* (Vishnu) his own, who is unobtainable to Brahmadev and others. 72. Then Tuka took water to clean his hands and ate *pansupari*. He stayed overnight there and performed a *kirtan*. Then taking leave of Dev (the Brahman), he started back to his own town. 73. First he bowed to Ganpati and then with his hands joined palm to palm he requested Dev to grant him leave to return to Dehu. 74. On this the Brahman requested him saying, 'Please let us see you here again. I will send you a message and then you come here with love.' 75. 'By all means,' replied the *Vaishnava bhakta* who at once departed.

A FARMER GIVES TUKARAM SUGARCANE

As he came near his town, a farmer came to him. 76. He prostrated himself before Tuka and requested him with joined hands, 'In my field the sugar-mill is working. Therefore please come as far as there.' 77. Seeing his good intention Tuka consented. And as he came into the field the farmer was very pleased. 78. He gave him a folded blanket to sit upon, and said, 'Blessed is my luck, for the Merciful to the lowly has come into my farm.' 79. Then he cut some sugarcane into pieces and gave Tuka the middle pieces. But Tuka had no taste for them. 80. For he who has tasted the juice of Brahm will never like other juices; just as in the sunlight, other lamps look without lustre. 81. One who is engrossed in spiritual knowledge, will he listen to the doctrines of an atheist ? When one has in his possession a wish-cow, who will care to have goats ? 82. So when one takes a liking for the name of God, other things to him are tasteless; therefore he did not know the proper taste of sugarcane. 83. But taking into consideration the good intention of the farmer he sat there for a while. Then the farmer brought some sugarcane juice in a clean pot for him to drink. 84. At the time of departure the farmer requested Tuka to take some sugarcane home for his children. 85. The farmer made a bundle of sugarcane and gave it to him. Taking it on his shoulder, Tuka set off. 86. As Tuka entered Dehu the children of the town asked him for sugarcane which he gave them, for he did not differentiate between his own and those of others; 87. just as to a lamp the master of the house and a thief are alike; or just as the sun shines equally on a prince and a pauper; 88. or just as the river Ganges makes no difference between a mango and a *babhul* tree which grow on its bank; 89. or just as on the earth there live both an ant and an elephant, but the earth is neither glad nor sorry, for it considers both of them alike; 90. or as there are innumerable water-animals in the ocean day and night, but the ocean shows no difference; 91. or as the moon at the time of the full moon shines alike on all; so also was Tuka's disposition; the marvellous state of his mind was incomparable.

TUKARAM'S WIFE BEATS HIM WITH SUGARCANE

92. He did not think of carrying the sugarcane to his house; for he was the friend of all beings; he had the same eye for the moveable and the immoveable. 93. After distributing the sugarcane among the children, there remained only one for him to carry home and when his wife saw it she flew into a rage. 94. The noble *Vaishnava* entered his house and spoke gently to his wife, but she returned harsh words in reply to him: 95. 'You distributed the sugarcane to other boys; did your own older children have the satisfaction of receiving it? At home our own children look so pitiful

for lack of food.' 96. Then she beat him on his back with the sugarcane and it broke into three pieces. Two of them fell on the ground and one remained in her hand. 97. In his usual quiet way the *Vaishnava* Tuka addressed his wife: 'Now the sugarcane is equally divided, because Pandurang is our Helper. 98. Your portion is in your hand. Two have fallen down and I shall lovingly divide them between myself and the children.' 99. The wife was astonished at this peace of his and said, 'He has become shameless and given up all thought for his family life. 100. Now what is the good of my clinging to affection for our family life and worrying him for nothing? He has given up all thought for family life and is indifferent to honour and dishonour.'

TUKA'S INCOMPARABLE PATIENCE

101. Thus thinking, his wife was silent. No simile can be found to describe Tuka's patience. 102. Then Mahipati thought for a while, and searched in the descriptions of ancient *bhaktas.* Among these he came across the story of the miser* in the eleventh part of the *Bhagwat* which was related to Uddhava by Shri Krishna. 103. The good people might have heard it from the commentary of Eknath. That place of the miser can be a fitting object for comparison with Tuka's peace. 104. But even this simile is inadequate, for the miser had become a *sannyasi* first and then came his persecution. 105. But the *Vaishnava bhakta* Tuka, although a householder, considered honour and dishonour alike. Even if his own wife beat him he was not at all angry. 106. Therefore I say that no simile can describe him. Can an ordinary ocean be compared with the ocean of milk? 107. Just as the fourth state of salvation (absorption), cannot be compared with the other states of salvation. Such was Tuka's

*See *Bhikshugita*, vol 3 in this series of 'Poet Saints.'

extraordinary state. May the fortunate listeners know it. 108. He who in the *Kali Yuga* posted a banner in *Vaikunth* (Vishnu's heaven) with his mortal body, that loving *bhakta* of God, the chief of the *Vaishnavas*, naturally became the *guru* of the world. 109. But it is useless to call him 'the great, the great.' What is the use of calling the ocean deep? Is it so for once only, and never otherwise? 110. Why should we say again and again that the sun is extraordinarily bright? We need not speak again and again of the moon as cool. 111. If we describe the forbearance of the earth, has it newly become so? No, it is naturally so. Then what is the good of praising it with one's lips? 112. In the same manner, Tuka was adorned for ever by thoughtfulness and peace of mind. Who is able to describe it? Only the knowing and holy ones understand it.

HIS BODILY, VERBAL AND MENTAL PENANCE

113. His bodily, verbal and mental penances were without comparison. Even when his very life was at stake he did not tell a falsehood. 114. We have described his verbal penance. Now listen to his mental penance. He had the same kindness for all beings without any distinction. 115. We described in short the mental penance of Tuka; and the bodily penance is effected by obliging others in bodily labour. 116. These three were the proper ornaments of Tuka. He walked to Pandharpur lovingly. 117. He made it a rule on the *Ekadashi* day of the fortnight to go to Pandharpur. He stayed at the temple of God for a day and started back the next day. 118. As he was going to Pandharpur he sang and danced in love and reached there on the seventh day. He remained there for three nights and then returned home.

TUKARAM IS AFFECTED BY MALARIA

119. In this way three years passed and after this he

was affected by malaria. Then seeing himself without strength he was much troubled. 120. He could not walk a single pace and he said to himself, 'The going to Pandhari is lost to me. I had in store some bad deeds in my former lives and therefore this interruption has arrived.'

TUKARAM'S LETTER TO VITHOBA

121. At that time the *Warkaris* (special pilgrims) were going as pilgrims to Pandhari and by them he sent a letter to Pandhari. 122. The *Vaishnava bhaktas* have heard the explanation of those twenty *abhangs*. If they are listened to lovingly, love for God is impressed on one's heart. 123. Bringing to his mind the image of Pandurang he said, 'O God of gods, the Husband of Rukmini, I have not the good fortune to pray to Thee in person. 124. But I make myself bold and write a letter with love. Even the *Vedas* and *Puranas* do not know Thy limit, then how can I describe Thee, sinful as I am? 125. But, O *Chakrapani* (Krishna), accept my uncouth speech. I made myself too familiar with Thy feet but I place my head on them. 126. Thou art the highest of all gods. O Madhava (Vishnu), Thou art the Lord of the cowherdesses in Thy *sagun* form. All describe the fame of Thy generosity and the glory of Thy good fame in the three worlds. 127. O *Hrishikeshi* (Lord of the heart), Thou destroyest heaps of sins by Thy name alone. By its power one's bad deeds will easily burn up, and one will not see poverty. 128. O Vithabai, all happiness clings to Thy feet. When *riddhi* (prosperity) and *shiddhi* (the accomplishments) become favourable, the four states of salvation become our slaves. 129. The position which is difficult to obtain, even to Indra and others, that becomes obtainable to Thy *bhaktas* through the knowledge of Thy love and by dancing with delight in Thy praise service and clapping the hands with joy.

130. There are many dull persons in the world and Thou, O Husband of Rukmini, art the life of these. But the store of my former deeds is not good and therefore Thou dost not invite me. 131. Art Thou treating me with indifference because Thou didst not get my message? And therefore didst Thou naturally become unkind and so hast left me here? 132. Or is there something more urgent for Thee, and so hast forgotten *me*, O Govinda? I have been anxiously waiting for Thee, O Mukunda. Show me Thy feet. 133. Or Thou didst think that something must be given to me as a gift? Perhaps this was the difficulty in Thy way, and therefore Thou hast neglected me and hast not sent me an invitation, O Vitthal. 134. If Thou hadst such a reserved mind, then why didst Thou give birth to children? To whom shall we go, and open our mouth to beg? 135. If Thou dost leave me, who is there to care for me? O Pandurang, who aside from Thee will do away with my fatigue? 136. Whom shall I wait for? Who is my dear friend? O *Shriranga* (Krishna) if Thou dost leave me, then how will this earthly life be destroyed? 137. Who will understand the trouble of my heart without my telling it? Apart from Thee I do not see anyone before or behind who will do away with my trouble. 138. O God of gods, the Husband of Rukmini, what wrong didst Thou see in me, and so mercy does not arise in Thy heart for me, and therefore Thou hast given me up, O merciful One? 139. At last look once at me. I do not wish to put Thee to an expense. I am muttering Thy names repeatedly day and night. 140. Whatever I may obtain by my fate, the same, whether solid or liquid, I will eat and pass my time, and give up the uneasiness of the heart. 141. But O Lord of Pandhari, I am resolved not to put my burden on Thee. Thou dwellest in the temple of my heart and knowest what is there. 142. But by nature we children long to see Thee,

therefore, O Husband of Rukmini, I am uneasy at heart. 143. Perhaps Thou hast a large number of children and Thou dost not like their peevish complaining, therefore Thou hast become cruel and hast abandoned me? 144. We children are quarrelsome and quarrel with Thee, O Husband of Rukmini. Hast Thou on that account given me up, O merciful One? 145. Or has Thy family become too large to support, and therefore Thou dost unkindly let Thy daughters remain at the homes of their husbands? 146. Or, O Lord of the World, didst Thou do suffer a loss in Thy trade, and so with a narrow mind hast put me in this disaster? 147. Or didst Thou lose credit with the public, and are Thy creditors dunning at Thy door and therefore, O Shri Hari, Thou hast forgotten me? 148. Well, if Thou hadst not anyone to send to give the invitation, Thou couldst at least have sent a message. That would not have cost Thee anything. Thou didst not like to accept this dry way of behaviour. Perhaps Thou art afraid at heart. 149. O Lord of the world, if Thou hast forsaken me, then who is Thy store for? Why dost Thou behave so niggardly that Thou dost not like the sight of Thy children? 150. Thou dost not like to speak just one word by Thy mouth, and thus accept thanks. Then to whom wilt Thou give the fortune which Thou hast so carefully kept? 151. Thy own children are not happy. By constant crying they feel hungry. Therefore act in such a way as will increase Thy reputation. 152. Please do not wait for our curse; it will do Thee no good. Therefore think well at heart and take care of the lowly. 153. Otherwise I will leave nothing reserved in my heart. I will disclose everything to the saints and rob Thee of all Thy gain. 154. I utter Thy name night and day, but I never again will utter it if Thou dost become so indifferent and dost make our longings vain, O merciful One. 155. Thou art the Lord of the world, so powerful, while we are born of Thee and yet are stricken with poverty. In this way Thou hast become notorious and wilt suffer disgrace in the world. 156. Then what is the good of sustaining life in a place where we do not obtain food to eat and have no invitation from our mother to come home ? 157. But O Husband Rukmini, at least remember me in the future, and send me some word. I am pining with sorrow day and night, therefore do not be unkind. 158. My life is in my throat and my mind has gone to cling to Thy feet. My heart is impatient to see Thee. 159. I am laying before Thee the difficulties of my family life, and as I am singing Thy praise I am waiting for Thee. Therefore look at me with a merciful eye and send for me at once. 160. I cannot have patience even for the twinkling of an eye. How can my mind be steady ? I restrain it over and over again, but it is not pure. 161. I am in such a condition. Thou knowest, O Pandurang. Therefore O Husband of Rukmini, cut asunder my earthly life. 162. I have never heard that Thou dost neglect Thy suppliants. Therefore I am thinking of Thy feet and lay my head on them. 163. I do not know when Thou wilt do what is proper. But I try to keep my heart tranquil and I sing Thy praises day and night. 164. O Holder of the *Sharang* bow (Krishna) give ear to this request of mine and send me the invitation. I shall be waiting till the *Warkaris* (pilgrims) come back. 165. Then I will go to receive them and devotedly lie prostrate at their feet, and will ask them the result of my message and what reward Thou hast sent for me ? 166. The step of the main door there is lying undisturbed and in the same way the saints will tell Thee of my prostrate *namaskar*. 167. If one should leave a stick standing without support it will of itself fall flat on the ground; in the same way the saints will tell Thee, O Lord of Pandhari, about my prostration (before Thee). 168. The saints will tell Thee that my prostrate *namaskar* is like an obstinate child rolling on the ground when persistently asking its mother to fulfil its wish'.

TUKARAM'S MESSAGE BY *WARKARIS*

169. Tuka then requested the *Warkaris* (pilgrims) as follows : 'Ask the god: "Why hast Thou cast away Tuka in a forest ? And what is his fault ? 170. Have pity for him in Thy mind." Then ask Him how many wrongs Tuka has done, and therefore why He has cast him away. 171. "Hast Thou forsaken Tuka, because he is not able to come to Pandhari, and is not able to see Thy parallel feet on the brick ? For what reason hast Thou forsaken him ?" 172. Then if the Lord of Pandhari mercifully calls me there, then I will come running, for I shall see the saints there. 173. The three kinds of fever which are in my mind will at once run away when I sing songs of Thy good deeds, and dance in the sandy bed there. 174. I shall come before my Mother and suck her breast. Listen to my pleading words and send me the message quickly. 175. O Ocean of mercy, the Life of the world, do not think of my merits or demerits. Destroy all my sins and show me Thy feet. 176. O *Hrishikeshi* (Lord of the heart), art Thou not able to destroy my sins, and therefore hast cast me away with cruelty in a foreign land ? 177. O Husband of Rukmini, as I hear of Thy reputation I feel penitent day and night. When I see Thee, surely Thou wilt intensely love me. 178. O Life of the world, my tongue is not able to describe Thy qualities. My mind has become impatient to taste the nectar of Thy love. 179. But the time is not favourable to me and I am sorrowing for nothing. My sorrow will increase in future, and there will be wrong thoughts which I shall not be able to resist. 180. O Shri Hari, Thou knowest my mind, therefore do what Thou likest. I have given up all uneasiness of heart and have become quiet. 181. But if Thou forsakest

me, then there will be a curse on Thee, and, O *Adhokshaja* (God), if Thou diest, I shall be an orphan. 182. Therefore I am sending Thee my blessing now, that I, O Husband of Rukmini, may live happy and that Thou mayest some time have mercy for me and accept me. 183. Although Thou forsakest me at a distance, still Thou wilt inquire after me. When Thy heart does not contain affection for me, then Thou wilt show me my mother's home. 184. O Ocean of mercy, Lord of the world, now listen to my request. Do as thou wilt, and henceforth I will not cry in complaint. 185. O Lord of Pandhari, send me Thy message just as Thou dost prefer. Whatever I have spoken, knowingly or unknowingly, forgive me that wrong, O *Ananta* (infinite One). 186. At first Thou didst treat me, Thy child, with indulgence, and didst fulfil my wishes. Now grant me a sight of Thee and destroy the disturbance of the snare of earthly existence.' 187. Tuka wrote such compassionate words and sent the letter by the hands of the *Warkaris* (pilgrims).

MAHIPATI DEFENDS HIS OWN LITERARY METHOD

Listeners should not feel troubled by this lengthy description. 188. You might say that I deviated from the relation of the regular story, that I have made the book too large unnecessarily, and that in the fit of intense delight and love, I was not mindful of any sense of proportion. 189. But it is not quite like that. I have not enlarged the book for nothing. I simply looked at the *abhangs* in the letter and commented on them in brief. 190. My talent falls short in describing Tuka's love. A painter may draw the sun, but he is not able to depict the light. 191. A river may overflow, but it cannot vie with the ocean. A cow giving a large quantity of milk cannot be compared with a wish-cow. 192. Brass may shine from a distance, but it cannot become pure gold. The power of nectar cannot be found in medicinal herbs. 193. The peacock dances at the sight of the cloud, but if the peahen tries to do the same there is a vast difference between them. The knowing ones understand this. 194. In the same way, in describing the love of Tuka, all my talent has become wearied. At the rise of the sun, all the stars become invisible. 195. If musk falls on the earth, it will be sold at the same rate *as* musk. Similarly my composition has been sanctified without effort in praising the saints. 196. Well, let us resume the thread of our narrative. The *Vaishnavas*, the pilgrims, started for Pandhari and Tuka sent by them the letter which he had written in love. 197. Then the *Warkaris* (pilgrims) bade farewell to Tuka and took the way to Pandhari, the narration of which the clever *bhaktas* should listen to with intense love in the next chapter; 198. just as a miser while counting his money does not let his mind be divided; or as a crooked-minded person becomes absorbed in the censure of another person; 199. Likewise, if the listeners pay attention with love to this story, the Husband of Rukmini will be pleased. Therefore Mahipati requests the listeners to listen to the narrative with devotion.

200. Swasti (Peace)! This is the *Bhaktavijaya* book, by listening to which the Lord of the world will be pleased. Therefore, O pious and loving *bhaktas*, listen to this very delightful chapter fifty.

CHAPTER LI

TUKARAM

(*Continued*)

Obeisance to Shri Ganesh. Obeisance to Shri Gopal Krishna.

MAHIPATI'S PRAYER TO GOD

1. Victory, victory to Thee, O *Hrishikeshi* (Lord of the heart). Merciful to the lowly, Dweller in the hearts of Thy loving *bhaktas*, Husband of Rukmini, the Lord of Pandhari, the Prime Cause of all, and the *Guru* of the world. 2. Victory, victory to Thee, whose *līlā* (voluntary deeds) are those of an actor in a play, Holder of the strings of the universe, Store of good qualities, the Lord of the Yadavas. Thinking in her heart of Thy feet, the daughter of the ocean (Lakshmi, the goddess of wealth) has become Thy suppliant. 3. O Knower of the heart, Pervader of the moveable and the immoveable, Primal Form of the universe, possessing form but without the three qualities, Giver of the promise to Pundalik, the supreme Lord! Victory to the Indestructible, Who exists as *Atmarupa* (in the form of the soul)! 4. Victory to Thee, O Ocean of mercy, Lord of *Vaikunth*, O Thou of immense form, who didst appear as Vaman (the dwarf) and as Parashuram (holder of the axe). Thou didst remove from the earth the Kshatriyas (the warrior caste) and didst establish the Brahmans. 5. Victory to Thee, Destroyer of the demons, Founder of religion, Lord of the worlds, Father of Brahmadev, Relative and Friend of Thy loving *bhaktas*, for aside from Thee they have no one else. 6. Should I attempt to praise Thee by my own mouth, my intellect has not sufficient inspiration. If I should think of worshipping Thee with love, I have not the means. 7. Should I think of visiting the sacred places in repentance, my

body has lost its strength. Should I think of giving to deserving persons, I lack money. 8. If I should think of practising religious rites, my life becomes uneasy through hunger. If I think of bowing down to all beings, their good and bad qualities arise in my mind. 9. O Shripati, if I wish to study the *Shastras*, my life is not in my power. If out of repentance I think of giving up worldly affairs, *vairagya* (the ascetic spirit) does not possess my mind. 10. If I think of meditating on Thee all alone, my reason cannot control my fickle mind, and instead of thinking of Thy form it wanders everywhere. 11. If I wish to restrain my senses, my tongue is not in my control. So am I environed by bad qualities. Thou knowest this secret of my heart. 12. Therefore, O Husband of Rukmini, I pray to Thee. As Thou lovest Thy *bhaktas*, grant me Thy loving inspiration to describe the fame of their good qualities. 13. With body, speech and mind I ask for the gift of this favour only. Aside from this I have no other wish. Therefore fulfil my desire.

TUKARAM'S SICKNESS AND LETTER

14. O listeners, you hearkened with reverence to the beautiful story in the preceding chapter how Tuka with his heart full of love sent a letter (to Vithoba) 15. Taking this letter of twenty-four *abhangs*, the *Warkaris* (special pilgrims) at once started on their way to Pandhari. As they marched on their way, waves of delight arose in their hearts and they wagged their heads to the loud clamour of the praise (of God). 16. Thus happy in each other's company the *Vaishnavas* arrived at Pandharpur. All others (at Pandharpur) as they saw them bowed prostrate at one and the same time at their feet. 17. They embraced each other and from their eyes flowed tears of joy. They lovingly waved lights over Shripati (Vithoba). 18. Then

choirs with banners in their hands came to the bank of the Chandrabhaga and after bathing they performed their daily worship. 19. They visited the tomb of Pundalik, went round the sacred town, and with very many cymbals and drums they danced in full delight. 20. Then the noble *Vaishnavas* arrived at the chief door of the temple and as they saw before them the eagle platform they prostrated themselves before it. 21. The *Vaishnavas* began to sing the *abhangs* in the letter written by Tukaram. Hearing this piteous plea the Husband of Rukmini was overcome with grief. 22. Tuka was not in good health, so the Lord of the heart was uneasy ; as is a doe at seeing her young one caught by a hunter in a net ; 23. or as a mother feels uneasy when she sees her child suffering from smallpox ; similarly, hearing Tuka's letter, the Life of the world became uneasy. 24. As the water-deities dry up the water the fish struggle ; in the same way, hearing the pitiful cry of Tuka, the Recliner on the Serpent *Shesha* was disturbed ; 25. or as a miser is disturbed in mind on learning that his hoard of money is being watched by a thief, so was the Holder of the *Sharang* bow (Krishna). 26. Then the Lord of *Vaikunth* addressed Rukmini thus: 'I feel anxious about Tuka's condition, therefore I am overcome with sorrow in my mind ; and tears stream from my lotus-eyes. 27. All the *Warkaris* (pilgrims) have come, and Tuka alone is missing from among them, therefore I do not feel at all happy. 28. We might go away from here, were it not that so many people have come ; so I ask you as to how we should act.'

GARUD TAKES VITHOBA'S REPLY TO DEHU

29. On this Rukmini replied: 'Send Garud (the Eagle) to bring Tuka here. He will seat him on his back and in less than a moment will bring him here. 30. When we possess so much power, why should we feel anxious at

heart ?' At this reply the Lord of the heart was gratified. 31. Then having called the Son of Vinata (the Eagle), the Lord of Pandhari ordered him this : 'Go at once to Dehu, and do this.' 32. Then taking a pen, the Life of the World began to write a letter. Oh you simple, good people, listen to it piously. 33. He said : 'As long as *Vaikunth* (Vishnu's heaven) and *Kailas* (Shiva's heaven) are in existence, may Tuka live and for ever remember me with love in the temple of his heart.' 34. As Vithoba sent this blessing (to Tukaram), Rukmini felt astonished at heart and said, 'These words from your lips can never be untrue.' 35. Pandharinath smiled silently and His heart could not contain His intense love (for Tuka). Then he wrote to Tuka: 'I feel so sorry at hearing of your strange sickness. 36. If you want to know how sorry I feel, your own heart will bear witness to it. For as the *Warkaris* (pilgrims) communicated to me your message, I became quite troubled at heart. 37. In fact, I ought to rush to meet you; but the pilgrims have assembled here in large numbers and so I have sent my Eagle there (to you) to fetch you here without fail. 38. Therefore without any reserve at heart sit on his back and come to Pandhari without losing a moment and meet me here at once.' 39. Having written thus, the Life of the world addressed the Eagle : 'Considering Tuka as Myself, seat him on your back and bring him here.' 40. 'By all means,' said the Eagle and placing his head at the feet (of Vithoba) he replied, 'He to whom my *Swami* (Lord) has given refuge, deserves to be bowed down to by me. 41. When Saraswati (the goddess of learning) favours a dullard, him the learned revere. When the ocean accepts a river flowing into it, naturally it does not reject the small rivulets (that feed the river). 42. If Mount Malaya (where sandalwood grows in abundance) with love lets *bor* and *babhul* trees grow in its neighbourhood, who will ever call them thorny bushes ?

For there is no lack of sweet fragrance in them. 43. When the Lord of speech (the guru of the gods) accepts anyone, all the multitude of gods respect him. Or if a rod of iron touches a *parīs* (a touchstone) then it can no longer be called rusty iron. 44. Thus seeing Tuka's pure mind, Thou art pleased with him; so I certainly have not the power to keep him at a distance.' 45. Saying this he placed his head at (Vithoba's) feet and then the king of birds got up quickly and started to go as fast as the wind.

GARUD MEETS TUKARAM

46. Now Tuka was feeling very impatient at heart, and with his hand on his forehead was waiting day and night (for the pilgrims' return), like a child when missing its mother; 47. or as the *chatak* bird when it is thirsty opens its mouth (towards the cloud), and as the hungry young ones of a tortoise look toward their mother. 48. If a miser loses all his money, he is restless day and night; as a fish struggles when water dries up. 49. In the same way, Tuka was uneasy day and night on account of his separation from Pandhari, when suddenly the Eagle stood near him. 50. At the sight of the Eagle, Tuka prostrated himself on the ground before him, embraced him with loving reverence, 51. and then asked him lovingly, 'Is the Husband of Rukmini happy ? I am uneasy day and night. I cannot say when I shall have a sight of Him ? 52. Why has the Life of the world been so cruel and hardened His heart ? Why has He thrown me aside in a strange land ? For these reasons I feel dejected. 53. Many *Warkaris* (pilgrims) must have assembled. Why has He forgotten *Me* ? What unbearable crime have I committed ? I certainly do not know.' 54. The vehicle of Vishnu (the Eagle) heard these words of Tuka, and replied, 'On account of your dejection of mind, the Life of the world has become very uneasy at heart; 55. as a mother is at

the separation from her infant child; or as the doe at the separation from her young one; or as a thirsty person is troubled at heart in the absence of water; 56. in the same way, the Husband of Rukmini thinks of you day and night and therefore has sent me to invite you and take you to Him.' 57. He read out the letter to Tuka sent by the Husband of Rukmini, at hearing which Tuka's eyes became wet with tears. 58. Tuka took the letter in his hand and again and again placed it on his head. Then holding the letter in his hand he pressed it to his heart and embraced it lovingly; 59. as a cloud showers water suddenly on a dry tree, in the same way Tuka felt happy at the sight of the Eagle; 60. as at the rising of the sun, the water lilies are happy, so at the arrival of the Eagle, Tuka felt happy; 61. as Bharata sat waiting for Shri Rama (his brother) at Nandigrama, and felt satisfied when the Son of Anjani (Maruti) delivered the message of (Shri Rama) to him, 62. in the same manner when the Husband of Rukmini sent the letter and the king of birds (Garud) delivered the message, Tuka's heart became quiet.

TUKARAM REFUSES TO RIDE ON GARUD

63. Then Garud in sweet words said to Tuka, 'Now please sit on my back and in less than a moment I will show you Pandhari. 64. Your body is emaciated by disease, and has not strength to walk, so the Lord of Pandhari has kindly sent me immediately. 65. Now, therefore get up quickly, and don't delay.' Hearing these words, Tuka said in answer, 66. to the King of Birds, 'You are my Master's vehicle and so an object of reverence to me, His slave, you wise one. 67. Shoes are to be put on the feet and not to to be placed on the head. A wise man must consider when he places ornaments for the feet (*wale* and *nepur*) on the head. 68. How can the step of stone at the main door of the temple be installed in the place of the image?

A royal menial, although he is the king's favourite, is not to be placed on the throne. 69. Therefore, O vehicle of Vishnu, hear me. I will never sit on you. I surely do not know how to describe the glory of your greatness. 70. You carry on your back the Ancient of Days and the Enjoyer of *Vaikunth* (*Vishnu*) whose belly contains limitless universes. This is a thing simply to be admired. 71. He is invincible to the gods and the demons, still you conquered Him, and moreover yielded to Him, and eventually became His vehicle, and you stand before Him with folded hands. 72. Therefore, to worshippers like me the Lord and His servant are the same. So I will never come by riding on your back. 73. Now therefore this is my earnest request to you. Think in your mind of my condition and go back to Pandhari at once and bring the Husband of Rukmini here.' 74. Then Tuka touched Garud's feet, prostrating himself before him and saying, 'The Life of the world is in your power, please bring Him here that I may meet Him.' 75. 'Surely,' said the son of Vinata (Garud the Eagle) and quickly started, determined in his mind to bring about a meeting between the Lord of Pandhari and Tuka. 76. With this resolve at heart, Garud arrived at Pandhari, and the Lord of the heart (Krishna) became anxious at not seeing Tuka on his back. 77. As when a man sent to fetch a daughter returns without bringing her, any mother feels sorry; just so was it with the Husband of Rukmini. 78. Then Garud approached and placed his head at His feet and said: 'O God of gods, Shri Hari, Tuka would not ride on me. 79. But, O Husband of Rukmini, on account of Thy separation Tuka feels sorry night and day. Now, O Lord of *Vaikunth*, kindly come and meet him.' 80. 'Of course,' said the Life of the World who embraced Garud, then called to Rukmini, and told her the secret of His heart. 81. On this the Mother of the universe replied, 'The *Vaishnava bhaktas* have assembled here for the pilgrimage. It is not proper for you to leave this festival and go. 82. As a house looks empty without a wife, or as a river without water, so Pandhari will appear without you, O Lord of *Vaikunth.* 83. As an army and fortune without a king, or as the multitude of stars without the moon, or as ornaments without the saffron mark (on the forehead of a woman whose husband is living); all these look ugly. 84. Likewise if you are not here on this occasion, Pandhari will appear forlorn. We shall go to meet Tuka after the *Gopalkala* ceremony '

NIMBARAJA'S STORY

85. Hearing this appeal of Rukmini, the Life of the World said, ' By all means. ' Just then saints came there to visit Him. Listen to their names:— 86. Shaikh Muhammad, Ganeshnath, Bodhla, and the well known Nimbraja, Santoba Powar, these *Vaishnava bhaktas* came there to visit Him. 87. Cymbals, vinas and drums were sounded, and the *Vaishnavas* sang in love. Banners were beautifully unfurled amongst which shone those with the emblems of the eagle. 88. All the people prostrated themselves on the ground when the Life of the world said to Rukmini: ' Nimbaraja has come rolling on the ground thus far; and so he must be very fatigued. 89. Therefore I must give him some suitable boon.' At this point the listeners may have a doubt, and with love raise a question. 90. They may ask ' Who is this Nimbaraja, and to what place does he belong? Describe him in detail. ' As they thus question, the mind of the speaker is filled with delight. 91. The question is like the moon to the *chakor* bird, or like a sudden shower of nectar to a hungry person as a result of good fortune; 92. or as when a wish-cow comes and stand in the yard of a pauper, or as when a *paris* (touchstone) by chance falls into a box of iron; 93. or as when a cloud showers on a crop about to ripen, then the

kernels increase twofold (fortunate are they who obtain this); 94. in the same way the speaker feels happy at heart at the question of the listeners, and replies: 'Listen with love to the detailed life of Nimbaraja. 95. In our own country there is a town called Devadaithan, and Nimbaraja was by a very old inheritance the accountant there. 96. Although he had children and others in his family, yet Nimbaraja called himself a *Vaishnava bhakta*, and as he was in the habit of worshipping the saints with devotion, repentance arose in his mind. 97. Then he said, 'Enough of this worldly life; the *maya* of God is uncontrollable, and all life is wasted when carrying on worldly affairs.'

NIMBARAJA VISIT THE *JYOTIRLINGAS*

98. With repentance at heart, he started out to visit sacred places. On visiting the twelve *Jyotirlingas** his mind was comforted. 99. He visited all the beautiful sacred places on earth, hard to travel to; then after visiting the seven* salvation-giving sacred towns he went into the Himalayas. 100. To describe the glory of the travel, the story would be far too long drawn out, therefore I will abbreviate. Let the listeners understand it. 101. Thrice he took a *kavadi* (sling) full of the water of the Bhagirathi, and in it bathed the god Rameshwar with love. Thus accumulating good deeds, he returned quickly home. 102. Now he wished to utter the names of Hari with his lips, and with this longing at heart he kept on repeating God's names. 103. One who has performed religious rites and austerities without the desire of their fruit, he alone out of repentance gives himself up with love to the praise of Shri Hari. 104. Visits to sacred places, performance of sacrifices, and the study of the *Vedas*, fructify only when one sings of the good qualities of Shri Hari with an unreserved mind. 105. Now

---

* See *Appendix* on 'Words With Numerical Significance' under 12, 'The Twelve *Jyotirlingas*'; and under 7, '*Saptapuris*.'

enough of this lengthy talk. The *Vaishnavas* know the lovely secret. They abandon all sense of honour and dishonour, and sing the praises of God day and night. 106. When one does not give himself up solely to singing the praise of Shri Hari all other means become useless as a deep well without water; 107. or as in a grain field there are a large number of ears without kernels; or as when a village officer is successful in acquiring a hereditary office, but is without an issue; 108. or as though one should study a good deal, but is not able to make a timely use of it; or as the sitting of a king on a throne is vain without power; 109. or as plates with various kinds of dainty food without any *ghee* (melted butter) on them; so all religious means become useless without the description of Shri Hari's doings. 110. Therefore Nimbaraja had a desire to sing the praise of God. So one day the Lord of Pandhari gave a command to Gajavadana (Ganpati). 111. Said He, 'Give Nimbaraja the boon that with inspiration he will sing My praise.' As the Husband of Rukmini gave this order, Ganpati replied 'Verily, verily.' 112. One night while Nimbaraja was asleep, the son of Parvati appeared to him in a dream in the guise of a Brahman. 113. He stroked him to rouse him and said, 'Accept this boon of mine.' Saying this He put on his palm a *vida* (rolled betelnut leaves). 114. Nimbaraja in a drowsy state threw it into his mouth. Then Gajavadana (Ganpati) said: 'This is an everlasting boon. 115. Now without study you will be able to delineate Hari's good actions. The genius of pleasure will everlastingly be present at your performance.' 116. The son of Parvati offered this boon and at once disappeared. When Nimbaraja awoke he brought to his mind the dream. 117. He did not see the Brahman near him, but there was the *vida* in his mouth. He swallowed it, and got up and sat down. 118. As he looked at his palm he found on it a red stain. He tried to wash it with water, but could not get rid of it; 119. just as the ocean supplies the well with water and it does not get dry even in a drought or as a person with divine knowledge satisfies a *Yogi* and he is no more troubled with the hunger; 120. or as iron with the touch of the *parīs* (touchstone) becomes gold, and no more can rust remain; or as when the Ganges accepts an insignificant rivulet, it becomes sacred to all; 121. or if Brahmadeva gives one a long life, he is unhindered by fear and disease; or if a prince supports a pauper, his fortune knows no decrease; 122. or when the sun gives one a physical lustre, how can it be impaired by cold ? So the stain of the *vida* could not be washed off. 123. From that day Nimbaraja began to perform *kirtans.* The *Vaishnavas* who listened to him were engrossed. 124. Having given up all idea of shame, honour, and social etiquette, and having forsaken all ties of hope, and discarded all differences, he enjoyed the pleasure of the love of God.

RUKMINI OFFERS A FORTUNE TO NIMBARAJA

125. In this natural state of mind, Nimbaraja went to Pandhari. The listeners should remember that it was at this point that they questioned me. 126. The Life of the world said to Rukmini, 'Give some boon to Nimbraraja.' At this the Mother of the world was astonished. 127. The Mother of the universe took the form of a female gardener and sat on the way with a basket full of carrots cut into pieces. 128. As Nimbaraja was returning from the temple she said to him in a gentle tone, ' My child is crying at home; I must go and fetch it. 129. So do me a kindness and sit here for a while. I will bring my babe and return immediately. 130. If you do not grant my request, who will take care of my carrots ? Many men are wandering in the bazar and they might take them away .' 131. As the Mother of the universe said this, his mind was filled

with pity and he said, 'I will sit here, but return quickly.' 132. The female gardener gave the basket in his custody and going to the temple, did not return for three long hours. 133. Then as Nimbaraja removed the cloth from the basket and looked into it he saw lumps of gold and not a simple carrot. 134. He was astonished and said, 'The Primal Mother (Lakshmi) wants to put me into temptation. This cannot be called gold but a great calamity. So it seems to me.' 135. Disgust arose in his mind, just as a Brahman on entering a Mahammadan's house will feel sick at the sight of the flesh there; 136. or as a beautiful person will not look at a leper; or as at the sight of liquor in front of him a repentant man will walk away from the place; 137. so when Nimbaraja saw the gold inside the basket his mind felt disgust. Then he returned to the temple and prostrated himself reverently before God. 138. He joined his hands palm to palm and pleaded, 'O God, why dost Thou put me into temptation? I wish Thy favour, and no fortune or wealth.' 139. Then he made a namaskar to Rukmini and returned to his lodging, and began lovingly to repeat the names of Hari without interruption. 140. Here in the temple Rukmini said, 'Oh Life of the world, I obeyed your order and gave gold to Nimbaraja, but his mind does not take to it.' 141. The Pervader of the world smiled and said, 'My *bhaktas* are pleased with my worship. Temptation, greed and avarice have no effect on them. 142. The showers of rain do not penetrate a mountain; and the sky cannot be painted black; nor does cold affect the sun; and heat has no effect on the moon; 143. thirst does not trouble the ocean, and food does not trouble fire. O you wise one, how can wind be shut up in a gaol? 144. So my *bhaktas* are indifferent; snares of temptation do not affect them.'

NIMBARAJA AT THE CHANDRABHAGA

While the Lord of *Vaikunth* thus spoke, Rukmini greatly wondered in her mind. 145. The next morning the saints started for the Chandrabhaga to bathe, with Nimbaraja in their company. 146. Then the Lord of Pandhari thought to himself, 'I must give Nimbaraja some imperishable reward by which in full love he will be engrossed in my praise.' 147. Saying this, He who was as dark as the *tamal* leaf took the garb of a Brahman, put garlands of *tulsi* around His neck and arrived there. 148. He had a cap on his head and a belt around His loins, on His forehead was the odorous black powder (*buka*). Listen to what the one dark as a cloud said to Nimbaraja at that time: 149. 'I am going to bathe in the Bhimarathi ; thieves are wandering here and there in the fair, therefore keep with you the belt, the cap, and the garland.' 150. Saying this, the Husband of Rukmini handed over to him His ornaments and in the twinkling of an eye disappeared. 151. As Nimbaraja looked about he could nowhere see the Brahman. For three hours he sat waiting for him. 152. Still he did not return. Then he communicated the news to the saints : 'A Brahman came here and listen to what he said. 153. Said he, " I am going to bathe, so keep my ornaments with you." Then he took off his garland, cap and belt, and handed them over to me. 154. Within the twinkling of an eye he disappeared then and there and I have been anxiously waiting for him. 155. He has not as yet returned ; so please tell me what should be done now.' The saints wondered as they heard this. 156. All the *Vaishnava bhaktas* said, 'He is not a Brahman but the Husband of Rukmini. He gave you these as a reward and disappeared. 157. Therefore without any scruple in your mind, wear these ornaments.' As the saints thus spoke he prostrated himself before them. 158. Then the saints fastened the belt on his loins and around his neck put the beautiful garland of tulsi and the cap on his head.

On his forehead they applied the black powder. 159. The *bhaktas* gathered in the sandy bed and said to Nimbaraja, '*Vanamali* (Krishna) has given you a reward, and has created a festival as delightful as *Divali* to the pious. 160. Therefore, you perform a *kirtan* on this bed of sand. Our ears are eager to hear you, please satisfy them. 161. Then the *vina* was set in tune with the drum. Collecting cymbals quickly, they unfurled the banners. 162. Brahmans well versed in the *Vedas*, *Shastras* and *Puranas*, many saints and *Mahants* and *Vaishnavas*, and men of all the eighteen castes came there to listen. 163. At sunset the *kirtan* began. Nimbaraja sang the obeisance with the clapping of hands and repeating the names of Vitthal. 164. As he thought of the Husband of Rukmini in his mind, tears of joy flowed from his eyes. The gods came there on their chariots of light to watch the wonderful event. 165. As people listened to his simple and loving singing their hearts were touched. Knowers and critics were absorbed in it. 166. When the speaker has only love in his mind, there the supreme Being finds comfort. Skill, cleverness and wisdom are unessential. 167. Singing without love is as the body without life, or as food cooked without salt. It does not give any taste at all. 168. Of what value is musk without fragrance? It should be thrown into the fire. A beautiful woman without a child cannot truly be called a mistress of the house. 169. Of what use are the fair complexion and a beautiful face without a nose? So also it cannot be a real *kirtan* in which the singing is without love. 170. 'O Krishna, Rama, *Meghashyama*, Govinda, Gopala, Purushottama, *Achyuta*, Narahari, and Atmarama, give me love in Thy worship.' 171. Nimbaraja uttered these names and danced. *Garudadhvaja* (the eagle-bannered one, Vishnu) was pleased, and what did He do then? 172. Shripati became a child, took peacock feathers in His hand, and did a very wonderful thing, which you listeners should listen to with reverence. 173. Shri Hari stood on the shoulders of Nimbaraja and waved with His own hand the wisp. Listen to this, O devout listeners. 174. He Who dwells in the ocean of milk, Who reclines on the serpent Shesha, Who is the very life of the Daughter of the ocean (Lakshmi), He, the Life of the world, waved the wisp lovingly on His *bhakta.* 175. Although *Yogis* with perseverance sit on the *vajrasana* (the bed of iron spikes) still He does not show Himself to *them.* He stands on the back of Nimbaraja and waves the wisp of peacock feathers. 176. He is not attainable to those spiritual aspirants who perform many sacrifices, religious rites and heaps of austerities. He, the Merciful to the lowly, *Hrishikeshi* (the Lord of the heart), reveres His *bhaktas.* 177. He whom the god Shiva (*Virupaksha*), restraining His mind, contemplates in solitude, He the Ornament of His *bhaktas*, the Husband of Rukmini, pays respect to His servants. 178. In a *kirtan* where the One who is like a cloud is present, there the sixty-four arts and fourteen sciences are favourable. This the wise can discern. 179. The audience looked on steadily; the *kirtan* lasted for four watches, but no one felt sleepy or wearisome. 180. The Ocean of milk knows no famine, and with nectar there can be no disease. Wise listeners, how can darkness visit the house of the sun ? 181. In the same way in the *kirtan* of the loving, sleep and sloth do not come. All forget caste-differences and become one. 182. The audience in supreme Brahman joy clapped hands in tune with the sound of cymbals and *mridang.* They forgot all differences and dualities and rocked themselves as they repeated God's names.

KRISHNA ON NIMBARAJA'S SHOULDERS

183. When there still remained four *ghatikas* of the night a wonderful event took place. The wife of a rich

person covered with a cloth was going to bathe. 184. She suddenly saw before her the Lord of Pandhari Himself. Then running quickly she arrived at the *kirtan*. 185. As she came near Nimbaraja, and began to look for the Husband of Rukmini, He disappeared, at which she wondered. 186. She wept loudly and clasped the feet of Nimbaraja. The people asked her as to why she came running there. 187. 'What wonderful sight did you see? Tell us at once.' She bowed to all. Listen to what she said, 188. 'Just now I saw Shri Hari on the shoulders of Nimbaraja, waving the wisp of peacock feathers lovingly with His own hand. 189. So I came running, but I don't see Him here now. I certainly do not know where the Husband of Rukmini has gone. 190. I wanted to see once more the beautiful and tender Lord of the world, therefore I am sorry at heart that He does not grant me this sight. 191. The people wondered and exclaimed, 'This wonderful event cannot be explained.' The wise ones came near, desiring to see some evidence of the event. 192. *Chakrapani* (Krishna) had disappeared from the shoulders of Nimbaraja. But on the black powder which the good people had thrown the tiny feet (of Krishna) were impressed. 193. Noticing this evidence, saints and other good people wondered. Embracing one another they prostrated themselves on the ground. 194. They bowed to the lady who had seen the Lord of Pandhari and said, 'Because you were in possession of some good deeds (in your former births), you saw the Husband of Rukmini.' 195. As the men and women were singing in this way the sun arose. Then Nimbaraja waved lights over the Holder of the *Sharang* bow (Krishna). 196. On the full moon day, the *Gopalkala* ceremony was performed and then the crowds of pilgrims began to disperse. Therefore the Brother of the lowly was sad. He was overcome on account of His own love. 197. When a helpless daughter goes to her husband's home, her mother weeps through grief. The same was the state of the Lord of Pandhari as the fair broke up. 198. Shri Hari said to Rukmini, 'This Pandhari now looks sad. My *bhaktas* have gone to their homes. So I find no rest. 199. Now we must hurry up and go to see Tuka.' Saying this the Lord of the world became very impatient. 200. Garud was sent for, and the god assumed a *sagun* form which the Husband of Aparna (Shiva) for ever contemplates with a pure heart. 201. Hari rode on the back of the Son of Vinata (Garud) with Rukmini, and arrived at the town of Dehu with the velocity of a wish.

TUKARAM MEETS VITHOBA AT DEHU

202. The grocer *Vaishnava* Tuka sat impatiently waiting. Said he, 'When will *Chakrapani* (Krishna) come with Mother Rukmini? 203. Today my right eye throbs and every now and then my right hand also throbs. These good omens comforted him all the time. 204. Just then, suddenly, he beheld the shining banner with an emblem of the eagle on it, and he went in front of it and in love prostrated himself. 205. Seeing the loving devotion of His *bhakta*, the god of gods manifested Himself. Even Brahmadeva and others are unable to understand Him. 206. The form of the god was beautiful and tender. He had worn the yellow garment. On His ears were the crocodile earrings and on His breast shone the *kaustubha* jewel. 207. On His head was a resplendent crown studded with divine gems. The Life of the world had put around His neck the *padak* and *ekavali* ornaments. 208. On His feet were the *nepur* and *wale* which made a tinkling sound. Hearing that sound the *Vedas* felt shy. The Lord of the world manifested Himself with Rukmini. 209. At the sight of this form, Tuka was delighted at heart. Then he embraced (the god) with love and held His feet.

210. In the next chapter there will be a conversation between the god and his *bhaktas* in a language full of pathos. Let the saints and others lovingly listen to it. 211. It is a delicious draught from the Ganges of love, like the nectar churned out of the ocean of joy. Mahipati requests the listeners to taste it quietly with love.

212. *Swasti* (Peace) ! This book is the *Bhaktavijaya*, hearing which the Lord of the world will be pleased. O ye loving and pious *bhaktas*, listen to it. This is the fifty-first very delightful chapter; it is an offering to Shri Krishna.

CHAPTER LII

TUKARAM

(*Continued*)

Obeisance to Shri Ganesh. Obeisance to the Lord of the world.

INVOCATION

1. Victory, victory to Thee, the Ocean of mercy to Thy *bhaktas*, the Imperishable, the Indestructible, the Saviour of the world, the Primal-Pillar, Generous in giving final deliverance, the Husband of Rukmini, O Shri Vitthal. 2. At whom Thou dost look with a compassionate eye, the snares of the worldly life are destroyed for him; Thou dost wean him from his worldly affairs, and eventually dost give him final deliverance. 3. Even the thousand-hooded Shesha is at a loss for words in the endeavour to describe Thy generosity. The talent of a great poet is wearied. There I am a mere gnat. 4. But the way of love is like this. Children speak to their mother in words without meaning, but she is not sorry at hearing them. On the other hand on account of her own affection she is pleased. 5. So also out of compassion, the Life of the world should accept my uncouth language. This is the only gift I ask of Thee, through Thy own inspiration, O merciful One.

GOD'S POWER SUPREME

6. Clouds obtain water from the ocean; rivers take the rain-water and pour into the ocean; then what obligation can there be when the thing is returned to Him to whom it belongs? 7. If the sun is to be seen, it is to be seen by its own light. In the same way, O Lord of the Heart, the power to praise Thee is not ours. 8. We bow down to the earth and the weight of our body falls also on the earth; likewise, to praise Thee, we have no independent power. 9. If we praise the wind it is through its power that we

breathe; in the same way Thou dost cause Thy own deeds to be uttered by my tongue. 10. If we wave incense over fire, it is through the power of the fire that the smoke comes up; in the same way it is through Thy power that the mind becomes quiet and Thy deeds are spoken. 11. If *abhisheka* (sprinkling water on a deity by reciting Vedic hymns) is made on the Ganges, the water taken for that purpose is taken from the Ganges itself; likewise it is through Thy inspiration that the poets speak in various ways. 12. When the moon rises it is visible by its own light. If a mother is served, the server's own body has come from her. 13. We sit under a wish-tree and water it by our imagination. A wise person feels shy to talk of his obligation. 14. Through Thy power, O Husband of Rukmini, the *Vedas* have praised Thee without limit; but after profound thought the *Vedas* said; '*Neti, Neti*' ('It is not that; it is not that').

TUKARAM'S PLEADING FOR INSPIRATION

15. Thou, O *Adhokshaja* (God), dost know the innermost secret of Thy *bhaktas*. Now grant me a boon and say 'Fear not' and cause me to relate the stories of Thy *bhaktas*. 16. At the close of the previous chapter the Husband of Rukmini went to Dehu and in a *sagun* form met Tuka lovingly. 17. The Life of the world was pleased and said, 'Ask for some boon and I will give thee such a boon as even Brahmadeva cannot obtain despite His effort.' 18. Tuka replied, 'That I should never forget Thee, that I should always sing of Thy deeds with a loving heart; 19. that I should for ever have the company of Thy loving *bhaktas*: this is the gift I ask for. Do not disappoint me, O merciful One. 20. That I should have love for Thy worship. I do not want a fortune. Thou mayest offer the four kinds of salvation; but I do not care for these. 21. An uninterrupted company of saints;

and Thy name ever on the tip of my tongue. If I have these, even rebirth will always be acceptable. 22. This is the only boon I ask for, O Husband of Rukmini.' Saying this he bowed down to God. The Lord of *Vaikunth* (Vishnu's heaven) wondered as He heard this.

23. The Friend of His *bhaktas* said to Garud, 'The loving Tuka is indifferent to worldly things, unattached to them and full of love. He has abandoned everything and he worships only. 24. On account of the pain of My separation from him, he has given up even food and water. Therefore his body is emaciated.' 25. On this the Son of Vinata (Garud) said, 'In Thy letter Thou hast given him the blessing that as long as *Vaiknuth* (Vishnu's heaven) and *Kailas* (Shiva's heaven) exist, Tuka shall live. 26. O Lord of *Vaikunth*, Thy promise will never prove untrue. Then why art Thou so sad at seeing him so emaciated? It is only out of Thy love for him. 27. As his mind is absorbed in Thy worship, he has overcome *Kali* (the Dark Age) and *Kāl* (god of death). He is truly the *avatar* of Nama. The saints know this secret. 28. He has worshipped Thee through several of his former births, and steadying and concentrating his mind has made Thee his own and sings lovingly of Thy deeds.'

29. On this the Lord of the world said to Tuka, 'I am very hungry. Without eating anything I hurriedly started to meet you. 30. Whatever food is ready in your house bring it on a plate. Don't you hesitate to bring it as it is, either dry or with sauce.' 31. The readers are likely to raise the question as to why *Chakrapani* (Vishnu) came hungry even when Rukmini was near. 32. Tuka intended to feed the god, and knowing it the Lord of Pandhari said so. For the Lord of the lowly does a thing by which the desire of His *bhakta* is fulfilled. 33. Then Tuka fetched water and washed the lotus-feet of the god; and at once

put around its neck a garland of tender tulsi leaves. 34. Then with great love he bowed to Him, and brought food on a plate, and dry bread with some vegetable and salt. 35. The Life of the world ate it with great relish. Good people may have a doubt as to how Narayan (God), the Dweller on the ocean of milk, ate dry and coarse bread. 36. But Shri Hari feels hungry when He finds sincere devotion. He cares for love only, and does not think of caste or race.

GOD CARES FOR LOVE, NOT FOR FOOD

37. The evil-minded Duryodhana had many dainty dishes and was waiting for Shripati to come and dine at his house, but He did not dine there but ate kernels at Vidur's. 38. When Draupadi with sincere devotion was anxiously waiting for Him (in her trouble), He put aside His own plate while dining (at His own palace) and rushed to help her, sat beside her, and asked for at least a twig of the vegetable to eat. 39. The *Yadnya Purusha* (Vishnu, the Lord of sacrifice), who is entirely pure, insisted on eating the food left over by the cowherd boys on their plates. The One dark as cloud also ate with love the fruit tasted by a Bhil woman. 40. So if He ate coarse food at Tuka's house, what wonder can there be? The listener should have no scruples as he hears these stories of old. 41. Well, the Life of the world sat there with Rukmini and dined. Tuka poured water on their hands to wash them and ate the food left over on their plates. 42. Tuka then gave them leaves of Tulsi to clean their mouths, and the Merciful to the lowly, seeing Tuka's love, ate them with great respect. 43. Thus pleased, the Lord of the world therefore said to Tuka, 'Now keep Me in your heart, and do not be sorry at separation from Me. 44. Whenever you call Me, I will meet you in My *sagun* form.' Saying this, *Adhokshaja*

(Vishnu) went away. 45. Tuka ran after Him and placed his head on His lotus-feet. Then *Vanamali* (Vishnu) returned to Pandharpur with Rukmini.

A FASTING BRAHMAN REJECTS TUKARAM'S FAVOUR

46. A Brahman with a desire for skill in reading the *Puranas* sat performing austerities at Alandi. This desire was ever present in his mind. 47. Then Dnyaneshwar said to him in a vision, 'Go at once to Tuka. He will give you a favour with his own hand and thereby your desire will be fulfilled.' 48. The Brahman thought it over and quickly went to Dehu. There he met Tuka and explained to him his heart's desire. 49. Said he, 'I was performing austerities at Alakavati (Alandi); but Dnyandev has sent me to you.' Hearing these words, Tuka was astonished. 50. Thought he, 'I do not possess a store of good deeds that I may spend on his account. Dnyandev has merely created a nuisance for me.' 51. He said to himself, 'This man has no learning in his luck. Therefore Dnyandev through disgust has sent this dogged fellow to me. 52. I am ignorant. I don't know *japa* (muttering God's names), *tapa* (penance) and austerities. Why has Dnyandev given *me* this honour ?' 53. Then he gave the Brahman eleven *abhangs* and a cocoanut and told him, 'When you eat this you will at once gain knowledge.' 54. The Brahman's mind was suspicious and he thought, 'Eating a cocoanut will not bring knowledge, and of what good to *me* are these *abhangs* written in Marathi ?' 55. With this suspicion in mind the unlucky fellow threw these away and went off; as if one should come across a wish-jewel, but sling it away as a mere pebble. 56. If an unlucky fellow finds a store of wealth, it appears to him as charcoal. A patient finds dainty foods bitter. 57. A drunkard considers any bottle containing the water of the Bhagirathi (the Ganges) as a

bottle containing wine. A poverty-stricken person will discard a grove of wish-trees. 58. In the same way, the Brahman threw away Tuka's favour then and there. Tuka then wrote and sent this letter to Dnyanraja of Alakavati (Alandi): 59. ' You have honoured an insignificant person such as I am, and have sent a fasting Brahman to me. I took your command on my head and at once gave him a favour. 60. But he doubted it and threw away the eleven *abhangs* and the cocoanut and walked off.' 61. This message which he had already planned in his mind he sent to Alandi. Then bringing *Hrishikeshi* (the Lord of the heart) into his mind, he began to repeat His names.

THE SAME FAVOUR TRANSFORMS A DULLARD

62. King Shivaji had in his service a person well versed in the *Shastras* and *Puranas.* This person had as his servant a Brahman who was a great dullard and ignorant. 63. He once came to Tukoba and bowed down to him. The noble *Vaishnava* took up the same cocoanut and gave it to him. 64. He also gave him the eleven *abhangs* which he had already written out. The Brahman cracked the cocoanut and ate the kernel then and there with love. 65. As he returned home he found that a *Purana* was being read. Among the audience were learned men well versed in the *Vedas* and *Shastras.* 66. There were other knowing and clever persons who listened to the reading. Just then the Brahman entered and addressed the reader: 67. ' You have not explained the words of the verse which you read just now. ' As the learned men repeated the question all others thought that he was quite right. 68. They exclaimed, ' This is really a great wonder for he does not even know his *a. b. c.* We are at a loss to understand how he should so suddenly understand the meaning of the *Puranas.* ' 69. On being asked to explain, he told the whole story in detail. Said he, ' Tuka gave me eleven

abhangs and a cocoanut. 70. As soon as I cracked it and ate the kernel of it, I could understand Sanskrit.' As the audience heard him they were wonder-struck. 71. Then the reader kindly asked him to come near him, and handing him a leaf of the book, said, 'Read this to us, then only shall we have clear evidence of what you say.' 72. Then in his mind bowing down to Tuka's feet, he began to explain the meaning of the *Purana*, at which the learned men in the audience were wonder-struck. 73. Said they, 'The doings of Vishnu's *bhaktas* are wonderful. They can make possible the impossible. With undivided love they have made *Chakrapani*(Vishnu) their own. 74. Like an actor in a play, Bhagwant (God) creates a mountain out of a mustard seed. The life of His *bhaktas* whom He loves passes all wonder.'

BRAHMANS OF CHINCHWAD SEND FOR TUKARAM

75. The wonderful news that a dullard had gained knowledge reached Dev at Chinchwad. The Brahmans then assembled together and naturally spoke to one another. 76. 'We censure Tuka out of pride. He should not be called a man, to be sure.' 77. Someone said, 'Let us call him here some day and ask him to explain who he really is. 78. He is a loving worshipper of the Brahmans. He will at once explain to us.' Thus the Brahmans of Chinchwad thought. 79. Then they hired a man and told him to go to Dehu and bring Tuka to Chinchwad at once. 80. They said, 'Tell him that Dev has called him to Chinchwad.' Hearing this the man went immediately. 81. Then he went to Dehu and prostrated himself before Tuka. There a praise-service of Hari was going on and many good people had gone there to listen. 82. With loving devotion and great regard men and women were listening. The sky was filled with the loud sound of God's names. The audience became bodily

unconscious. 83. No one thought of his worldly affairs. Even the eyelids did not close. The mind was absorbed in the name and form of God. All felt deep satisfaction. 84. The players of cymbals and drums forgot themselves. Every kind of distinction was lost. Love for God alone was in every mind. 85. Even the torch-bearer had lost bodily consciousness. His mind was engrossed in the name and form of God. He forgot to think of himself. 86. As he raised his torch it touched the canopy.

SHEKH MUHAMMAD EXTINGUISHES A DISTANT FIRE

Here another story begins. May the wise listen to it with due respect. 87. In Chambhargonde there lived the well known Shekh Muhammad. He was performing a *kirtan* with great delight for his love of God's name. He was an ocean of knowledge. 88. Men of all the eighteen castes, great and small, sat there to listen. There were also learned and rich persons, very wise and knowing Brahmans. 89. With concentrated mind all listened. The performance was exceptionally delightful and unbelievers could not find a word of contradiction. They became perfectly silent. 90. Just then the performer jumped and rubbed the canopy with his hands. All wondered at this strange sight. 91. Then those who sat in front asked. 'Why did you rub the canopy, O *Swami*? 92. Seeing this strange action, our mind is confused?' Then Shekh Muhammad explained: 93. 'At Dehu the *Vaishnava* Tuka is performing a *kirtan* in love. No one noticed that the burning torch had touched the canopy. 94. I saw it on fire, and I extinguished it from here.' On hearing this the listeners felt dubious. 95. No one could believe it and they said, 'The town of Dehu is very far from here. How did you get the news of the distant fire? 96. There also must be there a crowd of listeners. Could *they* not notice it? How do you say that you put out the fire in the canopy?

97. Then Shekh Muhammad replied, 'There were men listening to the *kirtan* of Tuka, but while they listened to the life deeds of Hari they forgot themselves. 98. Their minds were absorbed in the name and form of God and all were in a subconscious state. The torch touched the canopy and set it on fire, and I at once put it out.' 99. On this the listeners asked, 'In the *kirtan* there was the Lord of Pandhari. Why did He not avoid this accident when he saw the canopy burning? 100. Shekh Muhammad replied, '*Hrishikeshi* (the Lord of the heart) forgot Himself through love. He did not think of His divine state and *bhaktas* forgot their state. 101. Both had become one. So who was to protect, and whom? When two lamps are burning they do not appear to be different. 102. When they live in one place they mingle one with the other. This state of their unconsciousness I could mentally understand. 103. If there are two islands in a river the stream is divided in two. Afterward when they join, no difference is visible. 104. The idol of a god and the utensils of worship are made of the same brass. If they are melted in a crucible, no difference is seen. 105. If clarified butter and any other butter are boiled in one pan, no difference is noticed. 106. So when God and His *bhaktas* become one, who is to know another's pain? On account of this identity of essence, there is joy eternal, and differences sink. 107. The Husband of Rukmini forgot His divine state and Tuka no longer thought himself to be a *bhakta*. The same was the condition of the listeners. I understood this state. 108. If you do not believe what I say, then send someone to Dehu to bring the news.' The listeners considered this reply as satisfactory. 109. Then they wrote a letter to the *Patil* (village officer) of Dehu and sent it by a camel-rider. In the letter they said, ' Please explain at full length the marvel we saw last night.' 110. At sunset the

reply came, 'At night as the *kirtan* was going on with full din, the torch touched the canopy and set it on fire. 111. It made a very large hole in it, but no one knew of it that night. In the morning it was noticed. This made all wonder.' 112. As they read this letter, they considered Shekh Muhammad's explanation as true. Then going to him they prostrated themselves before him. 113. Said they, 'How you could understand the wonderful miracle at Dehu astonished us all very much. It is really a matter for wonder.' 114. At this he said, 'How can I explain this to you? Fish swim straight up the stream which is impossible for others. 115. There are many water animals but none can course through water as fish can. In like manner the secret of a *bhakta* is not understood by anyone else but a man of real devotion. 116. Ants alone can pass along the path that they know. So the secret of a *Vaishnava* is known only by one endowed with sincere devotion. 117. How can the path of a bird's flight be determined in the sky? Birds alone fly that way. Others do not at all understand. 118. The frogs which are accustomed to live in a well, do they know what an ocean is? So the secret of a *guru* and his *bhaktas*, the worldly-wise can never comprehend.' 119. Saying these words, Shekh Muhammad was silent.

MANY MESSENGERS GO FROM CHINCHWAD: NONE RETURN

120. Now to resume our story partly related some time ago. Let the listeners pay attention to it. The man who had come from Chinchwad sat listening to Tuka's *kirtan*. 121. His devotion became fixed there and he forgot to deliver the message. Therefore he did not think of any worldly affairs, for his heart felt so happy. 122. He did not think of returning home. As he lovingly beheld Tuka he became absorbed in his *kirtan*. 123. At Chinchwad, Dev was waiting for his return. Said he, 'It is

many days, but neither Tuka nor the messenger has come back. I cannot say what has happened to him. ' 124. Then the men (the Chinchwad Brahmans) sent another messenger. He also happened to listen to Tuka's *kirtan* and fell into the same subconscious state. 125. When after a further long delay he too did not return, a third man was sent. But he also lost regard for his body and his heart was full of love. 126. Then all the worshippers of *Gajavadana* (Ganpati) wondered and exclaimed, ' Three men went to Dehu, but none returned.' 127. As streamlets on joining the Ganges forget their former state; or as fragrance from various flowers identifies itself in essence with the wind; 128. when a wave is united with water, or a cloud disappears in the sky, or as borax in a crucible, these never appear again in their original forms; 129. such was the state of the messengers; they did not come back at all to report the result of their mission. As they listened to the loving *kirtan* of Tuka they were lost in it. 130. Had they but delivered the message to Tuka, he would not have hesitated to come; for no better worshipper of Brahmans, or better *Vaishnava* or knowing one, could be found than he.

CHINCHWAD BRAHMANS AND TUKARAM MEET

131. They (the Chinchwad Brahmans) thought among themselves, ' Now we must abandon all pride of caste, and visiting him tell him the secret of our heart, and have our doubts cleared.' 132. Thus thinking the Brahmans started for Dehu. Tuka, without any one telling him of this, knew it mentally. 133. Said he, ' The Brahmans sent messengers, but none of them gave me the message. Now they themselves are kindly coming to meet me. 134. If I do not go from here to meet them, it is insulting them. For the Husband of Lakshmi (Vishnu) wears as an ornament the impression of a Brahman's kick [Bhrigu's kick] on His breast. 135. Before they reach this place, I must

start.' Saying this in his mind he quickly started. 136. Just as when a *chatak* bird is thirsty, the clouds immediately come to it; or just as the ocean rises up at the sight of the full moon; 137. or when seeing a beautiful bit of diamond dust, a diamond comes up from the anvil [see also chapter 13 verse 204]; both give evidence of their attachment for one another; 138. because of the attraction of the magnet the particles of iron go to it; similarly Tuka knew at heart the great love of the Brahmans for him. 139. Therefore the *bhakta* of Vishnu at once started. On his way he loudly sang with great love the deeds of Shri Hari. 140. After travelling half the way he suddenly noticed the noble Brahmans coming towards him and Tuka prostrated himself before them.

141. On this the earth-gods (Brahmans) said, 'You are without doubt Vishnu's *bhakta*, therefore with a desire to see you we were coming. 142. But our desire is fulfilled just here.' So saying, they gave him a loving embrace and took their seats. Listen to what they said to Tuka: 143. 'You have assumed an *avatar* in the *Kali Yuga* and displayed an unprecedented character. We have witnessed this with our own eyes, at which we simply wonder. 144. Taking advantage of an opportunity, we have come to ask you privately as to who you are. Please explain to us.' 145. Hearing this speech of the Brahmans, he thought to himself, 'Unless I give them evidence, their doubt will not disappear.' 146. Then catching hold of the skin of his thigh, he ripped it open then and there. Inside there was pure, carded cotton. 147. At this sight the Brahmans wondered inwardly and said, 'We are at a loss to understand how Tuka lives as a man. 148. How can life be supported without flesh and blood?' One said, 'It is a work of *maya* (illusion). God's doing cannot be fathomed. 149. The jugglery of the five elements

through the love of worldly life has made men crazy for earthly enjoyments, and this craziness in men increases the love of the earthly life. 150. Tuka, who is Vishnu's *bhakta*, is beyond this. We knew this from experience. He cannot be called an ordinary man. He is really the *guru* of the world as an *avatar*. 151. The water of the Ganges should not be called ordinary. *Paris* (the touchstone) is not an ordinary pebble. Gold should not be compared with other metals. 152. The wish-tree is not a simple tree; the ocean is not a tank and Mount Meru is not to be compared with other mountains. 153. Garud, Vishnu's *bhakta*, was born from a species of bird. So this *Vaishnava* was born in a *Sudra* caste. But this is a poor simile. 154. Garud became Vishnu's vehicle, and thereby his body became pure. Tuka performs *Hari-kirtan*, and fully saves the dull and ignorant. 155. In future by listening to his poems, *Vairagya* (the ascetic spirit) will arise in the minds of evil men. He has shown a clear path to the ascetic *bhaktas*.' 156. Saying this the noble Brahmans bowed down to Tuka. He raised up their hands and fell at their feet. 157. He said to the Brahmans, ' This is not proper for you. Our Lord (Vishnu) still wears on his chest the impression of Bhrigu's kick. 158. You are fit to be worshipped even by the God of gods, the life of the world. Out of mercy you glorify me. In fact I am low-born and humble.' 159. On this the noble Brahmans replied, ' To call one who is lovingly devoted to Vishnu's worship as of a low caste is not right. For in praising Him, even the *Vedas* became wearied. 160. Monkeys worshipped Shri Ram; and therefore Valmiki has described them in his *Ramayana*. Shri Vyasa has written down in the *Bhagwat Purana* the glorious deeds of the cowherd lads. 161. Therefore we have a right to praise you. For the wonderful fame of Vishnu-*bhaktas* has more than filled the three worlds. 162. For a long time we have had a desire to see you and to-day it is fulfilled. You ripped open your thigh and gave us evidence.' 163. Then the Brahmans embraced Tuka and said, 'Please come to Chinchwad and perform a *kirtan* there some night.' 164. In order to show respect to their desire, Tuka went into the town (of Chinchwad) for a night.

Meanwhile the people of Lohagaon thought among themselves, 165. 'We should bring Tuka into *our* town and listen to his *kirtans* to our heart's content. If we drink the waves of love-nectar, our worldly life will be fruitful.' 166. Then they humbly approached Tuka, took him to Lohagaon, and with love always listened to his *Hari-kirtan*. 167. The pious and good people fed the Brahmans with many daintily cooked foods. 168. They erected a beautiful canopy. They worshipped the *Vaishnava* Tuka with garlands of flowers and fragrant sandal paste.

THE DESPONDENT *HARIDAS* AT LOHAGAON HELPED

169. For a month in Lohagaon every day there was a festival during which a *Haridas* from Pandharpur was going to collect money, there (at Lohagaon). 170. At that time a merchant was going into the bazaar on his horse. The *Haridas* accosted him. 171. You are travelling on a horse and we wonder how you can sleep here! 172. In reply the merchant said, 'Tuka has performed *kirtans* for a whole month and we were awake during the four watches of the night.' 173. When the *Haridas* heard this he felt anxious and said, 'I must not go into Lohagaon at all. 174. Where a *kirtan* of the God-loving (Tuka) is being performed, there the people will not like *my* skill; for a patient will never accept a drug when he can obtain divine nectar. 175. Before the lustre of a diamond the beads of glass do not shine; and at the rise of the sun the light of lamps fades. 176. Where there is the Ganges

flowing close by, who will care for wells ? So also, when one listens to an inspired *kirtan*, he will not like any artificial singing. 177. Let me avoid Lohagaon now and go to some other town. So thinking to himself, the *Haridas* turned back.

178. The people of the town at once went and reported to Tuka the matter which they had witnessed. 179. On hearing this, without a moment's delay he got up and said, 'Let us go to receive the *Haridas* and request him to come into the town.' 180. Tuka walked on hurriedly for joy at heart. The citizens also accompanied him to receive him (the *Haridas*). 181. Said they, 'The *Haridas* of Pandharpur being sad at heart is going away. Let us therefore invite him, and bring him into the town.' 182. Then they sent runners ahead and got him to turn back. He was told that the *Vaishnava* Tuka was coming to meet him in love. 183. As he heard this message he at once returned. Then Tuka bowed to the *Haridas* and embraced him. 184. The inhabitant of the sacred town (the *Haridas* from Pandharpur) said, 'I am going to get money. In the coming month of *Vaishakh* (May) I have to marry my son.' 185. 'Very well,' they said, and took the *Haridas* back into the town where he was given good lodging and also provisions of food. 186. After dinner at night he perfromed a *Hari-kirtan*. This went on for a month, and all felt joyful.

187. Then the *Vaishnava* Tuka ordered the pious citizens to raise a subscription for the *Haridas* and to see him off. 188. 'You may think it a matter of glory first to accept the labours of a Brahman and then to pay him for his labour, but thereby you do not acquire any store of good deeds. 189. There are citizens in this town, both rich and poor; raise money from them according to their ability.' 190. Hearing this command of Tuka, they

agreed. Then taking an inkpot, pen and paper, they wrote down names. 191. There were three sorts of people in the town, the best, the medium, and the ordinary type, and they requested Tuka to write figures against their names. 192. Tuka at once put one rupee against the best, eight annas against the middle men, and four annas against the ordinary. 193. The citizens did not agree to this, so Tuka told them to do as they pleased. 194. They themselves then wrote five rupees against the best and three rupees against the middle ones. 195. Only four annas had been charged the ordinary men but this amount was changed to one rupee. They showed the list to Tuka and got up at once. 196. Going into the town they raised the money. Then the chief citizens 197. piled the money before Tuka in a heap and said, 'Did not we adopt a good plan? Now pay the *Haridas* yourself.'

PRIDE OF DONORS EXPOSED BY TUKA

198. As they said this, Tuka knew in his mind that the demon of egoism had taken possession of their hearts. 199. It was as if a fly should fall into dainty food, or a bit of salt into milk, or as if a crooked-minded person should come and sit amongst the devoted; 200. or as if one should have tuberculosis in youth, or as if a Mang should enter an assembly of Brahmans, or as if one indifferent to worldly things should come in contact with a woman on account of some bad deeds done in his former birth; 201. or as if a swarm of locusts should fall suddenly upon a field at the point of ripening; or as if disease should attack the later crops in the month of *Margeshvar* (December); 202. or as when showers of rain are noticed in the sky but a sudden South wind should sweep them away; or as when the full moon rises it should be eclipsed by Rahu (darkness); 203. so, as the people

gave money in charity, pride their enemy occupied their hearts. Tuka thought of a remedy to destroy it. 204. The *Vaishnava bhakta* said to them, 'You have raised the money but be careful that you do not have any town-citizen out of the list.' 205. The people then said, 'There is a very poor weaver who is a reviler, a villain and very wicked. He has no love at heart whatsoever. 206. He alone is left out of the list. Others have given as their ability permitted them.' On this the loving *bhakta* said, 207. 'You go to his house and tell him from me, that you are to get from him the smallest coin which he can spare in charity.' 208. They wondered as they heard Tuka say this. Then they went to the house of the weaver and stood in his yard. 209. But he did not speak with them. He was engaged in warping. He did not ask them as to who they were or why they had come. 210. The citizens in wonder looked at one another and made signs to indicate that they had come to a fool just out of regard to Tuka. 211. Said they, 'A *Haridas* from Pandharpur has come here and has performed *kirtans* for a month. 212. Tuka has sent us to you to ask for some money.' At these words the fool was cross. 213. Said he, 'Since Tuka has begun his nonsensical talk, you have been mad. Without regard to public opinion you dance in his *kirtans* openly. 214. You have bid adieu to your worldly affairs. But why do you come to bother me? I have not in my house even a plate or bowl, then what should I give you?' 215. At these words of the fool his wife said to him, 'Out of regard for Tuka's words these great man have come and stood in our yard. 216. You are a great reviler and a villain. You never speak sweet words. At your house the visitors do not get even a clean seat. 217. Now have some consideration, and give them something.' Hearing his wife, the fool flew into a rage. 218. Angrily he said, There is a pot in our house. Give it them at once and send them away.' 219. Hearing her husband, the wife felt comforted. Then she brought a water-pot and cleaning it handed it to him. 220. He gave it with his left hand (Indian symbol of an evil heart) but in their hearts the men considered it a gain. They at once took the pot and left the place. 221. All began to wonder and said, 'This villain is pleased. It is as if a forest fire should cool, or the *sher* tree should bear fruit. 222. To-day a dry wood has sprouted, a stone is wet with perspiration. *Rahu* (darkness) has become white and thrown its light on the world. 223. It was just like this when the villain showed so much generosity.' One of them said, 'It was because our luck was favourable.' 224. In this way conversing between themselves they returned quickly to Tuka. They placed the water-pot before him and bowed to him. 225. Looking at it the noble *Vaishnava* said to the people, 'The weaver is very generous. He has subscribed largely.' 226. Then he took the pot in his hand, and said, 'This is a gold pot. You did not know it. Unless you test it you will not know.' 227. The men said, 'This pot is only of pure brass. It was rubbed clean and therefore it *looks* like gold.' 228. But as they heated it in fire they found it to be pure gold. At this wonderful sight all were amazed. 229. They said, 'The doings of (this) saint are indescribable. He has rid the brass vessel of its impurity. His love for worship cannot be described. It is incomparable.'

230. Then the *Haridas* was sent for. His feet were washed, garlands of flowers were put around his neck, and clothes were given to him and his party. 231. Then the citizens placed before him the money collected by them, and requesting that it be accepted, all of them bowed to him with respect. 232. Then the *Vaishnava* Tuka said, 'The citizens are very generous. They have collected

this money and have given it to you. 233. There is a poor weaver, an inhabitant of this town, who is supposed to be a first class knave. But he with his heart and soul has given you this gold pot. 234. Please accept this gift which, in fact, is as small as a tulsi leaf. With this you can marry your son.' Saying this he (Tuka) bowed reverently to his feet. 235. The men who were proud to think that they alone were generous, were enraptured as they beheld this wonder. 236. The *Haridas* was greatly satisfied and left for Pandharpur at once; and the God-loving Tuka, indifferent to all worldly things, returned to Dehu. 237. Without regard to worldly honour, he contemplated *Adhokhshaja* (Vishnu) in his mind. In his sight the indigent, the helpless and the king were alike.

TUKARAM'S MYSTIC-MANTRA AND GURU-LINEAGE

238. One day this loving *bhakta* was taking a nap when he had a vision. O pious listeners. hear what the dream was. 239. As Tuka (in his dream was going to the Indrayani to bathe, the Lord of Pandhari assumed the dress of a Brahman and suddenly met him. 240. Tuka as he saw him prostrated himself before him. Then the Lord of the heart placed His hand on his head mercifully (i. e., gave him the mystic *mantra*). 241. As he received the message he bowed to the Brahman and requested him, 'Come to my house to dine with love.' 242. The Brahman said to Tuka, 'I want a quarter seer of ghee. If you promise to give me that, I will come to your house at once.' 243. 'Granted,' said Tuka and holding him by his hand he brought him home and said to his wife, 244. 'The Brahman has not eaten anything. He is hungry. So give him provisions of food and a quarter seer of ghee every day with a loving heart.' 245. As she heard these words she flew into a rage and said, 'Where have you brought the Brahman from, and how am I to give

him ghee ? 246. At this angry reply of his wife, the Holder of the *Sharang* bow (Krishna), who is as an actor in a play and the Lord of all, vanished out of sight. 247. After having experienced this dream, Tuka awoke. Love for God could not be contained in his heart. This wonderful sight was without comparison. 248. Said he, 'The Lord *Sadguru* has done me a favour. But I have had no occasion to serve him. He found me as I was going to bathe in the Indrayani. 249. He placed his hand on my head and asked for a quarter-seer of ghee. But seeing a quarrel in my house he at once went away. 250. My *Sadguru* described to me his ancestral line: Keshava Chaitanya, Raghava Chaitanya; and gave his own name as Babaji Chaitanya. 251. He gave me the favourite mystic *mantra*: *Rama-Krishna-Hari*, which the Enemy of the demon Tripur (Shiva) constantly repeats in love. 252. The day was Thursday, the bright tenth of *Magha* (February) when I was so favoured, and then the *Sadguru* went away.' 253. In such a faith he lovingly worshipped *Hari*, and at night with delight and devotion performed *kirtans*. 254. The fortunate people were enraptured as they heard the various illustrations and the pleasing and inspired poems. 255. They said. 'He is not a common man. He is God's *avatar*. Through him the Husband of Rukmini saves the world.

TUKARAM'S ABHANGS THROWN INTO THE RIVER

256. As Tuka's reputation was thus increasing, the evil-minded were burning inwardly with rage. They said, 'Leaving aside the path of the *Shastras* he is preaching heterodox principles. 257. He has destroyed the *Karma Marg* (law of works) and made pious people worship God through the *Bhakti Marg* (law of love.) Excepting *Bhakti* (love) he does not utter anything else.' 258. The evil-minded determined to tie in a cloth all his manuscripts of poetry and threw them into the water; 259. just as seeing

the image of *Shaligrama* (Vishnu), the Muhammadans burn with anger at heart and with an evil intention think of breaking it; 260. as a parrot sits in his cage, singing the praise of Rama, but hearing such words, a hawk flies into a rage. 261. Ambarisha, on account of his observance of the *Ekadashi* (the 11th day of every fortnight), obtained great fame, but Durvas became jealous of him and came to persecute him; 262. in the same way the evil-minded entered Tuka's house and said, 'You teach principles contrary to religion and lead people to accept *bhakti* (the law of love). 263. That language of yours is Marathi and therefore impure. It should never be heard'. Saying this the villains took away with force his manuscripts of *abhangs*. 264. They made them into a bundle and put stones into it, and taking it to the bank of the River Indrayani they sank it in the river. 265. The Brahmans said, ' If within thirteen days the Life of the world takes them out dry, then only we shall honour them. ' 266. Having said this they went to their houses. But Tuka's heart was full of grief; 267. just as when one makes a bottle of glass and it gets broken; or as when a folded silk cloth takes fire; 268. or as when a *bakul* tree is cut down by a goatherd and the gardener grieves at its loss; such was the condition of Tuka. 269. As a generous person feels sad when he sees wells filled up with earth in a forest without water; or as a *Vaishnava bhakta* feels sad at the destruction of Tulsi plants by a goat; 270. or as the cooking woman feels grieved when a dog touches daintily cooked food; 271. or as the jeweller is sad at heart when one throws a pearl into the fire thinking it to be a pebble; 272. in the same way Tuka's heart felt when the villains threw his manuscripts into the river. This mighty calamity was a severe blow to his love of God. 273. Tuka went into the temple and sat at the main door persistently, just as the stone step before the door knows not how to stir. 274. Tuka cried, 'O Lord of Pandhari, Merciful to the lowly, why didst Thou cause me to labour for nothing? At last Thou didst permit this distress, the sinking of my manuscripts into the water. 275. Thou *Vanamali* (Krishna) didst appear to me in a dream and didst order and inspire me, ignorant as I was, to write the remaining verses of Namdev. 276. This being so, O Husband of Rukmini, why hast Thou brought this calamity on me? Well, do whatever Thou desirest, O Lord of Pandhari.' 277. Saying this, he contemplated Hari's form in his mind, and with his mouth repeated the mystic *mantra*, *Rama-Krishna-Hari*, with a heart full of love. 278. He ate no fruit, root, or any other food, and talked to no one. He gave up all desire and hope for his body and did not even drink water. 279. When the Life of the World saw Tuka in such extreme distress, He assumed the beautiful *Sagun* form of a child and the Husband of Rukmini came to console him. 280. He placed His assuring hand on his head and said, 'Quiet your mind. I, the Holder of the *Sharang* bow (Vishnu), will rid you of any grievous calamity.' 281. Saying this He whose complexion is as dark as the *Tamal* leaf disappeared. Perhaps he found the pure lotus-heart of Tuka a fit place to sit upon. 282. *Chakrapani* (Krishna) disappeared just then and was happy. I think it was in the evening.

TUKARAM'S MANUSCRIPTS RECOVERED

283. In this way thirteen days passed, and lo and behold! the revilers saw the manuscripts of Tuka floating on the water and the water had not touched the writing. 284. They said, 'We have unknowingly wronged and persecuted a *bhakta* of Vishnu. But the Life of the World is his Helper and He has freed him from this calamity 285. With a repentant heart they went to the main door

of the temple, and said to Tuka, 'Shri Hari is pleased with you. 286. Your papers have come up dry. Now open your eyes and see.' Saying this, all the men bowed to him, 287. and added, 'What can we do to a man whose helper is the Husband of Rukmini? In a bottle of nectar, diseases cannot enter. 288. Into the abode of the sun, darkness will have no entrance. Into the lunar circle, heat cannot find a way. 289. Likewise, calamity will have no effect on a Vishnu-*bhakta*, even with great effort.' In this way, talking between themselves, they sang the names of God. 290. Tuka opened his eyes, and saw his manuscripts which the Brahmans had brought to the temple dry. 291. At this wonderful sight his mind was consoled; as the mind of a blind man is enraptured on obtaining his sight; 292. or as on pouring nectar into the mouth of a corpse, it breathes and sits up; so was Tuka delighted at heart and exclaimed, 'The Dweller of Pandhari has favoured me.' 293. He joined his hands, and uttered seven *abhangs*. That incomparable pleasure of love can hardly be described. 294. But listen to the purport of it with love. Tuka shut his eyes and overcome with love at heart he said, 295. 'Victory, Victory, O Shri Vitthal, I am a great sinner. In regard to people's censure I put my burden on Thee. 296. I gave Thee a great deal of trouble. I am a sinner, and low-born. I closed my eyes and sat at Thy door for thirteen days. 297. O Shri Hari, I put the distress of hunger and thirst on Thee. O Murari (Vishnu), Thou didst sit in the temple of my heart and didst preserve me, 298. Thou didst keep dry the papers and didst avert the public censure. O merciful One, Thou hast proved to be true Thy proud title, "The Helper of the helpless". 299. Assuming the form of a child, O Husband of Rukmini, Thou didst console me and with Thy own hand didst give me an assurance. 300. Now let them cut my throat and let the wicked heap calamities on me; but never, never will I put Thee to trouble.'

TUKARAM PLEADS FOR PARDON

301. 'As for me, I am very wicked, impure and a sinner. I have certainly erred for once on this occasion. I made Thee stand in the water to protect my manuscripts. 302. I had no right to put my burden on Thee, the All-powerful. I a sinner did not know this, and acted without consideration. 303. O Shripati, what is done cannot be undone. But in future, O Husband of Rukmini, I will not put Thee to trouble. 304. O Shri Hari, I created trouble for Thee before anyone had placed a knife on my throat, or before I received a blow on my back. 305. Thy mind was divided in two places, in me and in the river. Thou didst avoid both the calamities, and hast increased my reputation in the public. 306. Should I say that Thou didst act as parents ! Nay, for they, even for a less' cause, would kill their child. I have acted horribly: still Thou, O Life of the world, didst help me. 307. O *Chakrapani* (Vishnu), Thou art an Ocean of mercy. I do not see anyone like Thee in the three worlds. If I mean to praise Thee with love, my tongue becomes wearied. 308. Thou art the Brother of the helpless and merciful. Thou art cooler than the moon and as kind as a mother. Waves of love rise in me. 309. Thou art beyond speech, O Lord of gods. I find no simile befitting Thee. Thou art the Life of all beings. Shiva became quiet on muttering Thy name. 310. Thou art the source of the five chief elements. If I should say that Thou art as sweet as nectar, it is nothing. Thou, O Life of the world, art beyond it. 311. I will not say anything now. Silently will I place my head at Thy feet. I am a sinner without limit, O Vithabai. Pardon me, O loving One. 312. I am full of bad qualities and very unrighteous. How often shall

I say, "Enough, enough of this worldly life." It does not let my heart rest. 313. Scruples without end arise in my mind. Their forms change every moment. If I come in contact with them, my mind gets fastened on them. 314. O God of gods, O Lord of Pandhari, destroy all my anxiety. O Limitless One, put an end to the snare of my destiny, and dwell in the temple of my heart.'

315. In this way Tuka pleaded with the Husband of Rukmini. Then going into the inner apartment of the temple, he embraced the god. 316. His eyes were fixed on the *Sagun* form of God. With his lips he was repeating the names of God.

TUKARAM'S SPIRITUAL INFLUENCE

Then (later) Tuka went to *Vaikunth* (Vishnu's heaven) with his body. 317. If I intend to write in detail that story, the Husband of Rukmini who is in my heart tells me, 'Tukaram still lives in this world.' 318. He visits his devoted and loving *bhaktas* in their dreams just as Dattatreya, the son of Anasuya, roams on earth at His will. 319. If the saints and good men doubt this, they should hear as evidence that he (Tuka) favoured Niloba with the mystic *mantra* in his dream. 320. If one's heart has pure love then Tukaram gives him the mystic *mantra*. That *guru* of the world is without comparison and still living. 321. He favoured me in solitude and caused me to write this work. Let not the wise entertain a doubt about this. 322. Tukaram, who pervades the whole universe and is a cloud of intelligence, is my *Sadguru*. I, Mahipati, am his sole suppliant without regard to my body.

323. *Swasti* (Peace)! This book is the *Shri Bhaktavijaya*. Hearing it the Lord of the world will be pleased. Listen to it, O pious and loving *bhaktas*. This is the fifty-second very delightful chapter; it is an offering to Shri Krishna.

CHAPTER LIII

MANKOJI BODHLA THE *PATIL* OF DHAMANGAON

Obeisance to Shri Ganesh. Obeisance to the Lord of the three Worlds.

GOD AS CONTROLLER OF THE UNIVERSE

1. Victory to Thee, Ornament of the universe, Feeder of the universe. Thou art beyond *maya*, O Saviour of the World. Assumer of a *sagun* form, unchangeable, generous in giving the final deliverance, O *Guru* of the World! 2. Victory, victory to Thee, Controller of the wheel of *maya*, Wearer of a yellow silk garment, Lord of *Vaikunth* (Vishnu's heaven), Father of the Lord of creation (Brahmadeva), the Saviour of the *Vedas*, O Pandurang. 3. O Lord of the world, Thou art alike to an elephant and an atom. The gods and Purandar (Indra, Lord of gods) obey Thee. 4. The sun and the moon traverse the sky, but Thou art their Regulator, just as a doll-player pulls the strings and makes the dolls dance. 5. The wind alone puts all trees into motion. Similarly, O Gopal, with Thy skill Thou dost give a turn to the universal globe. 6. The pores of Thy body contain the moveable and immoveable creation, O Lord of the World. It being so, Thou didst stand with Thy hands on Thy hips at the back of Pundalik. 7. Brahmadev and others do not know Thy limit; still Thou dost obey Thy *bhaktas*. Thou dost first throw them into various difficulties and then dost rush in person to their help. 8. Thou dost recline on the serpent Shesha, and on Thy banner is the emblem of the eagle. Lakshmi wishes for the dust of Thy feet. Still Thou dost stand to accept the worship of Thy *bhaktas*. 9. Although *Yogis* practise *vajrasan* (the spiked bed), still they cannot comprehend Thee. Thou dost dance without reserve, in the *kirtans* of

Thy loving *bhaktas.* 10. The lives of these *bhak'as* are wonderful, and Thou dost cause even me to describe them Otherwise I am dull and have no independent talent to sing their praise. 11. In the previous chapter I related the wonderful story as to how the Lord of Pandhari was pleased with Tuka, and kept his papers dry for thirteen days in water.

MANKOJI BODHLA'S PHILANTHROPIC SPIRIT

12. Now let the listeners pay attention to the following interesting story. The saints know in Baleghat that there is the well-known town called Dhamangaon. 13. The *Patil* (official) of the place was Mankoji Bodhla, a loving *bhakta* of God. He was a *Shudra* by caste, and was surnamed 'Jagtap'. 14. Mamatai was his loving and dutiful wife. She did not do anything in her domestic affairs without her husband's consent. 15. Their first son was Yamaji by name and he was indifferent to worldly things. Their daughter-in-law, Bhagirathi, was a mine of good qualities. 16. These four lived in unity. In their domestic affairs they were quite indifferent to worldly things. Day and night they thought of the Lord of Pandhari and sang His praises. 17. In their house there was an abundance of wealth and grain. They were influential and commanded respect. Their cattle-shed was full of cows and oxen. 18. On every *Ekadashi* (11th day of every fortnight), he devotedly went on a pilgrimage to Pandhari without fail. 19. On the sacred twelfth day, he fed the Brahmans and distributed food to the poor and hungry beggars. 20. On the thirteenth day he got up early, and returned to Dhamangaon. In this way many days passed, but finally there was a famine in the land. 21 The famine was very dreadful and grain was six seers a rupee The poor could not afford to buy food. 22. Seeing this dreadful famine, pity arose in Bodhla's heart.

He said, 'The Lord of the world pervades all being. 23. Bodhla took his wife aside and advised her, 'Give food and drink to the poor as our means permit.' 24. To give food to the hungry, water to dry trees, clothes to the poor in the cold season, 25. to give medicine to travellers and sick persons, to pull out a drowning person, to marry a poor Brahman, 26. to save a house on fire, to cremate the dead for whom there is no one to help, to give water to the thirsty, 27. to stroke the weak cattle, to free ensnared game, to speak kindly to beggars, all these are means of storing up imperishable good deeds. 28. Such a possession of good deeds begets righteous indifference to worldly things and takes one to the feet of Shri Ram; and hindrances arising from sensual desires vanish. 29. Many others practise severe austerities. Their good deeds come to an end as soon as their fruit is enjoyed. But indifference to worldly things, arising from doing good to others, is permanent.' 30. In this way Bodhla advised his wife privately. The wife consented and behaved accordingly. 31. Kindly disposed to all beings, she distributed food to the famine-stricken. Her reputation spread in the whole country and beggars came rushing. 32. On a pile of sugar, ants and flies flock. Travellers go running under the shade of trees. 33. Beasts eagerly resort to the water near a mountain; similarly the hungry and thirsty came in large numbers to Bodhla's house. 34. Bodhla loaded his horse with provisions of food, on the tenth day of the fortnight started for Pandhari, and arrived there on the eleventh day and bathed in the Chandrabhaga. 35. With cymbals and *Vina* in his hands he visited the tomb of Pundalik. Then singing loudly the names of Hari he circumambulated the sacred town. 36. Lovingly he prostrated himself at the main door, entered the temple, and with full open eyes looked steadily on the form of God. 37. He embraced the god, and related his heart's secrets like a girl when she returns from her husband's home opens her heart to her mother. 38. He placed his head at the god's feet and performed a *Kirtan* in the audience hall with the full din of delight during the four watches of the night, all awake. 39. He had the cooking performed by Brahmans and gave food to the hungry. Then taking leave of the god he returned home.

BODHLA'S POVERTY AND CONTENTMENT

40. Many days went by in this way and Bodhla spent in charity all his wealth and grain. He sold the jewellery of the house, he gave food to beggars. 41. His cows and oxen had to starve for want of fodder, so he distributed them to the people. In this way he sang the praises of God unhindered. 42. He earned his living by personal labour, and even out of this he gave something to satisfy the persons who came at meal-time, and also maintained his family. 43. Although reduced to poverty, Bodhla did not give up his resolve. With sincere love he pleaded with Govind and sang of His deeds. 44. The Husband of Rukmini was pleased at his devotion and privately manifested Himself to his sight. 45. The God of gods is not seen unless there is love in one's heart. Of what use is knowledge, without love and devotion ? 46. Where there is pride of knowledge, sincerity of mind never comes at all. A grown-up tree does not know how to bend. 47. A grown-up Brahman finds it hard to commit to memory the the hymns of the *Vedas*. A grown-up acrobat finds it difficult to bend his body. 48. When an earthen pot is well baked in fire, it cannot again be reduced to clay. Burnt seeds will never sprout. 49. So on account of knowledge sincerity disappears. Without love and faith *Hrishikeshi* (the Lord of the heart) cannot be attained. 50. Therefore saints disregard pride of knowledge. The wise will never go near a *hivar* tree. 51. If I go on dilating upon the charac-

teristics of saints this book will tremendously increase. Seeing the sincere love of Bodhla, the Lord of Pandhari met him.

BODHLA'S *BHAKTI*

52. On an *Ekadashi* day (the 11th day of a fortnight), Bodhla started on a pilgrimage to Pandhari. He had no money to spend on his journey and his wife became very anxious. 53. 'After I bathe in the Chandrabhaga I shall have no money to give to a Brahman in charity. How can I feed the Brahmans on the twelfth day, O dear wife? 54. But I will fetch firewood and sell it in the bazaar of Pandhari.' Saying this he at once started for Pandhari. 55. His feet were without shoes and his blanket and other clothes were in tatters. He had rags around his head; still he sang the praises of Shri Hari. 56. He exclaimed, 'It is a great comfort that my house is swept clean of fortune. God has removed the snares of *maya* and freed me from earthly affairs. 57. The sky looks fair when clouds melt away. The Ganges flows steadily after mighty floods. 58. In the same way Bodhla's heart became quiet at the loss of his property and with love in his heart he continued to sing God's praises. 59. As he came near Pandhari, he took a load of fuel on his head. and sold it for three pice. 60. With a repentant heart he bathed in the Chandrabhaga. He gave one pice to the Brahman who recited the bath-*mantra*. 61. With another he bought dry dates, the fragrant black powder (*buka*) and garlands of flowers. He then went into the temple and worshipped with love the cloud-complexioned One (Vithoba). 62. At night he listened to the *Hari-kirtan* and was awake during the four watches of the night.

KRISHNA AS A DECREPIT BRAHMAN APPROACHES BODHLA

Then on the twelfth day he sat still with a sad heart. 63. Said he, 'I am unable to-day to give provisions of food to a Brahman.' With three pies he bought half a seer of flour. 64. He tied it in the end of his blanket and sat on the bank of the Chandrabhaga thinking, 'I will consider myself fortunate if a Brahman comes to me. 65. I have no pulse, rice or salt. Who will accept the food of a poor man, when rich men come on pilgrimage and feed Brahmans in large numbers? 66. Who will lodge in a hut, leaving beautiful houses? Diners will not accept sour milk instead of good milk. 67. Why should Brahmans come to me. and set aside their rich patrons?' In this manner in spite of his dejection, he went on singing Shri Hari's praises. 68. The Merciful to the lowly and the Helper of the helpless seeing Bodhla's pure love came to him as a decrepit Brahman. 69. With stick in hand, cap on head and a worn out cloth around His waist, all trembling and in a hurry, the Lord of the world appeared in the sandy bed of the river. 70. The Life of the world said to Bodhla, 'You are my old patron. I live in the sacred town of Pandhari and bless you. 71. There are many other Brahmans who have rich patrons. I am weak and poor, and therefore none cares for me. 72. So, O Bodhla, I am hungry, and have come to see you. Whatever provisions you may have, give them quickly to Me.' 73. Bodhla felt satisfied when he heard the Brahman speak thus, and he said, 'The Husband of Rukmini is pleased with me.' 74. He untied the knot of his blanket, took out the flour and gave it to the Brahman, but at heart he felt abashed. 75. Said he, 'O *Swami*, there is only this flour without pulse or salt.' Listen to what the Dweller in *Vaikunth* replied: 76. 'Whatever you were able to give at this moment, you have given. Pulse and salt are not necessary,' said the One dark as a cloud. 77. Bodhla had a great desire to see the Brahman dine in his presence and the Lord of Pandhari knew this secret of his heart. 78. So the Husband of Rukmini said, 'I live in the temple. There is no room to cook there. 79. If you collect some cowdung cakes for Me, I will prepare cakes just here and eat.' On hearing this, Bodhla was greatly pleased. 80. Then he thought to himself, ' The Brahman, as it were, has expressed my heart's desire;' and in the hollow of his blanket be collected some cowdung cakes.

VITHOBA AND RUKMINI COOK FOR BODHLA

81. The Brahman having bathed he wore a wet and worn-out cloth, and Bodhla brought fire from other pilgrims. 82. The Dweller in *Vaikunth* (Vishnu's heaven), Who is as beautiful as a cloud, and seeing Whose fortune Lakshmi became the slave of His lotus-feet, sat to cook cakes. 83. He to Whom the Rishis in sacrifices give oblations by reciting the *Vedic* hymns, He, for the love of His *bhaktas*, is kneading flour with His own hands. 84. When Rukmini knew this, she came as an old woman to the spot where the Lord of Pandhari was cooking. 85. When the flame of a lamp is lowered, the light becomes dim; when a tree becomes old, creepers on it look yellowish; 86. as the drum is, so is the sound; as the flower, so the fragrance; among the clouds the lightning shines beautifully; 87. the colours suit a picture; the body is in likeness to one's disposition; the bean of *moog* (a sort of grain) grows as thick as the seed; 88. the sky becomes like the season; the river follows the stream; so on this occasion mother Rukmini assumed a likeness to suit her Husband's. 89. She had a mouth without any teeth and had earrings in her ears. She wore ornaments befitting her happy state of wifehood, saffron on her head, 90. and a white and worn-out garment. Supporting herself on her staff and stopping at intervals, she came along the sandy bed to search for the Life of the world. 91. She noticed *Chakrapani* (Krishna) in the act of kneading the flour in a pan and at this the Mother of the world chuckled.

92. 'Your patron has come for the pilgrimage; you left me behind, and have come here to cook all alone. 93. Here I am now to do the cooking.' Saying this Rukmini bathed and sat beside her husband. 94. 'You like to dine alone but now your wife has come to join you,' said the Mother of the world. At this Bodhla's heart became greatly satisfied.

VITHOBA AND RUKMINI DINE WITH BODHLA

95. Bodhla thought to himself, 'The food is very scanty. How can two have a meal ? I cannot really understand.' 96. Where there is the Mistress of limitless powers, there all *siddhis* (accomplishments personified) come to serve, so at the mere touch of Her hand the food increased to abundance. 97. When the Bhagirathi (the river Ganges) places itself in a large earthen pot, how can the water become scanty ? In the cowpen of wish-cows, there can be no lack of fodder. 98. At the wedding of the earth there cannot be any lack of room. So also where there is mother Rukmini present, nothing will be lacking there. 99. She thought to herself, 'If I cook any dainties, Bodhla's mind will be hurt.' Therefore she cooked only cakes but they tasted more delicious than nectar.

100. Three plates were ready with food on them and the Life of the world said to His *bhakta*, 'You also accompany us at dinner, and receive a favour.' 101. Bodhla replied, 'O noble Brahman, I will not dine just yet. You both dine first and then give me the food left over on your plates.' 102. 'Very well,' said *Hrishikeshi* (the Lord of the heart) and at once started to dine. The gods assembling in the sky watched the wonderful sight. 103. Invisible to men they conversed between themselves. They said, 'The Lord of the world Who is loving to His *bhaktas* goes after them. 104. Despite our efforts to persuade Him He never drinks nectar; seeing the love of Bodhla, He is eating

coarse food with love in his heart.' 105. After the Brahman and the *suvasini* (a woman enjoying the happy state of wifehood) had dined, Bodhla was given the food left on their plates, and in the twinkling of an eye the Holder of the *Sharang* bow (Krishna) vanished out of sight.

KRISHNA EJECTED FROM A DINNER PARTY

106. Then only it occurred to Bodhla that *Chakrapani* (Krishna) had come dressed as a Brahman, and after making him happy had gone away. 107. So Bodhla lovingly ate the food left on the plates as a favour. Then he went to the temple and thus addressed the god: 108. 'O Life of the world, Thou who art loving to Thy *bhaktas*, today Thou didst enjoy coarse food. Forsaking rich and large dinner-parties Thou in Thy great mercy hast honoured me, humble as I am.' 109. The Husband of Rukmini replied, 'I go also to that place where the Brahmans are fed with dainties, but no one cares to feed Me.' 110. To Bodhla, Vithoba said in addition, 'Tomorrow I will show you a wonder.' It chanced that a rich person had planned to feed a thousand Brahmans 111. Preparations having been made day and night, invitations were given to the Brahmans. A list of their names having been prepared, 112. a large canopy with cloth sides was put up in the sandy bed and the next day cooking was in progress. The Brahmans who had been asked to be ready bathed and occupied their places opposite their plates. 113. As they examined the list the number came to a thousand. Then *Adhokshaja* (Krishna) said to Bodhla, 'Now I will show you a wonder.' 114. Then the Life of the world dressed Himself as an old Brahman. Around His waist was a worn-out garment. He had a staff in His hand, and His neck trembled. 115. In this guise He started off and said to Bodhla, 'Mark the wonder from a distance.' 116. Coming near to the lines of the Brah-

mans the Life of the world and said, 'I am a hungry Brahman and wish for a dainty dish.' 117. They replied, 'Get away, you cannot be accommodated here.' Hearing this the Recliner on the serpent Shesha said, 118. 'Here there are a thousand Brahmans. Cannot *one* uninvited guest be cared for?' As the Lord of *Vaikunth* (Vishnu's heaven) said this, hear what the rich men said to Him in return: 119. 'When the invited Brahmans are present, where is the necessity of anyone uninvited? Many such as you will come; how are we to supply them with food?' 120. The Lord of the world then obstinately sat before a plate. Bodhla was watching this wonderful sight and become astonished. 121. The rich man then ordered his servants to throw the Brahman out. No one had any sort of consideration, and they forced the Lord of *Vaikunth* to leave His place. 122. Some held him by his hands and feet and others pulled him by his hair, saying, 'This Brahman is a great bully; he comes and sits before a plate obstinately.' 123. In this way they talked between themselves and pulled the Brahman away but the Life of the world managed to remain. 124. In the meantime ghee was served on the plates, the priest offered the opening prayer and the Brahmans sipped water and began to dine. 125. The Sporter in (or Enjoyer of) *Vaikunth* (Vishnu's heaven) as He saw it started to return, just as the Enemy of the Demon Tripur (Shiva) gets angry with an ascetic and is off.

DINNER PARTY IN DISASTER AFTER KRISHNA LEFT

126. When life leaves the body the latter is in extreme distress. So as soon as the Husband of Rukmini turned His back a great disaster took place. 127. A violent wind broke out, the sky was filled with dust, the plates were thickly covered with earth and they flew in all directions. 128. The canopy with its wall of cloth fell down, and all the Brahmans were scattered. God showed this wonderful

sight to Bodhla at which he felt astonished. 129. As soon as the Life of the world turned His back all the Brahmans got up and left the place. If roots are not watered how can any branches grow? 130. If the mother of the bridegroom leaves the wedding canopy, how can the females in the wedding party dine? If the cow does not give milk to its calf, how will the master of the house milk the cow? 131. The One dark as a cloud enjoys food through the mouths of Brahmans, and Him the god Shiva contemplates at heart. But when He was displeased, a great disaster at once fell. 132. Then the Lord of *Vaikunth* thus addressed Bodhla:—' All these men are hypocrites. I saw your pure love and I ate the coarse food with relish. 133. I refused Duryodhan's invitation to dine and ate kernels at Vidur's house. For the sake of a vegetable leaf of chaste Draupadi I went to her as a guest at midnight. 134. With love did I eat the food left over by the cowherds. The food brought to me by the wives of *Rishis* I ate with great delight. 135. The cowherds first ground the morsel in their mouths and then put the same into My mouth and I considered it as very pure.' As the Life of the world thus spoke, the loving *bhakta* was greatly pleased 136. and Bodhla said, 'O Life of the world, Thy limit is not known to anyone.' Saying this he clasped His feet. 137. Chokhamela was a loving *Vaishnava bhakta* and the One dark as a cloud ate the ghee offered by him. He also ate with loving delight the tasty fruits of a female Bhil.

THE WONDER ON BODHLA'S RETURN JOURNEY

138. Then taking leave of God, Bodhla returned to Dhamangaon and on his way he came to a barren tract of land. 139. Overcome with hunger and thirst, he did not see that a town was close by. The Life of the world knowing the heart of His servant came there to help him.

140. By a mere wish He created a garden at the sight of which the traveller felt relief. 141. The Lord of *Vaikunth* became the gardener and began working a *mote* (the bucket of a bullock-drawn well) at the well, while the chaste Rukmini became the female gardener and sat waiting for the *bhakta.* 142. Bodhla saw this but he felt in no way inclined to go into the garden. He considered cold, heat, sorrow and joy as equal and sang God's praises. 143. Then Rukmini put some bread, sour milk, fruits and roots in a basket, took it on her head and came before him. 144. She said to Bodhla, 'Why do you not come into our garden? The gardener saw you from a distance and is waiting for you. 145. You are a *warkari* (pilgrim) of Pandhari. Just come and sanctify our home. If you are thirsty or hungry you need not feel any reserve.' 146. Bodhla was astonished at heart, saying 'Nobody has ever lived in this place.' He entered the garden and rested there awhile. 147. After eating some roots and fruits he set off for Dhamangaon, but as he looked over his shoulders he could see nothing.148. Said he, 'Because I was very hungry, the Lord of Pandhari created this illusory scene.' When he reached home, he related to his wife the whole event.

THE PLEA OF BODHLA'S WIFE

149. One day Bodhla was watching his field. Contemplating *Adhokshaja* (Krishna) in his mind he began to repeat the names of God. 150. Said he, 'When they put a handful of grain into the seed-box of a drill-plough, then only the world prospers. So why should I drive away the birds? It is merely giving them pain. 151. They who are destined to have their food in the farm, let them with pleasure eat it. For the Husband of Rukmini is in all beings; so the ancient saints have said. 152. Tying the sling around his head, with a repentant heart he began to repeat the names of God. In the meantime his wife arrived

there with bread in a basket. 153. After serving him with food, Mamatai said to him, 'If you give the green pea to beggars, what will be our condition? 154. We have as yet to pay the government revenue. Besides, we need the grain for our maintenance. Therefore, O husband, bear my advice in mind. 155. I request you in the name of Vithoba that you do not give away any more pods.' Saying this she returned home.

BODHLA LETS PILGRIMS EAT UP HIS GREEN PEAS

156. At the same time a great number of pilgrims were going to Pandhari singing the praises of Hari with delight. As Bodhla saw them he felt glad at heart. 157. He got down from the loft and prostrated himself before them when a Brahman who was walking in advance said, 'The heart of this man is very tender.' 158. Then the Brahman said to him, 'O you Vishnu-*bhakta*, you are our feeder in famine. If you give me some pods I shall be glad, for I am hungry.'

159. As he heard the noble Brahman's request, pity arose in his mind and he said, 'My wife has just warned me in God's name not to give the green pods to anyone and has gone home. 160. However, you can go into the farm and take as many pods as you like.' The Brahman was glad at heart as he heard this 161. and while he was plucking the pods, the other pilgrims saw them in his hands. 162. Loudly shouting the names of Vitthal they requested Bodhla, 'If you give us some pods too, Shri Hari will favour you. 163. There is a great scarcity of grain in the land and the corn is three *payalis* (a measurement) a rupee. If you give grain in charity at this critical time you will surely store up good deeds without number.' 164. Bodhla was glad at heart on hearing them and said, 'Blessed is this day for I have met with saints.' 165. Then he said to the pilgrims, 'You can

pluck the pods yourselves; although my wife has warned me in the name of God (not to give them away).' He then returned home. 166. There were two hundred pilgrims who all entered into his field and stripped clean the *jondhala* (cereal grain) before they left. 167. The news that Bodhla's field had been stripped of its grain reached the town, hearing which all men and women there were astonished. 168. Some called him very generous; others a profuse squanderer; while some said that the Husband of Rukmini cared for his domestic life. 169. Knowing that his wife and son would worry him he did not go back into the town, but contemplating in his mind the Life of the world he began to sing His praises with love. 170. When the eldest son came there to ascertain the news he saw the stalks without ears, and was very sad at heart. 171. He sat there overcome with sorrow and as the father knew of it he advised his son in an *abhang*.

BODHLA'S COUNSEL TO HIS SON

172. Said he, 'O my dear son, listen to the definition of life. Your mind is very narrow. The bees store honey but starve themselves. 173. Then the forester comes, drives away the bees and takes away the comb of honey. The bees thus go into a forest and struggle for nothing. 174. In the same way, people with stinginess carry on their worldly affairs but when the hour of spoiling comes, they will at last give away their weath and grain. 175. To-day the produce of the field is spent on worthy men. Then why should you have any anxiety about this ?' As the loving *bhakta* of God thus spoke, repentance was impressed on the son's heart. 176. Young deer do not require a lesson in springing; the young ones of birds do not find it hard to fly; 177. and there is no necessity of a raft for the young fish; in the same way Yamaji's repentance was no difficult matter.

178. Yamaji then fell at his father's feet, and holding his hand, took him home and related the whole story to Mamatai his mother. 179. The wife felt satisfaction as she realized that the grain in their field had been distributed amongst the pilgrims. She felt the distribution of grain had been in a good cause, and that it was the result of good deeds stored up in their previous births.

VILLAGERS CONSPIRE AGAINST BODHLA

180. The wife was satisfied, no doubt, but the evil-minded and the revilers said amongst themselves, 'We do not know how he will pay the Government revenue.' 181. The villagers prepared a list of revenue payers and fixed seven *hons* (silver coins) against Bodhla's name. Listen to what they said among themselves: 182. 'In his state of pecuniary disability, Bodhla has his field stripped of its produce (by the pilgrims of Pandhari). He shouts God's names day and night and plays with cymbals lovingly. 183. Therefore first recover the *hons* (revenue) from *him*, and then *we* will all pay ours.' With this firm resolve they forwarded the report to the Government. 184. They said, 'If anyone opposes this proposal, he will have to pay for Bodhla.' Then they sent the *havaldar* (revenue officer) to his house, who said, 'Pay the *hons* at once.' 185. But there were only three *hons* in his house and despite very great effort he could not obtain a fourth.

NAGAU THE WOMAN MONEY-LENDER

In the town there was a Brahman lady by the name of Nagau who was a money-lender. 186. After the night had advanced three hours Bodhla went to her house and said, 'Take the interest in advance, but lend me four *hons* at once.' 187. 'Certainly,' said the money-lender; 'to-morrow morning I will lend you the *hons*.' Bodhla then left and returned to his house. 188. A big pot full of money she had buried underground she at once dug out and took four *hons* out of it.

189. Next day she heard in an indirect way in the town how he had had his field stripped clean of its corn by the pilgrims. 190. Then Nagau thought to herself, 'If I lend him the *hons*, they may never come back. If I lend, being tempted by the interest, the principal itself may be lost. 191. If I care for the chaff, the bullocks may eat the grain. If I take care of the pot of sour milk, the good milk may be spoiled. 192. A maund is thus lost for half a maund. "Penny wise, and pound foolish" is a popular saying.' 193. Well, the next day Bodhla went to Nagau and asked for the *hons*. She replied, 'I depended for them on another person and I promised you, 194. but now he refuses to lend. How can I help it? And there is no other money-lender in the town of Dhamangaon.'

195. At this reply of Nagau, the God-loving *bhakta* left the place and returned home. With an anxious mind he said to his wife, 196. 'I am in great trouble on account of the revenue. I can nowhere borrow four *hons*. So I will now go to Raleras at once and try to find out a money-lender.' 197. So addressing his wife, Bodhla at once started. As he was journeying, in his mind he sang Shri Hari's praises. 198. 'O Govind Gopal, Shripati, Saviour of the world, the image of Brahma (which is wanting in form), O Thou of *Sagun* Form, let me have love for singing Thy praises for ever.'

KRISHNA AS A MAHAR HELPS BODHLA

199. A rumour was afloat in the town that Bodhla had absconded. Therefore a bailiff came and blocked his door. 200. The cattle and calves were shut up in the house and He would not let in fire or even water. 201. As the evil-minded got up such a disaster the Lord of Pandhari was full of compassion. Said he, 'My *bhakta* is in danger,

So I must do something to free him from it. 202. Had he not had his field plundered, this calamity would not have happened.' Then assuming the form of an out-caste the Husband of Rukmini came. 203. The Holder of the *Sharang* bow took the form of Vithya Mahar who lived in the town. He took seven *hons* and went to the *chawdi* (village office). 204. 'Johar, my mother and father, Mankoji Patil sends these *hons* by me.' Saying this the Life of the world handed over the money to the *Chaugula* (village revenue officer) and was off. 205. Then the villagers collected the revenue and sent it in a bag to the Government Treasury at once. They said between themselves,) 'Where could Bodhla have had this money from at this difficult time ?'

206. On the day following the loving *bhakta* returned with the hons. As the Government revenue was paid up no complaint was heard in the town. 207. The Chaugula then said to him,'You sent by a Mahar the money which as soon as we received it, was sent to the King's Treasury.' 208. He asked his wife and son about it but they replied that they did not know. Then Vithya Mahar was sent for at once, and asked. 209. He said, 'I have not food enough even for a day in my house. How is it possible that I should pay the revenue for you at the village office ?'

210. As Bodhla heard what the Mahar said, he understood in his mind that it was the Husband of Rukmini who had lovingly come to relieve him of his distress. 211. His throat was choked with emotion, tears ran from his eyes, and he cried, 'O Merciful to the lowly, and the Lord of the helpless, Thou didst worry Thyself for my sake. 212. O Dweller on the ocean of milk, O Lord of Pandhari, why didst Thou take the guise of an out-caste ? I have given up all affection for the earthly life and come to Thy feet. 213. The singing of Thy praise has made me crazy; and I do not care for what the people say. I have

no regard for this perishable and solid body. 214. Now come and meet with me in Thy *sagun* form.' Seeing Bodhla's pure devotion the Lord of Pandhari fulfilled his wish. 215. Bodhla met with God and asked Him how He had paid the revenue for him. Listen to what the Friend of the helpless replied to His clever *bhakta*: 216. 'After your departure to Raler, the villagers created a great nuisance to your household. Then I stole away four *hons* of Nagau. 217. I added three which I found in your house to these, and thus paid seven *hons* at the village office.' As the Lord of Pandhari said this Bodhla laughed, 218. and said, 'O Merciful to the lowly, Lord of Pandhari, why didst Thou take the poor woman's *hons*? Now I will give her these which I have brought as a loan.' 219. The Life of the world then said, 'If you give her back the *hons* I will do away with her buried treasure in a moment.' 220. At this Bodhla clasped God's feet and said, 'Might is right.'

After this the Recliner on the serpent Shesha performed another miracle at Dhamangaon. 221. The green pods were stripped off by the pilgrims; but now the stalks were full of ears. The grain cellars which were lying empty for a long time were all filled with grain. 222. At this wonderful sight all the people were astonished and said, 'It seems the Life of the world is pleased with Bodhla.' 223. The Merciful to the lowly, the Husband of Rukmini, increases the reputation of His *bhaktas*. Mahipati, His badge-bearer, extols the virtues of saints.

224. *Swasti* (Peace)! This book is the *Bhaktavijaya*. The Lord of the world will be pleased as He listens to it. O ye loving and pious *bhaktas*, listen to it. This is the fifty-third very delightful chapter.

CHAPTER LIV

MANKOJI BODHLA THE PATIL

(Continued)

Obeisance to Shri Ganesh. Obeisance to the Husband of Radha

INVOCATION

GOD'S GRACE WORKS WONDERS

1. Victory, victory to Thee, Pervader of the Universe and Husband of Rukmini. Thou surely art my fortune, my mother, father and brother. Without Thee there is no rest. 2. Thou art my object of listening and thinking. Thou art my Sanskrit and Marathi languages also. 3. Thou art my skill, the speaker, and the One who causes me to speak. O beautiful as a cloud, Thou art the object of my love, O Merciful to the lowly, Shripati. 4. Thou art the unerring writer, Thine is vast ability, O Lord of *Vaikunth* (Vishnu's heaven). Thou art my eternal happiness, my *Sadguru* and Saviour. 5. Thou art my loving listener, the Giver of timely memory, O Infinite One. Avarice and attachment do not trouble one where there is Thy mercy. 6. O Husband of Laxmi, Thy grace makes the fool wise, just as at the sudden rise of the sun the darkness of night disappears. 7. Then darkness turns to light, without doubt. In the same way ignorance is uprooted by Thy grace. 8. When the *paris* (touchstone) comes in contact with iron, how can iron rust exist ? When a streamlet flows into the Ganges it becomes sacred. 9. In the same way, on whom Thou dost look of Thy own free will with an eye of grace, his fame will spread in the three worlds and will have no comparison. 10 Thy *bhaktas* who are God-loving and indifferent to worldly things do not forget Thee even for a moment. Cause me to write the marvellous lines of those saints.

PRECEDING CHAPTER REVIEWED

11. At the end of the previous chapter the Life of the world showed a miracle. In a moment he filled up all the grain-cellars of Bodhla. 12. The green grain in his field was distributed amongst the pilgrims and the stalks became full of ears. At this extraordinary miracle all wondered. 13. They said, ' Bodhla is an *avatar* of God. He should not be called an ordinary man. We are ignorant and mean and therefore we persecuted him. 14. The grain-cellars formerly empty were now filled with grain, and Bodhla had them looted by the Brahmans; as the *mogra* (fragrant flowering tree) when it has flowers gives them to those who like to enjoy them ; 15. as honey accumulates in lotus-flowers, they give it to the bees; or as clouds pour the water accumulated in them on the earth, 16. in like manner, *Hrishikeshi* (the Lord of the Heart), being pleased, gave corn to Bodhla. He became indifferent to earthly things and distributed corn amongst the Brahmans. 17. The stalks were full of ears and people rushed to see them. Bodhla's reputation travelled from country to country so that people said, ' Extraordinary is the power of saints.'

THE STORY OF HANSI

18. One day while the loving *bhakta* sat watching his field, Hansi, a female slave, suddenly came and fell at his feet. 19. If you want to know who she was just listen to her story. At a distance of four miles from Dhamangaon there was another village called Raleras. 20. The *Patil* or *Mukaddam* (two titles for the chief man) of that place was Bodhla's father-in-law. When he died and went to the home of salvation Mamatai was deprived of her mother's home. 21. She had two brothers, evil-minded both of them. They never inquired about Mamatai. They were very proud and their actions were very bad.

22. Hansi was a slave at their house. Her heart was very pious and she was ever in the habit of singing Hari's praises while she did her household work. 23. The boundaries of Raleras and Dhamangaon were near each other. The Vaishnava *bhakta* (Bodhla) was once cultivating the field near Raleras. 24. The fields of the two impious brothers of Raleras and that of Bodhla were side by side. They had employed Hansi the slave solely to watch the field. 25. Bodhla every day sat on the high seat in his field and sang the praises of Hari. The slave Hansi came there, and listened to him with love.

BODHLA ON WOMEN AND SLAVES

26. She at once clasped the feet of the loving *bhakta* and said, 'Tell me some means by which my earthly life will be fruitful.' 27. Bodhla heard her and thought to himself, 'She is bodily dependent. She is not able to repeat the praises of God or practice austerities, or meditate, or visit sacred places. 28. The lives of male and female slaves and of a wife are entirely dependent and can only be compared with the lives of cows, bullocks, and horses. 29. Because they had in store a great quantity of bad deeds they were born as such. They are not able to practise any vow without interruption. 30. If I should observe silence her love will suffer.' So thinking the *Vaishnava* addressed her: 31. 'O Hansi, hear what I say. You asked me about the means of salvation. As you perform the household work, just be thinking of Shri Hari. 32. On every *Ekadashi* (11th day of the fortnight) observe a fast, and in the evening come to Dhamangaon to listen to the *Hari-kirtan.* 33. After listening to it for four watches, return to your village the next morning. Take the permission of your master and continue this as a practice. 34. Your life will be fruitful and you will attain to the feet of Pandurang, and

will have a *sagun* manifestation of God. Have no doubt about this. 35. Hansi clasped the feet of Bodhla as she heard his advice, and said, ' On *ekadashi* I will come to Dhamangaon.'

SAINTS' ADVICE ADAPTED TO NEEDS

36. Saints advize means of salvation according to one's worth. A good physician first thinks of the disease and then administers medicine. 37. A king sits on his throne and commands each minister his duties. The mistress of a house with wisdom controls her daughters-in-law. 38. A wise lender of money lends in accordance to one's business. A clever speaker first looks at his audience and then performs his *kirtan* to suit their ability. 39. The sculptor first examines the softness or the hardness of a stone and then uses his chisel. In the same way, the saints first see the worth of their disciple and then advise as to the means of salvation. 40. Well, Hansi bore in in her mind the advice of Bodhla and as she did her household work with love, she repeated the names of God. 41. On the day of *Hari* (*Ekadashi*) she got up early and after performing quickly all her work with the permission of her master she went to Dhamangaon to attend the *kirtan* there.

A MAN BITTEN BY A SERPENT RESTORED TO LIFE

42. Bodhla's *kirtan* was very interesting. Even the ignorant could understand it thoroughly. The inhabitants of Bhovargaon came to listen to it with great love. 43. So many men and women came to listen that his house could not contain them. Therefore he stood in the public road and performed his *kirtan* there with love. 44. Hansi filled two large earthen vessels with water for the use of the people and herself swept the place of the *kirtan* clean. 45. The sky was the canopy, the earth served as a large carpet, and at hearing the loud sound of Bodhla's

kirtan the gods were delighted. 46. On an *Ekadashi* day as the villagers of Raleras were going to the *kirtan*, just near the village one of them was bitten by a snake. 47. At once the man vomited blood and died on the spot. The men who were with him lifted him up and seated him in the *kirtan*. 48. They thought among themselves that the secret should not be divulged to anyone. Bodhla was explaining the power of the name of Rama to the people. 49. He said, 'By the power of Rama's name the *bhakta* Pralhad was not burnt to death when thrown into fire. Even a poison turns to nectar; such is the evident power of God's name.' 50. The people who brought the dead man thought: 'We shall lay the blame at his (Bodhla's) door. We shall say, "This man's life left him just in the *kirtan*. If you bring him to life again, then only will we consider as true the power of the name of God."' 51. Saying this, they listened to the *kirtan* in silence, while Bodhla explained to the people the incomparable power of the name of God. 52. Said he: 'Hear, hear all of you the name of God costs nothing and is very purifying. It is sweeter than nectar. This I say from personal experience. 53. Therefore let all clap their hands, and shout loudly the names of Vitthal.' As the audience heard him say it, they lovingly shouted (the names of Vitthal). 54. The men who had seated the dead body in the *kirtan* said to Bodhla, 'This man who is sitting in front of us does not utter Hari's names.' 55. Bodhla did not know that he had died of a serpent-bite. Then listen to what the God-loving *bhakta* said to the corpse: 56. 'Bapa, you have obtained a human body, so do not neglect singing the praises of Hari. Now clap your hands and repeat loudly the names of God.' 57. The Lord of Pandhari who acts as one in a play, as He heard what His *bhakta* said to the dead body, thought to Himself, 58. 'Bodhla does not know that he is without life, and if he does not repeat the names of

God, his (Bodhla's) mind will be sad. 59. I Pandurang, am near him, and the pleasure of the *kirtan* will melt away if I do not help him.' Then the Husband of Rukmini with His own mouth commanded *Yamadharma* (the god of death), 60. 'At once bring back the life into the dead body that is sitting in the *kirtan.*' Hearing the speech of the Ocean of mercy, the god of death said 'Surely.' 61. At once the dead body got up and clapped hands and clasped the feet of Bodhla. 62. Then his companions got up and told Bodhla the whole story. As the listeners heard it they all wondered. 63. With shouts of 'Victory, Victory' they clapped their hands, the *bhaktas* of God were delighted, and from the lotus-eyes of Bodhla gushed out streams of tears. 64. Said he, 'O God of gods, Merciful to Thy *bhaktas*, Thou helpest me in my *līlā* (doings), helpless as I am. Had I known of the accident I would have felt sad. 65. As a mother picks out a fly from the food of her child without letting it know of it; in the same way, Thou Husband Of Rukmini, without letting us know about it dost prevent disaster to us.' 66. In this way pleading with the Husband of Kamala (Vishnu), he waved over the Husband of Shri Rukmini auspicious lights and prostrated himself before Him in love.

HANSI TO BE SOLD

67. The inhabitants of Dhamangaon said that Bodhla was a divine *avatar* and that he had come to the world of mortals to save mankind. 68. Hansi's love increased day by day after she saw with her own eyes the bringing to life of a dead body. 69. Every fortnight she went to Dhamangaon to listen to the *kirtan.* This went on for three years but suddenly an impediment occurred. 70. As a candidate in spiritual life (*sadhaka*) is performing the praise-service of God, and a great disaster comes upon him ; or as a

cat to overcome a pot of milk; 71. or as all diseases appear as a result of unwholesome diet; or as death watches for ever the body; or as a practiser of *yoga* is privately ensnared in this power by his very accomplishments; 72. or as a thief watches a store of wealth; or as a tiger tries to catch a wild animal; or as *Rahu* (darkness) comes in the way of the queen of the night (the moon) 73. so in (Hansi's) service of God a disaster was about to intrude. Now let the listeners pay loving attention to her story. 74. The slave, as she had Bodhla's favour, had complete spiritual knowledge. She used to listen to the *kirtan* on every *Ekadashi* and go back all alone. 75. She had a belief in the name of God and was for ever intent on meditating Him. Thus passed three years when suddenly a great disaster befell her devotion.

76. Hansi's sister, Mamatai, had two brothers-in-law who wanted to live separately. So they offered their slave Hansi for sale. 77. The news indirectly spread in the town, and had reached her ears. She was worn out with anxiety and said, 'Powerful is my fate indeed.' 78. She finished her duties, however, went on to Dhamangaon and when alone with Bodhla clasped his feet. 79. Her throat was choked with emotion. From her eyes tears flowed. Seeing her in such a condition the loving *bhakta* addressed her thus: 80. 'O Hansi, at seeing your pitiful condition I am very much perplexed. Explain the anxiety of your heart to me.' 81. Hansi said, 'O dear Bodhla, you are my father, my mother, and my dear friend. From to-day I am to be separated from Your feet. 82. My masters have offered me for sale, and a customer also has come from a distance. Now, O Swami, how will your *kirtan* fall on my ears?' 83. Bodhla said, 'O mother, hear me. You must go to the place where the deeds in your former life will compel you to go. Then why are you sorry for nothing? 84 Waves of water in the ocean

flow about, but they are not apart from the water, as all witness. 85. In the same way Shri Pandurang is the Ocean of delight. and we human beings are its waves. Try to understand this in your mind. Then you will not feel sorry on account of our separation.' 86. To this Hansi replied, 'I do not weep for this. I enjoyed your company on the boundaries of both the towns, but I shall now have no more of it.' 87. Saying this much she fainted and then collecting herself, she went into the house to talk. 88. She said to Mamatai, 'Your brothers have offered me for sale, therefore, O mother, I am fallen into an ocean of sorrow. 89. Please keep me in your house and pay them my cost.' Saying this she prostrated herself at her feet. 90. Seeing the condition of the slave, pity arose in Mamatai's heart, and she said, 'She must be freed by some means or another. 91. If we have not money (to buy her), we will sell our hereditary property at Dhamangaon.' But she determined to free the helpless one.

BODHLA OFFERS TO BUY HANSI

92. The kind Bodhla went into the house and gave to Hansi an assurance of security. Said he, 'You go ahead to your master's house and I will follow you quickly.' 93. This promise gave her a great comfort, just as the sprinkling of nectar on a dead body would give it; 94. or as when clouds pour their water on a forest fire, the fire is put out and the trees gain coolness and sprout newly; 95. in the same way the slave was comforted at the assurance of Bodhla. Then she at once returned to Raleras. 96. Then dear Bodhla followed her there and said to her brothers-in-law, 'I indirectly hear that you intend to sell your slave. 97. If that is true, then send her to my house. I will pay you whatever you ask for her.' 98. As they heard Bodhla, evil-minded as they

were, they flew into a rage and said, 'We won't let our slave into *Your* house, to be sure. 99. You have your ancestral property just near the boundary of our village. We will give her to someone else for nothing, but never to *You.*' 100. As the Vishnu *bhakta* (Bodhla) heard this arrogant reply, he was silent. Hansi who was weeping bitterly in the house said, 'Adverse is my fate ! 101. Then kind Bodhla said to Hansi, 'I will request Vithoba and take you to my house. This I say in the presence of my relatives.' 102. Saying this he returned to Dhamangaon and related to his wife everything that had happened. 103. A great fear arose in the minds of the evil-minded at Raleras. They thought that Bodhla would request Vithoba and have her killed by Him. 104. 'He has uttered his promise here, and that will never be untrue. Therefore a customer should be immediately sent for and she should be sold to *him.*' 105. The buyer who belonged to another town came there that very day and bought Hansi and her daughter. 106. They paid twenty-five *hons* (silver coins) and took in writing the sale-deed. The slave Hansi cried bitterly and said, 'O Lord of Pandhari, why dost Thou not come? 107. O Merciful to the lowly, Lord of Pandhari, rush to my help. Otherwise I shall give up all affection for my body, and commit suicide. 108. Bodhla has said to me that Vithoba will come and take me away. I think his words will not come true to-day.' 109. But the Lord of Pandhari knows the desire of His *bhaktas*, and in a Brahman's garb *Ananta* (the Infinite One) appeared there. 110. *Adhokshaja* (Krishna) stood in the yard of the evil-minded brothers and said to Hansi. 'Bodhla calls you.' 111. Hearing the words of the Brahman, the slave was delighted at heart and she clasped the Brahman's feet lovingly. 112. O pious *bhaktas*, listen with reverence to the wonder that now took place. The Lord of Pandhari disappeared there, taking the slave Hansi with

Him. 113. Hansi had a small daughter and she also was taken to *Vaikunth* (Vishnu's heaven). The relatives of Bodhla as they saw the wonderful sight were very much astonished. 114. They exclaimed, ' It is a great wonder. Where could she have gone to along with her body ? ' The customer replied, ' I clearly see that luck is not favourable to me. 115. I did not take the slave to my town, for she disappeared just here. Therefore return my money.' 116. The evil-minded said, 'We have given you the deed of sale, and now we are not at all responsible. 117. The Brahman who had come to invite (the slave) gave the name of Bodhla, so you go to Dhamangaon and complain to him.' 118. On this the customer said, ' We have heard indirectly that Bodhla asked you to sell the slave to him. 119. But you did not give her to him; then at the time of departing he said that Vithoba would certainly take her away. 120. It has happened just as he said it would; therefore I need not go to him to complain. You at once pay me back my money.' 121. In this way a quarrel ensued between three men. The Lord of Pandhari is the Advocate of His *bhaktas*. He increases the fame of His servants.

A MAHAR REFUSED A MYSTIC *MANTRA* BY VITHOBA

122. You pious *bhaktas*, 'listen to another wonderful account. In Dhamangaon there was a Mahar (an Untouchable), a very mischievous and garrulous fellow. 123. He said to Bodhla privately, ' Please give me the mystic *mantra*. I have deep love for your feet and therefore I make this request. 124. The loving *bhakta* as he heard him said, 'It is not to *anybody* that I give the mystic *mantra*. If the Lord of Pandhari permits it, well and good; I will ask Him in private.' 125. Then he brought the Lord of *Vaikunth* into his mind and said, ' O God, hear a request of mine. The Unmentionable (a Mahar) of my village seems to me to be a simple-minded man. 126. For many days he

has been after me to place my hand on his head. If You permit, then only will I accept him (as my disciple). 127. The Life of the World said to Bodhla in reply, 'We must not give the mystic *mantra* to a man of the low caste, 128. one who is always a disbeliever at heart and who does not like to listen to the *Shastras*; to such a man a *Sadguru* ought not to give such a favour. 129. He who first sees the *practical* outcome of the sacred books and then reads them time and again for the purpose of fulfilling his sensual desires, a *Sadguru* should not give the mystic *mantra* to such a disciple. 130. He who with a mischievous heart asks the reader again and again the explanation of the thing read, a *Sadguru* should not look upon him with an eye of mercy. 131. The disciple should be a knowing one, and indifferent to worldly things, or he should at least be a simple and a loving *bhakta*.' In this way the Husband of Rukmini advised Bodhla in private. 132. 'As for this man, he is *Anāmik* (Unmentionable) and of a low caste, very wicked, cruel and evil-minded. If you do not believe what I say, you try him just once. 133. Tomorrow, O chief of my *bhaktas*. perform the worship of the heap of thrashed corn in your field, send for the Mahar and have a bullock of yours killed by him; 134. show him in kind words that he should not divulge the secret to anyone, and if he keeps it a secret, then give him the mystic *mantra*.' 135. Bodhla replied, 'O Lord of Pandhari, I will never arrange a slaughter. Why should I have a bullock killed for nothing? I do not like it.' 136. At this the Husband of Rukmini said, 'My command is your authority. I will not let the blame of killing attach to you.' 137. The next day the Mahar came to Bodhla and held him by his feet and said, 'Please give me that favour now.' 138. Mankoji Bodhla said to the Mahar, 'Listen. On the heap of corn in my field kill one of my bullocks, but let no one know of this.

Then only will you be my true disciple.' 139. 'Surely, replied the Unmentionable who then killed a bullock. Then he had the beef cooked in a different house from his and had bread and rice cooked. 140. Bodhla got together his relatives to pay worship to the heap of corn, and as they were served with the beef and bread they very much wondered. 141. They said, 'Bodhla's conduct is changed. He practises slaying. He has killed a goat, and has given a dinner to the *kunbis* (or farmers) tonight.' 142. But no one knew that he had had a bullock killed, and all dined and went back to their homes. 143. Bodhla said to the Unmentionable, 'Hide the head of the bullock in the heap of corn and bury the skin in the chaff, and let no one know about it.' 144. The Unmentionable's mind becoming puffed with pride, he said, 'As soon as it is morning, I will go and tell the people about this.'

THE MAHAR BETRAYS BODHLA

145. While he was thus thinking, the sun arose and the malevolent Mahar went into the town at once and asked for bread from house to house. 146. He went into the *kunbis'* (farmers') houses, and sat by them. Then when they requested him to keep himself at a distance, and asked why he entered their houses, 147. he began to argue with them: 'What difference is there between you and me? The well-known Bodhla had a bullock killed beside the heap of corn yesterday. 148. You ate the beef, and why now keep me at a distance?' In the same way he went on repeating the same story from house to house. 149. There was then a whispering among the people that Bodhla had done a wrong thing. They said, 'He calls himself Hari's *bhakta* but he has ceremonially defiled his relatives.' 150. Some said, 'This is a false rumour.' Others said,' It is quite true, for Bodhla's bull is not seen in the cowpen.' 151. His caste people and relatives then gath

ered together and quietly thought the matter over saying, 'Let us go and ask Bodhla as to why he has polluted us.' 152. They then asked the Mahar to show them some evidence of what he had told them and he replied that he had hidden the head of the bull in the heap of corn, 153. and the skin in the chaff, and that he would show them the evidence if they would follow him. As they heard the malevolent Mahar all the men became very angry. 154. They said, 'Let us go and take Bodhla's life and if the king asks us about it we will pay the fine.' 155. Saying this the wicked people came and stood near Bodhla with sticks in their hands. 156. He had closed his eyes, was meditating at heart on the image of Shri Vitthal, and was all alone repeating God's name with love. 157. The people said, 'Open your eyes; we have come to kill you What a rascal you are that you have openly polluted all of us.'

A MIRACLE IS PERFORMED AND THE MAHAR PROVED FALSE

158. Bodhla said, 'O Lord of Pandhari, come to my help at this critical time. Apart from Thee, O merciful One, who is there to protect the lowly?' 159. On that the evil-minded said to him, 'The Husband of Rukmini will not come to your help now. You had a bull killed and you gave us its beef, and have thus practised pollution.' 160. Then turning to the Mahar they said, 'Bring your evidence and show us.' 'Surely,' he said and then went to look for it in the heap. 161. Now in the heap of corn there *was* the head of the bull, but the Lord of Pandhari had turned it into that of a goat. In the same way the skin was changed and all saw it as he drew it out. 162. As the Mahar took it in his hand, he bent his neck in shame. Said he, 'I killed a bull. This is indeed very strange.' 163. Then the villagers asked Bodhla, 'Where is your bull?' And the Lord

of Pandhari worked a wonder which no other can do. 164. The bull which had been butchered was brought back to life and the people wondered and exclaimed, 'The Mahar is a liar.' 165. Then the villagers addressed the Untouchable and said, 'We will kill *you.* You made a false allegation against Bodhla and made us persecute him.' 166. As the Mahar heard the angry talk of all he began to tremble all over and fell flat at the feet of Vishnu's *bhakta.* 167. He said, 'I am most guilty. I am a low caste, very wicked and evil-minded. Now forgive me my fault and save my life.' 168. As he (Bodhla) heard the evil-minded thus speak, pity arose in his mind and he requested the villagers not to kill him. 169. Then the Mahar abandoned all pride and prostrated himself before Bodhla, for he was overcome with shame at heart that he had wronged all of them. 170. In the meantime the Husband of Rukmini said in a whisper to Bodhla, 'I had told you the secret and you have experienced the truth of it.' 171. Bodhla then said, 'O Life of the world, no one understands Thy utmost reach.' Saying this he clasped His feet and the Lord of *Vaikunth* (Vishnu's heaven) smiled.

A GOOD CROP IN A FAMINE

172. You pious *bhaktas*, listen to another story about Bodhla with reverence. The inhabitants of Dhamangaon witnessed Bodhla's life in various ways. 173. They said, 'Bodhla is not a common man, he is really an *avatar* of God. He carries all safely through their earthly life.'

174. One year there was no rain at all. Therefore the sowing of seeds in Dhamangaon was not done for the first crops. 175. The absence of rain lasted until the month of *Ashvin* (October), then in the following month *Kartik* (November) there fell the rain of the *Swāti* (the name of one of the twenty-seven lunar changes) in abundance. 176. Bodhla borrowed money and bought seed, and the villagers

went to work as labourers. 177. Crowds of pilgrims with banners in their hands were going to Pandharpur. Seeing them Bodhla was pleased at heart. 178. With devotion he prostrated himself before the pilgrims and said, 'My Fate is favourable and therefore I see the saints.' 179. Among them were some Brahmans. They said to Bodhla, 'We hear that in famine time you give grain to the poor and therefore we have come here.' 180. Hearing what the Brahmans said he thought to himself, 'There is no grain in my house. If the saints and good people go away empty-handed my reputation will surely suffer.' 181. Then he called his son aside and told him to bring seed home and give the saints a dinner: 182. 'If seed is sown in the lifeless earth it yields crops; then what of saints who have life? If seed is sown in their stomachs, what will it not yield?' 183. Yamaji was greatly delighted at hearing his father's words and the labourers who had gone to work in the field were sent back into the town. 184. The seed was a maund and a quarter; this was ground and the pilgrims were fed. Seed of bitter pumpkin had been sown in his field, 185. and God's miracle is wonderful, for it now yielded many pumpkins. The villagers laughed and said, 'This is very strange. 186. Why did he feed the pilgrims with seed? And why did he sow the bitter pumpkin?' In the meantime a reviler came there; hear what he said: 187. 'Bodhla the *Patil* is our king and we are his subjects. He thinks that we should give up all sense of public shame, 188. therefore he is going to give every one of us a pumpkin to use as a begging bowl and therefore he has sown them here.' All laughed at what the bad man said. 189. Then all of them replied, 'Let us go to the field of Bodhla, and see the wonder. Let us all see what sort of a nice crop he has.' Saying this they all got up. 190. When they went into the field they saw innumerable pumpkins and they broke one of them open. 191. There they saw a wonderful sight, for the pumpkins yielded wheat. Then they said, 'God's miraculous deeds are unfathomable.' And the hearts of all were filled with wonder.

BODHLA ARRESTED

192. There was a *Havaldar* (village officer) present who said, 'This must be reported to the king.' He then wrote a detailed report to the Muhammadan king. 193. On reading the report the king said, 'Some magic has been practised.' Then he sent five armed soldiers to Dhamangaon. 194. They arrested Bodhla and took him to the royal court. When the king asked him about it he gave a detailed account. 195. The king grew angry and asked, 'How did wheat come into the pumpkin?' Bodhla said, 'I do not know. It is the doing of the Dweller at Pandhari.' 196. The king heard what God's *bhakta* said but he could not believe it, just as when hearing the life of Shri Ramchandra the evil spirits burn inwardly; 197. and as when Sanjaya read the *Bhagavadgita* to King Dhritarashtra he had no faith in it; just so the Muhammadan king could not believe the words of Bodhla. 198. The king flew into a rage and said, 'Make Mankoji Bodhla a Muhammadan.' At once a dish of cooked flesh was brought, 199. and Bodhla was compelled to eat it. Suddenly the flesh turned to flowers and *tulsi*, and the king at once got up and bowed to Bodhla.

MANKOJI BODHLA'S TRUE *BHAKTI*

200. The king said, 'Ask for as much wealth as your mind may desire.' At this Bodhla's mind was disgusted and he at once walked off. 201. To the king he said, 'I have no wish in my heart. When there is the wish-cow in one's house, why should he go begging from house to house? 202. When there is the wish-tree in one's yard, why should he plant trees of *sindi*? It is unseemly to

ride a donkey when one can afford to get the elephant of the god Indra. 203. Why should one abandon the shade of a mango tree and go and sit under a *hivar* tree? Why should one be tired of a human body and wish for that of a beast? 204. Why should one abandon the *bakul* tree and the *shevanti* and accept a *pungal* creeper (a stinking plant)? Why should one leave the company of saints and love revilers? 205. Why should one give up the praises of Hari and go to hear an obscene song? When there is abundance of curds and of milk in one's house, why should he go in search of sour milk? 206. Those who have attained the higher order of a *Paramhansa* (a class of ascetic), they will never return to the state of a householder. In the same way, when one has a deep love for the worship of Shri Rama, he will never accept a royal honour.' 207. Saying this he returned to Dhamangaon. He had in him a deep love for God and he was not proud. 208. When a *bhakta* is devoted to the name and form of God, then the *bhakta* forgets he is a *bhakta.* So also the Husband of Rukmini forgets His own divinity. 209. If a gold crown and an anklet are melted in a crucible then both lose their names. 210. In the same way while Bodhla sang the praises of Pandurang he forgot himself. Then thinking of the Life of the world in his heart he sang the praises of non-duality. 211. By dint of his good devotion, he changed Dhamangaon into Pandhari; and in various ways he brought his life to the notice of the people and by his love saved the dull and the ignorant.

212. In the next chapter there is the wonderful story of the loving *bhakta*, Ganeshnath. His life is very sweet. May the loving *bhaktas* listen to it with love.

213. The Merciful to the lowly, the Husband of Rukmini, through His grace causes me to explain the

right meaning of this book. I Mahipati am His suppliant and sing His praises with love.

214. *Swasti* (Peace) ! This book is the *Shri Bhaktavijaya*. The Lord of the world will be pleased to listen to it. O ye pious and loving *bhaktas*, listen to it. This is the fifty-fourth interesting chapter; it is an offering to Shri Krishna.

CHAPTER LV

GANESHNATH

Obeisance to Shri Ganesh. Obeisance to the Lord of the world.

INVOCATION

1. Victory, victory to Thee, the Imperishable, the Indestructible, the One without name and form, the supreme Being, the Lord of the Universe, the Pervader of the world, the Lord of his joy, O Shri Hari! 2. Thy *bhaktas* think of Thee; their meditation is on Thee, just as the *chatak* bird and the cloud live as friends. 3. A child longs for its mother, for the mother has love for her child; so the Husband of Rukmini follows the inclination of His *bhaktas*. 4. The ocean at the sight of the glorious moonlight on the full moon day is delighted. In the same way, O Life of the world, Thou takest delight in listening to the fame of Thy *bhaktas*. 5. Thy *bhaktas* praise Thee and Thou art also fond of their reputation. Therefore Thou hast caused me to write their lives in this book, the *Bhaktavijaya*.

GANESHNATH'S CHARACTER

6. In the previous chapter it is related that Bodhraj gave evidence to the Muhammadan king and then discarding all earthly riches, lovingly gave himself up to the worship of Hari. 7. Now listen to the wonderful life of Ganeshnath, ye pious *bhaktas* of God. He was knowing, thoughtful, very indifferent to worldly things, and a true worshipper of his spiritual *Sadguru*. 8. In the province of Baleghat there are two towns, Sarase and Ujjani. He lived there and performed *kirtans* with love. 9. He wore with love a riband around his neck, wooden earrings in his ears, a piece of cloth as a clout, and was content. He wished for nothing that would disturb his mind. 10. In the daytime he lived in the forest all alone, singing the

praises of Shri Hari, and coming back into the town at night sang of the deeds of God. 11. He did not care about receiving any honour, nor did he like the earthly way of worship, the hypocritical singing of the praises of God, fine clothes or riches, or dainty foods.

KING SHIVAJI VISITS GANESHNATH

12. Once on a time King Shivaji went on a pilgrimage to Pandharpur and hearing of Ganeshnath's reputation he went to visit him. 13. Falling prostrate before him he sat listening to his *kirtan*. Ganeshnath's knowledge was extensive and his poetry inspiring. 14. Using many illustrations he composed *abhangs* like arrows (which pierced the heart of the listeners), and made the ears of his audience very happy. 15. He (King Shivaji) had a new bedstead made for him and he longed to request Ganeshnath to sleep on it the very first day.

16. With hands joined palm to palm he said, 'O *Swami*, kindly spend a night in my camp. I have a new bedstead made for you.' Saying this he fell at his feet. 17. Seeing the respect paid him by Ganeshnath, the king was in a great difficulty, as when a tiger is about to carry away a doe, her heart trembles. 18. Knowing the difficulty, the ascetic said, 'Surely.' Then he collected small pebbles in the cavity of his hands and tied them in the end of his cloth. 19. Seeing those pebbles the king asked, 'Why have you picked up the pebbles ?' The latter replied, 'To count the names (of God)'. 20. The king then seated him in a palanquin and took him to his camp. He prepared a bed of flowers and requested Ganeshnath to sleep on it. 21. *Vidas* (rolled betelnut leaves) with the thirteen ingredients were arranged on a plate. Lamps were lighted and hangings were let down on all sides. 22. The king left there many fragrant things and various means of enjoyment and fortune and then came out.

GANESHNATH'S DISLIKE OF EASE AND SENSUAL OBJECTS

23. At the sight of sensual objects he felt repentance in every limb; just as a worshipper of fire finds himself pent up in the house of a Muhammadan; 24. or as a tiger takes a living cow into his cave and she with a fearful heart tries to come out of it as soon as she can; 25. or as a deer brought from a forest and tied up in a palace wishes at heart to be able to get away quickly; 26. or as a living fish struggles in ghee ; just so did Ganeshnath feel about the attractions in the royal palace. 27. As a parrot is put into a cage for the first time, and he does not like the food and drink given to it ; in the same way the one who was indifferent to worldly things felt disgusted. 28. He had taken with him some pebbles and had spread them on the bedstead where he slept for four *ghatikas* (one *ghatika*=24 minutes), when the sun arose. 29. When the king came to visit him he saw the pebbles spread on the bedstead. He felt astonished at heart and prostrated himself before him. 30. With hands joined palm to palm, he asked Nath of this and he replied, 'Had I slept on the comfortable bedstead, the sleep would have been too sound; 31. therefore in order to satisfy your real aim for me, I spread the pebbles on it and slept; for if the body is permitted to enjoy itself it will have to experience a proportionate amount of grief in the future. 32. You go on scratching the itch and feel very pleased at the time, but when the scratching ceases there is no relief; 33. we take pleasure in eating, but feel it troublesome to vomit; in the same way the pleasure derived from sleep is very sweet in the beginning, but in the end it is harmful to the body. 34. *Bachanag* (poisonous *gloriosa superba*) is sweet to eat but the eater loses his life; in the same way, O king, there is great danger in the enjoyment of sensual

objects.' 35. As the king heard this advice he repented and vowed never again to sleep on a bedstead.

GANESHNATH AS A SPIRITUAL *GURU*

36. In accordance with his resolve the king gave away in charity the bedstead to a Brahman. Such is the glory of the company of saints that even Brahmadev and others do not know. 37. Ganeshnath's state of life was like this: He was completely ascetic in relation to the three states of human life [referring either to waking, dreaming and sound sleep; or to infancy, youth and age]. He did not live in the town but roamed about in a forest. 38. As he performed his *kirtans* in his own country many pious people came to listen. Every day he gave the mystic *mantra* to anyone who might wish it. 39. As the disciple felt his hand on his head, his inclination for the earthly life left him. He gave up all family affairs and wandered about from forest to forest. 40. If the disciple was a very bad man, a reviler, or a designing one, as soon as Ganeshnath touched his head the complete spirit of asceticism came to him. 41. In this way a year passed and he had three hundred and sixty disciples. They wore clouts (i. e., were celibates), were strictly ascetic, and had full spiritual knowledge. 42. The people of different towns discussed them differently. Some said, 'Those who receive his mystic *mantra*, their attachment to worldly affairs at once disappears, and they follow their *Sadguru.*' 43. Some said, 'He is a horrible sorcerer;' or, 'He practises witchcraft;' or 'He is a great adept in spiritual knowledge;' 44. or 'He is Pandurang Himself;' or 'He is an outright hypocrite;' or 'His company destroys the earthly life;' 45. or 'Let no one go to visit him;' or 'What is in one's Fate is sure to happen;' 46. or 'Let us see him and give him a piece of advice; he has spoiled the lives of many and has spread destruction in many families.'

47. Saying these things they went to visit Ganeshnath one day and saw him deeply engaged in meditation under the shade of a mango tree. 48. As he finished his mental worship Ganeshnath looked around to see if there was anyone who wished to be his disciple so that he could place his hand on his head.

A MANGO TREE GIVEN A *MANTRA*

49. Revilers came and stood there and said, 'You have made simpletons your disciples, and made them wander about after you. 50. You have destroyed the family life of many and hence the people are very displeased. Now we request you to do something and please do it accordingly. 51. You saints are endowed with spiritual knowledge. In your sight the four classes of creatures are alike. Therefore from to-day graciously bestow your mystic *mantra* on the vegetable kingdom. 52. 'By all means,' he replied and exhibited a wonderful visible manifestation, which in this world of mortals is not possible to others though using various means. 53. There was an old mango tree there and he gave his mystic saying (*mantra*) to it, and placed his hand upon it. 54. When he made it his disciple the people saw the wonder with their own eyes and said, 'When you give your mystic *mantra* to human beings they give up their worldly affairs. 55. How are we to know that the tree is influenced by your *mantra* ? Therefore kindly perform some other miracle by which our doubt will be dispelled. 56. Someone had brought bread and vegetables to offer him. Ganeshnath picked some up and held them in his hand. 57. He thus addressed the tree which had received his *mantra*: 'This is God's favour, open your mouth and lovingly eat it.' 58. As the *Sadguru* uttered these words, a most wonderful sight occurred. The trunk of the tree split in two before all. 59. The bread was put into the

gap, and at that very moment it became just as before, at which all of them wondered, their minds becoming absorbed therein. 60. The wise and the revilers who were there prostrated themselves before Ganeshnath and said, 'There is no *bhakta* like you, so God-loving, so knowing and so pure. 61. Full of pride we troubled you for nothing. Saying this they went to their homes.

STONES CLAP HANDS

62. One day Ganeshnath was performing a *kirtan* in a forest and to listen to it there came the wise, the learned, the *bhaktas* of Vishnu and the thoughtful. 63. There were also men well versed in the *Vedas* and *Shastras*, and pious men of the eighteen castes had gathered there to experience the pleasure arising from the love of the *kirtan*. 64. Cymbals, *vinas* and drums were sounded. The sky re-echoed with the shouts of the names of God. 65. Ganeshnath put up his hands as if they were banners, to motion to the people to clap their hands. Hear what the wise and the learned said to him then: 66. 'You are a *Bharādī* (an order of *Gosavis*) and of a low caste. We Brahmans belong to the highest class. At *your* order we never will clap our hands.' 67. On this Ganeshnath replied, 'The palm tree is very tall but its shade is of no use to anyone. 68. You Brahmans are really the highest and most respectable amongst the eighteen classes, but your hands are not useful for clapping in a *kirtan*. 69. Now with a quiet heart just listen to the *kirtan*. By your favour, O masters, stones will clap hands.' 70. As he who had the ascetic spirit thus spoke, all witnessed a very wonderful sight. Suddenly there was an upheaval of the stones on the plain. 71. They fell on each other just like hands and created a clapping sound at which the people were wonder-struck 72. They said, 'This wonder is quite new. How did he

cause the stones to be full of life ? Ganeshnath's devotion is without comparison. His *maya* (or power over illusions) will not be known even to Indra (king of the gods) or to others.' 73. Then with a repentant heart the Brahmans all clapped hands and with this Ganeshnath was satisfied. 74. By this time the sun was in the meridian. Auspicious lights were waved over the god. Sweetmeats were served to the audience and the people went home. 75. On their way home the people said among themselves, 'Out of pride we persecuted him in vain.' In this way conversing with one another they praised Ganeshnath: 76. 'Ganeshnath is a loving *bhakta* of God.' He had a promise from the Lord of Pandhari and even until the present day there is a fair at Ujjani and Sarase. 77. Saints, *mahants* and loving *Vaishnavas* go there and the place is still awake to the possibilities of wonders occurring there. Thus the Merciful to the lowly for ever increases the reputation of His *bhaktas*.

KESHAV SWAMI & THE SLEEPY GROCER'S BLUNDER

78. Now ye pious ones, listen to the life of Keshav Swami who was very pious and not at all touched by the mire of sensual objects. 79. Wandering at will about the country, he once went to Vijapur and on an *Ekadashi* day performed a *kirtan* in the public square. 80. Hearing the reputation of Keshav Swami, many people came to listen. Among them there were saints, *mahants*, many others who were indifferent to worldly things, Brahmans well versed in the *Vedas*, and the learned. 81. There were men and women of the eighteen castes, the inferior, the higher and the most ignorant castes, and the crowd was so thick that the bazaar was overflowing. 82. Torches were lighted and the din of the cymbals and drums was heard there, Keshav Swami dancing with a loving heart full of delight in the *kirtan*. 83. He had an old Brahman

as his disciple to whom he said, 'Today is a great *Ekadashi* day and all have observed a fast. 84. Therefore you go to the grocer's and buy some dry ginger and sugar. When the people are about to disperse, distribute the same amongst them as a favour.' 85. At this order the Brahman went quickly to the market to the grocer's shop, but the grocer was sleeping. 86. Shouting out to him the Brahman said, 'Give me ginger and sugar.' 'Very well,' said the grocer who got up. It was dark in the shop 87. and when he felt for the ginger, he came across a bag of *bachanag* (*gloriosa superba*, a poison) and gave the Brahman seven seers of it, for (on account of darkness) he could not make out *bachanag* from ginger. 88. The same amount of sugar was given and the grocer said to the Brahman, 'My son has gone to market (at some other place), therefore I cannot come to the *kirtan*. 89. There must be many men there and this ginger will not suffice.' Saying this he put in just as much more as his two hands could contain. 90. His action was like one who gives a blessing which turns to pride; or like bad words for prayer; or like putting around one's neck a great snake which is mistaken for a garland of flowers; 91. or like practising magic in the place of austerities; or like giving a patient a disease instead of medicine; or instead of clouds, letting fire devour a forest 92. without the forest knowing; the grocer acted in the same way. He gave poison instead of ginger. He was overpowered by the effects of sleep, so he did not know what he was doing. 93. The buyer also did not know it. He returned home and with a crusher he broke it into pieces.

KRISHNA AVERTS DISASTER BY TAKING POISON

94. Now this mishap happened without the knowledge of anyone. The Lord of Pandhari knew it,

however, and said, 'If the listeners eat it, a great disaster will take place. 95. They have already fasted on account of *Ekadashi* and if they eat *bachanag* they will die; and no one will listen to My *kirtan* in future. 96. No one will believe the words of my *bhaktas*, and the people will consider as false My past delightful fame.' 97. Saying this the Lord of Pandhari thought to himself, 'I must prevent such a disaster.' Then he swallowed up the whole of the poisonous *bachanag*, 98. and turned the poison to nectar. The Life of the World acts in a manner which gives happiness to His *bhaktas*, whereby their births and deaths are destroyed.

A GRATEFUL GROCER

99. To return to our story. The *bhakta* Keshav was dancing with loving delight in his *kirtan* and clapping his hands while singing of the deeds of Hari. 100. The *kirtan* went on through the four watches of the night, lights were waved over the Husband of Rukmini, and the sweetmeats of *bachanag* were distributed to all. 101. Some tied it as Hari's favour in the end of their cloth, but several ate it on the spot and then went home. 102. At sunrise the grocer got up in his shop, and suddenly he saw before him the sack of *bachanag*. 103. He said 'A great disaster has occurred. What shall I do? I sold *bachanag* for ginger. 104. Many loving saints, God's *bhaktas*, must have come to listen to the *kirtan* and must have died, and I am the cause of it. 105. If the thing is known in the town who will save me (from death)? And even after death I shall be thrown into a horrible hell. 106. Bad as I am, I am shut out from this world and the next. No sinner like myself will be found in all three worlds. 107. Among animals the donkey and the pig are the two kinds that are considered the lowest, but I am worse than these.' In this way the

grocer repented. 108. 'Then why should I now live? I must drown myself in a well.' With this determination he left his shop and started off. 109. As he enquired in the town he learned that none had died. He attentively listened but he found none weeping. 110. He asked the people whether they had gone to the *Hari-kirtan*, and if they had taken any of the sweetmeat favour. 111. They said, 'We had observed a fast on account of *Ekadashi*, so we ate the favour of ginger and sugar just there and came home.' 112. On that the grocer said to them, 'You had a fast yesterday, so you must be very hungry now, therefore dine at once.' 113. They replied, 'We observe religious rules. We are not as anxious for food as you are, for we hope to be able to fast yet for one more night.' 114. At this answer he went away and inquired of others indirectly. Then he went to the cemetery and looked about. 115. But he saw not a single dead body. At this the grocer very much wondered and said, 'The Lord of Pandhari has prevented a disaster and saved many from it.'

KRISHNA'S IMAGE BECOMES BLACK

116. After his bath Keshav Swami looked at the metal image of Krishna. It appeared black at which he was astonished; 117. just as in an eclipse the moon loses its brightness, in the same way the Husband of Rukmini looked dark. 118. Seeing this the *bhakta* Keshav wondered in his mind and said, 'The image was very bright. How has it become so intensely black today.' 119. Hearing his wonderful account of this, men and women rushed there to see it. In the meantine the grocer came there and addressed Keshav Swami: 120. 'As I was feeling for the sack of ginger in the dark at night I happened to go to the sack of *bachanag*. I measured seven seers of it and gave it to the ma . 121. But that disaster

has been warded off by the Lord of Pandhari, and all the listeners have been saved. Now, O Swami, tell me how I should atone for it.' 122. Keshav Swami heard him and tears of joys streamed out of his eyes. His voice was choked, and he addressed God thus : 123. 'Victory, victory to Thee, O Mother Vitthal, Merciful to the lowly. Thou hast today averted a great calamity and preserved Thy reputation, by Thy favour protecting Thy servants. 124. The terrible poison of *bachanag* has affected Thee but Thou didst save the lives of many by Thyself becoming black. 125. By the taking of Thy name, the deadly poison which was given to Thy *bhakta* Pralhad changed to nectar. Then how could a bit of the poisonous *bachanag* harm Thee to-day ? 126. Thou art the highest and the God of gods. By singing Thy praises Shiva had his burning heat cooled. That the poison of *bachanag* should harm Thee today is a new thing, O Shri Vitthal. 127. Thou didst easily trample upon the serpent Kaliya (in the Yamuna river). His poison did not affect Thee; and that the poison of *bachanag* should turn Thee black is a wonder, O Shri Hari. 128. The demoness Putana with her breasts full of poison nursed Thee. Is *bachanag* deadlier than that poison, that Thou hast become dark ? 129. Has nectar suffered death today or has darkness swallowed the sun, or has the river Bhagirathi by its own sins become foul by the sins she has washed away? 130. Or has the earth felt the burden of grass, or has the adamant (of Indra) feared a mountain and run away ? Or has the sky been covered by dust?' It is just like that. 131. Can one imagine the round moon to feel the heat, or the ocean of milk to feel hungry, or the Husband of Parvati to be harmed by devils ? 132. Or can one imagine that Kuber (the god of wealth) could be poverty-stricken, or the word of Brahmadeva be false, or the sky lose its brightness ? 133. O Govinda, all the foregoing impossible things may be possible but Thou canst not be harmed, for in order to increase the reputation of Thy servants Thou dost reveal Thy *sagun* form. 134. Thou art without birth and unconquered, O Lord of Pandhari. Thou art the Controller even of *Kali* (the Dark Age) and *Kal* (god of death). O Lord of the helpless, kindly be bright again as before.' 135. Hearing this praise, the Husband of Rukmini was pleased and the metal image looked bright again. 136. As the people saw this miracle with their own eyes they very much wondered and said, 'In the *Kali Yuga* there is no better means of salvation than the *kirtan.*' 137. The grocer greatly repented and gave up all his worldly affairs, and in the company of Keshav Nath he listened to the stories of Hari.

GOMAI THE BRAHMAN WIDOW

138. May the listeners attend to the delightful story of Gomaiawa, a Brahman widow who started for Pandharpur. 139. She was very weak and very poor. She did not get sufficient food to eat. She wore worn-out clothes and begged for grain from house to house. 140. She soon reached Gulsare, where the river Chandrabhaga was in flood. She felt anxious at heart and said, 'Who will take me to the other side ?' 141. On the bright 10th of *Ashadh* (July) the pilgrims fasted. Gomai said to the boatman, 'Please take me to the other bank.' 142. There was a very large number of pilgrims and rich persons paid money to the boatmen and sat in the ferry boat. 143. As Gomai went near the boat she was pushed back into the water. Her clothes became wet and she came out weeping. 144. She wept loudly, saying, 'Who will take me to the other side now ?' The boatmen said, 'You old hag, pay us money and we will take you to the other side.' 145. Gomai said in reply, 'I will give you a handful of flour instead. Accept it quickly and take me to the other side of the

Bhivara (Bhima) river. 146. I cannot pay you in money.' In this way she pleaded in various ways with the boatmen but they had no compassion for her. The men at sacred places are hard-hearted and evil-minded. 147. All the pilgrims got to the other side but Gomai remained on this side. She did not know what to do. Then she began to weep sitting alone. 148. Said she, 'I shall not see the Husband of Rukmini. In vain did I come so far. The men at sacred places are very wicked. Their hearts will never melt.'

KRISHNA HELPS AS A BRAHMAN

149. Seeing her state, the Lord of Pandhari became a boatman and went to her quickly. He the Helper of the lowly, had a raft of pumpkins. 150. Shri Hari went near Gomai and said to her, 'Old lady, if you want to go to the other side of the river, get up quickly.' 151. She said, '*Bapa* (father), I am poor, I have no money to pay you. So if you accept a handful of flour and take me to the other side I will come.' 152. On this the Recliner on the serpent Shesha said, 'I do not take anything from anyone. I take the wretched to the other side. 153. Just for this reason, I have been staying a long time in Pandharpur.' As he said this, Gomai was very pleased at heart. 154. She said, 'O boatman, hear what I say. The night has advanced three hours. I have no other clothes to wear.' 155. On this the Lord of Pandhari said, 'I will not let anything of yours get wet, not even your hands and feet. I will take you on my shoulders, and take you to the other side.' 156. Saying this, the Merciful to the lowly lifted up Gomai and in a moment's time took her to the other side of the river. 157. Gomai asked the boatman, 'How is it that your body has not got wet? It is indeed very wonderful that you brought me to the other bank of the river (without getting wet yourself)!' 158. On this

Chakrapani (Krishna) said, 'I am not an ignorant boatman. I take my *bhaktas* quite dry to the other side of the ocean of worldly affairs.' 159. Gomai then said, 'You have laid me under an obligation; therefore take this handful of flour and tie it in your cloth.' 160. God replied, 'I do not take anything from anyone. Make cakes of it on the twelfth day and give them to the Brahmans.' 161. Saying this the Life of the world disappeared in a moment and the old woman went to the main door of the temple and had a vision of God.

KRISHNA AND RUKMINI DINE WITH GOMAI

162. On the *Ekadashi* day she listened to the *kirtan*, bathed in the Chandrabhaga, and sat on the sandy bed with the flour tied in a cloth. 163. She said, 'Today is a festival, the twelfth day of the fortnight. I should like to give dry provisions of food to a Brahman, but I have no pulse or salt. 164. If I see a Brahman, I shall speak humbly to him and say, "Kindly accept this handful of flour."' 165. But no Brahman came near her. Every one said, 'Right at the beginning I had the ominous sight of this widow, so now there is no possibility of obtaining a patron in her. 166. For who is going to accept only flour without coarse sugar, rice and ghee?' Saying this to himself, no Brahman came near her. 167. Gomai said, 'O Lord of Pandhari, what shall I do now? If I am not able to feed a Brahman on the twelfth day I will not eat food.' 168. Seeing her firm devotion the Lord of Pandhari, the God of gods, as an old Brahman went to her. 169. He said to Gomai, 'Today is the festival of the twelfth day; I am a poor Brahman and have come to you. 170. If you have at least flour enough for one cake, give it to me with good devotion.' As Shri Hari thus spoke the old woman was greatly delighted at heart. 171. The noble Brahman moreover said, 'I have no place to lodge in. I stay in the temple

and I am very hungry. 172. If you bake the cakes for me here, I will eat them just here with delight.' As the Lord of Pandhari thus spoke Gomai was joyful at heart. 173. Then she collected some cowdung cakes, bathed and baked the cakes and Pandurang with great liking and love began quickly to eat. 174. Just then Mother Rukmini as an old woman appeared there and said, 'O *Chakrapani* (Krishna), you came here by yourself to dine without my knowledge.' 175. Then the Brahman said to Gomai, 'Now feed the *suvasini* (a woman enjoying the happy state of wifehood). You are very lucky. Without any trouble you reap the benefit of dining a couple.' 176. There was flour enough for only two cakes but it increased in quantity and Rukmini and the Lord of Pandhari dined with Gomai. 177. Having taken a leaf of *tulsi* for cleansing the mouth, the Merciful to the lowly disappeared. Listen to another narrative which is most interesting, O loving and pious ones.

LATIBSHAH A MUHAMMADAN *BHAKTA*

178. Latibshah was a Muhammadan, a very pious *Vaishnava* who listened to the reading of the *Gita* and the *Bhagwat*, and sang the praises of Shri Rama day and night. 179. He gave up his own Muhammadan religion and took an intense liking for *kirtans*. With limitless love he performed his daily worship. 180. Then all the Muhammadans reported to the king that Latibshah worshipped Shri Rama day and night. 181. The Muhammadan king was very thoughtless and sent men to loot the cottage of Latibshah and utterly destroy it at once. 182. Immediately at the king's command all his officers went to the cottage but at the sight of him they all gained peace and happiness of heart. 183. They heartily repented and said, 'We will no more serve the king. We will stay just here, listen to the *Bhagavadgita*, and stay here for ever.' 184. The king was very much astonished at heart and said, 'No one has

come back. Therefore let me go in person to persecute him.' 185. Latibshah mentally understood that the king was coming to persecute him and he therefore took out the book of the *Bhagwat*, and sat reading it near the altar of the *tulsi* plant.

186. Latibshah was surrounded by loving and pious men who were listening to his reading with love. In the meantime the Muhammadan king hastened and sat down. 187. As he looked round he found the place scrupulously clean. Right in the middle was the *tulsi* altar and around it were many fragrant flowering bushes which filled the place with their perfume. 188. The walls were covered with mortar and were very smooth and pictures were beautifully drawn on them. On them were the pictures of the ten principal *avatars* of Vishnu. 189. There were also pictures of sacred rivers and towns, and *Kailas* (Shiva's heaven), and *Vaikunth* (Vishnu's heaven). The drawings were in fast colours. 190. The Muhammadan flew into a rage as he saw this lovely place. Then he commenced his persecution.

A MUHAMMADAN KING'S PENITENCE

191. The painter had drawn the pictures of Radhika and Krishna at Vrindavan. Radha had in her hand a *Vida* (rolled betelnut leaves) and she was in the act of putting it into the mouth of Krishna. 192. The king asked Latibshah angrily, 'Who are these two in the picture? Tell me quickly.' 193. Latibshah replied, 'They are Radhika and Krishna.' 'What is that in her hand?' the king asked him. 194. The Vishnu-*bhakta* told him that Radha was offering a *Vida* to Krishna. At this answer the Muhammadan was greatly enraged at heart. 195. Said he, 'If Radhika is offering a *Vida* to him, why does not your Krishna eat it?' At this question the loving *bhakta* got up. 196. He joined both his hands palm to palm and began

to plead with Krishna. 'O Thou, the Advocate of Thy *bhaktas* and Enchanter of the world, hear my humble request. 197. With *Vida* in her hand here is Radhika standing devotedly, then O *Hrishikeshi* (the Lord of the heart) please take it into Thy mouth.' 198. The God of gods was pleased by the loving devotion of His *bhakta* and through His *maya* worked a great wonder. 199. The picture of Krishna drawn on the wall opened its mouth at once and Radhika at the same time put the *Vida* into its month. 200. The evidence left there was that the green colour of the *Vida* which was noticed in Radhika's hand suddenly faded away. 201. As the king witnessed this marvel he bowed to Latibshah and said, 'Blessed is your pure worship, I vexed you for nothing.' 202. Saying this the king returned to his palace. Through pride of His *bhakta*, Shripati assumed a form. 203. The lotus-eyed One has *bhaktas* without end. His stories are without end. His *avatars* are without end. Mahipati is His suppliant and sings of His deeds.

204. *Swasti* (Peace)! This book is the *Shri Bhaktivijaya*. In listening to it the Lord of the world will be pleased. May the pious and loving *bhaktas* listen to it with love. This is the fifty-fifth delightful chapter.

CHAPTER LVI

SANTOBA POWAR : NILOBA : UDDHAVA CHIDGHAN

Obeisance to Shri Ganesh. Obeisance to the Lord of the lowly.

GOD'S LOVE

1. Victory to Thee, the Inhabitant of *Vaikunth*, the Attracter of the mind, the Husband of the Daughter of the Ocean (Lakshmi), the Imperishable, the Wish-tree, the best being, O Pandurang. 2. O Krishna, Vishnu, and the Supporter of all beings, the Mine of mercy, O God of gods, Thou art the only Treasure of one's happiness. 3. Thou art the Help of the helpless and generous to the unlucky. When the evil-minded persecute Thy *bhaktas*, Thou comest in person to advocate their cause. 4. Thou art the Friend of the friendless, Thou dost follow those who are free from desires. Thou givest an uninterrupted love for Thy worship and destroyest the earthly ties of thy servant. 5. Thou art the Lord of the helpless and the honoured Guest of the lowly. Thou dost grant assurance to the helpless. O Life of the world, I am dull of intellect, therefore help me to compose the book.

6. At the conclusion of the preceding chapter, as the king began to persecute Latibshah, the pictures on the walls became endowed with life on account of the loving devotion (of Latisbshah).

SANTOBA POWAR'S RENUNCIATION

7. Now listen with respect to the story of Santoba Powar who was the noblest of the *Vaishnavas* and the great pillar of ascetics. 8. At his house there were horses, elephants, and fortune. He was honoured by

the king. As he once listened to the *kirtan* of Tukaram, repentance arose in his heart. 9. Said he, 'The worldly life is unsubstantial and illusory. The human body is perishable. Then why should I waste my life for nothing?' 10. Under his command there was an army which he sent for, paid off and dismissed. 11. Then he sent for the Brahmans and had them take away all his fortune and distributed among them his horses, elephants and chariots. 12. He put on a scanty and torn cloth, and being free from hindrances he gave himself up to the repetition of God's names. 13. He was the inhabitant of Ranjangaon Sandas and as soon as the ascetic spirit was established in him, he danced in the *kirtan* without any sense of shame. 14. He sat on an island, in a wood situated at the junction of the Mula, Mutha, and Bhimarathi; just as a parrot as soon as it is free from a cage flies away and sits in a tree; 15. or as a bee falls into temptation (for honey) and is shut up in a lotus-flower, but after a time it makes a determined effort and comes out full of repentance for having yielded; 16. or like an old serpent which after leaving its skin looks bright again; in the same way did Santoba feel as he gave up all attachment to his worldly life.

17. This news became known in the town. The people wondered and his mother wept out of affection and exclaimed, 'How unfortunate! 18. My son dismissed his army, and distributed his fortune, and has now become unconscious of his body! Our ancestral reputation will suffer and the evil-minded will laugh at us.' 19. She then put ornaments on her daughter-in-law and seating her in a palanquin said, 'When he sees his young wife he will return to his domestic life. 20. In the temple of Shiva on the island, Santaji sat alone in meditation when his wife suddenly appeared there in a palanquin. 21. He opened

his eyes and asked her, 'Why have you come here? Go back at once without saying a word.' 22. The wife answered, 'I cannot be separated far from you. If the water animals leave the ocean they have no other course. 23. It is useless to try and separate the bark from the tree, or the splendour from gold. 24. In the same way if one leaves his faithful wife what course on earth is open to her?' As Santoba heard his wife he said, 25. 'You see that my condition is one of being indifferent to all worldly things. You have many garments and ornaments and therefore I feel ashamed to call you my wife. 26. If you like to harden your heart against them, then give away your garments and jewellery to the beggars; or get up at once, and go straight home.'

SANTOBA'S REPENTANT WIFE

27. As the wife listened to her husband she repented of the way she was living and cast away her garments and jewellery. 28. The beautiful garments which she had on her she threw away on the trees. By this action of hers the goddess of rags was pleased. 29. Santaji had a *dhotar* (a male's garment) and half of it he gave to her. Now both of them were indifferent to worldly things and sat there meditating God. 30. He now felt so hungry that he was overcome by hunger. Then he said to his wife, 'Go into the town to beg for food. 31. In Pargaon of Salomalo we have many relatives, but now give up all sense of shame, and go there at once. 32. If the people address you kindly, do not say anything in reply. If anyone gives you a whole loaf do not accept it.' 33. 'Of course, my lord,' replied the faithful wife who started to go. Giving up all sense of public shame and affection she entered the town of Pargaon. 34. As she begged from door to door the men and women said, 'Asceticism has become fixed in you on account of your good deeds in

your former births.' 35. As she went from one house to another she uttered the words, 'Hari Vitthal!' If alms were not given her immediately she went onward at once.

36. On one occasion she went to the house of her sister-in-law and shouted the words 'Hari Vitthal' at the door. 37. Santaji's sister lived there and she came running out. Putting her hands around her neck she said affectionately, 38. 'Sister, you are very refined and very beautiful. I do not understand why God is angry with you so suddenly? 39. You were in the habit of sitting in a palanquin; the pebbles must now be paining your feet as you walk. You have cast away bright ornaments and have accepted indifference to worldly things. 40. Leaving aside gold-bordered garments you are now wearing tatters. You have given up eating the dainty foods of your house and go begging dry food.' 41. Then she brought out two cakes mixed with coarse sugar and ghee and insistently put them into her bag at once. 42. Seeing the food Santaji's wife said, 'Why do you give so much food? If the Lord of my life knows it he will be angry with me.' 43. The sister with a choked voice said, 'My dear, I give this out of affection. So go to your cottage and both of you eat it.' 44. Because she bound her by an oath her brother's wife returned. Coming to the island (she) requested her husband, 'Now dine, my lord.' 45. She laid before him the bag which contained the food obtained by begging. He could see there all the cakes. 46. When he who was ascetic in spirit saw this he enquired of his wife the reason of so much food and she explained everything to him. 47. With repentance he said to his wife, 'Go back to Pargaon and return the food to whom it belongs. 48. If you do not obey me, I will never dine.' Seeing her husband's resolve she returned there, 49. and related to her sister-in-law what had happened. As soon as she

reached the Bhivra river, the sun had set and darkness had filled the sky.

SANTOBA'S REFUSAL OF ALL FOOD

50. At the source of the river it had rained very heavily and the river was suddenly in flood. She was anxious at heart and did not know what to do. 51. 'The one who is my God, or *Guru*, or husband, is far away on the other side of the river. I have lost my family life. Fate is, indeed, insurmountable and mighty. 52. If one has not good deeds in her store she is not able to serve her husband. Now, O Keshav, rush to my help, and favour me.' In this way she pleaded with God. 53. The Lord of Pandhari seeing her trouble, rushed there at once and the Lord of the lowly as a boatman addressed her thus: 54. 'You are sitting here in anxiety, while on the other side is Santoba Powar. If you want to go there, I will take you across the river.' 55. Santoba's wife said to the boatman, 'Consider me as your sister and take me at once to the other side of the river.' 56. As she said this, Shri Hari seated her on His shoulders and in the twinkling of an eye took her across. 57. From a distance the Lord of Pandhari pointed out Santoba to her and the Husband of Rukmini disappeared just there. 58. When she went to her husband she related everything to him and He said, 'You met with the Lord of *Vaikunth* (Vishnu's heaven). Why is He then trying me to the uttermost? 59. If I do not see Shri Hari I have resolved not to eat food, O my wife.' 60. Now in Pargaon there was a grocer who was a pious *bhakta* of God and the Lord of Pandhari gave him an order the next day in his dream as follows. 61. 'Cook dainty foods in your house and feed Santoba. Because you possess good deeds I have shown Myself to you.' 62. As the grocer saw this wonderful dream he at once got up and had dainty dishes prepared in his house, and he

took them to Santoba. 63. Telling him everything that had happened he said, 'The Lord of Pandhari has commanded, so therefore please dine.' Saying this he fell at his feet, 64. The *bhakta* Santoba then said, 'You saw the Husband of Rukmini. What sins do I possess that He is trying me to the uttermost? 65. For until I have a sight of Shri Hari I will never eat food.' Seeing this was his resolve the grocer went away. 66. They say that in the *Kali Yuga* life depends upon food but Santoba's resolve was very strange. Knowing his heart the Husband of Rukmini gave him a *direct* manifestation.

A VEXATIOUS BRAHMAN HUSBAND OF RANJANGAON

67. After this, Santoba every day went to Ranjangaon to beg. Here there lived an impious Brahman who was always cross with his wife. 68. He was most provoking and quarrelled with his wife constantly. If the wife said anything to oppose him he frightened her by saying, 69. 'I shall become a *Bairagi* (an ascetic) like Santoba Powar, and when I give up my family affairs you will be in a sad plight.' 70. He said this boastfully and then his wife remained silent; just as an acrobat flourishes a weapon without bodily braveness; 71. or as a barren woman describes her longings without being pregnant; or as the shadow and roar of the clouds in the sky are in vain without rain; 72. or just as eunuchs assume artificial breasts; or just as an actor acts as a king without an umbrella and a throne; 73. in the same manner, those who talk about asceticism and peace, without possessing those, belong neither to the family life nor to the spiritual life. 74. That Brahman was always frightening his wife, so the poor thing felt anxious and kept silent. 75. One day the *bhakta* Santoba came to her house to beg and she related to him in detail everything about her husband. 76. 'O Swami, my husband says that he will become crazy like you.

If you will give me some suggestion I will follow it out.' 77. The Vishnu *bhakta* replied to her, 'If after this he quarrels with you, let him act as he pleases and send him to me. 78. I will give him a piece of advice and send him back to you. Afterwards he will become as manageable as a monkey which is taken from house to house by its *darvesh* (monkeyman). ' 79. ' Very well, ' said the Brahman woman as she bowed to him. Santoba accepted the alms and returned to his Ashram. 80. In a moment's time her husband returned home and said, ' Why are you late in cooking ? I am very hungry. 81. I will give up my family life and become like Santoba and go wherever I like. ' When he began to quarrel in this way, 82. the wife replied, ' Then why do you delay ? Become like him at once. '

SANTOBA'S *MANTRA* FOR AN IRRITABLE HUSBAND

83. Hearing his wife's reply the Brahman began to think, ' Why should I now live ?' and he flew into a rage. 84. He then took his clothes and a pot and at once went on to the island and said to Santoba, ' I have given up my family life and have come to you. 85. Now I am like you, to be sure. I will never give up your company. Now favour me (with your mystic *mantra*) and show me the way to spiritual riches. ' 86. The Vishnu-*bhakta* said, ' Surely I am fortunate to have your company without any effort. I do not see any ascetic so indifferent to worldly things as you are in the three worlds. 87. Now take this gourd and fetch me water. Leave your turban and other clothes here, for there are thieves on the watch.' 88. ' Very well, ' said the Brahman who at once went to the bank of the river, feeling very much troubled by hunger. 89. As soon as he had turned his back, Santoba tore to pieces the clothes the Brahman had been wearing and threw them on the bushes; he also hurled the man's pot into

the deep part of the river. Then the Brahman returned. 90. Santoba said to him, 'Wear a string and a clout around your loins.' So the Brahman with a sense of shame put away his *dhotar*. 91. Then he wore a clout and said to the *bhakta* of Vishnu, 'I feel so hungry. My life is in my throat.' 92. He plucked some wild fruits and began to eat with his wife. The Brahman said, 'This is very bitter. I don't like it.' 93. Santoba said in answer, 'As you have come to me so willingly, why should you care so much how things taste? 94. Well, I will give you something cool and will satisfy your hunger.' As he heard this reply of Santoba he was very much comforted. 95. Then he plucked some leaves of the bitter nimb and began to eat. The Brahman said to himself, 'My fate is not favourable to me. 96. I was quite happy in my house, even when eating coarse food. But I had a foolish idea and I left my home.' 97. He wept silently and said, 'What plan shall I now adopt? I feel the cold intensely, and am worn out with hunger.'

THE REPENTANT HUSBAND RETURNS TO HIS WIFE

98. Santoba could see the condition of his heart and so he asked him, 'Why were you regardless of your home and why have you come here?' 99. The Brahman replied, 'My fortune has taken an evil turn. I quarrelled with my wife for nothing. Thereby I felt sad at heart and came to you. 100. But your company is very hard. You tore away my clothes. Now if I intend to go home, shame overcomes me. 101. If I go at night, my wife will not let me in. She will say, "Who is this *gosavi* (a mendicant) in a clout?"' 102. The Vishnu-*bhakta* answered, 'You always said to your wife, "I will become indifferent to worldly things like Santoba and go into a forest." 103. Now vow by God that from to-day you will not say so again Then I will take you to your house without anyone's

knowledge.' 104. The Brahman at once clasped Santoba's feet and said, 'If I quarrel again with my wife, may my tongue wither. I say this with God as my Witness.' 105. At night the *bhakta* Santoba went to the Brahman's house and said to the latter's wife privately, 106. 'I have given your husband my *mantra* (advice) and now I consign him to your care. I will send him presently, therefore do not quarrel with him now. 107. He will come here in a clout, therefore you give him a new cloth to wear.' Hearing this her heart was comforted. 108. Having advised the man's wife in that way he returned and told the Brahman to go safely home. 109. 'Mind, if you again quarrel with your wife, you will not find so harsh a person as myself to deal wlth.' The man placed his head at Santoba's feet and started homeward at once. 110. For fear of being seen he entered the town at night in the dark. Said he, 'If the Brahmans see me, they will excommunicate me.' 111. Therefore he entered his house quickly and tremblingly, and from that time he never again quarrelled with his wife.

SANTOBA AS A PANDHARPUR PILGRIM

112. After this event Santoba started for Pandhari as a pilgrim in the month of *Ashadh* (July). He was as delighted as a girl is when she visits her mother's home. 113. In the same way the *Vaishnava bhakta* went on singing and dancing full of love and two thousand pilgrims joined him on the way. 114. On the tenth bright (night) of *Ashodh* the *Warkari* (pilgrims) arrived at Narsinhapura where there is the junction of the Nira and Bhivra (Bhima). 115. It was the month of *Ashadh*, the rainy season, and the river was in high flood, its bed overflowing with water. Seeing this all became anxious. 116. They said, 'If we are not able to cross the river to-day we shall not be able to reach Pandharpur tomorrow. It seems the Husband of

Rukmini will not let us have the vision of him on the *Ekadashi* day.' 117. While they were talking in this way they reached the bank of the river and said, 'If there were at least one boat, we would all go over to the other bank of the river.' 118. At this the *bhakta* Santoba thought to himself, 'If we care for our body how shall we be able to see Bhagwant (God)?' 119. Therefore, having decided in his heart that Shri Hari (God) is both the Saviour and also the Killer, he went into the water at once and walked on. 120. A Vishnu-*bhakta* is devoted and loving and water cannot drown him. The water reached to his calves only. 121. Santoba took his *Vina* in his hand and began to sing the praises of God and he was able to cross the river at once. 122. When the other pilgrims saw this wonder they began to say, 'How are you going alone to the other side of the river and leaving us all here? 123. Believing you to be the image of God Himself we came in your company. But fate destines it otherwise, for we have not the good fortune (to go to the other side). 124. We had heard of your incomparable reputation and thus intended to go to Pandharpur in your company. Now we will all go back.' 125. Hearing the pilgrims' statement he stood in the water and put up his hands. Listen to what he said! 126. 'O men and women of all castes, even the quadrupeds, the great and the small, do not ponder, but follow me at once. 127. Entertain no fear at heart, for the Lord of Pandhari will save you.' At this assurance all were comforted. 128. They said to one another, 'Because Santoba is going to Pandhari he found the water knee deep only. Let us follow him.' 129. They put their loads on their horses and all the pilgrims got up in a moment and went one after the other until they reached the river. 130. Seeing this the Lord of Pandhari thought to Himself, 'The river is in flood and all will be drowned. 131. Santoba repeats My names, therefore he could get across, but all are not like him. They will not float like wood but will sink like stones. 132. If I do not rush to their help My *bhakta's* promise will be falsified. And if the pilgrims are drowned who will come to visit Me? 133 The wise will then consider the words of past saints as false.' Hear what the Life of the world did after saying this!

GOD AS A TORTOISE CARRIES PILGRIMS ACROSS A RIVER

134. The God of gods, by Whose help all beings in the universe live, became a tortoise in order to take all the pilgrims on His back over to the other bank. 135. The bed of the river was very wide, therefore the Husband of Rukmini became as large as that. The Lord of the world evades the disasters of His *bhaktas* in various ways. 136. The Lord of the world is revered by Brahmadev and others and Shiva contemplates Him at heart. He carried the pilgrims on His back. This to me is most wonderful. 137. Well, all the men and women, the small and the great of all the eighteen castes, loudly shouted the names of God and walked all together. 138. The *Vaishnava bhaktas* loaded their horses and bullocks and shouted loudly the names of God and went into the water. 139. They found the water only knee deep, at which all wondered and said, 'We were detained for nothing.' 140. Some clapped their hands saying, 'Blessed is the company of saints. Then with peaceful hearts they arrived on the other bank of the river. 141. But they did not know that it was God Himself who had saved them in the form of a tortoise. By the wonderful *maya* (of God) all beings are enveloped in an illusion of ignorance.

142. Then the *Vaishnava bhakta* with the other pilgrims reached Pandharpur, bathed in the Chandrabhaga river, and performed a *kirtan* with love. 143. All went to the main door, prostrated themselves before God and embraced Him,

and with sincere devotion bowed to His feet. 144. Santoba said, 'O Shri Hari, Thou dost protect Thy *bhaktas* in various ways. In praising Thee the tongue of the serpent Shesha became weary. 145. O God, Thou didst take the form of a tortoise and didst save the ignorant on Thy back. Now give me a refuge at Thy feet.' In this way Santoba pleaded with God. 146. At this the Merciful to the lowly smiled and said, 'You are My loving *bhakta*. Remain with me for ever.'

NILOBA AND HIS DAUGHTER'S WEDDING

147. There is another very interesting story. May the fortunate listeners pay attention to it with reverence. 148. O pious ones, listen to the sweet life of him (Niloba) to whom Tukaram, bestowing a great favour, gave the mystic *mantra* in a dream. 149. Niloba did not know what public honour and hypocrisy were. He performed the *kirtan* of Hari with devotion. He used to describe the lives of saints by quoting the words of the ancient saints. 150. He had children and other relatives. Even then he was far away from egoism. He accepted what was given him without begging, and with what he received he was hospitable to guests who came to him. 151. One day he planned the wedding of his daughter. His relatives were impious and hypocrites, and at his house there were no provisions of food, and so forth. 152. His wife said to him, 'You are indifferent to worldly things. In the end the evil-minded will make fun of us; so I think.' 153. The Life of the world knew this and assuming the form of a old Brahman he wore a torn cloth and came to their house. 154. He had a scarf on his shoulder at the end of which some small provisions of food were tied. In this way he went to Niloba and said, 155. 'I am a poor and weak Brahman. I have some provisions of food on me. Take them and give me a dinner.' 156. Niloba

bowed to the Brahman and said, 'Your provisions are not needed. Now at dinner-time make an offering of food to God and dine just here.' 157. On this Shri Hari said, 'I long to eat a stuffed cake, for I like sweet food. Therefore get the cooking ready at once and give me a meal to my heart's content.' 158. Niloba told his wife, 'Keep aside the provisions of the Brahman. Cook the food at once and feed the Brahman.' 159. 'By all means,' she said and took the provisions in her garment. She added, 'These provisions are too scanty; then how will you get full satisfaction?' 160. On this the Husband of Rukmini said, 'You put this in the provisions of the wedding, and take your own provisions and quickly satisfy my hunger. 161. If you do not accept my provisions I will not dine at all.' On this the loving *bhakta* said to his wife, 162 'What difficulty can there be in feeding one Brahman? Now quickly do the cooking and satisfy the Brahman.' 163. Then the Husband of Rukmini said, 'Cooking will take a long time. Therefore I will eat with love just what is ready.' 164. Then the Pervader of the world dined with His *bhakta* and at night while He was sitting quietly He said to Niloba Bowa, 165. 'Tomorrow is the wedding of your daughter. In your house there is no Brahman to fetch water, therefore if you keep Me (to do the work) I shall be able to prepare dainty foods. 166. Just for the love of God, I will fetch water.' 'Very well,' said Niloba who fell at His feet. 167. The next morning *Vanamali* (Krishna) got up quickly and without the knowledge of anyone performed the sweeping, also sprinkling the ground with water. 168. In the meantime the father of the bridegroom arrived with five hundred men as his wedding party. The bridegroom was honoured at the boundary of the town and then all his party went to lodge in a house assigned to them.

WHEN GOD PROVIDES NOTHING IS LACKING

169. Because the Life of the world was the Provider there was no lack of provisions. Who will have to remain fasting under the shade of a wish-tree ? 170. If the sun comes as a guest to one's house there will be no lack of light. If the river Ganges itself sits in a pot of water there will be no lack of water. 171. If clouds themselves do the sprinkling of water how can there be a dry place left? If *Gajavadana* (Ganpati) gives a lesson how will the pupil remain dull ? 172. The palmist cannot find any defects in the signs of one's personal beauty when the Creator Himself has created it? When Sarasvati (goddess of learning) does the writing herself what possibility of a mistake can there be ? 173. In the same manner, since *Hrishikeshi* (The Lord of the heart) personally came to the wedding, how could the provisions fall short ? He took the sling on His shoulders and brought water. 174. The provisions of the Brahman were put in with the household provisions and thereby these increased to abundance. Five hundred men dined regularly but even then they were not lacking. 175. Even in the hurry of other work, He quickly gave the provisions. He removed the plates after dinner without any delay and swept the yard clean. 176. If any of the diners lacked anything, the Life of the world at once served it to him. He joined His hands and requested the party of the bridegroom to dine quietly. 177. Niloba wondered in his mind and said, 'This Brahman is a very good man. The ceremony has passed off successfully. He lets nothing be lacking'. 178. Then the loving *bhakta* said, 'You were very useful to me in the wedding. Kindly tell me your name.' 179. On this the Life of the world said, 'Vithoba is my name. I ate to my content sweet food in your house for four days of the wedding.' 180. Niloba said to himself, 'I am not able to repay his kindness. But I think I should

cordially give him a cloth at the time of his going.' 181. Well, Shri Hari lived in his house for five days as a Brahman and personally laboured in the house of His *bhakta*. 182. On the sixth day after seeing the wedding party off, Niloba returned home and *Hrishikeshi* (the Lord of the heart) accompanied him.

183. In the presence of all, the Brahman went into the god-room (i. e. the room containing the idol-shrine) and in a moment's time disappeared. Niloba said, ' I will call Vithoba now.' 184. With a new gold-bordered scarf in his hand he called to Vithoba in order to put it on him (as a marriage gift and thanksgiving), but the lotus-eyed One could nowhere be seen. 185. At once he understood in his mind what it was and said, ' I put to trouble the Lord of Pandhari. May fire burn up my attachment to family life. To-day I have done a very wrong thing.' 186. Then the Husband of Rukmini appeared to him in a dream and placed His hand on Niloba's head saying, ' I will for ever remain with you with My hands on My hips.' 187. For his love of him, Shri Hari is still at Pimpalner. On the second day of the dark half of the month of *Phalgun* (March) there is a great and clamorous festival.

THE STORY OF UDDHAVA CHIDGHAN

188. There is another most interesting narrative of Uddhava Chidghan, an inhabitant of Dharur. He went from country to country lovingly performing *kirtans*. 189. As the result of his experience he had composed many interesting poems in which his audience, consisting of loving, unworldly and pious *bhaktas*, were absorbed. 190. By chance he happened to go to Bedar on the first day of the bright half of *Chaitra* (April) and performed a *kirtan* in the town that day with great *eclat*. 191. Many wise and learned men and the pious *bhaktas* of other castes full of love listened to his *kirtan* and their

minds were absorbed in it. 192. The people intended to hold his *kirtans* in succession, but Uddhava said to them, 'I have to go back quickly to Dharur for the festival of *Shri Ram Jayanti* (the festival of Rama's birth).' 193. The people requested him to perform that same *Ramanavami* festival just there, and considering their intention he acquiesced. 194. Then a capacious house was found and a canopy was erected, and in it a chair of state was prepared in which the Lord of Ayodhya (Rama) was seated. 195. He invited *Vaishnava* performers of *kirtans* and had *kirtans* performed. Brahmans were fed with various kinds of daintily cooked foods. 196. On one occasion the noble *Vaishnavas* were going in a procession in bands of singers with banners in their hands. In front of them musical instruments were sounded; and thus there was a great and delightful scene. 197. The *Haridases* (leading singers) went on singing with love near to a mosque where some Muhammadans were sitting at ease. Evil-minded as they were they said between themselves, 198. 'Uddhava Chidghan invites many *Haridases*, and has started a great heathenish nuisance; we will disgrace them by throwing dirt and dung on them.' 199. In those days the Muhammadans were very powerful and none cared to see what was just or what was unjust. Five hundred sly and arrogant Muhammadans of the town were sitting there. 200. The *Haridases* went on singing and dancing and the musical instruments were sounded in front of them. In this way the procession arrived before the mosque.

MUHAMMADANS BEAT *VAISHNAVA BHAKTAS*

201. The mischievous Muhammadans at once rushed at them and threw cowdung and earth on the *Vaishnavas*. They snatched the banners from their hands and beat them soundly. 202. They broke the strings of the *vinas*

and broke the *mridang* (drum). All fell in confusion, and the *Haridases* returned homeward. 203. The disciples of Uddhav Chidghan at once reported the sad event to him. As he heard it he felt very sad at heart; 204. as a bit of salt falls in milk, and it is spoiled; or as the cook feels restless when a dog touches the cooked food; 205. or as the mother of the bridegroom is sad at heart when the light is put out by a moth (a bad omen) while the bride and bridegroom are dining; in the same way he felt sad; 206. or as when a hungry person puts a mouthful of food into his mouth and at the same time a fly goes in with it; in the same manner when the Muhammadans disgraced the *Haridases*, Uddhava Chidghan felt. 207. Then he went near the state chair of the image and said 'Victory, victory to Thee, O Raghunath. If Thou didst not like this, then where was the necessity of so much ado? 208. Thou art the Soul of the universe and the Husband of Janaki. Thou dwellest in the hearts of all, then why should I lament for nothing? The saints have been dishonoured.' 209. Then he lifted the image of Raghunath and kept it in the god-room. He destroyed the state chair and pulled down the canopy. 210. He bowed to the *Haridases* and sat singing the praises of Shri Rama.

MARUTI DESTROYS A MOSQUE

Maruti became full of anger and said, 'I will turn Bedar (a Muhammadan city) upside down. 211. My Swami is Shri Raghunath, and His *bhaktas* were celebrating His festival. If the *Vaishnavas* are disgraced here in this manner then my life is good for nothing.' 212. Then the son of Anjani (Maruti) stood on the mosque in which the five hundred arrogant and mischievous Muhammadans were sitting. 213. Maruti took hold of a wall of the mosque and shook it with his hands. Close by there was a cottage of a Muhammadan *fakir* (a mendicant) who saw it. 214. The *fakir* was a very knowing man and understood what it meant. Maruti was angry because the *bhaktas* of Rama had been disgraced. 215. He therefore joined his hands palm to palm and he said to Hanumant (Maruti), 'Close by is my cottage which must be saved.' 216. When the mischievous men heard the words they said between themselves, 'The *fakir* seems to be crazy. We do not know to whom he is talking.' 217. He replied, 'A monkey has come and is about to pull down the mosque. Therefore you get up at once and hurry out.' 218. The mischievous men then said, 'The mosque is built of stones and surely even the father of a monkey will not be able to pull it down.' 219. At this the Servant of Rama (Maruti) flew into a rage and in the twinkling of an eye he brought down the mosque. 220. An uproar of sorrow arose and they said, 'A very astonishing event has taken place.' Then some reported the matter in the Muhammadan square. 221. The report said, 'The mosque suddenly fell down. Many of the mischief-mongers died. Those who survived had a severe internal pain and they rolled on the earth restlessly. 222. The *fakir* who saw the monkey hastened to tell the Muhammadans that Uddhava Chidghan was a great *bhakta* of God, and that they had persecuted him. 223. The mischievous fellows had thrown on them dung and dirt. Therefore it was that the monkey Maruti resolved in his mind to destroy the mosque.'

MUHAMMADAN KING'S PENITENCE

224. Hearing this news, the Muhammadan king was frightened and came to Uddhava Chidghan and bowed to his feet with sincere devotion. 225. He placed at his feet a thousand rupees and said, 'Perform your festival without any fear. 226. The men who persecuted you have gone to the home of death. Now request Maruti to

save us.' 227. The townsmen then assembled together and again put up the canopy. The state chair was decorated and the Husband of Janaki was seated in it. 228. Then with cymbals and drums the *Vaishnavas*, moved by love, sang and danced with delight. They performed the ceremony with great *eclat* again until the twelfth day. 229. Those who hate saints are unhappy all their life. Disasters hunt them out in various ways. 230. All disasters disappear at the remembrance of the feet of Shri Vitthal and bodily afflictions depart at once. 231. On the thirteenth day there was a dramatic performance and the *bhaktas* of Hari were all honoured. Mahipati says that the favour of singing God's praises is the fittest reward to the saints.

232. *Swasti* (Peace)! This book is the *Shri Bhaktavijaya*. The Lord of the world will be pleased to listen to it. Therefore, O pious and loving *bhaktas*, listen to the fifty-sixth interesting chapter.

CHAPTER LVII

VISOBA SARAF

Obeisance to Shri Ganesh. Obeisance to the Inhabitant of the Ocean of Milk.

GOD THE REAL ACTOR

1. Victory, victory to Thee, Whose abode is the ocean of milk, dark as a cloud, of various forms and names, and assuming *avatars* without end, O Good Being. Thy glory is not known even to the *Vedas*. 2. Victory, Victory to Thee, the Enjoyer of *Vaikunth* (Vishnu's heaven), Ocean of virtues, and Home of mercy. Knowing Thy glory, the Daughter of the ocean has become a suppliant at Thy feet. 3. Victory to Thee, Dweller at Gokul, Whose complexion is as blue as a cloud, the Stealer of milk and curds, Attracter of the Heart, Inhabitant of Mathura, the Killer of Kansa, and the Founder of religion, O Shri Hari ! 4. Victory to Thee, the Inhabitant of Dwarka, Whose banner is with an emblem of the eagle, and who dost act as in a play O *Adhokshaja* (God), Thy glory is without comparison, and only the daughter of King Bhimaka (Laxmi) knows it. 5. Victory, victory to Thee, Whose abode is on the bank of the Bhima river, O Giver of the blessing to Pundalik, and granting assurance to Thy *bhaktas* Thou lettest the shadow of Thy mercy rest on them. 6. O Husband of Rukmini, Thou hast done a wonderful thing in helping me to write this book, dull as I am. Thou hast as it were granted an assurance to a moth, and enabled it to lift (Mount) Meru. 7. Thou didst collect bears and monkeys, and through them didst effect the capture of (the ancient) Lanka city (in Ceylon); as Dnyandev granted a blessing to a buffalo and caused it to recite the

Vedas. 8. As a *paris* (touchstone) lends its virtue to iron and turns it to pure gold; or as the Ganges gives its sacredness to a streamlet; 9. or as musk might cause the earth to be weighed with it as of equal value; in the same way, O Lord of *Vaikunth* (Vishnu's heaven), through Thy mercy Thou hast caused my words to be written in a book. 10. O *Adhokshaja* (Vishnu), Thou art the highest of all. With love Thou dost worship Thy *bhaktas*, but Thou dost not come to them when various means of coaxing are used. 11. Thy *bhaktas* sing Thy praises. Thou dost like their lives. Thou hast placed me in the front as Thy instrument; but in reality Thou art the independent speaker.

MAHIPATI'S VALUATION OF HIS BOOK

12. Now let the listener pay attention. The book has come to the last chapter. It is as if while churning the curds one should see butter suddenly; 13. or as if one might see nectar fruit on a mango tree while being watered by him; or as if a medal of gold studded with jewels should itself come and hang around one's neck; 14. or while occupying oneself in cooking one should suddenly obtain a dish of dainty food; or while labouring in a field a dense crop should suddenly appear. 15. I think the last chapter is like the *Gopalkala* on the full moon day at the end of the festival at Pandhari. 16. In this book there are stories of many saints. The chapters thus far are fifty-six in number. These are, as it were, great jewels of fifty-six countries, which shine by their lustre. 17. Or this book, the *Bhaktavijaya*, is as it were the collection of fifty-six languages. Need I myself tell you that merely by listening to it the pious ones become victorious. 18. They are, as it were, the sharp weapons of fifty-six countries. The goddess Kalika (wife of Shiva) in the form of forgiveness wields them in Her hands, and on the

buffalo called anger comes riding along, so I think; 19. or they are the rivers of fifty-six countries which bring the water of love and are in loving search of the ocean of delight called Shri Pandurang; 20. or they are, as it were, the kings of fifty-six countries who with victorious flags in their hands easily destroy the army of the enemy of mankind, viz. *maya* (illusion), and enjoy the happy state of the fourth form of salvation, absorption in God. 21. Listen now to the fifty-seventh chapter which is the jewel crowning all the fifty-six chapters; just as the rich lovingly eat cooked rice with curds at the end of their dinner. 22. In the preceding chapter are related the persecution of Uddhava Chidghan by the Muhammadans, the miracle worked by Maruti, and the completion of the festival.

VISOBA SARAF DURING FAMINE

23. Visoba Saraf was a loving *bhakta* of God. He lived in the sacred city of Pandhari. Although a banker, he was indifferent to worldly things. 24. He had four sons and a faithful wife who was favourably inclined to him. She never opposed the order of her husband even in hard times. 25. Visoba never told a falsehood either in his family life or in business. He gave food to the hungry with respect. 26. There was a dreadful famine in the land and grain was sold at two *payalis* a rupee. Hungry Brahmans came and sat in his house. 27. All his wealth and grain were consumed in charity, but the beggars knew nothing of the donor's own condition. 28. A child struggles at its mother's breast, even though there is not a drop of milk in it. Although the subjects suffer many losses, still the king considers them as false. 29. A child cannot realize the ability or inability of his father. Likewise a beggar does not understand the personal difficulties of One who befriends him. 30. The hungry therefore came

and sat at Visoba's door and he gave food to all these as his means permitted. 31. When he could help in no other way, he sold his jewelry and valuable household vessels and thereby gave food to the beggars. 32. He cared nothing at all for popularity or affection; he had given up all care about his domestic life: he was even negligent of his body; and he meditated on the Lord of Pandhari. 33. He had no food for the hungry and no one in the town could give him a loan. People said, 'He has ruined his business and has become notorious as a bankrupt.' 34. Some said, 'He is a fool. He does not understand his own benefit. There are wise men who achieve both worldly gain and spiritual riches. 35. Now those who will believe Visoba will themselves come to the same sad state.' Men and women talked in this manner and all called him names. 36. Some of them said, 'His fate is not favourable to him, for although he had wealth and grain, he never became wearied in using them for pilgrims.'

VISOBA LOANS MONEY FROM A PATHAN

37. In Kasegaon there was a Pathan who did not know Visoba's condition. He (Visoba) borrowed money from him and again gave food to the hungry. 38. He borrowed time and again and the loan amounted to seven hundred rupees. He executed a loan-bond in writing at an interest of two per cent and gave it to him. 39. There was an ascetic of superhuman power by name of Rampuribawa. He had gone to Pandhari on pilgrimage and in order to test Visoba he had assumed a very dirty appearance. 40. He thought to himself, 'I must see his condition, wheter he is the same to all beings (or whether he makes any distinction). 41. He took the filthy mud from the sewer and smeared his person with it. He fastened a string of tatters around his waist and wore a dirty clout.

42. He took an earthen dish to eat from, and when the night advanced three hours he went to his house. 43. Like one crazy he called out to Visoba and said, "I am hungry." When Visoba heard him he came out. 44. Although he did not recognize him as an ascetic of superhuman powers, yet he requested him, 'O *swami*, dine here and then go back to your ashram. 45. Then he (Rampuribawa) placed a dish of food before him, and himself sat in front of him (Visoba). He had dirt on his person and it stank horribly. 46. Visoba with warm water washed him with his own hands. Then quietly wiping him he put on him a new clout. 47. He offered him sandalwood paste and rice and worshipped him, and put around his neck garlands of *tulsi* leaves; then fed him and prostrated himself before him. 48. He gave him a leaf of *tulsi* for cleansing the mouth and saw him off. Rampuri thought to himself, 'He (Visoba) is surely an adept in the knowledge of the soul. 49. He has the same eye for the tiger, the cow, and the scorpion. If an expert in such matters were to search for another man like him he could hardly find one. 50. For he honours in the same way a prince and a pauper. Even if searched for on the earth there cannot be many like him 51. He looks on the wealth and wife of another person as a vomit. There are not many like him, even if the three worlds were searched. 52. The Husband of Rukmini stays day and night at the house of him who pays the same respect to the helpless, to beggars and to Brahmans. 53. Such is the state of mind of Visoba and therefore he worshipped me.' So thinking the ascetic went to the ashram.

VISOBA'S BANKRUPTCY

54. Then an evil-minded person went to the Pathan of Kasegaon and told him the news of Visoba's insolvency. 55. He said, 'Go and ask for your money now.' Then

he went to Pandhari at once and addressed Visoba. 56. 'Pay back my money without delay or else I will sit dunning at your door.' 57. Hearing what he said, the loving *bhakta* felt very concerned and said to himself, 'I have no money at hand to pay you, what shall I do?' 58 Then bracing his mind with courage he told the creditor that he would send him the money after seven days. 59. He said, 'O Brahman, I cannot put faith in you, therefore let there be someone as security.' Then he invited some persons and told them of the agreement. 60. The men assured the Pathan that Visoba never told a lie and that on that day he was sure to send the money to him. 61. At this assurance the creditor got up and said as he went that he should think well and pay off the money. 62. Saying this the Pathan went back to Kasegaon and he determined to recover the money as soon as the period was over. 63. The six days went by and Visoba was very anxious in his mind. He said, 'The creditor will be waiting for the money, what shall I do now? 64. I have never told a falsehood, but now the time has unfortunately come at last.' He was sad at heart and looked very grave. 65. He was engaged in the worship of God but his mind was not at rest. The creditor was before his mind's eye and he could not restrain his restlessness.

VISOBA'S UNEXPECTED HELP

66. When the Husband of Rukmini saw this difficulty of Visoba's He assumed the form of his old secretary. 67. The Lord of Pandhari took the principal, viz., rupees seven hundred, and its interest, went to Kasegaon and said to the Pathan, 68. 'You know me as the old secretary of Visoba. He sends me here as the seven days are at an end. 69. Now you reckon up your account, together with the principal and its interest.' The creditor was astonished

at heart as he heard *Chakrapani* (Vishnu) saying this. 70. Then the Pathan asked the Brahman, 'He could not obtain a loan. Where has he found a creditor? I really wonder.' 71. On this the Husband of Rukmini replied, 'Visoba is very righteous; he never tells any lie whatever.' 72. The Life of the world sat near him, asked him to fetch the loan-deed and said, 'Ask some men to come here and in their presence square your accounts.' 73. The Friend of His *bhaktas* paid the money in the presence of some of the men of the town and took the deed from him. 74. He went to Visoba's home in Pandharpur, and tearing the deed a little at the top, left it in his book.

75. As he untied his *Bhagavadgita* he saw the deed executed in his name. He made out his own handwriting and felt very much astonished. 76. Said he, 'I have not returned the loan of the Pathan, then who has destroyed the deed?' He asked his wife and sons about it. 77. Then he patched the deed on the back and joined it as before. 'It must go to him to whom it belongs,' he said. 78. The pious *bhakta* of God went to Kāsegaon and saw the Pathan in the bazaar who enquired, 'Why have you come? 79. Your old secretary came to me this morning in a hurry, paid off my money with interest and took away the deed.' 80. Visoba replied, 'I do not know anything about it, but just to-day I saw the deed quite accidentally in my book. 81. I had no money to pay you but I had the destroyed deed. Therefore I came to tell you about it.' 82. When the God-loving *bhakta* said this the creditor answered, 'No, it is a lie.' Then he asked the men to come in whose presence the money had been paid off. 83. They also told the same story which made him wonder very much. Then he immediately returned to the sacred city of Pandhari. 84. He sent for his secretary and asked him about it. 'How did you pay off my loan? Tell me the truth.' 85. He said, 'I swear

by Pandurang that I know nothing about it.' As he said this, tears streamed from the eyes of Visoba. 86. He exclaimed, 'O Ocean of mercy, the Lord of the world, Thou didst worry Thyself for my sake.' Saying this he clasped the feet of God and was overcome with love. 87. The Husband of Rukmini said to Visoba, 'This is known all over the sacred town. Men and women have seen the evidence and wonder at it.'

GOD HELPS HIS *BHAKTAS* IN THEIR DIFFICULTIES

88. When a God loving *bhakta* is in difficulty, the One Who is as blue as a cloud comes to his help at once. The Merciful to the lowly does not think of time. 89. In the past, during the *Krita*, *Treta*, and *Dwapar* Ages, there were real *avatars* of God, and Bhagwant (God) saved His *bhaktas*. Can there be any wonder in this? 90. In the *Kali Yuga*, Shripati is personally present in an image of stone, and in His Buddha (silent) form He still gives various evidences to His people and increases the reputation of the saints. 91. But the *Kali Yuga* is better than all the past three Ages, for in the *Bhagwat*, Shuka has said that the Lord of *Vaikunth* (Vishnu) meets with His *bhaktas* within three and a half *ghatikas*. 92. But there is one difficulty. The *bhakta* must be pious and simple. Bhagwant (God) helps him who is not entangled in the snare of wrong conceptions. 93. 'It may be, or it may not be,' he who with such a doubt at heart, worships God, becomes an enemy of his own interest, and remains at a distance from the feet of Hari. 94. The Husband of Rukmini heartily wishes that His *bhaktas* should fall into difficulties, and then that He should rush to their aid and thus increase their fame; 95. just as a boatman at the bank of a river thinks, 'I should like to see a drowning person, and then I will jump into the water at once and pull him out.' 96. A generous person starts

a charitable dining house and day and night just wishes that a hungry person would come to him and then he could feed him to satisfaction. 97. A good physician thinks, 'The king should have some disease and then I will treat him for my own benefit and cure him of his disease.' 98. A wise speaker thinks in his mind, 'Someone should come with his difficulties and then with many illustrations I will solve all his doubts.' 99. In the same manner, with both His hands on His hips, the Husband of Rukmini thinks in His mind, 'The *bhaktas* should throw their burden on Me and give themselves up to meditation ; 100. then I will help them and increase their reputation in the world.' Shripati always thinks like this but no one else has the courage to do it.

CHAPTER LVII

(*Continued*)

SUMMARY OF THE *BHAKTAVIJAYA*

101. Thus far the good people have listened quietly to the interesting stories of *bhaktas* who had severed the snares of desires and had cast away all love for their perishable persons.

CHAPS : 1–3 JAYADEV & TULSIDAS

102. Now I will recapitulate the contents from the beginning of the book. In the beginning, I bowed to Ganesh and Sarasvati and then meditated on the feet of my *Sadguru*. 103. Many sins were committed in the *Kali Yuga*. This was known in the ocean of milk. Then the Husband of Lakshmi told His *bhaktas* to become *avatars* in the world of mortals, 104. in order to explain the glory of God's name to the people and make them worship God. This all have listened to in the *first chapter*. 105. That the thieves persecuted Jayadev, that Padmavati lied, and that the Life of the world brought her back to life, is all related in the *second chapter*. 106. A stone bull was made to eat food, a dead body was made alive by a blessing, and Tulsidas met with Raghunandan (Rama): all this is described in the *third chapter*.

CHAPS : 4–15 NAMDEV, KABIR AND DNYANESHWAR

107. Nama was found in a shell at which Damasheti greatly rejoiced, and the conversation between the Lord of Pandhari and Gonai is given: these things are

told *in the fourth.* 108. Kabir's birth by means other than the womb; his bringing up in a Muhammadan family; how the Holder of the *Sharang* bow (Krishna) wove the gold-bordered scarf for him ; and made him righteous by His own mercy; 109. that he committed a theft for the saints and killed his own son,Kamal, with his own hand ; how the king hanged Kamal, and how the saints brought him to life again ; 110. the assembling of saints in his yard ; and the help which the Lord of Ayodhya rendered Kabir by assuming his form in countless ways : with these stories there *ends the seventh chapter.* 111. Nivritti, Sopan and Dnyaneshwar were born as *avatars* from a *sannyasi* ; the Brahmans excommunicated them; these beautiful things are related in the *eighth chapter.* 112. In the *ninth chapter* is related the well-known story of how Dnyaneshwar made a he-buffalo to recite the *Vedas* ; how he worked a miracle by feeding his ancestors by *mantras*; 113. Dnyandev takes Nama from Pandhari with him to sacred places : and Nama brings to life a dead cow in his *kirtan* at Hastanapur (Delhi); all this is described in the *tenth chapter.* 114. Kabir's wife was very virtuous ; this made the grocer repent ; his meeting with Nama ; these things are described in the *eleventh chapter.* 115. How in Marvad the people were troubled by thirst and there gushed out water from the well, and how the god Naganath made the temple turn round, are related in the *twelfth chapter.* 116. In the *thirteenth chapter* we see the Lord of Pandhari dining with Nama in the dark half of *Magh* (March) and therefore the Brahmans excommunicated God. 117. *Adhokshaja* (Krishna) tells Rukmini that He likes His *bhaktas* very much and Satyabhama asked a secret of Narad; these things are related in the *fourteenth chapter.* 118. God assumed a *sagun* form and manifested Himself to the Brahmans and consigned them to the care of Dnyandev: this story is related in the *fifteenth chapter.*

CHAPS: 16–21 KURMADAS; RAKA & GORA; NAMDEV; JAGAMITRA NAGA; JOGA PARAMANAND; NARAHARI & NAMDEV; NAMDEV & JANABAI

119. God went to meet Savata who hid Him in his stomach; this wonderful sight was shown to Nama; and then God met Kurmadas; these narratives are given in the *sixteenth chapter*. 120. Gora the potter trampled on his own child; the Lord of the heart was pleased with him in his *kirtan*; the stumps of his hands were made whole; the child (being brought back to life) was given to its mother; 121. the kittens were put in the furnace, and the Lord of Pandhari saved them; Raka the potter had a remarkable ascetic spirit: these stories are described in the *seventeenth chapter*. 122. In the *eighteenth chapter* there is the wonderful story of how all the saints laughed at Nama, how the Lord of Pandhari then pointed out Visoba as his guru, 123. how at Nama's touch the particles of sand turned to so many touchstones, how Nama showed this wonder to Parisa Bhagwat and gave him the favour (the mystic *mantra*). 124. In the *nineteenth chapter* is related how Jagamitra was tormented by the *Havaldar* (or village officer); the Lord of the heart then appeared as a tiger, and showed the wonderful sight to the people. 125. In the *twentieth chapter* is related how Joga (Parmanand) felt great repentance, tied himself to bullocks, and in this way mortified himself; how the Holder of the *Sharang* bow (Krishna) met with him, and assured him with a blessing; 126. how Narhari Sonar observed a difference between Shankar (Shiva) and Hari (Vishnu); and how Murari (Vishnu) met with him in one form, are related. 127. In the *twenty-first* chapter is described the story of how the Lord of Pandhari ground corn with Jani, and Himself wrote the *abhangs* composed by her at which the saints laughed joyfully.

CHAPS: 22–30 MATSYENDRANATH, GORAKNATH & CHANGDEV; CHOKHAMELA, NAMDEV, JIVA & TATVA; PADMANABH & KABIR; ROHIDAS; KING PIPAJI; NARSI MEHETA & THE MATURITY CEREMONY OF HIS DAUGHTER

128. How Shankar (Shiva) gave the mystic *mantra* to Parvati; how it produced Matsyendra from the womb of a fish; how through God's *lila* (sport) Goraksha was produced from the ashes of a dunghill; 129. how Changdev made a tiger his vehicle; and how Dnyandev made a wall move, and met with him under the *Vishrantvat* (a banian tree under which they rested); these are narratives found in the *twenty-second chapter.* 130. In the *twenty-third chapter* the story of Chokhamela is given and two Brahmans, Jiva and Tatva, were ex-communicated by their caste because they had become Kabir's disciples. 131. In the *twenty-fourth chapter* the story of Padmanabha is given, his disease destroyed as he simply uttered 'Shri Rama,' and how Kabir 'sold' his wife to a grocer, are all related in this chapter. 132. The *bhakta* Rohidas was troubled by the Brahmans because he had put Shaligram (God) in a skin; he ripped open his stomach and showed them the sacred thread: this is related in the *twenty-fifth.* 133. Pipaji out of repentance abandoned his kingdom, and while Ramkrishna was coming from Dwarka he gave the mystic *mantra* to a tiger, all this is related in the *twenty-sixth.* 134. Narsi Meheta's life is very lengthy and his story is *ended in the thirtieth chapter;* Shri Shankar met with him and showed him the *Rasmandal;* 135. his son was married and the Life of the world cashed his cheque; in the maturity ceremony of his daughter He provided clothes and ornaments.

CHAPS: 31-36 RAMDAS OF DAKUR; KALYAN & NIRADHAR; BLIND SURDAS; SENA; KING SATVIK & KARMABAI; JANAJASWANT & SURDAS MADANMOHAN

136. Seeing the devotion of Ramdas, Chakrapani came to Dakur; this is related in the *thirty-first chapter*; may good people know it. 137. In the *thirty-second* the image of Mathura walked as far as Hardwar. In the *thirty-third*, Shripati (Vishnu) met with Surdas at Mathura. 138. In the *thirty-fourth chapter* the Husband of Rukmini assumed the form of the barber Sena and the Holder of the *Sharang* bow (Krishna) shaved the head of the (Muhammadan) king and captivated his mind. 139. In the *thirty-fifth* there is a wonderful story of how the king had his hand cut off, and how the Lord of the world was pleased with him and made it as it was before; 140. and seeing the devotion of Karmabai, the image of stone dined with her, and the worshippers of God had a dream of this at which they very much wondered. 141. In the *thirty-sixth* two biographies are given: Surdas Madanmohan, and how Shri Raghunandan (Rama) rescued Janajaswant who was being drowned in a pond.

CHAPS: 37-44 RASIK MURAR; MIRABAI; KANHOPATRA; DAMAJIPANT; MRITYUNJAYA; BHANUDAS; AND BAHIRAMBHAT

142. In the *thirty-seventh chapter* is the beautiful story of the loving *bhakta* Rasik Murar; to the elephant he gave the mystic *mantra*, and the king he enraptured in a moment. 143. Poison was given to Mirabai, a loving *bhakta* of God, but it turned to nectar: this story is described in the *thirty-eighth chapter*. 144. The meeting of Kanhopatra with the Lord of Pandhari, and the Husband of Rukmini saved the *bhakta* Damajipant; these stories are related in *chapters thirty-nine* and *forty* respectively. 145. In the *forty-first* the glory of Mrityunjaya is related;

he made dogs vomit emblems of Shiva. In the *forty-second* is described how Shripati sat holding the horse of Bhanudas, and their meeting. 146. God had gone to Vidyanagar, and Bhanudas brought Him back to Pandhari; the impaling stake sprouted into leaves; good people have heard all this related [in the *forty-third chapter*]. 147. In the *forty-fourth chapter* Naganath gave Bahirambhat a second birth, and dispelling his doubts taught him the knowledge of the soul.

CHAPS: 45-52 EKNATH & SHRI KHANDYA; RAMDAS ; TUKARAM

148. In the *forty-fifth* there is the story of Eknath who went as a suppliant to Janardan; he brought about a meeting between him and Shri Datta, and thus favoured him. 149. In the *forty-sixth* we read that in the guise of a Brahman the Lord of Dwarka served him, and that Eknath came to knew about it twelve years later. 150. Chapter *forty-seven* tells how Ramdas was a real *avatar* of Maruti, ran away from behind the marriage curtain, and how the Husband of Rukmini met him in the form of Rama at Pandhari. 151. In the *forty-eighth* is the story of how Tuka became an ascetic and how the Lord of the heart came into his *kirtan* and drove away the enemy's army. 152. In the *forty-ninth* we see how Tukaram gave a piece of advice to his wife, and through her generosity had her loot her house by Brahmans. 153. In the *fiftieth* is the interesting story of how Tukaram's wife beat him on his back with a piece of sugarcane, and how he wrote a letter full of the sentiment of compassion and sent it to Pandhari. 154. In the *fifty-first chapter* may the wise know that God stood on the shoulders of Nimbaraj in the *kirtan*. 155. Shekh Muhammad knew that the canopy (where Tukaram was performing his *kirtan*) was on fire by the touch of a burning torch; and Tuka's

manuscripts of *abhangs* floated dry on the river; these stories are described in the *fifty-second chapter.*

CHAPS: 53-57 MANKOJI BODHLA; GANESHNATH; KESHAV SWAMI; GOMAI & LATIBSHAH; SANTOBA POWAR; NILOBA; UDDHAVA CHIDGHAN; VISOBA SARAF; SUMMARY

156. Bodhla has his farm plundered and the revenue of his land is paid up by the Lord of Pandhari; the stumps of corn are full of innumerable ears; these stories are given in the *fifty-third chapter.* 157. In the *fifty-fourth* we read how a dead body was brought to life in a *kirtan*; how the slave Hansi was put out of sight; and how a Mahar was disgraced. 158. Hearers must have listened to the four stories described in chapter *fifty-five*, including the story that Ganeshnath out of mercy gave the mystic *mantra* to a tree; 159. in the *kirtan* of Keshav Swami the saints were saved, even though they had eaten the poisonous *bachanag*; the Lord of Pandhari took Gomai to the other bank of the river, and ate her cakes with love; 160. seeing the devotion of Latibshah, the picture (of Krishna) at once ate the *vida* (rolled betelnut leaves); and the Muhammadan king came as a suppliant and then went back to his place. 161. In the *fifty-sixth* there is the singular story how the God of gods in the form of a tortoise, seeing the devotion of Santoba Powar, took all the pilgrims to the other side of the river; 162. how at the time of Niloba's daughter's wedding God provided him with the materials of food; and how at Bedar, Maruti destroyed a mosque and gave provisions of food to Uddhava Chidghan, this is related in the *fifty-sixth chapter.* 163. Visoba Saraf was perfectly pious, and God paid off his loan (according to what we read in chapter *fifty-seven*): this all the listeners have recently heard. 164. These (*fifty-six chapters*) are, as it were, the royal swans of fifty-six countries. They, with bunches of pearls in the form of the stories of

God's *bhaktas*, assembled at the Manas Lake in the form of chapter *fifty-seven* to have sport. 165. (In the world) the earthly and spiritual lives were mixed together like water and milk. The royal swans put their beaks into it and separated milk from water. 166. These *fifty-six chapters* are, as it were, precious and divine gems, and the *fifty-seventh* is as it were a plate of gold; the plate is studded with jems, and with it God Whose abode is in *Vaikunth* (Vishnu's heaven) was worshipped. 167. The *bhaktas* who are lovers of God and free from desires are as it were the tender sprouts of *tulsi*; and stringing them into a garland the Merciful to the lowly is worshipped. 168. Or these are as it were pure stones of fifty-six countries; and fixing the *fifty-seventh* as the best place, a temple was erected on it, and in it was installed Him who is as blue as a cloud.

OTHER SAINTS CHARACTERIZED

169. There are many other *Vaishnava saints* and *Mahants* and well-known *bhaktas*; they are as it were handfuls of flowers which should be offered to God: 170. Bhartrihari and Jalandhar, Sadanand and Shankaracharya, and the generous King Gopichand and the thoughtful Narsinhanagar. 171. Hirasing, a grocer of Gujerat, Malukdas and Gangakavishvar, Charpati and Chaurangi, all these great *bhaktas* made the Holder of the *Sharang* bow (Krishna) their own. 172. Dhanajat, Bajidkhan, Baba and Nanaksadan, and Narsinhabharati Narayan and the thoughtful Achyutashram; 173. Halsi, Avaghad, and the *bhakta* Mudhaya, and Mukundraj of world-wide fame who composed the *Viveksindhu*, a philosophical work, by personal intuition; 174. Krishanambhat Yadnyavalki and the thoughtful Krishnadas Mudgal; Kanhaya, Haridas and Namapathki, these *bhaktas* of God are known in the world; 175. Lolimbraj, Chandbodhla, and the well-

known Shaikh Farid, and Shaikh Husen of excessive righteousness, these are the *bhaktas* whom God loves; 176. Narahari, Jayaram and Malopant, and the loving *bhakta* Narsinhasarasvati, and Mahamudgalbhat of world-wide renown who made the Husband of Janaki his own; 177. Ekling Mairal, who was an ascetic of superhuman power, and the well-known Sumati Kamalakar, Renukanandan the root of joy, whose *līlā* (deeds) are unfathomable; 178. Shripati and Dasopant, and Madhavdas of world-wide renown; Pralhad Badve and Papujipant were very much liked by God; 179. Gosavinandan and Vamansvami, Giribai, Chinmaynandan; the Life of the World was pleased at listening to the *kirtan* of Basvalinga; 180. Antoba and Bhagvantbhat, and the solely devoted Vitthal Purandar; God, whose abode is in *Vaikunth*, was pleased with the urgency of Mainavati; 181. Lalunkhoji Paramanand and Dadu Pinjari of perfect delight, seeing the intense love of Bahinabai, Govind danced in her *kirtan*; 182. Shridhar Swami of Nazre, the inhabitant of Pandharpur and the author of the great works of the *Harivijaya*, the epitome of the *Ramavijaya*, and the *Pandavpratap*; 183. Shivram Gosavi of Paithan, the son of Narayan Nimbaya whose enthusiastic *kirtan* the Husband of Rukmini rejoiced to listen to; 184. Tuka had a brother by name of Kanhaya, and his younger son, Narayan, who abandoning his wife went to Dwarka; 185. Bhagvantbawa the grandson of Bodhla, so also Narobababa of Paithan, had an immense liking for a *kirtan*, and love for the praises of God; 186. Anandtanay, of world-wide renown, and Raghupatishesha who possessed perfect knowledge, listening to whose *kirtan* the wise became wholly absorbed; 187. Madhvamunishvar, a great *bhakta* and inhabitant of Shendurvadiya, had great skill in composing *padas* (songs), which enraptured the Holder of the *Sharang* bow (Krishna); 188. Shakarjibava of Shiur, who performed a *kirtan* with great enthusiasm, was also an adept in philosophical knowledge and was as a lion to the non-believers; 189. Amritray was a loving *bhakta* of God, his poetry very sweet and appealing, listening to which even the revilers and the wicked were at once melted through his love. 190. There have been such loving *bhaktas* in the world, who possessed the boon of God's grace; I prostrate myself at their feet. 191. I bow repeatedly to the feet of Moreshvarbava of Tambve, who was a great follower of the Bhagvat religion.

WARKARIS OF PANDHARI AND FUTURE SAINTS

192. I bow to the feet of the loving *bhaktas*, who became the *Warkaris* (pilgrims) of Pandhari. 193. With love and delight I bow to those *bhaktas* who live in Pandhari, the inhabitants of the sacred town. 194. There will be many more *Vaishnava bhaktas* in the future, who will disappear and appear again at their feet; I prostrate myself with devotion. 195. There are innumerable *avatars* of God. It is beyond our power to count them, just as the drops of rain which fall on the earth cannot be counted. 196. There are plants on the earth which cannot be counted. How can the waves of the ocean be counted? 197. The Actor as it were in a play, the Husband of Rukmini, became Himself both the God and His *bhakta*. If we visit Him we naturally visit all saints. 198. The sight of the ocean means the sight of all the rivers. When you bow to the sun you see all his rays. 199. When you circumambulate the pipal tree, all its branches are included. In the same way there is no duality between the *bhaktas* and the Lord of *Vaikunth* (Vishnu's heaven). 200. As a skilful person cannot differentiate between sugar and its sweetness, so consider the Dweller on the banks of the Bhima and His *bhaktas* as one in heart.

THE GLORY OF THE SAINTS

201. The *Bhaktavijaya* is the result of these two (God and His saints). The listeners will obtain their wishes by just listening to it. 202. Those who continually sing of the lives of the *bhaktas* will be endowed with a wonderful spiritual knowledge. The Lord of Pandhari will favour them and meet with them of a certainty. 203. If one has this book in his house hindrances will never enter there, for Vishnu will turn the *Sudarshan* wheel of God round him ; bear this well in your mind. 204. The most emphatic thing in this book is that the Life of the World was pleased with His *bhaktas*. Therefore the Husband of Rukmini protects both the speaker and the listeners. 205. The wise should not consider the lives of the saints of *Kali Yuga* as commonplace. Great *munis* will sing of the saints of the *Kali Yuga*, the *Krita* and *Dwapar Yugas*. 206. The gods were greatly delighted at the commencement of the *Kali Yuga*. For if one concentrates his mind for only three *ghatikas* and a half he will meet with the Lord of *Vaikunth*. 207. Then the Muni Narad did a very wonderful thing. He held his tongue and his sexual organ with his hands, at which all the gods were astonished and they asked him the explanation of it; 208. on this the son of Brahma (Narad) replied, 'These two will not be restrained in the *Kali Yuga*.' As the gods heard it they were full of concern. 209. Then Narad told them that those who will listen to the lives of the *Vaishnava bhaktas* of the *Kali Yuga*, the Lord of *Vaikunth* (Vishnu) will meet with them. 210. As the son of Brahmadev (Narad) thus spoke, all the gods were delighted and said, ' We like this simple means (of salvation).' 211. Therefore the lives of God's *bhaktas* purify even the great sages and Indra and other gods. May the wise listen to these assertions and entertain no doubt.

GOD THE INSPIRER OF THIS BOOK

212. I have written in this book as much as I was ordered by the Husband of Rukmini. The musical instruments accompany their tunes with the musician. 213. We sow the seed in fields, but its sprouting depends on rain, just as the dancing of the wooden dolls depends on the pulling of the strings. 214. In the same manner, in writing this book, the *Bhaktavijaya*, the Inspirer of the intellect is the Husband of Rukmini. He sharpened my intellect and caused me to write this work as He wished.

DATE OF THE COMPOSITION

215. In the Shalivahan era 1684 (A. D. 1762), in the Chitrabhanu *samvatsar*, on the twelfth dark of *Vaishakh* (May), the book was completed. 216. To the South of the Pravara river there is the town Taharabad at a distance of ten miles. This very interesting *Bhaktavijaya* was composed there.

MAHIPATI'S CONCLUDING PRAYER

217. Now, O Lord of Pandhari, listen to my final request. Thou art the Speaker and the Listener and the Protector of the book through Thy mercy. 218. Thou art the only imperishable *Guru* of the whole world. Thou art beyond *maya* (illusion) and art Lord of all. Thou art the Refuge of the helpless. Thou dost enable Thy servants to cross over the ocean of this worldly existence. 219. Thou dost fulfil the cravings of Thy *bhaktas* in a moment. Seeing their pure love Thou dost dwell in their lotus-hearts. 220. To some Thou hast given the knowledge of the soul. Some asked for the last stage of deliverance. My mind also wishes the same, so that I may be able to sing of the deeds of Hari. 221. Some sit on *vajrasan* (the spiked bed), and some are dwelling in the land of *Vaikunth* (Vishnu's heaven). As for me, out of love I take delight

in singing the praises of Thy servants. 222. With unwearied love in my heart I have praised Thy servants. I Mahipati ask for this one reward, that with abiding love for the saints I should praise Thy servants.

223. *Swasti* (Peace) ! This book is the *Bhaktavijaya*, by listening to which the Lord of the world will be pleased Therefore, O loving and pious *bhaktas*, listen to the very delightful fifty-seventh chapter. Here ends the *Bhaktavijaya*.

APPENDIX I

NOTES ON PAURANIC NAMES IN THE *BHAKTAVIJAYA*

AKRUR

One of the Yādavas, the son of Shvaphalka and Gāndini, and always taking Krishna's side. Considering him to be a faithful messenger, Kansa sent him to fetch Krishna to Mathura from Gokul and kill him. But he explained all Kansa's plans to Krishna. By many stratagems he had obtained the possession of the *Syamantak* jewel.

AGASTI

A well known *rishi*, the son of Mitrāvaruna. He made the Vindhyādrī mountain range lie flat and thus humbled it. At the request of great *rishis* he drank up the ocean at one gulp and thus destroyed the Kalkeya *asuras* (demons) who had hidden in it. It was he who gave to Rama a sword, a bow, and a quiver ever full. He colonized the Deccan. *Vide Appendix II p. 43*[illegible].

AJĀMIL

A Brahman of the country of Kanyakubja. He had abandoned his parents and wife, and spent his life in the company of a Shudra woman. He dearly loved the youngest child of the Shudra woman by name Narayan. In this state he happened to hear a discussion about him between the messengers of Yama (the god of death) and Vishnu. On this he repented and, discarding his Shudra wife and children, spent his remaining days at Gangādwar in the service of God, and thereby obtained *moksha* after death.

ARJUNA

The third of the Pandavas, the son of King Pandu, and born to Kunti as the boon of the god Indra. A favourite disciple of Dronacharya; expert in archery whereby at the *swayamvar* of Draupadi (choice of a husband ceremony) he won her. At the time of the royal sacrifice of his brother Yudhishthira he conquered the Northern country. He pleased the god Shiva in the form of a hunter and obtained divine missiles from Him. He acted as a female dancer while living in disguise at the house of Virāta. At the time of the great Indian Civil War Krishna explained to him his duty now embodied in the *Gita.*

ANASUYĀ

The wife of the *Rishi* Atri and mother of the *Rishis* Datta and Durvāsa, known also as a very faithful wife and a great female ascetic. Once upon a time the gods Brahmā, Vishnu and Mahesha (Shiva), in accordance with the hints of their wives came to test her wifely fidelity but by the force of her purity she turned them into children and then at the request of their wives she again gave them their previous forms; by her desire, portions of these three gods led to the *avatar* of Dattatreya being born. During Rama's wanderings she gave to Sita an ointment which kept her beauty ever fresh and protected her from wild animals and demons.

AMBARISH

A king of the solar race, very powerful and a great devotee of Vishnu. He observed a strict fast on *Ekādashi* (the eleventh day of every fortnight). Once on a time the *Rishi* Durvās suddenly came to him on the twelfth day just as the king was to break his fast. He therefore invited the *Rishi* to dine with him. The *Rishi*, however, went to the river to bathe ceremonially and as he was late in coming back, the time for the king breaking the fast was passing away. So the king, in order that his observance might not suffer, offered the food to God and broke his fast by drinking the holy water in which the gods were washed. When on his return from the river the *Rishi* learnt of it he fell into a great rage, and from a lock of his hair created a demoness and made her follow the king to persecute him. But meanwhile the disk of the god Vishnu, ever ready to protect him, destroyed the demoness and pursued the *Rishi* Durvas, who went to all the great gods for protection but none would vouchsafe it to him. Finally he went to Vishnu who asked him to go as a suppliant to the king who had fasted a whole year for him, and then only would he be free from the pursuit of the disk. He went to the king who on seeing him was pleased and prayed the disk to stop the pursuit. The king freed Durvās and dined in his company.

ABHIMANYU

The son of Arjuna and Subhadrā, and the nephew of Krishna and Balarām; a great warrior like his father. He valorously broke his way through the army of the enemy arranged in a circle but was unable to come back and was treacherously killed. He was the father of King Parikshiti.

ARUNA

The son of Vinatā wife of Kashyapa; also the charioteer of the Sun; the elder brother of Garud (the divine eagle, Vishnu's vehicle) and the father of Sampāti and Jatāyu. Vinatā broke the egg which contained him before maturity and therefore he was born without legs.

AHALYĀ

The wife of the *Rishi* Gautama, the mother of Shatānand, and the adopted daughter of the god Brahma

Through ignorance she cohabited with the god Indra, and so was cursed by her husband and was turned into a slab of stone. Rama restored her to life by the dust of His foot.

INDRA

The chief of gods. In one day of Brahmadeva there are fourteen Indras. The present one is called Purandar. The name of the wife of Indra is Indrāni. *Vide Appendix II p. 423.*

INDRAJIT

Son of Rāvana. By the performance of many sacrifices he obtained from Shankar (God Shiva) a divine chariot, weapons and missiles. He captured Indra in battle and made him captive and therefore is named as Indrajit. His former name was Meghanād. By the missiles of Brahma he fastened Māruti the monkey-god who had gone in search of Sitā, and brought him into the royal court of Rāvana. In three hours he killed sixty-seven crores of monkeys and had thrown Rama and Lakshman into a swoon, but ultimately he was killed by Lakshman.

UGRASEN

King of Mathura, Kansa's father. Kansa had imprisoned him, but Krishna killed Kansa and reinstalled Ugrasen.

UTTĀNAPĀD

A king of the solar race. He had two wives, Sunīti and Suruchi by name. Dhruva was his son born from Suniti.

UDDHAVA

The nephew of Vasudev, a great devotee of Krishna and always accompanied him. They loved each other very much. When Krishna departed from Gokul to Mathura he sent Uddhava to console the *Gopis* and Nanda and Yashodā. Krishna explained to him the knowledge of the soul as he

(Krishna) passed away from this world. Then he went to Badrikāshram in accordance with Krishna's command.

UPAMANYU

The eldest son of Vyāghrapād *Rishi*, in the family line of Vashishtha; and elder brother of Dhaumya. His mother used to give him flour mixed with water instead of milk. Once when he had drunk real milk in a neighbour's house he obstinately asked for that kind of milk from his mother who felt sad and said, 'How can you obtain milk unless you please God? Our good deeds in our former births are not so strong as to give you milk.' Upon this he practised severe austerities and obtained the boon of mastery over the ocean of milk, and life as long as the world existed. He was a devotee of Shiva, and through him Krishna took the Shaiva vow.

URVASHI

A heavenly damsel born from the thigh of the *Rishi* Nārāyan of Badrikāshram, and the wife of king Pururavā, the first of the lunar race.

EKALAVYA

A fisherman by caste who made an earthly image of Dronācharya, regarded it as his *guru* and by dint of his great devotion learned from it the art of archery, becoming mightier than Arjuna. On one occasion Dronācharya witnessed his valour and made him promise as an honorarium to his *guru*, not to use his right thumb in archery. Even to this day the people of the hunter-caste stick to this promise.

KARNA

Born to Kunti before her marriage, through the *mantra* of the sun. For fear of public shame she put him into a box and threw him into a river. A charioteer

Adhirath by name found the box and brought up the child. His wife's name was Rādhā, and hence he himself was named Rādheya. Learning the art of archery with the Kauravas and Pandavas he became the rival of Arjuna in that art. Duryodhan then gave him the kingdom of Anga and formed friendship with him. He was a great donor, and when the god Indra went to him in the disguise of a Brahman asking for his armour and earrings, he gave these to him. In order to defeat Arjuna he went to Parashurām (the sixth *avatar* of Vishnu) as a Brahman and learned from him the use of missiles, but when Parashurām found out that he was a Kshatriya and not a Brahman he pronounced the curse that he would not remember the use of the art at the time of battle. While hunting he had once by chance killed a Brahman's cow who gave the curse that the earth would swallow the wheel of his chariot while fighting on the battlefield. Krishna and Kunti both narrated to him the circumstances of his birth, and sought to persuade him not to fight against the Pandavas, his brothers, but he did not listen to them and he was at last killed by Arjuna.

KADARYU

A Brahman inhabitant of Avanti (modern Ujjain), who was so miserly that his wife and children and other relatives robbed him of everything and drove him out of the house. On that account and also on account of the influence of the good deeds in his former births he turned an ascetic and obtained complete peace of mind. People tried their best to bring him down from that state, but in vain. Just for this virtue of his, Shri Krishna has related his story to Uddhava in the *Bhāgwat*.

KAYĀDHU

The wife of Hiranyakashipu, the daughter of Jambhāsura and the mother of Pralhād. When she was bearing

Pralhād her husband went away on austerities. Taking this opportunity Indra slew many demons and when he was taking her to heaven the *Rishi* Nārad met him and said, 'Her son will be a Vishnu-*bhakta* and will not hate you,' and thus freed her, and staying with her on the bank of the Bhāgirathi, gave her soul-knowledge. This knowledge Pralhād heard while in her womb and thereby became a *bhakta* of God Vishnu. After this the *Rishi* Nārad gave her back to her husband.

KANSA

The son of Ugrasen of the race of the Yādavas, a cousin of Devaki and the king of Mathura. In the ceremony of Devaki's marriage he heard a divine voice that he would be killed by her son, and therefore he killed her six sons. When Krishna was born and was sent to Gokul (surreptitiously), Kansa tried to kill him by sending many of his hirelings there, but failed in his attempt. Then finally Krishna and Balarām were brought to Mathura under the pretext of wrestling with his wrestlers, but they killed these wrestlers and Kansa as well.

KĀLAYAVAN

Born to a Yavan king's wife from the sage Garga for the purpose of defeating the Yādavas. He was a great warrior and invincible against the Yādavas. Krishna had him killed at the hands of the sage Muchakund.

KĀLINDI

The seventh wife of Krishna. She performed austerities on the banks of the Jumna river and married Krishna.

KUBJĀ

A maidservant of Kansa. She was personally crippled in three places. While at Mathura with his brother Balarām at the invitation of Kansa, Krishna healed her.

KUSHA AND LAVA

The sons of Rama, the son of Dashrath. They were born in the hermitage of the sage of Vālmiki, and were brought up there. The sage Vālmiki educated them in all arts. Both of them were very brave. After the royal horse sacrifice of Rama, the sage Vālmiki consigned them to their father's care and then Rama with his wife Sita and the children returned to Ayodhya.

KUNTI

The daughter of king Shur of the line of the Yādavas. She was adopted by King Kuntibhoja. She was the wife of Pandu. In her girlhood she had obtained *mantras* (charms) from the sage Durvās by which she could beget sons and so became the mother of Karna, Dharma, Bhima and Arjuna. They were portions of the four gods, the sun, Yama (the god of death), the wind, and Indra respectively. She gave two of her charms obtained from Ashvinikumār to her rival Mādri to whom two sons Nakul and Sahadev were born.

KUMBHAKARNA

The younger brother of Rāvana. He was very brave, and had an enormous person. He used to sleep for six months and was awake for one day only. He was killed by Rama.

KURMA *AVATĀR*

The second *avatār* of Vishnu. Vishnu assumed this *avatār* in order to support Mountain Mandār which was used as the churn at the time of churning the ocean.

KRISHNA

The son of Vasudev and Devaki, Kansa's cousin, the son of the maternal uncle of the Pandavas and the eighth *avatār* of Vishnu. Out of fear of Kansa, his father Vasudev stealthily took him to Gokul to Nanda who brought him up. He performed many wonderful things in Gokul in his childhood. He killed many giants who were sent by Kansa and in the end Kansa also. He was a great friend of Arjuna. Troubled by Kālayavan he forsook Mathura and founded the town of Dwāraka on the sea. He killed Narakāsur. He had eight chief wives, Rukmini, Satyabhāmā, etc. and 16,100 other wives besides. He went to the Kauravas as an ambassador from the Pandavas for reconciliation but failed in his attempt. He was given the highest place of honour in the royal sacrifice of King Dharma for which Shishupāl censured him; so he killed Shishupāl. He was the charioteer of Arjuna in the great Indian Civil War (between the Pandavas and Kauravas). He was an expert in soul-knowledge, explaining the *Bhagavadgītā* to Arjuna and soul-knowledge to Uddhava. He was killed by a hunter named Jarā. *Vide Appendix II pp. 424-429.*

KAIKEYI

The youngest wife of King Dashrath (Rama's father), mother of Bharat, and the daughter of the king of the country of Kaikeya. Incited by her maid Mantharā at the time of the installation of Rama as Yuvaraja, she demanded the exile of Rama and the coronation of Bharat in fulfilment of the two boons which her husband Dashrath had promised her long before. Rama therefore went into exile and grieved by his separation his father King Dashrath died.

KAUSALYA

The first wife of king Dashrath, and mother of Ramachandra.

GAJENDRA

At first king of the country of Pāndya. His name was Indradyumna.

GANIKĀ

A prostitute. She had a parrot which she taught continually to repeat 'Rama, Rama.' Thereby she also had to repeat this name of God and so attained final beatitude.

GARUD

The son of the sage Kashyapa and Vinatā; the younger brother of Aruna (the charioteer of the sun); the king of birds; also the vehicle of Vishnu. He was very powerful and brought nectar for the serpents and freed his mother from the slavery of his stepmother.

GAUTAMA

With severe austerities he brought the Godāvari river where it is. He was a great ascetic.

CHĀNUR

A great wrestler in the service of King Kansa. Krishna killed him when he had gone to Mathura with Balarām for the *Dhanuryāga*.

JATĀYU

The younger son of Aruna (the charioteer of the sun) a great friend of King Dashrath, who fought with Rāvana while he was carrying away Sita. But Rāvana skilfully contrived to cut off his wings, and left him in a dying condition. It was he who told Rama of Sita being carried away to Lanka.

JAMADAGNI

A *rishi* (sage), father of Parashurām, and the son of Richika from Satyavati the daughter of Gādhi. He was of a wrathful disposition. Once his wife was late in returning from the river for some reason so he had her killed by Parashurām. But at Parashurām's request she was again restored to life.

JĀMBUVATI

The daughter of Jāmbuvān, one of the eight chief wives of Krishna. She had six sons, Samba and others.

JAIMINI

A chief disciple of Vyāsa. He was the writer of the *Purvamimānsa.* He was an expert in debates. He was the author of the *Jaimini Ashvamedha.*

TĀRĀMATĪ

The wife of Harishchandra of the solar race. Their son was Rohidās. She was a very dutiful wife.

TUMBARU

One of the Gandharvas born from Prādhā. Rambhā was his wife.

TRIPUR

The three sons of Tarakāsur obtained from Brahmadeva the boon of three invulnerable cities. They were made of gold, silver and iron and rotated in the space on the sky and on the earth. The collection of these three is called Tripur. Shankar burned them and therefore he is called Tripurāri.

DATTA OR DATTĀTREYA

The son of Atri and Anasuyā. (See under *Anasuyā*).

DAMAYANTI

The daughter of King Bhima of the country of Vidarbha and as the wife of King Nala very dutiful.

DASHRATH

The son of King Aja of the Ikshvāku solar race, and the father of Rama. He had three wives, Kausalya, Sumitrā and Kaikeyi, but was without any issue. With the advice of his family *guru* Vashishtha he performed a son-giving sacrifice, through the *Rishi* Rishyashringa. Then four sons were born. From Kausalya Rama, from Sumitrā Lakshmana and Shatrughna, and from Kaikeyi, Bharat. He loved his sons very much. Rama was as it were his very life. Kaikeyi was his most beloved wife. Her obstinacy compelled Rama to go into the forest as an exile and King Dashrath died through mourning for his son.

DĀRUKA

The charioteer of Shri Krishna.

DURYODHAN

The eldest son of Dhritarāshtra and Gāndhāri, and an enemy of the Pāndavas. He was very skilful in mace-fighting. He devised many plans to destroy the Pāndavas. He tried to burn them in a lacquer house. He poisoned Bhima, and threw him into a river. But all his efforts proved fruitless. Finally defeating Dharma at dice he won his kingdom. He tried in an open assembly to strip Draupadi of her garment. He sent the Pāndavas into exile for twelve years, at the end of which they had to pass one year *incognito.* During this time he sent the sage Durvās to persecute them, and by carrying away the cows of King Virāta he tried to force them out of their disguise but he did not succeed. After the period of thirteen years Shri Krishna on behalf of the Pāndavas went to Duryodhan to bring about a reconciliation between him and the Pāndavas, but Duryadhan insulted Shri Krishna by telling him that he would not give to the Pāndavas even as much earth as would cover the point of a needle. He hid himself in the deep water of a pond after the death of his commanders Bhishma, Drona, Karna, Shalya and others during the great Indian Civil War. Bhima went to the pond, and challenged him to fight. He struck him on the thigh with his mace which made him senseless. Duryodhan then appointed Ashvatthāmā as the commander and he at dead of night killed all the warriors of the Pāndavas such as Dhrishtadyumna, etc., while they were asleep. Duryodhan died cheerfully when he heard this.

DURVAS

A *rishi*, son of Atri and Anasuyā. He had given to Kunti (the mother of the Pāndavas) at an early age, five *mantras* (charms) to beget as many sons. He was very wrathful. Once Duryodhan sent him to the Pāndavas and asked him to demand from them at midnight a dinner for him and his thousand disciples with a view to humiliate them. He went but was defeated in his attempt on account of the cooking pan which the sun had given to Draupadi producing any kind of food when required.

DUSSHĀSAN

One of the hundred sons of Dhritarāshtra, and the younger brother of Duryodhan. Like Duryodhan he was a brave and powerful warrior but was very wicked. He tried to strip Draupadi of her garment, and so Bhima vowed to kill him and drink his blood, a vow Bhima fulfilled in the great Indian Civil War.

DRAUPADI

The daughter of King Drupad, and wife of the Pāndavas. She was born from a sacrificial fire. In her *svayamvar* (choosing of husband ceremony), Arjun killed the fish on the target and won her. As soon as Kunti said the prize should be divided equally she became the wife of all the five and also lost her liberty along with the Pāndavas at the game of dice. When Duryodhan through Dusshāsan tried to strip her of her garment in the open royal court Shri Krishna provided her with innumerable garments and thus preserved her modesty. In her life of retirement she lived under the name of Sairandhri as the handmaid of Queen Sudeshnā. She was a most virtuous, noble and dutiful wife.

DHARMA OR DHARMARĀJA

The eldest son of King Pandu, and born to Kunti by the *mantra* (charm) of Yamadharma. He was extremely god-fearing and kind towards all beings and so was called *Ajātashatru* (one without an enemy). He was a great lover of truth, and even in times of adversity he did not swerve from it, although he was sharply reproached by Bhima and others. When first the plans of the Kauravas for the destruction of the Pāndavas were frustrated, King Dhritarāshtra gave him half of his kingdom. Afterwards he made conquests in all quarters of the world with the help of his brothers and with the fortune thus amassed he performed a royal horse sacrifice. This made Duryodhan jealous of him. He was very fond of gambling. Taking advantage of this Duryodhan gambled and cunningly defeated him, taking all his kingdom and sending him into exile. In the year of his life *incognito* he stayed at the court of Virāta as a player of dice assuming the name Kanka. He tried his best to make peace with Duryodhan but was unsuccessful. He defeated the Kauravas after his return from exile and ascended the throne. When Drona, lying on his deathbed of arrows, asked him whether it was Ashvatthāmā his son or elephant that was dead, Dharma replied that he did not know and so Drona forsook his bow. This was the only time in his life when he did not speak the truth. He performed a horse-sacrifice and ruled well. In the end, he seated Parikshiti on the throne and with his four brothers and Draupadi went into the Himalayas to perform austerities. An era named Yudhisthira was started in his name after him.

DHRITARĀSHTRA

Grandson of Shantanu in the lineage of Puru. Born

to Vyās through Ambikā, a wife of Vichitravirya. He was blind from birth, and therefore his brother Pandu received the kingdom. He had a hundred sons (one being Duryodhan) and one daughter. His wife was Gāndhāri. He also had a son named Yuyutsu born from a Vaishya woman. When Duryodhan, Shakuni and others lied and did other wicked things to destroy the Pāndavas he never forbade them. When finally all his sons died in battle he lived with Dharmarāja for fifteen years. During that period he was always vexed by Bhima with curt remarks which disgusted him and so he became an ascetic and went to the Himalayas, taking with him Gāndhāri and Kunti, and there they all died.

DHRUVA

The son of king Uttānapād and Suniti. His stepmother insulted him in his childhood and through anger he left his father, went into the jungle and performed severe austerities. Vishnu was pleased with these and so He gave him an eternal place.

NAKULA

The son of King Pandu and Madri, and fourth of the Pāndavas. He was a portion of the *Ashvinikumars*, the heavenly physicians, and was extremely handsome. He conquered the west. In his retirement he lived with King Virāta under the name of Granthik and was in charge of his horses.

NANDA

The chief of Gokul. He was a great friend of Vasudev. His wife was Yashodā. He brought up the brothers Balarāma and Krishna from their infancy.

NANDI

The bull of Shiva. His vehicle. The son of the wish-cow. His form is that of a human being except the head which is that of a monkey. He has short arms.

NALA

The king of the country of Nishadha the son of Virasen, and the husband of Damayanti. He was very handsome, truthful and an expert in the knowledge of horses. His brother Pushkar won from him in gambling all his royal fortune and drove him into the forest. One night Nala abandoned his wife in the forest in the hope that she would go and live with her parents and not suffer with him. She first went to King Chedi, then to her father when he came to know of her whereabouts. Nala then took refuge with King Rituparna of Ayodhya. When Damayanti knew it she invited Rituparna to Kundinpur to the choosing of her husband a second time and Nala accompanied him as his charioteer. Nala and Damayanti recognized each other and again lived together. From Rituparna Nala learnt the art of gambling and then won back his kingdom from Pushkar.

NAKRA

A divine chorister Huhu by name. Through the curse of a *rishi* he had become a crocodile; but along with Gajendra was saved by Vishnu.

NĀRAD

A famous celestial *rishi* (sage). He was one of the seven sons produced by the will of Brahmadev. He performed the song-service of Hari (God) and his favourite musical instrument was the *Vinā*. He was very fond of picking quarrels. He had access to the three worlds, viz., the heaven, the mortal world and the nether regions.

NRISINHA

The fourth principal *avatār* of Vishnu. In form he was half man and half lion, hence his name *Nrisinha* (lion-man.) He killed Hiranyakashipu, and protected Pralhād.

PARASHURĀM

The son of the *Rishi* Jamadagni and the sixth principal *avatār* of Vishnu. King Kārtavirya took away the cow of Jamadagni, and so Parashurām killed him. Kārtavirya's sons killed Jamadagni in vengeance for the death of their father. On this Parashurām vowed to annihilate the Kshatriyas; and on twenty-one occasions he rid the earth of all the Kshatriyas, doing this as a gift to Kashyap; and creating a new country near the sea-coast he lived there. This country is the modern Konkan. He was deprived of his divine power by Rama (son of Dasharath) as he acted disrespectfully towards him. By the command of his father he beheaded his mother. Bhishma, his disciple, had once defeated him in battle.

PĀNDAVAS

The sons of Pandu born from his two wives Kunti and Mādri. They were Yudhisthira (or Dharma), Bhima, Arjun, Nakul and Sahadev. Each is called a Pāndava.

PĀRVATI

Sati the wife of Shiva, who having abandoned her body in the sacrifice performed by Daksha was reborn as the daughter of the Himalaya mountains and so received the name Pārvati; other names Haimawati, Girija, etc have the same sense.

PULASTYA

The will-born son of Brahmadev. His wife was Havirbhuvā. He had two sons by name of Agastya and Vishravā.

PUTANĀ

A demoness sent by Kansa to nurse Krishna with her poisoned breasts and thus kill him. But Krishna sucked up the poison and killed her.

PRALHĀD

The eldest of the four sons of Hiranyakashipu born from Kayādhu. While he was in his mother's womb he became a devotee of God by hearing the discourses of Nārad. As he was a born *bhakta* of Vishnu his father persecuted him very much. At last Vishnu assumed the *avatār* of Narasinha and killed his father, and thus protected him.

BALI

The grandson of Pralhād, and son of Virochana, and the father of Bānāsur. He performed a sacrifice on the north bank of the Nurbada river in Bhrigukachcha. There Vishnu went in the form of a dwarf Brahman *Vāman* and begged of Bali a gift of three paces; with two paces he occupied the heaven and the mortal world and with the third sent Bali to the lower regions. Vishnu became his doorkeeper to make amends to him. He (Bali) is deathless.

BIBHISHAN

The brother of Rāvana. He remonstrated with his brother for kidnapping Sita and advised him to return her to her husband. Rāvana did not like the advice, so Bibhishan went over to the side of Rama. On the death of Rāvana, Rama seated him on the throne of Lanka (Ceylon). He is deathless.

BUDDHA

Founder of Buddhism. His original name was Shākyasinha. He was born at Kapilvastu. He is regarded as the ninth *avatār* of Vishnu.

BHAGIRATH AND BHĀGIRATHI

Bhagirath, the great-great-grandson of King Sagar. He performed severe austerities and brought the heavenly Ganges to the mortal world to save his sixty thousand ancestors, the sons of Sagar who lay in the form of ashes under the curse of the *Rishi* Kapil. Having been brought by King Bhagirath, the Ganges is called the Bhāgirathi. *Vide Appendix II p. 432.*

BHARAT

The son of Dasharath born to him from Kaikeyi. He loved Rama very much, and therefore went to the forest to request Rama to come back to Ayodhya to reign, but Lord Ramchandra did not come. Then Bharat kept the sandals of Rama on the throne, and for fourteen years reigned in his name, and when Rama returned from his exile gave him his kingdom.

BHASMĀSUR

A demon created by God Shiva from a lump of holy ashes. He was given the boon that the person on whose head he kept his hand would be turned to ashes. He began to trouble each and every person and so Vishnu took the form of a beautiful young damsel called Mohini and caused Bhasmāsur to keep his hand on his own head and thus turned him to ashes.

BHIMA

The second of the Pāndavas and born to Kunti from the *mantra* (charm) given her by God (the wind). Even as a boy he was very powerful and even in play threatened Duryodhan and others. He learned the art of wielding the mace from Balarām, Krishna's brother. He had the strength of ten thousand elephants. He killed many demons such as Baka, Hidimb, Jarāsandh and Kichak. He lived with king Virāt in his retirement as Ballav, and was in charge of the royal kitchen. He killed all the hundred sons of king Dhritarāshtra, viz., Duryodhan, Dusshāsan, etc.

BHĪMAK

The ruler of Vidarbha, known also as Bhīshmak. He was the father of Rukmi.

BHISHMA

The son of King Shantanu of the lunar race born to him from the river Ganges. At the desire of his father he vowed not to claim the throne and remained a bachelor till death. His father was pleased with his vow, and gave him the boon that he would die at will. He was a disciple of Parashurām but had defeated him once. When Arjun hit him in battle from behind Shikhandi he lay on a bed of arrows till the sun entered the summer solastices and then died. After the war (the Indian Civil War) he preached Dharmarāj (the duties of a king) and about religion.

BHRIGU

A Brahman *rishi* (sage), the will-born son of Brahmadev, of the line of Jamadagni. Once there was a dispute among the *rishis* as to who was the highest amongst the three gods, Brahma, Shankar (Shiva) and Vishnu. Bhrigu, who was sent to decide, treated Brahma and Shiva disrespectfully for which they were angry with him. Lastly he went to Vishnu, but finding him asleep he kicked him on His chest. This did not anger Vishnu, and this test made Vishnu the highest of the three. The mark of this kick is called the *Shrivatsa*. *Vide Appendix II p. 432.*

MADHU AND KAITABHA

Demons born from the dirt of the ear of Vishnu and whom Vishnu killed.

MATSYA (the fish *avatār*)

Vishnu became a fish in order to kill a demon called Hayagriva who intended to steal away the Vedas from Brahmadeva when he slept at the end of the *Kalpa*.

MĀRUTI

The son of Anjani, a female monkey and the wind. As a loyal servant of Rama he crossed the ocean and in

Lanka (Ceylon) found Sita. He was extremely powerful and ever celibate and one without death. Rama being greatly delighted taught him the knowledge of Brahma. *Vide Appendix II p. 422.*

MITRAVINDĀ

The daughter of Jayasena, King of Avanti. Krishna carried her away from her *Svayamvara* (choice of a husband ceremony) and married her. She was one of the eight chief wives of Krishna.

MUCHUKUND

He was much fatigued on account of his assisting the gods in their battles and the gods insisted on his taking rest. He asked for a boon of the gods for a secluded place to sleep in and that the man who tried to awaken him should meet with death as soon as his eyes fell on him, while he himself should have a *darshan* (vision) of Vishnu. Krishna cleverly caused Kālyavan to disturb his sleep and by him he was burned to ashes.

MENAKĀ

A heavenly damsel. She interrupted the austerities of Vishvāmitra who was attracted towards her and from her Shakuntalā was born.

YASHODĀ

The wife of Nand the chief of Gokul. She brought up Krishna.

YADNYAJITI

One of the chief eight wives of Krishna.

RAMA

The son of King Dasharath and Kausalya, and the seventh *avatār* of Vishnu. He was an expert archer and when Vishvāmitra took him from Dasharath to protect his sacrifice, he slew several demons, went to Mithilā (the capital of Janak), and there broke the bow of Shiva in two and thus won Sita as his wife. Parashurām came to fight with him for breaking Shankar's bow but Rama defeated him. Dasharath meant to give Rama the kingdom but Rama was sent into exile for fourteen years in fulfilment of his stepmother's (Kaikeyi's) previous boon from Dasharath. In his forest life his wife was kidnapped by Rāvana the king of Ceylon. While wandering in search of Sita he met Hanumān, Sugriva and other monkey chiefs and made friends with them. He crossed the sea by building a bridge, killed Rāvana, and then returned with Sita to Ayodhya and ascended the throne of his father. He had only one wife, used only one arrow and was true to his word. He had two sons, Kusha and Lava. In the forest by the touch of his foot, he restored to life Ahalya who had been cursed by her husband and was lying in a petrified state.

[Mr. Romesh C. Dutt, C. I. E., I. C. S. (retired), gives the following summary in volume 1, page 87, of *The Encyclopædia Of Religion And Ethics*:—'Rama, the prince of Ayodhya or Oudh, was banished by the king (Dasharath) his father for fourteen years, and came and lived in a forest near the sources of the Godavari, accompanied by his wife Sita and his younger brother Lakshman. During the absence of the two brothers from their cottage, Sita was taken away by Ravana, King of Ceylon. After long search Rama got news of Sita, and determined to cross over from India to Ceylon with a vast army of monkeys and bears to recover her. It was for this purpose that the causeway across the ocean (Adam's Bridge, or *Ramasetu*, Rama's Causeway) is said to have been constructed. Rama crossed over with his army, defeated and killed Ravana, recovered his wife, and returned to Oudh. The period of exile had expired; Rama's father was dead; and Rama ascended the throne.' Dr. Arthur Anthony Macdonell. who was Boden Professor of Sanskrit in the University of Oxford, in the article *Ramayana* in volume 1 of *The Encyclopædia Of Religion And Ethics*, attempted an estimate of this great Sanskrit epic of ancient India, in which he distinguished two parts: 'the first an ordinary narrative of human life without any admixture of mythological elements, beginning with the intrigues of a queen (Rama's stepmother Kaikeyi) at the court of Ayodhya to ensure the succession of her son (Bharata) to the throne.... Had the poem ended with the return of Rama's brother Bharata to Ayodhya after the death of their father, King Dasharath,' it might have passed for an epic based on historical events. But the second part has many mythological, and possibly allegorical, elements.]

J. F. E.

RĀVANA

The King of Lankā (Ceylon). Mandodari the daughter of Māyāsur was his wife. He obtained various boons from Brahmadev with his severe penance. He had imprisoned all the gods and made them his slaves. From Kuber the treasurer of the gods he had obtained the Pushpak *viman* (aeroplane). Bibhishana was his brother. He had kidnapped Sita, Rama's wife. So Rama besieged his city defeated and killed all the Rakshasas including Rāvana and rescued Sita. Rāvana had ten heads and was therefore called Dashamukha. He was a great devotee of Shiva, divided the Vedas in parts, and explained the syllables of the Vedas. He initiated the three methods of the study of the Vedas, viz. *Krama*, *Ghana* and *Jatā*.

RAMBHĀ, URVASHI, TILOTTAMĀ

Heavenly damsels.

RUKMĀNGAD

A great devotee of Vishnu, and a strict observer of *Ekādashi* (the eleventh day of every fortnight).

RUKMINI

The daughter of King Bhishmak of Vidarbha and Krishna's chief wife. It had at first been decided that she be given to Shishupal, but on account of her love for Krishna, she wrote him a secret letter asking him to take her away. So Krishna deceived everybody, defeated Rukmi and the other kings and carried her away. She had a son by name Pradyumna. When the Yadavas were all destroyed she burnt herself. *Vide Appendix II pp. 426–428.*

RUKMI

The son of Bhishmak of Vidarbha and the elder brother of Rukmini. He hated Krishna and wanted to marry Rukmini to Shishupal. A battle was fought between him and Krishna but he was defeated. Later Balarām, Krishna's brother, killed him.

RENUKĀ

The mother of Parashurām (wielder of an axe) and wife of Jamadagni. Because on one occasion when she saw Chitraratha Gandharva sporting with his wives, her passions were roused, her son Parashurām, at the desire of his father, killed her.

LAVA

The younger son of Rama and the younger brother of Kusha. (See under *Kusha*).

LAKSHMAN

The son of King Dasharath and his wife Sumitrā. He loved Rama very much and accompanied him into his exile. He killed Indrajit, the son of Rāvana.

LAKSHMANĀ

One of the eight favourite wives of Krishna.

LAKSHMĪ

The wife of Vishnu. The story goes that she was churned out of the ocean.

VARĀHA (BOAR)

The third *avatār* of Vishnu. He came out of the nostrils of Brahmadev, killed the demon Hiranyāksha and saved the earth by holding it on his tusk.

VASHISHTHA

A great Brahman *rishi* (sage), the son of Mitrāvaruna. He had a wish-cow which Vishvāmitra demanded but the cow was unwilling to go. When he used force, from her body she produced various kinds of soldiers and extirpated the army of Vishvāmitra. So they became enemies. To gain such spiritual power as that of Vashishtha, Vishvāmitra practised severe austerities. Because Vishvāmitra was a Kshatriya, Vashishtha would not acknowledge him as a Brahman sage though everyone else did. So Vishvāmitra killed his hundred sons. But when he really acquired that worth he was accepted by Vashishtha as a Brahman sage. *Vide Appendix II p. 431.*

VĀMAN (DWARF)

The fifth *avatār* of Vishnu. In order to help Indra he sent Bali to the lower regions. (See under the word *Bali*)

VĀLMĪKI

The well-known writer of the great epic *Rāmāyana.* While going to practise austerities he was abandoned by his parents in a forest. *Kirātas* (forest hunters) took him and brought him up as a robber. He became clever at archery and once when going to kill a sage he asked him to go and ask his wife and children if they would share his nefarious deeds. Being convinced that they would not, he repented and practised severe austerities by repeating the two letters in the word 'Rama' in the reverse order until he was enveloped by *valmik* (an ant-hill) and therefore he was called Vālmiki. Once moved through pity he cursed a hunter who had killed a pair of *kraunch* birds. The curse was in the form of a couplet which came naturally from his lips. Brahmadev asked him to compose the *Rāmāyana*. When Rama abandoned Sita in the forest he took care of her and when Kusha and Lava were born he educated them and sent them all to Rama.

VIDUR

The son of a female slave of Ambikā, the wife of Vichitravirya, the father of Dhritarāshtra. He was begotten by Vyāsa, the well-known writer of the *Puranas*. He was very righteous, unbiassed, of right judgment and wise. He advised Dhritarāshtra not to hate the Pāndavas, and to let them have their share in the kingdom, but his advice was disregarded. He put the Pāndavas on their guard as they were about to be burnt in the lacquer house especially created for their destruction by their cousins the Kauravas. He had gone to perform pilgrimages when the battle took place between the two parties. After the battle he went to live in a forest and died there. *Vide Appendix II p. 429.*

VISHVAKARMĀ OR TVASHTA

The architect of the gods.

VISHVĀMITRA

The son of King Gādhi of the lunar race. Although a born Kshatriya, by his severe austerities he became a Brahman *rishi* (sage). He had many sons including Yādnyavalkya. He hated Vashishtha. In order to interrupt him in his austerities Indra sent Menakā a heavenly damsel. She accomplished her purpose and from her Shakuntalā was born to him. Because the gods refused to admit King Trishanku with his mortal body into heaven, Vishvāmitra created a separate world for his (Trishanku's) residence. (See under *Vashishtha, p. 413 & Appendix II p. 431.*)

VYĀSA

Son of Pārāshara from Satyavati born in her maidenhood. He made the divisions in the *Vedas.* He wrote the *Mahābhārata.* From him were born to Vichitravirya's wives Dhritarāshtra and Pandu, and Vidur from a slave of Ambikā. He is also known as Dvaipāyan, Krishnadvaipayan, etc.

SHAKUNI

The son of King Subal of the country of Gāndhār, the brother of Gāndhāri, the wife of Dhritarāshtra, and Duryodhan's maternal uncle. He induced Duryodhan to gamble with Dharma. He was an expert deceitful gambler. He was killed by Sahadev.

SHABARI

A female Bhil, and the maid of the sage of Mātang who lived near the Pampā lake. She was a great devotee of Rama.

SHATRUGHNA

The son of King Dasharath of his second wife Sumitrā. He killed Lavanāsur. While Rama led the life of an exile he reigned in his name like Bharat. He founded the country of Shurasen and made Mathurā its capital.

SHISHUPĀL

The son of Damaghosha, and Vasudev's sister's son, and the king of the country of Chedi. Rukmini was his betrothed wife, but Krishna took her away and after that he became Krishna's enemy. At the royal sacrifice of the Pāndavas, Krishna was given the first honour, therefore he (Shishupāl) insulted Krishna, and the latter killed him.

SHUKA

Son of Vyāsa. He was a born philosopher and a celibate till death. Rambhā a heavenly damsel was frustrated in her attempt to seduce him. Vyāsa taught him the *Bhāgvata*, and he read it to King Parikshiti.

·SHUKRA

The son of the *Rishi* (Sage) Bhrigu and Pulomā. He was the preceptor of the *Daityas* (demons). His daughter was Devayāni born from his wife Jayanti, the daughter of Indra.

SANAK

One of the first will-born sons of Brahmadev. Sanatkumār, Sanatsujat, and Sanandan were his brothers. All of them were expert in the knowledge of the Supreme Spirit.

SAHADEV

The fifth and last of the Pāndavas, Mādri's son was very beautiful. Was very skilful in sword-fight, and was a great astrologer. In his retirement he was in charge of the cattle of King Virāt.

SAHASRĀRJUN

The son of Kritavirya of the Yadu line, and therefore was called Kārtavirya. He had a thousand arms. He had obtained them as a boon of the god Dattātreya. His capital was Māhishmati. He took away the wish-cow of the father of Parashurām who therefore killed him. He ruled justly.

SANJAYA

The son of a charioteer by name of Gavalgana. He was the charioteer and adviser of King Dhritarāshtra. Through the favour of Vyās he was able to understand all that happened in the war just from where he sat, and he explained the same to King Dhritarāshtra.

SATYAVATI

The daughter of Uparichara born from a fisherwoman. She was also known as Matsyagandhā, Yojangandhā, and Gandhavati. Before she was married, Vyāsa was born to her from the *Rishi* (Sage) Parāshar. Afterwards she was married to King Shantanu, and had from him two sons, Chitrāngad and Vichitravirya.

SATYABHĀMA

One of the eight chief wives of Krishna, the daughter of Satrājit. After the death of Krishna she burnt herself on his funeral pyre. *Vide Appendix II p. 426*

SATYAVĀN

The son of Dyumatsen of the country of Shālva. He was also known as Chitrāshva. He was the husband of Savitri, the daughter of King Ashvapati and through her power he became long-lived although destined to die early.

SATRĀJIT

The eldest grandson of King Anamitra of the Satvat race of the Yadu family line. He gave his daughter Satyabhāma to Krishna. He was killed by Shatadhanva.

SĀVITRĪ

Daughter of King Ashvapati of the Madra country. Wife of Satyavān and famous as a dutiful wife. Born as the fruit of eighteen years' worship of the goddess of the same name. Savitri was a child of wondrous beauty and lustre and hence no prince dared to wed her but at last after wandering in various countries at her father's suggestion she herself chose Satyavān in marriage. Though Nārad the Rishi told her that Satyavān would be short-lived, she nevertheless remained loyal to her choice. After her marriage she rendered the highest service to her mother-in-law, father-in-law and husband. Going into the forest with her husband on the appointed day of his death, she followed Yama (the god of death) as he was taking her husband away, saying 'Wherever the husband goes, there goes the wife also.' She followed singing the praises of Yama, and finally obtained the threefold boon, viz., that her blind father-in-law should receive sight, that to her father and herself should be granted a hundred sons, and that her husband should return to her.

SĀNDIPANI

The son of a sage by name of Kāshya. He lived in Avanti, the modern Ujjain. Krishna and Balarām learned from him all sciences and arts including the knowledge of the Supreme Spirit. Kuchail (or Sudāmā) was also studying there. As an honorarium to their *guru*, Balarām and Krishna brought back to life the dead sons of their *guru*, and then went to their home.

SITĀ

The heroine of the *Rāmāyana* and the adopted daughter of Siradhvaja Janaka who found her while ploughing the ground. The breaking of the Shiva-bow was the condition to be fulfilled by the man who should become the husband of Sitā. Rama broke it, and Sitā became his wife and was a model of a faithful wife. She followed him in his exile. While Rama was away, Rāvana kidnapped her and tried hard to induce her to yield to his sensual wishes but she did not. After her rescue from Rāvana, Rama would not admit her to his house, so she threw herself into the fire and came out of the test safe and sound. After the accession of Rama on the throne she was great with child, but Rama abandoned her on account of the calumnious language which a washerman used in connection with her, and she took refuge with the *Rishi* (Sage) Vālmīki in the forest. There Kusha and Lava were born to her. Vālmiki taught them the *Rāmāyana* and everything that was fit to be learnt by Kshatriya children. He sent all the three to Rama, and convinced him of Sitā's purity, but she instantly disappeared in the earth. (See under the name *Rama* for other details.)

SUDĀMA

A poverty-stricken Brahman, Krishna's school-fellow. Persuaded by his wife he went to Krishna with a handful of parched rice. Krishna was pleased on seeing him and raised him to a great and a glorious life.

SUMITRĀ

The daugter of Shur, king of Magadha. The second wife of King Dasharath, and the mother of Lakshman and Shatrughna.

HAYAGRIVA

A demon who tried to carry away the *Vedas* from Brahmadev. But Vishnu took the Matsya (fish) *avatar* and killed him. This *avatar* is also known as Hayagriva, hence an epithet of Vishnu.

HARISHCHANDRA

A king of the Ikshvaku family line, and the eldest son of King Trishanku. Vashishtha praised him in the court of Indra, and therefore Vishvāmitra tried various means to test his goodness, but he bravely endured every test.... One of the most memorable incidents of the entire narrative about Harishchandra describes the moment when his Dom master commanded him to slay his wife Taramati, and her last prayer was : 'In every birth let there be a king like Harishchandra, a son like Rohitha, a *guru* (preceptor) like Vashishtha, and a beggar like Vishvāmitra.' (Abbreviated from the *Abhinava Bhaktavijaya* account, pp. 673–674.)

[This ancient king 'is said to have lived in the *Treta Yuga* or Silver Age. Many legends are recorded concerning him....He is best known for his piety and his suffering. He was a sort of Indian Job, who passed through inconceivable and undeserved woe, and had to sell even his wife [Taramati] and child [Rohith] in order to pay the dues of the rapacious saint Vishvāmitra. He finally sank to be the servant of a Dom, his duties being to collect the clothes that covered the corpses at the Benares place of cremation, and to deliver them to his master. At the climax of his sufferings in this degrading occupation, he had to steal the clothes from the corpse of his own son, which was brought thither for cremation by his mother, Harishchandra's long-parted wife. The parents resolved to end their sorrows by dying on the son's funeral pyre. The gods then intervened. His Dom master, who was really the god Dharma, or Virtue, taking human form on purpose to test Harishchandra's sense of duty, expressed himself satisfied. Harishchandra and his wife were translated to heaven, and his son was resuscitated and restored to his kingdom, where he reigned in his father's stead. The whole story is told with much pathos in the seventh and following chapters of the *Markandeya Purana*. The story also occurs in the *Padma Purana*, and is a favourite subject of modern vernacular literature. The *Harishchandis* are nearly all of very low caste, mostly Doms. They claim to practise the tenets handed down to them from Harishchandra's Dom master; who was taught piety by his servant in the intervals of his employment. They worship Vishnu as the Creator of the universe; and if they have any other definite doctrines, they are those of the *Bhakti Marga*.'*] *J. F. E.*

---

* Dr. Sir George A. Grierson in the *Encyclopædia of Religion And Ethics*, vol. VI, page 517.

APPENDIX I

HIRANYAKASHIPU

The father of Pralhād, a great devotee of Vishnu. He pleased Brahmadev and got from Him the boon that he would not suffer death at the hands of a man or a beast at night or in daytime or on earth or in water. So Vishnu took the form of Nrisinha, half man, half beast, and killed him in the evening, a time between day and night, and under the door, that is, neither in the house nor outside.

HIRANYĀKSHA

The younger brother of Hiranyakashipu. Vishnu became *Varāha* (a boar) and killed him.

APPENDIX II

PAURANIC NARRATIVES REFERRED TO IN THE *BHAKTAVIJAYA*

AGASTI'S DRINKING THE OCEAN

Supported by the power of the demon Vritra, the demons Kālakeya often fought with Indra. When with much effort Indra killed the demon Vritra, the Kālakeya demons hid themselves in the ocean, and at night devoured the *rishis* and impeded their religious functions. Thereupon Indra and other sages prayed to Brahmadev who asked them to go to the sage Agastya. They went, and in compliance with their request the sage Agastya with his power of penance drank the ocean at a gulp, and thus the demons were destroyed.

INDRA'S THOUSAND PHYSICAL HOLES

Brahmadev gave his adopted daughter Ahalyā in marriage to the sage Gautama. Indra wished to have her for his wife as she was very beautiful, and being foiled in his attempt he resolved to enjoy her by some means or other. Once when Gautama was away from his house on account of the solar eclipse, Indra went in the disguise of Gautama to his house and enjoyed Ahalyā. Just then the real Gautama returned, found out Indra, and cursed him saying, 'You will have a thousand holes in your body.' Ahalyā too was cursed and turned into a slab of stone. When appeased by her and the gods he again said that she would be restored to life by the dust of the feet of Rama, and that Indra would have a thousand eyes.

A HUNTER BITTEN BY A SNAKE WHILE IN THE ACT OF SHOOTING BIRDS

While wandering in a forest to secure some game a hunter beheld a male and a female pigeon on a tree. He aimed his arrow at them, but in the meantime a hawk noticed the two birds and intended to pounce upon them. The birds were thus between two fires, and they prayed to God to save them and a wonderful thing occurred. A snake came out of its hole and bit the hunter, so the arrow he had aimed at the birds hit the hawk instead, and thus the two birds were saved, and they thanked God.

KRISHNA SHOWS HIS INNUMERABLE FORMS TO COWHERDESSES

One day a cowherdess caught Krishna while stealthily eating butter in her house, and notwithstanding his prayers she dragged him to his adopted mother Yashodā; on the way many cowherdesses joined her. As they saw Krishna's mouth smeared with butter they all exclaimed, 'The robber is well caught. Now we shall have him punished soundly by Yashodā.' All then started to go to Yashodā to complain against Krishna, and when Krishna found his escape impossible, he performed a miracle. Every cowherdess had in her hand a Krishna with his mouth smeared with butter, and every cowherdess had in her hand a pot of curds as she was going to complain to Yashodā. In the meantime another Krishna was playing in the yard of Yashodā with other cowherds. Just then Nanda arrived there with his relatives, and each of them was carrying a Krishna in his hand. In this way when the cowherdesses found all space filled with Krishna they were amazed and forgetting their complaint went away.

KRISHNA TAKES THE FORMS OF COWS AND CALVES

Once on a time Brahmadev wanted to see whether or no Krishna was a perfect *avatār* of God and he therefore carried away all the cows, calves, cowherds, etc., into his own land, the *Satyaloka*. Krishna knew this and for a whole year he took their forms and everything seemed as usual. After the end of a year he (Brahmadev) being convinced, went to Nanda and returned the real cows, calves and cowherds, and the ones that were acting in their stead inmediately disappeared. All were astonished at this miracle.

THE SLAYING OF THE SERPENT KĀLIYĀ

In a deep place in the waters of the Jumna river there lived a very venomous serpent by name Kāliyā and all the water of the river on his account had become poisonous. Some cowherds drank it and died at once, at which Krishna was much enraged; in order to punish Kāliyā he jumped into the river and straightway entered his house. His wives, as they saw the tender form of Krishna, began to persuade him to leave the place at once and not fall a victim to the anger of the serpent who would kill him. But notwithstanding their entreaty he began to play his fife. At its sound Kāliyā coiled himself around Krishna, and tried to suffocate him to death. But Krishna swelled His body enormously so that Kāliyā's bones were broken and in an agony of death he uncoiled himself. In the meantime Krishna jumped on his head and began to play His fife and to dance. Kāliyā began to pant in distress and supplicated Krishna. His wives also pleaded with Krishna for their husband's life and Krishna spared his life on condition that he leave the place and resort to the ocean. Krishna came out and consoled those who were lamenting for Him as dead, and restored to life all the cowherds who had lost their lives on account of the poison of the serpent.

KRISHNA AND THE WIVES OF THE *RISHIS*

When the *rishis* knew of the various sports which Krishna played with the cowherdesses, a sort of disrespect about Him arose in their minds, as they thought that defilement would thereby spread everywhere. Understanding this, and in order to explain Himself to them, he went to them and asked for food saying that he was hungry. They replied that no food could be given Him unless it was first offered to the fire, and thus sent Him away. Then Krishna sent some of His companions to the wives of the *rishis* to beg for food. As they had heard of His many sports, they had great regard for Him and thought him to be the divine soul and without the knowledge of their husbands they prepared many dainty dishes and took them to Krishna. Seeing their devotion He was much pleased and giving them His blessing He sent them away with His assurance of impunity. One of those wives was caught by her husband as she was going to Krishna. She was brought back and tied to a post, and died while being beaten by her husband. The other *rishis* not seeing their wives in their houses went to Krishna, but to their astonishment found that they had already left the place, except the one who had died owing to her husband's beating. All had seen her tied to a post, and all saw her here also. This struck them as very wonderful, and they became convinced of the spiritual power and purity of Krishna. Krishna also instructed them in various ways and taught them the principle of humanity towards all creatures.

KRISHNA HUMBLES THE PRIDE OF NĀRAD

Nārad was present at the wedding of Krishna with Jāmbawanti. He was very proud of his singing, and thought there was no equal to him in that art. To humble his pride Krishna devised a plan. Said he to Nārad, 'Everything is in abundance here except singing, so it would be well if you would sing a little.' Nārad replied, 'What is the good of singing in an assembly of bears? (Jāmbawanti was the daughter of a bear, Jambawant.) It would be looked on as a matter of jest.' Then Krishna looked at a bear and ordered it to sing. Taking the *vina* of Nārad it sang so beautifully that all wondered. Not only so, but the singing left its effect even on the slab of stone on which the bear had been sitting, and it melted, and as the singing stopped it became solid again, and the *vina* of Nārad stuck in it. As the singing ended, Nārad got up and began to take up his *vīna*, but it would not move. Then Krishna said, 'O king of *munis*, it will come out only if you will melt the slab by your singing. Just try.' At this Nārad was overcome with shame, and confessed that his singing was deficient and that his pride had been humbled. Then he praised Shri Krishna and requested Him to give him back his *vīna.* Krishna then ordered another bear to sing, and as it began to sing the slab melted and Nārad got his *vīna* back.

GIVING UP OF KRISHNA AS A GIFT

Satyabhāmā was very proud of her beauty, and thought that it had the power to keep Krishna under her thumb. Once when Krishna was in her mansion she said to Him, 'Rukmini does not possess so much beauty nor love nor devotion for you as I do, nevertheless you stay with her longer and love her more, which is not good. You should always stay with me.' Krishna replied, 'I love a person as much as he loves me.' Then they had a talk on other subjects and Krishna under the pretext of sleeping lay down quietly with his face covered. Just then Nārad the *muni* came there. Bhāmā offered him a seat and pleased him with her worship. In the course of conversation she said to Nārad, 'Krishna loves me exclusively, but tell me some means by which I shall be able to enjoy the same love for ever in my future births.' Nārad said in reply, 'If one gives a thing which one loves most as a gift to a Brahman, the same will one possess in the future births.' Bhāmā replied, 'I see no better deserving to receive the gift than yourself. So you accept the gift please.' Being always ready to make fun, Nārad at once consented, and told Satyabhāmā that just then was the most auspicious time for the gift. Bhāmā made all the preparations, and Krishna was already there. He laughed to Himself at seeing what was going on. Bhāmā told Him that she was going to offer Him as a gift to Nārad. Krishna said, 'But before you act up to Nārad's advice, you should first consult all my other wives, for if you do not, there will be great unhappiness. Think well of this.' Bhāmā replied that she had already thought of it,and worshipping Nārad in accordance with religious rites she gave Krishna to him as a gift. The delight of Nārad could not be contained. He at once took Krishna; and Bhāmā now became impatient. She entreated Nārad to leave Krishna there but Nārad took Krishna into the mansion of Rukmini who requested Krishna to sit on the sofa. But Krishna replied, 'Now I have become the property of Nārad. Without his order I cannot do anything.' As Nārad repeated what had happened, Rukmini fell into a swoon. At the news of Krishna's having been given as a gift, all His thousands of wives and his father Vasudev assembled there. Bhāmā was sent for, and when she came they all asked her, 'What right have you alone to give away Krishna as a gift ?' In thus addressing her they made her miserable and all requested Nārad to give up Krishna but he would not listen. Eventually it was settled that if Nārad received Krishna's weight in gold he should leave his claim and give back Krishna. Bhāmā was also proud of her fortune, so she put Krishna in one of the scales and her ornaments in the other, but in no way would the scale with ornaments go down. She was very much dejected at heart at this, and hung down her head through shame and disappointment. All the other wives of Krishna following the example of Bhāmā put their ornaments into the scale but with the same result. Finally all the gold in Dwārakā was put into the scale and even then the scale would not go down. At last Rukmini said, 'How can the Supreme and complete *Brahma*, Lord Shri Krishna, Who at His will can create and destroy in a moment innumerable universes, how can He be weighed against gold? He can be weighed against *bhakti* alone.' So removing all the gold she put a leaf of *tulsi* into the scale, and mentally pleaded, 'O God, consider me as your humble handmaid and preserve my shame.' Just as she finished her prayer, the scale in which Krishna had been placed flew up, and the people made joyful acclamations in the name of Shri Krishna and Rukmini. God hungers after devotion, and it was made evident that Rukmini's devotion was unexcelled. In this way Satyabhāmā's pride was humbled.

DRAUPADI RECEIVES FOUR ARMS AND ASSUMES INNUMERABLE FORMS

In the royal sacrifice of the Pāndavas many Brahmans dined daily. After them dined the kings and then the others. Draupadi used to serve all these and when she felt wearied she looked at Shri Krishna and His glance relieved her of her weariness. Many days passed in this way. On one occasion as Draupadi was serving the kings, Krishna praised her for her hard work and she became choked with emotion at realizing that she was so much loved by Krishna. Just then the knot of her jacket became loose and her upper garment also slipped. At this critical moment Duryodhan and others asked her to serve them many things at once, and began to treat her without modesty. In her dfficulty she invoked Krishna and through his favour received two more arms. With these she knotted her jacket and straightened her garment and began to serve. Just then the evil-minded men saw before each one of them a Draupadi being helped by Krishna. At this the righteous felt delighted and the evil-minded ones were put to shame, and all were convinced of the power of Draupadi's devotion to God.

KAURAVAS' ATTEMPT TO BURN THE PĀNDAVAS IN A LACQUER HOUSE

The Kauravas could not bear to see the respect given by the people to the Pāndavas on account of their good nature, learning, and modesty. They therefore asked their father, King Dhritarashtra, to order them to go to live in Vāranāvat. The house which had been prepared for them to live was stuffed with combustible things such as lac, resin, etc., and a *Yavan* Purochan by name, had been kept there with orders to set fire to it on an appointed day, and thus burn the Pāndavas to death. The Pāndavas set out to go and live at Vāranāvat, but Vidur had apprized them of the danger awaiting them by sending a secret message in a secret language, and for their escape he had also prepared a passage underground which was pointed out to them at the proper time. But Dharmarāj behaved as if ignorant of anything and was waiting for the day on which the house was to be set on fire. Dharmarāj was very generous and many people came to him and went away fully satisfied by his gifts of food and money. On the day on which the house was to be set on fire a Bhil woman had come to live there with her five sons, and she dined and slept on the spot. As Bhima had been warned beforehand, he was on his guard. At midnight the *Yavan* by name Purochan got up, but before he could set fire to the house, Bhima caught him and tied him to a post, and taking all his brothers and his mother, got out of the house by the secret passage underground. The house was then set fire to by Bhima, destroying with it Purochan the *Yavan* and the Bhil woman with her five sons. In the morning people saw six corpses there, and all thought that the Pāndavas were burned to death and therefore all lamented. When the news reached Hastinapur the people there felt very sad, and Dhritarāshtra with his sons outwardly bewailed. But after the *Svayamwar* of Draupadi (choice of her husband ceremony) the Pāndavas appeared openly, and came again to live in their kingdom.

THE COMING OF THE HEAVENLY GANGES TO THE MORTAL WORLD AS BHĀGIRATHI

Bhagirath was the son of King Dilip of the line of the Ikshvakus. In order to save his ancestors, the sons of Sagar, who were sixty thousand in number burnt to ashes by the sage Kapil, he wanted bring down to the mortal world the heavenly Ganges. In order to accomplish this he practised severe austerity, and the Ganges being pleased consented to do as he wished. It came to the mortal world, and saved Bhagirath's ancestors, and since then has remained here under the name of Bhāgirathi (by which it is often known) as the result of Bhagirath's efforts.

BHARATA HUMBLES MĀRUTI'S PRIDE

In the battle between Rama and Rāvana, Lakshman fell down in a swoon by a missile hurled at h im by Rāvana To bring him to life Māruti went to bring Mount. Drona on which many efficacious herbs grew. While carrying it he felt proud of his strength. As Māruti was passing Nandigram where Bharata was reigning he saw Māruti, and taking him to be a demon shot him with an arrow which threw him on the ground. Māruti was sorry, for he thought that he would not be able to reach the place where Lakshman lay unconscious, before sunrise and therefore would not be of any help in restoring the life of Lakshman. When Māruti met Bharata he related his errand. Bharata at once put him on the tip of his arrow which had the name 'Rama' on it and shot him to where Rama was. In this way Māruti's pride was humbled.

VISHNU HOLDS BHRIGU'S KICK (ITS MARK) ON HIS CHEST AS AN ORNAMENT

Once in an assembly of *rishis* a question arose as to who among the three gods was superior. Some favoured Brahma and some Shiva and Vishnu and the question could not be decided. So it was decided that he would be called the best of all who had forgiveness and peace of mind. Bhrigu went to Shiva and Brahma and purposely insulted them on which he was driven away by both. Lastly he went to Vishnu, but He was asleep. So Bhrigu gave Vishnu, a sharp kick on his chest, but instead of getting angry, Vishnu humbly said, 'I am sorry I was sleeping and thus could not welcome you.' This was held to prove Vishnu's superiority. The mark of Bhrigu's kick is called *Shrivatsalanchhan* and god Vishnu wears it as an ornament to show what respect he has for Brahmins.

VISHVĀMITRA'S NEW CREATION

Trishanku, a king of the Ikshvaku family line, wanted to perform a sacrifice with the help of Vishvāmitra, desiring to go to heaven with his mortal body. As Vishvāmitra was of the Kshatriya race, and the host Trishanku had become a *chāndala* (untouchable) by Vashishtha's curse, no Brahman would go to take part in the sacrifice. But with great difficulty some Brahmans did come, though the gods would not take their oblations. At length Vishvāmitra said, 'By the power of my own good actions, you go to heaven, O king'. As Vishvāmitra said this, the king began to fly up like a bird heavenward, but Indra (the chief of gods) would not allow him into heaven. Trishanku began to fall but as he was falling, Vishvāmitra said, 'Stay just there, for your sake I will create a new heaven and there I will locate you.' So Trishanku remained hanging in space and Vishvāmitra commenced a sacrifice as he had resolved and created somethings. But Indra became frightened at it and prevailed on Vishvāmitra to stop his further creation. Indra caused Trishanku to give up his mortal body and took him to heaven with a divine body.

[VASHISHTHA AND VISHVĀMITRA, OR BRAHMAN'S POWERFUL STICK

As Vishvāmitra was once on a hunting expedition he halted at the hermitage of Vashishtha who showed him and his army every kind of hospitality with the help of the wish-cow which he possessed. Vishvāmitra asked him to give him the cow, but when Vashishtha refused, Vishvāmitra began to drag away the cow by force, but the cow created four kinds of armies from her body and defeated him. Feeling deeply mortified he went into the Himalayas, and there practised severe austerities and obtained many weapons and missiles which he used on Vashishtha, but the latter took his *Brahma-dand* (the Brahman's stick) in his hand and assuming a huge form swallowed them.]

[Another narrative about the *Brahma-dand* reads as follows :—Once on a time there was a dispute between Vashishtha and Vishvāmitra as to their superiority, and in order to settle the question both of them went to Brahmadev. He asked them to produce some witnesses in whose presence the decision would be given. Vashishtha first went to the sun and requested him to come. The sun said that he had to give light to the earth and consequently could not come. But Vashishtha placed his *Chati* (a sannyasi's upper garment) in the place of the sun, and told him that it would do his work until he returned. Then he went to the serpent Shesha who holds the earth on his head. There Vashishtha placed his stick (the Brahma-stick) which would support the earth until Shesha returned. He then went to the moon, and in its place kept his water-gourd to work for it until it returned. Vishvāmitra could not obtain any such witnesses, and this established the superiority of Vashishtha over him.]

[VISHNU IN THE FORM OF A SWAN

Once upon a time the sages Sanak and others asked Brahmadev in the *Satyaloka* (Brahmadev's heaven) a philosophical question. His mind was at that time otherwise engaged and so he could not answer. Just then Vishnu appeared on the scene as a swan and removed their doubts.]

APPENDIX III

WORDS WITH NUMERICAL SIGNIFICANCE USED IN THE *BHAKTAVIJAYA*

Words Under Numeral 3

Tritāp or *trividhatāp*:—the three classes of affliction, indicating their origin, seat or nature, viz , *Adhyātmik*: psychical (as sorrows, sickness), (2) *Adhibhautik*: physical or material (as earthquake, conflagration, inundation); (3) *Adhidaivik*: from the gods or devils or fate (as injury from lightning, pestilence, blight).

Three kinds of actions:—(1) *Kāyik*=bodily, (2) *Vāchik*= verbal, (3) *Mānasik*=mental.

Tribhuvan:—three lands, viz., (1) *Svarga*, heaven, (2) *Mrityu-loka*, mortal world, (3) *Pātāl*, hell, or lower regions.

Words Under Numeral 4

Four kinds of sin:—(1) bodily, (2) verbal, (3) mental and (4) *Sansargik*, contagious.

Chaturmāsya:—a period of four months, commencing from the bright 11th of *Ashādha* (July), and ending on the bright 11th of *Kārtik* (November).

Char avasthā :—four states: (1) *Jāgriti*, wakefulness; (2) *Svapna*, dreaming; (3) *Sushupti*, sound sleep without dreaming; (4) *Turya* or *Turiya*, simple consciousness, the state of abstraction from without and of absorption in the contemplation of one's own spirit.

Char khani:—the four classes of the animal and vegetable kingdom: (1) *Andaja*, oviparous, (2) *Jāraja*, viviparous, (3) *Svedaja*, sudoriparous, (4) *Udbhijja* ground-bursting (vegetating).

Char ashram:—The four religious orders referring to the four stages of life: (1) *Brahmacharya*, celibate life,

(2) *Grihastha*, householder, (3) *Sannyas*, abandonment of all worldly possessions and earthly affections; (4) *Vanaprastha*, forest life.

Char mukti:—The four stages of salvation: (1) *Salokatā*, residence in the heaven of a particular deity: Brahma, Vishnu, Shiva, Devi, Indra; (2) *Samīpatā*, nearness to the deity; (3) *Sarupatā*, assimilation to the deity; (4) *Sāyujyatā*, absorption into the essence of Brahma.

Char mudra:—an air or disposition of countenance during abstract contemplation, four such are enumerated: (1) *Bhuchari*, (2) *khechari*, (3) *chachari*, (4) *agochari*.

Char yuge:—Four eras: (1) *Krita*, (2) *Treta*, (3) *Dvapara* and (4) *Kali*.

Char varna:—The four castes or orders: (1) *Brahmans*, the priestly class; (2) *Kshatriyas*, the warrior race; (3) *Vaishyas*, traders; (4) *Shudras*, servants.

Char vani:—four kinds of speech:-(1) *Parā* (ear) (2) *Pashyanti* (eyes), (3) *Madhyama* (nostrils) (4) *Vaikhari* (the tongue).

Char Veda:—the four *Vedas*:—(1) the *Rig Veda*, (2) the *Yajur Veda*, (3) the *Sama Veda*, (4) the *Atharva Veda*.

Char purusharth:—The four principal objects of human life: (1) the acquisition of merit by pious and virtuous acts; (2) the pursuit of fame, riches, or power; (3) the enjoyment of the pleasures of sense; (4) the seeking and working out for final emancipation.

Words Under Numeral 5

Prana:—a vital air. Five are enumerated: (1) *Prāna*, this has its seat in the lungs preeminently, and is expressed as life or vitality; (2) *Apāna*, this has its seat in the anus; (3) *Vyāna*, the vital air diffused throughout the body; (4) *Udāna*, the vital air that rises up the throat and passes into the head; (5) *Samāna*, that vital air which is considered essential to digestion.

Panchakannya :—the five most chaste wives, (1) Ahilyā the wife of *Rishi* (Sage) Gautama, (2) Draupadi the wife of the five Pāndav brothers, (3) Sita the wife of Rama the seventh *avatar* of Vishnu, (4) Tārā the wife of Vali (monkey king), or of Brihaspati, the preceptor of the gods, (5) Mandodari the wife of Rāvana the ten-headed monster.

Pancha gandha :—(1) *Kapur*, camphor, (2) *kankol*, all spice, (3) *lavang*, clove, (4) *jayaphal*, nutmeg, (5) *supari*, betelnut.

Pancha gavya :—the five products of the cow :—(1) *gomutra*, cow's urine, (2) *gomaya*, cowdung, (3) *dudh*, cow's milk, (4) *dahi*, curds, (5) *tup*, clarified butter.

Pancha tatve or *pancha mahabhute* :—the five natural elements:—(1) *Prithvi*, the earth, (2) *Āpa*, water, (3) *Tej*, fire, (4) *Vāyu*, the wind, (5) *Ākāsha*, cavity.

Pancha tanmatra or *pancha vishaya* :—(1) *Shabda*, sound, (2) *Sparsha*, touch, (3) *Rupa*, form, (4) *Rasa*, juice, (5) *Gandha*, smell.

Pancha Pāndava :—The five Pandav brothers, the sons of King Pandu:—(1) Dharma, (2) Bhima, (3) Arjuna, (4) Nakul and (5) Sahadev.

Panch mahāyadnya :—The five oblation services. This presentation of food, before beginning the meal, to the gods, saints, demons, manes of ancestors, and men, is a part of a Brahman's daily course. The five terms are: (1) *Devayadnya*, (2) *Pitri-*

yadnya, (3) *Bhutayadnya*, (4) *Manushyayadnya*, (5) *Brahmayadnya*.

Panchakshari mantra :—A mystic formula of five letters. *Namas Shivaya*, a bow to God Shiva.

Panchamrita :—The five nectarous substances: (1) *Paya* milk, (2) *dahi* curds, (3) *ghrita* clarified butter, (4) *madhu* honey, (5) *sharkarā* sugar. In a mixture of these five elements of immortality an idol is bathed.

Panchagnisadhan :—Performance of a particularly austere devotion consisting of sitting in the midst of four fires burning northwards, southwards, east-wards, westwards, and the fifth the sun through his day's course.

Words Under Numeral 6

Shadguna :—The six attributes of God: (1) *Samagra aishvarya* all sovereignty or lordship, (2) *Samagra dharma* all goodness or excellence, (3) *Samagra yasha* all glory, majesty, or power, (4) *Samagra shri* all opulence or fulness, (5) *Samagra dnyāna* all knowledge or understanding, (6) *Samagra vairāgya* absolute exemption from desire or affection (i. e. all-dispassionateness.)

Shadras :—The six flavours or tastes : (1) sweet, (2) sour, (3) salt, (4) pungent, (5) astringent, (6) bitter.

Shadripu :—The six enemies of the soul: (1) lust, (2) anger, (3) covetousness, (4) love or affection, (5) pride, (6) envy.

Shadvarga :—A class of six vices or blemishes: (1) sexual passion, (2) anger, (3) cupidity, (4) natural affection, (5) pride, (6) jealousy or envy.

Shashthipujan :—Worship performed of *Shashthi* (Durga)

and other goddesses by a woman on the sixth day from her delivery.

Shat shastras:—The six *shastras* as ascribed to the *Rishis* (Sages) Kanad and Gautam:— the two *Nyāya*, the two *Mimānsa*, the *Sānkhya* and the *Yoga*; or according to another enumeration; *Nyāya*, *Vaisheshika*, *Mimānsa*, *Vedānta*, *Sānkhya*, *Patānjala* (*Yoga*).

Shadurmi:—The six waves. The six excitements of the *shadripu* (six enemies), *shadurminadi* being the river agitated by these waves, viz. man, (1) *Shoka* sorrow, (2) *Moha* temptation, (3) *Jara* old age, (4) *Mrityu* death, (5) *Kshudhā* hunger, (6) *Pipāsā* thirst.

Shadaksharimantra:—A mystic formula of six letters, *Om Namas Shivaya.*

Shat darshanas:—The six schools of Hindu philosophy.

Words Under Numeral 7

Saptapuris:—The seven salvation-giving cities: (1) Ayodhya (Oudh), (2) Mathura, (3) Maya, (4) Kashi (Benares), (5) Kanchi, (6) Avantika (Ujjain), (7) Dwarawati (Dwarka).

Saptachiranjiva:—Seven ever-living persons: (1) Ashvatthama, (2) Bali, (3) Vyās, (4) Hanumān (Maruti), (5) Bibhishan, (6) Kripācharya, (7) Parashurām.

Saptadhatu:—1. The seven elementary substances of the body, viz., (1) *Rasa* chyle, (2) *Rakta* blood, (3) *Mansa* flesh, (4) *Meda* fat, (5) *Mājja* marrow, (6) *Asthi* bone, (7) *Shukra* semen.

2. Seven metallic substances: (1) *Suvarna* gold, (2) *Rajata* silver, (3) *Tamra* copper, (4)

Vanga lead, (5) *Naga* tin, (6) *Tikshnaka* iron, (7) *Kansya* bell metal.

Saptapadi :—A ceremony during the solemnization of marriage, the bridegroom taking seven steps on rice with his bride; this makes the marriage irrevocable.

Saptaloka:—The seven *loka* or worlds: (1) *Bhurloka*, the earth, (2) *Bhuvarloka*, the region between the earth and the sun, the world of the *muni*, *siddhis*, etc., (3) *Svarloka*, the heaven of Indra, betwixt the sun and the polar star; (4) *Maharloka*, the sphere of the sun and luminaries; (5) *Janaloka*, the abode of the sons of Brahma, (6) *Tapoloka*, the heaven of beings mighty in *tap* or austere devotion, (7) *Satyaloka*, the heaven of Brahma and the *rishis* (sages).

Words Under Numeral 8

Ashtabhava:—the eight affections of the body considered as indications of the prevalence of *satvaguna* (the quality of goodness). These are: (1) *Stambha*, stupefaction, (2) *Sveda*, perspiration, (3) *Romancha*, errection of the hair of the body, (4) *Svarabhanga*, or *vaisvarya*, fluttering of the voice, (5) *Vepathu* or *kampa*, trembling, (6) *Vaivarnya*, change of colour for the worse, (7) *Ashrupata*, flowing of tears, (8) *Pralaya*, syncope or swooning.

Ashtavidha yoga :—the eight modes of *yoga* or self-restraint in profound contemplation: (1) *Yama*, restraint or government of the senses; (2) *Niyama*, a religious observance; (3) *Āsana*, posture or attitude; (4) *Prānāyam*, breathing; (5) *Pratyāhar*, withdrawing or restraining the organs from the objects of sense; (6) *Dharanā*, suspending the breath, abstracting the mind and restraining all mental wants; (7) *Dhyāna*, profound and abstract contemplation; (8) *Samādhi*, deep contemplation, abstracted or absorbed state.

Ashta siddhi:—The eight supernatural powers or capabilities: (1) *Animā*, infinite minuteness; (2) *Mahimā*, greatness; (3) *Garimā*, gravity; (4) *Laghimā*, lightness; (5) *Prapti*, faculty of obtaining everything. (6) *Prākāmya*, irresistible will; (7) *Ishitva*, supremacy; (8) *Vashitva*, holding in command by magical means.

Ashtāng :-Eight parts of the body: (1) *Shira* the head; (2) *Vaksha* chest; (3) *Hridaya* heart; (4) *Bāhu* arms; (5) *Uru* thighs; (6) *Jangha* legs; (7) *Dhopre* elbows; (8) *Padānguli* toes.

Words Under Numeral 9

Navavidha bhakti :—The nine kinds of worship (of the supreme God or of an idol representing some god). These are: (1) *Shravan* hearing (the attributes, excellencies, or wondrous achievements of, as read or recited); (2) *Kirtan* reading or reciting (these attributes, etc.); (3) *Smaran* calling to mind or meditating upon (the names and perfections of); (4) *Pādasevan* washing, kneading or shampooing, etc., of the feet of; (5) *Archan* outward worship or common service, consisting in washing, anointing, presenting *naivedya* (gifts etc.); (6) *Vandan* adoration or performing *namaskār*, etc.; (7) *Dāsya* service in general in or about the temple; (8) *Sakhya* cultivating friendship or familiar intercourse with; (9) *Ātmanivedan* consecration of one's self.

Nava indriyas : nine organs :—two ears, two eyes, two nostrils, one mouth, the urethra, and the anus.

Nava ras :—the nine sentiments or passions : (1) *Shringār* love; (2) *Hāsya* mirth; (3) *Karun* pitifulness or tenderness; (4) *Raudra* anger; (5). *Vira* heroism; (6) *Bhayānak* terror or fear; (7) *Adbhuta* astonishment or surprise; (8) *Bibhatsa* disgust; (9) *Shānta* tranquillity.

Words Under Numeral 10

Dashāngadhupa :—an incense composed of ten fragrant ingredients: (1) *Devadar*, (2) *Motho*; (3) *Uplata*; (4) *Chhali*; (5) *Ala*; (6) *Jula*; (7) *Nakhla* (8) *Ral*; (9) *Lakh*; (10) *Harada*.

OR

(1) *Koshttha*; (2) *Gula*; (3) *Lakh*; (4) *Haritaki*; (5) *Ral* ; (6) *Jatamasi* ; (7) *Shilaras* ; (8) *Sākhar* ; (9) *Moth*; (10) *Guggul*.

OR

(1) *Nakhla* ; (2) *Vala* ; (3) *Chandan* (sandal); (4) *Uda* ; (5) *Vishesh* ; (6) *Agar* ; (7) *Tup* (clarified butter); (8) *Kāpur* (*camphors*); (9) *Honey* ; (10) *Roses*.

Dasha avatār :—the ten principal *avatārs* of Vishnu: (1) *Matsya* fish; (2) *Kurma* tortoise; (3) *Varāha* boar; (4) *Nārasinha* half man, half lion; (5) *Vāman* dwarf; (6) *Parashurām* the axe wielder; (7) *Rama*; (8) *Krishna*; (9) *Buddha*; (10) *Kalanki*.

Ten characteristics of a Brahman :—(1) *Shama* a restraint of passions; (2) *Dama* curbing the passions; (3) *Shauch* purity; (4) *Dāna* giving; (5) *Santosha* satisfaction; (6) *Kshamā* forgiveness; (7) *Ārjava* straightforwardness ; (8) *Bhakti* devotion to God ; (9) *Dayā* kindness ; (10) *Satya* truthfulness.

Dasha grantha :—The ten books of the Rigveda : (1) *Sanhita* ; (2) *Brahman* ; (3) *Aran* ; (4) *Shiksha*;

(5) *Kalpa*; (6) *Vyākarana* (grammar); (7) *Nigantu*; (8) *Nirukta*; (9) *Chhanda* (prosody) (10) *Jyotisha* (astrology or astronomy).

Words Under Numeral 12

The twelve marks of the *gopichandan* clay :—(1) Forehead; (2) throat; (3) chest; (4) naval; (5) right flank; (6) right arm; (7) right ear; (8) left flank; (9) left arm; (10) backbone; (11) neck; (12) left ear.

The twelve *Jyotirlingas* :—In the following twelve places there are temples dedicated to Shiva: (1) Kashivishveshwar (Benares); 2. Tryambakeshwar (at Trimbak near Nasik); 3. Rameshwar (Ceylon); 4. Malikarjun (Srishela, Madras Presidency); 5. Kedareshvar (in the Himalayas); 6. Mahakaleshvar (Ujjain); 7. Onkareshvar (Māndhata on the banks of the Narmada) 8. Ghrishneshvar (Ellor); 9. Nageshvar (Avandhya) 10. Somanath (in Kathiawar); 11. Bhimashankar (Poona District); 12. Vaijanath (Parali, District Thana).

Dvādashākshari mantra :—a mystic formula containing twelve letters: *Om namo bhagavate vāsudevāya*

Words Under Numeral 13

Trayodashguni vidā :—rolled betel-leaves with thirteen ingredients: (1) betel-leaves; (2) lime; (3) betelnut; (4) catechu; (5) clove; (6) nutmeg; (7) nutmace; (8) saffron; (9) all-spice; (10) cocoanut kernel (11) camphor; (12) cardamon; (13) almond.

Trayodashākshari mantra :—a mystic formula with thirteen letters: *Shri ram jayaram jaya jaya ram.*

Words Under Numeral 14

Chavadā ratne :—The fourteen precious things obtained from the ocean on churning it; viz., (1) *Lakshmi*

(Vishnu's wife); (2) *Kaustubh* (Vishnu's ornament); (3) *Pārijatak* (the wish-tree): (4) *Surā* (wine); (5) the moon; (6) the wish-cow; (7) *Airavat* (Indra's elephant); (8) *Apsaras*, the heavenly damsels such as Rambha, Urvashi, Tilottamā, Menakā, etc. (9) a *horse* with seven mouths (belonging to the sun); (10) the deadly *Hūlāhal* (poison); (11) Hari's (Vishnu's) *dhanu* (bow); (12) *shell*; (13) *nectar* (the drink of the gods); (14) *dhanvantari* the physician of the gods.

Chavadāve ratna:—A fourteenth precious thing is *chavadāve ratna*, a sound flogging or beating.

Chaudā vidyā:—1. The 14 divisions of science: (1-4) the four *Vedas*, (5-10) the six *angas* (grammar, prosody, astronomy, pronunciation, interpretation of usual terms, the Hindu ritual,) (11) the eighteen *Puranas*, (12) *mimānsa* or theology, (13) *nyaya* or logic, (14) *dharma* or law.

OR 2. (1) Spiritual knowledge, (2) chemistry, (3) music, (4) the *Vedas*, (5) astronomy or astrology; (6) grammar, (7) archery, (8) swimming, (9) logic, (10) an indecent treatise on the art of love, (11) equestrian skill or horsemanship, (12) dramatic acting or assuming many disguises, (13) husbandry, (14) medicine.

OR 3. (1-4) The four *Vedas*, (5-8) the four minor *Vedas*, (9-14) and the six *Shāstras*.

Words Under Numeral 16

The sixteen purificatory rites: (1) *Garbhadhan* sacrifice on or before conception; (2) *Punsavan* sacrifice on vitality in the foetus; (3) *Anavlobhan* sacrifice in the third month of pregnancy; (4) *Vishnubali* sacrifice in the seventh month; (5) *Simantonnayan* sacrifice in the fourth, sixth or eighth months; (6) *Jātakarma*, giving the infant clarified butter out of a golden spoon before dividing the naval string; (7) *Nāmakarana*, naming the child on the tenth, eleventh, twelfth, or the 101st day; (8) *Nishkraman*, carrying him out to be presented to the moon on the third lunar day of the third light fort night; (9) *Suryavalokan*, carrying him out to be presented to the sun in the third or fourth month; (10) *Annaprashan*, feeding him with rice in the sixth or eighth month, or when he has cut teeth; (11) *Chudakarma*, tonsure in the second or third year, (12) *Upanayana*, investiture with the sacred string in the fifth, eighth, or sixteenth year; (13) *Mahanamya*, instruction in the *Gayatri* after the *munj* thread ceremony (14) *Samavartana*, loosening the *munja* from the loins; (15) *Vivāha* marriage; (16) *Svargarohana*, obsequies.

Shodashopachāra:—the performance of sixteen points in idol-worship: (1) *Avahana*, summoning or invoking; (2) *Asana*, offering a seat; (3) *Padya*, water for cleaning the feet; (4) *Arghya*, an oblation to gods or venerable men, of rice, *durva* (grass), and flowers with water only; in the palm of the hand or in a small vessel; (5) *Achaman*, sipping water before or after religious ceremonies or meals, from the palm of the hand; (6) *Snana*, bathing; (7) *Vastra*, offering a garment; (8) *Yadnyopavita*, the sacred thread, (9) *Gandha*, sandalwood paste; (10) *Pushpa*, flowers.(11) *Dhupa*, incense; (12) *Dipa*, light; (13) *Naivedya*, offering of some eatable; (14) *Dakshina*, offering of money; (15) *Pradakshina*, circumambulation; (16) *Mantrapushpa* the gowpen or double handful of flowers; accompanied by the recitation of a *mantra* thrown on the idol's head (as at the conclusion of worship).

Words Under Numeral 18

The eighteen *Puranas*:—(1) *Matsya* ; (2) *Markandeya* ; (3) *Bhavishya* ; (4) *Bhagavat* ; (5) *Brahmanda* ; (6) *Garuda* ; (7) *Linga* ; (8) *Padma* ; (9) *Vaman* ; (10) *Agni* ; (11) *Kurma* ; (12) *Skanda* ; (13) *Narad* ; (14) *Vārāh* ; (15) *Brahmavaivartak* ; (16) *Vayu* ; (17) *Brahm* ; (18) *Vālmīki*.

The minor eighteen *Puranas*:—(1) *Brahm* ; (2) *Vishnu* ; (3) *Shiva* ; (4) *Brihda Narad* ; (5) *Laghunarad* ; (6) *Narasinh*. (7) *Bhagvat* ; (8) *Renuka* ; (9) *Yamanarad* ; (10) *Hansa* ; (11) *Nandiprokta* ; (12) *Vayuprokata* ; (13) *Vishnurahasya* ; (14) *Talvasar* ; (15) *Bhagwati* ; (16) *Pashupat* ; (17) *Bhavishya* ; (18) *Brahmand*.

Words Under Numeral 24

The twenty-four elements :—(1–5) *The five natural elements*; viz., the earth ; water; fire ; wind ; space or cavity; (6–10) *The five objects*; viz., sound, touch, form, juice, smell, referring respectively to the ear, the skin, the eye, the tongue and the nostrils ; (11–20) *Ten organs* :—five organs of sense and five organs of action ; (21) the mind ; (22) egotism, self-love considered as spiritual ignorance ; (23) intellect ; and (24) *maya* (illusion).

Words Under Numeral 33

The thirty-three gods : viz., 12 *Aditya* (suns); 11 Rudra ; 8 Vasu ; one Indra ; one Prajapati ; total 33.

Words Under Numeral 64

The sixty-four arts or accomplishments :—(1) *Gita* singing or song ; (2) *Vādya* instrumental music ; (3) *Nritya* dancing ; (4) *Natya* union of singing, dancing and instrumental music; (5) *Alekhya* writing or drawing; (6) *Visheshakachhed* tatooing or the making of spots, lines and figures on the person by puncturing and staining; (7) *Tandulkusumbaliprakar* investigating and arraying (an idol etc.) with rice and flowers; (8) *Pushpastaran* spreading and arranging a couch of flowers; (9) *Dashanvasanangarag* painting, staining, dyeing, colouring (of teeth, clothes, body); (10) *Manibhumikakarma* fixing of gems or stained glass into a floor, mosaic work; (11) *Shayanarchan* laying and disposing of beds, sofas, reclining carpets and cushions; (12) *Udakvadya* playing on musical glasses with water; (13) *Nepathyayoga* scenic representation, stage-playing; (14) *Udakaghat* arresting and accumulating water in aqueducts, cisterns or reservoirs; (15) *Chitrayoga* picture-making, limning, decorating etc.; (16) *Malyagrathanvikalp* stringing of rosaries, necklaces; garlands, wreaths; (17) *Karnapatrabhanga* art of making ear-ornaments; (18) *Panakarasaragasavayojan* preparing of lemonades, sherbets, acidulated drinks, spirituous extracts with due flavour and colour; (19) *Suchiranakarma* needlework, tailor work, sewing; (20) *Sutrakrida* making of parrots, flowers, tufts, tassels bunches, bosses, kops, etc. out of yarn or thread; (21) *Sugandhyukti* art of making perfumes; (22) *Vinadamarukavadyani* drum and tabor beating; (23) *Prahelikakutavanidnyana* solution of riddles, enigmas, covert speech, and verbal puzzles; (24) *Pratimala* casting images into a mould. (25) *Durvanchakayoga* device or strategy for outwitting and overcoming the wicked; (26) *Pustakavachan* or *pustakavachashakti* reading, including chanting or intoning; (27) *Natakakhyayikadarshanam* histrionic or scenic representation; (28) *Kavyasamasyapuran* completing stanzas upon receiving a part; (29) *Pattikavetrabanavikalpa* practice with sword, single stick, quarter-staff, bow and arrow etc., fencing archery etc., (30) *Pushpavatika* flori-culture; (31) *Yantramatrikadharan matrikasanvachyam* art of forming mystical diagrams and of addressing spells, binding amulets etc.; (32) *Manasikavyakriya* poetic creation or invention; (33) *Chhalitayoga* art of deceit and trickery; (34) *Tarkakarma* reasoning or inferring, weighing, pondering, considering; (35) *Takshana* chopping, paring, planning, carpentry work; (36) *Vastu* architecture; (37) *Raupyaratnapariksha* knowledge of coins, metals, and jems; (37) *Dhatuvada* chemistry or minerology; (38) *Maniragadnyan* colouring (by foil or *upadhi*) of gems and beads; (39) *Balakridana* skill in youthful sports; (40) *Akardnyan* judgment (i. e. of appropriate places and of the nature, quantities and qualities of contents of) mines and quarries; (41) *Vrikshayurvedayoga* art of determining the age of trees and plants; (42) *Meshakukkutalavakayuddhavidhi* urging goats, cocks, quails, etc. to fight one another. (43) *Shukasarikapralapana* teaching of starlings, parrots etc. to speak; (44) *Utsahan*, setting on, stirring up, inciting, animating, stimulating; (45) *Keshamarjan*, kaushala dressing the hair with unguents and perfumes; (46) *Abhidhanakosha* knowledge of the dictionaries or many vocables, languages, dialects; copia verborum vel fandi; (47) *Shekharapidayojana*, binding of turbans and chaplets, and forming of crests and top-knots;

(48) *Gandhayukti*, art of preparing perfumes and odours; (49) *Bhushanayojan*, disposing of ornaments and decorations; (50) *Aindrajala*, magic or sorcery; (51) *Krauchamaranayoga*, art of assuming disguises, characters and deceptive forms; (53) *Hastalaghava*, dexterity or manual skill; (53) *Chitrashakapupabhaktavikarkariya*, culinary art, cookery; (54) *Aksharamushtikakathan*, art of diving the contents of a closed hand; (55) *Deshabhashadnyana*, knowledge of one's own tongue and of its dialects; (56) *Chhandodnyana* knowledge of scanning or construing verse; (57) *Kriyavikalpa* knowledge of processes and methods in general (58) *Vastragopana* art of disguising and falsifying cloths(making cotton to appear as silk, and what is common to appear as fine or good); (59) *Dyutavishesha* art of playing with false dice etc, gambling roguery; (60) *Akarshakkrida* art of drawing into one's possession (as by *mantras*) of the property of others; (61) *Mlechhitakavikalpa* discrimination of foreign languages (from the Sanskrit); (62, 63, 64) *Vainayikavidyadnyana* or *vaijayikavidyana* or *vaitalikavidyadnyana* knowledge of the several departments of conjuration, charming, and devil-craft.

The following are also enumerated :—

(1) *Nritya*; (2) *Chitra*; (3) *Vaditra*; (4) *Mantra*; (5) *Tantra*; (6) *Ghanavrishti*; (7) *Sanskritajalpan*; (8) *Kriyakalpa*; (9) *Dnyana*; (10) *Vidnyana*; (11) *Dambha*; (12) *Ambustambha*; (13) *Gita*; (14) *Talaman*; (15) *Akaragopan*; (16) *Aramaropan*; (17) *Kavyashakti*; (18) *Vakrokti*; (19) *Naralakshana*; (20) *Gajapariksha*; (21) *Hayapariksha*; (22) *Vastushuddhi*; (23) *Laghubuddhi*; (24) *Shakuna*-

vichar; (25) *Dharmachar*; (26) *Andajachurnayoga*; (27) *Natya*; (28) *Grihadharma*; (29) *Suprasadanakarma*; (30) *Kanakasiddhi*; (31) *Varnikavriddhi*; (32) *Vakpatav*; (33) *Karnalaghava*; (34) *Lalitacharan*; (35) *Tailasurabhitakarana*; (36) *Bhrityopachar*; (37) *Gehachar*; (38) *Vyakarana*; (39) *Paranirakarana*; (40) *Vinanad*; (41) *Vitandavad*; (42) *Ankasthiti*; (43) *Janachar*; (44) *Kumbhabhram*; (45) *Sharirshram*; (46) *Ratnamanibhod*; (47) *Lipiparichhed*; (48) *Vaidyakriya*; (49) *Kamavishkaran*; (50) *Ranahan*; (51) *Chikurabandhan*; (52) *Shalikhandan*; (53) *Mukhamandan*; (54) *Kathakathan*; (55) *Kusumagrathan*; (56) *Varavesha*; (57) *Sarvabhashavishesha*; (58) *Vanijya* (59) *Bhojya*; (60) *Abhidhanaparidnyan*; (61) *Vastrabharan*; (62) *Yathasthan*; (63) *Antyaksharika*; (64) *Prashnahepralika*.

Words Under Numeral 84

Chauryāshīcha-pherā or *garkā*:—the round of eighty-four lakhs of births, rebirths or transmigration.

APPENDIX IV

EPITHETS OF VISHNU FOUND IN THE *BHAKTAVIJAYA*

THESE EPITHETS ARE ALSO APPLICABLE TO VISHNU'S *AVATARS* SUCH AS RAMA, KRISHNA AND VITHOBA

(Alphabetically arranged)

A

Achala :—One whose form is unchanged.

Achintya :—One who is beyond thought and meditation.

Achyuta :—One whose form is unvarying.

Aja :—One without birth.

Ajita :—Unconquered one, invincible.

Antaka :—The destroyer of beings.

Atīndriya :—One who is not an object of sound, touch, etc.; one beyond the sense organs.

Adhokshaja :—One who occupies the space between the sky and the earth with a universal form.

Anagha :—Free from sin.

Ananta :—(1) Infinite, without end; (2) *Ananta-shāyi* (*Ananta* the serpent *Shesha*, and *shāyi* recliner): Recliner on the serpent Shesha. (3) *Anantātmā* Infinite soul.

Anekamurti :—One who assumes various forms.

Amurti or *Amurtimān* :—One without form.

Amrit :—One without death or one who gives salvation to beings.

Aravindāksha :—Lotus-eyed one.

Avyakta :—One without form.

Avyaya :—One without change.

Ashoka :—One without sorrow, or One who dispels the sorrows of beings.

Ashvattha :—Unsteady.

Akshara :—One without waste; One whose form suffers no change.

Adideva :—The primal cause of the universe and the home of resplendent qualities.

Ananda :—Giver of joy to beings ; One of delightful form.

B

Bija-avyaya :—Unchanged cause of the universe.

Brahm :—The greatest of the great; increaser of the world; the all-pervading element.

Brahmanapriya :—One loved by the Brahmans and who loves the Brahmans.

Bhaktavatsala :—One who is kind to His *bhaktas*.

Bhagavana :—One possessed of the sixfold fortune : (1) All-sovereignty, (2) All-excellence; (3) Allglory; (4) All-opulence; (5) All knowledge; (6) Absolute exemption from desire.

Bhayakrit :—Creator of danger to His *bhaktas* who have gone astray.

Bhyanashana :—Dispeller of the disasters of His *bhaktas*.

Bhutatma :—One who resides in the heart of beings.

C

Chakradhara or *Chakri* :—Wielder of the *Sudarshan* disk.

Chaturbahu or *Chaturbhuja*, *Chaturbhava* :—One having four hands indicating, as it were, the four principal objects of human life : (1) The acquisition of merit by pious and virtuous acts; (2) the pursuit of fame, riches or power; (3) the enjoyment of the pleasures of sense; (4) the seeking and working out of final emancipation.

D

Damodara :—One who was fastened by a rope by Yashoda in his Krishna *avatar*.

Devakinandana :—The son of Devaki–Krishna.

Devesha :—God of gods.

Dharanidhara, Dharadhara :-Who in the form of the serpent Shesha supports the earth on his hood, or as a *Varāha* (boar) *avatar* held it on its tusk.

Dhata :—Holder of the earth in His various forms as Shesha, etc.

G

Gadadhara :—Holder of the *Kaumodaki* mace, an indication of intellect.

Garudadhvaja :—Whose banner bears the emblem of Garuda, the eagle, Vishnu's vehicle.

Gopati :—(*Go*, cow or the earth; *pati*, supporter) Supporter of cows or the earth.

Govinda :—Protector of cows, speech and the earth.

H

Hari :—Destroyer of sins or of a desire for earthly life.

Hrishikesha :—The Lord of the senses and of the heart.

I

Ishvara :—Lord of the whole universe and possessor of all-opulence.

J

Janardana :—Punisher of the wicked; Giver of benevolence to beings.

Jaya :—Restrainer of anger, and subduer of all beings.

K

Karta :—Creator of the world.

Kama or *Kanta* :—The most beautiful, as beautiful as a hundred gods of love put together.

Kala :—Destroyer of everything.

Keshava, Keshiha:—One who has beautiful hair, or is the destroyer of the Keshi demon.

Krishna:—Dark-complexioned one, the eighth *avatar* of Vishnu.

Kanta, pati, nayaka, vara, vallabha, nath, dhava, ramana, priya: These words following a female noun mean the husband of; e.g. *Ramakanta*, the Husband of Rama. *Rukminipati* the Husband of Rukmini, etc.

L

Lokabandhu:—Brother of other beings.

Lokanath:—Lord of the universes.

M

Madhusudana:—The destroyer of the demon Madhu.

Mahadeva:—The greatest of the gods.

Mahabhaga:—Highly fortunate.

Manohara:—The attracter of the minds of beings by his qualities, such as beauty, etc.

Mahabhuta:—One who does not suffer by the change of time, or who is the elementary truth.

Mahidhara:—One who supports the earth.

Madhava:—The Husband of *Ma* (the goddess of wealth); one born in the Madhu family line.

Mukunda:—Giver of salvation to His *bhaktas*.

N

Narayana:—Pervader of the five elements such as the earth, the water, the fire, the wind and the space; or One who has for His abode the water.

Paramatma :—One beyond cause and effect, One most pure, One ever free.

Parameshvara :—Lord God, the highest of all, and who resides alike in all beings.

Pundarikaksha :—One who lives in the lotus-heart of beings or One whose eyes are like a lotus.

Pushkaraksha :-Lotus-eyed One; One occupying the space.

Purusha :—One who resides in the human body, a town with nine doors, or the Ancestor of all beings.

Purushottama :—The best of all males.

Putatma :—One having a pure soul, or one who is himself pure.
Purna :—One whose desires and powers are complete.
Prakashatma :—Whose soul is full of light.
Prabhu :—Most powerful, resplendent.
Prana :—The Giver of life or the life itself.

R

Rathangapani :—Holder of a wheel-disk.
Ravilochana :—The witnesser of the whole universe, or whose eye is the sun.
Rama :—In the contemplation of whose form the *yogis* are delighted.

S

Satya :—One who is truth, intelligence, infinite and the all-pervading element *brahm*.
Sarvadnya :—The All-knowing.
Sarveshvara :—The Lord of all.
Sudarshana :—Whose form is beautiful to look at ; whose sight gives joy to the eyes.
Suresha, *Sureshvara* :—Lord of all gods.
Svayambhu :—Spontaneous, free.
Srashta :—The creator of everything in the world.
Sharangdhara :—Holder of the *Sharang* bow.
Shiva :—Giver of happiness.

T

Trilokesha :—The Lord of the three worlds.

V

Vatsala :—Kind to all.
Vanamali :—The wearer of garlands of wild flowers.
Varada :—Giver of a boon; fulfiller of a wish.
Vāsudeva :—The son of Vasudeva; who lives in all beings and in whom all beings live.
Vijaya :—Who is victory in form.

Vishnu :—Pervader of the moveable and immoveable creation.

Vishvatma :—The Universal Soul.

Veda :—Who is Himself the Vedas; the Giver of knowledge.

Vaikunth :—One who has free movement; whose movement is unimpeded.

APPENDIX V

POETIC FANCIES USED IN THE *BHAKTAVIJAYA*

1. Chakor (a particular bird) is fond of the rays of the moon.
2. Chatak (another kind of bird) drinks only rain water.
3. There is a jewel in the hood of a cobra.
4. Rarely are pearls found in the temple of an elephant.
5. A female tortoise feeds her young ones simply by steadily looking at them.
6. Pearls are produced in the ocean if it rains while the *svāti nakshatra* (cluster of stars) is in the ascendant in the sky.
7. If a diamond is stuck in an anvil it comes out only at the sight of diamond dust. *Diamond* (a masculine noun), *diamond dust* (feminine noun). The idea is that a male is attracted by a female.

INDEX OF TECHNICAL WORDS, NAMES OF PLACES AND PERSONS

A

D

E

F

G

H

J

M

Q

R

S

U

W

Y